THEORIES OF REVELATION

THEORIES OF REVELATION

An Historical Study

1700-1960

H. D. McDonald

BAKER BOOK HOUSE
Grand Rapids, Michigan

One-volume edition issued 1979
by Baker Book House with permission
of copyright owner.
ISBN: 0-8010-6081-8
Formerly published under the titles,
*Ideas of Revelation, An Historical Study,
A.D. 1700 to A.D. 1860* © H. D. McDonald, 1959
and *Theories of Revelation, An Historical
Study, 1860-1960,* © H. D. McDonald, 1963
Printed in the United States of America

PREFACE

When the two books that comprise the present volume first appeared, they were successively hailed by reviewers as important contributions that provided the background for the then-contemporary debate on revelation and the Bible. In his foreword to the earlier volume, Professor D. E. Nineham of the University of London thought himself not ill-advised to state, 'No great rashness is needed to predict that in the coming decades one of the most debated theological questions will be how the Bible is to be understood and approached if it is to be a vehicle of revelation for our time'.

Those acquainted with the contemporary theological scene will know how truly this prophecy is presently being fulfilled. The whole subject of the proper valuation of the Scriptures in and by the church has become central. Especially to the fore in the discussion are such questions as the Bible's inspiration, infallibility, and inerrancy. Yet in some quarters it seems to be supposed that the latter issue in particular is a new subject of debate. But the only new feature relative to the subject of inerrancy, as this historical study will make clear, is that it has now become a matter of concern among those who wish to be classed as conservative evangelicals. It was an issue over which controversy raged from well back into the nineteenth century; and it was throughout the main cause of the division between liberal and conservative scholars and theologians, as well as the characteristic mark of identification of each, the liberal admitting errors in the Scriptural revelation and the conservative stoutly contending for an inerrant Bible.

One of the main purposes in issuing a new edition of this work is to have in hand, in historical sequence, the extended debate respecting the status of the Bible, and so to provide the right perspective for an understanding of the present controversy. For it is surely necessary to have some knowledge of how and why there first arose within the church such questions as: Is the Bible a divine revelation? Is it the Word of God? Is it inspired? Is it inerrant?; and so to be informed as to how and why they were sometimes answered with a blank denial, a halfhearted acknowledgement, or a full affirmation.

Prior to the year 1700, when the volume begins, all these questions would have been answered in such a manner as to equate the Bible with God's special revelation. And on this account it was held to be rightly designated 'the Word of God', and in consequence fully inspired and totally trustworthy. In the aftermath of the Enlightenment, however, with its emphasis on reason that gave birth to Deism, the serious question was posed for the church whether there was indeed any such special revelation of God as was presupposed by the Biblical record. How Christian apologists faced this fundamental question is discussed in the earlier part of the present volume. It is there noted how two broad and quite opposing views developed within the church. There was, on the one hand, an extreme emphasis on revelation as the communication of certain truths about God given in strict propositional fashion. In this context faith was generally conceived as the mere assent to a set of doctrinal statements. Such mental acknowledgement, it had to be admitted, had little effect on the total life of the individual. It was something without heart and spirit: and especially did it appear to be very much without the Holy Spirit of God. On the other extreme there developed the idea of revelation as something altogether subjective. God was to be sought and found, neither in the starry skies above nor yet in the sacred Scriptures without, but in the mystic depths of a man's own soul. It is something deeply inward. This understanding of revelation left it without any truth-content and tended to substitute individual feelings for historical facts.

Such extreme views could not, however, be long upheld, so others not so clean-cut were naturally advanced. But even here the opposition continued between the ideas of revelation as truths presented to man's reason and as an inner feeling of the divine. And this led inevitably to a discussion of the relation between the Scripture and the Spirit. On the one side were those who emphasized the objective Word as having creative power in itself. On the other side were those who claimed to be so led by the Spirit that they had no need of the dead letter of the Scriptures. Neither of these views was given credence by the great evangelical leaders of the time. So Charles Simeon, who contended strongly for the objective Word, saw also the need for the inner action of the Spirit; and John Wesley, while emphasizing the Spirit's work, did not fail to insist on the need for the Word without.

While these ideas were to remain throughout the whole period — and are still with us today — the middle of the nineteenth century witnessed other influences that were to have an important bearing on the subject of revelation in general and that of Scripture in particular. The controversies initiated by Darwin's evolutionism and the coming of the Higher Criticism focused attention on the Scriptures and raised the question of their place in the scheme of revelation. The Bible, in fact. became the storm centre; and the problem of the period — which is our problem still — was to give a convincing statement of its significance.

Since an influential body of church opinion, both Roman Catholic and Protestant, has proposed that the Bible can no longer be regarded as an objective, infallible authority, the whole question of religious authority is again in debate. But it can hardly be denied that historically Christian faith has been related in some definite way to the Biblical record. The question is, How is the Bible so related? And if it is related in such a way that it is the ground of faith — the norm and source of faith — then must it have a real authority? But to have such authority it must come to us as 'the Word of God'. Thus are we brought back again to inerrancy and inspiration, which were much discussed in the period following the publication of Darwin's *Origin of Species* and the introduction into Biblical studies of the critical methodology.

As we have sought to trace out what writers on each side of the controversy had to say, we have deemed it right to let them state their case, as much as possible, in their own words: especially is this so with regard to the subjects of Biblical inerrancy, inspiration, and authority. Nonetheless, we have not hesitated at various places to give our own criticisms, seeking to give, as far as we conceive it, a positive statement. In taking such an attitude we have not been unmindful of the subtitle, which announces the whole as 'an historical study'. But we know that it is quite impossible to approach a subject without any presuppositions. This is especially so in theology, where a man's convictions should be deep and meaningful. Even in the realm of science, which once claimed to be the most objective of studies, it is now admitted to be no longer a tenable view that the scientist, so to speak, stands over against his data with no postulates. Indeed the whole scientific endeavour would be fruitless if this were so.

It is in the light of this observation that we have thought it right not only to criticize negatively where we have considered it necessary, but also, especially when dealing with the three related subjects referred to above, to give a positive account of our own convictions. In this way we have sought to avoid giving a mere, dry catalogue of facts, like those scientists whom Lord Rutherford used to describe as 'stamp collectors': they lose themselves in their finds and admire their collection just as would any contented philatelist.

Christ is, of course, the Lord of Scripture, as He is Lord of history and of total life. But the Christ Who is Lord is truly the Biblical Christ, for there is no other. The Christ Who is final for world history and saving faith is not the Christ of subjective experience, nor the Christ of personal encounter, nor the Christ of church declaration — except insofar as these are identical with the Christ set forth in Scripture. The Christ Who is God's last revelation to us is the Biblical Christ, no more and no less. This is the Christ Who Himself in authenticating this conclusion, at the same time authenticated the Bible as fully 'the Word of God': '. . . beginning from Moses and from all the prophets, he interpreted to them in all the scriptures the things concerning himself' (Lk. 24:27 R.V.).

Maybe we should add that we are aware of some misprints and a few inaccuracies in dates and the spelling of names in the pages that follow. Because of the methods of modern reprinting, these have not been corrected; but they should not have any serious effect on the whole account.

I should like to take the opportunity to thank Baker Book House for reissuing these two books, which have been out of print for some time. They have been the subject of constant enquiry; so it is our hope that they may be of use to those who are concerned to understand correctly how to regard the Bible in the church.

IDEAS
OF REVELATION

An Historical Study

A.D. 1700 to A.D. 1860

BY

H. D. McDONALD

B.A., B.D., Ph.D.(Lond.)

LECTURER IN HISTORICAL THEOLOGY
LONDON BIBLE COLLEGE

FOREWORD

'Whoever would take the religious literature of the present day as a whole, and endeavour to make out clearly on what basis Revelation is supposed by it to rest, whether on Authority, on the Inward Light, Reason, Self-evidencing Scripture, or on the combination of the four, or some of them, and in what proportions, would probably find that he had undertaken a perplexing but not altogether profitless inquiry.'

These words, written by Mark Pattison almost exactly a century ago, are in his usual ironical vein. But, ironical or not, the Anglican bishops who have been discussing the authority of the Bible at the 1958 Lambeth Conference, will no doubt testify that they are as applicable to-day as they were when they were first written. And the very fact that the Lambeth Conference has raised this question as one of the major items on its agenda is evidence that modern Christians by no means regard it as an 'altogether profitless inquiry'; on the contrary, Christians of all kinds are becoming increasingly concerned with it. No great rashness is needed to predict that in the coming decades one of the most debated theological questions will be how the Bible is to be understood and approached if it is to be a vehicle of revelation for our time.

Mark Pattison's contribution to the discussion in his day was to write a history of how the matter had been viewed between 1688 and 1750. Dr McDonald has sought to make a similar contribution, though his work is on a larger scale and brings the history of the discussion down far enough to include the views of F. D. Maurice. If Dr McDonald's writing avoids the ironical vein of Pattison's, it is based on the same exhaustive study of the original sources, and Dr McDonald seems to have a special gift for singling out the telling quotation which sums up in memorable form the quintessence of a writer's argument.

If we can ever learn anything from history, this book should help us to do so, so far as its subject is concerned, the sense in which the Bible is, or yields, revelation. For the most part the reader is left to draw the moral for himself, but there are not lacking definite hints

that Dr McDonald has his own ideas on the contemporary relevance
of his researches, and these hints the reader will find it worth his
while to follow up.

D. E. NINEHAM

UNIVERSITY OF LONDON
KING'S COLLEGE
1958

PREFACE

THE subject of Revelation is of special interest to-day. Recent writers have been concerned with such subjects as the fact and focus of the divine self-disclosure. This pre-occupation with the problems of revelation is, however, no new thing, for it is the purpose of the following pages to show that the ideas which in recent years have come to prominence are the very ideas which were forced into the foreground in a past period. It will be necessary to mark out this era and to show how these several different views of revelation came about.

Much which has of late appeared on the subject is, we believe, not as original as it is stated. Claims and charges are made which we think would never have been made if writers had come to their subject aware of the historical background of their own particular view. The fact is, of course, that there is no helpful volume to supply this information. There are Histories of specific Christian Doctrines, as, for example, the Atonement and the Person of Christ, but there is little on the subject of Revelation as such. This is an omission which it is the purpose of the present volume to remedy. Apart from the last two or three pages, the remainder constitutes a thesis approved for the Degree of Doctor of Philosophy in the University of London.

The work should have a special interest for serious students of theology. But it should appeal also to the informed general reader who is concerned to know how Christian men have regarded Divine Revelation.

A work of this nature has demanded a good deal of withdrawal to the seclusion of the study and for this reason the author would like to acknowledge the co-operation of his wife and family who did not lay claim to his presence and help when they were rightly demanded.

A special word of thanks must be recorded to the Rev. Professor D. E. Nineham, Professor of Biblical and Historical Theology, King's College, University of London, who read through each section as it was completed. His criticisms and suggestions were of the greatest help and many of them have been acted upon. Professor Nineham has continued his kindness by writing a 'Foreword'.

I am further indebted to two of my friends and colleagues of the London Bible College for their help: to the Principal, Rev. E. F. Kevan, M.Th., B.D., for his unfailing interest, and to the Rev. J. C. J. Waite, B.D., for reading through the page proofs.

Grateful acknowledgement is also made to a number of publishers for permission to use copyright material: to the Epworth Press for Edwin Lewis's *A Philosophy of the Christian Revelation* and C. R. North's *The Old Testament Interpretation of History*: to the Lutterworth Press for Auguste Lecerf's *An Introduction to Reformed Dogmatics*; Alan Fairweather's *The Word as Truth*; and Wilhelm Niesel's *The Theology of Calvin*: to the S.C.M. for Emil Brunner's *Revelation and Reason*: to the Princeton University Press, for R. Bretall's *A Kierkegaard Anthology*: to Wm B. Eerdmans for Louis Berkhof's *Systematic Theology* (Introductory Volume, 1932), E. J. Carnell's *A Philosophy of the Christian Religion*, and E. J. Young's *Thy Word is Truth*: to Messrs Faber and Faber for Donald Baillies' *God Was In Christ*; Reinhold Niebuhr's *The Self in the Dramas of History*, and J. V. Langmead Casserley's *The Christian in Philosophy*.

A final word of thanks is due to the publishers for their kind co-operation during the process of publication.

H. D. McDONALD

London Bible College

CONTENTS

CHAPTER   PAGE

I   THE BOUNDARIES OF AN AGE   1
- (i) The Interest of the Age   1
- (ii) The Confines of an Era   4
- (iii) The Change of an Emphasis   6
- (iv) The Contrasts within the Period   14

II   THE MANIFESTATION OF AN ANTITHESIS   17
- (i) The Philosophical Background: Descartes   19
  - (a) Reason and Feeling   21
  - (b) Objective and Subjective   24
  - (c) Inference and Intuition   28
  - (d) Facts and Values   30
- (ii) The Religio-Philosophical Background: The Cambridge Platonists   31

III   THE SUPREMACY OF THE RATIONAL   35
Revelation as Infallible Reason
The Deistic Dogmatism   36
- (i) A Summary of the View   36
  - (a) Reasonableness of Christianity — Locke   41
  - (b) Christianity not Mysterious — Toland   43
  - (c) Christianity as Old as Creation — Tindal 47
- (ii) A Criticism of the View   51

IV   THE AUTHORITY OF THE SUBJECTIVE   63
Revelation as Indwelling Light   63
- (i) An Understanding of the View   63
- (ii) The Weaknesses of the View   69

V   THE THESIS OF THE ORTHODOX   75
Revelation as Communicated Extras   76
- (i) The Basis of Revealed Religion   77
- (ii) The Need for Revealed Religion   89
- (iii) The Proofs of Revealed Religion   96

VI THE CHANGE OF AN EMPHASIS   117
   Revelation as a Body of Revealed Doctrines   120
     (i) The New Enemies   121
     (ii) Contrast with the Earlier Polemic   125
     (iii) The Bampton Lectures and the Biblical Revelation   129
     (iv) General Literature and the Biblical Revelation   140

VII THE FOCUS ON THE INWARD   149
   Revelation in the Immediacy of Experience   149
     (i) The Background of Idealism — Berkeley   151
     (ii) The Rejection of Reason — Dodwell   154
     (iii) The Immanence of the Eternal Christ — Law   158
     (iv) The Apostle of the Christian Consciousness — Erskine   162
     (v) The Supremacy of the Subjective — Coleridge   171
     (vi) The Victory of Faith — Hare   179
     (vii) The Meaning of Revelation — Maurice   181

VIII THE TEACHING OF THE EVANGELICALS   195
   Revelation in the Word through the Spirit   195
     (i) The Background of their View   195
       (a) The View-point of the Puritans   196
       (b) The Work of the Westminster Divines   205
       (c) The Position of the Reformers   206
       (d) A Statement on the Evangelicals   212
     (ii) The Exponent of their View   213
     Charles Simeon
       (a) Natural Religion   215
       (b) Reason — Natural and Enlightened   219
       (c) Revelation and the Scriptures   224
       (d) The Scriptures and the Spirit   233

IX THE DOCTRINE OF A LEADER   245
   John Wesley
   Revelation by the Spirit and through the Word   245
     (i) The Source of Wesley's Faith   245

(ii) The Statement of Wesley's Teaching   246
      (a) Reason and Revelation   246
      (b) Revelation and Scripture   255
      (c) Scripture and the Spirit   259

X THE NEED FOR A UNIFICATION   266
   (i)   The Objective and Subjective   266
   (ii)   The Mediate and the Immediate   270
   (iii) The Scriptures and the Spirit   273
   (iv)   The Words and the Word   276

   CONCLUSION   283

   ALPHABETICAL LIST OF BOOKS MENTIONED   289

   ALPHABETICAL INDEX TO WESLEY'S WORKS QUOTED   299

CHAPTER I

THE BOUNDARIES OF AN AGE

The purpose of the following pages is to single out various views of revelation which came to the fore within the period of history from 1700 to 1860. In addition, an endeavour will be made to find a starting point, and to trace out the developments of each separate doctrine.

Questions concerning how and why and where God has revealed Himself must ever be of fundamental importance. Yet, as the student of historical theology will have observed, the problems raised by the idea of a disclosure of God were not early discussed. Centuries of theological debate, created by other needs, were to pass before attention was focused upon the subject of revelation as such.[1] It is living issues, after all, which call for immediate investigation. Abstract problems, unrelated to pressing needs, do not claim the attention of the generality of men. In the history of Christian doctrine it has been the urgent problems which have claimed the concern of the Church at large. Theological debate has sprung out of the necessities of experience or been entered upon to meet a challenge to the faith.

(i) *The Interest of the Age*

In the post-apostolic period problems specifically theological became central. Questions concerning the relation of the one God to the world and of Christ to the one God had to be solved. Following from and arising out of these discussions were the great Christological controversies which for many years agitated the Church. Attention was here fixed upon the inner nature of Christ's Person. In the process of these debates the Church elaborated its creeds and fenced itself off from those anathematized as heretics. The ecclesiastical and hierarchical system developed as a result.

---

[1] The discussion by Irenaeus on the subject of Inspiration may be quoted as an exception. But an exception to the general truth stated above it most certainly was.

Ecclesiology was therefore the dominant interest of the mediaeval period. The Church regarded as the gift of God and the guardian of truth claimed to be the arbiter in the affairs of the soul. The Church was believed to be a divine institution in which alone men and women could be guaranteed eternal life. This conception taking priority and pre-eminence, was defended with all the weapons of warfare, legitimate and illegitimate, spiritual and carnal. Both intellect and instrument were called upon to maintain the autocracy of the papacy believed to be established by divine decree.

This notion was, however, soon to be dispelled. An interest, at once spiritual and personal, was to turn men's attention from the institution to the individual. The whole stately edifice of ecclesiasticism which had been built up by tools provided by Aristotle was shattered by the dynamic discovery of Luther. Now became central the soteriological question concerning the significance and sufficiency of Christ's work and the right of each man to stand alone, *coram Deo*, and secure the saving benefits of the only Redeemer. How can a man be just before God? such was the pressing issue of the period. The answer of the Reformation was that a man is declared righteous by faith.[1] And this answer, vindicated in the actuality of experience, was believed to be validated in the writings of the New Testament.

From the question of justification by faith, circumstances, particularly in England, were to force upon men another interest. From the problem of personal salvation attention was turned to the problem of divine revelation. The Deists of the early eighteenth century refused to allow that God had given any special message to man beyond those indications of Himself set upon the original creation. It was, therefore, the denials of the Deists which raised the issue. 'Books on evidences had been written before this time, but it is to the rise of the Deists that we owe nearly the whole of our evidence literature.'[2]

Difficulties of a new kind were being raised. The intellectual atmosphere at the turn of the eighteenth century called for a fresh

[1] It must, of course, be allowed that the problem which became a personal one for Luther was an inevitable one arising out of the prevailing Zeitgeist. Harnack has a discussion on how far Luther's significance is rightly to be understood as a rediscovery of the Pauline doctrine of justification by faith. A. Harnack, *History of Dogma*, vol. 7, p. 206 f.
[2] J. Hunt, *Religious Thought in England* (1873), vol. 3, p. 97.

type of literature. It was the realization of this that made Robert Boyle found his lectureship and so anticipate the problems which the discoveries of the Royal Society might raise.

The first of the Boyle Lectures was delivered in 1692 by Richard Bentley under the title, *The Folly of Atheism and Deism even with respect of the Present Life.* Thus was begun that extensive literature for which the period is noted, all dealing with evidences of Christianity, or to be more exact, using the title given by the same Bentley to his Boyle Lectures in 1693, *The Christian Revelation.*[1]

The idea of revelation was, therefore, the dominant one of the period. Put generally it may be said that it was the purpose of the orthodox apologists to prove the need for a special revelation to

---

[1] This series of lectures was never published. It is of interest to note how many of the Boyle Lectures (or Sermons) for the first half of the eighteenth century treat of the subject of Revelation. In 1699 the preacher was Dr Samuel Bradford, later Bishop of Carlisle, and then of Rochester. He discoursed on *The Credibility of the Christian Revelation from its Internal Evidences.* His approach was that God authenticates His revelation to all who are in the right attitude to receive it. The one who is willing shall know of the doctrine. He shall be taught of the Father. This knowledge of the Father comes by 'studying the works of creation, by the suggestion of conscience, and by the inward teaching of the Divine Spirit'. Bradford goes on then to expound those doctrines of Christianity involved in the knowledge of the Father.

In 1700, Blacknell, afterwards Bishop of Exeter, was the lecturer. His first sermon on Luke 16. 30, 31, entitled, *The Sufficiency of a Standing Revelation,* appears to cover the whole series. Blacknell argues that the Scriptures are that 'Standing Revelation', and that the authority and genuineness of its several books are sufficiently established. So complete is the evidence that it is 'an unreasonable request to ask for more'. In 1710 Dr Josiah Woodward preached on *The Divine Original and Incomparable Excellency of the Christian Revelation.* His argument is that Christianity must be true because it is founded upon Scripture and the Scripture must be true because it is God's Word. The general tone of the lectures had already been set in 1705 by Dr Samuel Clarke who followed his series of the previous year with the subject, *The Unchangeable Obligation of Natural Religion and the Truth and Certainty of the Christian Revelation.*

William Denham's *Physico-Theology* (1711) and (1712) also bears upon the subject. So also does Benjamin Ibbot's *Free Thinking* of the years 1713 and 1714. It is indeed Ibbot's purpose to maintain the reality and sufficiency of the Christian revelation. Dr John Leng, who was later to become Bishop of Norwich, explicated the *Natural Obligation to believe the Principles of Religion and Divine Revelation* in 1717 and 1718. In 1721 and 1722 Brampton Gurdon dealt with *The Pretended Difficulties in Natural Religion no excuse for Infidelity.* Dr Burnet's subject for 1724/5 was *The Demonstration of True Religion.* William Berriman took the years 1730, 1731, 1732 to explain the sufficiency of *The Gradual Revelation of the Gospel for the time of Men's Apostasy.* In the lectures of 1739, 1740, 1741 Dr Leonard Twells spoke about miracles and prophecy. Henry Stebbing sought in the years 1747, 1748, 1749 to rout the Deists. His title was *Christianity Justified upon the Scripture Foundation, being a Summary View of the Controversy between Christians and Deists.* After the half-century had passed the Boyle Lectures seemed to excite little attention. During the next fifty years six of the lecturers only put their work in print.

those who questioned it, as it was the desire of those, who for want of a better designation may be called the Evangelicals, to show the sufficiency of it to those who sought it.

Had the two, however, worked together head and heart might have been satisfied. But trouble arose because those who essayed to meet the enquiries of the mind did not always remember that man was more than mind. On the other hand, those who endeavoured to bring the saving revelation to the heart were inclined to forget that man had a head as well as a heart.

In this way the protagonists of each view were at odds. Opposing doctrines were brought into conflict. And on each side there were those ready to press the idea accepted by this group or that to its logical conclusion. Some fell naturally into a position of compromise. The consequence was that a variety of views can be disentangled from the literature of the period each giving a different understanding of the doctrine of revelation.

The period, then, is characterized by a deep interest in the subject of revelation. This indeed is its distinctive feature.

Yet certain as this fact seems to be, there has been no serious attempt, as far as we can discover, to trace out the various views of revelation which came into prominence at the time. Certain aspects of the period are, of course, well known, and brief summaries of the general concepts can be found. On the whole, however, specific note has not been taken of the ideas with which we are concerned. Histories of Christian Doctrine pay scant attention of the views of revelation which characterized the era.[1]

(ii) *The Confines of an Era*

It is regarded as a truism to-day that there are no breaks in history; that the past is not isolated from the present, and that the present is creative of the future. This being so there will be, necessarily, a certain artificiality about all suggested divisions of history. For the convenience of study, however, there must be a cleaving of the centuries into periods. Yet each era must reveal its own special characteristics. At the same time, it must be observed, that the views which become dominant in any one period

---

[1] Harnack's *History of Dogma* ends at the Reformation. The works of Dorner and Hagenback are mainly concerned with German theology. Fisher's, *History of Christian Doctrine* passes lightly over the period. Something of more detail, but not from the point of view that we have adopted can be found in Hunt's, *Religious Thought in England* (3 vols., 1873).

are those very tendencies which stirred in the underground of that which precedes. It is these creative undertones, understood by men of deep insight, which indicate the pattern of the dawning era.

It has been observed, however, that from the point of view of Christian doctrine history can be divided according to the prevailing theological interest: and the interest of our period was certainly focused on the problems of revelation. But these very questions were themselves raised by the deistic claim that reason was of itself sufficient and that no special word from God was needed. It was in this way that the deists initiated the period known in history as 'the Age of Reason'.

It is usual to place its start at the beginning of the eighteenth century and the whole of that century is then generally so designated. The Bampton Lectures of the year 1805, given by Edward Nares, Rector of Biddenden, Kent, were published under the title, *A View of the Evidences of Christianity at the Close of the Pretended Age of Reason*. Nares considered himself to be placed at the end of an epoc, an era which 'has ostentatiously indeed been denominated the Age of Reason'.[1] Throughout the previous years, the Christian revelation, he asserts, has been assailed with every weapon which reason could rally to the battle, 'the heavy artillery of learning and criticism, as well as the lighter weapons of wit and ridicule have been repeatedly brought into the field.'[2]

Although Nares places himself at the end of the Age of Reason and thus marks the beginning of the nineteenth century as that end, for the purpose of our investigation it is extended down to 1860, for the reason that discussion concerning revelation was still to the fore. However might be the reactions to rationalism in the first half of the nineteenth century, the period can still broadly be referred to as the *Saeculum Rationalisticum*. We thus find Herbert Spencer in the middle of the century becoming enthusiastic in denouncing reason's tyranny. 'Reasoning', he says, 'has come to excite an amount of faith greatly in excess of that which is its due.' There has arisen, 'an awe of Reason which betrays many into the error of supposing its range unlimited'. 'By extinguishing other superstitions,' he adds, 'Reason makes itself the final object of superstition.'[3]

---

[1] Edward Nares, *A View of the Evidences of Christianity, etc.*, p. 17.
[2] Op. cit., p. 11.
[3] *Principles of Psychology*, pt. vii, ch. 2.

Yet it must be acknowledged that there were, particularly in England in the second half of our period, other influences which were challenging the dominant rationalism. Coleridge's insistence on a more spiritual philosophy, for example, was a vigorous protest against the sufficiency of mere reason: as was the Christian idealism of F. D. Maurice. This philosophy of opposition was itself bound to create its own understanding of revelation.

There were other influences, too, which were calling in question the omnipotence of reason. In the realm of a more theoretic philosophy the ideas of Kant were being understood. Kant's significance for theology was to put God outside the range of reason. In his book, *The Critique of Pure Reason*, Kant reduced to impotence the whole array of theistic proofs, and there as 'a grim, inexorable iconoclast', as Heine expresses it, he left men with no reasoned God at all. He then, however, in his *Critique of Practical Reason*, endeavours to find an argument for the existence of God based upon man's moral need. He thus 'as with a magic wand, revives the corpse of deism which theoretic reason has slain'.

While Kant thus emphasized the limitation of knowledge to the phenomenal, Sir William Hamilton insisted upon its relativity. Neither philosopher, it is true, sought to weaken belief in God, but rather to put such belief on a foundation that lay outside the power of reason to undermine. Yet the conclusion of each philosophy was the creation of a new agnosticism: it is to express and confess with Tennyson,

> '*We have but faith: we cannot know;*
> *For knowledge is of things we see.*'

(iii) *The Change of an Emphasis*

The middle of the nineteenth century has been noted as marking a new stage in theological discussion, and this fact makes more explicit the reason why the date 1860 has been chosen as the close of a period.[1] It is distinctly the start of the modern scientific age which initiated the conflict between religion and science. Here indeed lies the contrast between the two periods. The former was concerned with specific problems of a special revelation, while the latter was concerned with the serious question whether there was

---

[1] Cf., V. Storr, *The Development of English Theology in the Nineteenth Century from 1800 to 1860*, and L. E. Elliot-Binns' *English Thought*, 1850–1900.

any revelation at all. Two influences brought about this change which threw into such sharp contrast the two periods.

1. The Influence of Darwin

In 1859 Darwin's *Origin of Species* made its appearance. As gradually the implications of the work became evident, it was seen that theology was being forced out of its isolation, and that it could no longer maintain a divorce between sacred and secular knowledge. The view was taken that the new apologetic, unlike the old, cannot be concerned with such items as the reasonableness, the content and the sources of a special revelation *per se*. A challenge had been issued to the very existence of theistic belief itself. Whereas the earlier apologetic made it its task to prove the necessity and value of a special revelation to those who believed that God need not and could not make any such, it was the task of the newer to indicate the evidences for an actual God Who could reveal Himself to those who believed that there was nothing above, beyond or other than the system of nature which alone is self-evident and self-explanatory.

However true it may be that Darwin's work was the climax of a movement, it certainly is to be marked as the commencement of an era.[1] Reinforced by the philosophies of Comte, Bain and Spencer, and by the researches of Tyndall and Huxley, and by the historical studies of Buckle and Taine, the movement reached its dogmatic position and took up a hostile attitude to theology. From now on the battle between science and religion was joined, and the next few decades saw it waged with not a little fury on each side.

The theory of Darwin was eagerly grasped as providing unbelief with its decisive weapon. 'The plain truth is', declares Wildon Carr with evident enthusiasm, 'that the evolution theory has antiquated all theodicies.'[2] Intoxicated with its early success the new view confidently announced mechanism, not merely as a scientific method, but as a body of doctrine adequate to explain the whole universe. Banished now were all notions of teleology and axiology. The whole domain of life was subjected to the rigor of mechanism and the hypothesis of vitalism which had been allowed in the early

[1] Cf., 'Doubtless the greatest dissolvent of contemporary thought of old customs, the greatest precipitant of new methods, new inventions, new problems, is the one effected by the scientific revolution that found its climax in the *Origin of Species*.' J. Dewey, *The Influence of Darwin on Philosophy*, p. 19.
[2] *The Changing Background of Religion and Ethics*, p. 75.

years of the century as necessary to account for the behaviour of living organisms was abandoned.

'The scientific interpretation of natural phenomena', declares Wildon Carr again, 'has made the interest of God more remote, God's existence more problematical, and the idea of God unnecessary. Mathematics and physics are making it increasingly difficult to assign a place for God in our co-ordinations and constructions of the universe, and the necessity of positing a first cause or of conceiving a designer, a necessity which seemed *prima facie* obvious to a pre-scientific generation, does not exist for us.'[1] This certainly was what many of those who lived in the immediate post-Darwin period believed.

Darwin, then, initiated a new climate of opinion. His doctrine was eagerly accepted.[2] Anyone rash enough to call this thesis in question was brushed aside as *impos animi*, or, as a man *hors de saison*. His notion of natural selection was held to play havoc with the spiritualistic understanding of the world. Natural theology had no possible foundation.[3]

It was, strangely enough, in the year 1859, the year of Darwin's *Origin of Species*, that there appeared the *Political Economy* of Karl Marx. Whereas Darwin was over-awed by the misery in nature, Marx was overwhelmed by the misery in society. Darwin sought to explain the riddle by the principle of the development of organic nature, while Marx proclaimed his famous dialectic of

[1] *The Changing Background of Religion and Ethics*, p. 71.
[2] Cf., Du Bois Reymond's feeling for Darwin's view. He compares it to the feeling of a drowning man to whom a plank was pushed out. 'When', he adds, 'the choice is between a plank and destruction, the advantage is on the side of the plank.' *The Seven Enigmas*, pp. 78, 79.
[3] Cf., Fiske's *Outlines of Cosmic Philosophy*. 'From the dawn of philosophical discussion, Pagan and Christian, Trinitarian and Deist, have appealed with equal confidence to the harmony pervading nature as the surest foundation of their faith in an intelligent and beneficent Ruler of the Universe . . . . One and all . . . they challenge us to explain, on any other hypothesis than that of created design, these manifold harmonies, these exquisite adaptations of means to ends, whereof the world is admitted to be full, and which are equally conspicuous among the phenomena of life. Until the establishment of the Doctrine of Evolution, the glove thus thrown, age after age, into the arena of Philosophical controversy was never triumphantly taken up. It was Mr Darwin first, by his discovery of natural selection, supplied the champions of science with the resistless weapons by which to vanquish, in this their chief stronghold, the champions of theology. . . . It needs but to take into account the other agencies in the organic evolution besides the one so admirably illustrated by Mr Darwin, it needs but to remember that life is essentially a process of equalibration, both direct and indirect, in order to be convinced that the Doctrine of Evolution has once and for all deprived natural theology of the materials upon which until lately it subsisted.' Op. cit., vol. 2, pp. 366–9.

history and announced his doctrine of the evolution of human society. The concurrence of these two works was dramatic. The immediate disciples of Darwin believed that the new empirico-scientific world-view had banished for ever all notions of deity, purpose and miracles. Marx and his adherents considered themselves to have discovered the key to inevitable social progress and to have swept aside the theological superstititions of basic social moralities. Gone for ever, it was announced, was the old dualistic notion of two orders of existence, a natural and a supernatural. In such a context there was no place for another world; no existent and active God. Any idea of revelation was, therefore, sheer illusion. Nature was all and there was nothing else. Renan thus states it to be a fact that none could dare be temerarious enough to deny, 'Il n'y a pas de supernatural.'

From the middle of the nineteenth century there was, therefore, a totally different view of the world, which is characteristically modern. This Weltanschauung is essentially antisupernaturalistic. The religious interpretation of the world had given place to the scientific. A. M. Fairbairn spoke of this Zeitgeist as a 'heathen revival'.[1] He does not use the term as one of reproach but as an endeavour to indicate its main feature. 'Its characteristic is naturalism, the expulsion from thought, not merely of the supernatural, but of the ideal, of the transcendental and spiritual, and a return to a nature sensuously interpreted. This naturalism is so marked as to constitute the differentiating element of our intellectual movement. The thought of the Christian centuries, even where it has been least Christian, has still been penetrated by the ideal and theistic elements. Theism has been, as it were, its common basis.'[2] The Renaissance indeed was a classical not a pagan revival. Even deism, although it moved away from Christ, did not discard God. By relieving Him of the care of the universe it gave Him little to do. Still God was necessary for thought, and reward for keeping His laws essential for the life of reasonable religion.

The concept of evolution as such was not, of course, new. Hobbes, Voltaire, Rousseau and Kant, to mention but a few, had already taught that man arose out of a prior animal state. But with these thinkers the notion was philosophical, and, as such, did not

[1] *Studies in Theology and Religion*, p. 80.
[2] Ibid.

make any great impact upon general thought. Darwin, on the other hand, was believed to have given to the speculative ideas of the philosophers a basis in scientific fact. From now on it was hailed as the only scientific account of the world and consequently naturalism was the apparent logical conclusion. There therefore arose a host of writers who conceived it to be their special prerogative to show how impossible it was to believe in any God or any revelation at all. The progress of science, it was declared, had rendered all such beliefs invalid, since, as T. H. Huxley contended in his *Lecture on the Physical Basis of Life*, 'the extension of the province of what is called matter and causation' means 'the concomitant gradual banishment from the region of human thought of what is called spirit and spontaneity'. So great a difference then did Darwin make in the interpretation of the world, that whereas the advocates of essential Christianity between the years 1700 and the middle of the nineteenth century were concerned to show that God had given a special word, those who followed had to prove that He was there to speak any word. This means that the earlier writers considered it their business to maintain the value of a special revelation. With the later apologists interest turned to the vindication of the reality of a general revelation.

2. The Introduction of the Historical Method

Just as Darwin was thought to have given to evolution a basis in scientific fact, so the introduction of the so-called historical method was held to justify the criticisms which the deists maintained against the Bible.[1] The deists, observes Professor Norman Sykes, 'hit upon some of the agreed conclusions of the higher critics of the nineteenth century.' Yet they did so 'by chance rather than by scientific research'.[2]

---

[1] Collins maintained that the religion of Israel was a combination of Egyptian and Chaldean theologies. He dated the book of Daniel in the Maccabean period and considered the greater portion of the Old Testament to be a reconstruction by the scribe Ezra. Toland anticipated the Tübingen School of Baur by proclaiming that there were in the early Church, two parties, the Ebionites or Judaizers, and the liberal party of Paul, which somehow became fused into a unity. On the Continent, Lessing turned attention to the New Testament. In a posthumous work, entitled, *A New Hypothesis concerning the Evangelists regarded merely as Human Writers* (1788), he raised the question of the origin of the Gospels; his critical work was carried on by Herder and Reimarus. Reimarus is referred to by A. M. Fairbairn as the last representative of the 'dying Deism'.
[2] N. Sykes, *The English Religious Tradition*, p. 61.

It was because the criticism of the Bible was associated with deism that the conclusions of Bishop Colenso were greeted with such antagonism, although his views, in comparison with later critical writers were modest indeed. The Church felt bound, in the earlier period, to reject the valuation of the Scriptures associated with deistic scepticism. It was only in the second half of the nineteenth century, and especially after the publication of the *Essays and Reviews* in the year 1860, that the opinions which the deists expressed gained a firm foothold in the Church itself.

It is, of course, true that the beginnings of historicism are to be found prior to the middle of the nineteenth century. This understanding of history as something dynamic, was itself a reaction from the account of it as artificial and sterile which had earlier prevailed. The earlier writers were indeed completely indifferent to the significance of history. Their view was merely the prolongation of the Enlightenment's repudiation of the historical in the interests of the rational.

An impetus towards this newer appreciation may be found in Leibniz's exposition of the law of continuity in the theory he set forth of the gradation of the monads. 'Nature', he declared, 'never makes leaps.'[1] The whole universe is to be viewed as a living thing 'like a garden full of plants and like a pond full of fish'.[2] There is therefore nothing sterile or static in the universe. There is the appearance of chaos and confusion, but appearance only.

But of the individual monads which make up the totality of existences, each is complete in itself, occupying itself with itself alone. Each is *Einmalige* (singular). 'The monads', he writes in an euphistic manner, 'have no windows through which anything may come in and go out.'[3] At the same time the whole army of monads cannot exist without contact. They are therefore brought into union by his principle of pre-existing harmony.

In Leibniz, then, two principles, namely that of continuity and that of connection are seen. By Lessing these twin fundamental ideas were taken as providing the key to the understanding of history. Lessing brought into being 'a deeper sense of the meaning of the historical'.[4] In his *Education of the Human Race* a break is made with the Enlightenment. The rationalist, it has been

---

[1] *The Monodology*, tr. R. Latta, p. 376.
[2] *Discourse on Metaphysics*, tr. G. R. Mackintosh, p. 266.
[3] *The Monodology*, p. 219, cf., *Discourse on Metaphysics*, p. 252.
[4] A. K. Rogers, *A Students' History of Philosophy*, p. 410.

observed, could not find any middle ground between the truth of a religion based upon reason alone, and its falsity, and therefore its beginning in fraud and priestcraft. Lessing refused to accept the antithesis. For him absolute truth was outside the range of man's ability: but so, too, was absolute falsity an impossibility. This meant for Lessing that God sought to educate men by a progressive revelation, moving from the less adequate to the more effective. God was not, therefore, outside the world in solitary isolation. He is within the movement of history and the events of experience, as the immanent God, energizing and unifying. With Lessing the emphasis which Spinoza had earlier given to the immanence of God as ἕν καί πᾶν, and which failed of immediate influence, was now made effective. Even Lessing in his famous dictum that 'Accidental truths of history can never yield proof of necessary truths of reason', far from denying the cogency of history, was actually seeking, as Karl Barth has shown, to evaluate its true significance.[1]

This understanding of history was extended by Herder. Not only, as in Lessing, was the concept of development to be applied to religion, but all life grows and develops. Thus we find Herder turning his attention to the folk origins of national cultures. It was in this way that the Leibnizean hypothesis of external connection was exchanged for an inner principle of development.

Together, the notion of connection and continuity were to change the whole understanding of history. All life began to be regarded as the unfolding of the one divine ζωή. History is all of a piece. No single event stands apart from the rest. No hiatuses are to be observed, since past and present are bound together in a living union. History reveals, it was claimed, an evident development, a process from a lower to a richer and fuller life.

By such ideas theology was necessarily influenced. The clear-cut distinction between natural and revealed religion was now abandoned. This meant that no single people and no special history

---

[1] Cf., *Die protestantische Theologie im 19 Jahrundert*, p. 209 ff. See also, *Church Dogmatics*, vol. 1, i, p. 166. 'Lessing recognizes perfectly well a proof of Christianity by history.' But it must be 'the proof of the Spirit and power'; i.e., history proves us no truth, so long as it is 'accidental truth of history', truth merely told us by others but not as such 'felt' and 'experienced' as such by us, experienced in the way the 'paralytic feels the beneficent shock of the electric spark'. 'Religion is not true because the evangelists and apostles taught it, but they taught it because it is true. By its inner truth must Scriptural traditions be explained, and all the Scriptural traditions in the world cannot give it inner truth if it does not possess it,' op cit., ad loc.

could be claimed as the specific sphere of the divine activity. All religions developed from one common origin. There were cruder religious ideas suited to the underdeveloped state of the religious instinct. But, as the *sensus numinis* grew, so too did religion; from the natural to the spiritual, from the tribal to the universal. In all religious groups the one true religion finds expression more or less.

It is in this context that Kant is to be found refusing to set Christianity over against other religions as the only true one. He distinguishes between the various religious creeds and religion *per se* in a manner characteristic of the earlier Lessing. 'There is', writes Kant, 'only *one* true religion, but there can be many varieties of religious creeds . . . . It is, therefore, more appropriate to say: this man is of the Jewish, Mohammedan, Christian creed, than he is of this or that religion.'[1]

It is against the background of such views of the divine immanence that we will have occasion later to refer to the understanding of revelation by men like Coleridge and Maurice.

With Hegel the new historical sense adumbrated by Leibniz and advanced in Lessing found its most thorough philosophical expression. Here the concept of development was raised to provide the key to the riddle of existence. Man was conceived to be but a part of the one divine life, a temporary manifestation of the one divine spirit. In this context all was supernatural because everything is but a transitory expression of the Eternal Absolute. To such a conclusion was the historical method driven under the influence of an idealistic philosophy.

A new twist was given to historicism after the middle of the nineteenth century. The principle of continuity was now reinforced by the Darwinian biological theory. Historical occurrences must be conceived consequently as the outcome of mechanical processes. All life can be explained as the product of natural laws. Thus some writers sought for the creative causes of historical events in man's physical environment, and endeavoured to base history upon anthropogeography. Others looked to the social environment for an explanation. Spencer, Comte and a host of like-minded writers conceived of society as somehow itself a higher organism which, like other living things, is subject to biological laws and will

[1] *Religion within the Bounds of Pure Reason*, p. 108. Cf., 'The distinction between natural and revealed religion is impossible . . . Christianity is not the one religion, the only one, but simply the most complete species of the genus', W. Bousset, *What is Religion?*, pp. 8, 9.

eventually come to perfection in the struggle for existence by natural selection and heredity. Consequently, whereas for the earlier idealism all was supernatural, for the new materialism all was natural.

(iv) *The Contrasts within the Period*

The discussions of the previous section will have revealed that the age under consideration was dominated by two main influences, the deistic and the idealistic. In the earlier period there was the deistic emphasis upon the remoteness of God, while the later part, in which idealism was in the ascendancy, accent was on the nearness of God. This means that the first was generally rationalistic and the second broadly mystical. The contrast is not, of course, absolute, as will be seen later, since, as always, however sharply it may be drawn, there is still the tendency for an opposition quickly to appear.[1] A comparison between Clarke and Coleridge will confirm the general truth of this statement.

Objectivity and abstraction are, then, the characteristics of the first half of the eighteenth century. Operating with Aristotelian categories of thought, the reasoning by which its theology was maintained was discursive. God was detached from the individual consciousness and viewed as a mere transcendent Object. He was removed beyond the bounds of the universe. He was to be sought, not in the depths of man's consciousness, but in the heights beyond man's vision. God, in this conception, is the Altogether Other; the great Exception not the close Example. The divine was so separated from the human in the rational theology of the time, that there was no God near enough to be worshipped. There were abstract conceptions of Him conjured out of its own grandiose dialectic. God was consequently objectified, externalized and intellectualized. The result was that the theology of the period was the product of a sort of conceptual self-hypnosis.

On the other hand, and by contrast, the sort of view that developed as a reaction was a type of philosophical mysticism. Here God was sought, not above but below, not without but within. He

[1] Cf., 'It is no accident that in the *saeculum rationalisticum* the heyday of Deism and of the Wolfian philosophy saw the rise of a series of strongly emotional religious movements, of Pietism, Moravianism, Methodism in Protestant Europe, and in Catholic Europe of the devotion (presenting marked affinities with these) of the Sacred Heart; while, outside the Churches, close upon the heels of Voltaire there came Rousseau.' C. C. J. Webb, *Problems in the Relations of God and Man*, p. 73.

was not detached from the human consciousness. He is the Eternal Subject, occupying the innermost shrine of man's spirit to be discovered by an intuitive awareness. Emphasis is here placed upon the 'kinship' between man and God; upon the divinity of man and the humanity of God.

The rational theologians tended towards the mechanical. The order in the objective world was made the basis of the large quota of religious knowledge to be gained from general revelation. While the Church, as heir to the special revelation made to the Jews, was conceived to be the custodian of those extra doctrines which were to be believed. Thus faith was regarded as intellectual assent to the revelation, objective as a concept and stereotyped into a dogma, which were to be accepted as of binding authority.

For men like Coleridge and Maurice, on the other hand, the external was rejected as a tyranny. Man's own spirit was the sphere of the divine operation, and faith was a coming to the awareness that in the depths of his soul man is akin to God. This discovery of God within one's own being, is revelation: this is the ultimate authority for the individual man.

Some writers would characterize Eastern theology as mystical and the Western as rationalistic. The East followed the lines of the Platonic thought and tended to emphasize the inward.[1] The West, on the other hand, more influenced by Aristotle, was inclined to accentuate the objective. There is, of course, some justification for this wide generalization, but it is so general as to have no real value. The truth is that in Western theology itself there is the same tendency, at one time to stress the objective, and at another time the subjective. This fact can be illustrated by the doctrines of the atonement which can be, and, indeed, have been divided into objective and subjective views.

The relationship between subject and object is an issue of fundamental importance. Whenever the correct balance between the two is upset some element of the full truth must be lost. This observation holds good in all realms of knowledge, and theology is not an exception.

---

[1] Cf. Berdyaev's rejection of 'creationism' and acceptance of Origen's 'pre-existence' doctrine. 'The traditional opinion, according to which each human soul is created by God at the moment of physical conception, is such a lamentable one that we need not stop to consider it . . . . The pre-existence of the soul (sc. spirit) in the spiritual world is an indispensible truth, for the soul (sc. spirit) is, not the child of time but of eternity.' N. Berdyaev, *Freedom and the Spirit*, p. 326.

'Theology is certainly a human enquiry, whether or not it be more, whatever its assurance of a more than human reference and validity in the objects with which it deals or the methods by which it deals with them. It is to be expected, therefore, that theology, too, will share in that error which is common to humanity, and that sometimes such error will be the result of a disproportion of the subjective and objective factors in its special kind of knowledge.'[1]

[1] James Brown, *Subject and Object in Modern Theology* (The Croall Lectures given in the University of Edinburgh, 1955), p. 12.

CHAPTER II

THE MANIFESTATION OF
AN ANTITHESIS

The period, then, which has been marked out reveals, in the main, two sharply opposed views of revelation. These may be described, broadly, as objective and subjective.

It was against the background of deism that the first view was elaborated, and it is in this context it must be understood. It was essentially a rationalistic doctrine of revelation basing itself upon the Aristotelian principle of the sufficiency of reason. It demanded assent to certain doctrinal propositions. As a theory of revelation, it was psychologically unsound because it failed to take account of the other constituents of man's psychical nature. As a polemic against deism the orthodox arguments became nugatory. The battle waged against the deistic opponents, indeed, could never be decisive for the origin and weapons of both were the same. Each was the product of that estimate of the natural man characteristic of the Enlightenment with its fundamental principle of 'sound common sense'. So closely akin, in this respect, were the deists and their opponents, that the former could refer to Archbishop Tillotson as their spiritual father. On the fly-leaf of Toland's, *Christianity not Mysterious*, there is a quotation from the Archbishop which serves as a text for all that follows. Tindal has some fourteen extended passages from Tillotson's works in his, *Christianity as Old as Creation*. In one place he refers to the renowned ecclesiastic as 'the incomparable Tillotson'.[1] Anthony Collins, likewise contends that Tillotson is the one 'whom all English free-thinkers own as their head'.[2] On the other hand the general position of Tillotson is the same as that adopted by the orthodox in the next century.

This fact means that each side was hindered from dealing a decisive blow on the other. It is for this reason that the arguments of the orthodox apologists were for the most part nullified, and the

[1] *Christianity as Old as Creation* (3rd edition), p. 197.
[2] *Discourse of Freethinking*, p. 171.

battles which they waged against the deists, in their defence of revealed religion were so much 'sound and fury, signifying nothing'.

It was inevitable that the era should give birth to a doctrine of protest. The inevitable reaction soon set in. There thus developed, in opposition, a doctrine of revelation which sought its origin and authority within each individual soul. Attention was directed to the inner life of man. It was consequently an understanding of revelation as something subjective in contrast with the objective view of the anti-deistic apologists. Here we have an idea of revelation as something based upon the inner experience of the individual. Whereas the objective doctrine has affinities with Aristotle, this view is more akin to Socrates.

There are broadly two movements in philosophical thought running through history which may be called the Aristotelian and the Socratic. The first of these was more concerned with the external world. It began with physical facts and based its inferences by way of abstraction upon the data they provide. Much was made of the logic of analogy. This was the view which dominated Mediaevalism and found a supreme advocate in Aquinas. The orthodox apologists were in line with this conception. They consequently made much of external proofs and were more concerned with propositions than with persons; more interested in the niceties of exact logic than in the necessities of human lives.

Socrates, on the other hand, gave attention to the individual, to the truth already held. He began with self-consciousness. The second view of revelation which took its rise as a doctrine of protest is in line with this philosophic emphasis. It would find its certainty, neither as a formal result of the principle of analogy nor as a conclusion to a chain of syllogistic reasoning, but as a fact already given in self-conscious experience. It was therefore argued that the array of proofs so carefully marshalled by the writers on 'evidences' can bring no assurance to the doubting mind. There is in the obscure retreat of the human heart an *aliquid inconcussum*, an unshaken somewhat, independent of and undisturbed by the finest and fiercest intellectual arguments. The attitude of those who advocated this view is well expressed in a letter by Principal John Cairns to George Gilfillan in 1849. Gilfillan had written expressing the wish for some great minds to appear to confound the arrogant pretences to knowledge claimed by unbelievers.

Cairns replies: 'I cannot share your longing for intellectual giants to confound the Goliaths of scepticism — not that I do not think such persons useful in their way, — but because I think Christianity far more impressive as a life than a speculation, and the West Port evangelism of Dr Chalmers far more effective than his Astronomical Discourses.'[1] Cairns allows that such apologists are 'useful in their way', but many of those who adopted the view that the orthodox doctrine was sterile and that vital Christianity is a datum or revelation made immediately to a spiritual faculty of the soul were far from granting that it had any value at all. It was the inward assurance of God's immediate presence which provided for these writers the *point d'appui*. Here was a certainty which no metaphysical speculation could injure, for this *aliquid inconcussum* was for them akin to the *Cogito, ergo sum*, of Descartes. Faith bore its own signature and the assurance of its authenticity was within. That this understanding of revelation did justice to the important psychological element of affection is undoubted, thereby correcting an obvious deficiency of the propositional doctrine. But the view thus elaborated is itself, none the less, theoretically and spiritually insufficient.

A reading of the period, then, reveals an antithesis between the objective and subjective estimates of revelation. The doctrine of revelation as a body of divinely mediated truths to which assent was to be given was advanced against the deists and maintained against the 'Enthusiasts'. The idea of revelation within the immediacy of experience gave exclusive emphasis to the subjective side. This doctrine developed as a conscious repudiation of the propositional view. Each suffers, therefore, from the defects of onesidedness.

(i) *The Philosophical Background*
DESCARTES

Put into a more immediate context these opposing views can be seen to derive from the dualism left by, and the antitheses latent in the philosophy of Descartes. When Descartes was, as he tells us, 'shut up in a stove',[2] it was out of that day's meditation there was

---

[1] Professor MacEwen, *Life and Letters of John Cairns*, p. 307, cf., John Cairns, *Principal Cairns*, p. 84.
[2] *The Discourse of Method* (tr. John Veitch), p. 10. Veitch translates the passage '. . . a whole day in seclusion'. A footnote explains, 'in a room heated by means of a stove.' Bertrand Russell (*History of Western Philosophy*, p. 581),

begun a fresh departure in philosophic thought. Repudiating the grand system of doctrine set up on the authority of the Church, Descartes, with no tradition behind him, had to find the starting-point for his philosophical reconstruction 'within himself'. The *Discourse of Method* was the 'trumpet-note for the resurrection of the human mind from the death of formalism'.[1] Descartes says that his 'design was singly to find ground of assurance'.[2] He believed he had found this in what has come to be called the principle of 'Cartesian doubt'. Let all else be considered unreal, the existence of the 'I' which doubts must remain an undisputable fact. 'But immediately upon this I observed that, whilst I thus wished to think that all was false, it was absolutely necessary that I, who thus thought, should be somewhat: and as I observed that this truth, I think, hence I am, was so certain of such evidence, that no ground of doubt, however extravagant, could be alleged by the sceptics capable of shaking it. I concluded that I might, without scruple, accept it as the first principle of the philosophy of which I was in search.'[3]

Descartes gives to the concept of self as a 'thinking thing' a connotation wider than the modern psychological use of the term. A thinking being is one which 'doubts, understands, (conceives), affirms, denies, wills, refuses, that imagines also, and perceives'.[4] It is from this, *Cogito, ergo sum*, that Descartes builds up a new superstructure of knowledge, moving from man to God.

For Descartes there was first of all stress upon 'clear and distinct ideas' as the only justifiable assurance of certainty. Reason, he says, 'is by nature equal in all men.'[5] Thus 'we ought never to allow ourselves to be persuaded of the truth of anything unless on the evidence of our reason, and it must be noted that I say of

comments, 'Descartes says it was a stove (poêle), but most commentators think that this is impossible. Those who know old-fashioned Bavarian houses, however, assure me that this is entirely credible.'

[1] J. P. Mahaffy, *Descartes*, p. 70.

[2] Op. cit., p. 23.

[3] *Discourse of Method*, p. 27.

[4] *Meditations*, p. 89. Cf., *Principles of Knowledge*, 1, 9. 'The ordinary translation of *cogitare*, to think (*denken*) is liable to occasion misunderstanding since *denken* in German (and the same is true of *think*, in English, at least in philosophical terminology) signifies a particular kind of theoretical consciousness. Descartes himself elucidates the meaning of cogitate by enumeration: he understands by it to doubt, affirm, deny, understand, will, abhor, imagine, feel a sensation, etc. For that which is common to all these notions we have in German scarcely any word but *Bewesstein* (consciousness).' W. Windelband, *History of Philosophy*, p. 391.

[5] *Discourse of Method*, p. 3.

reason, and not of our imagination or our senses'.[1] Then, secondly, Descartes makes the individual consciousness the secure beginning of the process of knowledge. An application of this principle of knowledge by doubt, is found in Butler's, *Analogy*. 'The very act of doubting religion', writes Butler, 'implies some evidence for that of which we doubt.'[2]

This double aspect of the Cartesian Philosophy is noted by Hegel, who, however, does not follow through its implications. To Descartes, observes Hegel, 'nothing is true which does not possess an inward evidence in consciousness, or which reason does not recognize so clearly and conclusively that any doubt regarding it is impossible.'[3] These two principles, once stated, soon diverged and became hostile. The necessity for clear and distinct ideas gave rise to the demand for mathematical certainty. On the other hand, by seeking a basis in the individual consciousness there developed a feeling for, what may be called, mystical assurance. Thus it came about that two views which were to influence the understanding of revelation were brought into opposition: an antithesis was set up between reason and feeling, between external and internal, between object and subject, between deductions from the facts of experience and inductions from the realities within experience.

(a) Reason and Feeling

The side of the Cartesian philosophy which bore immediate fruit was the insistence upon the supremacy of reason. Religious truths must be demonstrated after the strictest Euclidean fashion. Windelband declares that, 'it was in this direction that the influence of the Cartesian philosophy proved strongest in the following period. In all the changes of epistemological investigation until far into the eighteenth century, this conception of mathematics was a firmly established axiom of all parties.'[4] Not only upon Continental writers, but, as Professor Mahaffy contends, in no less measure upon English thinkers is the influence of Descartes to be noted: 'the theological arguments of Clarke on the Attributes, and of Butler on the doctrine of the future life, are framed on the model of Descartes.'[5] But apart from these specific instances, the

[1] Op. cit., p. 32.
[2] *Analogy* (New edition), p. 266.
[3] S. W. F. Hegel, *History of Philosophy*, vol. 3, p. 227.
[4] W. Windelband, *History of Philosophy*, p. 395.
[5] J. P. Mahaffy, *Descartes*, pp. 202-3.

whole apologetic of the anti-deistic apologists was dominated by
the idea that the exactitude of the mathematical method should be
applied to metaphysical speculations and theological doctrines. The
object was to construct a train of reasoning so compact that there
should be no flaw in the train. It goes without saying that for the
deists the principle of clear and distinct ideas was absolute. The
rule is: 'whatever is evidently repugnant to clear and distinct Ideas,
or to our common notions is contrary to reason.'[1] In these words
Toland, for example, considers reason to be not only the ultimate
ground of knowledge, but, besides, the only test of certainty.
Tindal, too, makes it 'His grand design to prove, that there neither
hath been, nor possibly can be Revelation at all: And the main
Principle on which he builds is this; That the Light of common
Reason is abundantly sufficient without it'.[2]

There is no need to ransack the literature of the orthodox
apologists to see that the same idea there prevailed. A. A. Sykes
declares it to be his purpose 'to treat of Religion both Natural and
Revealed, as to deduce it from its first Principles, and to show that
they are both strictly Rational'.[3] Later in the same book, he avers
that, 'the Light of Reason is not that uncertain, weak, insufficient,
inconstant thing, that is by some pretended: nor ought it to be
treated as something carnal and dim.'[4] In language no less strong,
Bishop Browne asserts that the orthodox are no whit behind their
opponents, the deists, in 'the use of reason in religion'.[5] Dr Clarke
considers that the doctrines disclosed by special revelation, when
taken together, present a scheme more 'confident and rational . . .
than any of the wisest of the Ancient Philosophers ever did, or
the cunningest of the Modern unbelievers, can invent or con-
trive'.[6]

In the same vein Bishop Butler, although he allows that there
must be in the scheme of Revelation much that the human understanding cannot grasp, will not 'vilify reason', since reason alone
is competent to judge of the credibility and consistency of revelation. Emphasis was thus placed upon the cogency of the theistic

---

[1] J. Toland, *Christianity not Mysterious* (1696), pp. 23–4.
[2] J. Conybeare, *A Defence of Revealed Religion*, pp. 4, 5.
[3] A. A. Sykes, *The Principles and Connection of Natural and Revealed Religion,
Distinctly Stated*, Preface, viii.
[4] Ibid and p. 385.
[5] P. Browne, *Answer to Toland*, p. 120.
[6] *A Discourse Concerning the Unalterable Obligation of Natural Religion, and the
Truth and Certainty of the Christian Religion* (9th edition), p. 370.

proofs and the ability of reason to reach certain conclusions regarding God's existence and attributes.

Turning to the other side of the Cartesian doctrine, namely, the teaching that the basis of certainty is to be found within the individual consciousness, it was inevitable that sooner or later theology would be affected thereby. Descartes asserted that 'nothing is true which has not this inward evidence in consciousness'.[1] Nature itself could only be assured on the grounds of an existent God Who could not deceive; it followed therefore that no argument for God's existence could be based thereon. The proof must rest, not upon things without, but upon things within, upon ideas rising out of the individual consciousness. Here was a change of emphasis, which under the influence of men like Coleridge and Maurice gave impetus to the notion of revelation as the feeling of God's indwelling presence. No longer was appeal to be made to the concinnity of nature but to the immediate consciousness of God native to the individual soul.

Certainly F. D. Maurice realized this creative significance of Berkeley's philosophy. He regarded Berkeley 'as the strongest and honestest thinker among our English metaphysicians' yet, although he 'missed the circumference', 'found the "centre" in the heart.'[2] In his, *Christianity not founded on Argument,* H. Dodwell contends for 'a constant and particular Revelation imparted separately and supernaturally to every individual'.[3] It is a revelation of this nature which alone is effective. It was by a flash of divinely given insight that Peter made the Great Confession. When once it comes there is no need any further for subtle sophistries and conceited casuistries. Here is absolute certainty, not built upon the credit of ancient literature, for each possesses his own contemporary proof. What need now to 'apply to Libraries for a more compotent Information and Discovery'?[4] Each has his own divine literature written upon the tables of his heart, which time cannot destroy, nor change render useless. 'Now,' asks Dodwell, 'what a very different prospect this, and Ground of Security from the empty Notion of mere manuscript Authorities and Paper-Revelations?'[5]

Opposed thus were two views of revelation each of which could

---

[1] S. W. F. Hegel, *History of Philosophy,* vol. 3, p. 232.
[2] *Life of F. D. Maurice* (by his Son), vol. 1, pp. 82, 83.
[3] *Christianity not founded on Argument,* p. 58.
[4] Op. cit., pp. 59, 70.
[5] Op. cit., p. 60.

find its source in Descartes: the one basing itself upon reason and the other on feeling.

(b) Objective and Subjective

By his sharp distinction between extension and thought, Descartes accentuated an antithesis between the object and the subject. As a result 'in its quest for truth the seventeenth century discovered two main kinds of certainty, one objective and external, the other subjective and internal'.[1] With Descartes, then, 'the subject and object, always interconnected in man's actual experience, were thus severed from each other in the very starting-point of philosophy.'[2] This antithesis between the two gave rise to the tension which later developed into the antagonism between the religion of authority and the religion of the spirit. A time came when, in Protestant theology, any reference to objective proof was wholeheartedly repudiated. A point was reached when Sabatier can say: 'The two methods are so radically opposed that to accept the latter (the subjective) is at once to mark the former as insufficient and outworn.'[3]

For the anti-deistic apologists stress was laid upon external proofs. On the other hand 'in finding the ground and type of all certainty in his own existence, Descartes was shutting himself up within his own subjectivity',[4] and, as a consequence, gave rise to the subjective criterion. The assumption of the externalists was that revelation consisted in a system of supernatural notions and inspired doctrines authenticated by clear and discernable objective evidence. The assumption of the subjectivists was that all external proofs were unnecessary and useless. For those who emphasized this side of the Cartesian dualism 'the living centre, the luminous focus, of the Gospel is the inner and immediate sense of the divine sonship'.[5]

The literature of the period reveals how great was the attention given by the externalists in collecting and collating evidences. To them the world existed, 'out there', as God's world, since He

---

[1] B. Willey, *The Seventeenth Century Background*, p. 76. Cf., 'The two orders of certainty, objective and subjective, correspond to Descartes's division of reality into Extention (matter) and Thought (mind, soul).' Ibid.

[2] Baron von Hügel, *The Reality of God*, p. 188.

[3] *Religions of Authorities and the Religion of the Spirit*, (E.T.), p. 15.

[4] J. Baillie, *Our Knowledge of God*, p. 152.

[5] Prof. Lobstein, *Introduction to Protestant Dogmatics* (tr. A. M. Smith), p. 159.

could not deceive us. It is a divine creation and bears upon itself evidence of God's image and superscription. Let men behold the ordered mechanism, the intricate combination of cosmic order, let them but see the delicate arrangements of the several parts, and they must believe. It was the firm conviction of the apologetic writers that when the evidences were marshalled and indicated, assent could not be withheld.

Before the eighteenth century dawned Joseph Glanvill wrote: 'When God himself would represent his own Magnificence and Glory, he directs to his Works.'[1] Nature, he says later, 'is no Holy Mount, which ought not to be touched; yea, we are commanded, To search after Wisdom and particularly this, when we are so frequently called to celebrate our Creator for his Works.'[2] In the same spirit Paley began his *Natural Theology*, by making effective the illustration of the watch found on the heath, giving it a sense of originality.[3] The finder of such a watch, observing the delicate arrangements of its works, the intricate union of its several parts under the control of an over-arching purpose, must, Paley asserts, be led unerringly to the idea of a maker. The conclusion is not invalidated if one had never seen a watch constructed, or if the precise duties of each part is not understood. The watch is not explained on the suggestion that it is the product of metallurgic laws. The world, like the watch, presents evidences of design, and the question 'is not shaken off',[4] by supposing an endless succession. To believe it just came to be without art or skill is manifestly absurd. 'This is Atheism: for every indication of contrivance, every manifestation of design, which existed in the watch, exists in the world of nature.'[5] The Atheist is the one who fails to see the design or acknowledge the Designer. It was along this line of 'Evidences for Christianity' that the whole apologetic of the orthodox was conducted with

'*The repetitions wearisome of sense*
Where soul is dead, and feeling hath no place.'[6]

[1] J. Glanvill, *Essays on Several Important Subjects in Philosophy and Religion*, Essay 1, p. 15.
[2] Op. cit., p. 38.
[3] The watch illustration is used by Tucker, *The Light of Nature*, 1, 523; 2, 82; Bolingbroke, *Works*, 3, 188; Clarke, *Works*, 1, 6; Burnet, *Sacred Theory of the Earth*, 1, ch. 4.
[4] *Natural Theology*, p. 12.
[5] Op. cit., p. 14.
[6] Wordsworth, *Excursion*, 4, 620.

The same exclusive emphasis on the objective element is made
by the anti-enthusiasts. The position taken up by Knott in the
Bampton Lectures of 1802 was maintained by John Bidlake nine
years later. One of the most extraordinary works of the period
comes from George Lavington, Bishop of Exeter, entitled, *The
Enthusiasm of the Methodists and the Papists Compared*. The book
called out a reply from John Wesley himself. Wesley not unjustly
charges Lavington with stabbing 'Christianity at the heart, under
cover of opposing enthusiasm'.[1] It was Lavington's conviction that
any emphasis upon the inner and individual would disturb the
stately edifice of doctrine which the Church declared to be revealed.
It was in such a 'climate of opinion', to quote a phrase from Glanvill,[2] made popular by W. N. Whitehead, that the works of Butler
and Paley came to be regarded highly and were studied with a
reverence born of their assumed finality.

This reference to Glanvill recalls us back to this author who nigh
a century and a half earlier classed 'enthusiasm' with Atheism as
'another dreadful Enemy . . . a false conceit of inspiration'.[3] Its
worst feature being its disparagement of sober reason. The enthusiast 'having heard great things of the Spirit's immediate
Motions and Inspirations cannot well fail of believing himself
inspired, and of entitling all the excursions of his Fancy to the
immediate Acting of the Holy Ghost'.[4]

The subjective emphasis took longer to gain position and
popularity, but its significance lies in its wholehearted repudiation
of all external evidences. F. D. Maurice, for example, grounds
revelation in the being of the individual which is divine in its inner
essence. He can thus say of Renan that although he took 'the
supernatural out of the Gospels, he cannot take it out of his own
life'.[5] It is his charge against Dean Mansel that, because he
'differs from St Paul and St John he must deal unfairly with the
witness in our hearts'.[6] External evidences are merely learnt off;
the conclusion is reached: all is clear. Young men are made to
'take Paley's evidences for granted as if they were divine'.[7]

---

[1] Wesley, *Works*, vol. 13, p. 22.
[2] *The Vanity of Dogmatizing*, p. 227.
[3] *Essays on Several Important Subjects in Philosophy and Religion*, Essay 4,
p. 17.
[4] Op. cit., p. 18.
[5] *Life of F. D. Maurice* (by his Son), vol. 2, p. 463.
[6] *What is Revelation?* p. 444.
[7] Op. cit., p. 453.

Thomas Erskine allows that a just appreciation of the created universe and its providential arrangement should lead men to the necessity of conforming their lives thereto. But the fact is it never does. Men are content to speculate as long as they are not challenged to alter their lives: 'men are in general so much occupied with the works that they forget their great Author: and their characters are so opposed to his, that they turn away their eyes from the contemplation of that purity which condemns them.'[1] Inevitably natural theology becomes a subject for metaphysical speculation. It can be evaluated without enthusiasm: 'it would be difficult to find a devoted natural religionist.'[2] It creates no sense of need; it gives no feeling of urgency; it has no moral constraint. Mere abstract principles can be admired, and will be, as long as they remain so. It is when they take breath, when they become the incarnate realities of a human life, that they become challenging. A corrupt politician may speak loudly in the admiration of the abstract idea of integrity, but when the idea takes the form of a man and a course of action, then it is transformed from a principle to be lauded into a person to be lashed. Then it becomes obvious that the proclaimed love of the abstract principle was sheer illusion, for the man who really loves the abstract principle, cannot but love it when it is embodied and exemplified. Man can easily profess high esteem for harmless generalities. They will 'admit the abstract ideas of a God of infinite holiness and goodness: and will even take delight in exercising their reason or their taste in speculating on the subject of his being and attributes; yet these same persons will shrink with dislike and alarm from the living energy which these abstract ideas assume in the Bible'.[3]

S. T. Coleridge sweeps aside the whole array of external proofs. On Paley he is specially severe, for it is Coleridge's teaching that Christianity is spirit and life. 'Hence,' he writes with vigour, 'I more than fear the prevailing taste for books of Natural Theology, Physico-Theology, Demonstrations of God from Nature, Evidences of Christianity and the like. EVIDENCES OF CHRISTIANITY! I am weary of the word. Make a man feel his WANT of it: rouse him, if you can, to the self-knowledge of his NEED of it, and you can safely trust it to its own Evidence — remembering only this the

[1] *Remarks on the Internal Evidence for the Truth of Revealed Religion*, p. 48.
[2] Op. cit., p. 51.
[3] Op. cit., p. 79.

express declaration of Christ Himself: No man cometh to Me, unless the Father leadeth him.'[1]

Such then was the message of those who valuated revelation in its subjective action. It is because the divine message appeals to the heart and there authenticates itself that it does not call for mental gymnastics. The divine author 'must have known that not one out of a hundred who ever heard of it could ever have leisure or learning to weigh its external evidences'.[2]

(c) Inference and Intuition

It will have become obvious that the Cartesian dualism created the opposition which more recent philosophical theology has discussed under the question: Does the knowledge of God come by Inference or by Intuition? The rationalists and objectivists necessarily maintain the former. Professor A. Lecerf insists that 'with the first successors of Descartes we find ourselves still in the full floodtide of rational dogmatism'.[3] Arising therefrom there will be denial of all ontological arguments. Stebbing consequently emphatically declares that 'there are no innate ideas of God, so likewise we can have no proof of such a being *a priori*'.[4] Emphasis is thus placed upon the sufficiency of external evidence. Bishop Browne, in a later book, takes up a point made in an earlier, and announces as 'a sure and incontestable Truth, that we have no immediate proper Idea of God at all, or of his Attributes as they are in themselves; or anything else in the world'.[5] Analogy is therefore the only acceptable method for the attainment of divine knowledge. This idea is not to be set aside as 'strange and new'. It is as old as the Fathers.

On the other hand Bishop Berkeley rejects analogical knowledge and insists upon immediate revelation. He refers to Browne as a 'minute philosopher' who lived 'not long since'. In his book with that title, one of its characters, Euphranor, confesses that the idea of divine knowledge gained by means of analogy is new to him. Crito tells that he entered into an investigation as to 'what foundation there is in the Fathers and Schoolmen' for the view. He con-

---

[1] *Aids to Reflection* (new edition), p. 272.
[2] Thomas Erskine, *Remarks on the Internal Evidences for the Truth of Revealed Religion*, p. 186.
[3] A. Lecerf, *Introduction to Reformed Dogmatics*, p. 45.
[4] H. Stebbing, *An Enquiry into the Evidences of the Christian Religion*, p. 10.
[5] *The Procedure, Extent and Limits of the Human Understanding*, Intro., p. vi.

cludes that the idea 'owes its original to those writings which have been published under the name of Dionysius the Areopagite'.[1]

By insisting upon certainty within the individual consciousness, Descartes gave rise to the 'so-called immediate and inward revelation which in modern times is so highly regarded'.[2] Those who follow this line contend that the awareness of God wells up from within. Mansel had condemned any assertion of the immediate knowledge of God. F. D. Maurice retorts that this doctrine which has 'fallen into oblivion in the last century',[3] is what earnest and religious men require. However Mansel may limit the soaring spirit of man, however he may clip the wings of the soul to hinder its flight to realms divine he cannot obliterate the human feeling of God, nor banish the truth that the real meeting-place between God and man is the inner arena of the human spirit. In a note dedicating the *Theological Essays* to the poet Laureate, Alfred Lord Tennyson, Maurice says: 'I maintained in these Essays that a Theology which does not correspond to the deepest thoughts and feelings of the human being cannot be a true Theology.'[4] It is from this standpoint that Maurice rejects, what he calls, all 'notional' views of revelation. He argues that there is a manifesting of God in every striving for good, in every fight against evil. 'God manifests Himself in every act distinguishing the man from the evil which has possessed him.'[5] Revelation is, in fact, the unveiling to man of his divine origin; the casting out of the foreign spirits, the awakening of man to his own divine humanity. Revelation is not, therefore,

---

[1] *Minute Philosopher*, p. 164. This claim by Berkeley is, I think, justified by the historical facts. It is the purpose of the pseudo-Dionysian writings of the fifth and sixth centuries to effect a synthesis between the prevailing neo-Platonist philosophy and orthodox Christianity. This fact is seen more especially in the work entitled the Divine Names. The true Godhead according to 'Dionysius' is super-personal and undifferentiated. The Scriptural titles for God refer to the whole nature of the godhead. But as the godhead is itself beyond knowledge the undifferentiated names cannot give adequate understanding of God as He is in Himself. 'The Scriptures lead man along the affirmative path as far as he is able to go, but such conceptions of the Divine nature they give are to be regarded in the form of metaphor and analogy. In His essential nature, God is above and beyond all beings, sensible and spiritual.... All perfections of creatures can be attributed to God to a superlative degree, but, as the cause always remains superior to the effect, the Supreme Cause can only be described in analogical fashion.' S. J. Curtis, *A Short History of Western Philosophy in the Middle Ages*, p. 22. Cf. C. E. Rolt, *Dionysius the Areopagite on the Divine Names and the Mystical Theology*, (S.P.C.K., 1920), Introduction.
[2] S. W. F. Hegel, *History of Philosophy*, vol. iii, p. 226.
[3] *What is Revelation?*, p. 134.
[4] *Theological Essays*, Preface.
[5] *What is Revelation?*, p. 77.

regulative injunctions, but redemptive inspiration. The former is powerless, since it is like announcing elaborate instructions on good swimming to a drowning man. Those who specify revelation as merely regulative axioms are asked: 'Has not Methodism vanquished you, and Puritanism vanquished you before?'[1]

Julius Hare goes so far as to contend for this inwardness of revelation amongst the heathen and specifically amongst the Jews. There was a feeling after and a desire for God as the living one to be trusted. To the patriarchs of Israel God was intimately near. He lit the light of faith in the heart of Abraham. 'It was by a direct, special revelation of Himself, that God awakened the life of faith in Abraham.'[2] True faith is not belief in a Book, it is not assent to propositions but a 'living personal relation' with God. The upholders of 'notional faith' usually regard those who testify to this 'living personal relation' as 'enthusiasts' and 'fanatics'. Some may, indeed, have overstepped the bounds of propriety, failing to wed caution to their zeal, but their real offence, in the eyes of their critics, 'was the witness they bore in behalf of a living as opposed to a notional Faith.'[3] For Coleridge, Christianity is an affair of the heart. His position is that of St Bernard, 'We must retire inward, if we would ascend upward.'[4] Coleridge, says Dr Marsh, 'boldly asserted the reality of something distinctively spiritual in man, and the futility of all modes of philosophizing in which this is not recognized, or which is incompatible with it.'[5]

(d) Facts and Values

The man whose interests lie in the rational, the objective, the inferential, will of necessity be concerned with 'facts'. To him, as to Plato, poetry will be anathema. His concern will be with cold proofs. Such a man will talk, as Locke does, about the *Reasonableness of Christianity*. To him the mysterious will be suspect. That which is another's glory is to him repugnant. Thomas Browne had written with obvious exhilaration, 'I love to lose myself in a mystery, to pursue my Reason to an O altitudo! . . . I can answer all the Objections of Satan and my rebellious reason with the old

---

[1] Op. cit., p. 87.
[2] *Victory of Faith*, p. 145.
[3] Julius Hare, *Victory of Faith*, p. 73.
[4] Quoted in Marsh's *Preliminary Essay*, p. xxv. (This essay by the Rev. D. J. Marsh, President of the University of Vermount, U.S.A., was published with the first American edition of Aids to Reflection, 1829.)
[5] Ibid., p. xxxi.

resolution I learned from Tertullian, *Certum quia impossibile est*.'[1] '*Credo quia impossibile est*,' retorts Locke, 'might be a good rule for a sally of zeal, but would prove a very ill rule for men to choose their opinions or religion by.'[2] The man of reason concerned with facts cannot be carried away from the world of hard facts.

The subjectivist will be more concerned with the appreciation of facts, than with their investigation. He will be more of a poet. Thus we find Locke a master of prose and Coleridge an authority on poetry. In the Cartesian philosophy, therefore, there is latent this further opposition 'which has become so troublesomely familiar to us since, between "values" and "facts"; between what you *felt* as a human being or as a poet, and what you *thought* as a man of sense, judgement, enlightenment'.[3] How sharply opposed these two became later is well known. It was the boast of the scientists of the new age that they had successfully eliminated all values from their consideration. On the other hand, theologians like Ritschl made it their glory to state religion merely in terms of value apart from any basic facts.

(ii) *The Religio-Philosophical Background*
THE CAMBRIDGE PLATONISTS

A further accentuation of these antitheses can be traced to a group of thinkers known to us as the Cambridge Platonists or Latitudinarians. From a more pronounced religious standpoint these writers of the seventeenth century provide a background for the oppositions which came into sharp focus in the next era. The most prominent members of the Cambridge Platonists were Whichote, More, Cudworth and John Smith. Their supreme significance, it is agreed, was to stress the rationalistic appreciation of Christianity. Whichote refers constantly to reason as 'the candle of the Lord'. Allied to the Cambridge men were preachers like Tillotson and Stillingfleet. Their views on reason, however, differed. For Tillotson it was a ratiocinative process; the latitudinarians, on the other hand, conceived of it in the Platonic fashion as a means whereby direct contact could be made with spiritual reality. 'In the Cambridge Platonists the spirit of Plato aids the spirit of Descartes in the task of reducing the imagery of religion

[1] *Religio Medico*, i, p. 9.
[2] *Essay on the Human Understanding*, 4, 18, sect. ii.
[3] B. Willey, *The Seventeenth Century Background*, pp. 87, 88.

to clear and distinct ideas.'[1] Whichote advocated a liberal policy towards men of good will whatever their persuasion. 'Let all uncertainties lie by themselves in the catalogue of disputables; matter of future enquiry.'[2] Cudworth was undoubtedly the most renowned of the group, as he was the most exclusively ethical in his teaching. He conceived of good and evil as grounded in the reality of things and cognizable by reason. They are objectively existent and 'the knowledge of them comes no doubt to the human mind from the divine; but it is from the Divine Reason in whose light man imperfectly participates, not merely from the Divine Will of each. Ethical, like mathematical, truth relates properly and primarily not to sensible particulars, but to the intelligible and universal essences of things, which are as immutable as the Eternal Mind whose existence is inseparable from theirs: ethical propositions therefore, are as unchangeably valid for the direction of the conduct of rational beings as the truths of geometry are.'[3]

It is in John Smith, the clearest speculative thinker of the Cambridge Platonists, that we find, not only the rationalistic element strongly stated, but the feeling antithesis very definitely implied. The very first property of religion, Smith contends in his *Discourses*, is to widen and enlarge a man's mental capacities. 'A good man, one that is actuated by religion, lives in converse with his reason; he lives at the height of his own being.'[4] In common with the other writers, Smith evinces an evident belief in the ability and dignity of reason. However their interpretation differed from that of their contemporaries: their emphasis upon the sublime quality of reason was of supreme significance. It was to give impetus to that rationalism which prevailed throughout the Age of Reason.

There was, however, another message, found especially in Smith which led to another conclusion. This is confirmed by the fact that Coleridge acknowledges his indebtedness to the Cambridge Platonists. There are numerous passages in the *Discourses* where Smith repudiates the rationalistic and objective views. Divine truth, he tells us, 'is not to be discerned so much in a man's brain,

[1] Op. cit., p. 151. Cf., 'The Cambridge Platonists were in fact more influenced by Descartes than by Bacon,' C. E. Raven, *Rational Religion and Christian Theology*, vol. 1, p. 109, Gifford Lectures, 1951. They were not slow, of course, as Raven goes on to point out, to observe his weakness.
[2] *Moral and Religious Aphorisms*, p. 547.
[3] H. Sidgwick, *History of Ethics* (5th edition), pp. 170, 171.
[4] *Discourses* (4th edition, edited by H. G. Smith, 1895), p. 376.

as in his heart.'[1] 'It is but a thin, airy, knowledge that is got by mere speculation.'[2] In this way Smith undermines the rationalism which he has already asserted. The knowledge 'ushered in by syllogisms and demonstrations' is of least value. In language that could well have been taken from Pascal, and which can be paralleled in Coleridge, Dodwell and Maurice, he proclaims religion to be 'a heavenborn thing, the seed of God in the spirits of men'.[3] It is from the hidden depths of the individual soul that divine knowledge springs. 'Therefore to seek our divinity in books of writings, is to seek the living among the dead: we do but in vain seek God many times in these, where His truth too often is not so much enshrined as entombed: — no; *intra te quaere Deum*, seek *God within thine own soul.*'[4]

In a section in the *Discourses* entitled, 'Of Legal and Evangelical Righteousness,' Smith condemns the legalism of Judaism with its notion of salvation by obedience to precepts as 'an external and lifeless thing'.[5] He contrasts this with the gospel which 'is not so much a system and body of saving divinity'.[6] Should it be turned into an external administration 'credenda propounded to us to believe',[7] it becomes as killing as the law itself. The old covenant 'was only externally promulgated, wrapt up, as it were, in ink and parchments, or, at least, engraven upon tables of stone, whereas this new covenant is set forth in living characters engraven upon the vital powers of men's souls'.[8]

In the *Discourse*, 'Of the Existence and Nature of God,' a note characteristically modern is struck. Smith asserts that it is his purpose not 'so much (to) demonstrate THAT (God) is, as WHAT He is'.[9] Although 'God has copied Himself out in all created being' it is still true that certainty is not found by the mere contemplation of the external world, but the world within. Within the individual is to be found, not simply an image of the divine, but 'the Deity itself'. It will follow then that 'whenever we look upon our soul in a right manner, we shall find a Urim and Thummim there, by which we may ask counsel of God Himself, who will have this always borne upon its breastplate'.[10] There is, he asserts, that which is the best and truest knowledge of God, which is not discoverable by the

[1] *Discourses*, p. 300.   [2] Op. cit., p. 4.
[3] Op. cit., p. 390.   [4] Op. cit., p. 3.
[5] Op. cit., p. 323.   [6] Op. cit., p. 339.
[7] Op. cit., p. 328.   [8] Op. cit., p. ibid.
[9] Op. cit., p. 329.   [10] Op. cit., p. 128.

labour and sweat of the brain, but 'that which is kindled *within* us by a heavenly warmth in our hearts'.[1]

For the godly man this is the highest assurance. No external evidences and no elaborate arguments are needed by those whose hearts are thus 'strangely warmed'. The one so assured 'will find satisfaction within, feeling himself in conjunction with truth, though all the world should dispute against it'.[2]

Although it was the purpose of the Cambridge Platonists to rescue religion from all meaningless additions and to set forth its essentials in clear and distinct ideas, it is, at the same time, equally true that the aim of all these writers 'was to "call men off from dogmas and barren speculations" . . . affirming values where the orthodox affirmed facts'.[3]

[1] Op. cit., p. 3.   [2] Op. cit., p. 13.
[3] B. Willey, *The Seventeenth Century Background*, p. 138.

CHAPTER III

THE SUPREMACY OF THE RATIONAL

The antithesis, then, which revealed itself in the preceding period, and which was accentuated by the work of the Cambridge Platonists, developed, in our era, into the rationalism of Deism, on the one hand, and the enthusiasm of the Quakers, on the other. Here can be seen two opposite views of revelation, the rational-objective and the mystico-subjective. It is against the background of both these that the 'orthodox' apologists justified their understanding of revelation.[1] It is this fact which accounts for the seeming contradictions which pervaded their writings. Against the deists, who resolved revelation into truths of natural reason, they had to humble reason from its exalted position: against the enthusiasts they had to exalt it from its humble position.

The battle which had been earlier fought out in the field of politics was now transferred to the sphere of religious thought. The deists conceived of reason as an absolute sovereign, whereas their opponents would make it a limited monarchy. In the eyes of both, the enthusiasts were rabid republicans, if not absolute anarchists. The contradictions inherent in the orthodox literature of the eighteenth century are due to their effort to find an argument against these two, Dogmatism and Enthusiasm. Even before the century had begun Glanvill gave expression to the opposition. In his *Essays on Several Important Subjects in Philosophy and Religion* (1675) he castigates the Enthusiasts because they argue 'for the Universal Inability of Reason in the things of Religion'.[2] Against them, he replies: Reason is 'in a sense, the Word of God . . . written upon our Minds and Hearts; as Scripture is that which is

---

[1] The term 'orthodox' is used in a broad sense throughout these pages to describe those who were active in the defence of the accepted doctrines of the Church. They were content with the established order and stood against innovations in theology. They were, for the most part, apologetic and evidence writers. Cf., V. Storr, *Development of English Theology in the Nineteenth Century*, p. 79; J. H. Overton, *The English Church in the Nineteenth Century*, p. 24.

[2] *Essays on Several Important Subjects*, etc., Essay 5, p. 16.

written in a Book'.[1] Depraved in some sense the reason may be, but, his conclusion is: 'Follow reason, for no article of faith can contradict it, and every article of faith must agree thereto.'

On the other side, in his *Vanity of Dogmatizing*, Glanvill seeks to weaken the sovereignty of reason. The Preface tells us: 'It is levied against Dogmatizing, and attempts upon a daring Enemy, Confidence in Opinion.' On Aristotle he is especially severe. His works comprise, 'a huddle of words, and terms insignificant.'[2] He asserts that Aristotle drew a veil over nature and upon theology has had a damaging effect, so that Luther's censure is neither unjust nor uncharitable. 'While Aristotle is made the centre of things there is little hope.'[3] He thus concludes, 'It is shallow, unimproved intellects which are the confident pretenders to certainty.'[4] Since, then, both rationalism and enthusiasm had a specific doctrine of revelation, it is important that the ideas of each should be drawn out so as to understand the significance of the orthodox reply.

REVELATION AS INFALLIBLE REASON

THE DEISTIC DOGMATISM

(i) *A Summary of the View*

One of the most important influences of the Renaissance was to give man complete confidence in himself as a rational being. The human individual was believed to possess a faculty capable of searching into the ultimate mysteries. In this way, as Berdyaev says, the 'Renaissance once more discovered the natural man, the old Adam of the pre-Christian world, for whom Christianity had substituted the new Adam or the spiritual man'.[5] The Erasmic view of man as a creature of reason issued in the Deistic, Enlightenment and Illumination ideas of which 'the distinctive mark was the conscious rejection of all external, authoritative infallibilities'.[6] The general view that developed therefrom was that religion consisted in a few simple truths which were of its very essence, and, which were available to all men, since all possessed the sovereign faculty of reason. 'The Enlightenment', observes Professor Tillich, 'fore-

---

[1] Op. cit., p. 20.
[2] Op. cit., p. 150.
[3] Op. cit., p. 166.
[4] Op. cit., p. 15.
[5] N. Berdyaev, *The Meaning of History*, p. 131.
[6] J. Oman, *Grace and Personality*, pp. 3, 4.

shadowed by Erasmus' fight with Luther, and by theological humanism . . . believed in the possibility of inducing the great majority of individuals to follow the demands of an integrated personal and social life by education, persuasion and adequate institutions.'[1]

It was in this context that man's estimate of himself as a rational being became absolute. He was able to penetrate to the last secrets of the universe. There was no island of knowledge he could not explore. The most thorough application of this doctrine of reason's sovereignty is seen in the deistic movement which opened the modern era of rationalistic criticism of the Bible.

Descartes, as has been shown, gave philosophical justification for this high estimate of man's ability. His view-point was adopted by the theologians of the seventeenth century. To Glanvill, a Fellow of the Royal Society and Rector of Bath Abbey, Descartes is the 'great', the 'renowned', the 'unparalleled'. He thus announces that 'reason is certain and infallible'.[2] Nothing, he insists, has done more harm to religion than the disparagement of reason.

The apologists in our period, as staunch Churchmen, were interested in defending institutional religion. This conception went back to Bishop Hooker. In his *Ecclesiastical Polity*, Hooker introduced a doctrine of conformity based upon an ecclesiastical theory. He sees God as the supreme keeper of law and order. He thus considers all human law to have as its purpose the curbing of man's outward actions for the sake of the common good.[3] As the angelic host reveal their perfection by their unhesitating obedience to the divine will, so submission to the 'saving legislation' which God gave to the Church is the ordained way of salvation. The state has therefore the duty to maintain the authority of the Church, since the two are but different aspects of the one reality. This point is made in Book 8 of the *Polity*. 'We hold', he says, 'that there is not any man of the Church of England but the same is also of the commonwealth, nor any man a member of the commonwealth, which is not also of the Church of England . . . .'[4]

There is, according to this thesis, a law of society, namely,

[1] P. Tillich, *The Protestant Era*, Preface, p. xxxv.
[2] *Essays on Several Important Subjects, etc.*, Essay 5, p. 20.
[3] *Ecclesiastical Polity*, vol. 1, 10, 1, 2.
[4] Op. cit., vol. 2, bk. 8, ch. 1, 2. These words may not be Hooker's own. Isaak Walton in his *Life of Hooker* prefixed to vol. 1, refers to Hooker as 'the happy author of five (if not more) of the eight books of the Laws of the Ecclesiastical Polity'.

'consent to some general bond of association,' and, in addition, certain divine imperatives to fill up 'the defects of those natural ways of salvation'. The Church therefore unites within itself 'a law of reason and a law supernatural'.[1] Here God's saving legislation is looked upon as the supernatural addition to the natural laws of society.

Accepting this conception of the Church as coextensive with the state and the distinction between natural and supernatural laws, the deists went on to deny the need for these asserted divine extras. They consequently argued that the natural laws of society, unfolded by reason, were sufficient, and that they themselves were true Christians.

It was, however, as has been earlier indicated, to Archbishop Tillotson that the deists looked as their head. Tillotson was the foe of all irrationalism. Mysticism and enthusiasm were anathema to him. He laid stress upon the sufficiency of reason, first to comprehend natural religion and then to judge of revealed. He begins his series of sermons on, 'The Miracles Wrought in Confirmation of Christianity,' with the observation 'Whosoever impartially considers the Christian Religion, cannot but acknowledge the Laws and Principles of it to be reasonable'.[2] By giving special insistence to the subject and scope of natural religion, and by putting strong emphasis upon the adequacy of human reason, Tillotson gave the impression that Christianity was a matter of mere common sense. All immediacy in religion was regarded as either a futile enthusiasm or a fatal superstition. To say with Tertullian, *Certum est quia impossibile*,[3] is to utter the utmost blasphemy, for reason is God-given and whatever is not of reason is not of faith. It was thus evident that: νοῦς ἐστί βασιλεὺς ἡμῖν οὐρανοῦ τε καί γης.[4]

Tillotson, of course, still gave allegiance to the prevailing view of revelation as the disclosure of certain divine truths. But he regarded these extras as a sort of republication of natural religion. They served, with their promises of rewards and threatenings of punishments, to enforce those obligations of which all men, as reasonable beings, were aware. For Tillotson this meant that nothing could be received as revelation which contradicted the natural truths of reason. It is clear that Tillotson was anxious to

[1] *Ecclesiastical Polity*, vol. 2, bk. 1, 15, 2.
[2] *Sermons*, vol. 2 (3rd edition, 1727), p. 494.
[3] *De Carne Christi*, 5.
[4] Plato, *Philebus*, 28.

stress the importance of the Christian revelation. But he still maintained that both natural and revealed religion were grounded on reason.

He illustrates from the story of Abraham. It was, he asserts, only after he had 'reasoned with himself', and based his conviction on the omnipotence of God, that the patriarch's readiness to act passed from the realm of credulity to that of faith. This understanding of faith will be seen to be in line with that of revelation. There is no faith, Tillotson declares, where there is no sufficient reason. Faith implies conviction, and conviction, in its turn, is based upon rational evidence. Teaching like this, it will be obvious, undermined the old view in which special revelation was allowed to contain mysteries which reason could not fathom.

Tillotson, indeed, goes to extremes in condemning those who, in their zeal for revealed religion, overthrew natural. He is convinced of the binding obligations of natural religion. This principle is carried so far that Tillotson places the natural duties of nursing mothers above the laws of revealed religion.

'This I foresee will seem a very hard saying to nice and delicate mothers', he writes, 'who prefer their own ease and pleasure to the fruit of their own bodies, but whether they will hear or whether they will forbear, I think myself obliged to deal plainly in this matter, and to be so faithful as to tell them that this is a natural duty, and because it is so, of a more necessary and indispensable obligation than any positive precept of revealed religion, and that the neglect of it is one of the great and crying sins of this age and nation.'[1] Statements like this, with the whole drift of Tillotson's teaching, seems to justify Charles Smyth's remark that, 'The content of his preaching was little more than a prudential morality, based rather on reason than on revelation, and appealing deliberately to sober common sense.'[2]

Already before the eighteenth century had begun, the notion that true religion was the intellectual discovery of certain fundamental axioms had been set forth by Lord Herbert of Cherbury. Leyland with some reason refers to Herbert as the first of the

[1] *Works*, vol. 4, p. 452 (edition, 1741).
[2] In the light of what is here said it will be easy to understand the high place accorded to Tillotson by both the deists and their orthodox opponents. A very different estimate is given by Whitfield and Wesley. During his stay in Georgia in 1740 the former declared that Tillotson knew no more of Christianity than Mahomet. He sought to justify his statement in two pamphlets in which it is asserted that 'all natural men speak well of his works', and that the archbishop

deists. In his book, *On Truth as it is distinguished from Revelation, Probability, Possibility, and Falsehood*, Herbert seeks to discover what he regards as the essentials of true religion. He draws up a list of five articles,[1] or 'common notices', as he calls them. These are innate, and therefore discoverable by all men everywhere. Because they are disclosed directly to the mind they are the only necessities and the only certainties. When all religions are stripped of their priestly additions, then, Herbert declares, we are left with the absolute requirements, 'the only true catholic religion.'

Herbert does not, indeed, deny the possibility of a revealed religion. There are some truths which have been revealed, but these do not possess the same certainty as those 'derived from the faculties'. These revealed truths depend for their authority upon the revealer. They are not certain truths of the mind. Herbert specifies certain criteria by which external revelation is to be tested, but these are so strict that there is no authority left for any revelation except those cases of immediate disclosure to the individual himself. This last point justifies Herbert's own assertion that on 'one fair day in summer', when the sun shone clear and no wind stirred, it was revealed to him that it would benefit the world if his book, *De Veritate*, were published.

This idea was later reasserted by Charles Blount in a volume of papers published in 1693 under the title, *The Oracles of Reason*. Blount denied that there was any other revelation beyond that which man's unaided reason could discover. If such a revealed religion existed it would of necessity need to be universal, since 'no Rule of Revealed Religion was, or ever could be made known to all Men'.[2] There must, therefore, be no such thing. He contends that 'what is not universal and equally known to All Men, cannot be needful for Any'.[3]

had 'no other than a bare historical faith'. It was the restraining influence of Lady Huntingdon which kept Wesley from making an open attack upon Tillotson and Bishop Bull in his Oxford University sermon of 1741. The position he intended to take was found among his papers after his death, and is now number CXXXIV of his published sermons.

[1] The five fundamental truths of religion, according to Herbert are: (1) Belief in the existence of a Supreme Being; (2) The duty of worship; (3) The Obligation of virtue and piety as service due to the Supreme Being; (4) Necessity of repenting of sins and forsaking them; (5) Rewards and punishments in this life and the next.

[2] A supposed Letter from A. W. to Charles Blount, Esq., 'Of Revealed Religion as opposed to Divine Revelation', published in *Oracles of Reason*, No. 14.

[3] Ibid.

(a) Reasonableness of Christianity — Locke

It is John Locke, however, who took up a position fruitful alike for the deists and their opponents. This point is illustrated by the references to Locke made by different writers. E. S. Waterhouse, for example, considers Locke to have been a 'powerful supporter' of the deistic position.[1] G. Fisher, on the other hand, maintains, 'Of the writers on the anti-deistic side, there was none abler or more eminent than John Locke (1632–1704).'[2] The fact is that each of these writers is correct in his estimate. Under the influence of the deistic onslaught, Locke felt that the interests of orthodoxy would be best served by 'rationalizing' theology and thus make it less vulnerable. This was the purpose of his *Reasonableness of Christianity*. The result was, that in seeking to make Christianity 'easy' of acceptance, Locke really robbed it of its worth, and consequently his work which was meant to be a sword against deism became a powerful weapon in its hands.

Standing as he does on the threshold of the new century, his work is at once the conclusion of the ideas which revealed themselves in the seventeenth as well as the starting-point of the enquiries which occupied the eighteenth century. Locke's 'influence pervades the eighteenth century with an almost scriptural authority'.[3]

It has been usual to speak of Locke as the founder of rational theology in England. This is not strictly exact since he says no more than the most orthodox theologians in the preceding period. He was, however, more thorough in the application of accepted principles. He pressed the claims of reason so as to leave no room for the background of traditional superstitions and unfathomable mysteries. Locke was, in fact, so complete in his reasoning that he was often carried logically far beyond the position that he desired to establish.

In his *Reasonableness of Christianity*, he assures us that belief in Jesus as the Messiah is the only thing needful. To believe this is to believe all that God has demanded as necessary. While Locke allows that revelation discloses truths beyond the compass of reason, there are still passages in which he comes near to the true deistic position. 'Reason must', he says, 'be our last judge in

---

[1] *The Philosophical Approach to Religion*, p. 151.

[2] *History of Christian Doctrine*, p. 374.

[3] *Spectator*, No. 387, quoted by B. Willey, *The Seventeenth Century Background*, p. 269.

everything.'[1] Like Whichote he refers again and again to reason as 'the candle of the Lord'. True religion cannot be out of reach of the common man, for plain men form the generality of mankind: the majority 'have not leisure for Learning and Logick'. The one who asserts that God has given a long catalogue of things to be believed will run into infinite absurdities. God has made no such demand, for He is a compassionate Father. To man 'He has given Reason, and with it a Law. That could not be otherwise than what Reason should dictate; unless we should think, that a creature (reasonable) should have an unreasonable Law'.

In the fourth edition of his *Essay Concerning Humane Understanding*, which appeared in 1700, there was added a chapter, on 'Enthusiasm', in which Locke approximates more closely to the true deistic standpoint. This chapter now forms an integral part of the fourth book, and with the one preceding, entitled, 'Faith and Reason,' gives a fair indication of the drift of his argument.

It is first laid down, in a manner followed later by Mansel, that the boundary between Faith and Reason should be drawn. Those ideas 'beyond the discovery of our natural faculties and above reason, are, when revealed the proper matter of faith'.[2] Nothing contrary to reason can be accepted on the supposed authority of revelation; 'if anything shall be thought revelation which is contrary to the plain principles of reason and the evident knowledge the mind has of its own clear and distinct ideas, there reason must be harkened to as to a matter within its providence.'[3] Revelation itself must have the approval of reason; it is not a matter of faith. Faith 'can never convince us of anything that contradicts our knowledge'.[4] The sum of the matter is, 'Whatever God hath revealed is certainly true; no doubt can be made of whether it be a divine revelation or no, reason must judge; which can never permit the mind to reject a greater evidence to embrace what is less evident, nor allow it to entertain probability in opposition to knowledge and certainty.'[5]

It is the folly of Enthusiasm that it asserts revelation without reason. It takes feeling for seeing, and can itself be no proof. Locke reiterates that 'Revelation must be judged by reason',[6] indeed reason alone is the true judge. No prophet is a mere complex

---

[1] *The Reasonableness of Christianity*, sect. 14.
[2] *On the Human Understanding* (New edition, 1894), p. 587.
[3] Ibid.   [4] Op. cit., p. 586.   [5] Op. cit., p. 588.
[6] Op. cit., p. 595.

of unreasoned emotions. 'God when He makes a prophet does not unmake the man: he leaves all his faculties in their natural state, to enable him to judge of his inspirations, whether they be of divine origin or no. When He illuminates the mind with supernatural light, He does not extinguish that which is natural.'[1] In another passage in the same chapter there are statements which come still nearer to deism, and may be regarded as the occasion for some writers putting him in their company. 'Reason', says Locke, 'is natural revelation, whereby the Eternal Father of Light and Fountain of all Knowledge, communicates to mankind that portion of truth which he has laid within reach of their natural faculties. Revelation is natural reason enlarged by a new set of discoveries communicated by God immediately, which reason vouches the truth of by the testimony and proofs it gives that they come from God.'[2]

The eighteenth century, then, opened with an unbounded confidence in reason, and the 'immediate offspring of Locke's book was Toland's, *Christianity not Mysterious*'.[3] By exaggerating some of the statements of Locke's, *Essay*, and applying them in his own way, under cover of Locke's authority, Toland led on naturally to the true deistic position, in which revelation is regarded as infallible reason.

(b) Christianity not Mysterious — Toland

In the Preface of Toland's book the basic assumptions of deism are stated. Toland, it should be observed, did not regard himself as a deist. He certainly did not deny the possibility of revelation. He boldly contends that it is the rejection of his views which is the occasion of so many becoming 'Deists and Atheists'.[4] He is to be regarded as a disciple of Locke who consistently applied the philosopher's logic. Toland's fundamental assumption is that all that is essential in Christianity must be understandable. It is, therefore, impossible for reasonable men to receive mysteries on the proclaimed authority of the Early Fathers,[5] particular Doctors pronounced orthodox,[6] a general Council or an infallible pope.[7] Toland announces the sincerity of his purpose with the information that reason and its uses have been 'the happy instruments'[8] of

---

[1] Ibid.   [2] Op. cit., p. 591.
[3] B. Willey, *The Seventeenth Century Background*, p. 280.
[4] *Christianity not Mysterious* (3rd edition, 1696), p. 176.
[5] Op. cit., p. 2.   [6] Op. cit., p. 3.   [7] Op. cit., p. 4.   [8] Op. cit., Preface, p. ix.

his own conversion. The reference is to his renunciation of Roman Catholicism and his acceptance of Protestantism.

The gospel contains nothing obscure, for 'religion must necessarily be reasonable and intelligible'.[1] He thus makes the equation: 'Religion is always the same like God its author,' and, 'Truth is always and everywhere the same.'[2] It is no objection to urge that reason is depraved. Toland denies that it is. The rationality of the divine image has not been impaired. Revelation, Toland argues, is a removal of the veil. It is a disclosure of the true meaning of religion, which reason must appreciate and approve. Faith and knowledge are thus identified and faith is consequently defined as 'a firm persuasion built upon substantial reason'.[3] Toland avows it to be an article of his faith that he can believe only that which is reasonable. Reason, he asserts, tends to 'confirm and elucidate' revelation. He will dispense with the varied opinions of sects and parties and consider only 'those of Jesus Christ and his apostles'.[4] The element of mystery, he boldly declares, must be eliminated from Christianity because it is not only an easy refuge for the unthinking, but a real stumbling-block in the way of its acceptance.

To be sure, mysteries have crept into Christianity, but the advice that 'we must adore what we cannot comprehend' is impossible. Some assert that the Scriptures contain mysteries: they would have us 'believe what the literal Sense imparts, with little or no Consideration for Reason, which they reject as not fit to be employed about the revealed Part of Revelation. Others assert, that we may use Reason as an Instrument, but not as a Rule of our Belief. The first contend some mysteries may be, or at least, seem to be received by Faith. The second that no mystery is contrary to Reason but above it. Both of them from different Principles agree that several Doctrines of the New Testament belong no further to Enquiries of Reason, than to prove them divinely revealed, and that they are properly Mysteries still. On the contrary, we hold that Reason is the only Foundation of all Certainty: and that nothing Revealed whether as to its Manner or Certainty is more exempted from its Disquisitions, than the Ordinary Phenomena of Nature. Wherefore, that there is nothing in the Gospel contrary to Reason, not above it; and that no Christian Doctrine can properly be called a Mystery.'[5]

[1] Preface, p. xxvii.   [2] Preface, p. xx.   [3] Op. cit., p. 138.
[4] Op. cit., Preface, p. ix.   [5] Op. cit., pp. 5, 6.

Scripture itself must be subjected to the test of reason since it is the reason which must judge of what is figurative and what is literal; 'otherwise, under the pretence of Faith in the Word of God, the highest Follies and Blasphemies may be deduced from the Letter of Scripture; as that God is subject to passions, is the author of sin, etc.'[1] Seeming contradictions are to be patiently worked out in the assurance that they are not ultimately real. The purpose of the gospel is to dispel ignorance and eradicate superstition, herein lies the evidence of its own rationality. Toland considers that the Mystery Religions disguised 'naked religion' under all sorts of rituals which became the selfish concern of priests. He investigates the meaning of the word 'mystery', and concludes, rightly, that it connotes the disclosure of a secret. Things hidden from the philosophers of Greece and the people of Israel are now plain to those instructed of God. It is absurd to think of Paul saying that the Gospel is the mystery 'made known unto all the nations' if it is still incomprehensible.

No wise man would assert that a substance like water was above reason because he has never enquired into its parts and properties. This means for us: 'First, that no Christian Doctrine, no more than any ordinary Piece of Nature can be reputed Mystery, because we have no adequate or complete Idea of what belongs to it. Secondly, that what is revealed in Religion as it is most useful and necessary, so it must and may be easily comprehended, and found as consistent with our Common Notions as what we know of Wood, or Stone, or Water or the like. And, thirdly, that when we do as familiarly explain such Doctrines as what is known of Natural Things, (which I contend we can) we may then as properly be said to comprehend the one as the other.'[2] The real essence of things, is after all, unknown to us.

The question remains, How were mysteries introduced into Christianity? Broadly, according to Toland, the process was, what we may describe as, firstly natural, and then, secondly, deliberate. To begin with, the converts from Judaism 'who continued mightily fond of their Levitical Rites and Feasts',[3] retained their rituals. These, being at first tolerated by the stronger brethren, soon became part of Christianity itself and apostolic sanction sought for them, Then, too, the Gentile converts, 'not a little scandalized at the Plain Dress of the Gospel,'[4] brought with them

[1] Op. cit., p. 34.　[2] Op. cit., p. 80.　[3] Op. cit., p. 159.　[4] Ibid.

the pomp and secret mysteries of their old religion. The Christians, eager to win them, did not oppose their additions. Philosopher and 'wise man' saw it worth their while becoming Christians, and they soon made unintelligible puzzles out of what was originally plain. To crown the process, when the Emperor Constantine became a Christian, 'multitudes then professed themselves of the Emperor's Persuasion, only to make their Court and mend their fortunes thereby, or to preserve those Places and Preferments whereof they were possessed.'[1] All the paraphernalia of the heathen temples were thus sanctioned and sanctified for the service of the Church and multitudinous accretions were added to the primitive simplicity of the gospel, which was already overlaid with Jewish and Gentile excesses.

Over against this more natural process went the deliberate. Toland puts it like this: 'Now their own advantage being the Motive that put the Primitive Clergy receiving Mystery, they quickly created themselves, by its existence, into a separate and politick Body.'[2] In this way there grew up grades and distinctions in their ranks till at length they claimed the sole right of interpreting the Scripture. Thus they became apart from, above, and authoritative for the rest. Ceremonies are, therefore, the source and cause of mystery. Let them but be eliminated, and reason be free to exercise its native ability, and then, so Toland assures us, we will come to the pure essence of Christianity, the true understandable revelation of God — the revelation of reason.

Collins presses Toland's ideas to their logical conclusion. Whereas Toland sought to dissociate himself from deism, Collins had no such hesitancy. The very titles of Collins' five major works gave all a fairly accurate indication of his position. The first, *An Essay on Reason*, appeared in 1707. This was followed two years later by *Priestcraft in Perfection*. His most important work, *The Discourse of Freethinking* came out in 1713, eleven years later came his, *Grounds and Reasons of the Christian Religion*. His last work, *Scheme of Liberal Prophecy*, is dated 1727. In *The Discourse of Freethinking*, Collins argued for the identity of revelation and reason. In no way was reason to be restricted, for by it alone can truth be discovered and error detected. For Collins the adoption of rationalistic principles meant the abandonment of supernaturalistic

[1] Op. cit., p. 162.
[2] Op. cit., p. 170.

THE SUPREMACY OF THE RATIONAL

religion. It was at this point he left himself open to an attack which his many enemies were not slow to press home. Amongst his more formidable foes are to be found Bentley and Swift.

It was a strange irony which called down upon Collins' head the biting sarcasm of Dean Swift. Collins in his *Discourse of Freethinking* had made the injudicious jest that certain 'zealous divines' should be shipped abroad to convert the heathen. Their absence would result, not only in the spread of Christianity elsewhere, but in freedom from faction at home. Among the divines designed for this export, Collins names Swift. The Dean of St Patrick's, Dublin, was not the man to take such a remark lightly; soon the 'freethinker' was made to feel as diminutive as one of the Lilliputians of the *Gulliver's Travels*. Swift's retaliation came in the form of a tract entitled, *Mr Collins' Discourse of Freethinking put into plain English, by way of Abstract for the Poor*.

In the tract Collins' arguments were restated but the result was a fantastic burlesque. The Bible is set over against the statements of the 'Freethinker', and it is easy to draw the conclusion that the 'Freethinker' is both knave and fool. One example of Swift's method will indicate how crushing was the result. 'The Bible says the Jews were a nation favoured by God; but I who am a freethinker say that cannot be, because the Jews lived in a corner of the earth and freethinking makes it plain that those who live in corners cannot be favourites of God.'[1]

(c) *Christianity as Old as Creation — Tindal*

It is in Tindal's, *Christianity as Old as Creation* that we have 'the culminating point of the whole deistic controversy'.[2] A sermon preached by Dr Sherlock, Bishop of Bangor, before the Society for the Propagation of the Gospel gave Tindal the title for his book. The bishop argued that the religion of the Gospel is the true original religion of reason and nature. The gospel of repentance assured a restoration to that position from which man by transgression fell. Thus 'the Gospel was the Republication of the Law of Nature, and its Precepts declarative of that original Religion, which is as old as Creation'.[3] It is Tindal's starting declaration that the only true religion is that discoverable by reason. The notion

---

[1] Swift's *Works*, vol. 2 (edition, 1859), p. 185.
[2] L. Stephen, *English Thought in the Eighteenth Century*, vol. 1, p. 134.
[3] *Christianity as Old as Creation* (3rd edition), p. 60.

that there are two, one a natural and the other a revealed, is rejected at the outset. Natural and revealed religion are in fact but
different aspects of the one rational religion. The two are alike in
the manner of their communication. 'The one being the Internal
and the other the External Revelation, the same unchangeable
Will of a Being, which is alike at all times infinitely wise and good.'[1]

From the beginning God has given a rule or law of conduct, and
what He has given can be neither imperfect nor incomplete. It
being God's will that 'all men should come to a knowledge of the
truth', it follows that He, at all times, must have given the means
whereby they should find those laws which they should profess
and practise. Christianity is, therefore, true, because it must be
regarded, and only in so far as it is regarded, as a republication of
natural religion.

The laws of conduct are based upon the unalterable principle
of things. Thus the revelation of nature is absolutely perfect so that
external revelation can add nothing to it. The gospel must thus be
grounded in the same eternal necessity. If this were not so God
could be condemned as arbitrary. 'If He once commanded things
without reason, there can be no reason why He may not endlessly
change His commands.'[2] No special revelation can be claimed as
enlarging or ennobling the revelation of nature, since this would call
in question the perfection of what has been given by nature. The
voice of nature issues its convincing demand that God should be
worshipped. The method of such worship is left to man's convenience. Man alone has 'issued out commands which have no
Foundation in Reason'.[3] The benevolent God, Tindal argues, has
granted to men senses to make them aware of that which is hurtful
or helpful to their bodies. It cannot be supposed that He has less
regard for their souls. Adopting a hedonist ideal, he concluded
that reason is given 'to discern what Actions make for and against
Happiness'.[4]

It is by fulfilling their duties that men are 'made partakers of the
divine nature'. No written book could contain the precepts and
prescriptions for every need. And certainly no atonement is required by God for men's transgressions. 'A mediatory conception
of God', he says, 'led the heathen to think that He delighteth in the
butchery of innocent Animals; and that the stench of burnt Flesh

[1] Op. cit., p. 2.   [2] Op. cit., p. 52.
[3] Op. cit., p. 101.   [4] Op. cit., p. 18.

should be a sweet-smelling Savour to his nostrils as to atone for the Wickedness of Men.'[1] Tindal asks, in words akin to Socinius: 'How sins freely pardoned could want any expiation? or how after a full equivalent paid and adequate satisfaction given all could be mercy and pure forgiveness?'[2] All that is required of men is summed up in the Sermon on the Mount, although Tindal makes the audacious claim that its precepts are better expressed by Confucius.[3] The epitome of true religion is, therefore, 'Do all the good we can, and thereby render ourselves acceptable to God in answering the end of creation.'[4]

He sees rituals and ordinances, 'the Borders and Fringes' of religion, raised by human authority to the status of essentials. Thus is the indifferent made the binding. But all that is needful is to follow reason, for therein lies true religion. 'As long as Men believe the Good of Society is the supreme Law, they will think it their Duty to be governed by that Law: and believing God requires nothing of them than what is for the Good of Mankind, will place the whole of their Religion in benevolent Actions, and to the utmost of their Abilities copy after the divine Original; but if they are made to believe that there are things which have no relation to their Good, necessary to Salvation; they must suppose it their Duty to use such means as will most effectually serve this Purpose; and that God, requiring the End, requires all those means as will best secure and propagate it.'[5] There is nothing left but to trust reason and 'every attempt to destroy reason by reason is a demonstration that Men have nothing but Reason to trust to'.[6]

Where reason is set aside the way is left open for a host of impostures all claiming to umpire in the life of man. No book can be regarded as infallible because of the human means of transmission; 'the Probability of Facts depending on human Testimony must gradually lessen in Proportion to the Difference of Time when they were done.'[7] Tindal refers to several 'orthodox paradoxes', like the doctrine of the Trinity, which are beyond the common people. He insists that the accumulating of external marks like 'uninterrupted Tradition, incontested Miracles, Confessions of Adversaries, Numbers of Proselytes, Agreement among themselves',[8] are not sufficient to establish a particular religion. Prophecy cannot be

[1] Op. cit., p. 78.
[2] Op. cit., p. 419.
[3] Op. cit., p. 310.
[4] Op. cit., p. 18.
[5] Op. cit., p. 133.
[6] Op. cit., p. 158.
[7] Op. cit., p. 163.
[8] Op. cit., p. 211.

appealed to, since, he contends, the Apostles' expectation for an immediate return of Christ was proved false.

Variant readings, and according to Bentley there are 30,000 in our 'present best editions',[1] make the Bible unreliable. To say that most of these are insignificant is no sufficient reply, since in a book in which most things are regarded as of the greatest moment it is impossible to accept so much as of no importance. The truth of a doctrine cannot be established by all the 'plain texts' adduced in its favour. In Augustine's time all the 'plain texts' were on the side of predestination: it is now contended that they are on the side of Free-will. Nor, indeed, can the commands of the Bible be observed in present society. Who, for example, will refrain from eating black-puddings because of the injunction to abstain from blood?

Tindal repudiates a Book religion, because, he argues, the greater part of humanity has no knowledge of it; while those who have, owing to the imperfections of language cannot understand it. Following Locke[2] he urges that an attested copy of an original only is permitted as evidence in law: 'and a Copy of a Copy never so well attested, and by never so many credible Witnesses will not be admitted as Proof in Judicature.' No refuge can be sought in appointed teachers, for to place the necessities of salvation in the hands of the local clergy is only to set up a pope in every parish. Then, too, the Reformers' doctrine of the *testimonium Spiritus sancti internum* only leads to an unhealthy subjectivism. Difficulties and alterations in theological views, Tindal takes as evidence that there is no secure special revelation. 'There are twenty several Opinions concerning Justification all drawn from the Scriptures by men only of the Augustine Confession; and there are sixteen several Opinions concerning Original Sin; and as many Distinctions of the Sacraments as there are Sects of Men that disagree about them.'[3]

Having in Tindal the best exposition of the deistic dogmatism it is unnecessary to follow their literature any further. What followed was but a less vigorous reiteration of *Christianity as Old as Creation*. How the orthodox met the challenge of Tindal will be seen later: it is estimated that one hundred and fifty replies to him were forthcoming.[4] Fortunately most of these, which were mere repetitions

[1] Op. cit., p. 294.
[2] *Essay on the Human Understanding* (2nd edition), pp. 276–7.
[3] *Christianity as Old as Creation*, p. 261.
[4] *Bibliography of British History*, ed. by Pargellis and Madley (1714–89), p. 150.

of the greater works, have long since passed into oblivion. The fact is, as C. E. Moore rightly observes: 'The arguments of the deists were never successfully refuted. On the contrary, the striking thing is that their opponents, the militant divines and writers of numberless volumes of 'Evidences of Christianity', had come to the same rational basis as the deists. They referred even the most subtle questions to the pure reason, as no one now would do. The deistic movement was not really defeated. It largely compelled its opponents to adopt its methods.'[1]

(ii) *Criticism of the View*

Leaving, then, until a later chapter an investigation of the mode and method of the orthodox reply, we purpose here to make some criticism of the deistic presuppositions.

To begin with, the basic notion of the whole deistic movement was the Cartesian doctrine of the equality of reason in all men. 'Reason', observes Toland, 'is the Foundation of all Certainty.' It is not just an instrument of the self, but the very essence of the self, consequently, reason does not operate merely to make discriminate judgements but is the only source of religion and virtue. Setting out from this premise, the deists believed that sure and certain knowledge was truly attainable by all without too much effort. They thus proclaimed that since the world is the creation of a deity of absolute rationality, then men made in His image are also supremely rational beings who can follow God's plan in the created universe. 'The intellect cannot question the truth of what it apprehends as necessary; and the only necessity it recognizes is the necessity of what is intelligible.'[2]

A. Starting then from this premise that reason is equal in all men the logical results for deism must be an unhealthy individualism. Each man is king in his own domain; each recognizes no other authority but the findings of his own unstained and unstunted reason. There is no objective standard, for the criterion of truth lies in the knowing subject, not in the object to be known. By exclusive emphasis on the divine transcendence, deism repudiated any idea of the divine immanence which, in some sense, can be held to interrelate the individual units.

On the other hand, by separating man from God, deism made

---

[1] *Christian Thought since Kant*, p. 24.
[2] W. de Burgh, *Towards a Religious Philosophy*, p. 138.

the relation between man and man a purely pragmatic one. There was no real binding link. This deistic conception is in line with the Leibnizian doctrine of monads each separate and self-sufficient. Leibniz had insisted that the individual entities which make up the totality of the universe is each complete in itself. Each monad is 'big with the future', thus having its explanation within itself. For the deists, then, the single individual, with his 'clear and distinct ideas' was his own authority. He has no connection with and no responsibility to, another. The deistic position was a mere doctrinaire one, only possible on the basis of a complete misunderstanding of the human individual.

In the rejection of the Leibnizian doctrine there is no need to go to the other extreme and advocate the Humian denial of an existing self. Nor, on the other hand, need it be maintained that the individual is the result of the interplay upon some neutral 'stuff' of social forces. Personality is not created by the environment. Because it develops in a social content it does not follow that it is produced by it. It is true that human beings do become aware of their own personalities by association with others. But it is also true that there is a 'self' which becomes aware; an 'I' that takes notice. 'Because we arrive at the knowledge of our own personalities through contact with others,' observes Dalgairns, 'it does not follow that personality itself is constituted by the sharp shock which comes of knocking our own self against another self.' The paradox exhibited by the fact of personality is, that, while it has a centre all its own, a private world of thought and feeling which others cannot penetrate, yet, because we are persons, we can transcend our isolation. As Professor John MacMurray remarks, 'The more universal a person becomes in his self-transcendence, the more unique does he become in his individuality.'[1]

The deists failed to grasp the fact stated by Aristotle in his definition of man as a 'political animal', or as we might say to-day, a 'social being'. In a recent book Reinhold Niebuhr has pointed out that each individual is 'unique', and that the 'internal dialogue of the self' is beyond the penetrating analysis of any 'depth psychology'. There is an internal self which cannot be invaded by the most formidably armed host of psychoanalysts. At the same time, just because man is a social being, the self cannot be complete in isolation. 'The self is engaged in a perpetual dialogue with other

[1] *Adventure*, ed. by B. H. Streeter, p. 193.

selves in which its dependence upon others becomes apparent.'[1] The more real an individual knows himself to be the more related does he recognize that he is. Even Leibniz, who had insisted so strongly upon the separateness of the monads, could not leave it at that; he thus reintroduced a principle of unity by the back door in his artificial doctrine of pre-existing harmony. But the deists had nothing to bind together the isolated selves: they viewed each individual as an all-knowing, centre, adequate in its own self-sufficiency. Such was the result which followed from its own failure to understand the fact of man's social nature.

B. It must be pointed out further, that when once the fundamental assumptions of deism are accepted then naturalism and scepticism must inevitably result. Man by his own unaided reason can find out all the truth that he needs. God has apparently nothing to add; no new truths to disclose. The order of nature is thus a closed system in which there is no need for, and no possibility of, a rift. The veil is in no place rent, for God cannot reveal anything more of Himself than that which is already written into the laws of nature.

Tindal insists that God Himself is bound by this inflexible necessity. The will of God is always determined by the 'nature and reason of things'.[2] Therefore, 'Individual wisdom can have no commands, but what are founded on the unalterable reason of things.'[3] It is to be concluded, Tindal affirms, that 'God's will is so clearly manifested in the Book of Nature that he who runs can read it'.[4]

But the question arises, To what purpose would it be to read God's signature upon the universe when He stands beyond it in solitary isolation unknown and unknowable by any intimate acquaintance? The deists, in this respect, unlike Kant, did not even require God as a Dispenser of Happiness, as a Paymaster of Pleasure, renumerating those who obeyed the dictates of the categorical imperative. Tindal finds a natural connection between goodness and pleasure. Rewards and punishments, he contends, are the inseparable attendants of virtuous and vicious actions. God is consequently pushed aside as unnecessary. In this context a retort by Leyland can be appreciated, 'I do not see that he leaves

---

[1] *The Self in the Dramas of History*, p. 42.
[2] *Christianity as Old as Creation*, p. 65.
[3] Op. cit., p. 247.
[4] Op. cit., p. 24.

God anything at all to do in the matter.'[1] God has no finger in the pie; has nothing to do with rewards for virtue. The biblical assertion that we must all appear before the judgement seat of Christ to give an account of the deeds done in the body, is meaningless. As a result ethics have no divine standard. There is no ultimate reference. All is natural.

God is conceived to be a purely ornamental Being having no present or future significance for the world; but many people feel no sentiment for the purely ornamental. God may have started the world, but He no longer steers it. He moved it, but He does not now mind it. He is, as Carlyle says, 'An absentee God, sitting idle ever since the first Sabbath at the outside of the world and seeing it go.' A God so indifferent and inactive will soon not be believed in at all. Thus with a world rationally sufficient and a God completely indifferent, the logical result is naturalism and scepticism. As J. V. Langmead Casserley has observed, 'The deists saw that, although the physical science of their time required the idea of God as Creator, it could not tolerate the conception of any further divine interference with the course of the creation. Once the universe had begun to exist, all further explanations of what happens in it must be couched in scientific terms alone.'[2]

C. This leads to another important theoretical defect of which the deistic teachers were unaware. In a world of regularity and order the deists found the one sufficient reason for their idea of a Creator in the argument from Design. It was, indeed, logical enough to suppose, *a priori*, that the world could only continue without 'any further divine interference' if it followed an ordered plan. And the deists had no doubt here. They were optimistic about everything, for the world to them was flooded by an excess of light. They were content in their faith that the universe was brought into existence by a Happy Being, and it is, therefore, the best of all possible worlds. But what if God is no longer amused by it? That matters not, since all creation is good and beautiful and man reasonable and wise: then all is well. The evidences of design are so abundant, so the deists believed, that there need be no doubt about a Master Mechanic Who set it all agoing.

It was in this context that the deists proclaimed and maintained the authority and sufficiency of the teleological argument for the

[1] *Answer to Tindal*, p. 234.
[2] *The Christian in Philosophy*, p. 104.

existence of their transcendent Creator. The 'proof' was used of course with equal emphasis by their opponents. But there are two points to be made against the deist's gay use of the argument.

First, their optimism was not justified by all the facts. There is more in the world than the deists were ready to acknowledge. There is a sterner side of nature which must not be overlooked in the interests of a theory. The mood of deism was too gaily cavalier: 'all's well with the world'. But deism is not a true induction from the facts. Its major premise was a sweeping generalization which took no account of the negative instances. Those of deistic outlook should not have had to wait for John Stuart Mill's essay on nature to have been made aware of the evidences of dysteleology.[1] It is against the background of this emphasis of deism that the importance of Butler's *Analogy* is to be seen. Butler, by way of correcting the shallow optimism of the deists, may have gone to the other extreme, but he was certainly right to accentuate the gloomy aspect in contrast with the gaiety of deism. Against Tindal's assertion that nature is an open book in which anyone can read the facts of the Creator's existence, Butler showed that nature itself is mysterious and mystifying. Herein lies the supreme significance of the *Analogy*. It is important to remember that 'he is not arguing with atheists, but with Deists'.[2] The deists may reject vital doctrines of Christianity because they consider them to be unreasonable and mysterious, but if understandability and absence of mystery are the criteria, then, How can the deists be so sure that God created the world and set it off on its ordained path when there is so much evidence for the cruel, the unreasonable and the haphazard? Read in this context Butler's argument is certainly valid. If there is so much mystery in nature, is it not reasonable to suppose, on the principle of analogy, that there will be mystery also in God's special revelation? Divorced from its historical setting the *Analogy* is a weary and a dreary book. 'If we come to its perusal fresh from a course of reading in deistic literature; we should thankfully imbibe its teaching as a wholesome tonic after dipping into the honey-pots of optimism.'[3]

Then, secondly, by putting God out of touch with the world and beyond the experiences of men, it followed that the deists should

---

[1] Cf. 'In sober truth nearly all the things which men are hanged for or imprisoned are nature's everyday performances.' *Three Essays on Religion*, p. 28.
[2] C. D. Broad, *Religion, Philosophy and Psychical Research*, p. 20.
[3] A. B. Bruce, *Apologetics*, p. 126.

give exclusive place to the teleological argument for the existence
of God. They failed to appreciate that there were other points of
view. All 'transcendental theologies', indeed, seem committed to a
denial of the validity of the ontological proof. In this respect both
deist and orthodox alike followed Aquinas. The 'Angelic Doctor'
held that God is not the first to be known, but that we arrive at a
knowledge of Him by inference from the created world. E. L.
Mascall claims that this rejection of the ontological proof and
acceptance of the cosmological and teleological arguments as adequate is the 'traditional approach'.[1] His attempt to justify this
position in the 'Preface' cannot be considered convincing. To refer
to the Thomistic method as the 'traditional approach' is surely
straining the evidence. It was not, as a matter of fact, until the
time of Aquinas, for whom Aristotle was the supreme master, that
the idea of argument from nature to God found any significant
place. It has but to be remembered that the works of Aristotle had
only come to light again in the preceding century or two. The first
reaction to the rediscovered works of the Greek philosopher was so
much one of fear that the University of Paris solemnly condemned
them in 1215. It was not until we come to the time of Aquinas that
we find the heathen Greek baptized into the service of Christian
theology.

The Thomist, Gilson, rejecting the ontological argument, points
out that in Greek thought there is no trace of it. He explains the
fact like this, 'Thinkers like Plato and Aristotle, who do not identify God and being, could never dream of deducing God's existence from his idea; but when a Christian thinker like St Anselm
asks whether God exists he asks, in fact, whether Being exists, and
to deny God is to affirm that Being does not exist.'[2] His point,
however, proves something other than he intended. It shows that
the Greek approach of Aquinas is the essentially rationalistic
approach in distinction from the Anselmic. But as the Greek
approach of Aquinas was necessarily late it would be more just to
argue that the Anselmic is the specifically Christian 'traditional
approach'. Certainly Augustine, like Anselm, did not interpret
God through nature. For both, all experiences were to be understood in the light of the inner realization of God given in self-
conscious experience. All nature was to be understood through

---

[1] *He Who Is, A Study in Traditional Theism*, pp. 14–17.
[2] *Spirit of Mediaeval Philosophy* (E.T.), p. 59.

Him. 'How remarkable it is', exclaimed Pascal, 'that no biblical author makes use of nature to prove God!'[1] The traditional approach, then, seems to be, not through nature to God, but rather through God is nature interpreted and faith strengthened. However conclusive the Thomistic method has been considered in the past, and is still so to-day by such neo-Thomists as Maritain, Gilson, Box and Mascall, there are many not convinced that the conclusion is certain. There are those who maintain an opposite point of view.

Those, therefore, on the other side, whose religious philosophy gives greater emphasis to the immanence of God tend to make the ontological proof fundamental. Several writers would indeed maintain that all the so-called Theistic proofs begin from an already existing idea of Him. They contend that the proofs for the existence of God could never have been set on foot without prior belief in His existence, and the belief in His existence could never arise apart from God's own activity within. This means that some scholars can maintain that all cosmological arguments for the existence of God are based on the ontological, since there can be no belief in a transcendent Creator as such because that belief is itself evidence of His immanence.[2] Others press the point further and maintain that the ontological argument was not an attempt made by Anselm to prove the existence of God because it began with an already assured faith in Him. This is confirmed by the fact that Anselm's ontological argument occurs in his *Proslogion*, which is really a book of meditative prayer not a work on metaphysical philosophy.

Anselm himself, it is noted, affirmed that argument is belief in search of an understanding. The purpose of religious philosophy is not to originate a knowledge of God. Philosophy, indeed, in contrast with the exact sciences, does not lead to conclusions which lie in the realm of the completely unknown. Its purpose is rather to 'bring us to know in a different way things which we already knew in some other way'.[3]

The more writers on this side press the idea of the divine immanence the more they look within for the knowledge of God. Thus while all transcendent theologies make it a matter of

---

[1] Quoted in J. Baillie, *Interpretation of Religion*, p. 185.
[2] Cf. W. G. de Burgh, *Towards a Religious Philosophy*, ch. viii.
[3] R. G. Collingwood, *Philosophical Method*, p. 161.

inference, all immanentalist theologies make the knowledge of God
a matter of intuition. Here again two points of view come into
opposition.[1]

Our own conviction, however, believing as we do in the truth of
what Archbishop Temple has described as the 'immanence of the
Transcendence'[2] is, that this antithesis is false. The truth seems to
be that in the act of religious knowledge there is a union of the two.
There is, at the same time, an inference and an intuition. Rashdall
refers to the exclamation of Helmholtz who had made some
brilliant discovery: 'It was given me!' he said. But Rashdall's
comment is a virtual contradiction of the statement, 'it was not
true', he says, 'because it came to Helmholtz in this way, but because it was subsequently verified and proved.' This would seem,
however, to make truth to depend upon verification — ultimately
a pragmatist epistemology. Actually Helmholtz's words imply that it
was more than an immediate inspiration. 'It was given me!' united
with, 'I have got it!' There was both an intuition and an inference
combining in the one act. In so far, therefore, as this conclusion is
true, it means that the deist's complete repudiation of the intuitive
and exaltation of the inferential method is not exact.

D. The deists made man a mere creature of reasoning and they
failed to observe that, psychologically, religion is more deeply and
broadly based. To identify revelation and reason is really to equate
religion and philosophy. Herein lies one of the chief difficulties in
all rationalistic theologies. Our interest in this place is not in a discussion of how the two may be said to be conterminous. Since both
religion and philosophy are man's quest for ultimate reality it is
evident that they must have elements in common.

It is, however, important to observe that religion and philosophy
are not one and the same. 'The religious act or attitude,' says

---

[1] The same opposition has, of course, persisted. Cf., e.g. Hastings Rashdall,
'All religious truth, as I hold, depends logically upon inference,' again, 'I deny
that the truth of God's existence can reasonably be accepted on the basis of an
immediate judgement or intuition,' Hastings Rashdall, *Philosophy and Religion*,
ch. II, cf., p. 106. See also, J. Caird, *The Introduction to the Philosophy of
Religion*, ch. II. On the other side, cf., e.g. F. B. Jevons, 'All attempts to exhibit
the existence of God as an inference from experience are foredoomed to failure.'
Religion and Evolution, p. 134. Cf. also, 'The reality of the deity is not a *deduction* from religious experience, but the *content* of it — *that which is experienced*.
If the immediate reality of the higher principle be taken away there could be
nothing left of religious experience. It would no longer exist. But it does exist,
and therefore that which is given and experienced in it exists also. *God is in us,
therefore He is.*' Solovyof, *Justification of the Good* (E.T.), p. 164.
[2] *Nature, Man and God*, p. 277.

H. R. Mackintosh, 'is not merely a knowing act and attitude, otherwise it would be hard to distinguish it from science and philosophy.'[1] That the two are not to be equated should be obvious in spite of the rationalists' identification of them. There is a sense in which religion may be said to be, at the same time, narrower and wider than philosophy. One only needs to glance through the contents of any comprehensive text-book on Metaphysics to observe that there are many topics there dealt with which have no place in religion. Upon many subjects with which science has to concern itself, no Christian man would enter the claim that the interest is forbidden by religion. This does not mean that any doctrine of 'double truth' is permissible. Nor does it mean that religion is not concerned with the whole of life, but it does mean that there are provinces of philosophical enquiry and scientific investigation in which religion has no special concern.

On the other side of the paradox, it is equally true that religion is much wider than philosophy. If the two are to be identified then we would be committed to the fantastic position that the greater the philosopher the more truly religious he would be. This is obviously false. To be able to know is one thing, to be able to worship is another. A philosopher may seek to penetrate into the utmost secrets of the universe but the religious man must pray to the God of the universe. That which is the final problem for philosophy is the first assurance for the believer. Love, not learning, after all, is the primary truth about religion. The optimism which identifies knowledge with virtue has been so often proved false in the experiences of men that it is strange how it was raised by the rationalists to the final truth about human life.

The fact is that the religious kind of knowledge does not depend upon a man's metaphysical acumen. The peasant behind his plough may have a deeper religious understanding than the philosopher in his study. In the region of the spirit, the scientific and the academic are not the passport to greatness. As Schleiermacher long ago observed, if religion and philosophy were the selfsame thing then 'religion could be acquired by study — a thing not hitherto asserted'.[2] When one asks the question, To whom shall we go in our quest for an understanding of the deep things of the spirit? we are sure to be answered by the honest scientist and

---

[1] *The Christian Apprehension of God*, p. 36.
[2] *Reden*, tr. Oman, p. 102.

philosopher, who are only such, Come not to us for a knowledge of these things. We instinctively feel that one who is merely an adept in methodology is not the best man to meet the needs of an anxious enquirer. It was the washerwomen of Bedford who set John Bunyan on the way everlasting. This does not put a premium upon ignorance, but it is an assertion of the principle that it is the pure in heart who see God. It is to men of humble spirit that God discloses His secrets. On the final truths about God and man; life and death; sin and forgiveness; and the like issues of eternal significance, we rightly listen to the Man of Galilee rather than to the men of Greece. To Plato and Aristotle we may go if we would adventure into the secrets of metaphysical knowledge, but it is to Jesus Christ we must go if we would know of a Father and a Friend.

It is an error to take the thought-element in consciousness as the whole, since 'thought' and 'life' are not co-extensive. The human mind is not an active centre of energy which operates to trace out logical correlations or to observe uniform sequences. It is also a centre of value, or, perhaps more correctly, a subject of value. Religious knowledge cannot be limited to that which can be logically explained or expressed. Its deepest certainties lie outside the realm of the scientifically verifiable. 'Where God is present, He is active, and where He is active He needs no testimonial of character.'[1] God ever comes to the total life of man, not to the reason only, but to the whole psychical nature of the responding individual. And because this is so, God's revelation of Himself will not be irrational, on the one hand, nor can it be identified with reason on the other.

The deists would eliminate all that cannot be understood and yet they themselves begin from that which is an ultimate mystery, the inexplicable self. The paradox which dominates our spiritual life is, as Schweitzer has indicated, that if rational thought thinks itself out to a conclusion, it comes to something non-rational. As long as religion remains truly religion it must contain something which reason cannot fathom. It is true that a religion all mystery would be impossible for rational beings, but it is also true that a religion without mystery would be equally impossible for creatures who are more than intellect. Because religion is essentially a relation between a human self and a personal God there will be more in it

[1] H. Wheeler Robinson, *Redemption and Revelation*, p. 8.

than the reason will ever be able to comprehend. It is thus possible to accept the remark of Dean Mansel, 'Let Religion begin where it will it must begin with that which is above reason.'[1]

E. With a God completely indifferent and man inherently good and the world perfectly ordered, the question for the deist must arise, What need and what possibility are there for religion?

There is no need seeing that man has no urgent want to drive him out in search for an understanding and undertaking God. It is only when the soul cries out, 'O wretched man that I am! who shall deliver me from the body of this death?' (Rom. 7. 24), that there is the 'stuff' of religion. It is only when one is aware of the fact, that 'In me, that is, in my flesh dwelleth no good thing' (Rom. 7. 18), will one seek a Redeemer. Where there is no feeling of guilt there can be no need for God. Knowledge of sin is, after all, as Kierkegaard says, 'possible only in the presence of God.'[2]

On the other hand there is no possibility of religion in deism with its 'God' on the limits far withdrawn. 'The God of Deism', says Emil Brunner, 'is one who, after the creation of the world, withdrew to His own heritage, He is a God who has said farewell and gone away,'[3] this is the conception of God lashed by the ridicule of Goethe:

> *'What kind of God were this, who only from without*
> *would move the world,*
> *Letting the universe flow in circles round his finger?'*

Certainly with a God of this kind revelation is impossible and prayer inadmissible.

The design of God, Tindal informs us, was to make men happy, and for this purpose the rules of rational religion were made known to all mankind. But, on the one hand, there is evidence enough that those who would live godly in the present world are not always happy; and, on the other hand, it may well be questioned if such a hedonist ideal is valid. Is it not more certainly the purpose of God to make men holy? The ultimate command of the Gospel is in fact: 'Be ye holy, for I am holy, saith the Lord.'

To such a statement, then, of revelation as infallible reason, a reaction was bound to set in. It was defective from every point of

---

[1] *The Limits of Human Thought*, p. 182.
[2] Quoted in E. Brunner, *Philosophy of Religion*, p. 78.
[3] E. Brunner, *Revelation and Reason*, p. 356.

view. 'Deism', says M. Reville, 'in sound philosophy is not tenable. It establishes a dualism, a veritable opposition between God and the world, which stand opposite to and limit each other . . . . A reaction in fact was inevitable. It was necessary that it should be at the same time philosophical and religious, and should come to the satisfaction of the needs that had been misunderstood or suppressed. In philosophy Deism could no longer hold up its head against the objections of reason. In religion, every one was weary of optimism and of empty declamations. Deism removed God so far from the world and from humanity that piety exhausted itself in the endeavour to rejoin Him in the icy heights of heaven, and ended by renouncing the attempt.'[1]

This discussion, it is worth while to point out, is not merely of historical interest. If deism, as such, quickly passed away, killed by the necessity for a religion to meet men's more fundamental needs, its main concepts found expression elsewhere. Its notion of God as remote and out of reach was erected into a more dignified philosophy by Kant. While its equation of religion and philosophy was given a more confident and a more plausible emphasis by Hegel. Today the same view is set forth with new vigour by the neo-Idealism of Benedetto Croce and Giovanni Gentile. These writers view religion as immature philosophy which is doomed to extinction when man reaches his intellectual stature. This excess of confidence in reason we have seen to be untenable. There is a knowledge wider and more satisfying than that which reason alone can discover.

[1] Quoted in J. Orr, *Christian View of God and the World*, p. 395.

CHAPTER IV

THE AUTHORITY OF THE SUBJECTIVE

It is now necessary, so that we may have a full account of the types of revelation in our period, and a better understanding of the orthodox apologetic, to refer to a doctrine which may be more familiar to the general reader. Because of this acquaintance, no prolonged exposition need be attempted. Certain criticisms, however, which the doctrine demands will be made and certain contrasts which were implied will be investigated.

REVELATION AS INDWELLING LIGHT
(i) *An Understanding of the View*

It is not easy for us at this distance either to appreciate, on the one hand, the desires which gave birth to the spirit of 'enthusiasm', or, on the other hand, the repugnance with which it was regarded by the orthodox. In what has come to be called 'Enthusiasm', there was a reaction, and at times a violent one, from all ruling objective standards, whether Church or Scripture. To those who repudiated such outside curbs, revelation was regarded as something internal. It thus appeared excusable for each individual to do that which was right in his own eyes.

In some cases this doctrine developed as an avowed rejection of the Calvinist teaching of an elect number of saved souls for whom alone an atonement had been made. To stress the universal influence of Christ, emphasis was placed upon the Johannine declaration that, He was the light that lighteth every man that cometh into the world. For this reason, Henry Denne, for ex-example, in a tract entitled, *The Draw-net of the Kingdom of Heaven*,[1] advocated the doctrine of the Indwelling Light. Denne is called by Thomas Edwards in his *Gangraena*, 'an antinomian and desperate Arminian,' who boldly asserts, 'that Jesus Christ has

---

[1] The full title of the work is, *Draw-net of the Kingdom of Heaven, or Christ Drawing all Men* (1646). Denne was a graduate of Cambridge who had received ordination into the Established Church. He later became a Baptist.

died for all men, Turks and Pagans' for 'Judas as well as Peter'.[1]

Numerous indeed were the companies of those who looked for the inner revelation of the light. Something of their variety can be found in a pamphlet which appeared in London in 1652, under the enchanting title, *The Pulpit Guarded by XVII Arguments*. The author, a Puritan Divine at Henley-in-Arden, volunteers the information; 'We have many sects now abroad, Ranter(s), Seekers, Shakers, Quakers and now Creepers.'[2] This list is by no means complete, for in another passage others are mentioned: and there are still to be added the Familists and Muggletonians and others of lesser account. But however these sects differed from each other, and whatever the precise relation between them, the general characteristic of all was that which goes under the description, given in opprobrium, Enthusiasm.

The doctrine of the indwelling light manifested itself in a particularly crude form among the Ranters, but in a more spiritual manner among the Quakers. The excesses of the Ranters were certainly abhorrent to the Friends, as their early literature abundantly testifies. A dark picture is given of the former in the *Ranters' Bible*, by one, Gilbert Roulston who, for a number of years, had been among them. They laid emphasis upon the sufficiency of the indwelling light, but were completely antinomian. That numbers of them were, what would be termed in these days neurotics, is beyond dispute. Ranterism was a 'Free Spirit' movement, which discarded all external standards. Unlike the Seekers, the Ranters did not allow to the Scriptures the position even of a 'secondary help'. They were thus their own sole authority, each finding, like Descartes, his sufficient assurance within his own subjectivity.

'The Seeker movement had undervalued objective religion and outward helps. The natural result was that those who pushed the ideas of the Seekers to their extreme limit and, throwing overboard all outward systems, acknowledged nothing Divine except the Spirit in themselves, had no fixed authority anywhere, no criterion of morals, no test of spiritual guidance, no ground and basis for goodness. Being "taught by the Spirit", they claimed that all

---

[1] Op. cit., p. 91. Edwards writes again: 'He professes all the Arminian Doctrines. That Christ died for all, and for Judas in particular and that he was confident: That he died for all, as well as for any,' p. 49. This page is out of place, following p. 76. In this the copy in Dr Williams' Library agrees with that in the British Museum.

[2] Op. cit., p. 15.

other teachings were of no use. They called the Scriptures "a
tale", "a history, a dead letter," "a fleshly story, a cause of divisions and contradictions." They looked upon Christ as a "figure"
or "type" of the TRUE DISPENSATION OF THE SPIRIT, upon which they
claimed to have entered.'[1]

Arising out of their doctrine of the indwelling light in all men,
the Ranters went on to assert a crude pantheism. 'There were
probably varieties of Ranters theologically. Pantheism, or the
essential identity of God with the universe, and His indwellings in
every creature, angelic, human, brute or inorganic, seems to have
been the belief of most of the Ranters that could manage to rise to
metaphysics.'[2] God was in all and thus was all good and nothing to
be refused. It was this conception which led the Ranters into the
excesses of antinomianism which spread throughout the land both
moral disease and religious fanaticism. So disturbing indeed was
their influence that Parliament had to act to curb the tendencies
which were making for 'the dissolution of human society'.[3]

It was perhaps such excesses which led Isaac Taylor, the recluse
of Stamford Rivers, in the first half of the eighteenth century, to
investigate the phenomenon. He published his conclusions in a
book entitled, *The Natural History of Enthusiasm*. Possibly a
statement by Locke concerning his *Essay on Enthusiasm* gave to
Taylor his inspiration for the work. Locke had excused his own
limited treatment of the subject by saying, 'To give an historical
account of the various ravings men have embraced for religion
under the name enthusiasm, would, I fear, be beside my purpose,
and be enough to make a huge volume.' It was left to Taylor to
supply this defect. The author certainly looked back to the past,
for, he observes, his own age cannot be considered 'eminently or
conspicuously an age of religious enthusiasm'.[4]

Some enthusiasm he traces to infirm constitutions,[5] other to an
over-lively imagination, and, yet other to an exclusive preoccupation with prophetical interpretation,[6] and so forth. 'A chronic

[1] Rufus M. Jones, *Studies in Mystical Religion*, p. 469.
[2] D. Mason, *Life of Milton*, vol. 5, p. 18.
[3] 'Preamble to act of Parliament of blasphemous and execrable Opinions, Aug.
9th, 1650,' Scobell's *Collection of Acts and Ordinances*, pt. ii, p. 124.
[4] *Natural History of Enthusiasm* (2nd edition), p. 16.
[5] Cf., 'There was an element of fierce fanaticism in the movement, and among
the Ranters there were some real lunatics.' R. M. Jones, *Studies in Mystical
Religion*, p. 469 (Footnote).
[6] Cf., 'The adoption of an exclusive theory of exposition will not fail to be
followed by an attempt to attach the special marks of prophecy to every passing

intellectual enthusiasm' he makes the source of heresy. In considering that unrestrained enthusiasm of which the earlier Ranters were such a tragic illustration, Taylor makes many cogent points. He who knows that he is really separated from God, not simply by means of distance which he can himself cross, but by a chasm which he cannot bridge, will not be tempted to give expression to the ravings of the enthusiasts. 'In a word,' he says, 'it may be confidently affirmed that no man becomes an enthusiast in religion, until he has forgotten that he is a transgressor — a transgressor reconciled to God by mediation.'[1] The great need of the enthusiast is for a profound awareness of his deficiencies. 'Genuine humility would shake the whole towering structure of this enthusiastic pietism.'[2] It is pride which inflates a person into enthusiasm. If, therefore, the sad error of the enthusiast lies in his thinking of himself more highly than he ought to think; the fundamental weakness is to be found in his 'outlawry from common sense and scriptural authority'.[3]

But it was in a form less violent and antinomian that the early Friends expressed their doctrine of the inner light. This milder manifestation was not however limited to the Quaker movement, since, as Dr Rufus Jones says in his Introduction to W. C. Braithwaite's, *Beginnings of Quakerism*, 'There were numerous persons, both outside and inside the Quaker group, who quite independently of George Fox, had the insight that religion, to be true and spiritual must be "well grounded in the witness of the Spirit".'[4] It is among the Friends, however, that we find societies organized to give expression and witness to the view. 'This doctrine of the inner light', it has been justly observed, 'was the only positive assertion that the Friends were prepared to make.'[5] But it is in the Quaker movement that it is seen at its best.

'The important fact is obvious enough, that here in the English Commonwealth there now appeared a group of persons — plain, simple, persons without technical learning — who succeeded in passing from knowledge about God, knowledge that consisted of demonstration from Scripture texts, "notional knowledge", they

event, and it is this attempt which sets enthusiasm in flame.' *The Natural History of Enthusiasm*, p. 115.
[1] *Natural History of Enthusiasm*, p. 49.
[2] Op. cit., p. 37.
[3] Op. cit., p. 79.
[4] *Beginnings of Quakerism*, Preface, p. xxviii.
[5] *Enthusiasm*, R. Knox, p. 156.

aptly called it, to inward, first-hand experience which was so vivid, so warm and intimate, so mightily transforming, that they one and all were convinced that they had found God in the present tense.'[1]

In the early pages of his *Journals*, George Fox tells how the understanding of the inner light came to him as a vivid and vital experience, an experience which put him, he believed, into marked contrast with the prevailing temper of his age. The period was one in which the idea of an immediate revelation was, for the most part, incomprehensible. Revelation was thought to be embodied in propositions to which an unquestioning assent had to be made; so ran the general view. Knowledge of God was thus second-hand, distant and dim. It was to the light within, George Fox asserts again and again, that he owed his understanding of God. He was led to see, he tells us, that the Light and Spirit had come before the Scripture, and, therefore, did not ultimately depend upon it. This light within, he proclaims, was given to all men. 'Now the Lord opened to me by his invisible power, that everyman was enlightened by the Divine Light of Christ; I saw it shine through all; and they that believed in it came out of condemnation to the light of life, and became children of it; but they that hated it, and believed not in it, were condemned by it, though they made a profession of Christ.'[2]

In the preface to the first edition of the *Journals* which appeared in 1694, three years after Fox's death William Penn lays it down as the Quaker's special contribution secured by their leader that, 'In his testimony on ministry he much laboured to open truth to the people's understandings, and to bottom them upon the principle, Christ Jesus the Light of the World, that by bringing them to something that was God in themselves, they might the better know and judge of Him and themselves.'[3]

Fox, according to his own story, had read the Scriptures, and listened to many preachers, but his spiritual condition was nothing bettered, but rather grew worse. He had to learn that God dealt with men directly and through the light within.[4] In the record of

---

[1] *Beginnings of Quakerism*, Preface, p. xxxvii.
[2] *Journal* (8th edition), p. 34.
[3] *Journal* (1st edition, 1694), Preface, p. xlvii.
[4] The following passage, taken without translation from Norman Penny's edition, 1911 (Cambridge University Press), illustrates Fox's position. 'I declared ye everlastinge truth of ye Lorde & ye worde of life (for severall houres) & y^t ye Lord & Christ Jesus was come to teach his people himselfe & to bringe y^m of all ye worlds ways & teachers to Christ there way to God: & layde open all

George Fox, then, we find him giving testimony to the universal indwelling light. 'In a day of shams,' writes William James with some warmth, 'it was a religion of veracity rooted in spiritual inwardness, and a return to something more like the original gospel truth than men had ever known in England.'[1]

It was twenty-five years before the eighteenth century dawned that Robert Barclay set forth this doctrine of the indwelling light in theological form. It is the mission of the Friends, he says, 'to preach Christ, and direct people to His pure Light in the heart.'[2] He finds, it is significant to observe, justification for his position in the writings of the Cambridge Platonist, John Smith, quoting from his *Discourses*, those passages in which a mere 'notional knowledge' of God is repudiated.[3] The tragedy of his day he sees in the rejection of the very doctrines for which he contends: 'nothing is less minded and more rejected by all sorts of Christians, *than immediate and divine revelation*; in so much that once to lay claim to it is matter of reproach.'[4] It is declared that the sons of God are led by the Spirit of God, yet anyone claiming to be so led is called 'an heretic' by the 'pretended orthodox'. It is this inner revealing of God which alone gives certain knowledge, for it is a direct manifestation of God within the heart; a very different thing this from 'soaring, airy head-knowledge'.

Passage after passage reiterates the thesis, 'that inner and immediate revelation is the only sure and certain way to the true saving knowledge of God.'[5] There is a knowledge of God claimed by some, but it is merely learnt off like the prattling of a parrot. The Socinians are rebuked for denying the inner operations of the Spirit and yet teaching that there is a light inherent in man. There is none however 'barbarous and wild' who has not 'found something in his heart reproving him for something evil which he has done'.[6] This 'something' is not to be equated with reason or conscience. It is a divine light, or, as he sometimes calls it, a 'seed' within the soul. The sum of what he has to teach is, he says, 'That

there teachers & sett uppe ye true teacher (Christ Jesus): & how they was judged by ye prophetts Christ & ye apostles & to bring y^m off ye temples made with hands y^t they y^{m}selves might know they was ye temples of God,' p. 42.

[1] W. James, *The Varieties of Religious Experience*, p. 7.
[2] R. Barclay, *Apology*, (10th edition, 1841), p. 169.
[3] Op. cit., p. 21.
[4] Op. cit., p. 17.
[5] Op. cit., p. 23.
[6] Op. cit., p. 126.

where the true inward knowledge of God is, through the revelation of his Spirit, there is all; neither is there an absolute necessity of any other.'[1] In every man, then, there is a light or seed of God; such did George Fox believe to be a true induction from his own experience, and such, too, was the view set forth by Barclay in theological form.

It was the conviction of the Quaker theologian that this doctrine of the indwelling light relieved men from 'the horrors of Calvinism'. But the escape was apparent only. In a manner which the Genevan theologian would have commended, Barclay stresses man's utter corruption and inability.[2] Even the light within is regarded as in no sense inherent in man *qua* man. It is to be likened to a candle in a lantern. But it is just here that 'the horrors of Calvinism' which Barclay had supposed himself to have escaped, is reintroduced by the back door, although Barclay, apparently, is unaware of the fact. All men have the indwelling light and by many it is rejected, with the consequence that the candle in the lantern goes black out, to leave the abandoned soul in the slough of eternal perdition.[3] Man can do nothing of himself to bring salvation within his reach. He must 'wait' the movement of the Spirit, and 'not resist' when it comes. But even these attitudes are not man's to achieve: they are the results of a supernaturally bestowed gift of faith. 'Faith', says Isaac Penington, one of the early Quakers, 'is not found in man's nature, so that it is a gift to be waited for and obtained from God.' Here we are back at a predestinarianism, no less strong, even if unconscious, as that of either Augustine or Calvin.

From this statement of the doctrine of revelation as indwelling light three deficiencies can be seen to follow. It falls, therefore, to consider

(ii) *The Weaknesses of the View*

A. First of all account must be taken of the total exclusion of reason. Barclay limits the activity of reason to 'things natural': it

---

[1] Op. cit., p. 24.

[2] Cf., *Proposition* iv, 'Concerning the Condition of Man in the Fall,' pp. 89–101. 'All Adam's posterity, or mankind, both Jews and Gentiles, as to the first Adam, or earthly man, is fallen, degenerated, and dead: deprived of the sensation of feeling of this inward testimony or seed of God; and is subject to the power, nature and seed of the serpent . . . , etc.'

[3] Cf., 'This divine and glorious life is in all men as a seed which of its own nature draws, invites, and inclines to God,' *Apology*, p. 129.

can have no place in 'things spiritual'. Indeed, in the realm of the spirit, reason is an obstacle, a stumbling-block, in the way of spiritual progress: 'the place where God dwells and manifests Himself was in men's hearts.'[1] Truth is consequently something experienced. It is significant that William James found the views of the Quakers congenial. His own *Pragmatism* is but the theoretic exposition of that which George Fox and his followers were here maintaining. Truth is based upon experience, it is, in fact, made by experience, and is estimated to be truth in so far as it does good to the soul. This is nothing other than the religious application of pragmatism; a principle valid enough in its way, but crippled by its complete subjectivity.

The early advocates of the doctrine of the indwelling light failed altogether to understand the place of reason in religious experience. The reason for this failure on their part may be twofold. The position they took up was one of reaction from the 'intellectualism' of the orthodox. But they were, as well, certainly hampered by their environment of ideas. It was the general notion that reason and reasoning were to be equated, and its only function was regarded as the setting forth of clear and distinct ideas. The Quakers had therefore no true psychology; no sufficient understanding of man's psychical make-up. Perhaps it is too much to expect that in the period in which they lived they should have grasped that 'there is no separate organ for the apprehension of divine truth, independent of the will, feeling and thought. Our knowledge of God comes to us in the interplay of those faculties'.[2] They did not see the full significance of the very chapter in John's Gospel to which they made such constant appeal: not only is Christ there revealed as the Light; He is the Logos also. It was this exclusion of reason which made inadequate their religious psychology. Although their misological attitude was limited to 'things spiritual' it is clear that it is just here that the real place of reason must be understood. Religion is essentially a relation, a relationship with God; it is, therefore, a relationship which involves the whole man in all the elements of his psychological nature. If it is not a contradiction in terms, it should be stated that there is no true religious epistemology which excludes from its account the activity of reason in the experience of religion.

[1] W. C. Braithwaite, *The Beginnings of Quakerism*, p. 34.
[2] W. Inge, *Personal Idealism and Mysticism*, p. 3.

B. Consequent upon this exclusion of reason and emphasis upon the indwelling light there followed an assertion of individual infallibility. When once all objective standards are swept aside and the subjective criterion is installed and crowned as all-sufficient, there seems little possibility of escape from the claim to personal infallibility. The early Quakers found themselves the object of such an accusation. The charge was not indeed without some real support, since some, at least, of the original Friends did not hesitate to make the claim. 'They believed', observes Braithwaite, 'that inspiration gave infallibility.'[1] That which others regarded as limited to the writers of the Scriptures they believed that they themselves possessed. 'In the light I met with infallibility,' says Penington, 'there the light of God's spirit is a certain infallible rule, and the eye that sees is a certain eye.' Justification for the view seemed clear enough. The indwelling light came from above, from God. Those who followed the light were 'the children of God', and it increased more and more until the perfect day. By coupling their experience of the indwelling light with their doctrine of Perfectionism there was the resultant notion of an almost complete identification with God. Thus George Fox can say 'he that hath the same spirit that raised up Jesus Christ is equal with God . . . which is a mystery . . . . According to the flesh I am the son of Abraham, According to the Spirit the Son of God, saith Christ'. Such an assertion was bound to lead to misunderstanding. He found it hard to explain himself and was, as a matter of fact, charged with blasphemy for making himself equal with God. That Fox was well satisfied with his own interpretation there can be no doubt, but his distinctions were not easily grasped by men of the world. As the quotation given above indicates, his point was that it was the spiritual man which is from above, that is one with God in Christ. Speaking in the saints, the Man from Heaven is the infallible one. But however much the position may be 'explained' and 'illustrated' it remains true that the early Friends, or some of them at least by actual claim, and all of them by the logic of their doctrine, did think of themselves as possessing infallibility. This was the natural conclusion to their teaching of revelation as indwelling light.

C. From the two points we have already made it was a further natural consequence that among the Friends there should be a

[1] *The Beginnings of Quakerism*, p. 109.

depreciation of the Scriptures. Fox stressed that the light came to him apart from the Scriptures. Barclay refers to those who agree that God is known only by an inward revelation but assert that such knowledge is mediated through the written word. He sees no possibility of, and no need for, such documentary mediation. Since all is ascribed to the action of the Spirit, the Scriptures are not to be given this intermediate position: 'the Spirit, and not the Scripture, is the foundation and ground of all truth and knowledge, and the primary rule of faith and manners.'[1] He uses a number of arguments designed to remove it from the exalted position given to it by the orthodox: arguments which were used later with such eloquent force by the deist, Tindal. Barclay would prove that God acts apart from the Scriptures since there are unlearned men who cannot read, and numbers of variant readings which put ordinary folk in doubt.

He will, however, allow to the Scriptures a 'second place'. Scripture would seem to be for Barclay as it is for Karl Barth a mere 'witness' to revelation as God chooses to make it. It is an attestation that God speaks and acts because it is a record that He has spoken and acted in the past.[2] Like Barth too, Barclay seems to teach that revelation is an act of God apart from the written word. Revelation is essentially and at all times *Dei loquentis persona*. It is God speaking, or, alternatively, Christ speaking.[3] In a manner, too, worthy of Brunner, Barclay likens the Scriptures to a 'looking-glass' and a 'window'.[4] Consonant also with his thesis, and like Brunner, he sees no conclusive reason to believe in a 'filled canon'.[5]

This doctrine of revelation which received its more spiritual significance and expression in the Quaker movement was, how-

---

[1] *Apology*, p. 67.
[2] Cf. K. Barth, *Church Dogmatics* (E.T., Professor G. T. Thomson), 1, i, pp. 57 f., 125 f., etc.
[3] Cf., *Church Dogmatics*, 1, i, p. 155 f.
[4] Cf., 'Just as the windowpanes are not there to be looked at, but to enable us to look through them at the view beyond, so we are not commanded to believe the Bible, but, through the window of the Bible, to see God's light,' E. Brunner, *Revelation and Reason*, pp. 181–2.
[5] *Apology*, p. 86. Cf., 'The dogma of the canon, like every other ecclesiastical decision of faith is not final and infallible, but it is possible and right continually to reexamine it, test it, and revise it.' Brunner acknowledges that the canonical decisions of the Early Church are not to be lightly set aside; and that there is a strong presumption that its decisions are likely to be accepted. He asserts however, that 'It would be easier, indeed, to envisage a reduction of the New Testament canon, such as Luther suggested'. *Revelation and Reason*, p. 132.

ever, in a very real way conditioned by the prevalent philosophical and religious Weltanschauung. It is this fact which distinguished it from a view which came afterwards into prominence, and which will be discussed later under the title, Revelation as Immediate Experience. The background of the doctrine here under review, Revelation as Indwelling Light, was the accepted dualism of the day, in which God and man, spiritual and natural, stood apart from each other. The Light or Seed within was, as we have seen, no part of man's nature. It was a foreign element. The line between human and divine was sharply drawn, and it was believed that never the twain could meet.[1]

Any suggestion that the light of God's spirit belonged to man's nature *per se* was obnoxious to the early Friends. It was a satanic temptation to be resisted. George Fox tells how he passed through such a period of darkness in which the devil had unleashed all his fury. But he came through to noonday and victory. On another occasion, in the Vale of Belvoir, a dark cloud overshadowed him and so completely obliterated was the world of spirit that, almost overwhelmed, he was tempted to say, 'All things came by Nature.' To speak thus was tantamount to declaring, 'There is no God.'

It was only as he sat still and gave no heed to it, that at length hope arose within him, and the steadying assurance returned, 'There is a living God Who made all things.'[2]

It was the constant affirmation of William Penn, in his *Primitive Christianity Revived*, that the light within is, 'in man but not of man.' It is natural to men, he asserts, to have a supernatural light.[3]

'The light of which we speak', declares Barclay, 'is not only distinct, but of a different nature from the soul and its faculties.'[4] The relation of the divine to the human was conceived somewhat

[1] It would be interesting to draw out further parallels between the Quaker theologian and Barth. For Barth, God is conceived to be 'actus purus' (*Church Dogmatics*, 1, i, p. 44). Like Barclay he teaches that there is no continued and natural relation between God and man. Both begin from the idea of the divine transcendence. It would compromise the sovereignty of God if He were involved in the worldly process. It is incorrect, therefore, to speak of God as 'immanent' in the sense of a continuity between the divine and the human. More correct is it as W. F. Camfield interprets, to speak of the idea of 'immanence' as meaning that 'there is transcendence in the world'. (*Revelation and the Holy Spirit*, p. 157, cf., K. Barth, *Credo*, p. 34.) This means for Barth as it does for Barclay that there is no real identity between the word of Scripture and the Word of God (cf., *Church Dogmatics*, 1, i, pp. 310–11).
[2] *Journal*, p. 26.
[3] *Primitive Christianity Revived* (1606), 3, i, 2.
[4] *Apology*, props., 12, 14, 16.

after the fashion of a lighted candle within a darksome cave, or a lamp in a dismal dungeon. Those who preached the doctrine of a light within could not conceive of it as in any sense natural to the human spirit: to have done so would have been for them the denial of revelation and the expression of an undisguised Pelagianism. Thus while in their theology they repudiated any idea of a divine immanence, in their experience they allowed its reality. But it was just here, in the next era, those who emphasized the subjective element, in opposition to the sterile objectivity of the orthodox, found the starting-point of their view. Under the influence of a rising idealistic philosophy, the dualistic conception of the universe was giving way. Stress was put upon the divine immanence, and the clear-cut separation between natural and spiritual was abandoned. Neither nature nor man was considered to have existence apart from God. There was a natural unity between the divine and human; and it was urged that in the inmost depths of his being every individual was akin to God. The Spirit of God was immanent in the life of man, not as an alien element, but as a natural reality. It was, then, under the impact of an idealistic philosophy that later writers are to be found expounding their view of revelation within the immediacy of experience.

With the triumph of idealism, a point was to be reached when Sabatier could maintain: 'Supernatural gifts become natural; or rather, at this mystic height, the antithesis becomes meaningless and obliterated.'[1]

[1] A. Sabatier, *Religions of Authority and the Religion of the Spirit* (E.T.), p. 307.

CHAPTER V

THE THESIS OF THE ORTHODOX

Those who, in the period of our review, have come to be designated, *The Orthodox*, regarded both Dogmatism and Enthusiasm with unaffected horror. The orthodox apologists saw in deism an impossible exaggeration of reason, while the Methodist Movement was considered to be a new exhibition of enthusiasm. Thus, Bishop Butler, for example, in an interview with John Wesley dismissed the leader of Methodism as one such misguided fanatic. 'Mr Wesley,' said the bishop, 'I will deal plainly with you: I once thought you and Mr Whitfield well-meaning men, but I cannot think so now, for I have heard more of you — matters of fact, Sir. And Mr Whitfield says in his *Journal*, "There are promises still to be fulfilled in me." Sir, this pretending to extraordinary revelation and gifts of the Holy Ghost is a horrid thing, a very horrid thing.'[1]

Against these two branded enemies the orthodox felt it necessary to enter into battle. To undermine deism they had to exhibit the reality and utility of a revealed religion; to the enthusiast they had to prove its objectivity and authority.

Broadly the deists argued that the only revelation men were given or needed was the moral dicta written into the constitution of the universe, and discoverable by all rational beings. What the intelligence could not encompass cannot belong to the essence of religion. Opposing deism, the orthodox apologists sought to defend revealed religion by reason, and at the same time to indicate the defects of reason as an instrument.

The two fundamental assumptions of deism, namely, that reason was in no way inadequate, and that revelation was in no way limited were the focal points of the orthodox attack. Apart from the negative method of demolition, the two main positive arguments towards the establishing of a revealed religion, were, first, to show that reason itself could not go the whole way. Then, secondly,

[1] Quoted in Overton and Relton, *History of the English Church*, vol. 7, p. 93.

to show that the element of mystery was no objection to revealed religion since, 'as large a bill of complaints,'[1] can be brought against natural religion. This argument was pressed with polished vigour by Butler. The central problem of the discussion 'was to discover the valid, rational grounds for belief in Christianity, and to decide between rival claims of reason and revelation'.[2]

The general view taken by the orthodox was that revealed religion was a necessary adjunct to natural religion. They thus argued for

REVELATION AS COMMUNICATED EXTRAS

In two respects there was not much to choose between deism and its orthodox opponents. Firstly, neither side had any real insight into the meaning of history. The problems of theology were constructed in the abstract; they were unrelated to the development of the past. The defenders of revealed religion viewed history as divided into two separate periods, with revelation the special characteristic of the earlier. Since revelation was indicated in prophecy and attested by miracles, questions concerning both came necessarily into prominence.

Then, secondly, in the statement of their case both sides gave to reason the prior place. Already before the eighteenth century dawned, Tillotson, as we saw, gave expression to views which led directly to deism. At the same time he is to be found setting down the lines which the orthodox apologists were to follow. 'Natural religion', he says, 'is the foundation of revealed, and revelation is designed simply to establish its duties.'[3]

The battle with the deists had been joined and the method of attack made clear before the eighteenth century began. A year after the publication of Toland's *Christianity not Mysterious*, in 1696, came such replies as Browne's *Answer to Toland*, Prideaux's *Letter to the Deists*, and Leslie's *Short and Easy Method with the Deists*. Leslie's reply is neither short nor easy and it worked no magic in demolishing deism. Prideaux asked his opponents, 'whether the Christian religion be in truth really given by divine revelation from God our Creator; or else a human invention contrived by the first propagators of it to impose a cheat upon man-

[1] William Law, *The Case of Reason*, p. 66.
[2] V. Storr, *The Development of English Theology in the Nineteenth Century*, p. 46.
[3] *Works*, (Edition, 1857), vol. 2, p. 333.

kind?'[1] He concludes that there is only one answer, for Christianity bears all the marks of its supernatural origin.

(i) *The Basis of Revealed Religion*

The fundamental importance and the prior position of natural religion is axiomatic to the apologists. Thus Bishop Butler can say, 'Natural religion is the foundation and principal part of Christianity.'[2] Ably as Butler answered the deists, he worked from the same premise as they. His position is that Christianity is essentially a republication of natural religion, with the exception that revealed religion adds some essentials which natural religion lacked. It is by the medium of natural religion, Butler argued, that the significance of the divine Fatherhood is discovered. The further relationship to the Son and the Spirit is brought about by revealed. Reason constitutes the prior relation, revelation indicates the second. 'The essence of Natural Religion may be said to consist in religious regard to God, the Father; and the essence of revealed Religion, as distinguished from Natural, to consist in religious regard for the Son and the Spirit.'[3]

In the Boyle lectures of 1705, Dr Samuel Clarke likewise based the extras of revealed religion upon the assurances and obligations made certain by natural religion. H. Stebbing in his *Defence of Dr Clarke* writes of the Gospel as 'an Instrument to restore Natural Religion'.[4] To believe it to be anything other than this would be to misunderstand the significance of both. Leyland, who became Butler's successor in the bishopric of Bristol, believed that reason itself could discover with certainty the facts of God's existence and attributes. He maintained that God's moral attributes are also fully comprehensible to the human understanding. Equally known to the single individual, without any special revelation, is his duty towards God and man. Even the meanest of men have sufficient knowledge of the general points of morality.

Sykes insists that there is an unchangeable law of action to which all reasonable beings are necessarily committed. The law of human action is the eternal law of truth to which even God Himself must conform, for 'the will of God itself is governed and

[1] *Letter to the Deists*, p. 5.
[2] *The Analogy* (New edition), p. 195.
[3] Op. cit., p. 202.
[4] *A Defence of Dr Clarke's, Evidences of Natural and Revealed Religion*, p. 5.

directed by Truth'.[1] To conform to this law, which reason can discover, is the whole duty of man. Indeed man's actual conformation to this law is itself religion. Sykes seems to make little, if any, distinction between religion and morality. 'Nor ought Religion', he writes, 'to be distinguished from Morality, as if it had no Relation or Concern with it.'[2] It is known by all people in every age that virtue should be practised. 'The Gentiles had not their moral knowledge from Revelation.'[3] Yet they still knew God and His attributes; their social relation and their duties; the truth of a future state and the reality of punishments and rewards. 'And if it appears that they had right Notions concerning their Duties, and had right Principles sufficient to lead them to right Action, it will follow, that the Light of Reason is not that uncertain, weak insufficient, inconsistent thing, that is by some pretended; nor ought it to be treated as something carnal and dim.'[4] Sykes sets out a long catalogue of items which the moral philosophers of heathendom designated either good or bad. It was the light of reason which was for them the sufficient guide. He goes so far as to contend that the gospel has nothing to add to the eternal rules of truth. 'Jesus Christ never particularly or directly intimated any Design to vary from the Law of Nature; Nay, by his preaching upon the Doctrine of Repentance, he called Men back to that Law, as what they had violated by Sin.'[5] Revelation is therefore but a reinforcing argument providing new motives for the fulfilment of natural duties.

Sykes, it must be allowed, goes further in his approximation to deism than most of those who were its opponents. Nevertheless it was the fundamental assumption of all the orthodox apologists that natural religion is no meagre affair. It has provided men with a large quota of religious necessities.

In proclaiming that natural religion is the basis of revealed the apologists of the eighteenth century were merely reiterating the traditional Thomistic doctrine. It is well known that Aquinas in the thirteenth century, by the use of the Aristotelian logic, built up his natural theology in the confidence that reason could go a long way along the road to a knowledge of God. Revelation comes in then to fill up that which is behind in the searchings of reason.

[1] *The Principles and Connection of Natural and Revealed Religion, etc.*, p. 19.
[2] Op. cit., p. 94.
[3] Op. cit., p. 434.
[4] Op. cit., p. 385.
[5] Ibid.

For Aquinas there is no ontological argument possible, for that would start from a prior recognition of God's existence. The mind, to begin with, has no innate ideas; knowledge is built up, little by little, on the basis of sense experience. A divine intuition is for Aquinas in this life impossible. 'In those things which we hold about God there is truth in two ways. For certain things that are true about God wholly surpass the capability of human reason; for instance, that God is three in one: while there are certain things to which even natural reason can attain; for instance, that God is, that God is one, and other like things, which even the philosophers proved demonstratively of God, being guided by the light of natural reason.'[1]

The eighteenth-century apologists, then, began with the acceptance of this Thomistic dichotomy of natural and revealed religion, in which division of labour, each part contributes its own separate elements. They wholeheartedly believed that reason was sufficient of itself to discover certain fundamental truths to which other knowledge is added as a divinely disclosed extra, a *donum super-additum*. Revealed religion was like a second volume designed to extend the knowledge already given in the first. As volume one was the foundation and principal part of religion attention was naturally focused upon it. Were not the main facts of religion, after all, matters of general concern? And thus they must be capable of advocacy and proof by plain common sense. Common sense was indeed the watchword of the age. 'The defect of the eighteenth century', observes Mark Pattison 'was not in having too much good sense, but in having nothing besides.'[2] It was as a result of this that natural and revealed religion were somehow brought into opposition. 'Revelation may serve, perhaps, to introduce the conclusions of natural religion to people who are too simple and uneducated to excogitate them for themselves, although, even so it must function within the limits of reason, but revelation confronts the mind with no new facts with which the philosopher must wrestle and by which his thought may be fertilized and inspired. There are no mysteries. This post-Cartesian rationalism moved in a world in which all, even in religion, is rather insipidly clear and distinct.'[3]

It was, as has been noted, Butler's interesting contention that

[1] *Contra Gentiles*, 1, 3.
[2] *Essays and Reviews*, p. 297.
[3] J. V. Langmead Casserley, *Retreat from Christianity*, pp. 43, 44.

'the relation we stand to God the Father is known by reason, the relation we stand to Christ by revelation only'. The question, however, arises, What connotation has the term 'Father' for Butler? Is it used as a synonym for Creator? This would seem to be the case. But there are many who would be ready to repudiate the suggestion that natural religion can give a certain idea of a creator. Kant later argued that the only conclusion possible from the data provided by the observation of physical phenomena is that of a 'Cause' and an 'Artificer'. Certainly Butler's view that natural religion brings us into religious regard to God the Father is too sweeping. It may be questioned whether experience confirms or the evangelical records countenance the doctrine that such a knowledge of God as Butler suggests comes through the activity of human reason. The finest ratiocination does not lead men into a filial relationship. It is, we believe, the central message of the New Testament that it is in the Sonship of Christ that the Fatherhood of God is known. It is in and through Jesus Christ that we have the right to say, Abba, Father.

It is no mere accident that the apostle Paul gives the words of his benediction in 2 Corinthians xiii. 14 in the order he does. By putting the grace of the Lord Jesus Christ before the love of God, Paul is being true to the facts of experience. It is by the grace of Christ that the love of God is known. 'The order of the clauses in the great Trinitarian benediction,' observes Professor James Stewart, 'where "the grace of the Lord Jesus Christ" stands first, followed by "the love of God", may be taken as a transcript of Paul's own experience: it was through this meeting with Christ, a Christ Who was all grace, that he entered on the knowledge of love divine.'[1] Dr James Moffatt in a comment on the same passage says, 'Grace is put first, since it is through this manifestation that the divine love is realized.'[2] Butler's neat arrangement of natural and revealed religion and his clear-cut attribution of separate relationships arising from each have, we believe, little justification.

The whole notion that revealed religion is to be conceived as a number of divinely communicated extras to natural religion calls for some general criticisms.

A. Influenced as they were by the scholastic tradition and Cartesian rationalism the 'evidence' writers appear to have had too

[1] *A Man in Christ*, p. 140.
[2] *Grace in the New Testament*, p. 151.

optimistic a view of man's natural ability. Whatever interpretation is to be put upon the idea of the *Imago Dei*, it is impossible to give to reason the credit the apologists were wont.[1] Man does not see through the unclouded glass of an impartial reason. There is this truth in the Freudian thesis that all reason is fundamentally rationalization, that it is natural for man to seek the things which self-interest dictates. No single individual is completely exempt from that irrationality which has its source in man's selfish desires. There is a sense in which every man is 'eccentric', is 'off the centre'. Refusing to have God in their knowledge, men were given over to a 'reprobate mind' (Rom. 1. 28). Man whose original position was to be relationship-in-love is now, in some sense, existence-in-hostility. In this respect we think Brunner's words are correct. Maintaining that man is a being capable of responsive love to a holy and divine Father, he declares that he 'has set himself in opposition to his origin'.[2] In the light of all the facts we are convinced that the notion of the apologists that there is a large quota of knowledge of God to be gained by man's native rationality was too extravagant.

B. By the orthodox apologists the notion of religious knowledge was too metaphysically conceived. It was as a result of their conception of man's reasoning abilities that the anti-deists were able to regard natural religion as the result of man's unaided intelligence. The Cartesian doctrine of man as a rational being whose reason could bring out clear and distinct ideas lay behind their polemic. They accepted the definition of man as a rational animal; and they followed Aristotle in the place he gave to reason, and reason 'meant for Aristotle and for all Western thought since his day, the logical and analytical faculties of the mind'.[3] God, it was believed, could be confined in man's neat syllogism. The apologists never seemed to understand that man is not all mind; they never seemed to grasp that there are more ways of knowing than

---

[1] Irenaeus' doctrine that the 'Fall', which meant for man the loss of a superadded gift of righteousness with his essential rationality left undimmed is, to us, unacceptable; so, too, is the opposite view that the 'image' was completely defaced and effaced. To maintain that the 'image' is totally destroyed is to put man so out of touch with God that he could not ever be aware of the separation. To say that the Imago Dei is altogether destroyed involves a contradiction since a recognition of God is implied in the statement.

[2] *Man in Revolt*, p. 114. Cf., 'Man is a sinner, i.e. his actual existence is diametrically opposed to his origin.' E. Brunner, *The Christian Understanding of Man*, Essay, p. 161.

[3] *The Self and the Dramas of History*, Reinhold Niebuhr, p. 15.

the 'scientific'. It is the perpetual fallacy of rationalism to assume that, 'it is, *prima facie*, of the nature of a thinking being to frame true and adequate thoughts.'[1]

To raise here the question of the character and the channel of religious knowledge would be to go beyond our purpose. It is, however, relevant to point out that because they did not understand the fact that religious knowledge is conditioned in a religious way that the work of the opponents of deism was for the most part ineffective. Spiritual things are not merely observed *ab extra*. There is a sympathetic union which gives a deeper assurance. Spiritual things are spiritually discerned. We cannot refer to God as *das Ding*. God is personal and we can therefore know Him only by the direct communion of sympathetic intercourse. It is this personal intercommunion which is the fundamental certainty in religion. Where this is, the most flawless 'proof' of the sceptic cannot disturb, and where it is not, the most carefully marshalled 'evidences' are no substitute for it.

If this is called 'mysticism', then mysticism we must have, for man is more than a creature of reason. The alternative to this is scepticism. If religious knowledge depends upon reason alone, then the result must be agnosticism since man by reason cannot find out God. 'Certainly the sense of awe, derived by the religious soul from its vivid apprehensions of the greatness of Reality, a Reality experienced as so much deeper than the soul can ever express, is specifically different from any sense of uncertainty as to the existence and the super-human nature of Reality underlying this apprehension.'[2] This, indeed, is, as von Hügel goes on to say, 'healthy mysticism'.

C. The apologists do not seem to have been able to find a satisfactory account of the significance of natural religion. The paradoxical fact is that, on the one hand, it was given far too exalted a position, and, on the other hand, it was not given a place important enough.

Anyone acquainted with the works of Clarke, Stebbing, Conybeare, Butler and Paley will agree that they made natural religion fundamental. So evident is this that Collins could make the scathing retort that no one disbelieved in the existence of God until

---

[1] Quoted from Spinoza by B. Bosanquet in *The Meeting of Extremes in Contemporary Philosophy*, p. 82.
[2] F. von Hügel, *Essays and Addresses on the Philosophy of Religion*, p. 21.

Clarke set out to prove it in his Boyle Lectures. Paley raises the question concerning the usefulness of his *Natural Theology*. He allows that most of those who will read his book will have no uncertainty regarding the existence of the Divine Being. Nevertheless the argument, he thinks, will not even then be in vain, for it will give stability to those whose faith is challenged, and it will give support to those who have believed on authority. Paley, however, goes further and asserts that the supreme value of proving the existence and character of God is, not only that human speculation may be satisfied, but that the foundation is laid for a fuller disclosure of God which the knowledge gained by natural religion assures. He writes; 'we may well leave to Revelation the disclosure of many particulars, which our researches cannot reach, respecting either the nature of that Being as the original cause of all things, or the character and designs as a moral governor, and not only so, but the more fuller confirmation of these particulars, of which, though they lie beyond our reasonings and our possibilities, the certainty is by no means equal to the importance.'[1]

Paley here refers to 'many particulars' which it is the province of revealed religion to add to the discoveries of human reason. Others were not so generous in their estimation of the extras so disclosed. John Foster, for example, is content with a small sum of additions. Christianity, he informs us, has 'two or three plain and useful positive duties',[2] which are given to supplement those already found by the light of reason. The more important place was thus given to natural religion, and, as a result, in 'the eighteenth century even what passes for orthodox religious thought was closer to and more sympathetic towards deism than "enthusiasm" '.[3]

Natural religion held such a large place in the thinking of these writers that we are left with the impression that it was only a matter of time before sufficient knowledge would have been gained. However, as things were, revealed religion has added its limited particulars. So large an amount is supplied by natural religion that it appears to be well nigh enough.

On the other side, however, it was this very magnifying of natural religion which resulted in the minimizing of it. Natural religion was not really important enough, restricted as it was to

[1] 'Natural Theology', *Works*, vol. 4, p. 424.
[2] *The Usefulness, Truth and Excellency of the Christian Religion*, p. 302.
[3] J. V. Langmead Casserley, *Retreat from Christianity*, p. 45.

those very realities which were not of primary value. It is but a small thing to be convinced of the existence of a mere Designer or Conserver of values. But it is not a First Cause the human heart needs but a Father's heart, 'a Friend behind phenomena.'

'It is common to hear proofs offered in support of the claim there is "a God",' observes W. N. Clarke, 'but to say, "I believe in a God," may mean much or little. "A God" may be simply a creator, or a first cause, concerning whose character or relation to man little or nothing is asserted. Only unsatisfactory proof of the existence of God is possible while the idea of God is undefined and the name ambiguous. To prove that there is a God, is far less than to prove that God as now conceived is a living Being; and the question in Christian Theology is the same as that which is vital for all mankind, whether the good God is real.'[1] It is the deep things of God's being — things which are of eternal significance for man — which the apologists, for the most part, left outside their reckoning. By accepting the clear-cut division between natural and revealed religion the orthodox failed to apply their own presuppositions. They ought to have carried through their fundamental principles and maintained the exclusive supremacy of reason. Instead they began with the existing dichotomy and confined themselves to those truths believed to be proper subjects for reason's investigation. Their purpose doubtless was to leave the other beliefs aside as irrational and to eliminate them from the possibility of intellectual enquiry. As a consequence, natural religion was rigidly confined, and the very themes of deepest significance to man were excluded from review. 'Thus it could come about that David Hume should compose his Dialogue on Natural Religion, so cogent in argumentation, so urbane, so devastatingly polite, at a moment when John Wesley was altering the characters of thousands and the course of English History by preaching salvation through the Precious Blood — a theme which one suspects that Hume and his friends would have thought ill-suited for refined conversation. If Natural Theology is restricted, or restricts itself, to the study of what has never been of a supposed revelation, then it is concerned with what is very unimportant alike to its own students and to all mankind.'[2] The paradox, then, revealing itself in the literature of those whose concern it was to keep faith alive in a period of indifference

---

[1] *Outlines of Christian Theology* (2nd edition), p. 103.
[2] W. Temple, *Nature, Man and God*, p. 9.

and attack is that natural religion was accorded a place in excess of its importance, and yet, because it was limited to what was least significant, it was not given a place important enough.

The trouble arose, of course, from the stress laid upon the divine transcendence by both the deists and their opponents. The latter were unable to see that the sharp division between natural and revealed religion was ultimately unsound. Instead of looking upon natural and revealed religion as two-distinct volumes (although the first was regarded as a tome and the second as a pamphlet), with man the author of the former and God of the latter, they ought to have observed as Augustine had done earlier, that God was in a real sense the author of both. This does not mean that revelation is all of the same sort, but it does mean that in a significant way all knowledge of God is revealed. 'All religious knowledge of God, wherever existing, comes by revelation; otherwise we should be committed to the incredible position that man can know God without His willingness to be known.'[1]

It is incorrect, therefore, to speak as the apologists did, of a natural religion resulting from man's intellectual discovery and a revealed religion resulting from God's self-disclosure, as if the two were somehow unrelated. The notion that revelation is a mere addition to the discoveries of reason does not fit the facts. It is more in accord with the facts to conceive of special revelation as illuminating and vindicating the truths given in general.

It was the conviction of Augustine, as Professor B. B. Warfield has shown, that 'all knowledge rests ultimately on revelation'.[2] Augustine's problem was 'not how to supplant a strictly natural knowledge by a strictly supernatural knowledge'. His concern was with the restoration of those capacities whereby man could regain that knowledge described as natural. Man *qua* man cannot profit by general revelation: God must come creatively to bring about this result. 'The intervention of God', according to Augustine, 'by a special revelation works, therefore, harmoniously into a general scheme of the production of knowledge of God through general revelation.' This harmonious union of natural and revealed religion the anti-deists failed to achieve.

The Old Testament is the historical account of the dynamic belief that God is known only as He makes Himself known. It is

[1] H. R. Mackintosh, *The Christian Apprehension of God*, p. 65.
[2] *Studies in Tertullian and Augustine*, p. 222 f.

the assurance of its religious men that God must remain forever in unknown isolation unless and until He reveals Himself. 'If men know God, it is because He has made Himself known to man. The idea of men reaching to a knowledge or fellowship of God through their effort is foreign to the Old Testament.'[1] The very fact that man has 'The Instinct for Transcendence',[2] means that eternity is set in the human heart. However foolishly men may have expressed their fundamental longings they are testimony to his nostalgia. He is aware of 'the Beyond that is within', and he is sure of what Dr Matthews calls 'the Beyond that is akin'.[3] It is this very fact that makes man a religious being. 'He carries within himself a supernatural reference, and he cannot rescind it; or if excision there be, a scar is left, and the scar is testimony.'[4]

Revelation is a disclosure of God to man, whether it be termed general or special. God is the source of it; man is the object of it. It is from God, it is for man.

This means that there will be a revelation of God in nature because it is man's environment. Man is in God's world, and it cannot be doubted that He has written His signature upon His vast works for all men to read. He has never left Himself without witness; 'on each of His works', says Calvin, 'His glory is engraven in characters so bright, so distinct, and so illustrious, that none, however dull and illiterate can plead ignorance as their excuse.'[5] But while none can plead ignorance, all must confess blindness. 'It is true', observes Paul Tillich, 'that the history of culture is a history of permanent demoniac distortions of revelation and idolatrous confessions of God and man.'[6] God's signature and hallmark were set upon the spacious firmament, but man has sought to erase them, to carve his own instead. But they are there still for all to read; and they can be read still by those who stand within the full light, evidences of God's eternal power and divinity.

It can be asserted further that there must be a revelation of God in history because it is man's story. The apologists, no less than their opponents, had no sense of the historical; they had no idea of the meaning of history. Yet history in general is a revelation of the

[1] *Hastings Bible Dictionary*, vol. 2, p. 197.
[2] Evelyn Underhill, *The Mystic Way*, ch. 1, sect. 1.
[3] *God in Christian Thought and Experience*, p. 10.
[4] E. Lewis, *The Philosophy of the Christian Revelation*, p. 28.
[5] *The Institutes of the Christian Religion* (Beveridge's translation), vol. 1, p. 51.
[6] *The Protestant Era*, Preface, p. xliv.

divine purpose. In history God is active, and it is this 'actuality'[1] of God in history which constitutes it as revelational, it unfolds the deeds of God. We cannot agree with H. A. L. Fisher that history is without 'a plot, a rhythm, a pre-determined pattern'.[2] History is no accident, its web is woven on the loom of a divine purpose.

But the key to history is not found within history itself. Nor yet can history be interpreted through nature. This is the fallacy of the Marxian dialectic which conceives of history as due to the human machine's need of fuel. 'The truth is', says Alan Richardson, 'that the meaning of history will not be found within.'[3] It thus becomes impossible 'to interpret history at all without a principle of interpretation which history as such does not yield'.[4]

This understanding of history as somehow revelational is itself derived from revelation. It was the prophets of Israel who first made the bold announcement that Jehovah (Yahweh) was Lord of History. This means that the appreciation of all history as a medium of revelation was brought to light through special revelation. The prophets saw God active within the history of their people. This was indeed the stand-point from which they surveyed their national events. They saw God as having a personal interest in affairs, 'The Jews were the first to introduce the principles of the historical and a keen feeling for historical destiny into the life of mankind.'[5] It was indeed out of this understanding of the historical as the sphere of the divine activity that the God of history was seen to be the God of nature. Nature was consequently viewed religiously in the context of the 'divine history'. For the people of Israel there was really no clear-cut division between 'history' and 'nature'. 'In emphasizing "history" as the primary field of God's revelation we must not imply that "nature" is excluded. It is excluded as the primary field but included within "history" as part of the Living God's revelation to his creatures.'[6] The fact is, as Dr H. Wheeler Robinson has pointed out the Hebrew people lacked a word for 'nature'. The reason is, of course, that they allowed no 'middle neutralities'; so that when modern man talks of 'nature' the Hebrew would have spoken of 'God'.

---

[1] H. Wheeler Robinson, *Redemption and Revelation*, chs. iv, vi.
[2] *The History of Europe*, (1935, Miffin), p. vii.
[3] *Christian Apologetics*, p. 99.
[4] Reinhold Niebuhr, *Nature and Destiny of Man*, vol. 1, p. 151.
[5] N. Berdyaev, *The Meaning of History*, p. 86.
[6] W. J. Wolf, *Man's Knowledge of God* (The Christian Faith Series), p. 73.

But while all history was seen to be the workshop of God, in the light of God's dealing with the chosen people of Israel, this 'special' history, in its turn, is seen to be more vividly and dramatically God's workmanship in the historical Person of Christ. It is 'only through Jesus Christ that history can be defined as world history'.[1] God's supreme revelation has taken place in time. The gospel story is dated: it is grounded in history. Here is special history, significant history, saving history. Thus is Christianity not a fleeting theosophy, but a final theophany; it is not a philosophical concept, but a historical culmination. Here the process found fulfilment — the progressive revelation through the Old Testament story is fulfilled and filled full, ἐφάπαξ, 'once and for all,' in God's ultimate and best disclosure, His own Son — a historic Person. It is in the light of the special historic revelation in Christ that the whole drama of history is seen to be the activity of God.

This means that in the final disclosure, God has revealed Himself in Personality because it is man's essence. In man, made in the image of God, there must be some revelation of Him. Man still contains within him, as Bacon says, 'the sparkle of his first purity.' 'What shall we say,' exclaims Calvin, 'but that man bears within him a stamp of immortality which can never be effaced?'[2] Man's conscience, sometimes excusing and sometimes accusing, is an inward witness to God. Although 'man is a god in ruins' as Emerson remarks, he is still, out of the wreckage, aware of a glory that was meant to be his. But once again it is in the Personality of God made Man that human personality itself is understood.

As personality is the essential thing in man it is just here that God has disclosed Himself in His clearest and final form — in a Face like my face. It is for this reason that the Christian points to the living Personality of Christ as the final Exegete of God. Here is God speaking in word and deed. 'Incarnation is the highest possible form of divine revelation to us since human personality is the highest created form of existence known to us.'[3] The fullness of time had come in the fifteenth year of Tiberius Caesar, when Pontius Pilate was governor of Judaea. Then God at last spoke in One Who is Son of God: then was the Life manifested. The Truth of God was embodied in a life. God had appeared on the arena of

---

[1] E. Brunner, *Revelation and Reason*, p. 405.
[2] *Institutes of the Christian Religion*, vol. 1, p. 54.
[3] W. Y. Mullins, *Freedom and Authority in Religion*, p. 315.

human experience. The Word was made flesh. The literature of Heaven was translated into the language of earth. Hitherto, in history, in conscience, God had revealed His hand. Now in Christ He has laid bare His heart in a final unfolding of Himself for which He had been preparing through the selection of Israel.

Since this is, we are persuaded, the true understanding of God's unveiling of Himself, it means that special revelation is no mere appendage to general. The position is rather that special revelation is 'the means by which the truths given in general revelation can be adequately apprehended and known to us'.[1] It was such facts as these that the anti-deists failed to appreciate: and by failing to appreciate them they made their doctrine of revealed religion trivial and unconvincing.

(ii) *The Need for Revealed Religion*

In order to make secure their polemic against the deists, it was necessary for the apologists to indicate the value of a revealed religion. It is here that something of a contradiction is to be found. The reason which has been earlier so highly estimated is now to be shown, by some to be inadequate, and by others to be distorted.

Clarke contended that an understanding of early philosophy and an observation of the human heart would indicate that a revelation was 'plainly wanting'.[2] The early philosophers show the need for the extras which are given by revealed religion. They had their certainties regarding morality, immortality, and so forth, but their greatest and best were 'never able to frame to themselves any complete, regular and consistent system or scheme of things: but the truths which they sought were single and scattered, accidental, as it were, and hit upon by chance, rather than by any knowledge of the whole true state of things; and consequently less universally convictive'.[3] The ultimate end the chiefest philosophers of ancient days could not see, while the multitudinous differences between them gave them no sure resting-place. The duties of life of which they were certain they had no authority to enforce. They could approve the best, they could not achieve it. They were aware of a malady which afflicted mankind but they had no idea from whence it came. They were 'entirely ignorant of some Doctrines absolutely

[1] A. Richardson, *Christian Apologetics*, p. 134.
[2] *Discourse concerning, etc.*, p. 306.
[3] Op. cit., p. 301.

necessary to bring about this great End of the Reformation and Recovery of Mankind'.[1] Philosophy was for the Greek, as the law was for the Jew, their schoolmaster to bring them to Christ. The rest of men, he sees involved in 'nothing but Words and Subtility, and Strife, and Empty Contention'.[2] So indolent the nature, so violent the passions that the majority of men show little eagerness to discover and little desire to understand. Only a few select souls have been able to penetrate far into the divine secret of the universe. The rest of men 'have great need of particular Teaching and much Instruction, not without some weight of Authority as well as Reason and Persuasion'.[3]

In the first of his eight sermons, published under the title, *The Use and Necessity of Divine Revelation*, Dr John Rogers, Canon of Wells, argues that revelation is essential to fix a rule of morality. He asserts that God constantly gave particular revelations until Christ appeared. He expresses amazement that there should be those, at so late a date, who, having witnessed the progress of Christianity, can believe that God left men 'without any other Rule than the Collections of Natural Revelation'.[4] God Who has given ample evidence of His existence and His concern for men's happiness, has in revealed religion, not only clearly exhibited the duties requisite for the fulfilment of that happiness but has also supplied therein a motive.

Those who hold the sufficiency of reason must suppose it equal in all men. Experience does not confirm this; and allowance must be made for the passions and lusts which discount its effectiveness. Philosophy cannot reform the libertine — ' 'tis vain to expect that the generality of man will ever be governed by sober and dispassionate Reason.'[5] Hobbes' social contract theory is not adequate for the regulating of man's selfish motives. Some guiding authority there must be, but no human one is without impossible difficulties. 'If, therefore, human laws are the ultimate Rule and Standard of moral Good and Evil, if nothing is Good but what they direct, and nothing Evil but what they forbid, Men are left in these cases without Rule, without any Motive or Obligation to these Duties, or any Restraint from acting contrary to them.'[6] If, however,

---

[1] *Discourse concerning, etc.*, p. 290.
[2] Op. cit., p. 289.   [3] Op. cit., p. 280.
[4] *The Use and Necessity of Divine Revelation*, p. 4.
[5] Op. cit., p. 11.
[6] Op. cit., p. 19.

an additional urge to the fulfilment of the good. If some follow virtue from the belief in God assured in nature then, 'If a Revelation were to supply us still with more and different Arguments to practise what is right, it would not but be of singular advantage.'[1]

It was this statement of the case which called out against Sykes the criticism of Warburton who charges him with supposing 'Obligation without Law, a revelation of Natural Religion without a Deity'.[2] Sykes makes a gallant effort to rebut the charge and to justify his position that there is an eternal law of things to which even God Himself must conform. God, he insists, is necessarily good. He will ask his opponent, Is this not so? He will go on pressing the question; 'I shall continue "teazing" him, till I force him to prove that God is necessarily good.'[3] Sykes assumes that if this is allowed then his own case is proved.

In a chapter entitled, 'The Advantages of Revealed Religion,' Sykes raises the question concerning the usefulness of a particular disclosure of God in view of the undoubted sufficiency of reason. It is not right, he thinks, to decry revelation. On the other hand it is folly to seek to undermine reason in order to enhance the benefits of revelation. Revelation does not fix a rule of morality for such was known prior to its coming. Neither does it assure religion, for religion consists in doing our duties from a sense of God's being, and this the natural light of the understanding gives. To answer the question, then, Sykes specifies the advantages of revelation to be that, 'It contains Motives and Reasons for the practice of what is right, more and different from, what Natural Reason without its help can suggest.'[4] These motives and reasons are to be found in the several particulars peculiar to the New Testament, as, for example, the final triumph of God's kingdom through Christ, the doctrine of the Trinity, the positive institutions of Baptism and the Lord's Supper.

In order to indicate the necessity for a revealed religion, Butler bids his readers contrast the state of religion where it is enjoyed with that where it has not come. The greatest of the ancients, the bright lights of antiquity, reveal how urgent was the need for the

[1] Op. cit., p. 101.
[2] *The True Foundation of Natural and Revealed Religion Asserted, Being a Reply to the Supplement of a Treatise entitled, The Nature, Obligation, etc., of the Christian Sacraments*, p. 5.
[3] Op. cit., p. 24.
[4] *The Principles and Connection, etc.*, p. 244.

republication of the obligations arising out of natural religion and the giving to them a new authority. Butler draws a contrast between moral and positive commands. The former are superior because they are the ends to which the positive precepts are directed. Between the two there can be no ultimate opposition. Yet the positive commands are as binding as the moral the moment they are seen to be the word of Him with Whom we have to do. Thus, while positive duties are, 'those the reasons of which we do not see'[1] and are 'external commands', they demand unhesitating obedience when they are recognized to be God's.

To see, then, revealed religion as the anti-deists did, as a reinforcement of natural religion, or as a source of inspiration for morality, or as a standard by which deviations from natural morality is to be judged, is not a very convincing account of the usefulness of a revealed religion. The statement of these particulars is itself sufficient to exhibit the defectiveness of the whole polemic. There is nothing here to grip. Revealed religion merely adds a number of extra 'positive commands' to which obedience must be given. The Person of Christ becomes almost lost in the precepts for conduct. The Sermon on the Mount is of more significance than the Sacrifice on the Hill. Jesus is regarded as the publisher of extra moral dicta. The whole attitude results in giving a false view of the Person and place of Jesus Christ.

The anti-deistic literature, from Browne to Butler, is vitiated by the untenable notion that Jesus set out a number of additional propositions to which assent was to be given. Bishop Browne misconceives the real essence of the Gospel when he writes of faith 'as an Assent to a revealed and express Proposition upon the Testimony of God; and till something be so revealed by him there could be no assent by us to any such Proposition; we cannot believe in his express Word before he spake to us by the Prophets and His Son. And now that all these things concerning himself and us are delivered to Mankind, Men still have it in their own natural Election whether they will either Consider them, or give Assent to them; but we are told that he that Believeth them shall be Saved, and he that Believeth not shall be Damned.'[2]

This notion makes the Christian gospel regulative but not redemptive. Jesus appears as a lecturer in ethics Who propounds a

---

[1] *Analogy*, p. 206.
[2] *The Procedure, Extent and Limits of the Human Understanding*, p. 335.

system which all must acknowledge as being in accord with the reason of things. It regards the words of Jesus as single pieces of an artistic mosaic instead of diamond rays flashing from a divine personality. It makes faith mere assent to certain formal propositions instead of warm and living trust in a present Saviour. The doctrine of these apologists may be Scholastic, but it is not Scriptural: it may claim to be Thomistic, but it cannot claim to be Pauline.

What the period needed, and, alas, what the period lacked, was a man like P. T. Forsyth to write with conviction and appeal upon the Person and Place of Jesus Christ. In Christ God did not simply countersign the best intuitions of the heart or the highest productions of the reason. It is only in faith that the final significance of Christ is understood, not a believing *as* Christ, nor yet a believing *with* Him, but a believing IN Him. 'The deity of Christ cannot be proved, to either the lower or the higher rationalism, either to the deistic or the idealistic, the Wolffian or the Hegelian.'[1] The question must face us as the most urgent, the most critical and the most far-reaching: Did Jesus connect His saving mission with His Person or with His precepts? With His ideas or with His work? 'Is saving faith a Rationalism, i.e. a faith in universal ideas, intuitions, or processes, which have no exclusive relation to a fixed point in history?'[2] Are we to start with the World or with the Word. 'Are we to demand that Christ shall submit to the standard of certain principles or ideals which we bring to him from our human nature at its heart's highest and its thought's best? Or as our new creator is he his own standard, and not only so but both judge, king, and redeemer of human nature, and the fountain of new life, autonomous in Him, and for all the rest derived? Is he the prophet and champion of man's magnificent resources, or is he the redeemer of man's spiritual poverty and moral wreck? Did he come to transfigure before men the great religious and ethical ideas, or to infuse into men new power, in the thorough, final, and godlike sense of endowing them with a new and ransomed life? Did he refurbish Humanity, or redeem it? Did he release its best powers, or bestow them? This is the last issue, however we may blunt its edge, or soften its exigency in particular cases. It is between a rational Christianity and a redemptive. And it is not to be obscured by

[1] *The Person and Place of Jesus Christ*, p. 94.
[2] Op. cit., p. 95.

extenuations which plead that the function of ideas is redemptive, or that redemption is the profoundest rationality in the world, the "passion which is highest reason in the soul divine". That was the line that nearly lost Christianity to the pagan public in the old apologists, whose great object was to make their religion stand well with the Universities and the State — a perilous attempt for Christianity.'[1]

(iii) *The Proofs of Revealed Religion*

It was the business of the orthodox, not only to show why a revelation was 'plainly wanting', but also to adduce evidence that it was actually given. Having set forth the advantages that would result from a revealed religion, it was asserted that this divine revelation was given in the truths of the gospel. But a revelation supernaturally given must be supernaturally guaranteed. There must be infallible signs to attest its divine origin: there must be adequate and authentic 'external evidences' which will assure that it is not unreasonable to accept the truths disclosed by revealed religion.

Dr Clarke thus asserts that revealed religion 'to the judgement of Right and Sober Reason, appears of itself highly credible and probable'.[2] He goes on to declare that Christianity 'as taught by the Holy Scripture, has all the Marks and Proofs of it being actually and truly a Divine Revelation'.[3] There are truths which reason itself cannot discover and these have been made known by a particular revelation of God, and as these revealed truths were demonstrated by divine testimonies it was no longer unreasonable to accept them. By these external signs their authenticity was assured. The special authenticating proofs by which revealed religion was established are miracles and prophecies. In the polemic of the period, therefore, we find long and laboured sections devoted to the argument from miracle and the argument from prophecy.

The case is put in an almost naïve manner by Stebbing. He premises that man's happiness depends upon his doing good according to nature. To forbear to do good is 'contrary to Reason, and if it is contrary to Reason it is contrary to our own happiness'.[4]

---

[1] *The Person and Place of Jesus Christ*, pp. 95, 96.
[2] *A Discourse concerning, etc.*, p. 157.
[3] Op. cit., p. 155.
[4] *An Enquiry into the Evidences of the Christian Religion*, p. 38.

It is agreeable to the nature of God to disclose to man those particulars requisite for his happiness. But the question must be asked, Has this revelation been made? A divine doctrine, Stebbing says, is not only 'suitable to the Divine nature',[1] but it is also in harmony with the knowledge of God assured by natural religion. A fuller certainty is, however, required, for, 'if God has given us a revelation, he has given us full Evidence that it is his Revelation.'[2] The first of these sure proofs is miracles. To this is to be added one other crowning and conclusive proof, for 'we have another key given to us to detect the Imposture, if it be one; a key put into our hands even by the Founder of this Religion himself; and that is, a Pretence in him to fulfill Prophecies'.[3]

Sykes refused to make an exact equation between the Scripture and revealed religion. The Bible, he maintains, contains, besides general facts of history and social life, a large number of moral maxims which the light of reason discovered. He leaves us with a small residue of revealed items. He then asks, 'how are we to distinguish Matters of Reason from those of Revelation, or how are we to know which facts are wrote [sic] from human Testimony, and which are wrote [sic] by the Inspiration of God.'[4] Sykes considers that inspiration and revelation are one and the same reality; he therefore asserts that there must be sure and certain evidences both in the man himself and in the matter of his claim.

With regard to the first, if the truth is discoverable by reason then the claim to a particular revelation can be set at nought. But inspiration itself is an occasional matter. The man inspired is not always so, consequently there must be some way to distinguish between what is spoken under the urge of God and what otherwise. God, when He makes a prophet does not make a puppet. On the other hand, nothing is to be regarded as revealed which contradicts the natural reason. It is only the credible which has consequence for us.

There are, however, some truths assured by prophecy. If matters are before announced as of extraordinary nature and later history records their fulfilment, then there is a powerful evidence of their truth. Sykes meets the deistic argument against prophecy and its evidential value. The deists urged that those passages which the orthodox adduced as prior disclosures of events yet to be, are

---

[1] Op. cit., p. 47.   [2] Op. cit., p. 50.   [3] Op. cit., p. 73.
[4] *The Principles and Connection of Natural and Revealed Religion*, p. 114.

really later interpolations, deliberate fabrications or *post factum* accounts. All these assertions Sykes meets with real ability.

He notes, for example, the objection to the Book of Daniel on the hypothesis that he wrote, or rather that the book was written, after Antiochus Epiphanes' reign. The argument, he observes, is taken from Porphyry, the heathen critic of early Christianity. This source must be held to destroy its strength.

He meets, too, the notion that certain prophecies are merely 'Theological or Poetical method of conveying Religion to Mankind'.[1] Prophecy is not to be regarded as 'an art or science', as some would maintain on the basis of those passages which refer to 'the schools of the prophets'. Prophecy, Sykes teaches, is due to God's will and design Who inspired men as He saw fit. With the gift of prophecy there goes also the confirming evidence of the ability to perform miracles.

The positive evidences for Christianity, Butler likewise considered to be miracles and prophecies. They are, indeed, the 'two direct and fundamental proofs'.[2] For the first Christians miracles and the dynamic influence of the gospel message on its first professors provided strong evidence, whereas 'we or future ages', from conformity between prophetic history, and the state of the world, and of Christianity, 'may possibly have proof of it, which they could not have.'[3]

Such then were the proofs adduced for the reality of a revealed religion by the anti-deistic apologists. What was said by Clarke, Stebbing and Butler was reiterated by the others. Reason assured natural miracles and prophecy authenticated revealed religion. For the deists natural religion was alone sufficient, consequently miracles were unnecessary. With them there was begun the first all-out attack upon the miraculous. Yet their assault was based upon some very definite philosophical presuppositions. Miracles are swept aside because reason was considered to be adequate. There was no serious attempt made to discuss their historical evidence. The deistic rejection of the miraculous rested upon *a priori* considerations. 'The disavowal of the miracles by those who generally styled themselves Christians occurred first as the consequence of a view of our knowledge of God which set aside the

[1] *The Connection of Natural and Revealed Religion*, p. 164.
[2] *Analogy*, p. 275.
[3] Op. cit., p. 260.

classical Christian conception of a supernatural revelation and was itself derived from the rationalism of the new philosophy of Descartes and his successors.'[1]

(a) *The Anti-deists and the Argument from Miracles*

The apologists of the eighteenth century, in their use of the argument from miracles, continued the traditional statement. The special miracles of the Gospels were the divine attestation that the gospel itself was 'from above'. The miracles, it was believed, could be adduced as evidence that the authority of revealed religion was itself reasonable. The items which reason could not prove have been vouched for by miracles. What was thus confirmed by a special intervention of God was to have unqualified assent.

The general attitude was that it was only a revelation which had the higher evidence of the miraculous action of God could claim authority over the conscience of men. Thus while the deists would say that no reasonable person can reject the religion of reason, therefore no reasonable person can believe the miracles because, not only does the reason provide all that is necessary, but also because the miracles are not 'reasonable'; the orthodox replied that no reasonable person can refuse assent to a religion which has been so signally approved by God's special intervention.

This last term recalls us to the fact that the anti-deists by explaining miracles as a divine intervention were in line with the traditional doctrine which is accustomed to put the miracles among the external evidences for the truth of Christianity.

It is not until the time of Augustine that we find any attempt made to treat of miracles in a scientific manner. Prior to his day they were not strange phenomena. Origen, for example, asserts that the miracles wrought by Christ were still being performed in his day.[2] At the same time the reality of heathen miracles was allowed and Origen admits that in and by themselves the ability to work miracles and to utter prophecies is no infallible sign of divinity. The real tests are: Is the worker of miracles himself morally pure? and, Is the race of men made the better by their performance? So long as demoniac wonders were regarded as possible the 'argument from miracles' could not be pressed. By Augustine's day miracles seemed to have ceased, as he looks back

---

[1] A. Richardson, *Christian Apologetics*, p. 158.
[2] *Contra Celsus*, 1, 2, 26, cf., also, 3, 24, 26.

upon a period, now remote, when these strange happenings took place.

Augustine taught that miracles were not contrary to nature.[1] They were happenings which could not be fully explained because all the workings of the natural order were beyond the human understanding. They were not therefore irrational. He believed that some miracles could be interpreted on the hypothesis of the speeding up of natural processes. In the story of Moses' rod turned into a serpent there is an instance of this acceleration of the ordinary course of things. It was believed that in decaying wood serpents might quite naturally originate, and on this occasion the gradual process was, by divine action, made instantaneous.

Augustine goes into the subject of the nature of miracles with penetrating details, and his teaching was to shape the thinking of succeeding centuries. There are miracles, on the one hand, which are the outcome of inherent causes, or *semina occulta*, introduced by God at the first creation. There are those, on the other hand, which are mysterious happenings resulting from God's occasional intrusion into the natural order. Thus, briefly put, Augustine attributed miracles to the workings of either some inherent seed or an outside Sovereign. It was out of this distinction that two historic views developed. Some came to regard miracles as an extra work of God outside the usual activity of nature. This was the doctrine elaborated by the Scholastics and the anti-deistic writers of the eighteenth century. Others denied the need for any such extra divine works. They asserted that enough was introduced by God 'in the beginning'. All the events of the world result from *semina* inherent from the first creation. A deistic system, with a denial of the miracles in the strict sense, was the natural conclusion to this line of thought.

For the orthodox, then, that was to be designated a miracle which was the result of the transcendent God breaking into the natural order. Thus Stebbing defines a miracle as 'an Intrusion of the Divine Being to change the Laws of Nature'.[2] The miracle is an abrupt act.

Beginning with this conception of a miracle as 'a violation of the Laws of Nature',[3] Hume set out to upset the whole orthodox

---

[1] *De Civ. Dei*, bk. xxi, ch. viii, cf., as well, *Contra Faust. Manich.*, xxvi, 3.
[2] *Enquiry into the Evidences of Christianity*, p. 53.
[3] *Essays* (Edition, 1788), 2, p. 19.

apologetic. The task was not, indeed, difficult for, as Johannes Wendland has observed, 'A wrong idea of miracle is the necessary result of conceiving of God's relation to the world as exclusively transcendent; for then His action must come breaking in upon the phenomenal order in miracles which are isolated and abrupt. This is the point of view which leads inevitably to the idea of "violation of the laws of nature", "abrogation of the natural order," "breach of the causal nexus." And the polemic against the miraculous justly makes positions of this kind an object of attack.'[1]

The apologists, like Aquinas, restricted miracles to events within the sphere of sense. For the Thomists such realities as, for example, the Incarnation and God's redeeming action in human lives, are not miracles, since they are not a departure from the natural order. By thus restricting miracles within the area of the sensory the 'argument from miracles' advanced by the anti-deists was without spiritual appeal.

Luther gave to these external evidences a place of little value. For him, the supreme miracle was Christ Himself, His words and His works are divine wonders. He points out that, although the world demands outward signs, it refuses to receive them, whereas, miracles of greater and more striking worth are all the time taking place in the moral experiences of men.

An examination of the New Testament will reveal, we think, that there the miracles are mainly subservient to the saving work of Christ. It is in the light of His redeeming activity that they are to be understood. They are not presented as isolated events, and their unusualness, as such, is not generally adduced as proof of a Divine activity. 'Christ and His works are all of a piece, and he who has apprehended Christ, or rather been apprehended by Him, will not seek to reduce the self-manifestation of the Saviour to the measure of humanity. To prove the miracles one by one is as impossible as to disprove them in the same way, but they unite with the Person and the words of Jesus into one divine whole through which God reveals His very heart to men.'[2]

The miracles of the New Testament are outflashings of Christ's divine Person. They are no mere wonders. The whole of Christianity rests upon a supernatural basis and the gospel story unveils a supernatural Person, not only when, what are called miracles are

[1] *Miracles and Christianity* (tr. H. R. Mackintosh), p. 3.
[2] James Denney, *Studies in Theology*, p. 208.

being wrought. The anti-deists failed to observe that the 'question is not about isolated "miracles", but about the whole conception of Christianity — what it is, and whether the supernatural does not enter into the very essence of it? . . . Is there a supernatural Being — God? Is there a supernatural government of the world? Is there a supernatural relation of God to man, so that God and man may have communion with one another? Is there a supernatural Revelation? Has that Revelation culminated in a supernatural Person — Christ? Is there a supernatural work in the souls of men? Is there a supernatural Redemption? Is there a supernatural hereafter? It is these larger questions that have to be settled first, and then the question of particular miracles will fall into its proper place.'[1]

(b) The Place of Analogy

Since they began with the world rather than from the Word to arrive at a knowledge of God, it was inevitable that the apologists should give a supreme place to the argument from analogy. This position, fundamental to the anti-deists as a whole, is set forth in the clearest manner by Bishop Browne. He states quite emphatically that analogy is the only method for the attainment of divine knowledge. Whilst the real nature of the Christian mysteries cannot be understood, Browne asserts that 'all can both Know and Believe them under Analogical Representations and Conceptions'.[2] The purpose of his book, he says, is 'to trace the whole Extent and Limits of the Human Understanding; to trace out its several steps and degrees of its Procedure from the first and simple Perception of sensible Objects, thro' the several Operations of the Pure Intellect upon them, till it grows up to its full Proportion of Nature; And to shew how all Conceptions of things Supernatural are then grafted on it by Analogy; and how from thence it extends itself immensely into all the Branches of Divine and Human Knowledge.'[3]

The knowledge of God, like any other knowledge, Browne insists, is derived from the senses and the reason. The senses are the 'groundwork' of both. Rejecting the notion of innate ideas, and consequently the possibility of any ontological argument for the

---

[1] J. Orr, The Christian View of God and the World, pp. 10, 11.
[2] The Procedure, Extent and Limits of the Human Understanding, p. 30.
[3] Op. cit., p. 33.

existence of God, Browne asserts the empiricist's dictum, *nihil est in intellectu quod non prius fuit in sensu*; 'Nothing is more true to the fact,' he declares, 'than that we have no Ideas but of sensible Objects; upon these it is that the Mind begins to assert its Operations.'[1] Knowledge of God is not derived, therefore, from 'any Ideas we have of Him, or from any direct Intuition of the Intellect; but from Observations and Reasoning of the Mind upon Ideas of Sensation'.[2]

God is known in the 'mirror' of creation and of our own selves. Reference is made to the apostle's words, 'we see through a glass darkly,' in contrast with the face to face knowledge of the future life. The glass does not exhibit the reality and substance of the thing represented, and yet it is right to maintain that we see the thing, the face, the man. 'Thus we say we see a Man in a Glass, when we see no such thing: for the Appearance hath nothing of the real nature of the Man in it.'[3] But analogy is not to be confused with metaphor, although it must be insisted that analogy is 'absolutely necessary' for our knowledge of God.[4] Thus while knowledge of God is the 'mirror type' and is analogical it is not merely metaphorical. Metaphor is 'never used but to express something already known and conceived by the Light of Nature, or revealed by God with more Exactness through the Mediation of Analogy'.[5] It is the reason's operations upon the things of the senses which gives the certainty of God's existence and attributes.

There are, however, truths about God, like that of the Trinity in Unity, which 'could not have been the Invention of Man because it is itself altogether incomprehensible'.[6]

By giving analogy the supreme place Browne was merely carrying on the mediaeval tradition, in which Aquinas stands forth as the greatest of its teachers. It is Browne's contention that the 'incomprehensible things' are themselves revealed under analogy of such relations as are familiar to us, like that of Father, Son and Spirit. Only in this way, it is maintained, could an understanding of God be gained.

Hubert S. Box justifying the Thomistic teaching states that 'few philosophers other than scholastics have realized the necessity in metaphysics of analogical prediction. Because they have not

[1] Op. cit., p. 64. [2] Op. cit., p. 81.
[3] Op. cit., p. 116. [4] Op. cit., p. 134.
[5] Op. cit., p. 134. [6] Op. cit., p. 302.

grasped the analogical character of things, many thinkers are afraid of interpretating the Being of God in terms of human experience'.[1] Box, as a neo-Thomist, accepts the doctrine of Aquinas and denies that a knowledge of God comes in any other way except by the 'negative-positive' principle.

It is not our purpose to enter into a detailed investigation of the place of analogy in religion. The use of the principle in this realm raises fundamental and complex questions. So difficult is the problem that E. L. Mascall in his book, *He Who Is*, which is a study of the 'Five Ways' of Aquinas, makes this the excuse for avoiding a discussion of the method.[2] On the other hand, F. C. Copleston, S.J., in his exposition of the philosophy of Aquinas devotes a section of his book to the Angelic Doctor's use of analogy, but his exposition is far from clear.[3]

It is cogent, however, to point out that the eighteenth-century evidence writers who, in their understanding of the origin of religious knowledge, followed Aquinas closely and asserted the doctrine that our ideas of God are built up by way of the senses, could not conceive of any other position as possible. Obviously, where all ontological knowledge is denied, the conclusion follows. But it should be noted that Berkeley, to whom ontological knowledge of God was acceptable, rejects this application of analogy.

Those who developed, as a reaction from the objective view of the apologists, an understanding of revelation as given immediately within experience, also repudiated analogy as the method by which a knowledge of God is gained. A God inferred and invested with attributes on the principle of the extension of human qualities or the negation of these qualities, was considered to be too distant. Whereas, if God can be known 'face to face', then, it was argued, He reveals Himself immediately and directly to the trusting soul for Who He is.

In our own day there is a vigorous repudiation of the method of analogy as used by the Thomists. Professor James Baillie, for example, maintains that the idea of God as perfect is not the result of comparing the less perfect with the more, because the standard

---

[1] *God and the Modern Mind*, p. 247.

[2] Mascall, it is true, in a sequel to, *He Who Is*, entitled *Existence and Analogy*, has attempted to make up for the deficiency of his earlier work. The viewpoint is essentially Thomistic and consequently the supremacy of the *analogia entis* is asserted.

[3] F. C. Copleston, *Aquinas*, pp. 67–8, 129–36.

of perfection must be already apprehended before the comparison itself is instituted. A cannot be compared with B unless both A and B are somehow already known. Professor Norman Kemp Smith takes a similar position. He contends that God cannot really be known by analogy. He argues that, without antecedent or independent knowledge of God, it would not be possible to arrive at any knowledge of Him by the principle of analogy. He assures us that if we start with the creaturely as exhibited in man and nature, and, on the pattern of what is found in the creaturely, we endeavour to construe to ourselves concepts of the divine, we are foredoomed to failure.

Those who are not convinced by these arguments can with some justification, stress Aquinas' 'analogy of Being'. It certainly does seem possible, in some way, to argue from the known to the unknown, from, for example, the idea of man to that of super-man.

An opposition to the Thomists, latent, at least, in Calvin, has been taken up in recent times by the Barthians. Whereas the earlier rejection of the principle of analogy derived from an insistence upon the divine immanence, Barth's arises from an accentuation of the divine transcendence. Brunner credits Barth with being the first theologian who has seen in the application of the principle of analogy the main difference between the Roman and the Reformed theologies. For Barth God is the 'Wholly Other'. He is 'actus purus'.[1] Man, on the other hand, has lost all 'point of contact' with the divine: the Imago Dei is entirely effaced. He is without a trace of his divine original. Thus, if man would know God, it can only result from an inbreaking of God from without, an 'invasion' from above. This is the understanding of revelation of which, for Barth, the Bible is a 'witness'.[2] The Bible is the human testimony to the fact that God has spoken directly to men in the past, and that He will do so again.[3]

Clearly with such a doctrine there can be no place for analogy. No human being can gain any knowledge of God by the exercise of

[1] *Church Dogmatics*, 1, i, p. 44.
[2] Cf., *Church Dogmatics*, 1, ii (E.T., 1956), p. 457 ff.
[3] Cf., *Church Dogmatics*, 1, i (E.T., 1936), p. 125 ff. It is right, however, to point out that Barth, later in his *Dogmatics*, writes: 'Apprehension of the Word of God could not take place, where there is not in and along with this event something in common between God who speaks and man who hears, an analogy a similarity, for all the dissimilarity involved in the difference between God and man, a "point of contact" — now we may use this concept too — between God and man'. Op. cit., 1, i, p. 373. In this quotation the important words are 'in and along with the event', for they explain his view. Prior to the apprehension of the

a reason which is altogether distorted by sin. Any notions which men can construe will not be of the true and living God; they will be of 'no God', the very negation of the real. Thus for Barth the analogical method leads logically to a *theologia naturalis,* and therefore is anathema.[1]

It will be seen, then, that both the subjectivists, because of their emphasis upon the divine immanence, and the Barthians, because of their emphasis upon the divine transcendence, repudiated the method of analogy. On our view the exclusive application of the principle, on the one side, and the total rejection of it, on the other, are untenable. The use of the method is certainly beset with real difficulties especially when the resemblance 'is interesting or emotionally satisfying'.[2] Miss Stebbing contends that 'the greater our ignorance of the subject-matter, the more likely are we to be misled by a weak analogy',[3] and she quotes Dr J. M. Keynes' remark that 'the common sense of the race has been impressed by weak analogies'.[4] Such statements are, of course, no sufficient reason to repudiate the analogical method as such. They do serve, however, to show that it must be used with caution and understanding.

The fact that man is made in the image of God, and that however affected he may be by sin, some relation to God still persists, is adequate justification for the use of the method of analogy. 'We must think of the divine on the analogy of all that is richest and most human, not only in our actual character, but in the better we

'word', the 'point of contact' does not exist. It is in 'faith' that it comes to be. It is then and there restored. 'The reconciliation of man with God in Christ includes in itself or else begins with a fresh establishment of the lost "point of contact". This point of contact is, therefore, not real outside faith but only in faith. In faith a man is created by the Word of God for the Word of God, existing in the Word of God, not in himself, not in virtue of his humanity and personality, nor from the standpoint of creation, for what is possible from the standpoint of creation from man to God has actually been lost through the Fall,' *Church Dogmatics,* 1, i, p. 273. The whole section of the *Dogmatics,* entitled, 'The Word of God and Faith,' p. 260 ff., is intended to make this teaching clear. But it is still not clear how man, who has lost all natural *capax verbi divini,* now receives it in the act of faith. One is left wondering whose is the 'point of contact', Is it God's or man's?

[1] Barth, although he rejects the *analogia entis,* allows that there still exists the ἀναλογία τῆς πιστεῶς. 'We thus', he writes, 'do not oppose the Catholic doctrine of the *analogia entis* by a denial of the concept of analogy. But we say that the analogy in question is not an *analogia entis,* but according to Rom. 12. 6, ἀναλογία τῆς πιστεῶς.' *Church Dogmatics,* 1, i, p. 279.

[2] I. M. Stebbing, *A Modern Introduction to Logic,* p. 254.

[3] Op. cit., ibid.

[4] Op. cit., ibid.

aspire to be.'[1] Analogy certainly can be used to confirm and clarify our religious knowledge. It 'plays a part in suggesting ideas and in aiding our thought'.[2] So much, at least, may be granted. This means that the rejection of the principle, from either an idealist or a Barthian standpoint, is invalid. On the other hand, against the apologists, we feel bound to contend, that they were too optimistic and too dogmatic in their use of the method. They did not see, and they could not grant, that any other idea was possible.

There were two particular arguments used by the deists which their opponents had to answer. It was the contention of the former that there could be no revealed religion beyond that already provided for all in the dictates of natural religion. They argued, firstly, that there could be no disclosure of God limited in extent and action to a select section of humanity. They felt that the claim to a revealed religion which involved only a particular people would impugn the justice of God. Then, secondly, they rejected anything as revealed which had to be described as mysterious. Mystery was, for them, *per se*, proof that the claim could not be upheld. Only the understandable could be the revealed.

(c) Revealed Religion as Limited

Stebbing rejects the validity of the argument against a revealed religion on the grounds of its want of universality. He asks his opponent, 'If of two men you relieve one, Can it be said that one is not relieved?'[3] Revelation is, after all as Clarke has contended, an act of God's mercy, it is not a matter of justice. The necessities of men are not the sole reason for God's actions. Nor is the happiness of men the only consideration. If it were so, it might be argued that nature would have provided it, and omnipotence bestowed it. Conybeare urges as a justification for the limitation of revealed religion the absolute freedom of God. It is with Him 'to bestow or not bestow a revelation as he pleases', since He is 'the most proper judge when and to whom to grant it'.[4]

Foster attacks the deistic thesis, pointing out that reason itself is restricted. Some races are little more than brutes. It is said that God ought to give to all what he has given to some. The assertion, he agrees, is plausible, but we have to accept, not what we think

[1] A. E. Taylor, *The Faith of a Moralist*, vol. i, p. 62.
[2] G. Galloway, *The Philosophy of Religion*, p. 342.
[3] *Defence of Dr Clarke*, p. 80.
[4] *Defence of Revealed Religion*, p. 419.

God should have done, but what, as a matter of fact, He has done. It appears reasonable to argue that God should have made all men good logicians, yet He has made some 'downright idiots'.[1]

Butler notes the 'great weight' attached by the deists to the restricted nature of revealed religion. Butler replies to the deists by stressing the two main points of the Analogy. First, he observes, nature itself provides instances of the same restriction. Evidently the Author of nature 'bestows that upon some which he does not upon others, who seem equally to stand in need of it'.[2] As we cannot understand this in the natural sphere still less can we do so in the spiritual. Then, secondly, Butler would have us constantly to recognize our ignorance. Religion, he says, has not come to satisfy the curious mind, but 'only to regulate' the lives of men, and to 'teach them their duty'.[3] The judge of all the earth, we are to believe, will do right. For those who act in accord to the moral principles known to all men, God will make merciful allowance. And even if the deists were right in arguing that a revelation must be universal, there would still be disadvantages rising from man's capacities, length of days, education, external circumstances, and so forth.

According to Alan Richardson this conception of a limited revelation has special difficulties for the 'modern mind'.[4] It is therefore of interest to observe that it was a problem the anti-deistic writers had to face. They had insisted that God revealed Himself at a set period and to a selected people. We have seen how some of the apologists met the charge that this was arbitrary and irrational. Cogent as were some of the points made in their replies, their position would have been more secure if they had seen the significance of the message proclaimed by the Hebrew prophets. It was they who announced Jehovah as Lord of history. There was no favouritism in God's selection of Israel. The records of this people are not devoid of all that would glorify them. Indeed their sins are chronicled with a starkness and a vividness which startles. And upon the children of Israel the judgements of God are meted out with an unsparing severity. It was the prophets who were the true interpreters of Israel's history as significant.

'Taught by the prophets the Hebrew people of the Old Testa-

---

[1] *The Usefulness, Truth and Excellency of the Christian Religion*, p. 67.
[2] *Analogy*, p. 259.
[3] Op. cit., p. 361.
[4] *Christian Apologetics*, p. 139.

ment times, when they were true to themselves, were unique amongst the nations of the world in regarding themselves as bound in a Covenant-relationship to the God Who was discerned as the Lord of history and they thus recognized themselves to be committed to the realization of the will and purpose of God in their national life. In the great crises of Israel's history there arose a succession of prophets who interpreted to those who would listen what God was doing in the various upheavals and reconstructions of their life as a nation. It is an indisputable fact that such a prophetic interpretation of history arose in Israel and nowhere else. God indeed worked through Egypt, Babylon, Greece and Rome; but these nations and empires produced no prophets of the biblical type to interpret what God was doing; they remained blind to the operations of the Lord of history, and hence no special revelation came forth from them. The events of history as such do not themselves constitute a revelation; it is the prophetic interpretation of the historical events which is the vehicle of special revelation in the sense which the biblical and Christian tradition understands that conception. Where there are no prophets there can be no special revelation. And if the phenomenon of prophecy is found nowhere except in the Jewish-Christian tradition, then we must cease to complain about "the scandal of particularity" and resolve to accept the facts as facts, refusing to explain them away in obedience to a quite unscientific predilection for a general theory which was conceived before the facts were examined. If we ask why this special revelation and special type of knowledge of God active in history should have arisen in Israel only, or why other nations did not give birth to prophets of the biblical type, we are in the presence of mystery; we do not know the answer to this question, which must inevitably remain concealed within the secret counsels of God: this is the mystery of "election", which is not, after all, an invention of theologians but an admission that there are facts which we cannot explain but must not try to explain them away. That we cannot explain why God chose the Jewish people to be the special instrument of His purpose in history is no reason for denying the plentiful evidence that He did choose them.'[1]

(d) Revealed Religion as Mysterious

Once it is realised that reason does not hold the infallible position

---

[1] A. Richardson, *Christian Apologetics*, pp. 140, 141.

that the deists accorded to it, it naturally follows that there are some areas of knowledge beyond its scope. It was in this way that their opponents forced their point that it was no discredit to revealed religion to insist that all its items could not be reduced to clear and distinct ideas.

John Foster declared that the true attitude for men to adopt before God is an attitude of reverent agnosticism, and to confess that He may have reasons we know not of. It is unreasonable to reject the propositions of revealed religion because it sets forth in its agenda items which are beyond the researches of the understanding. God can give positive rules without clear reasons for them: the right is His, and His divinity is revealed in the exercise of it. God has rights beyond those which we credit to Him.

Rogers gives expression to the view, in opposition to the deists, which was later elaborated so eloquently by Bishop Butler. In nature, Rogers points out, there are things which we cannot understand. Of things remote we can but know one side, while things near are only known by appearance. There is a point beyond which we cannot go; 'Our Prospect is terminated by a narrow Horizon.'[1] 'The gradual Advancement of Human Reason in what it does know, the Boundaries that stop its Progress and confine its Perceptions, oblige us to conclude, that there must be many Truths beyond our Discovery or Comprehension.'[2] There must be, therefore, more in the attributes of God than the reason can discover, and, possibly others besides which it can never find out. Many of the propositions of revealed religion must consequently be unintelligible. There is no reason to reject them for they are guaranteed by the veracity of God. The positive ordinances of Christianity are not to be set aside because God 'may annex his Graces to what Ordinances he thinks fit'.[3]

It is, however, to Butler we must turn for the most telling use of the argument. Butler assures us that reason alone can judge of the credibility and consistency of revelation. But he goes on to maintain that if it be allowed that a revelation has been given then 'it is highly credible beforehand, we should be incompetent judges of it to a great degree'.[4] Of the scheme of nature we are not fully aware, and in the natural sphere there is much too deep to be fathomed,

---

[1] *The Use and Necessity of Divine Revelation*, p. 80.
[2] Ibid.
[3] Op. cit., p. 100.
[4] *Analogy*, p. 219.

too high to be understood. Thus, argues Butler, 'our being in-competent judges of one, must render it credible that we may be incompetent judges also in the other.'[1] In an apt illustration Butler clinches the matter. When a citizen of a kingdom reveals him-self an incompetent judge of how the laws should be carried on, there is no reason to think that he will be a fit one when extra-ordinary measures are needful. If we show our ability to be in-sufficient when natural instruction is concerned, it is unlikely that we can have any assurance of certainty in the supernatural realm. This being so we cannot lay it down *a priori*, the method, the measure or the meaning of revelation. This insistence on the inability of reason is stressed in a powerful sermon 'Upon the Ignorance of Man'. This is the last of Butler's sermons — fifteen in all — preached at the Rolls Chapel and published in 1726.

The text for the sermon is Eccles. viii. 16, 17, and the passage, attributed to Solomon, is made to express the king's 'great ignorance of the works of God, and the method of his providence in the government of the world'.[2] The limits of the human under-standing are clear. The world without and the world within are beyond our utmost reach. In the 'scheme of Providence, the ways and works of God are too vast, of too large extent, for our capacities'.[3] A veil has been drawn over God's power, wisdom and goodness. But this very ignorance is an occasion for faith, and those who obey the gospel, 'upon less sensible evidence than Thomas, earn the Saviour's commendation, "Blessed are they that have not seen, and yet have believed." '[4] Happiness does not consist in being well instructed. Virtue is the real source of man's true life; thus the lesson is, to depart from evil and to fear God. This realization of ignorance he finds to be 'the proper answer to many things which are called objections against religion'.[5]

Mystery is to be expected in religion as well as in nature, and it is the essence of folly to reject the evidence we have because it is not what we desired. It is unreasonable to scorn lesser lights to guide the way because the sun is not shining in its strength. If a man had to take a journey by night he would be thankful for any light to illuminate the darkness until the daybreak and the shadows flee away.

[1] Op. cit., p. 502.
[2] *Sermons printed with Analogy* (new edition, 1882), p. 531.
[3] Ibid., p. 533.   [4] Ibid., p. 535.   [5] Ibid., p. 537.

In the second part of the Analogy it is premised that 'Christianity is a scheme quite beyond our comprehension'.[1] Butler summarizes the main articles of the gospel and urges that Scripture itself indicates the incomprehensible nature of its revelation when it speaks in 2 Timothy iii. 16, of 'the great mystery of godliness'. When the separate particulars of the message are examined we 'immediately run up into something which shows our ignorance in it'.[2] The laws of God's general activities are but imperfectly known to us, and the laws which govern His extraordinary ways are entirely unknown to us. The whole scheme of divine revelation is disclosed only in part. In temporal affairs men must act on evidence which must necessarily be inconclusive. After all 'probability is the guide of life'.

There is much in this anti-deistic insistence upon mystery in revelation which cannot be denied. It is, however, not easy to approve of Butler's method. The question arises, Is the best way of meeting a problem to raise a crop of new ones in a related topic? Are we likely to accept revelation because we are told that we cannot explain nature? Yet it would appear that the method was the only one possible for the apologists beginning as they did with the notion of an exclusively metaphysical epistemology.

A survey of the foregoing pages will leave little room for doubt that the anti-deistic apologists somehow missed the mark. Not only were they too close to their deistic opponents for mortal combat, but they failed to get into contact with the deeper needs of the human soul for a religion more personal and more soul-satisfying. While the God of deism was heedlessly remote, behind the universe; the orthodox deity was helplessly confined within a logical system. The one was indifferent, the other was imprisoned. Consequently neither the one nor the other sufficed for the soul, sin-sick.

Deism was, therefore, not destroyed by the burning sarcasm of a Conybeare nor the brilliant argument of a Butler. It was to the preaching of Whitfield and Wesley that the heart of the people responded.

There is one name among the host of those who entered the list against deism whom we have left for special consideration because of his penetrating understanding of the deistic doctrine.

---

[1] *Analogy*, p. 233.
[2] Op. cit., p. 235.

(e) William Law's attack on Deism

In William Law's book, *The Case of Reason, or Natural Religion Fairly and Fully Stated*, there is a new depth of argument. The subtitle tells us it is directed against Tindal's *Christianity as Old as Creation*. Law comes to the attack with a forcefulness and originality which were lacking in the other writers on the same side as he. They, for the most part, gave the impression of half-accepting and half-protesting. Law does not repeat second-hand arguments and ineffective shibboleths. He attacks the central territory of his enemy. He directs his arrows to the heart. He comes, not to skirmish, but to slay. And it is beyond doubt that Law wins a decisive victory and remains a conqueror on the battlefield.

Tindal argued that God must act according to the fitness of things, if He did otherwise He would be arbitrary. Law replies that if the premise is accepted, the conclusion does not follow. The 'whole argument', contends Law, 'proves directly the contrary to that which the author intended to prove by it.'[1] The fitness to which God's acts must conform cannot be anything in nature, it must be grounded in His own being. To act in this manner means that many of His works must be incomprehensible. He would act arbitrarily if He did anything contrary to His nature. The reason of things cannot tell us why He created man as He has, or rules them as He does. No necessary fitness can be observed in many of God's ways. 'And don't you say', Law asks his opponent, 'that God has made you for your own sake, ought you not therefore to know the reasonableness and fitness of things?'[2] The fact is that there is much we cannot examine or explain. We must believe where we cannot prove. If reason and fitness are considered necessary to salvation they must likewise be considered so for nature. 'For it is just as wise and reasonable to allow of no mysteries or secrets in Creation and Providence.'[3] What is fit for God as Creator is as much above our power to understand as it is for us to govern the universe.

Law meets Tindal's objections to the atonement and shows the folly of rationalizing this central doctrine. 'He who rejects the atonement for sins made by the Son of God, as needless, because he cannot prove it to be necessary, is as extravagant, as he who would deny that God created him, by his only Son, because he did

---

[1] *The Case of Reason*, p. 62.
[2] Op. cit., p. 64.   [3] Op. cit., p. 66.

not remember it.'[1] And our memory is as proper a faculty in the one instance, as reason is in the other.

. Tindal errs in making God the slave of some outside fitness to which He must conform. There is no such prior pattern. God's attributes cannot be founded on anything outside Himself. God is Himself the ultimate cause of all; the final fitness, and 'we have not found out God, till we have found out a Being that has no cause'.[2] 'To ask, therefore, whether there is not something right and wrong, antecedent to the will of God, to render his will capable of being right, is as absurd as to ask for some antecedent cause of his existence, that he may be proved to exist necessarily.'[3] 'Dare anyone say that God's laws are not founded on the eternal reason of things?'[4] exclaims Tindal. Law dares to say it. God's existence is not founded on the eternal existence of things; to say that God's laws depend upon eternal reason is like saying that His power is founded on the eternal capacities of things. 'And as to the existence of God, because it contains all perfections, cannot, for that reason have any external cause; so the will of God, because it is all perfection, cannot, for that reason, have any external rule or direction.'[5] God's goodness *is* arbitrary, and His arbitrariness is His goodness.

Tindal lays it down that God must act according to the relation in which He stands towards His creatures. This relation, he asserts, is also based on the fitness of things. In other words, as Law shows, it is based upon God as He is in Himself, the omniscient Creator, the governor of all and so forth. These are items of the divine nature beyond our comprehension far. If then 'the relation itself is incomprehensible, then those actions that have their fitness in it, must surely be incomprehensible'.[6] This argument is forcefully pressed, and it is shown that none can tell the degree of reason which rational beings possess, or how much new and revealed knowledge God may see fit to add. Tindal thinks that if God designed good for His creatures He would not have deferred the communications of those requirements which make for their good 'till the time of Tiberius'. Law answers, but if God acts according to His relation with His creatures, then it must be concluded that this relation, directed by His foreknowledge, means that He was not acting other than for the good of men by giving

---

[1] Op. cit., p. 74.   [2] Op. cit., p. 86.   [3] Op. cit., p. 88.
[4] *Christianity as Old as Creation*, p. 385.
[5] *The Case of Reason*, p. 90.
[6] Op. cit., p. 93.

such a revelation, at such a time, and to such persons. His deferring it 'till the time of Tiberius' is, in fact, a supreme evidence of God's concern for His human family. God's foreknowledge took account of 'the actions and state of free agents, and of the effects of his revelation'.[1] His revelation was given at a time when its results would be greatest.

Since God's acts are grounded in the fitness of His own Being, then it was the fittest occasion for Him, Who is supremely good, to do good to all. From the state of the relation which exists between God and man, the reasons for the time, matter and manner of the divine revelation are beyond human discovery. It must be concluded that God's revealed truths are in fact mysterious and incomprehensible.

Law is ready to meet the question, How then can they be received as divine? He points out, as Butler did later, that the creation is accepted as the work of God although it abounds in mystery. 'And the relation itself is therefore, mysterious, because creation and providence cannot be delivered from mysteries.'[2] Instead of this leading to atheism it should lead to adoration.

Law appeals to miracles and prophecies on which, he declares, Christianity is founded, as a sufficient proof that it is a divine revelation. He does not accept the position of the other antideistic writers that a miracle cannot ever attest anything contrary to reason. Tindal asserted that since evil spirits are supposed to be able to work miracles then no value can be attached to them as proofs. Law retorts: 'if the creation must of necessity be allowed to be the work of God, notwithstanding any unknown degree of power in evil spirits; if we can as certainly ascribe it to God, as if we really knew there were no such spirits; then in some cases, miracles may be a full proof of the operation, or the inter-position of God, as if we really knew there were no such spirits in being.'[3] If God is to be accepted as the Creator, then it follows of necessity that He still presides over the universe. Providence attests His actions in things ordinary, and if God works in things ordinary then there is no reason to deny extraordinary activity to Him. But if the incomprehensible is attributed to evil spirits, then there is no reason why the ordinary should be attributed to God.

Law believes that miracles are absolute proof. 'It seems therefore

---

[1] Op. cit., p. 95.   [2] Op. cit., p. 103.
[3] Op. cit., p. 108.

to be needless, and too great a concession, which some learned divines make in this matter, when they grant that we must first examine the doctrines revealed by miracles, and see whether they contain anything in them absurd, or unworthy of God before we receive His miracles as divine.'[1] There is no appeal from the evidence of miracles. To judge a doctrine by reason, and then the miracles by the doctrines is to begin at the wrong end. The doctrines are revealed 'because of our ignorance of the nature and reasonableness of them', and the miracles are wrought with the purpose of preventing us from acquiescing in our judgement of the worth and value of the doctrines.

In another chapter Law turns the tables on his opponent. Free-thinkers make a great show of reason, they assume the position of champions, pretending to vindicate the right of all men to judge according to its dictates. Law replies with the observation that this is trite, for reason is the only way rational creatures can determine anything either theoretical or practical. 'It is not a matter of duty for men to use their reason, but of necessity.'[2]

The human reason, however, far from being, the be all and end all, is precisely that which renders men fit recipients for the revelation of God. It is as natural for men to use their reason as it is to see with their eyes. The unbeliever is opposed, not because he reasons, but because he reasons falsely. The question, then, is 'not whether reason is to be followed, but when it is best followed? not whether it is to be our guide, but how it may be our safest guide?'[3] And it is our best guide when it admits its imperfection and follows the light of heaven. It cannot ever be a true guide since, in his last chapter, Law sets out to show, 'that all the disorders of our passions, the corruptions of our hearts, all the reveries of the imagination, all the contradictions and absurdities that are to be found in human life, and human opinions, are strictly and precisely the mutability, the disorders, corruption and absurdities of the human reason.'[4]

[1] *The Case of Reason*, p. 109.   [2] Op. cit., p. 115.
[3] Op. cit., p. 116.   [4] Op. cit., p. 128.

CHAPTER VI

THE CHANGE OF AN EMPHASIS

The passing of deism gave the orthodox apologists opportunity to turn their attention to the Methodist movement, which was regarded as a recrudescence of 'enthusiasm'. There was an understandable anxiety among many convinced Churchmen lest the activities of Whitfield and Wesley should upset the ordered structure of the Established Church. It was feared that a schism, like that of early Montanism, would weaken the authority of this ordained institution, and give occasion for the rise of all sorts of irregularities, each claiming the sanction of an immediate revelation. It was out of this anxiety and fear that there appeared a flood of books and pamphlets all aimed at curbing the Methodist excess. Such works as Green, *On Enthusiasm*, and Bishop Gibson, *Against Enthusiasm*, had this avowed design.

The best known of these anti-enthusiast volumes — a work which John Wesley himself felt compelled to answer — was Bishop Lavington's *The Enthusiasm of the Methodists and Papists Compared*. The Bishop had written of Wesley as pretending to special and immediate revelations, and he likens enthusiasm to 'a kind of drunkenness'.[1] This charge, with a long list of others, Wesley denies, maintaining that, 'the Mystic Divinity was never a Methodists' doctrine.'[2]

But interest in the enthusiasm of the Methodists was soon turned, to what was regarded as another expression of the same spirit in a different realm. The beginning of the nineteenth century marked the commencement of a new state and stage in scientific activity. Not only had Dalton, in 1803, announced his atomic theory and Sir Charles Bell turned attention to the study of the brain to indicate the difference between the sensory and the motor nerve mechanism, but Lamarck had stood forth as the precursor of the scientific doctrine of evolution. The early years of the century

[1] Op. cit., p. 75.
[2] *Works* (1809), vol. 13, p. 55.

saw an increasing use made of the mathematical method in physics. There was everywhere a growing unrest with anything that savoured of the mysterious. The claim was being made that no province of the universe could be shut off from scientific investigation. Theologians were ordered to abandon their territory. Theological and metaphysical assumptions were not to be allowed to erect a 'No Thoroughfare' notice anywhere. Theologians were refused the right to say to the scientist, Thus far shalt thou go and no farther. The time had come, it was being announced, when science must free itself from the dictates of metaphysics.

Thus it was, with the stabilization of Methodism the orthodox turned their attention from the religious enthusiasm to the scientific. Yet the scientific world of the early nineteenth century differed only from the earlier deistic one in the fact that the God of deism was eliminated. The remote God of deism was now removed, and the throne of the universe was left unoccupied.

In this scientific climate there arose a fervent unbelief, eager to accost and attack the protagonists of revealed religion, ready to undermine the bulwarks of the faith. The Report of the Society for Promoting Christian Knowledge for 1832 gives the information that, in London, productions claiming to be directed towards the diffusion of science, but hostile to revealed religion, were disseminated to the amount of three hundred thousand a week. Their zeal on behalf of unbelief was regarded as another manifestation of the enthusiastic spirit. Here was 'an unauthorized outstripping of all rightful bounds of reason'. If the religious enthusiasm was responsible for incredulity, this new scientific enthusiasm gave vent to infidelity. Dr Bidlake in the Bampton Lectures of 1811, traces the fanaticism which springs from religious enthusiasm, and the unbelief in a divine revelation, which in the name of science, conceives of the world as a closed system, to the same root. 'Having therefore endeavoured', he writes, 'to show the regular consistency of all schemes of providence, and the demonstrative probability of the truth of the Christian religion; we must show the unhappy tendency of pretentions which would destroy all consistence, and render religion contrary to what God has designed it to be; making it, instead of a system of practical piety and goodness, a visionary illusion. It is highly probable that these opinions originate from the same strong and restless passions of the mind which influence other men to deviate into the extreme of infidelity. These extremes of error spring from the same evil root. The same principle of ambition is observable in both. If the infidel is gratified by assuming the solemnity of doubt, of suspicion, of scorn, and in thus defying the armies of the living God; the pride of the enthusiast is equally flattered by the idea of his being the chosen favourite of Heaven.'[1]

Both the fanatic and the infidel must be made to see that God's revelation is complete and final. While the latter treats Christianity with a cold indifference, the former 'ask for no evidence'. They 'trust only to certain inward and equivocal feelings'.[2] The infidel is disposed to believe nothing and to revile everything. The enthusiast acts under the sway of some internal and imaginary impulse. He impudently aspires to familiarity with the Sovereign of the Universe. But asks Bidlake, 'of what avail are ordinances, if men can be saved by instantaneous conversion?'[3] He thinks that the enthusiasts' sense of guilt is the offspring of mental gloom; while the assertion of the inner feeling of grace received is rejected because it is built upon the notion that 'good and religious conduct will not render him worthy of acceptance with God'.[4] Faith, according to Bidlake, is 'the assent the reason gives to the word of God'.[5] It is built upon the impartial weighing of evidence, and it is only the man of integrity who will give unprejudiced attention to the proofs. Indeed the evidence of his integrity is seen in the fact that he gives his 'Amen' to the doctrines as divine. The enthusiast, therefore, puts immediate inspiration in the place of patient instruction. The infidel, on the other hand, puts arrogant declamation in the place of reverent devotion.

Against the latter, Bidlake will show 'that the evidences of revealed religion are capable of a very high demonstration; that the scheme of divine revelation is grand, comprehensive, consistent and harmonious in its general design; agreeable to the attributes of the Deity, and to the analogies of his economy in the natural and moral world'.[6] He attributes the motives of unbelief in a 'superintending Providence' to apathy, impiety and pride. The desire for novelty is also a potent force. The bravery of the soldier in the

---

[1] *The Truth and Consistency of the Divine Revelation; with some Remarks on the contrary extremes of Infidelity and Enthusiasm* (2nd edition), pp. 154, 155.
[2] Op. cit., p. 153.
[3] Op. cit., p. 154.
[4] Op. cit., p. 169.
[5] Op. cit., p. 197.
[6] Op. cit., p. 6.

ranks can go unobserved, but he who meets the enemy single-handed is brought to the notice of every eye. Thus 'to tread in the accustomed path is to be lost in a crowd, men hope from every deviation to acquire a degree of pre-eminence or at least to attract attention'.[1]

In order to confound the infidel, Bidlake sets out to prove the reality of a particular providence. He uses the cosmological argument to secure his evidence for a 'superintending First Cause'. Reference to second causes is not sufficient to account for the continual adaptation of nature to an over-arching purpose. The Mosaic account of creation, the Fall, and the Deluge bears the marks of a divine disclosure, a fact made obvious when the account is contrasted with the mythologies and polytheism of other peoples. 'If then no conception of natural religion were so clear, no declarations so express, as are evident in the Jewish revelation, is it not to be concluded that the Scriptures must have derived their origin from a source superior to human?'[2]

There is much greater evidence for the New Testament, whose universal appeal, superior morality and central Figure give it a quality and an authenticity which none can gainsay. In the light of these overwhelming proofs, the infidel, like the enthusiast, is charged with blindly rejecting the reality and the authority of revelation as a body of revealed doctrines. The infidel would have us 'reject the promises of revealed religion, which alone afford rational hope and firm conviction'.[3]

REVELATION AS A BODY OF REVEALED DOCTRINES

Two enemies, then, the apologists at the close of the eighteenth and the beginning of the nineteenth centuries, felt themselves bound to combat. There were the enthusiasts who had to be restricted to the Scriptures as the full and final revelation, and there were the infidels who had to be convinced of the Scriptures as a real revelation. This fact can be illustrated by a comparison of two series of Bampton Lectures which appeared in the first half of the nineteenth century. In 1802, G. F. Nott took as his subject, *Religious Enthusiasm*, while in 1833, F. Nolan discoursed on *The Analogy of Revelation and Science*.

For Nott the tragedy of religious enthusiasm was that it upset

---

[1] Op. cit., p. 10.   [2] Op. cit., p. 92.
[3] Op. cit., p. 32.

the communicated body of revealed truths. Where there is a
desire for 'immediate revelation, rather than the study of Scripture,
it will be easy to trace the progress of enthusiasm'.[1] For Nolan the
tragedy of 'Scientific' infidelity was its rejection of revelation. 'In
the increasing ardour', he writes, 'with which scientific enquiry is
now pursued, when every facility is not merely afforded to individual exertion, but means are used to draw out the general
strength of combined operations; some anxiety, if not apprehension, may be felt, as to the direction in which this growing power
may be ultimately turned. When the interests of Philosophy are
exclusively advanced; there can be no room to attend to the un-
obtrusive claims of Religion. Experience has unfortunately proved,
that as the one advances its pretentions, the other is found to
decline in its reputation.'[2]

The works of Nott and Nolan are important, then, first, because
they indicate the awareness by the orthodox of their opponents.
In their view the religious enthusiast was guilty of the sin of undermining, while the scientific infidel was guilty of the sin of unbelief.
Against both, the apologists sought to defend Christianity as a body
of 'revealed truths from which it is impossible to deviate without
incurring guilt'.[3] To the first, therefore, had to be proved the
finality of the Scriptures as a system of doctrine, to the second the
actuality of revelation within the communicated word.

(i) *The New Enemies*
(*a*) *Religious Enthusiasm*

G. F. Nott began his series of Lectures with an investigation of
the meaning of the word 'enthusiasm'. It denotes, he concludes,
'that self-sufficient spirit, which placing the conceit of human
fancy on a level with real inspiration has ever proved by its results,
that it is not of God.'[4] He unhesitatingly attributes such enthusiasm to the ultimate agency of the devil. He will be content to
assert, however, that in men like Whitfield and Wesley it is due to
a vehement action of the imagination. 'The first conceit of divine
illumination in the mind of the Enthusiast is owing to the in-
ordinate action of imagination, which, when vehemently excited, is
known to represent ideal objects so vividly to the apprehension,

[1] G. F. Nott, *Religious Enthusiasm*, p. 48.
[2] *The Analogy of Religion and Science*, p. 33.
[3] *Religious Enthusiasm*, p. 324.
[4] Op. cit., p. 6.

that they are mistaken for material ones.'[1] The tragedy is that the enthusiast, while claiming to justify himself from Scripture, in reality denies its finality and authority. 'All pretence to rapturous communications of divine knowledge is enthusiastic delusion.'[2]

Enthusiasm is stimulated by pride, vanity and ambition. There is a curiosity which drives some to be wise beyond what is written; there is an unsanctified ambition for spiritual pre-eminence. Some have a consuming desire for immediate revelations, and seeing that no such private communications are possible, they are soon created by the obliging imagination and believed in as undoubted realities. 'If they did not think themselves inspired,' says H. More, 'they were not enthusiasts.'[3]

The most awful result of this fevered spirit is that it openly violates the unity of the Church. And the Church for Nott is a visible institution by law established. The providence of God has 'preserved among us the Established order entire'.[4] To be the occasion for schism is to be guilty of the darkest sin.

Having set forth the causes and the characteristics of enthusiasm, Nott goes on to apply his conclusions to Whitfield and Wesley. They are both to be designated 'enthusiasts' because they have pretended to special revelations, and by their conduct have separated from the established Church. They 'believe themselves, like the Prophets and Apostles of old, to have received a particular communication of divine authority'.[5] They believe themselves to be specially raised up of God to deliver the people, they fancy that God intervened on their behalf by miraculous interpositions, they arrogate to themselves words which should only be attributed to Christ and His apostles, they preach false doctrine. Concerning the last charge Nott singles out three 'errors' which are specially repugnant: (1) The assurance of salvation and forgiveness by the immediate activity of the Holy Ghost, (2) Perfectionism, (3) regeneration as a conscious act taking place in the heart, sometimes with an agony issuing in joyous peace. With these and other arguments Nott concludes, 'that the Authors of the Sect were, in the strict sense of the word, Enthusiasts.'[6]

Being thus deluded they must have been overcome by the passions of pride, vanity, and ambition. The works of Whitfield and

---

[1] *Religious Enthusiasm*, p. 37.   [2] Op. cit., p. 31.
[3] *Divine Dialogues*, p. 469.   [4] *Religious Enthusiasm*, p. 85.
[5] *Religious Enthusiasm*, p. 216.   [6] Op. cit., p. 251.

Wesley are made to yield the necessary proof, and, of course, use is made of Lavington to assure the correctness of the conclusion. Can there be any doubt that they grasped at public fame? If there should be any then Nott will remove it. Any admission of unworthiness, any claim to a divine guidance, any reference to extraordinary manifestations of the Spirit, and the like, are all laboriously marshalled and skillfully used to draw the same conclusion. Can their doctrines be true? it may be asked. How can they be? The test of true doctrines is that 'they are perfect at the very time of their delivery'.[1] But the leaders of this Sect have admitted to altering their views. They stand, therefore, self-condemned. 'For though the founders of this Sect asserted, that they were filled in a peculiar manner with the Holy Ghost; and that they were instructed of God, what they were to teach to mankind; they nevertheless contradicted not only themselves, and one another, but even the very Scriptures.'[2]

The result of such enthusiasm was inevitable. By following the dictates of their own inclinations they have repudiated the authority of the Church: 'if men believe that the Almighty communicates his will to them by impressing forcibly upon their hearts what in every situation he would do, they would naturally suspect that every strong impulse, or inclination which they feel may be a divine suggestion.'[3] They have lost sight of the fact that the complete system of religion has been communicated entire. They would add thereto the fancies of their own fevered minds and their own fictitious messages. 'How can it be a mark of a superior mind, to be indifferent as to the deviations which are made from the one unalterable standard of Revealed Truth.'[4] Religion of *this* enthusiastic origination is not from above.

When once enthusiasm is allowed to continue its disrupting influence it will be content, not merely to tear asunder the unity of the Church, but with nothing less than the break up of social solidarity, by dissolving the ties of natural affection and the harmonies of public business and private families. It will even extend its baneful influence further, and, by exciting public dissentions, lawful government itself will become impossible. To such a conclusion then, must enthusiasm lead; to such an awful end are carried those who seek personal revelations from God.

[1] Op. cit., p. 302.   [2] Op. cit., p. 305.
[3] Op. cit., p. 329.   [4] Op. cit., p. 380.

(b) Scientific Scepticism

Nott considered himself to be defending the fully-revealed scheme of doctrine from the attacks of the religious enthusiasts. But it was for Nolan to maintain the same position, some thirty years later, against the prevalent scepticism of his day. The task, he feels, to be of special urgency, and it is not to be 'looked upon as uncalled for at a time, when the interests of Revelation are not merely overlooked, but the subject deemed incompatible with the cultivation of Science'.[1] It is the purpose of Nolan to show that there is no disharmony between Revelation and Science. He therefore takes up the Biblical account of the Creation, the Fall, the separation of the races, and related topics, and maintains that nothing that a true science can discover has rendered these impossible. 'The sacred legislator, it is admitted, addresses us in a religious, not in a philosophical character; but in demanding our assent to communications, as delivered by inspiration, we have some right to expect, that as far as they extend, they should maintain their pretensions to infallibility.'[2]

Moses, he asserts, was no illiterate primitive, for 'he must have been sufficiently versed in the principle of science, to have accommodated his descriptions to the views entertained of it by the moderns'.[3] In these intricate lectures reference is made to ancient cosmologies, and recent advances in geological, physiological, zoological and geographical knowledge. It is concluded that 'the disclosures of Revelation, are consonant to the decisions of Science'.[4] Nothing has been discovered that renders a belief in a Deluge impossible. The longevity of the patriarchs is considered to be sufficiently explained on the hypothesis that an Egyptian scheme of chronology was used, in which, instead of a year of twelve months, seasons of three are computed. This means that the age of any one recorded individual is already reduced to one-fourth of that period. Methuselah's real age is consequently 242 years. When allowance is made for the relative purity and simplicity of their lives and the unhurried nature of their existence in a leisurely environment this number of years is not difficult to accept.[5]

---

[1] The Analogy of Religion and Science, p. 356.
[2] Op. cit., pp. 44, 45.
[3] Op. cit., p. 48.
[4] Op. cit., p. 314.
[5] In a footnote, Nolan quotes from the parish register of St Leonards, Shoreditch, London; Thomas Carn, died Jan. 28th, 1588, aged 207 years.

He is certain also that naturalists are agreed that the whole human race was developed from one human family. In Lecture 5 he states that, 'Whatever, therefore, be the test by which the scheme of Revelation is tried; whether it be estimated by the attributes of the Deity or the constitution of nature; by the immutable principle of good and evil, or the decisions of ethical and physiological science; under every trial it bears testimony to the goodness and benevolence of its Author, not less striking than the works of nature supply of his power and wisdom.'[1]

Christianity is clearly a body of revealed truths: and the authors of the sacred books 'deliver a communication from Him who can as little err himself as conspire in deceiving others'.[2] It is when the ablest systems which men have devised to solve the riddle of the universe are found to leave the reader as perplexed as before, that one turns to the Scriptures with the assurance of their divine origin. Problems which throughout the ages have agitated enquiring minds, like the origin of sin and the diversity of languages, are here solved. With a simplicity which is at the same time profound, its divine system of truth satisfies the most eager mind, and it is, at the same time in harmony with the best results of human knowledge. Nolan concludes his discussion with the hope that his endeavours will 'restore Revealed Religion to that importance which natural (religion) has engrossed'.[3]

(ii) *Contrast with the Earlier Polemic*

This last observation of Nolan provides us with the contrast between the earlier polemic against the deists and the present one against the 'enthusiasm' of the Methodists and the unbelief of infidels. Here there is little discussion of natural religion. Religion as revealed is the important thing, and this is no longer regarded as adding a few positive commands to natural religion. The whole concern is now with the reality and finality of that which God has specifically disclosed in a system of communicated truths. In George Chandler's brilliant work the point is made that true religion is from first to last revealed: 'knowledge of divine things was communicated, not by metaphysical arguments, not by subtle disquisitions on the nature and attributes of God, processes which our

---

[1] Op. cit., p. 192.
[2] Op. cit., p. 222.
[3] Op. cit., p. 357.

own experiences tell us are in the least degree suited to convey information on the subject to the immature mind, but demonstratively and palpably.'[1] What is called general revelation was communicated in common to the whole race of men. Religion was necessary to man, but it was something he was unlikely to discover, yet he was 'fully capable of receiving it, when imparted'.[2] God gave to the whole race knowledge of Himself as Creator and Judge, and the necessity of every man to live before Him in righteousness.

In addition He has given a particular revelation 'taking its rise from the Fall'. In increasing measure and at definite stages of man's development, as he was able to receive it, 'God established a direct communication first, with a particular individual; next, with the immediate descendants of that individual; and then, as those descendants multiplied into a people, with the people derived from the original ancestor.'[3]

With Abraham a new epoch was begun. Then again with Moses 'a highly interesting era commences' in which, for the first time, the divine words were preserved in written records. In between the periods when God made some new communication, there arose the 'testimony of prophecy' which acted 'at the time, to animate the passing generation with hope for the future; afterwards, to afford a retrospective argument for the truth of His words'.[4] At length, in the fulness of time, He appeared Who was the subject of all prophecy, and in His light, the race, which had reached the 'adult state of human reason',[5] saw clearly those truths which were but dimly apprehended in earlier days. From henceforth Christianity is confirmed, no longer by the continued exhibition of miraculous agencies, for man has learned to put away childish things: no longer is its truth impressed upon the mind by the strength of irresistible demonstration; but, since man has become able to weigh moral evidence, it requires to be investigated and examined. The divine word was embodied in a writing to become the building agency of the Church's life and the binding authority of the Church's doctrine.

---

[1] *The Scheme of Divine Revelation considered Principally in its Connection with the Progress and Improvement of Human Society*, p. 49.
[2] Op. cit., p. 6.
[3] Op. cit., p. 81.
[4] Op. cit., p. 96.
[5] Op. cit., p. 185.

With the passing years men invented ideas which they first set side by side with the Word, and then, inevitably, these human notions usurped the ruling place, claiming an allegiance which was never intended, thereby corrupting the pure faith. At length in the providence of God, at the Reformation, the authentic message was recovered, and the extraneous ideas swept away. It is the glory of the Reformation, that among other blessings of lasting worth, 'above all, it has established the grand, the fundamental doctrine of the supremacy of the scripture. It has pronounced the scripture to be the guide of life, the rule of faith, the test of truth. It has declared that no earthly power has authority in religious matters, unless that authority be given by the word of God.'[1]

The Principle of Selection

The nineteenth century had not far advanced before the Methodist movement showed that it would not fulfil the prediction that it would destroy the whole framework of Christianity. Its continued existence however was considered by some Churchmen to be a weakening of the revealed order. Although its enthusiasm might, in some measure, have 'cooled off', it was still regarded as an enemy, because its fundamental doctrine of immediate revelation was as opposed as ever to that of revelation as a body of revealed doctrines. At the same time, as we shall see later, there were within the Established Church itself, men who vehemently repudiated this view of revelation, and, by advocating a doctrine of revelation within the immediacy of experience, they found in the Methodist movement a natural ally.

It is for this reason that F. D. Maurice, for example, saw a significance in the Methodist teaching which was more akin to his own position than the cold assent to infallible truths which the orthodox appeared to demand. It was as a result of this that Maurice was plunged into the violent controversy with Dean Mansel, on the subject of revelation, which closes the period of our review.

But with the waning concern for the Methodist enthusiasm there went a growing awareness of the infidel challenge. The new world science had presented seemed to crowd out the possibility of revelation; or, at any rate, what was regarded as the 'assured results' of its discoveries, had rendered its claims and conceptions impossible. Scepticism was thought to be justified by science. Sir

---

[1] *The Scheme of Divine Revelation, etc.*, p. 231.

Oracle had spoken and no dog was supposed to bark. Of the growth
and influence of infidelity many believing men were aware. In the
introduction to a remarkable work, entitled *An Essay on the Nature
and Immutability of Truth in Opposition to Sophistry and Scepticism*,
Dr John Beattie, Professor of Moral Philosophy and Logic in the
University of Aberdeen, noted that 'Scepticism is now the profession of every fashionable inquiry into human nature; a scepticism
which is not confined to points of mere speculation, but has been
extended to the practical truths of the highest importance, even to
the principles of morality and religion'.[1] The same understanding
of the times is given in the General Appendix of Watson's *Apology
for the Bible*. 'The present', we there read, 'has been called — the
age of philosophy — the age of reason: if by reason and philosophy,
irreligion is understood, it undoubtedly merits the appellation;
for there was never any age since the death of Christ, never since
the commencement of the history of the world, in which atheism
and infidelity have been more generally professed.'[2] The Bishop of
London, Dr Porteus, in 1816, felt compelled to issue *A Summary of
the Principle Evidences for the Truth and Divine Origin of the
Christian Religion*, because it was a time, when, he says, 'new
compendiums of infidelity and new libels of Christianity are dis-
persed continually, with indefatigable industry, through every
part of the kingdom, and every class of the community.'[3]

The influence of Paine and Gibbon was apparent in all strata of
society. By many, both these opponents of a divine revelation were
hailed as the high-priests of a new worship of nature and as the
apostles of a triumphant infidelity. In the preface of Simpson's
Plea for Religion and the Sacred Writings — a work directed
especially against the daring unbelief of the author of *The Age of
Reason* — there is the observation: 'It will be allowed by every dispassionate observer, that if ERRONEOUS AND NOXIOUS TENETS were
ever diffused among men in every age, they are eminently so in the
present.'[4]

But the orthodox had men of no meagre ability who were eager
to meet the infidel challenge. A host came to their help against the

---

[1] *The Evidence of the Christian Religion*, (*A collection of Works, Tracts, and
Essays on the Subject, 1812*), vol. 3, p. 3.
[2] *Apology for the Bible*, p. 560.
[3] *A Summary of the Principle Evidences, etc.*, Preface, p. iv.
[4] *Plea for Religion and the Sacred Writings*, Preface, p. iii. Cf., also Publisher's
Appendix, p. 401.

might of the enemy. The evidence of their work can still be seen in a large, if little read, literature. Something of the extent of their labours is indicated by Jortin, 'Fabricus has reckoned up', he tells us, 'some hundreds and doubtless several treatises might be added which have escaped his diligence,'[1] all assuring the reality of a revealed religion.

A large number of volumes were added between the time that Jortin wrote and the end of the period with which we have to do. So large is the list that some principle of selection is needed, for these many volumes cover the same ground as an examination of their contents will reveal.

The following principle of selection is adopted. A number of the most important of the Bampton lectures on our subject and a number of the most cogent works from general literature have been singled out to illustrate the way the newer apologists sought to confound the infidel and incidentally to check the enthusiast.

Two titles, one from these Bampton lectures and the other from this general literature, will indicate the nature of the reply. In 1847, W. A. Shirley, Bishop of Soder and Man, was responsible for the lectures which were published under the title, *The Supremacy of the Scripture*.[2] Earlier Jacob Bryant, in a vigorous volume, entitled, *A Treatise upon the Authenticity of the Scriptures*, drew attention to what he referred to as the 'divine volume'. The very titles of these two books will make it clear that for these later apologists revelation was identified with its record. God's special disclosure was equated with the Scriptures. Consequently a defence of revelation and a defence of the Bible were the same thing.

(iii) *The Bampton Lectures and the Biblical Revelation*

The following five series of Lectures,[3] delivered over a period of half a century will help towards an understanding of the outlook

---

[1] *Discourse Concerning the Truth of the Christian Revelation* (2nd edition, 1747), Preface, p. iv.

[2] Only four of the eight lectures given by Shirley were published. As a matter of fact, only two of the four were delivered owing to the illness and the subsequent death of the lecturer.

[3] The five chosen are as follows: (1) James Williamson (Prebendary of Lincoln), *The Truth, Inspiration, Authority, and end of the Scriptures, Considered and Defended*, 1793; (2) E. Nares, *A View of the Evidences of Christianity at the Close of the Pretended Age of Reason*, 1805; (3) John Miller, *The Divine Authority of the Holy Scriptures Asserted, from Adaptation to the Real State of Human Nature* (2nd edition, 1817); (4) T. W. Lancaster, *Popular Evidences of Christianity Stated and Examined*, 1831; (5) W. A. Shirley, *The Supremacy of the Holy Scriptures*, 1847.

which prevailed in the first half of the nineteenth century. By identifying special revelation with the Scriptures it was immaterial as to whether the works of the era were entitled, *Evidences of Christianity*, or, *The Truth of the Bible*. The two stood or fell together. And as the Old and the New Testaments belonged together any error in the former would necessarily undermine the validity of the latter. If the foundations were insecure the superstructure could not stand.

(a) Revelation and the Scriptures

Those who discoursed on the subject in the late eighteenth and early nineteenth centuries saw it as their task to prove that the 'Scriptures are authentic', and with that established it must follow that 'Christianity is true'.[1]

James Williamson does not think of this as a 'blind and implicit acquiescence' in the Scriptures, because each man is 'at full liberty to examine with candour the grounds and evidences of Christianity'.[2] He proceeds then to draw together the proofs for the truth and authenticity of the Bible. A written revelation is a more secure method, he argues, than oral tradition, for the conveying of the pure doctrines of Christianity to distant generations. So strong are the evidences that we cannot refuse our assent to the whole of the divine revelation. The Jewish belief in their Scriptures as of 'heavenly origin' was confirmed by our Lord. 'The doctrines of Christianity, the predictions of the prophets, and the precepts of the law, which we are informed was our schoolmaster to bring us to Christ (Gal. iii. 24), cannot be denied to be of divine original by any, who does not wish to disbelieve all inspiration.'[3] None dare say that the 'holy penmen' mixed falsehood with truth.

T. W. Lancaster states that it is his purpose to deal with 'the proofs of revealed religion, as may suffice for the reasonable conviction of all men'.[4] It is only a small number of persons who can discover and estimate the whole body of external evidences adduced as proof of Christianity; and Lancaster refuses to believe that the faith of the many has to be built on the credit of the few. He asserts, therefore, with Athanasius that, 'The Christian faith

[1] W. T. Lancaster, *Popular Evidences of Christianity, etc.*, p. 155.
[2] *The Truth, etc., of the Scriptures*, p. 102.
[3] Op. cit., p. 61.
[4] *Popular Evidences of Christianity Stated and Examined*, p. 3.

carries within itself the discovery of its own authority, and the holy scriptures which God has inspired, are all-sufficient in themselves for the evidence of their own truth.'[1] No direct revelation has, or need, come to us. All that God has disclosed is found within the divine book.

This leads Lancaster to raise the question, Are these Scriptures really deserving of such high credit? The New Testament, he insists, must be authentic because it is not likely that the early believers were hoodwinked by forgeries. The Scriptures 'profess to deliver a doctrine on which the salvation of mankind depends, and which, on pain of eternal ruin, demands the obedience of all men. Such books would surely never get into currency, unless those who first received them were satisfied that they were written by persons duly authorized'.[2]

No one can think of an imposture beguiling all the people with a forged law as if it were an authentic act of Parliament. More especially would this be impossible if that 'law' demanded considerable sacrifices and required painful duties. Lancaster does not think that the usual way of proving that certain books were received as canonical to be the best. The usual method runs something like this: citations from the books now accepted are found in some early Christian writer or other, and it is then concluded that their authority is established. But, according to Lancaster, this does not follow, since the authority of the writings from which quotation is drawn must be first made certain. No such circuitous method is necessary.

If a question were raised concerning a person's title to an estate, who would be prepared to believe that there was a flaw in the grant five centuries back? 'Who does not see, that a title of this nature might be presumed to be good; that it would not have been admitted from the first, if its legality had not been fully proved; and that the evidence MUST, in the nature of things, have now perished, which formed its original basis? Why then desire to try over again, at this time, a question, the true grounds of which have been unavoidably swept away from human knowledge? Yet it is by such a process that we try the authenticity of the canon of Scripture: this is what the enemies of revelation demand; and it is a demand in which the advocates for revelation are too ready most judiciously

---

[1] *Popular Evidences, etc.,* p. 32.
[2] Op. cit., p. 62.

to acquiesce.'[1] But the question is already settled. Only those who were contemporary with the need to make the decision could do so. And they did. They were the only people, in the nature of the case, who could be vigilant against impostures. They were called upon to attest by pain and martyrdom the faith which they held, it was not likely, therefore, that in these circumstances, they would have accepted the fictitious.

It was, indeed, because they were so watchful that some books only gained recognition after long trial. This fact is itself testimony that not everything coming forth in the name of Christ was grasped at, and that the acceptance of any book is proof sufficient of its authenticity.

This genuineness has the moral attestation of every believing man. There is within man an intuitive faculty which under the influence of the divine Spirit can authenticate the revelation. God has given to the natural man senses to discern. This being so, 'it is only reasonable to think, that God, in offering a revelation to his accountable creatures, should both IMPRESS UPON THAT REVELATION the distinctive characters of his own wisdom and goodness; and also IMPART TO MAN an adequate and adapted faculty of perceiving and discriminating these characters.'[2] If bodily organs are given, can spiritual ones be denied? Those whose spiritual eyes are open will see God's own image and superscription on the Christian revelation. In the Bible he reads, he will discover a wisdom, a virtue and a doctrine not of this world.

But Lancaster goes on to insist that this inner persuasion does not lead to fanaticism (enthusiasm), which is a 'natural disposition of the mind, in which the imagination is strong, but the reason weak'.[3] A recognition of the Church as a divinely sanctioned institution, with a lawfully appointed order of bishops, 'whose authority, by legitimate succession, is derived from them to whom Christ first gave it,'[4] will curb fanatical excess. All uncredited pretentions to divine authority, all unauthorized administrations in the name of the Gospel, are invalid, and consequently 'wholly unavailing to the purpose of giving a title to God's covenanted mercies'.[5] Every claim to a 'special revelation' based upon an 'alleged inward light' is therefore to be set aside. Thus certain

---

[1] *Popular Evidences, etc.*, p. 78.   [2] Op. cit., p. 181.
[3] Op. cit., p. 219.   [4] Op. cit., p. 311.
[5] Op. cit., p. 326.

assertions of the Calvinists, and the Methodists are to be refused; as are those of the Arians, the Socinians and the Deists. While the 'Gnostick, in the primeval heresy', and the 'Evangelical, in these times', discover 'a fond allegiance to the same pretentions'.[1]

Shirley in his lectures rejects 'implicit faith' in any Church tradition. The essence of saving faith is a practical trust in God's revealed word. The Bible is, in itself, no 'dead letter' to be awakened to significance and relevancy by our own reason; such a view is 'essentially rationalistic'.[2] The purpose of his discourses is 'to maintain the SUPREME AUTHORITY OF HOLY WRIT against the claims of tradition and authority on the one hand, and presumptuous and rationalistic speculations on the other'.[3] John Miller sought to assure The Divine Authority of the Holy Scriptures, by arguing that its own internal evidence and authority are inescapable. Many persons matured in homes where the Bible is reverenced as the authentic revelation from God submit to it as an infallible guide. This devout reception of the Bible, as the Word of God, for the reason that it is presented as such from the first, is not to be swept aside as mere implicit faith. That such faith is real cannot be denied. After all, while it is a blessing to be able to enquire, not all have the ability to do so. But while all cannot enquire, all can experience the truth of the sacred volume, and it is, 'that which attests the divine authority of the holy Scripture to our own hearts.'[4] It is, indeed, the purpose of the discourses to stress the 'internal excellence and character of holy Writ itself'.[5] External proofs are not, of course, without value. They are, however, introductory; they are 'as it were, the title deeds of our inheritance'.[6] The Bible is, then, itself, 'the statute-book of an everlasting kingdom.'[7] First there is that which is 'natural', and such was the old Mosaic dispensation. Its concern was with the present and the palpable. Then there is the 'spiritual', the 'Evangelical', wherein man is addressed as a spiritual and immortal being. Yet the same divine Spirit is the author of both, and thus the substance of the divine plan was in each age the same. Their difference lies in the manner of their appeal. The Old appealed to the immediate and the external. Temporal blessings were its reward for good conduct.

[1] Op. cit., p. 327.
[2] The Supremacy of the Holy Scriptures, p. 5.
[3] Op. cit., p. 8.
[4] The Divine Authority of the Holy Scripture, etc., p. 15.
[5] Op. cit., p. 23.　　　　[6] Op. cit., p. 18.　　　　[7] Op. cit., p. 29.

The promised rest was expected by most to find its fulfilment in the present life. Because the appeal of the Old was to the sensuous, it followed that the 'apostasy of the Jews became IDOLATRY'.[1] The new order, bringing life and immortality to light, addressed itself to the spirit of man, to that which does not belong to time and which is not satisfied with the temporal. The present dispensation eclipses the ancient by reason of its spiritual pre-eminence. The rejection of revelation is the modern apostasy, it is 'the SPIRITUAL and INTELLECTUAL REJECTION of the Deity'.[2]

Because, therefore, the new is addressed to man as a morally responsible being 'we must receive it in that INNER MAN, to which it is so pointedly offered'.[3] The doctrine which has received such eloquent emphasis by Emil Brunner, trembles on the lips of the Lecturer. Miller sees man as a being of 'capacity' and 'destiny'.[4] Man *qua* man is a 'responsible' being.[5] Man is capable of making 'response'.[6] He is a creature 'addressed' by God,[7] to Whom he must make the response of faith.

Miller finds reason for 'the believer implicitly confiding in Scripture' in the consideration that what was said of Christ, can be said of it; it 'knew what was in man'.[8] Although a book of 'small substance' it is sufficient for every phase of man's existence and every contingency of man's experience. 'Were the BIBLE not divine, it would have failed by excess of precept. It would have attempted too much.'[9] Yet in a volume so limited, it presents man with a picture of himself that he could not have wished, with a remedy which he could not have devised and with a destiny which he could not originate. Here is a book of which each can say, it told me all things that ever I did. Is not this of God?

In every age Scripture was adapted to human needs. In the old

[1] *The Divine Authority of the Holy Scripture, etc.*, p. 44.
[2] Ibid.   [3] Op. cit., p. 49.   [4] Op. cit., p. 52.
[5] Cf., 'The kernel of man's being is responsibility and responsibility is the essence of humanity.' E. Brunner, *Scandal of Christianity*, p. 59. 'It is not that man receives responsibility as a quality to be added to his human existence; but responsibility is the same thing as human nature.' *The Christian Understanding of Man* (Church Community and State), vol. 2, p. 157; also, *Man in Revolt*, p. 102.
[6] Brunner argues that 'responsibility' implies 'respondability', i.e. 'the ability to respond'.
[7] Cf., 'Man's distinctive quality consists in the fact that God turns to him and addresses him. In this "address" God gives man his distinctive quality.' *The Christian Understanding of Man*, p. 156. Cf., God created man 'as one who can hear His call and answer it'. *Man in Revolt*, p. 75.
[8] *The Divine Authority of Holy Scripture, etc.*, p. 75.
[9] Op. cit., p. 78.

dispensation God taught man more by fear than by love. The supreme note was one of terror rather than of tenderness. When Christ came 'grace' and 'love' were the major themes. After Him there were the Apostles who spoke 'neither the denunciatory tone of the Prophets, nor yet the peculiar, unequivocal authority of their divine Master'.[1] They entreated and exhorted against the background of the grace and love which they had experienced in Him. Not only was the whole scheme admirably adapted to God's progressive unfolding of Himself, but the same scheme comes down to the experience of every individual. There is the denunciation of sin which reveals it for what it is. There are the conduct and the character of Christ, which come as power and pattern. There is the life which we are exhorted to follow in the 'apostolical writings'. Thus is the whole plan of revelation meant for ourselves. The law and the prophets speak to us: the gospel records have us in view: the letters which follow are for our lives. 'All are fresh, as applicable to the exigencies of our existing nature, as if they were fruits gathered into the storehouse of truth only yesterday.'[2] All vital truth is, therefore, to be sought in the Scripture alone, and 'the law of life proposed to us in the holy Scripture', is 'sufficient (a law) for the wants and wishes of every individual person called into obedience to it'.[3] For Miller, then, the process of the Scripture is the process of experience: first law, then love and finally learning. And it is this very fact which assures the book to be divine.

(b) The Mosaic Record as History

The special subjects central in the 'scientific' attack upon the Bible as the revelation of God, were the Mosaic account of the Creation and the Fall. It was to these themes, therefore, that the defenders of revelation had to give special attention. Each part of the Genesis story was regarded as historical and factual. The 'scepticism' of the day demanded a freer treatment of the Mosaic cosmology. In the Introductory Preface to Dr Geddes' version of the Pentateuch a plea is put forth for regarding the stories as non-historical. He asks his readers to 'weigh his arguments in the scale of reason, devoid of theological prepossessions'. The 'rude and

[1] Op. cit., p. 151.
[2] Op. cit., p. 170.
[3] Op. cit., p. 203.

unpolished' account, made up of 'popular traditions and old songs',[1] is not to be read as history. They are mythological representations; they are the means whereby a certain truth was conveyed to those in an earlier and non-scientific age.

But the stigmatization of the stories as 'myths' had in the early days, an origin outside the Church. Its source was the scientific scepticism of the day. It was a way of escape from 'literalism', and a method of 'explanation' whereby the Genesis stories could be fitted into the framework of the assumed finality of the scientific 'world-picture'. Thus would all Christians, but the most obdurate literalists, be satisfied. The apologists of the period certainly felt themselves under pressure from their sceptical opponents, in the urge to abandon their notion of Genesis as historical.

'It has been one of the concessions most peremptorily demanded of us of late', says Nares, 'that we should agree to acknowledge it (i.e. the account of the Fall) to be no better than a mythological representation of things, a description merely imagined to account for known phenomena.'[2] Nares, in common with those who were defending the Biblical revelation, could not agree to the demand. He contends, rather, for the historical reading of the stories. The Fall, he insists, was a real fact, and basic to the subsequent unfolding history of man's redemption. 'If we will not be informed of these matters historically,' he writes, 'and I may add, in regard to the creation at least supernaturally, we must be content to be ignorant.'[3] The historical, he feels, cannot be allegorized nor could the mythological be historicized: 'for it is certainly not a fanciful representation of the creation of man, and the origin of evil, that we want; but the exact and positive history of those events, as the first and indisputable foundations of religious and moral responsibility.'[4] Nares rejects the idea that the stories are 'representations of present appearances'. 'They are facts and events, certainly not capable of being explained by allegory; and a figurative representation of such things is altogether useless.'[5]

In no less vigorous language, James Williamson, the Prebendary of Lincoln, rejects all mythological interpretations of the Genesis records. The account, he asserts, bears the evidence of history.

---

[1] *Introductory Preface to the Pentateuch*, p. iii.
[2] *A View of the Evidences of Christianity, etc.*, pp. 110, 111.
[3] Op. cit., p. 121.
[4] Op. cit., p. 117.
[5] Op. cit., p. 155.

The stories 'cannot be perverted into allegory and hieroglyphic'. He regards it as of 'no small importance whether we believe or deny the truth of this history; since it is closely connected with Jewish and Christian doctrines'.[1, 2]

(c) Scripture and Tradition

W. A. Shirley raises the question of the oral tradition behind the Gospel records and he can be said to anticipate the work of the more recent Form Criticism. The Son of God proclaimed the Father's love 'by oral teaching, and did not during his personal ministration dictate any written document'.[3] The 'salvation spoken by the Lord' . . . 'was verbally handed on, and confirmed to the

---

[1] *The Truth, Inspiration, etc., of the Scriptures*, p. 72.

[2] This part of the discussion will be of interest in view of the modern concern with 'demythologizing', which has come into such vogue with the publication of Bultmann's essay, '*Neues Testament und Mythologie*, which initiated the lively Entmythologisierungs controversy.' Ian Henderson, *Listener*, March 15th, 1951. The defenders of Biblical revelation in the early nineteenth century could not have foreseen that the principle which they felt bound to reject would one day be extended, within the Church, into the New Testament itself. For Bultmann the whole New Testament is 'legend-tinted'. For the 'scientific sceptics' of the earlier period the Genesis stories certainly were. They were, therefore, not to be taken literally if they were to come to any sort of terms with science. Does not a certain scepticism actuate Bultmann? When his *Theology of the New Testament* (vol. 1) was published in English, the question appeared in the *Expository Times* (vol. LXIV, No. 4, Jan. 1953), 'Should we find in this book less of the thorough-going scepticism which marred his *History of the Synoptic Tradition* and his *Jesus* written more than twenty years ago? Had the most radical New Testament scholar since Strauss mellowed somewhat with the years? We are sorry to say that we cannot report any recantations. The passage of twenty years has not altered Bultmann's scepticism about the Gospels as historical documents. Scepticism, to be sure, has its value, if only it drives us to re-examine the historical foundations on which our faith is based . . . . But there is a scepticism which by its sheer extremeness overreaches itself and alienates the sympathy of reasonable men. And this kind of scepticism, alas, spoils Bultmann's book at the very beginning.'
Bultmann feels the need for 'demythologizing' to be a scientific necessity. 'When I demythologize the Bible,' he explains in a broadcast address, 'I reckon with the fact that the thinking of modern times has ceased to be mythological and is determined by science.' (*Listener*, Feb. 5th, 1953). He insists that he is seeking an 'explanation', but we feel, as did the earlier apologists against the scientific scepticism, that he is 'explaining away'. Bultmann seems too sensitive to the 'scientific' atmosphere, and almost assumes that 'modern science' is the final truth. The present writer regards his efforts to demythologize to be both impossible and unnecessary. It is impossible, because in whatever language he restates the Gospel, be it ever so 'scientific' is it thereby any the less 'mythological'? The world pictured by the scientist is no more 'real' than that of religion. Is there anything less 'mythological' in such notions as 'matter', 'atoms', 'protons' and the like? On the other hand we feel that there is too much talk about 'explaining' the Gospel for the sake of that fiction the Modern Man. The need is for pro-clamation not for explanation. 'Instead of demythologizing the Bible, every sound spiritual energy in contemporary society urges us to re-mythologize man.' U. E. Simon, 'The Unconscious Use of Myth,' *Listener*, Feb. 26th, 1953.

[3] *The Supremacy of the Holy Scriptures*, p. 13.

faithful by those who heard him.'¹ The question is not then between an oral and a written form, since in the later written documents we have a faithful record of the teaching already made known in oral tradition.

The written records become therefore the exclusive authority, since, the floating testimony of tradition is no longer a sure basis for doctrine. Therefore, 'when once we drift from the sure anchorage of God's written word, there is no saying into what ocean of superstitious reveries, mystical hallucinations, rationalistic speculations, and even of unlimited and bottomless scepticism, we may not be carried, before we are aware, and even while we deem ourselves most secure in the guidance of primitive orthodox and catholic consent.'²

God might have continued to convey His mind by an 'unwritten tradition', but the existence of the Bible is itself proof that He preferred it otherwise. The Roman Church claims to be in possession of a binding tradition to be given the same assent and unenquiring submission — *pari pietatis effectu* — as the written word; but such a claim cannot be granted, therefore such assent and submission are inadmissible. There is evidence enough in the Bible itself of the insecurity of tradition. Just as the five books of Moses, 'written by one to whom God had been so nigh, descended to us with a sanction to which no merely human document, written or unwritten can lay claim, and this divine record at once supersedes all reference to oral traditions which had gone before, and which are in fact embodied in its sacred and mysterious contents,'³ so is it with the rest of the Old and New Testaments. The attitude of our Lord Himself to the traditions of the elders of Israel is decisive. That He recognized the Old Testament 'as the oracles of God, the authentic exponent of the Father's will, and the supreme guide of man in all that he was to achieve, and do, and hope for',⁴ is, he thinks, beyond question. The elders had set up beside the written word an infallible tradition, and, as a result, 'made the word of God of none effect by their tradition.' In a way parallel the Roman Church has added traditions for which an equal reverence is demanded: thereby 'teaching for doctrines the commandments of men'.

Yet Christ did accept the restrictions of certain ecclesiastical

¹ Op. cit., p. 14.   ² Op. cit., p. 30.
³ Op. cit., p. 41.   ⁴ Op. cit., p. 48.

ordinances as of confessedly human institution. He thus set an example of good order in the Church to which all wise-hearted and humble people will submit; but with the realization that these are not 'a matter of divine command, and therefore essential to the very being of the Church'.[1]

The significance of this Shirley deems important. It is the essential and authentic word which is the rule and guide. He points out that in the great controversies within the Church, appeal was not made to oral tradition, to any special revelations, or to any mysteries reserved for the favoured elect. There is 'no reference to any authorized interpretation of Scripture, none to any authority in matters of faith, and still less to any one visible centre of Christian union, other than the living Head, even Jesus, and the one faith in Him'.[2] Shirley goes through the Apostolic Fathers and shews that since they did not appeal to any authoritative traditions the first link in the chain is missing. Some have argued that because the inspired interpreters of Scripture are no more, there must be some authority to fix the sense. The idea, however, not only 'discredits the promised aid of God's Holy Spirit to every devout and humble enquirer',[3] but has led to a 'crop of errors, as, for example, the notion of an infallible line of teachers and the practical infallibility of the universal Church'. The Fathers appealed to Scripture directly and not to any oral tradition. They gave their own understanding of the sacred words and they were not bound by any authoritative tradition, or interpretation. It was the Gnostics who were, perhaps, the first to seek for a seat of infallibility and they fancied they found it in a select body of intellectual speculators. But against their pretended secret knowledge and higher understanding the Fathers took their stand upon the Scriptures alone.

The Montanists, on the other hand, sought infallibility in an immediate revelation and thus went beyond what was written. 'The Gnostic obtaining authoritative interpretation, by a rationalistic tradition, and the Montanist obtaining an infallible guide by direct inspiration, but both explaining away, or superseding the written word, and leaving the Church practically to human guidance.'[4]

Shirley calls on those who would preach and teach the Christian

---

[1] Op. cit., p. 48.   [2] Op. cit., p. 64.
[3] Ibid.   [4] Op. cit., p. 128.

message to shut themselves up to the written word, and to treat the whole Bible as 'the very voice of God Himself'.[1] The Bible is the 'very book of God'.[2] It is still true that some wrest the Scriptures to their own destruction 'even as their table and the common daily mercies are a snare to many'. But this does not mean that the 'one standard of truth' should therefore be withheld. Rather is it to be widely circulated and continually preached. 'We can trust God with the effect of his own book on the souls of men'.[3]

(iv) General Literature and the Biblical Revelation

Turning to the general apologetic literature in the defence of the Scriptural revelation it will be found that, while there is not the same understanding of the issues involved, not the same hints at developments yet to take place, there is, broadly, the same appreciation of revelation as a body of communicated truths embodied in the Scriptures. Out of the large literature open for review five volumes have been selected as representative of the rest.[4]

Jortin's date puts him more akin to the earlier apologetic. He asserts that the 'Christian revelation is founded upon natural religion'.[5] He does not however enter upon any discussion of the latter. His concern is with revealed religion. He regards Christianity mainly as a body of doctrines and moral precepts. 'The Gospel', he tells us, 'promised eternal happiness to those who lead religious lives, and to impenitent sinners denounced the most dreadful punishments.'[6] The sacred books are amply attested by external evidences. The fact that the New Testament volumes were written by apostles and friends of apostles guarantees their integrity and supremacy. The writers did not invent discourses and attribute them to Christ. 'If they had followed this method, they would probably have made his discourses, exhorting to virtue and dissuading to vice, in general terms; it would not have entered into their thoughts to have crowded together so many allusions to

---

[1] Op. cit., p. 78.   [2] Op. cit., p. 66.   [3] Op. cit., p. 67.

[4] The five chosen are: (1) Jortin, *Discourse Concerning the Truth of the Christian Revelation* (2nd edition, 1747); (2) R. Watson (Bishop of Landaff), *Apology for the Bible*, 1796; (3) Edward Maltby, *Illustrations of the Truth of the Christian Revelation*, 1801 (2nd edition, 1803); (4) Jacob Bryant, Esq., *Treatise upon the Authenticity of the Scriptures, and the Truth of the Christian Revelation* (3rd edition, 1810); (5) Beilby Porteus (Bishop of London), *A Summary of the Principal Evidences for the Truth and Divine Origin of the Christian Religion*, 1810.

[5] *Discourse Concerning, etc.*, p. 73.

[6] Op. cit., p. 26.

time and place, and to other little occurrences, which nothing, besides the presence of the object, would suggest.'[1]

The gospel has taught truths we should not otherwise know. It declares that God is good, and we can therefore be assured that where there is a genuine effort to follow after righteousness He will reward with the remittance of punishment. Amendment of life is necessary to the attainment of truth. Most of those who came to accept Christianity were, he thinks, earnest seekers after the good. If it be urged that several 'had led bad lives before' it is to be remembered that 'there are degrees of wickedness, and there is no reason to suppose that these sinners were for the most part of the worse sort'.[2] Jortin seems to think that there is need to live well before the truth of Christianity can come to us. We are to understand 'that the practice of Morality leads to the practice of Christianity, and that, since conversion is brought about by stages, and revealed religion is founded on natural religion, he who is moved to embrace the Gospel must first be sensible of the difference between good and evil, truth and falsehood, virtue and vice, must love the one and abhor the other, must repent of his former transgressions and receive the sacred knowledge, which is offered to him, with gratitude and a firm resolution of performing his duty'.[3]

A reading of Bishop Watson's ten letters, in which he attacks the second half of Paine's *Age of Reason* makes it a matter of amazement that the Rationalist Press still persists in publishing the sceptical work.

Paine impugnes the morality of the Bible, and yet he professes to accept natural religion. But the 'morality' of the natural order can also be called in question. So Watson asks, 'Why do you not spurn as spurious, the book of nature in which the fact is certainly written, and from the perusal of which you infer the moral justice of God.'[4] Paine makes an attack on the several books of the Bible. He uses all the arguments, but without the inhibition and reserve, of the later liberal critics. The first five books of the sacred record are dismissed as 'spurious, and (that) Moses is not the author of them; and still further, (that) they were not written in the time of Moses, nor till several hundred years afterwards.'[5] Paine actually

---

[1] *Discourse concerning, etc.*, pp. 220, 221.   [2] Op. cit., p. 6.
[3] Ibid.
[4] *Apology for the Bible* (published with Simpson's *Plea for Religion and the Sacred Writings*, 1812), p. 423.
[5] Op. cit., p. 432.

assigns them to 'stupid pretenders to (Mosaic) authorship' at the time of Ezra. Watson repudiates the notion and meets the arguments one by one. The books of Joshua and Samuel are referred to a late anonymous writer: Paine, in fact, makes much of their anonymity. Watson replies that their authority is not lessened because of this. 'Doomsday Book is anonymous' and 'yet our courts of law do not hold it without authority'.[1]

Chronicles is put by Paine after the reign of Zedekiah and as there are verses found in Genesis similar to verses in Chronicles, he argues that therefore Genesis must be later still. Watson retorts; because there are 'a few verses in the book of Genesis which could not have been written by Moses; therefore, no part of Genesis could have been written by Moses; a child will deny your, therefore'.[2] On Isaiah, Paine is specially severe. He has an idea of what has later come to be referred to as 'deutro-Isaiah'. Parts of the last chapters must belong to the age of Cyrus since, of course, prophecy is not possible. The book of Jeremiah is disordered and is therefore to be distrusted. Daniel belongs to the Maccabean period. Watson recalls, in reply, a story of a 'learned Rabbi' who, presiding at a disputation with Christians, exclaimed, 'Let us shut our Bibles; for if we proceed in examination of this prophecy (viz. that of the Seventy Weeks), it will make us all become Christians.'[3]

Paine extends his critical work to the New Testament. The Virgin Birth, the genealogies, the massacre of the innocents, the words over the cross, the time of the Crucifixion among other items are all held to contain evidence of imposture. The phrase in Matthew 'unto this day' is made to prove 'that the book must have been manufactured after the lapse of some generations at least'. Paine will not believe in revealed religion because there is so much which cannot be revealed. 'What is there you can account for?' asks Watson. The germination of a blade of grass and the fall of a forest leaf are beyond comprehension. Thus Paine is asked, 'will you refuse to eat of the fruits of the earth because God has not given you wisdom equal to his own? Will you refuse to lay hold on immortality, because he has not given you, because he, probably, could not give to such a being as man, a full manifestation of the end for which he designs him, nor the means requisite for the attainment of that end.'[4] Watson then draws together natural and

[1] Op. cit., p. 450.   [2] Op. cit., p. 465.
[3] Op. cit., p. 490.   [4] Op. cit., p. 552.

revealed religion and states: 'For my own part, I can see no reason why either revealed or natural religion should be abandoned on account of the difficulties which attend either of them. I look up to the incomprehensible maker of heaven and earth with unspeakable admiration and self-annihilation, and am a deist, — I contemplate, with the utmost gratitude and humility of mind his unsearchable wisdom and goodness in the redemption of the world from eternal death, through the intervention of his Son, Jesus Christ, and am a christian.'[1]

Maltby's book is of considerable importance. For him the internal evidences for the genuineness and authenticity of the biblical record are conclusive. The language of the New Testament books is 'of a manner of thinking and expression very consonant with the opinions and practices of the inhabitants of Judaea'[2] at the time they were written. The vividness of the detail marks them out as the work of an eyewitness. They are free from party spirit. There is no attempt to panegyrize the central Figure or to palliate the failings of those who surrounded Him. In the several writings the same Personality is unveiled. The existence of the numerous apocryphal books is evidence that there were genuine ones. When once the canonical Scriptures are compared with these apocryphal works the reality of the counterfeit is not difficult to detect. The apocryphal works are evidently written with a purpose, and tend, like the so-called 'Epistle of Mary the Virgin to the Inhabitants of Messina and Florence', to justify some strange doctrine or other, as this fabrication does Mariolatry, and the worship of relics. The disgusting pomposity of some of this literature is in marked contrast with the natural simplicity and unadorned and unornamented style of the accepted books. The vulgar efforts to satisfy natural curiosity concerning our Lord's early years, seen in other apocryphal writings, just reveals how totally out of harmony they are with the real truth: 'the apocryphal writers have shewn themselves so little expert in their trade of fiction, that they have described this exalted character in a manner suited only to a vain and petulant boy, exerting his miraculous powers for silly ostentation, or the worse purpose of gratifying some malignant passion.'[3] Jesus resolutely refused to fit Himself into the Jewish pattern of the

---

[1] Op. cit., p. 554.
[2] *Illustrations of the Truth of the Christian Religion*, p. 4.
[3] Op. cit., p. 61.

Messiah. But this is what an impostor would have done. His final
claim to be the Holy One of God, if it were not true, was to add the
outrage of insult to the bitterness of disappointment. He made
Himself equal with God. His 'scheme' of doctrine is such that no
impostor could have adopted it nor any enthusiast conceived it.
Christianity could not have survived if it were not true since it cuts
across all that men hold dear. It was published to the world without
regard to men's cherished notions, and it has triumphed; 'it is to
the last degree improbable, if not morally impossible, that Christianity should have originated in mistake or artifice.'[1] The disciples found Christ's doctrine 'a hard saying'; it was only the
gradual acceptance of His message as true led them to abandon
their Jewish rituals and to accept the Gentiles as fellow-heirs of the
promises made to Israel.

Maltby, it may be observed, meets the argument of Bolingbroke
and Chubb who drew a distinction (which some deem modern)
between the Jesus of history and the Christ of Paul.

Bolingbroke conceived of Jesus as a religious Jew seeking to
revitalize Judaism and One whose interest was with the Jew only.
To Paul belongs the doubtful honour of 'universalizing' His
message and expunging from it the Jewish elements. Maltby shows
how Jesus, although He did send His disciples, in the first place, to
'the lost sheep of the house of Israel', yet by precept, practice and
parable He looked beyond the bounds of Israel to the Gentile
world. In His final commission He expressly states that His gospel
is for 'every creature'. At the same time Paul always made it his
business to address himself first to his own people. 'And this same
Apostle, who has been so unjustly accused of setting up his own
gospel in opposition to Jesus Christ, though he strenuously contends that there is no distinction between the Jew and the Greek,
yet, whenever a priority can be maintained pleads in favour of the
Jews: "to the Jew first, and also to the Greek." '[2]

A host of opponents of Christianity attest the purity of Christ's
character, and if His virtue be attested, How can His doctrine be
denied? As a man of acknowledged truthfulness Jesus could not
have taught that which was false. He certainly shared the Jewish
belief that the Mosaic law was divine. It is therefore relevant to
ask, Is it credible that being 'himself a believer in the law of

[1] *Illustrations of the Truth of the Christian Religion*, p. 85.
[2] Op. cit., p. 198.

Moses, he nevertheless attempted to supersede it by a system originating in fallible speculation and supported by groundless assertion'?[1] To suppose such a thing would be to deny that He was a man of virtue and make Him a schemer for the overthrow of the religion He Himself believed to be the revealed will of God. He who thus claimed to be 'of God', is thereby found undermining God's laws: 'this surely is to suppose him guilty of gross deceit. He frequently asserted its authority in such a way as to give the impression that He believed it to be a divine legislation. He solemnly asserted that He bore witness to the Truth and yet, How can it be held that He is virtuous still, if, while proclaiming the authority of Moses, He did not believe it were so?' Is it possible that such a character as this would have engaged in such a complicated scheme of cunning, hypocrisy and impiety?[2] There is no doubt that the Jewish was the best form of religious and civil polity then existing in the world. 'If Jesus overturned this merely to establish a code of his own fabrication, he cannot escape the charge of impiety. If we add too the fixed conviction of the Jews that their national prosperity and happiness depended upon their adherence to the commands of Jehovah, as delivered by Moses, there appears a degree of rashness and cruelty in thus destroying the palladium of the Jewish state, from which, on the infidel hypothesis, the character of Jesus cannot be exempted. Nor can it be regarded as more excusable in the means adopted, than in the ends pursued, if the religion he established had no warrant for its excellence or permanence than the sagacity of his own views or the comprehension of the intellect. The holy and venerable name of the Lord of heaven and earth was the cloak, upon this supposition, as the assumed cover of his fictions: and the intimate union and connection by which he professed to stand related to the Deity could only be an additional and unnecessary outrage against the divine majesty. To destroy the institution of this august and incomprehensible Being, under pretence of showing him greater reverence; to do away the peculiar rites with which he had signified his command that his people should honour him, under the fictitious assumption of authority from that very Being; especially when we consider the profound and unparalleled reverence entertained by all the Jews for that holy name and those sacred institutions; would have been a procedure at once so unaccountable and so

---

[1] Op. cit., p. 229.   [2] Op. cit., p .231.

desperate, that it would scarcely be imputed to any man, however audacious and however resolute in the prosecution of his purposes:— far less could it be imputed to the meek and unassuming, the spotless and irreproachable Jesus.'[1]

Jacob Bryant makes the point that rational religion has never been able to uplift a people. The most successful missionary method is to go straight to the wounds of Christ. The experience of the Moravian missionary Grantz is quoted to show that rational arguments for the existence of God and for His attributes, as the basis upon which to enforce resulting moral obligations, have been proved futile. He goes on to argue that the Old Testament prophecies concerning the Messiah, into which Christ so wonderfully fitted, cannot be the *post factum* work of biased Christian writers who sought biblical proof for their beliefs. The sacred books were, after all, in Jewish hands, and they were 'particularly scrupulous about the conservation of the sacred volumes so that they would not suffer a single word to be added or omitted'.[2]

The New Testament records are no less authentic and trustworthy. 'No histories have been transmitted with such incontestable marks of truth as the Evangelical writings.'[3] They bear the very stamp of divinity; the hall-mark of heaven. 'We have been told a great deal', observes Bryant, 'about nature, and the light of nature; and Christianity has been pronounced AS OLD AS CREATION. By this was meant, that all the essential truths, which were taught in the Gospel, were antecedently known by this light; and the Christian system, in consequence of it, was neither new, nor necessary.'[4] But how contrary to the facts is such a contention. The whole world groaned for some divine doctrine, for some infallible instruction, and God in mercy met the cry of the human heart. Thus the 'grand system' of inspired Scripture has been delivered to us. And if some difficulties remain for us after careful and prayerful study then 'it is our duty to acquiesce, and trust the word of God, which cannot deceive'.[5]

Bishop Porteus likewise maintains that the New Testament is a 'faithful history of Christ and his religion'.[6] He gathers together, for the help of those recently confirmed, all the lines of evidence into one grand summary. Indeed, in a masterpiece of compression,

[1] *Illustrations of the Truth of the Christian Religion*, p. 244.
[2] *A Treatise upon the Authenticity of the Scriptures, etc.*, p. 77.
[3] Op. cit., p. 117.   [4] Op. cit., p. 163.   [5] Op. cit., p. 180.
[6] *A Summary of the Principal Evidences*, p. 7.

he has presented all the arguments of the Bampton Lectures and the general literature as a sort of grand finale: 'when we consider', he writes, 'the deplorable ignorance and inconceivable depravity of the heathen world before the birth of Christ, which rendered a divine interposition necessary, and therefore highly probable; the appearance of Christ upon the earth, at the very time when his presence was most wanted, and when there was a general expectation throughout the East that some great and extraordinary personage was to come into the world; the transcendent excellence of our Lord's character; the calmness, the composure, the dignity, the integrity, the spotless sanctity of his manners, so utterly inconsistent with any idea of enthusiasm and imposture; the sublimity and importance of his doctrines; the consumate wisdom and perfect purity of his moral precepts, far exceeding the natural powers of man born in the humblest situation, in a remote and obscure corner of the world, without learning, education, language, or works; the rapid and astonishing propagation of his religion, in a very short space of time, through almost every region of the East, by the sole effort of himself and a few illiterate fishermen, in direct opposition to all the power, the authority, the learning, the philosophy, the reigning vices, prejudices, and superstitions of the world; the complete and marked opposition, in every essential point, between the character and revelation of Christ, and the character and revelation of Mahomet, exactly such as might be expected between truth and falsehood; the intimate description of all the most material circumstances of his birth, life, sufferings and death, and resurrection, given by the ancient prophets many hundred years before he was born, and exactly fulfilled in him, and him only, pointing him out as the messenger of the Jews and the Redeemer of mankind; the various prophecies declared by Christ himself, were all punctually accomplished, more especially the destruction of Jerusalem by the Romans; and many astonishing miracles wrought by Jesus, in the open face of day before thousands of spectators, the reality of which is proved by multitudes of the most exceptional witnesses, who sealed their testimony with their blood, and was even acknowledged by the earliest and most inveterate enemies of the Gospel; and, lastly, the most astonishing and well-authenticated miracles of our Lord's resurrection, which was the seal and confirmation of his own divine origin, and that of his religion: — when all these various witnesses are brought together, and impartially weighed, it seems hardly within the power of a fair and ingenious mind to resist the impression of their united force. If such a combination of evidence is not sufficient to satisfy an honest inquirer into truth, it is utterly impossible THAT ANY EVENT, WHICH PASSED in former times, and which we did not see with our own eyes, can be proved to have happened by any degree of testimony whatever. It may be safely affirmed that no incident can be produced by any one fact or event, said to have taken place in past ages, and established by such evidence as that on which the Christian revelation rests, that afterwards turned out to be false. We challenge the enemies of our faith to bring forward, if they can, any such instance. If they cannot (and we know it to be impossible), we have a right to say that a religion supported by such an extraordinary accumulation of evidences, must be true, and that all men, who pretend to be judged by argument and by proof, are bound, by the most sacred obligations to receive the religion of Christ, as a real revelation from God.'[1]

[1] *A Summary of the Principal Evidences, etc.*, pp. 40, 41.

CHAPTER VII

THE FOCUS ON THE INWARD

The orthodox apologists, as has been shewn, in the defence of their position against the exaggerations of the deists conceived of revelation as a limited number of moral dicta, extra to those already known by natural religion, and against the excesses of the enthusiasts they regarded it as a body of communicated truths demanding an unquestioning assent. The result of such views of revealed religion was to make the preaching of the period lacking in life and warmth. It was coldly apologetic and fiercely polemical. Religion was a matter of debate, the attainment of right notions. Thus in the pulpit, as Dr Johnson informs us, 'the apostles were tried once a week on the charge of committing forgery.' It was all wonderfully impressive, but weakly ineffective; there was certain evidence of learning, but little evidence of life.

When, however, a conception becomes dominant there seems to be an inevitable reaction. 'The type of view', observes Dr C. C. J. Webb, 'which makes feeling as opposed to reason the organ of religious experience usually appears as a reaction from some form of what is called Rationalism, and finds a relative justification for its existence upon facts which Rationalism has ignored.'[1]

REVELATION IN THE IMMEDIACY OF EXPERIENCE

Against the sterile rationalism of the orthodox doctrine of revelation there was a protest from two quarters. On the one hand, under the impetus of a rising idealistic philosophy (which from one point of view is only the theoretical expression of religious mysticism), and its stress upon the divine immanence, there was advocated a doctrine of revelation within the immediacy of experience. From an intellectual point of view there was seen to be need for a more personal contact with God than that knowledge about Him embodied in syllogisms. On the other hand, under the preaching of Whitfield and Wesley, there was an emphasis upon the inner

[1] *Problems in the Relations of God and Man*, p. 69.

action of the Holy Spirit. Both these views agreed in repudiating
the cold propositional rationalism of the orthodox. In some of their
statements, those who advocated revelation within the immediacy
of experience resemble the present neo-liberalism of the Barth-
Brunner school. They were also averse to the Evangelicals, while
the latter were little inclined to acknowledge any kinship.

That statement of revelation which found its most vehement
expression in Maurice began from the assumption of the immanence of God in every man, whereas the doctrine of the Evangelicals stresses the indwelling of God in believing men. Thus,
whilst both maintained the inwardness of revelation, they were, as a
matter of fact, really opposed. Only in their insistence upon the
inward were they alike, in no other sense were they identical.

That this last observation is true, is confirmed by a comment
made by John Wesley on Dodwell's book *Christianity not Founded
on Argument*. Dodwell in advocating the inwardness of revelation
denies that reason has any place in it. In the context of his remarks
Wesley makes it clear that he does not deprecate reason. At the
same time it is still a fact that you cannot reason concerning colour
if you have no natural sight, 'so you cannot reason concerning
spiritual things, if you have no spiritual sight: because your ideas
received by your outward senses are of a different kind.'[1] Wesley
then goes on to tell us that Dodwell's book was warmly recommended to him as stating the same position 'But', continues
Wesley, 'on a perusal of that piece (i.e. *Christianity not Founded on
Argument*) notwithstanding my prejudices in its favour, I could not
but perceive that the general design uniformly pursued throughout
the work, was to render the whole of the Christian Institution to be
odious and contemptible . . . the author . . . *makes a shew* of
defending an avowed doctrine of Christianity, namely, the supernatural influence of the Spirit of God.'[2]

At the close of our earlier investigation of the idea of revelation
as indwelling light, it was pointed out that the followers of George
Fox differed from the later school of Coleridge, in the fact that,
whereas the former began from an emphasis on the divine transcendence, the latter stressed the divine immanence. For the newer
teachers God's indwelling was not thought of as the visitation of
an Alien Spirit. By accentuating the kingship of God, the Friends

[1] 'An Earnest Appeal to Men of Reason and Religion', *Works*, vol. 12, p. 14.
[2] Op cit., *Works*, vol. 12, ibid.

conceived of God's indwelling as something apart from the human spirit; the residence of a 'Wholly Other'. Those who followed Coleridge stressed, with him, the kinship between God and man, and regarded the divine as immanent in all nature and in all men.

Its advocates were anxious to maintain that the divine and the human existed as one spiritual continuum. Even if it be maintained that they did not lay hold of the true connecting link, it is to their credit that they did see that a revelation is only possible if some 'point of contact' remains. A radical discontinuity renders a revelation impossible, or, at least, useless. If God speaks to men who are in no sense *'capax verbi Domini'*, the question may be asked, To what purpose is this waste? Whether indeed the writers with whom we are now to be concerned did overstate their case in their teaching of a continued kinship between God and man remains to be seen. They certainly did stress the idea of the unbroken Fatherhood of God, it is a question if they were equally aware of the fact of the broken sonship.[1] At all events, one thing is clear, their doctrine was conditioned and coloured by philosophical idealism. It was against this background that the understanding of revelation within the immediacy of experience must be presented.

The task, therefore, before us is, first, to give an account of the creative significance of the idealism of Bishop Berkeley, and then, to show how this conception influenced the idea of revelation. The doctrine of revelation which developed as a result will then be traced through representative writers until it reaches its strongest expression in F. D. Maurice.

(i) *The Background of Idealism — Berkeley*

The student of philosophy does not need reminding that it was the purpose of Berkeley to prove that unspiritual matter is nonexistent. He resolved to show the immaterialism of the external world. Berkeley was convinced that the notion that brute material substance existed as a reality apart from mind was 'the main pillar of Scepticism'. He thus argued that all that exists are ideas in the mind of God and that human ideas are produced by the direct action of God. This means that all ideas of the human mind are proof of God's existence and being, since all such ideas have their genesis in God.

[1] Cf., H. Wheeler Robinson, *The Christian Doctrine of Man*, p. 91 f.

'It is therefore plain', he writes, 'that nothing can be more evident to any one that is capable of the least reflection, than the existence of God, or a Spirit who is intimately present to our minds, producing in them all that variety of ideas or sensations, which continually effect us, on whom we have an absolute and entire dependence, in short, in whom we live, and move, and have our being.'[1] Berkeley concludes his *Treatise Concerning the Principles of Human Knowledge* with the assurance that God 'is present and conscious to our innermost thoughts; and that we have a most absolute and immediate dependence on him'.[2] Here then is an idealism which is at the same time an immanentalism. It is Berkeley's significance that he does not seek to provide new and novel arguments for the Christian apologist. He would have us see God; he would have us lift up our eyes and behold Him, for He is not very far from any one of us. The words of Acts xvii. 28, 'In him we live, and move, and have our being,' quoted by Berkeley in the passage above, constantly recur throughout his works. While it is not a verse used for any of his sermons, 'it occurs so often in his works', says Canon I. T. Ramsay, 'as to have been called his "favourite quotation." '[3] It is this 'favourite quotation' which is, indeed, Berkeley's real message, for here he finds an assertion of God as actual within. Berkeley's main doctrine was then, as A. D. Lindsay observes, 'an appeal to immediate experience.'[4] It follows, therefore, that he must reject the idea that a knowledge of God comes only as a result of 'resemblance and analogy'.[5] It is, in fact, this very doctrine that he puts into the mouth of an infidel in the *Minute Philosopher*.

Berkeley's Defence of Revelation

It is in *The Alciphron, or The Minute Philosopher*, that we have, what Dr Timothy Dwight describes as 'an able defence of Divine Revelation, by one of the first philosophers of any age and any

---

[1] *A Treatise Concerning the Principles of Human Knowledge* (Dent's edition), p. 191.
[2] Op. cit., p. 195.
[3] A sermon preached at Festival Service in the Chapel of Trinity College, Dublin, July 10th, 1953, by Canon I. T. Ramsay, Nolloth Professor of the Philosophy of the Christian Religion in the University of Oxford, reprinted from *Hermathena*, No. LXXXII, 1953.
[4] *Theory of Vision and other Writings by Bishop Berkeley* (Dent), Preface, p. x.
[5] These words from Archbishop King's sermon on Predestination were taken up and made the thesis of Bishop Browne's volumes.

country'.[1] This enthusiastic estimate of the book is not shared by all. Dean Swift thought it 'too speculative' to have real effect, while Bishop Hoadley spoke of it as 'the most plain attempt to bring obscurity and darkness into all science, as well as to make nonsense essential to religion, that this last age has produced'.

The book consists of seven dialogues in which Lysicles represents the light-hearted worldling. Here is 'refuted' Mandeville's *Fable of the Bees* in which the notion that 'private vices are public benefits' is proclaimed. Whether Berkeley was successful in his refutation is a matter of debate, at any rate, he was ably replied to by Mandeville in a *Letter to Dion*. In Berkeley's work, Alciphron upholds the moral theory of Shaftesbury with the idea of conscience as a form of taste, and the contemplation of the abstract beauty of virtue as its own sufficient reward. Euphranor and Crito announce Berkeley's own views. The main point he makes is that God is not a being whose existence can be proved apart from the world. His thesis is 'faith alone is required'. Since the whole material world is 'illusion' and the only reality IS GOD, it follows that God is nearer than breathing, closer than hands and feet. He does not, however, make faith irrational. He is ready to admit that 'The being of God is capable of clear proof, and the proper object of human reason'.[2] But while the reality of natural religion is open to the light of reason, it is 'limited to those who are capable of such proofs'.[3]

No sharp distinction is allowed between natural and revealed religion. Since God is the common Father of Lights all derived from Him, whether designated natural or revealed, springs from the same source.[4] Berkeley, it seems, was aware that a day would come when Laplace would eliminate the God of deism as an unnecessary preface to the world's history. He therefore resolved to meet the contingency by denying the reality of matter. In this way, he argued, the evidence for Christianity was not by means of logical demonstration. It is essentially moral and probable. The proofs are neither scientific nor demonstrative. The Christian message, in fact, is not directed to the reason, but to faith, although, it is granted, it is not opposed to reason. Revealed religion is not,

[1] 'Prefatory recommendation to the first American edition' (1803), by Dr Timothy Dwight, President of Yale College.
[2] Berkeley's *Works*, vol. 2 (Edition A. C. Fraser, 1871), p. 337.
[3] Op. cit., vol. 2, p. 182.
[4] *Minute Philosopher*, p. 183, cf., p. 335.

therefore, a category apart from faith, since faith is a fundamental factor in all our lives. 'Did minute philosopher but reflect, how rarely men are swayed or governed by mere ratiocination, and how often by faith, in the general and civil concerns of the world! how little they know, and how much they believe!'[1] Along with Berkeley's idealism, then, there went the doctrine that revelation was not something that the reason can discover, but which faith must accept. It is the immediate assurance and the direct awareness of God, Who thinks His own thoughts within us.

(ii) *The Rejection of Reason — Dodwell*

The contention of Berkeley that revelation is not addressed to reason but to faith was taken up by H. Dodwell to become the thesis of his volume, entitled, *Christianity not Founded on Argument* (1743). Dodwell contends for a 'constant and particular Revelation imparted separately and supernaturally to every Individual'.[2] It is in this personal and immediate relationship that, according to Dodwell, the true nature of Christian evidence is to be found. He goes beyond Berkeley, however, and maintains that the principle of faith is contrary to reason. 'I am fully persuaded', he writes, 'that the judging at all of religious Matters is not the Providence of Reason, or indeed an Affair where she has any Concern.'[3]

Dodwell advances three main arguments for his view.

1. He first asserts that the intellectual faculty of reason is unable, by virtue of its own nature, to act as the principle to lead into true faith. It was evidently never intended by God to be the method chosen. Infant baptism, he takes as proof that the whole rationalist position is false. Babies cannot rationally accept the terms of salvation, yet, 'they commence true Believers at once, and are made Heirs of Salvation.'[4] This means that salvation is not assent to certain propositions carefully marshalled and investigated. He asks those who would industriously seek for convincing proofs: 'Are you not at this Instant a baptized and covenanted Christian?'[5] In a manner worthy of Luther, Dodwell sees reason as an illustration of human arrogance. Rational religion is a form of pride. Man can take some commendation for having ascended

---

[1] *Minute Philosopher*, p. 258.
[2] *Christianity not Founded on Argument*, p. 112.
[3] Op. cit., p. 7.
[4] Op. cit., p. 9; cf., also, p. 69.
[5] Op. cit., p. 113.

the ladder of his carefully constructed syllogisms to bring God down. Dodwell will not however grant man this ability. For while baptism makes it evident that reason has no place in the commencement of the Christian life, prayer, as an activity in which reason has no real place, assures us that reason has no part in its continuation.

If assent to propositions, after patient investigation, is to be regarded as the faith of the gospel, then the question arises concerning the condition in which people are until the rational avowal be made. A position of indecision must be supposed; a place of neutrality: but is not this very term itself one of horror and detestation in a believer's ear? Even the very notion of examining evidence, suspending judgement, until all is clear to the mind, is an admission of, at least, a temporary disbelief. Then would religion be born out of pious doubt. It would be something we originate by our own fine arguments; except that there is always the difficulty of knowing when the great announcement shall be made. Who can take upon himself the fearful and fateful decision of saying that the last doubtful point has been settled, and no longer does he see through a glass darkly?

During the time of neutrality, when all the arguments are being surveyed, religion, which comes to influence our actions and direct our conduct, is not there. And supposing the conclusion should be reached 'too late', What then? 'As long as we are debating the Genuineness of our Rule, we have no Tie on us as respect its Authority?'[1] During the period of indecision, obedience is not necessary; thus the good works then and there performed are of no value, since, whatever is not of faith is sin. If in this 'Infidel interim', we should be caught unawares, like the fool of our Lord's parable, we should be likewise 'unfurnished of our Passport', we should be without an apology, without a wedding-garment.

Few men are qualified to reason accurately, and God cannot be so unjust as to require of all men that which so many cannot give. It would not become Him to make salvation a matter of such blind chance and guess-work, and to set the precious soul upon the hazard of a random conjecture. In the Gospels the one all-inclusive and the one all-conclusive command is 'to believe'. With clinching emphasis Dodwell asks, 'Will a faith, thus built upon Syllogisms, ever furnish out any of these miraculous Effects, which are described

[1] *Christianity not Founded on Argument*, p. 15.

to attend a just and furnished Belief?'[1] A rational orthodoxy can never administer comfort, never control the passions, never produce holiness of life. The forced acknowledgement of the mind is not the sort that creates heroes and martyrs. It is a warm, believing confidence that will, if occasion demands, strive unto blood, and open up heaven to those who are faithful unto death.

2. As a second disproof of mere rational assent, Dodwell notes that the Scriptures do not picture Christ as presenting His message for leisurely investigation. And His disciples were sent forth, not to argue, but to announce. Indeed, for the former they had neither the qualifications nor the time. Their message was a proclamation which carried its own demonstration and vindication. Christianity was not regarded as a useful scheme for the few who could be led to see how logical and consistent were its doctrines. 'And was it in Truth', asks Dodwell, 'can we suppose, for the sake of any such Conclusion, and to enforce such a Persuasion about his Errand, that the only Son of God, and Partner of the Divinity, could demean this exalted Nature, to struggle through a long course of human Passions and Temptations, and be content to expire at last under such accumulated Circumstances of long Anguish and Horror upon the accursed Tree, and all, as it seems, by this account to recommend his Doctrines only to the Opinions of a Few Men of Parts, who were happily formed with the Faculties to conceive his Proofs?'[2]

3. This leads Dodwell to stress his point that true Christianity is the result of an immediate divine illumination. As a result of which he maintains there is no need of 'mere manuscript authorities and Paper-Revelations'.[3] God addresses Himself to men whose 'will is by nature free', and it is this fact which makes the gospel so unique and urgent. Christianity did not sweep to such early success because of its reasoned advocacy. There were those, in fact, who could not but acknowledge the grandeur of its doctrines and the greatness of its results, and yet they stood still without. The gospel was first welcomed by ordinary people who possessed the minutest portion of human talents. What the philosopher could not penetrate, the pauper could rejoice in. A subtle spirit and an informed genius may be blinded, but he who would be a candidate for discipleship, must first renounce his reason.

---

[1] *Christianity not Founded on Argument*, p. 24.   [2] Op. cit., p. 44.
[3] Ob. cit., p. 59.

The positive proofs marshalled by the learned Dr Clarke in favour of revealed religion have but given birth to as many negative doubts. Argument cannot create faith, and where faith is, it can add nothing. 'For what can Reason's confirmation do for me here, but fix me where I am? and what can her assistance give me in the case more than I have already?'[1] A long comment by Bishop Beveridge on 1 Cor. 2. 14 is quoted to sustain the view that the human reason is at a discount as far as God is concerned. What is needed is a spiritual light within the soul, a divine infilling, an immediate revelation of God. Where this is nothing else is needed; 'however plausibly Christianity may be enforced as a Fact, it can yet never be true, as a Gospel, in Virtue of any Arguments deduced from Reasoning.'[2]

There are not two kinds of Christianity, one for the intelligentsia and the other for the ignorant: one based on reason and the other of faith. He thus concludes 'Be satisfied henceforth that there is a kind of Evidence of Power beyond which Reason can never pretend to Furnish such as brings with it that cordial Peace and Assurance of Mind to which all Conviction by human means is an utter Stranger, such as you can see enable your pious Mother without any of the reputed Advantages of academic Institution to pronounce with so much peremptory Justice on all Religious Causes, and reprove, with so good a Grace, all the well-glossed Heresies of a lettered Clarke.'[3]

It is not easy to estimate Dodwell's book. Wesley, as we have seen, regarded it with disfavour.[4] Leyland, from the standpoint of the rational orthodox saw it as an attempt to ridicule Christianity.[5] Whatever be the truth of the matter, Dodwell's position was undoubtedly an emphatic rejection of the view that Christianity could be disseminated and defended by rational arguments. And it was this very statement which called out the hostility of both the deists and the orthodox, for 'it was monstrous to overthrow that common ground of "reason" where Christian and anti-Christian liked to meet and fight their duels, under a set of rules both sides accepted'.[6]

[1] Op. cit., p. 87.
[2] Op. cit., p. 111.
[3] Op. cit., p. 115.
[4] See above, p. 150.
[5] See the *Oxford Young Gentleman's Reply to Dodwell and Two Letters from Dr Leyland, published together with Christianity not Founded on Argument.*
[6] R. N. Stromberg, *Religious Liberalism in the Eighteenth Century*, p. 108.

(iii) *The Immanence of the Eternal Christ — Law*

The importance of William Law in the development of the doctrine of revelation in the immediacy of experience cannot be overestimated. Insufficient account, we are convinced, has been taken of him. Law stressed the complete inadequacy of the external evidences for Christianity, and 'strikingly anticipates the teaching of the later school of theology, which traces its origin to Coleridge, and has a natural affinity to the mystical elements'.[1] An examination of Law's works will reveal how much Coleridge, Hare and Maurice but re-echo his thought.

Maurice, for example, begins with the same fundamental assumption. He writes to his mother: 'My text is, "Know ye not that Jesus Christ is in you?" . . . not to the faithful Christian or to the unfaithful one, "For in him we live and move and have our being" . . . . Christ is in every man . . . . The truth is that every man is in Christ; the condemnation of every man is, that he will not own the truth; he will not act as if it were true, he will not believe that it is true, except he be joined to Christ, he would not think, breathe, live for a single hour.'[2] This is a mere reiteration of Law's teaching that 'Christ is in every man'. 'Every one has Christ in his spirit, lying there in a state of insensibility and death.'[3] 'Every man hath the Spirit of God, The Spirit is in every soul.'[4]

By maintaining that the presence of Christ is in every man, Law can state categorically that the Church of Christ is therefore not limited to those who are called Christians. We are called upon to 'See here the extent of the Catholic Church of Christ! It takes in all the world'.[5] It is just this view which is further and more fully elaborated by Hare and Maurice.

Fundamental, then, for Law is the doctrine of the divine immanence, especially in the works just quoted where his position is virtually pantheistic.

It is, however, in the volume, *The Way of Divine Knowledge*, that he deals more particularly with the inner revelation of the

---

[1] L. Stephen, *Religious Thought in the Eighteenth Century*, vol. 2, p. 405.

[2] *Life of F. D. Maurice* (by his son), vol. 1, pp. 154, 155.

[3] *The Spirit of Love*, sect. 2, p. 34.

[4] *The Spirit of Prayer*, pt. 1, p. 63. Cf., 'No faith could ever begin, unless every man had Christ in him.' *The Spirit of Love*, pt. 2, p. 34. 'The birth of Christ is already begun in every one. Jesus is already within (whoever thou art,), . . .' *The Spirit of Prayer*, pt. 1, p. 55, 'Poor sinner, Christ dwelleth in the centre, the fund, the bottom of thy soul.' *The Spirit of Prayer*, pt. 1, p. 63.

[5] *The Spirit of Prayer*, pt. 1, p. 56.

indwelling Christ. As this work is specified by its author 'As Preparatory to a New Edition of the Works of Jacob Behmen; and the Right Use of Them', the mystical approach will be readily appreciated. In the form of a dialogue between Humanus, Academicus, Rusticus and Theophilus, Law makes his own position clear. Assent to the whole New Testament can never make one a Christian. True Christian faith is the direct contact of the soul with Christ, in God. It is the rising up within of the Christ-spirit. This is the doctrine that Humanus has been taught by Theophilus; now that he has so learned the truth he will no longer seek to make converts to Christianity by arguments and evidences. Twenty years of debate with the deists has convinced him of this folly. Each new book in the defence of Christianity just brings out new objections. Apologetics is like a lecture on anatomy in which the lungs, the heart, the liver and so on, are indicated in a dead body; but the body is lifeless still.

Academicus must therefore renounce his learning, for it is a mere human thing; 'it has no higher a Nature or Birth than Natural Doubting.'[1] But Christianity is not something learned. Indeed 'the Demonstrators of the truth and reasonableness of Christianity have betrayed their own cause, and left true Christianity unmentioned'.[2] Academicus will seek in vain to understand Behmen until he sits where the mystic sat. He seeks information, he needs illumination. He would receive good notions, but what is wanting is a new nature.

The experience to which Behmen testifies is only got by renouncing reason. The boasted knowledge of the natural man is to be put to death, for 'notional knowledge, the treasure of human reason, is the very builder of Babal'.[3] The man qualified by human learning to publish an edition of Homer with critical notes, may be quite unfit to write comments upon the spirit and meaning of Christ's words. The knowledge of logic does not give a blind man the ability to receive the light of the sun, while skill in Hebrew and Greek cannot open up the soul to the light of God.

When Academicus asked of learned divines the question, What must I do to be saved? he was recommended vast volumes and tedious tomes. He lit his candle early and put it out late. He waded through the literature of seventeen hundred years. And all

---

[1] *The Way of Divine Knowledge*, p. 120.   [2] Op. cit., p. 30.
[3] Op. cit., p. 93.

to fruitless result when he could have stood with the primitive
Christians who had none of these packed libraries. Had he stood
with them he would have heard these words; he would have learnt
that the light and life of God come immediately to the soul. They
well up from the depths of one's own being.

Two sorts of people fail to find any help in Behmen. Those who
are unregenerate still and those who follow the light of reason.
Reason, Law thinks, is rightly called by Behmen, the Antichrist.
It leads men from Christ. It is 'the old Serpent called Subtelty, the
first and last grand Deceiver of Mankind'.[1] But the true knowledge
of God is not got by searching or working. 'The Truth is nowhere
to be found by Man, but in a New Birth from above.'[2] This cannot
be 'till Christ, who is the one Fountain of Life and Light, be seen
in you; it is in vain that you rise up early, and take late rest, in
quest of Truth'.[3]

Law repudiates as saving faith a belief in the letter of Scripture.
Without the light of God even the instruction of an angel would be
fruitless and as the 'dead Paper on which the Scriptures are
written'.[4] For Law, as for the school of Barth and Brunner the
Word of God is Christ Himself; 'the Word of God which saveth
and redeemeth the Soul', he writes, 'is not the Word printed on
Paper, but is the . . . ever-speaking Word, which is the Son of
God.'[5] The new birth is God speaking and winning a response
from the soul. It is the immediate communication, or perhaps,
stimulation, within the individual of God's own divine nature.

The personal response of the will to the movements of God is
the 'magic power' of which Behmen speaks. But the ultimate fact is
the divine will, which, as will, is final 'magic', and is the 'mother of
us all'. For Law magic seems to be a synonym for mystery. Yet the
human will is in some sense identified with the immanent Christ.
It is the 'heavenly Will, which is the only Spark of the Deity in us,
given by the Free Grace of God to all mankind, as soon as fallen,

---

[1] Op. cit., p. 164.   [2] Op. cit., p. 134.   [3] Op. cit., p. 133.
[4] Op. cit., p. 137.
[5] Op. cit., p. 164. According to Barth revelation is the '*Deus dixit*' the 'one
Word of God within which there can be neither a more or less'. *Church Dogmatics*, I, i, p. 136. He maintains the two-way equation, 'God's Word is God's
Son' and 'God's Son is God's Word'. Op. cit., p. 156. On Brunner's view see,
e.g. his *Revelation and Reason*, pp. 118, 119. It may be pointed out that the same
idea of Christ's 'contemporaneity' (*Gleichzeitigkeit*) found in Barth and Brunner is
clearly taught by Law. For Brunner the idea derives from Kierkegaard. See
Brunner's *Revelation and Reason* and the latter's *Philosophical Fragments*, ch. 4,
and *Training in Christianity*, ch. 4.

and called in Scripture the inspoken Word of God in Paradise'.[1] The 'inspoken Word' is the Christ within every man; the Will that hath the power of salvation in it.

Like Dodwell and Berkeley, Law argues that all men live by faith. The important thing is the object of this faith; according to its object it can be divine or devilish, saving or sensual.

The deist who imagines that he follows reason lives in an illusion. 'He may indeed easily enough keep himself free from all Christian Faith; but whether he will or no, a Faith must do all in him, and for him, just in the same degree, as it does for the Christian.'[2] But equally the rational 'Christian' who merely assents to doctrine is outside saving faith. 'The Delusion of the Deist lies here; He refuses an Assent to the History of Facts and Doctrines of the Gospel; and this is *his* proof to himself that he lives by Reason, and that it is the Principle of his Life. On the other hand, he who assents to the History of Facts and Doctrines of the Gospel, is, by the Deist reckoned a Man of Gospel Faith, and lives by it. But this is all a Mistake on both sides. For this Assent on the one Side, and Dissent on the other, touches not the Matter of either Reason or Faith.'[3]

Law asserts that natural religion has been the cause of much evil. But he comforts himself with the reflection that in every age a few spiritual writers have witnessed to true 'Gospel faith'. Notional religion, he contends, was brought forth by a Church which had lost its life: its elaborate propositions arose from the contentions of sects. But the Bible is a 'witness' to genuine spiritual faith; it addresses itself to the heart and the conscience.

Reason having renounced the help of God has made shipwreck. Learned reason without the Church denies, and learned reason within builds up some rational interpretation on the letter of Scripture: but learned reason everywhere is of the earth earthy.

If mystery lies at the basis of all, then it is folly to argue either for or against. If there is no ultimate understandable premise, there can be no final sure conclusion. All things were created out of nothing, thus the possibility of giving a reasoned account of anything,

---

[1] *The Way of Divine Knowledge*, p. 158. Cf., 'When Adam fell, this centre of his soul became a prisoner in an earthly animal. But from the moment God spoke Christ in Adam, all the treasures of the divine nature, the light and Spirit of God came again into man, into the centre of his soul,' *The Spirit of Prayer*, pt. 1, p. 60.
[2] *The Way of Divine Knowledge*, p. 174.
[3] Op. cit., p. 176.

in man's nature or religion, is ruled out. As all things were created out of nothing, then, too, the new creation is not produced out of reason. Where the ground of truth is everlasting mystery the so-called art of disputation on either side is an absurdity. 'Why is not the learned Papist shocked at Transubstantiation,' asks Law, 'or the Protestant at Predestination and Reprobation?'[1] To his own question he makes answer, 'It is because each of them have enough of the Truth of Reason and Goodness of Criticism, to draw the Letter of Scripture to his Side.'[2] Literal learning, as Law calls it, does not lead to the inward knowledge which is the very essence of Christianity. What matters in the renewal of the soul is the immediate awareness of the immanent Christ. Without this all religious forms are inadequate. No specific form of religion is of any consequence if it fails to help towards the opening of the heavenly life in the heart; and no one form of religion is in itself necessary to the Truth. There can, therefore, be full acceptance of Behmen's words, 'A Christian is of no Sect, and yet in every Sect.'

Knowledge of the Christian way can become a snare and a delusion if the enquirer does not 'turn to Christ, as the one Way, the one Truth, and the one Life, and Salvation of the Soul; not as notionally apprehended, or historically known; but as experimentally found, living, speaking, and working in your soul'.[3]

An emphasis like that seen in Law upon the inwardness of Christian evidences was made by Vicesimus Knox, master of Tonbridge School, from 1778 to 1811. Knox felt that Paley's external arguments needed supplementing. However that may have answered the questions of gainsayers, it is, he insists, in the inner witness of the responding heart that we find the most persuasive proof. This is the thesis elaborated in his *Christian Philosophy*. Light and life, he urges, are their own clearest evidence: it is not easy to prove the reality of the first to a blind man, or the reality of the second to a dead one!

(iv) *The Apostle of the Christian Consciousness — Erskine*

Such is the title given to the versatile Thomas Erskine by Principal Tulloch.[4] Erskine, a layman, sided with MacLeod

---

[1] *The Way of Divine Knowledge*, p. 254.
[2] Ibid.
[3] Op. cit., p. 174.
[4] F. W. Cornish, *Quoted in History of the English Church*, vol. 8, pt. ii, p. 192.

Campbell and adopted a soteriology akin to that expounded by his Scottish compatriot, in the latter's book, *The Nature of the Atonement*. He, however, apparently went beyond MacLeod Campbell and asserted a universalist doctrine. All humanity, it seems, is ultimately to be restored to God's favour.[1] Erskine was a friend of F. D. Maurice and his influence upon him was profound. Avoiding, like Maurice, party attachment, he spoke of 'Calvinism as a sheep in wolf's clothing, and Arminianism as a wolf in sheep's clothing'.

It is in his book, *The Internal Evidences for the Truth of Revealed Religion* (1820), that he treats of our subject. At the end of his work referred to, he contends that the standpoint is not novel, but there is much fresh and original notwithstanding. 'The object of the Gospel', he tells us, 'is to bring man into harmony with God; the subject of its operations, therefore, is the human heart in all its various conditions.'[2] With this as the fundamental thesis, the author sets out to consider, what may be called, the 'moral influence' of the Gospel. The value of all the external evidences is repudiated.

The gospel does not address itself to men's reason as something to be leisurely investigated. It comes rather with a moral persuasion to the heart. Several telling illustrations are given to prove that a stirring deed can evoke a response of love and gratitude, and work for a change of life. A mere general amnesty, for example, would not have produced a hatred of sin and a love of God. 'A pardon without a sacrifice could have but a weak and obscure appeal to the understanding and heart.'[3]

God's aim in dealing with men is not to grant them pardon. Had this been so He could have withheld information on the subject until men stood before the judgement seat. God's great purpose was rather to transform men by weaning them from their sins. This is the moral intention of the gospel and the assurance of its truth lies in the attainment of that end. It is this inner transformation, under the moral constraint of the gospel, which is true faith. It is when, with joyous abandonment one gives himself to its influence that there comes 'a new birth'.[4]

The faith of the gospel, then, is not mere knowledge of doctrine. Abstract doctrines have become divorced from their moral biblical

---

[1] *Dictionary of National Biography*, vol. 6, p. 862.
[2] *Internal Evidences for the Truth of Revealed Religion*, p. 56.
[3] Op. cit., p. 71.
[4] Op. cit., p. 109.

purpose. They are isolated summaries, detached dogmas. In the
Bible, doctrine is the source of life. But as for our creeds and
articles, 'the doctrines contained in them are not stated with
reference to their great object in the Bible — the regeneration of
the human heart, by the knowledge of the Divine character.'[1] It is
only in 'gospel faith' that the creeds have any value. They give a
convenient summary, they act as warnings against danger, and
they stand as doctrinal landmarks. But knowledge of them however perfect is not Bible faith. 'The knowledge communicated by
revelation is moral knowledge, and it has been communicated in
order to produce a moral effect upon our characters; and a knowledge of the Divine essence would have as little bearing upon this
subject, as far as we can see, as a knowledge of the elementary
essence of matter.'[2]

The moral change effected in us by the gospel is the work
within us of the Spirit of God. And because this is so, no external
attestation of the gospel is required by an appeal to miracles. Some
miracles, like the resurrection of our Lord, belong to the very
essence of the gospel and cannot be detached and treated as
mandatory labels. 'The belief of the miraculous attestation of
the Gospel, then, is just so far useful as it excites our reverence
for, and fixes our attention upon, the truth contained in the
Gospel.'[3]

Erskine repudiates a religion imposed from without and by
authority. True Christian faith must be something rising up
within; it must be something to which the conscience can give its
assent, for whatever is not of conscience is not of faith. Like
Maurice, Erskine regards man as needing the assurance that he is
already reconciled to God. 'If the question is asked, "How can I
obtain God's mercy?" the reply must be given, "God has already
declared himself reconciled through Jesus Christ; so you may have
it by believing it." '[4] Like Brunner he regards men as responsible
beings committed to decision. 'We feel we are not unconcerned
spectators of these things. We are sure that, if there be a principle
which can explain and connect them all together, it must be a most
important one for us; it must determine our eternal destiny.'[5]

[1] *The Internal Evidences for the Truth of Revealed Religion*, p. 91.
[2] Op. cit., p. 95.
[3] Op. cit., p. 188.
[4] Op. cit., p. 194.
[5] Op. cit., p. 198.

Kant Undermines Rationalism

A new Copernecian revolution in thought was introduced by Immanuel Kant (1722–1804). In his *Critique of Pure Reason* Kant had argued that the ultimate postulates of religion cannot be rationally proved. But in his *Critique of Practical Reason* he allows that what cannot be proved by the pure reason is a necessity of the practical reason. For Kant the ideas of freedom, immortality and God were somehow necessities of a thinking being. It is as absurd by reason to prove there is a God, as to prove freedom, immortality and God to be unreal. 'For we can only say that we know anything by reason when we are somehow conscious that we know it even if it had not been given us in experience; hence rational knowledge and knowledge *a priori* are one and the same.'[1]

Since Kant's day, philosophy generally may be estimated by its agreement or disagreement with him. In the main, it can be said, that he gave rise, on the one hand, to a sceptical intellectualism, and on the other hand, to a practical anti-intellectualism. Re-opening the question of knowledge, in an effort to bring men out of the impasse created by Hume's scepticism, Kant postulated an existing 'ego', as more than the sum of sensations. He drew, also, a sharp distinction between the 'thing-in-itself' — the noumenon — which is beyond knowledge, and the thing-in-appearance — the phenomenon — which alone is the object of knowledge. This denial of any knowledge of the noumena led easily to the scepticism of Spencer, to whom God was the great Unknowable, beyond all predications.

But for two reasons Kant's critical philosophy, itself intellectualistic in the extreme, led to the defeat of intellectualism. First, Kant had argued that there was something which reason could not prove, namely, the reality of reason itself. There was thus that which lay outside its scope and criticism. 'Henceforth rationalism must efface itself in the presence of criticism. It has to reconcile itself to the inevitable: reason is losing its empire over objective external reality. Its proved certainties have collapsed. The Scottish David has vanquished the Goliath of dogmatism.'[2] This quotation from Lecerf introduces the second consideration. Kant, it is well known, made an onslaught on the traditional arguments for the existence of God. God could not be rationally

---

[1] *Critique of Practical Reason* (tr. T. K. Abbott), p. 97.
[2] A. Lecerf, *Introduction to Reformed Dogmatics*, p. 45.

proved to exist. Yet he will grant that the assurance of God's existence arises out of man's moral nature. With Kant then there was begun a new subjective emphasis. All externality is regarded with loathing. Man, for Kant, is essentially an autonomous moral being, and it is that which commends itself to this moral autonomy which is alone of value. Thus Kant can write in a letter to Lavater (24.4.1775), 'I distinguish the *teaching* of Christ from the *report* which we have of the teaching of Christ, and in order to get at the former I try above all to extract the *moral* teaching separated from all precepts of the New Testament. The former is surely the fundamental doctrine of the Gospel, the latter can only be auxiliary doctrine.'[1] For Kant the standard of judging between the 'moral teaching of Christ' and the mere 'report' was to be found within. With him, therefore, begins the rout of reason. 'Since the impressive efforts of Kant', observes W. E. Hocking, 'to mark out a strictly limited province which all our major human interests lie safely outside of, thinkers of the first rank (with exceptions, but with singular accord) have added some strokes to the picture of reason's retirement, representing it as servant to the will, or as a tool and creature of some darker and more primal reality — blind impulse, immediate feeling, the unconscious. . . . The whole apparatus of reason in religion has retracted in importance in favour of a more substantial basis — which we have agreed to call feeling.'[2]

Immediately, indeed, this side of Kant's teaching was taken up by Jacobi, the 'faith-philosopher' and used as a weapon against Kant's own 'rationalism'. In his book, *Of the Divine Things* we find Jacobi emphasizing 'feelings' as the source of religious knowledge.

The Background of the Theology of Coleridge

The place that Jacobi sought for the 'feelings' was secured in the theological system of Schleiermacher (1763–1834). Schleiermacher defined religion as the immediate feeling of absolute dependence upon God. This 'immediate feeling' he regards as the presupposition of all religions. In this way he announces, what Brunner calls, his 'relativistic conception of religion'.[3] The 'essence of religion',

---

[1] Quoted, S. Körner, *Kant*, p. 170.
[2] *The Meaning of God in Human Experience*, p. 37 f.
[3] *Revelation and Reason*, p. 219.

'the religion within the religions,' that which manifests itself in many historical forms, is this feeling of dependence. It is nothing accidental, but is 'a universal element in life'.[1] It is, in fact, one and the same, with what Schleiermacher calls, the God-consciousness: 'God-consciousness is always . . . the feeling of absolute dependence.'[2] This doctrine is, at bottom, the same as that worked out more recently by Otto under his 'Numinous' formula in his *Idea of the Holy*.

Those who become aware of this native God-consciousness need no other argument since 'the recognition of this fact entirely takes the place for the system of doctrine, of all so-called proofs of the existence of God'.[3] The important thing is this immediate or intuitive certainty of God. Indeed this feeling of dependence is nothing other than the immanence of God. This doctrine of 'God-consciousness' is really Schleiermacher's substitute for the Quaker doctrine of the 'inner light'. It is significant that the only English work quoted by Schleiermacher in his *Christian Faith*, is Robert Barclay's *Apology*. While it is true that on each mention of him it is to differ from him (which is understandable since both allusions have to do with the Ordinances, which, of course, Barclay rejected), it is indicative of how strongly was the mystic influence upon him.[4] Barclay, to be sure, sought to safeguard a distinction between the inner light and man's own spirit. But in the final exposition of Schleiermacher's views there is little distinction between the Spirit of God and the spirit of man. For Schleiermacher, the God-consciousness is one and the same with 'immediate self-consciousness'.[5] Even the contention of Otto is not true, the contention, namely, that Schleiermacher argued by inference from the feelings to a God beyond them.[6] He would rather have us assured of a God found within our feelings. For Schleiermacher Dogmatics is 'a statement about our feelings, not about God'.[7] But, ultimately, as any statement about the feelings is a statement about the God-consciousness, then for Schleiermacher, any statement about the God-consciousness as a reality of the feelings, is a statement about God.

---

[1] *The Christian Faith* (tr. from 2nd German edition, ed. by H. R. Mackintosh and J. S. Steward), p. 133.
[2] Op. cit., p. 260.   [3] Op. cit., pp. 133, 134.
[4] Op. cit., p. 625; cf., p. 643.   [5] Op. cit., p. 5.
[6] *The Idea of the Holy*, p. 10.
[7] H. R. Mackintosh, *Types of Christian Doctrine*, p. 60.

Schleiermacher on Revelation and Scripture

Reference must be made briefly to Schleiermacher's understanding of these two related subjects so as to appreciate the
position taken up by Coleridge and his followers. Schleiermacher
begins by stressing that revelation is not a human discovery, nor
yet, is it something 'excogitated in thought by one man and so
learned by others'.[1] Revelation is not an operation upon man as a
cognative being; 'For that would make revelation to be originally
and essentially *doctrine*.'[2] He views it rather as that which arises
within man himself like an heroic or poetic inspiration. It would,
he says, 'be difficult to draw any clear dividing line at all between
what is revealed and what comes to light through inspiration in a
natural way.'[3] This understanding of revelation, is, he contends,
illustrated in the Person of Christ. In Him dwelt the God-
consciousness in fullest measure. But the indwelling God-
consciousness belongs to man, *qua* man. He, therefore, rejects the
idea that the divine revelation in Christ was absolutely supernatural. Human nature has within it 'the possibility of taking up
the divine into itself, just as did happen in Christ'.[4]

Schleiermacher elaborates his thesis that there is in both the
Redeemer and the redeemed a 'supra-rational' element. In both it
is a veritable indwelling of God: in Christ in the form of the Logos;
in the redeemed as 'a movement of the Holy Spirit'. Yet he will not
allow any clear-cut distinction between the supra-rational element
and the common human reason. 'For', he says 'the highest goal
that is set before these workings of redemption is always a human
state which not only would obtain the fullest recognition from the
common human reason, but in which also it is impossible always to
distinguish, even in the same individual between what is effected
by the divine Spirit and what is effected by the human reason.
Inasmuch, then, as the reason is completely at one with the divine
Spirit, the divine Spirit can itself be conceived as the highest
enhancement of the human reason, so that the difference between
the two is made to disappear.'[5] This notion, when applied, means
for Schleiermacher, that there is nothing strictly supernatural, nor,
yet, is there anything specifically rational. The common idea, he
contends, that would draw a distinction between natural (rational)

---

[1] *The Christian Faith*, p. 50.   [2] Op. cit., p. ibid.
[3] Op. cit., p. 61.   [4] Op. cit., p. 64.
[5] Op. cit., p. 65.

and revealed (supra-rational) religion, errs. It is to him obvious that 'this can be no more than a juxtaposition, and that these two kinds of dogma cannot form one whole. Between the rational and the supra-rational there can be no connection. This further becomes pretty clearly evident in all treatises upon Christian doctrine which divide themselves into a natural theology, purely rational and thus valid not only within, but also outside of Christianity, and a positive supra-rational theology, valid only within the compass of Christianity. For then the two are and remain separate from each other'.[1] This division Schleiermacher will not allow, since, in the individual, the element of the God-consciousness is at the same time both divine and human, so in 'one respect all Christian dogmas are supra-rational, in another they are all rational'.[2]

All this means that Schleiermacher's position is, as Brunner does not hesitate to say, semi-pantheistic. 'If a man awakens to the fact that within his single life the Whole is living, that in his personal existence there is beating, vividly, vitally, the pulse of the Infinite movement, then in that man, Schleiermacher teaches, authentic piety is born.'[3] It will be granted that he made man look within for the spirit and the spring of religion. It is a category *sui generis*. God was not the conclusion of a chain of syllogistic reasons. He was there, immediately within the soul — so close that it seemed impossible to separate Him from self-consciousness and contemplate Him objectively. Instructed in Moravianism and influenced by Romanticism, Schleiermacher really gave doctrinal expression to both in his Christian Faith.

In the end the position is that Revelation is not an inbreaking of God, but an upsurging of divine humanity. It is a natural discovery. Such a view of revelation made it too weak to have any creative significance. 'If', says a living author, 'we accept the supernatural only as something too weak and passive to interfere with the natural, we had best call ourselves materialists and have done with it, — we shall gain in honesty what we lose in respectability.'[4] In the context of our period when idealism was in such vogue it would be better to substitute the word 'pantheism' for 'materialism' in the above quotation: with this done, the words are applicable, and the rebuke is warranted.

[1] Op. cit., p. 66.   [2] Op. cit., p. 67.
[3] Op. cit., p. 67. Cf. H. R. Mackintosh, *Types of Modern Theology*, p. 52, from which the quotation above is made.
[4] Joy Davidson, *Smoke on the Mountains*, p. 116.

When we turn to Schleiermacher's understanding of Scripture it will be found that the same subjective principle which runs through all his work is applied. It is that which commends itself to the believer which is of value. The peculiar authority accorded to the Scripture rests upon the faith of the believer in Christ.[1] He condemns those text-books and Confessions which begin with a doctrine of Scripture. He would have us accept the Scripture rather as a witness to the God-consciousness which is expressed in the feeling of dependence. A doctrine does not necessarily 'belong to Christianity because it is contained in Scripture'.[2] Like Tertullian he seems to be saying that the soul is by nature Christian. 'If faith in Jesus as the Christ', he writes, 'or as the Son of God and the Redeemer of men is based on the authority of Scripture, the question arises how this authority itself is to be based; for obviously the thing must be so done as to impress the conviction on unbelieving hearts, so that they too may by this path come to faith in the Redeemer. Now if we have no point of departure but ordinary reason, the divine authority of Scripture, to begin with, must admit of being proved on grounds of reason alone; and as against this two points must be kept in mind. First, this always involves a critical and scientific use of the understanding of which not all are capable; on this theory, therefore only those so gifted can attain to faith in an original and genuine way, while all others would merely have faith at second-hand and on the authority of others . . . . Secondly, if such proof could be given and if faith could be established in this fashion — if, that is to say, faith, given a certain degree of culture, could be implanted by argument — then on such terms faith might exist in people apart from repentance and change of the mind; which means that, having originated in this way, it would not be genuine faith at all. In other words, a conviction of this kind, gained through demonstrative proof,

[1] It is worth pointing out that the position adopted by Schleiermacher is the same as that followed by Brunner. Faith in Christ is prior to faith in the Scriptures, is the teaching of Brunner. 'Not because I believe in the Scriptures do I believe in Christ, but because I believe in Christ I believe in the Scriptures,' *Revelation and Reason*, p. 170. That this is a reversal of the historic 'orthodox' position Schleiermacher acknowledges. In a footnote Brunner maintains that M. Kähler was the 'first scholar to point out quite clearly this reversal of ideas'. It is strange that Brunner fails to note that the same line was taken earlier by Schleiermacher. Perhaps his own supposed repudiation of Schleiermacher's theology would not permit the reference. But we are of the opinion that Brunner is closer to Schleiermacher in his view of revelation than he would allow.
[2] *The Christian Faith*, p. 593.

would in itself have no value, for of itself it would not result in true living fellowship with Christ.'[1]

Although we are not concerned here with any criticism of Schleiermacher, it may be apposite to point out that in the passage just quoted, the author seems to argue that because reason cannot be given the supreme place, it cannot be given any. But this conclusion does not follow. At any rate, whether this be cogent or not, it is important to observe that these references to both Kant and Schleiermacher are necessary so as to provide the background for what follows.

(v) The Supremacy of the Subjective—Coleridge

In S. T. Coleridge, there is a strong emphasis upon the subjective element in revelation. Revelation is indeed a subjective matter. As a youth Coleridge had read much Neo-Platonic philosophy. With his friend Wordsworth he studied Spinoza and was greatly influenced thereby. It is recorded by Crabb Robinson that on one occasion Coleridge opened Spinoza's *Ethica* and kissed the portrait of its author, exclaiming, 'This book is gospel to me!' adding, the epexegetical remark, 'his philosophy is nevertheless false.'[2]

For a short time Coleridge joined the Unitarians but soon found himself out of sympathy with their doctrinal tenets. Abandoning them, he declared against all Socinian interpretations, and maintained belief in man's inherent sinfulness, and redemption through the Blood of Christ.

It was, indeed, the burdening reality of sin which conditioned his theological views.[3] A stay in Germany brought him into contact with the Kantian philosophy. Henceforth he forsook his earlier Spinozian necessitarianism and took account of the human will. Anyone who examines his own heart, Coleridge urges, will come to a realization of his own need. He will become aware of the sin for which his own will is responsible. The reality of original sin, he declares, is the primary fact: 'the doctrine of Original Sin gives to all other mysteries of religion a common basis, a connection of

---

[1] *The Christian Faith*, pp. 191, 192.
[2] *Diary*, vol. 1, p. 399.
[3] Cf., '. . . the conviction of sin . . . had for him more than for most philosophic theologians an awful pressing reality and he kept preaching it as the basis of all religion with energy . . . .', A. W. Benn, *History of English Rationalism*, vol. 1, p. 249.

dependency, an intelligibility of relation, and total harmony, that supersede extrinsic proof.'[1]

Kant had placed the origin of evil in the will and at the same time repudiated the Augustinian doctrine of heredity sinfulness and guilt. The same position is adopted by Coleridge. To be accountable man must be free. Positive evil 'follows necessarily from the postulate of a responsible will'.[2] 'Moral evil', he says again, 'is an evil that has its origin in the Will.'[3] Thus 'corruption must have been self-originated'.[4]

Yet an evil common to all must have a ground common to all. This ground cannot be the Divine Will. Coleridge, like Kant, identifies the Divine Will with the law of man's moral being. It is the categorical imperative, 'inasmuch as a Will, perfectly identified with Law is one with the Divine Will, we may say, that in the unfallen rational agent the Will constitutes the Law.'[5] But how man's common sin began in the individual Coleridge, having rejected the traditional doctrine, is unable to say. 'It is a mystery, that is, a fact we can see, but cannot explain.'[6] Coleridge maintains that all that takes place in the noumenal world is outside the range of the understanding. So the Work of Christ is like the origin of sin. Both can only be comprehended by their consequences. 'The mysterious act, the operative cause is transcendent, *Factum est*: and beyond the information contained in the announciation of the Fact, it can be characterized only by the consequences.'[7]

It is when a man feels the need which his own will has originated that he seeks a Saviour. He does not then want demonstrations and evidences. He is after that which can be transacted on the territory of his own spirit. Coleridge will not have this dismissed as 'transcendental trash', borrowed from Law and Behmen. He confesses to have read only Law's *Serious Call* and a 'small tract on Prayer'. So close, however, is Coleridge's thought to that of Law that we are tempted to think that he was more influenced by the 'small tract' than he cared to acknowledge. He sees Christianity as a 'divine rekindling'. It is not concerned with formal beliefs for 'religion has no speculative dogmas', he announces in true Schleiermacherian fashion.[8]

---

[1] *Aids to Reflection*, p. 198.   [2] Op. cit., p. 189.
[3] Op. cit., p. 192.   [4] Op. cit., p. 180.
[5] Op. cit., p. 192.   [6] Op. cit., p. 201.
[7] Ibid.   [8] *Table Talks*, p. 189.

Coleridge and the Bible

Having indicated Christianity as something essentially inward, Coleridge must inevitably say something about the Scriptures. He condemns out of hand all belief in their infallibility as 'if possible still more extravagant than Papal Infallibility'.[1] In his seven letters published under the title, *Confessions of an Inquiring Spirit*, he elaborates his subjective principle according to which the Bible is to be estimated.

Any identification of revelation with the words of Scripture is to be rejected. In a number of places he announces that the Scriptures 'contain' the Word of God. It is as the Bible 'finds me',[2] he says, that its truth is guaranteed. In the Bible there is 'something' experienced which is absent from every other book: 'the words of the Bible find me in greater depths of my being; and that whatever finds me brings with it an irresistible evidence of its having proceeded from the Holy Spirit.'[3]

Borrowing the term 'bibliolatry' from Lessing, he inveighs against what he regards as 'book worship'. He thinks that the doctrine of the 'verbal inspiration' of Scripture was borrowed from the Jews, who regarded their Pentateuch as so given. 'Now for "Pentateuch" substitute "Old and New Testament", and then I say that this is the doctrine which I reject as superstitious and unscriptural.'[4] Coleridge does not indicate that a doctrine is not necessarily false because it is 'borrowed from the Jews'. The argument could be dangerous if pressed too far, since the basic doctrine of the Gospels is the ethical monotheism of the Old Testament prophets.

There is a sense in which revelation must be understood as truth through history. But for Coleridge it does not seem to matter if the 'history' is a fictitious concoction or an altered sequence of events on the basis of some philosophical presupposition. The word of God is that which speaks, and is only that which speaks. Thus the Scripture is not the revelation; it is for Coleridge, as it is, in our day, for Brunner, the permanent possibility of revelation. Or, perhaps, even less specific than that, the Bible is for Coleridge, as it most definitely is for both Barth and Brunner, a 'witness' to the

---

[1] *English Divines*, vol. 1, p. 154. Cf., 'The idea of an infallible Scripture is to be paralleled only to the Romish tenet of infallibility', *Confessions, etc.*, p. 316.
[2] *Confessions*, p. 286.
[3] Ibid.
[4] Op. cit., p. 299.

actuality of revelation.[1] There is no reliance to be placed upon 'external proofs'. 'The truth revealed through Christ has its evidence in itself, and the proof of the divine authority in the fitness of our nature and deeds.'[2]

Revelation is, for Coleridge the welling up of the divine within, the springing into 'life' of the ever-active God, Who is the indwelling Life and Light of every human personality. Everyman shares the divine nature, and 'conversion' is really the rising to conquest of our native God-consciousness. It is just here that there is an interesting contrast between the school of Coleridge which begins with an emphasis on the divine immanence, and that of the neo-liberal school of Barth and Brunner which start with an exclusive emphasis upon the divine transcendence. For Coleridge and his followers, influenced by idealism revelation is really an upsurge of divine life; for the newer school it is an inbreaking of divine life. Revelation is to be characterized as the perpendicular from above, 'das Senkrecht von oben.'

An inevitable consequence of Coleridge's statement must be the obliteration of the distinction between natural and revealed religion. 'I know of no religion not revealed,'[3] he says. Like Kant he sees some of the truth in every religion; a truth according to the measure of God's grace. Coleridge could have used Kant's words, 'There is only *one* true religion but there can be many varieties of religious creeds . . . . It is therefore, more appropriate to say: this man is of the Jewish, Mahommedan, Christian creed, than, he is of this or that religion.'[4] There is no human soul, Coleridge teaches, unilluminated by the light of God. For the Christian when this light is turned on to the Scriptures, certain passages become radiative: and what becomes so illuminative becomes authenticated — for us.

[1] So many and so important are the parallels between what we may call the Coleridgean School and that of the neo-liberal school of Barth and Brunner that we are tempted to say that they have presented little that is new. This would, of course be too sweeping. The general difference, however, and the one that conditions their varied emphasis is that, while Coleridge gloried in the divine immanence and thus saw a certain 'identity' between God and man, the newer school repudiated Immanence as the 'deadly error of Hegelianism' and put their emphasis upon the 'otherness' of God. Although in the eyes of Barth, Brunner has compromised the position by giving away to 'a new version of Immanence' yet Brunner can still say: 'revelation is still a wonder ". . . that breaks into the world *from beyond the world*," ' cf., P. K. Jewett, *Emil Brunner's Concept of Revelation*, p. 18.

[2] *Confessions*, p. 299.
[3] *The Statesman's Manual*, Appendix B, p. 266.
[4] *Religion within the Bounds of Pure Reason*, p. 108.

Coleridge is considered by many scholars to be the real source of those views which found expression in, what has come to be called, the Broad Church. We have seen reason however to go back beyond him for the beginning of those ideas of which he was such a vigorous exponent. At the same time, those who developed his views, as did Arnold, Hare, Thirwall and Maurice, naturally looked to Coleridge as their chief. These men were either his disciples or his admirers. The tradition was continued by Stanley, Jowett, Kingsley and Robertson, 'while for every stage in the development of the school some hint or precedent or germ may be found in the recorded utterance of the master.'[1]

Opposing Theories of Inspiration

Coleridge's attack upon the doctrine of verbal inspiration demands a reference to the two theories which were now brought into conflict. The view of the inspiration of the Bible of which Coleridge was such an ardent advocate, has been suggestively called the 'Illumination Theory'. It is in line with Schleiermacher's view and was later maintained by F. D. Maurice and F. W. Robertson.

The Illumination Theory is an advance on the 'Intuition Theory' as taught by F. W. Newman, and in America by Theodore Parker. In this latter doctrine inspiration is regarded merely as the sharpening of powers possessed in some measure by all men. This statement naturally allies itself with Pelagian and Rationalistic views of man's dependence upon God.

The Illumination Theory is more obviously connected with an Arminian emphasis upon man's natural ability to co-operate with God. The Bible writers, it is said, were inspired as a result of the divine intensification and elevation of their religious preceptions, to a degree beyond that experienced by ordinary believers. This doctrine would limit inspiration to the writers, and refuse it to the writings. Thus the Scriptures are said to 'contain' the word of God; to contain that which their illumination had 'hit upon'.

This theory has the merit of taking account of the human element within the Scriptures. The personal idiosyncrasies of each writer are so obvious that the human individual was not lost in the divine indwelling. It is, of course true that there is an illumination

[1] A. W. Benn, *History of English Rationalism*, vol. i, p. 282.

of every believing man by the Spirit of God. But there is also a vital difference between the illuminated Christian and the inspired prophet. In the former case the Spirit works to give a vivid apprehension of truth already revealed; in the latter case there is a communication of new truth. This means that there is an activity of the Spirit in each case, not merely different in degree, but also different in kind. So completely dominated is this theory by the subjective principle that it is difficult to acknowledge any part of the Bible as absolutely dependable. As a consequence there is no reliable objective standard of truth and duty. Some canons must be given to detect which parts of the Scripture are to be received, and as these are not provided by the advocates of the Illumination Theory, then, it must be assumed, that that only is allowed which commends itself to the individual conscience and reason. The single individual thus becomes his own authority. The basis then of this Schleiermacherian and Coleridgean teaching is a pragmatist epistemology, which can be certainly valuable as a test of truth, but which is inadequate as an ultimate standard.

On the other side, the doctrine, against which Coleridge pronounced so vigorously, followed from an overstress on the divine transcendence and sovereignty. Here the Bible writers are regarded as passive instruments in the hands of God: His pens, not His penmen. This 'docetic view of inspiration', as Dorner calls it, virtually denies the inspiration of the persons in maintaining that of the writings. Thus we find Hooker saying: 'They neither spake nor wrote any word of their own, but uttered syllable by syllable as the Spirit put it into their mouths.'[1] Hooker's declaration was restated by others in such a way as to convey the notion that the process of inspiration was completely mechanical.

As so stated this theory cannot be made to square with the facts. That there are instances of a communication in a definite form of words cannot be denied.[2] But the exception must not be taken as the general rule. There are obviously 'human elements' in the Bible, in, for example, Paul's anacolutha and the expressions of grief and anger. Had mechanical dictation been the method used there would have been no need of eyewitnesses or the careful researches of a diligent historian like Luke.

While these objections are not of small moment it should be

---

[1] *Works*, vol. 2, p. 383.
[2] Num. vii. 7, 8, Rev. xix. 9, xxi. 7, etc.

observed that, as against the Intuition Theory, the 'Dictation Theory' sought to emphasize that inspiration is not a natural process: and against the Illumination Theory that it is not a partial process. The purpose was to insist that not a part of the Bible, but the Bible in all its parts, is the word of God. In maintaining that the Bible was verbally inspired the interest was not in the method but the result.

Whereas the Illumination Theory was right in stressing the human element, the Dictation Theory was no less correct in emphasizing the divine element. Any true view of inspiration like any true appreciation of the Person of Christ or any correct understanding of Christian experience, must make due allowance for both elements in the final unity. This will mean that inspiration is neither a discovery nor a dictation. It is easy to slide into a conception either too distinctly human or too exclusively divine. Coleridge erred on the one side, those he opposed erred on the other. Inspiration in one sense heightened and in another sense held the quickened powers of the man.

How, in the Person of Christ, the human and the divine were united in one Person is a mystery. So is it with the process of inspiration. It is easier to say what it does NOT involve than to clearly state what it does. The Bible is the most human of books as it is the most divine. And because experience attests this to be a fact, the reality of both the human and the divine elements must be given due recognition in any adequate theory of inspiration. Cogent in this respect are the words of Karl Barth when he writes, 'there is no point in ignoring the writtenness of Holy Writ for the sake of its holiness, its humanity for the sake of its divinity.'[1] At the same time, just as in the Person of Christ, so is it with the Scriptures, it is not easy rightly to unite the human and the divine. There is always the danger of making Christ, and the Bible too, either too much the one or the other, to detract from the human in the interests of the divine, or to accentuate the divine to the detriment of the human.

The old antithesis between the schools of Alexandria and Antioch has returned in the understanding of the doctrine of inspiration. There are some who adopt, what we may not unjustly call, an 'Apollinarian' attitude with regard to the agents of divine revelation. They see the human element, as it were, 'reduced' and

---

[1] *Church Dogmatics*, I, ii (E.T., 1956), p. 465.

its place taken up by the divine Spirit; only in this way, it is believed, can the Bible be secured from all error.[1]

Others, on the other hand, like Nestorius, set the human and divine in juxtaposition. By thus separating the human from the divine, they feel themselves able to regard the Biblical history and 'Wissenschaft' as subject to the defects of human imperfections.

It goes without saying that an exclusive emphasis upon the divine transcendence leads naturally, if not necessarily, to a 'mechanical' conception of inspiration, while an overstatement of the divine immanence tends to make inspiration little more than a matter of human insight.

No true understanding of the process of inspiration can, we believe, be entertained which does not do justice to the human and the divine in Scripture. There is 'something' in the Bible which can hardly be explained in words; there is an atmosphere, a potentiality, or whatever one may call it, which can, in the last analysis, be referred to only as 'its Divine Character'. This 'Divine Character', which can hardly be denied, must have an adequate cause, a Divine cause, God. But, at the same time, it is quite evident that the divine message was given to men of varying capacities and contrasting temperaments and at different times. What they have given bears the stamp of their personal idiosyncrasies and their own age. The agents of inspiration were clearly no passive instruments, no motionless recipients of the divine word. The individual was himself in the picture as an active participant. This double fact must be fully appreciated if we are to arrive at a true doctrine of inspiration. To ignore one side is, in fact, to invalidate the other.

Following Coleridge we find Archdeacon Julius Hare and F. D. Maurice acknowledge their indebtedness to those who had earlier taken the same line. More particularly, however, they both indicate that they had received much from Coleridge himself.[2] Educated under Vicesimus Knox at Tonbridge School, Hare later became a

---

[1] It was in this way that the Scholastics conceived inspiration, by regarding man as a 'deficient instrument'. This was the position taken by Aquinas, cf., 'In the case of Prophetic Revelation the Prophet's mind is moved by the Holy Ghost in the same way as a deficient instrument is used by the principal agent.' H. Pope, O.P., of the Collegio Angelico, Rome, 'Article on the Scholastic View of Inspiration,' *The Irish Theological Quarterly*, July 1911. (Produced by the Professors in the Faculty of Theology, Maynooth (St Patrick's College.))

[2] *The Mission of the Comforter* (1864), vol. 1, Preface. *The Life of F. D. Maurice* (by his son), vol. 1, p. 175 f.

tutor at Trinity College, Cambridge. The source and substance of Christianity, Hare argued, in his *Mission of the Comforter*, is in the inner workings of the Spirit. But His influence is not limited to the baptized; it is seen in all religions, and wherever righteousness is found.

(vi) *The Victory of Faith — Hare*

In 1839, Hare preached six sermons before his University, on the subject of 'faith'. These, with others, given at various times, were published in 1840, under the title, *The Victory of Faith*. Throughout the discourses he inveighs against the multiplicity of books on Evidences of Christianity, which have turned the news of the gospel into a philosophical system or a moral theory. He tells us 'we are inundated with dissertations on the external evidences of Christianity; in which it was treated like any other historical fact, and witnesses were sifted and cross-examined; but without regard to the main witness, the witness in the heart of the believer himself'.[1]

In a remarkable sermon preached at Hastings, May 19th, 1835, at the Archdeacon's Visitation, Hare took as his text the words; 'Lo I am with you always, even unto the end of the world.' The discourse is entitled, 'Christ's Promise, the Strength of the Church.' In it a contrast is drawn between the outlook of the divines of the sixteenth and the seventeenth centuries and those of the eighteenth. The preacher thinks of it like 'the transition in Pharoah's dream from the fat kine to the lean'. In the former preaching, he says, 'we find Christ, the Wisdom of God, and the Power of God unto salvation.' In the newer 'we read about the Infiniteness of the Divine Attributes, about the Benevolence of the Deity, about the Judgement evinced in the Dispensations of Providence, about the demonstrative evidence contained in the Resurrection'.[2] The clergy of the period 'preacht essays of heathen morality, with no trace of the Gospel in them, except the name of Christ awkwardly dragged into a peroration'.[3]

Rejecting all intellectualistic and notional definitions, it is Hare's purpose to stress the subjective element in revelation. This, he finds, to be 'faith', which he conceives to be essentially practical. He makes a similar comment as Dodwell and Law on I Cor. i. 7. Had Paul's purpose, in preaching the gospel, he says, 'been chiefly

[1] *The Victory of Faith*, p. 24.   [2] Op. cit., pp. 341, 342.   [3] Op. cit., p. ibid.

to convince the Understanding, the wisdom of words would have been the very means the best fitted "to accomplish" it.'[1] The God Whom reason constructs, has, however, no power over the heart. It is an arid abstraction, a mirage of the mind. He is not the living God for Whom the soul cries out.

Real faith is not the result of sweeping together the fallen leaves of the past. True faith is that which raises 'our hearts from visible things to the invisible'.[2] The heart is the real hub of religion. In this emphasis upon the inward, Hare claims that he is reasserting the authentic message of Luther. The volume is thus sent out with the prayer that the sermons in it 'might help some in embracing the truth which Luther taught'.[3]

But not only is faith a practical principle, it is also somehow a natural principle of life. It is not to be regarded 'as a totally new quality, a gift of the Spirit',[4] for no man can live without faith. It is in fact 'the ground-work of all that is distinctively human in man, of all his activities, of all his well-being and happiness even in this life'.[5]

To each individual man a special revelation is made. The soul's response to it brings the inner witness of the Spirit. The apostle to the Gentiles did not seek to win men's approval and assent. He sought to capture man's soul. Like Berkeley and Maurice, Hare refers to Paul's Athenian sermon, and says that he 'took occasion from the altar dedicated to the Unknown God, to declare that God to the Athenians, whom they were already worshipping without knowing him, so will every teacher, who has the spirit of St Paul, examine and interrogate the voice in men's heart, until he makes it bear witness to the truth of God's word'.[6]

Rightly does Hare refuse to see an antithesis between faith and reason. The real opposition, he insists, 'is not between Faith and Reason, but between Faith and Sight; or more generally between Faith and Sense.'[7] Faith and reason differ only in the method of their approach to the object. In any complete act of faith the three elements of man's psychical nature, knowing, feeling and willing, must have a place. Faith, therefore, he teaches, 'proceeds from the inmost depths of the soul, from beyond the firmament of Con- sciousness whereby the waters under the Firmament are divided

[1] *The Victory of Faith*, pp. 27, 28.   [2] Op. cit., p. 163.
[3] Op. cit., Preface, p. xiv.   [4] Op. cit., p. 70.
[5] Op. cit., p. 96.   [6] Op. cit., p. 140.
[7] Op. cit., p. 79.

from the waters above the Firmament. It is the act of that living principle, which constitutes each man's individual, continuous, immortal personality.'[1]

Real revelation according to Hare takes place within the individual soul. Whether the Scriptures are to be regarded as an objective standard, an external revelation, *per se*, he does not make clear. He certainly does not think of the Bible as containing truth stated in a formal creed. This, he argues, would be a bondage upon men's minds. He sees the Scripture as giving living examples of men, who, in the development of civilization, sought, through faith, a living personal God. His stress upon the inward seems rather to make him repudiate the authority of the external. 'Lovers of the Bible', he says, 'too easily degenerate into bibliolaters, lovers of the Church into ecclesiolaters'.[2]

(vii) *The Meaning of Revelation — Maurice*

The name of F. D. Maurice holds a secure place in the history of British theology. The son of a Unitarian minister he later became, by conviction, a clergyman of the Church of England. After service in a parish he was appointed Professor of theology in King's College, London. He lost this position as a result of a controversy concerning his orthodoxy. He was then appointed Chaplain to Guy's Hospital and at the same time held a professorship in Cambridge. The erroneous doctrines attributed to him were that he taught universalism and denied eternal punishment. A study of his works does seem to indicate that he did hold the opinions charged against him. According to his biographer, his own son, almost his last words were a comment on the passage, 1 Peter iii, 'the ark', Peter says 'saved the eight souls as a promise that ALL should be saved, so baptism saved those who were baptized, thus figuring God's salvation for all'.[3]

(a) *What is Revelation?*

On this subject Maurice's particular views are set forth in two volumes in which he attacks Dean Mansel's Bampton Lectures of 1859. The first book, entitled, *What is Revelation?*, appeared in the same year as the discourses he opposed. It comprises, first, a

---

[1] Op. cit., pp. 37, 38.
[2] *The Victory of Faith*, p. 321.
[3] *Life of F. D. Maurice*, vol. 2, p. 641.

series of seven Epiphany sermons, and then a number of 'Letters to a Theological Student'.

Maurice in opposition to the 'notional' doctrine of revelation advocated by Mansel, maintains that revelation is an immediate unveiling of God to the soul. Mansel's lectures 'were put forth at the time as the great bulwarks of orthodoxy against all assailants'.[1] But to Maurice their logical conclusion was Agnosticism.

Maurice begins his sermons with a discourse based on Luke ii. 32. He declares that in all men there is an inner feeling after God to which He responds. Revelation is the 'inward beholding' of God within. There can be no substitute for this, be it Scripture, or tradition or Church. 'No book can do it, be it ever so divine, no Church authority or tradition, can do it, be it ever so venerable.'[2] 'To substitute for this practical faith, which rests upon God Himself and His own manifestation of Himself in the Son of God and the Son of Man, a belief in a holy book, is to disobey all the warnings of that Book.'[3]

It is this view of revelation, underlying the theology of Maurice, which constitutes the grounds of his opposition to Mansel. Revelation is the unveiling of Christ within the heart.[4] Mansel has maintained that 'the only way . . . to confute Rationalism, to establish Christianity, is to affirm that God cannot be known, and that man is prohibited by his constitution from seeking such knowledge'.[5] Maurice, in reply, in a sermon on St Paul's words to the Athenians (we have seen this verse used by those who, before him, held the same view of revelation) pressed his idea of revelation as man's immediate awareness of God as reconciled. The apostle, he observes, did not begin with 'clearing the ground of all opinions and speculations'.[6] His method was, not to argue, but to announce. By giving his assent to the declaration of the heathen poet, Aratus, that man is God's offspring, Paul 'endorses the words of the poet'.[7] He confirmed to his listeners that their origin was divine and that God was in 'the strictest and fullest sense, their Father'.[8] They

[1] *What is Revelation?*, Preface. *Life*, p. 327.
[2] Op. cit., p. 8.
[3] Op. cit., p. 9.
[4] Cf., *Use of the Word Revelation in the New Testament* (F. D. Maurice), *Present Day Papers on Prominent Questions of Theology* (ed. by the Bishop of Argyle).
[5] *What is Revelation?*, p. 33.
[6] Op. cit., p. 37.
[7] Op. cit., p. 45.
[8] Op. cit., p. 46.

were spiritual beings created and redeemed; their feeling after God is God's revelation to them, the assurance that they would be all gathered to the Father of us all.

Man as God's offspring, redeemed in Christ, is the theme of Maurice's theology. He sees the incarnation as the manifestation of the sinless root of humanity. He expresses disapproval of the Evangelicals who 'still seem to make sin the ground of all theology, whereas it seems to me that the living and holy God is the ground of it, and sin the departure from the state of union with Him, in which He has brought us'.[1] Arising out of this conception we find Maurice proclaiming the gospel to be belief in the ever-present indwelling of God. In a letter to Miss G. Hare he writes: 'The kingdom of God is near you; the kingdom of God is within you. It is what all are longing to hear.'[2]

In his *Theological Essays* he exclaims: 'Thanks be to God for the witness which is borne in our day for the spirituality NOT of a FEW men, but of man as man.'[3] He asserts that the gift of the Spirit is not connected with a society but with the world, seeking to convince the world that has lost its true sociality. The world contains the elements of which the Church is composed, while the Church is 'a human society in its normal state: the world is that same society irregular and abnormal'.[4]

Maurice takes baptism to be a witness to the fact that all men are united by and united in Christ. To the Rev. Isaac Taylor he writes 'do not let us surrender the one great witness which we possess, that a nation consists of redeemed men, sons of God, that mankind stands not in Adam but in Christ; Give up the Prayer Book to an Evangelical or semi-Evangelical commission, and this witness will be eliminated by a thousand little alterations'.[5] Recalling his experiences among the labourers of his first curacy at Bubbenhall and the sick at Guy's Hospital, he says, 'It seems to me that except I could address all kinds of people as members and children of God, I could not address them at all.'[6]

(b) Maurice and Mansel

It is in his 'Letters to a Theological Student' that Maurice makes his attack upon Mansel. The thesis developed by Mansel is summarized in a quotation from Sir William Hamilton, made by the

---

[1] *Life*, vol. 1, p. 450.
[2] Op. cit., p. 528.
[3] *Theological Essays*, p. 3.
[4] Op. cit., p. 396.
[5] *Life*, vol. 2, p. 258.
[6] *Life*, vol. 1, p. 236.

Bampton lecturer himself: 'the last and higdest consecration of all true religion must be an altar, 'Αγνώστῳ Θεῷ, to the unknown and unknowable God.'[1] If this view were true, as a *Times'* reviewer of the *Limits of Religious Thought* pointed out, then all literature having a mystical tendency must be banished. No longer must Thomas à Kempis be read, and not for the reason that he was a 'Romanist', but because he assumes 'that there is a divine Teacher of Man's Spirit; that it is possible for man's spirit to have converse with that Teacher'.[2] With à Kempis must go Augustine's Confessions, the works of the Jansenists, the Puritans, Bishop Leighton's Commentary and a host of others. Besides, Whitfield and Wesley must be banished from the library of Christians and the Prayer Book will have to be drastically revised. 'All that is expressed in books of divinity by the union of the soul with Christ by living intercourse with Him, is impossible in the very nature of things, if Mr Mansel's mode of confuting infidels is the right one.'[3]

Maurice doubts Mansel's right to claim for his 'notional' doctrine of revelation the authority of Butler. At any rate, Maurice considers Butler useful as a study, or, perhaps, ammunition against the infidel, but he has no value in producing the beginnings of religion in the soul.

In the 'Letters to a Theological Student,' Maurice takes up the Bampton lectures one by one, and point by point. A formidable list of names has come under Mansel's condemnation in the notes to the lectures, as either Rationalists or Dogmatists: included are Schleiermacher, Anselm, Jowett, Priestly, Kant, Coleridge. Maurice retorts that the Bampton lectures themselves cannot be exempt from either charge. Indeed they are at the same time both rationalistic and dogmatic. In fact to be a man one must be both. There is, of course, a false rationalism and a false dogmatism, but to be both in the best sense is desirable and necessary. And we are both in the best sense when the Spirit has awakened us to the divine life within. This does not mean that the gospel must be presented in ponderous propositions and abstruse arguments. The Evangelist, who knows none of the clap-trap of philosophy, can speak and be understood. To put, therefore, faith outside the reason, as Mansel does, is false and fatal.

[1] *Limits of Human Thought*, p. 158.
[2] *What is Revelation?*, p. 134.
[3] Op cit., pp. 134, 135.

(c) The Theology of the Conscience

Maurice deals with Mansel's strictures on Schleiermacher. Maurice regards Schleiermacher as honestly reacting from the formal authority of the creeds. He does not, however, he is anxious to insist, accept the 'so-called Theology of the Consciousness'.[1] But his own might be aptly called the 'Theology of the Conscience'. He conceives of the 'conscience' as the light of God within; the divine witness to our natural kinship to God.

Mansel makes much of the Kantian distinction between noumenon and phenomenon. Maurice replies that the distinction is general to all philosophy from the earliest days. He repudiates the attempt to limit knowledge to the phenomenal, to the seen and the felt. Vital religion is not a discovery of God through experience, but a discovery of God in experience. For the fact is, he stresses again, we speculate about that which is distant from us. But the ground assumption of true education is, he claims, 'we are actually united to the Father of All, in His Son.'[2] He argues that 'the relation of the father and mother precedes all consciousness of it; the father and mother have a life of their own besides their relation to us. Their feelings to us are discovered first; then we seek to be acquainted with themselves, to know their minds, character, purposes. That relation to the Heavenly Father which is the ground of our relation to them, is unfolded to us in like manner, amidst the consciousness of disobedience, distrust, wilfulness, forgiveness.'[3]

Arguments for the 'faith' learnt off as if they were of unquestioned authority can lead to fatal results. Away from the class-room and the study they are assailable. In the world they possess no sanctity. Brought to collapse under the criticism of the sceptic, there is nothing left, and the result is a gnawing atheism. But had the lessons been otherwise learned, learned, that is, according to what Maurice understands to be the truth; had men been led to see God in the doubts and struggles of the individual heart, then there would have been no loss of faith when the enemy came in like a flood. Such a faith as this rests, not on 'arguments about the origin of documents', but arises out of life's experiences. Dogma there must needs be. But if there is a living God, 'surely to speak of Him is better than to speak of my notions about Him; or even my convictions which will be feeble or vital in proportion as they

[1] *Theological Essays*, p. 128.   [2] *What is Revelation?*, p. 352.
[3] Op. cit., p. 210.

are or are not divorced from that which calls them forth.'[1] True preaching, he thinks, begins with the Spirit, whereas the creeds begin with the Father.

(d) 'Realized Eschatology'

For Maurice the Incarnation reveals the 'sinless root of humanity'. It is the assurance of 'Regeneration as the restoration of human beings to their true filial position in Christ, of mankind to its unity in Him'.[2] This regeneration has to do with 'society': 'Phrases have been used by all parties', he writes, 'which seem to imply, that it is simply an operation of the individual.'[3] Christ is the 'regenerator' of society, and revelation is the awakening of society to that fact. In consequence of this teaching, Maurice anticipates the more recent doctrine of 'realized eschatology'. With humanity restored in Christ, a tribunal of judgement can no longer be placed in a distant future: 'it is one before which we in our inmost being, are standing now.'[4] It was for this reason that Maurice was charged with denying the doctrine of eternal punishment. Eternal life is likewise not something delayed to a future time but is discovered in the present.

(e) Where the Bible comes in

In the context of a doctrine of revelation as taught by Maurice the question naturally arises, What place has the Bible in all of this? In Letter xiv in the Sequel to What is Revelation, Maurice makes answer. The Bible apparently is a witness for him to this conception of revelation. Throughout its unfolding story, God was unveiling Himself, and every crisis of Israel's history is 'a day of the Lord'. In every event God was revealed, rebuking those who forgot Him, and assuring those who followed Him. The Bible is not to be equated with the revelation. Mansel had argued that the Bible must be taken as a whole or not at all. This Maurice takes as an indication 'that the book, merely, as such was taking the place in his mind of the Revelation whereof the book speaks'.[5]

He accepts the Bible, like Coleridge, because, as he puts it, 'I have heard Christ for myself, speaking to me out of this book, and speaking to me in my heart.'[6] He draws the now familiar distinc-

---

[1] Sequel to What is Revelation, p. 3.   [2] Theological Essays, p. 226.
[3] Op. cit., p. 232.   [4] Op. cit., p. 299.
[5] Sequel to What is Revelation, p. 280.   [6] Theological Essays, p. 340.

tion between the words of the Scripture and the Word of God in the Scripture. 'More and more' observes his son, 'he had come to look upon all expressions implying that the letter of the Bible is the word of God as denials of the living "Word of God" of Whom the Bible speaks.'[1]

In a letter to Charles Kingsley on the subject he writes: 'Why was it you received the Old Testament? Not because you heard stories about inspiration or cared a farthing for them, but because the Book spoke to you of a deliverer of the people, which no Greek myths spoke.'[2] He protested against a declaration by a group of clergy who maintained that the Bible not only contained, but that it IS the word of God. 'The Word of Truth, I believe, as St John taught and as George Fox taught, to be very much ABOVE Scripture, however, he may speak by and in the Scripture.'[3]

In F. D. Maurice the understanding of revelation which we have traced throughout this chapter may be said to have reached a climax, although, as indicated, the whole view has been revived again in a new context, by the neo-liberal school of Barth and Brunner. Maurice, however, emphatically does not belong to the modern period, although much of what he has to say is characteristically so. It was for him to insist more 'dogmatically' than those who preceded him, that religion is a matter of life and revelation has its 'locale' in the inner spirit. Maurice, above all, emphasizes the free Spirit of man, and he thus deprecates all unproductive disputes and subtle causistries. In his defence of his case, however, Maurice makes sweeping generalizations and pointless exaggerations, and, as a result, he does not carry conviction.

'Maurice', observes Professor A. K. Rogers, 'is not himself a controversialist, but the outcome of his case is perhaps even more dangerous in its ultimate tendency. It leads him, that is, to deprecate any disposition to put the issue sharply, or to allow the mind to range beyond what makes for religious edification. It is this dislike of facing issues, rather than any unavoidable obscurity in his positive beliefs, that is responsible for Maurice's pervading cloudiness. Thus his own views were strongly in the direction of the new and freer conception of the Scriptures. But instead of coming to the aid of Colenzo he takes the side of his enemies, not because Colenzo's criticisms are mistaken, but because the moral lessons of the Bible are so greatly more important than questions

---

[1] *Life*, vol. 2, p. 452.　　[2] Op. cit., p. 267.　　[3] *Life*, vol. 2, pp. 499, 500.

of literary accuracy, that doubts about the letter ought to be kept as much as possible in the background.'[1]

There is, of course, much in the statement of revelation we have just traced which is of practical moment and relevance. It was right to direct attention to the living Personality of Christ, and it was vital to stress the fact that the Christian Faith is more than mere assent to doctrines however authoritatively conveyed; and more than belief in writings however divinely revealed they may be conceived to be.

But, although our primary concern in this study is with the tracing out of developments, rather than with the criticism of theories, there is, nevertheless, one point above several others which could claim attention, which calls for special reference. In their understanding of revelation as an inward unveiling of the indwelling Christ, the 'Coleridgeans' (if we may coin a word to cover all those doctrines we have had in review) failed to make clear what, on their view, is the position of the Scripture. Dodwell scorns, what he called, a 'Paper-Revelation', Law condemns pre-occupation with the 'letter of the Scripture', and all of them repudiated a 'book-religion'. Yet they all appear to be left with a Bible on their hands with which they are not too sure what to do. To get rid of it seemed inadmissible, to hold on tightly to it seemed impossible. As far as the 'Coleridgeans' are concerned there was no satisfactory reply to the question, Where does the Bible come in? and especially none to the related question, What is the nature of its authority?

Having identified 'verbal inspiration' with a dictation or mechanical process, the idea of a verbally inspired book is rejected. It is not clear, however, whether the Bible is to be regarded as an inspirational book or as an inspired Scripture. If it is the former then the problem of the nature of its authority (if authority it has), remains. If, on the other hand, it is somehow regarded as an inspired Scripture then the problem of the relation of inspiration to the words of Scripture has to be faced. God has chosen human words to be, what Brunner calls, the 'locale of revelation'. He has not chosen music or painting. And if human words are the selected vehicle then it is required to be shewn how the assertion that God was not interested in the 'words' of Scripture is to be understood. It is trite to observe, as has been done, that Luke's words are

---

[1] *English and American Philosophy since 1800*, p. 119.

specifically, 'Lucan', and Matthew's are 'Matthean'; no one doubts that this is so. But Luke and Matthew and the rest had what Rudyard Kipling calls, in another context, 'the magic of the necessary word.' How they 'hit upon' the 'necessary word' to indicate and to illustrate that which is indeed almost beyond words is not told to us. These issues are not raised here to press any particular point of view, but because they are questions forced upon any thoughtful reader confronted with the doctrine of revelation as the immediate unfolding of the indwelling Christ.

Maurice, it may be observed, condemned Mansel for quoting a passage of Scripture at the opening of each of his Bampton lectures because these ornamental prefixes had no immediate and necessary connection with what followed. Maurice himself in his own sermons is at pains to point out the importance of every phrase in any true exposition of the Scripture. He uses his text, as historically it was meant to be used, as that which gives force and authority to his words. But it is not evident what force and authority the Scriptures he quotes are intended to give. The 'Coleridgeans' refer to certain passages, which, they hold, sustain their view of revelation. But suppose the one to be convinced and converted to their doctrine answers, 'Such passages have not "found me" ', — What then? Is it not obvious that something more than this subjective criterion is needed? For the rightness of this doctrine of revelation is made to depend upon the Scripture, upon the rightness of which, in its turn, we cannot depend.

One is aware of a zigzag of thought throughout the whole of the writings with which we have dealt. On the one hand, there is an appeal to Scripture as if it were considered sufficient. To those who are to be assured of the correctness of the position of the 'Coleridgeans' it is quoted as the word to silence all doubts and settle all controversies. It is enough that, 'It is written.' It was certainly enough for Christ, Who opposed His foes, whether Satanic or Sadducean, with the identical formula. But on the other hand, for all that, the Scripture which is quoted in this sufficiently authoritative way, is not to be regarded as the word of God. From whence, then, does its authority spring? The answer which seems to be in the thought of these writers is, that it gains its authority when it *becomes* the word of God within experience. But apart from the fact that the 'Coleridgeans' appear to deny their own thesis in the way they use the Bible, there is a difficulty which they failed to meet. Since, *ex hypothesi*, there is a sharp divorce between revelation, which is a coming to a knowledge of the Christ within, and Scripture as a record, a 'witness', perhaps, to this view of revelation, it would then appear that the divine revelation can well take place apart from the Scripture. This is indeed allowed as a possibility. But let the possibility be admitted, and it will not be long before the actuality be claimed. This means that we are thrown back (in theory at least) into all the vagaries of enthusiasm, in which each can assert the validity of his own private revelation.

The vehement rejection by the 'Coleridgeans' of the whole idea of a 'propositional' revelation is only possible on the basis of the assumption that revelation is illumination, never communication. Its concern is with 'light' rather than with 'truth'. But if there is a relation between the two: if, that is, the written word does not merely indicate the possibility of revelation, but in some way brings revelation to us, then there is a sense in which Scripture is revelation because therein God speaks in, by and with the written word thus bringing us into relation to His initial revealing acts. If the Scripture does not merely indicate where 'light' is to be found but does so 'in truth' then it is not easy to escape the fact that, in so far as revelation comes through 'the word as truth', it cannot be without 'propositional' form. 'We speak disparagingly about mere assent to propositions. But do we mean mere assent, or assent to mere propositions? Mere assent is possible and ignoble. Assent to a mere proposition is a monstrosity which cannot occur. For if assent is real, the proposition has done its work, and it is the ontological reality itself, whose nature the proposition has described to us, that we acknowledge.'[1] Let us be agreed that the Bible holds what Dr Temple calls an 'interim position'[2]; yet the fact remains that there is still a real relation between the words and the Word. It is this 'real relation' the 'Coleridgeans' did not, and, we think, on their premises could not, make clear.[3]

---

[1] Alan Fairweather, *The Word as Truth: A Critical Examination of the Christian Doctrine of Revelation in the Writings of Thomas Aquinas and Karl Barth*, p. 14.

[2] See *Nature, Man and God*, pp. 116–18.

[3] On several occasions throughout the previous exposition it has been suggested that much of what is being said by Barth and Brunner (with, of course, important qualifications) was already said by the 'Coleridgeans'. For this reason it has been thought to be useful in this footnote to indicate the main features taking Brunner as an example.

Brunner, like Coleridge, begins by insisting upon the identity of revelation with Christ the Word as subjectively apprehended. (Cf., *The Christian Doctrine of God*, p. 63.) He goes on to insist upon a vital point, the complete separation of Christ as the Word of God from the Bible as human testimony, or 'witness' (*Hinweis*) to that revelation. The divine Word of God, incarnated and unveiled (yet still veiled) in the human heart, which is properly revelation, belongs to the sphere of 'Thou-Truth' (*Du Warheit*), in contrast with the witness to that revelation, the Scripture, which is 'It-Truth' (*es Warheit*). For Brunner, too, the tragedy of all tragedies is to identify the two. This is the folly of the 'orthodox', the greatest and gravest of its manifold sins originating from the absurd doctrine of verbal inspiration. Brunner excells himself in his condemnation of this 'fundamentalist' error. As a witness to revelation the Scripture is mainly doctrines and revelation is not concerned with doctrine, for revelation itself is God's in-breaking in the personal heart, which is the divine Word of God, Jesus Christ. This is the revelation to which the Bible 'points'. But not every part of the Scripture bears witness with equal clarity: 'we cannot maintain that everything that is Biblical — not even everything in the New Testament — is in the same way, or to the same extent, the "bearer" of the word of God' (*Revelation and Reason*, p. 129). Some passages, indeed, but 'stammer' out His name (*The Philosophy of Religion*, p. 153). That which is on the 'rim' of the New Testament has little 'witness' value. While there are passages, like 2 Pet. ii. 4, which fall outside the 'rim'. For all that the Scriptures have an 'instrumental authority', although when it comes to matters of 'world-knowledge' what they have to say, has 'no doctrinal authority,' cf., *The Christian Doctrine of God*, p. 57.

Brunner has made the idea of 'verbal inspiration' the focus of his ridicule, but when he comes to find some authority for the Scripture, he cannot do so apart from the words. The human word can bear testimony to the divine Word because of the similarity between the two (cf., *The Christian Doctrine of God*, p. 184). God's revelation, in the last, must come through human language. 'Hence the Word of God is there in the form of revealed human words, not behind them . . . , but in direct identity, in a complete correspondence of man's word and God's word' (*The Christian Doctrine of God*, p. 26). This seems very much a falling back into a doctrine he has repudiated. He agrees that the idea of 'verbal inspiration' is the 'classical' doctrine, but it is an error withal, yet it is an error 'most comprehensible'. It would indeed be better to 'hold fast to it, than on account of its incorrect form, cast off its precious content, which is the Christian Church's principle of Scripture' (quoted by P. K. Jewett, *Emil Brunner's Concept of Revelation*, p. 159). Brunner's difficulty is that he desires to draw a sharp distinction between the Word and the words and yet he cannot maintain it. He observes, 'the written record is part of this revelation, it is not the whole' (*Revelation and Reason*, p. 12) and yet he says, 'Holy Scripture therefore does not only speak of revelation; it is itself revelation' (op. cit., p. 21). This is no isolated reference; 'In theory' he remarks again, 'there is no particular need to bring the Word of God and the written word into a specially close connection; quite the contrary' (op. cit., p. 125). Yet for all that, 'It is only through the written word that the testimony of Christ of the first witnesses has been maintained in its original and distinctive form' (p. 126). This means that 'the written Scripture, is the medium in which the word of God comes to us, since it alone contains the Apostolic word of revelation' (ibid.). These sort of statements could be multiplied, and they are not easy to harmonize. The same pendulum swing of ideas which we have seen in the 'Coleridgeans' is to be observed. Appeal is made to the Scripture because it contains, in its words, the revelation of God, on the other hand, no decisive appeal can be made to it just because the revelation of God in the Word is not 'connected' with the words of Scripture. In his little book *'Our Faith'* which appeared in 1936 Brunner likens the Voice of God in the Bible, 'His Master's Voice', to a voice heard on a gramophone record. It is the real voice of the singer which is heard, but there are noises and scratchings besides which are not the master's voice (cf., op. cit., p. 10). That is good as far as it goes. But there are two questions which arise. How can we be sure that the voice we hear is indeed the master's voice? When it appeals to me as such, and when it 'finds me'. Such answers are not too obvious. Again, How can we be sure that the voice heard was indeed the voice recorded? And especially how can we be sure if we accept that

Important, then, is, we believe, the question we have raised concerning the relation of revelation and record. The revelation is, of course, prior to the record. First the life then the literature which embodies and secures the original revelation for subsequent generations. If there were no adequate record then would each new age need again the revelation. Bethlehem and Calvary would need to be repeated to bring God to men. But the records become for the ages subsequent to the original revelation the vehicle of objective truth about Him of Whom was the disclosure. From this it follows, as Dr W. R. Matthews says, 'we are not free to construe our conception of God in abstraction from history. . . . Our starting point is a creative experience which comes to us mediated through human testimony.'[1] The record is necessary if the revelation is to be preserved. The revelation of God in Christ would not have been guaranteed to those who followed unless He completed it in an adequate medium of transmission. It would have been tragically still-born if it were not permanently safeguarded. The securing of this result will be assured 'either by a continuous Apostolate supernaturally secured in the *Charisma veritatio*, as Rome claims, or by a book which should be a real successor of the Apostles, with a real authority on the vital matters of truth and faith. But we discard the supernatural pope for the supernatural book'.[2] But not all that was revealed has been recorded. The apostle John refers to many things that Jesus did which have not been written down. In this sense, it must be allowed that there is a distinction between the revelation and the record, but, at the same time, all that is recorded has been revealed, and what is not recorded is as a matter of fact unknown to us. This fact means that no cleavage can be made between history and interpretation. It is impossible on

God was not active in the recording? The problem becomes more complicated when it is stated that the Bible is a 'witness' to a revelation, and more difficult still when so much is allowed as apparently incapable of ever 'becoming' the word of God; as ever being a 'bearer' of God. In this case the demand for some criterion to separate the voices on the record from the voice of the master becomes urgent. It is the impossibility of finding any such standard, other than one's own subjective appreciation of the 'one voice' that has made men like the ex Bishop of London, Dr Wand, write off the whole attempt to make such distinctions as folly. In his book on *The Authority of the Scriptures*, he writes, 'the title, Word of God, if it is to be used at all, as we hold it must, applies to the whole Bible and not to mere parts of it, however supreme their value may be.' It is impossible, he argues, to distinguish some short sentence out of the whole as having a divine character above the rest. 'The Word of God', he concludes, 'is heard both in the events themselves and in the record of them,' op. cit., p. 83.

[1] *God in Christian Thought and Experience*, p. 44.
[2] P. T. Forsyth, *The Person and Place of Jesus Christ*, p. 171.

certain philosophical presumptions to alter the facts and retain the interpretation. They belong together. So in the New Testament, the facts are not to be separated from the interpretation of those facts within the New Testament itself. 'In the actual history (it is said) God was at work revealing; but in the record, or commentary, it was man construing. In the transfer to writing much of the reality has vanished; and the living plant is even dried between the leaves of the book. So it is said. And thus our very exaltation of the personal revelation in Christ has led to a fatal depreciation and neglect of the Bible, as being a mere record, which we may use for our satisfaction but need not for our life.'[1] But, as we see it, the revelation in Christ is only final and full when it is seen not in this act or that, but in every deed and word and the application and interpretation of every deed and word: that is, in the whole Christ of the whole New Testament. Thus we learn from the New Testament of the Revelation incarnate, and we see in the New Testament Revelation interpreted, and we have in the New Testament Revelation preserved. The Bible in a real sense presents us with God-given facts and God-inspired valuations. Here we have the seamless coat of fact and value woven into a pattern so close that it is not possible to sever them. The Bible contains 'the record, the interpretation, and the literary reflection of His grace in history'.[2] The real message of the Christian gospel is not a bare fact but a revealed fact and an inspired interpretation. It is the whole record of facts and interpretations which constitute the story of redemption and which become saving history.[3]

This means that the authority of the Bible lies within its own sphere, namely, that of a redemptive relation with God. It is, at the same time, the avenue, the dynamic and the touch-stone of genuine Christian experience. This does not mean that the Bible is placed, obstructively, between the soul and God, and thus becomes a sort of 'paper pope'. The authority of the Bible, we have asserted, relates to the redemptive experience, and like all truth, to be of value it must be subjectively realized. Thus the correlative of

---

[1] P. T. Forsyth, *The Person and Place of Jesus Christ*, pp. 148, 149.
[2] A. B. Bruce, *The Chief End of Revelation*, p. 280.
[3] The point we make here is simply that God's final self-disclosure is not to be regarded as a single isolated 'event', as such, and on its own. The full and final revelation of God, for example, is not the 'event' of the Incarnation *per se*, but the incarnated life in its totality. But the incarnated life is the life of Christ as lived, and known to us by His words spoken and His deeds done as these were from the first interpreted and applied.

revelation is faith: of the Bible is the Holy Spirit. It is as Calvin says 'the secret testimony of the Holy Spirit', which seals the authority of Scripture to the believing heart. There must be the *'testimonium Spiritus Sancti internum'*. 'Let it therefore be held as fixed that those who are inwardly taught of the Holy Spirit acquiesce implicitly in Scripture; that Scripture, carrying its own evidence along with it, deigns not to submit to proofs and arguments, but owes the full conviction with which we ought to receive it to the testimony of the Spirit.'[1] This is a different thing from cold assent to external writings. The telescope before the eye of the astronomer is not a means of obstruction: it is a means of observation. By it the glories of the otherwise unknown sky are revealed. By it he learns what is there, and what without it he could never see. So is it with the written word, when once focused by the eye of faith: by it God is seen.

---

[1] *Institutes of the Christian Religion*, vol. 1 ,p. 72.

THE TEACHING OF THE EVANGELICALS

At this point it would seem that an enquiry is demanded into the understanding of revelation held by those who were described as the 'Evangelicals'. It will have been clear from the earlier pages that those who have been referred to as the 'orthodox', as well as their opponents who emphasized the subjective doctrine of revelation, both repudiated the title. The Evangelicals, therefore, stood apart from each of these two sections. They maintained, in opposition to both, their own doctrine of a divine disclosure which may be summarized under the heading:

REVELATION IN THE WORD THROUGH THE SPIRIT

It is, of course, only in what follows that this summary statement can be clarified and its adequacy justified. But to seek into the doctrine of revelation taught by the Evangelicals, two tasks are involved. On the one hand, it is necessary to find its origin since no special view comes into being, so to speak, overnight. The Evangelicals certainly did not think of their teaching as something new. They were emphatic that they were in line with the past. It will consequently be part of our present investigation to trace out the lineage which they claim. On the other hand, since the Evangelicals, though not without real scholars, were not specially interested in creating theological systems, we shall have to find from among them a teacher who shall best state their position. The first, then, of the two purposes of the present section is to seek:

(i) *The Background of their View*

The Evangelical party of the eighteenth century was the spiritual heir of the Puritans in their understanding of Revelation and the Scripture.[1] The concern of both was to declare the Biblical message

---

[1] 'Evangelical Churchmen trace their pedigree to the Puritans; and the Reformers . . . ,' G. R. Balleine, *A History of the Evangelical Party in the Church of England*, p. 1.

rather than to justify the ways of God to man. For this reason there is not, particularly among the former, much discussion concerning the necessity and nature of revelation. For both, the best proof of the existence of a special disclosure of God was the possession of the Scriptures. There was no great need to justify that which was so evidently and creatively existing. God had communicated His revelation which was confirmed by the presence and confined within the covers of the Bible, the Written Word of God.

It was this conviction which was the assurance and strength of the Puritans. To them is to be attributed that habit of Bible reading which became so characteristic of British Protestantism. By their example and teaching 'England became the people of a book, and that book was the Bible'.[1] The Puritans found in the Bible the source of their inspiration, and by laying stress upon the right of every man to its use they gave vitality to 'a wide spread "Bible religion" as distinct from a "Church religion" '.[2]

(a) The View-point of the Puritans

The Puritan literature is not, however, without reasoned statements concerning the very basis of their faith. There is, for example, the brilliant treatise by the learned John Owen, entitled, *The Divine Original of the Scripture.* The argument which he here sets out is extended in his *Reason of Faith.* A similar line of thought is developed in the appendix of Thomas Halyburton's posthumous work, *Natural Religion Insufficient and Revealed Religion Necessary.*[3] Chalmer's in his preface to his *Institutes of Theology* pays a high compliment to Owen's work. He declares that the Puritan theologian has given to those who desire a 'satisfactory conviction of the claims of the Bible', 'the most solid and indubitable proof.' Great as were the contributions of Leslie, Lyttleton, Dodderidge, Bates, Baxter, that of Owen was even greater, since, continues Chalmers, 'we hold Dr Owen to have rendered a more essential service to the cause of divine revelation, when, by his clear and irresistible demonstrations, he has proved that the Written Word itself possesses a self-evidencing light and power for manifesting its own divine original, superior to the testimony of eyewitnesses, or the evidences of miracles, or those

[1] J. R. Green, *A Short History of the English People* (1891), p. 460.
[2] D. C. Somervell, *A Short History of our Religion*, p. 239.
[3] Halyburton was made Professor of Divinity in St Andrews in 1710, but died in 1712, at the age of thirty-eight.

supernatural gifts with which the first teachers of Christianity were endowed for accrediting their divine mission.'

In his treatise Dr Owen sets out to prove that 'the whole authority of the Scriptures in itself depends solely on its divine original'.[1] The argument runs as follows: God, it is asserted, spoke IN the prophets, psalmists and preachers whose messages we have. What they had to say was not the result of their own insight and discovery. 'God was with them, and by the Holy Ghost so spake in them — as to their receiving of the Word from him, and their declaring of it unto others by speaking or writing — as they were not themselves enabled by any habitual light, knowledge, or conviction of truth, to declare his mind and will, but only acted as they were immediately moved by him.'[2] Accordingly the divine inspiration had reference, not simply to the men, but also to their words.

The inspired men were not left to record their message in any words they pleased. 'They invented not their words themselves, suited to the things that they learned, but only expressed the words they received.'[3] As regards matter and form they were under the influence of the Spirit, thus the whole product is the Word of God. This being the 'divine original' of the Scripture, its authority is assured. All God's revelations are self-evidencing. Nature, for example, 'declares itself to be from God by its own light and authority.'[4] In like manner do the 'innate light of nature, and principles of conscience of men'.[5] This fact is, however, more true and more obvious in the case of the Written Word which God has magnified above all else.[6] From the revelation of the Bible the authority of God speaks out clearly and convincingly. As authority can only operate is the sphere of personal relations, the authority of the Scripture, which is none other than the authority of God, means that it is to be acknowledged and obeyed. Those who profess to accept the authority of the Bible are compelled by that very profession to receive it as the Word of God. The Scripture declares itself to be Θεόπνευστος, and it is therefore to be attended to in the same manner as any person who was divinely inspired.

Our Lord reminded the rich man of the parable that his surviving brethren had the written word as the only and adequate ground of assurance. He indicates 'that those who will not own or

---

[1] *Works of Owen* (edited by W. H. Goold, 1853), vol. 16, p. 297.
[2] Op. cit., p. 298.
[3] Op. cit., 16, p. 305.
[4] Op. cit., p. 311. [5] Op. cit., p. 310. [6] Op. cit., p. 311.

submit to the authority of God in the Word, would not be moved by the most signal miracles imaginable'.[1] The apostle heard the voice of God on the mount, yet that same apostle 'tells us that, comparatively, we have greater security from and by the written Word than they had *in* and *by* that miraculous voice'.[2] Thus is the word of prophecy made more sure.

Owen proceeds to specify the 'innate arguments in the Scripture of its divine original and authority'. They are its 'light' and its 'power'. Light manifests itself. It needs neither argument for its presence nor witnesses to its existence. It is declared of the written word, as it is of God Himself, that it is the light. Scripture is the story of man's salvation. It is power — '*vis, virtus, Dei*'. The saving word is not only $\delta\acute{v}\nu\alpha\mu\iota\varsigma$ $\theta\epsilon\acute{o}v$ in itself; it is also $\delta\nu\nu\acute{\alpha}\mu\epsilon\nu o\varsigma$, 'able and powerful' in respect of us. The Scripture therefore shares that property which belongs to God.

Owen adds what he calls, 'the consequential considerations, for the confirmation of the divine authority of the Scriptures'.[3] These are the suitableness of its doctrines for the needs of all men and the harmony existing between its several parts.

The final assurance, however, that the Scripture is the word of God, is the testimony of the Spirit. The Spirit never 'speaks to us *of* the Word, but *by* the Word'.[4] 'That the Scripture be received as the word of God, there is required a twofold efficacy of the Spirit.'[5] On the one hand he acts upon the individual's mind. He communicates spiritual light, gives wisdom, and creates a spiritual sense and taste. On the other hand the testimony of the Spirit has reference to the Word itself. Here Owen has in mind the effectiveness of the word in other hearts because of the effectiveness experienced by the individual. In reference to the word, the testimony of the Spirit is 'a public testimony, which, as it satisfies our souls in particular, so it is, and may be, pleaded in reference unto the satisfaction of all others to whom the Word of God shall come'.[6]

This double testimony of the Spirit is, however, only formally distinguishable. In all grounds of assent, Owen argues, there unite in one the authority of testimony and the self-evidence of truth. So is it in reference to the Scriptures. 'In the same Word,

---

[1] Op. cit., p. 317.
[2] Op. cit., p. 317.
[3] Op. cit., vol. 16, p. 337.
[4] Op. cit., p. 326.
[5] Op. cit., p. 325.
[6] Op. cit., p. 328.

we have both the authority of the testimony of the Spirit and the self evidence of the truth spoken by him; yea, so that both these are materially one and the same, though distinguished in their formal conceptions.'[1] For Owen, the testimony of the Spirit is no 'private whisper, word or voice, given to individual persons',[2] but, 'the public testimony of the Holy Ghost, by and in the Word, and its own divine light, efficacy and power.'[3]

A less usual attitude to the Scriptures is taken by John Goodwin, who, although generally reckoned among the Puritans, yet, in this respect, as in others, stands outside the main stream.[4] Daniel Neal refers to John Goodwin as 'a learned divine and a smart disputant, but of a peculiar mould'.[5]

In his *Divine Authority of the Scripture Asserted* Goodwin takes up a point made in his earlier *Hagiomastrix, or Scourge of the Saints,* which had laid him open to the charge of denying the Scriptures to be the Word of God.[6] Goodwin had stated that the word of God was something different from the written Scripture. It is the purpose of his *Divine Authority of the Scripture Asserted* to amplify and justify his position. He therefore maintains that the divine word is not to be identified with the written record. It certainly cannot be equated with any one translation, since there is no translation without defects. Translations are, after all, as Jerome long ago remarked 'muddy streams or rivulets, in comparison with the Originalls'.[7] Neither can the word of God be identified with the original manuscripts themselves. These are unknown, and even among the oldest and best there are variations.

The real word of God, on the other hand, is incorrupt and incorruptible, consequently, observes Goodwin, 'the true and proper foundation of the Christian Religion, is not inke and paper, not any book, or books, not any writing, or writings whatsoever, whether Translations, or Originalls; but that substance of matter, those gracious counsells of God concerning the salvation of the World by Jesus Christ, which indeed are represented and declared, both in Translations, and Originalls, but are effentially and really distinct

---

[1] *Works of Owen*, vol. 16, p. 328.   [2] Op. cit., ibid.
[3] Op. cit., ibid.
[4] Goodwin's strong Arminianism to which Wesley acknowledges his debt puts him also outside the general Puritan tradition. Cf., J. R. Mersden, *The Early Puritans*, p. 348 f.
[5] *History of the Puritans*, vol. 3, p. 362.
[6] *Hagiomastrix* (1647), sect., 28.
[7] *Divine Authority of the Scripture Asserted* (1648), p. 7.

from both, and no waies, from their natures and beings, depending on either of them.'[1]

According to Goodwin, then, here is the authentic Word, the true Scripture, which like water in a cup is to be distinguished from the vessel which contains it. This is the Scripture, the divine authority of which can be established by two modes of arguments, the 'intrinsical' and the 'extrinsecall'. The former of these is of two types, the one 'which respects the planning, phrase, language, and manner of indighting or framing the Scripture'. The other 'which respects the matter or substance of them'.[2] The 'extrinsecall' is likewise of two sorts; '1. such remarkable passages or acts of Divine Providence, whereby God plainly owns the Scriptures as his, and from himself. 2. Into such doings, or sayings of men, which were so far confederate with those Providences of God, as to joyn in testimonies with them on the behalf of the Scriptures.'[3]

This sharp divorce between the Word of God and the written Scripture was vigorously and vehemently opposed. It ran counter to the prevailing view. The doctrine generally accepted was that, although the method of inspiration might not be explicitly stated, it nevertheless resulted in language which was rightly to be designated the 'word of God'.

In such a manner did men like Matthew Henry, the commentator son of Philip Henry, understand the Scripture to be the revelation of God. He states in his Ordination Confession, 'I believe: "that this book of Scripture was given by the inspiration of God, holy men speaking and writing as they were moved by the Holy Ghost," "And that this foundation of all revealed religion, is a perfect, sufficient rule of direction for all the children of men." '[4]

In his *Commentary on the Scriptures* the same understanding of the written record is maintained. He observes in reference to 2 Tim. 3. 15–16 that, 'Those who would acquaint themselves with the things of God, and be assured of them, must know the Holy Scriptures, for these are the summary of divine revelation.'[5] He

[1] *The Divine Authority of the Scripture Asserted*, p. 17. Cf., 'I conceive the matter of the Scriptures, I mean those glorious and Divine Truths, those holy and righteous commands, those great and precious promises, those astonishing and dreadful threatenings, conteined and expressed, as well in Translations, as in the Originalls were of greatest pregnancie and power both to discover and assert their royall Parentage, and descent from God.' Op. cit., p. 16.

[2] Op. cit., p. 31.

[3] Op. cit., ibid.

[4] May 9th, 1687, cf., J. B. Williams, *Life of Matthew Henry*.

[5] Matthew Henry's *Exposition of the Old and New Testament*, ad. loc.

goes on to say that the excellency of the Scriptures lies in their divine inspiration. The Bible is therefore 'a divine revelation, which we may depend upon as infallibly true. The same God that breathed reason into us, breathes revelation among us'.[1]

In another comment on 2 Peter 1. 19–21, he is more definite and explicit concerning the activity of the Holy Spirit in the inspiration of the Scriptures. His words on this point may be taken as representative of the general view. 'The prophets and penmen of the Scripture', he writes, 'spake and wrote what was the mind of God, and though, when under the influence and guidance of the Spirit, it may be well supposed, that they were willing to reveal and record such things, yet it is because God would have them spoken and written. . . . That the Scriptures are the word of God, is not only an article of the Christian's faith, but also a matter of science and knowledge. . . . As a man not barely believes but knows assuredly, that that very man is his peculiar friend, in whom he sees the proper, peculiar, distinguishing marks and characters of his friend; so the Christian knows that *book to be the word of God*, in and upon which he sees the proper marks and characters of a divinely inspired book. He tastes a sweetness, and feels a power, and sees a glory, in it truly divine . . . . To call off our minds from all other writings, and apply them in a peculiar manner to these as the only certain and infallible rule, necessarily requires our being fully persuaded that these are divinely inspired, and contain what is truly the mind and will of God.'[2] He goes on to refer to the Holy Spirit as the 'Supreme Agent' in inspiration. The writers were 'but his penmen'. They were His 'instruments'. 'The Holy Ghost', he declares, 'inspires and dictates to them what they were to deliver of the mind of God . . . so that the very words of Scripture are to be accounted the words of the Holy Ghost.'[3] The Bible is, therefore, to be esteemed and reverenced as the book of the Holy Ghost, its very words proceeding from God.

The same estimation of the Scripture is declared in the context of controversy, by one of the earlier Puritans, William Whitaker (1547–95), who was Regius Professor of Divinity in Cambridge for sixteen years.[4] In his *Defence of the Authority of the Scriptures* he

---

[1] Matthew Henry's *Exposition*, ibid.
[2] Op. cit., ad. loc.
[3] Op. cit., ibid.
[4] Whitaker was honoured by the degree of Doctor of Divinity by the University of Oxford, for his learning.

maintained against Bellarmine, the divinity and sufficiency of the Bible as the rule of Protestant faith.

The Puritans, therefore, did not regard the Bible as a mere record of revelation. It is itself the revelation of God in which and through which God comes savingly to the soul.

John Arrowsmith, who at a later date than Whitaker, occupied the Regius chair of divinity at Cambridge, writes: 'The Scripture is of divine authority: Holy men of God (saith Peter) spake as they were moved by the Holy Ghost. They wrote accordingly. All Scripture, saith Paul, was given by inspiration of God . . . they have God for their author . . . . It is a thing wherein the Son of God, who indited the Scripture gives abundant satisfaction on the spirit of goodly men, as to make other arguments, though not useless, yet to them of less necessity; He alone bearing witness to the divinity of holy writ, and to the truth of his own testimony, so putting a final issue to that controversie.'[1]

Henry Palmer, who in 1644 became master of Queen's College, Cambridge, like Arrowsmith equates revelation with the Scripture.[2] He asks in his catechetical fashion '29 Q. From whence must we learne to know God and serve him rightly?' He gave the reply, '29 A. To know God, and serve him rightly, wee must be taught of God's word.' '30 Q. Which book is God's Word?' '30 A. The Bible or the Scriptures of the Old and New Testament is the very word of God.'[3]

In a sermon on 1 John 4. 1, A. Burgess observes, 'That therefore we may not split ourselves upon inevitable Rocks: God hath left us his word as a Rule, *by which all revelations and operations* of his Spirit are to be tryed. All the Scriptures are $\Theta\epsilon\acute{o}\pi\nu\epsilon\nu\sigma\tau o\iota$, by divine inspiration; and therefore the breathings of God's Spirit are to be expected in this Garden: and those commands of *attaining to the Scripture only* and to observe *what is written*, are a plain demonstration that God hath tyed to the Scriptures onely.'[4]

John Ball was held in high esteem by the Westminster divines. He asks the question, 'What is it to be immediately inspired?' He

---

[1] *A Chain of Principles* (1659), pp. 103, 104. Cf., 'The Scriptures in like manner contain the minde of Jehovah . . . . Somewhat of *his nature* we may learn from his *creatures*, but should have known little or nothing of *his will*, had not the canonical *Scripture* revealed it,' op. cit., p. 86.

[2] Benjamin Brook, *Lives of the Puritans*, vol. 3, p. 76.

[3] *An Endeavour of Making the Principles of Christian Religion . . . plaine and easie, etc.* (1644), p. 7.

[4] Sermon xxiii, *Spiritual Refining* (1652), (2nd edition, 1658), p. 132.

answers, 'To be immediately inspired is to be, as it were, breathed, and to come from the Father by the Holy Ghost without all means.' He goes on to assert that in this fashion the original Scriptures 'were inspired both for matter and form'.[1]

One of the most important, as well as one of the most interesting writers of the Puritan period was William Bridge. His three sermons on 2 Peter 1.19 are of major importance for an understanding of the prevailing doctrine of revelation and the Scriptures. The purpose of Bridge in these sermons, is to set forth the sufficiency and supremacy of the Scripture. In comparison with the voice that spoke from the excellent glory, 'the Word of God written is surer than that Voice they heard in the mount (whereof he spake in the former verse). More sure is the Written word, than the Voyce of Revelation; not *ratione veritatis*, not in regard to the truth uttered, for that Voyce was as true as any word in Scripture; but more sure, *ratione manifestationis*, more certain, more settled, and established.'[2] Like John Owen he sees the Scripture as a self-manifesting light. It is more sure, more pleasant, and satisfying than all those claims to light advanced by men. The light of the Scripture is perfect. It is therefore more to be relied upon than immediate revelations, than dreams, than visions, than direct impressions made upon the heart whether with or without the Word, than experience, than the law and light within, than 'Judicial astrology'. 'The written word of God is our appointed Food, our daily Food.'[3]

While Bridge puts the Bible above the 'law', the 'light' and the 'Spirit' within, he does not mean it to be understood that he gives no place to the testimony of the Spirit. The reverse is the truth. The need of the Spirit to enlighten both the mind and the book is insisted upon. At the same time he maintains that the Spirit never by-passes the Scripture. The Holy Spirit is 'sent to open the Scripture to you, not to take away the Scripture from you'.[4] He points out that our Lord, in the days of His flesh, referred to and deferred to the written word. He argues that as a consequence 'Christ in us, is not more privileged than Christ without us; but Christ without us, was tied by the Scriptures, therefore Christ within us much more'.[5]

---

[1] *A Short Treatise, etc.*, pp. 7, 8.
[2] William Bridge's Works (Twenty-two several books of Mr William Bridge ... collected in two volumes), 1657 Scripture Light, the Most Sure Light, Ser. 1, vol. 2, p. 4.
[3] Op. cit., p. 23 (Sermon 2).   [4] Op. cit., p. 29.   [5] Op. cit., p. 30.

Bridge will not allow the application of the term 'the word of God' to be applied to Christ exclusively, and as a pretext for refusing its application to the Scriptures. 'Some there are', he writes, 'who say, That Christ only is called, the Word, or the word of God; and that the Doctrine preached or Written, is not the Word or the Word of God, But though Christ is called the Word, John 1, yet I do not find in all the New Testament, that he is called the Word of God in the present.'[1] This designation, Bridge contends, is for Him when the kingdoms of this world become the kingdoms of our God and His Christ. Then shall He be King of Kings and Lord of Lords, 'the Word of God'.

This means then that the Scripture is to be regarded in itself as the very word of God. It is therefore necessary 'to hold fast the very letter of it'. At the same time it has to be made clear that the true Scripture is not the letter by itself, since the 'Letter with the true sense and meaning of it, is the Word'.[2] The letter and the sense belong together as do the body and the soul. Does not the sense lie 'wrapped up in the Letters and Words thereof'?[3] The words of 2 Cor. 3. 6 may be quoted against him. But Bridge replies that in this passage the contrast is not between the letter and Spirit of the Scriptures, but between the law and the gospel. The apostle calls 'the Ministration of the Law, the Letter; and the Ministration of the Gospel, the Spirit'.[4] Thus to preach from the letter of Scripture is not to preach the letter, or to be ministers of the letter.[5] For this understanding of revelation and Scripture, Bridge claims the authority of Luther.

Yet the Puritan divines, in their teaching that the Bible was, *in toto*, the word of God, differed from the non-Puritan Churchmen only in the extent of its application. The Puritans considered that all matters relating to the worship, constitution and discipline of the Church were set down in its pages.[6] Their opponents, on the other hand, were ready to admit that there was much in the

---

[1] *Scripture Light, the Most Sure Light*, Ser. 3, p. 40.
[2] Op. cit., p. 46.
[3] Op. cit., ibid.
[4] Op. cit., p. 47.
[5] It is surely in this way that the famous saying of Luther is to be interpreted. The Scriptures, he declared, are the crib that contains the Christ. But to separate the Christ from the crib is to fall a victim to, what a later period spoke of as 'enthusiasm'. Whereas to give attention to the crib (mere intellectual assent to the propositions of the Scripture) and miss the Christ is but another species of rationalism. Crib and Christ, letter and sense, word and Spirit belong together.
[6] J. R. Green, *A Short History of the English People*, p. 460.

Church's life for which the Scripture had made no provision. Tradition and convenience were therefore a sufficient justification in these cases. For the non-Puritan, the Scripture, as far as it went, was still the word of God; both its message and its words being given by the Holy Ghost. So certain is this that Archbishop Parker could deprive a vicar of his benefice for denying the verbal inspiration of the Bible.[1]

(b) The Work of the Westminster Divines

The Puritan attitude to the Scriptures found expression in the work of the Westminster Assembly. This statement finds justification, not only from the fact that Arrowsmith and Bridge, whose words have been quoted above, belonged to the small committee which prepared the material and sketched the outline of the Confession, but also from an examination of the work produced and a comparison of it with the Puritan literature.

The opening section of the Confession, 'Of the Holy Scriptures', declares them to be the 'written word of God', and 'divinely inspired'. For a 'full persuasion and assurance of the infallible truth, and divine authority thereof', there is, however, needed the inner witness of the Holy Spirit.[2] It is declared that there is no appeal from the Scripture. The Larger Catechism asks the question, 'What is the word of God?' The answer given is, 'The holy Scriptures of the Old and New Testament are the word of God, the only rule of faith and obedience.'[3]

The Westminster divines maintained that the Bible was authoritative and infallible because it was inspired. Only because it is a product of the Spirit's action can the Scripture be regarded as possessing the authority of God. Because it is born of the Spirit's inspiration it needs no certificate of approval from any man or Church.[4]

In their declarations on this subject the Westminster divines felt themselves to be expressing the attitude of the Protestant churches as a whole. More particularly, however, as Professor Benjamin Warfield writes: 'the chief source of the Westminster doctrine of the Holy Scripture is the general teaching of the Reformed

[1] Op. cit., p. 471.
[2] Confession, ch. 1, v.
[3] The Larger Catechism, Q. 3 and Answer.
[4] Cf., J. Macpherson, The Westminster Confession of Faith, with Introduction and Notes, p. 35.

theology.'[1] The Puritans did, in fact, believe that their doctrine of revelation and the Scripture, which gave birth to the Westminster Confession, was itself based upon that of the Reformers. They considered themselves to be stating essentially, although, perhaps, more formally, the teaching of Luther, Calvin and the rest.

Warfield gives an extended quotation from Heppe's profound study of the doctrine of the Scripture in the Continental Reformers in his *Die Dogmatick der evangelisch-reformirten Kirche* (1861). Heppe has shewn that they regarded the Bible as authoritative and infallible because of its divine inspiration. 'Since the authority of Scripture coincides with the authority of God, it is absolute authority.'[2] No sharp distinction was allowed between Scripture and the Word of God. The canonical Scriptures, it was held 'not only contain the word of God, but are themselves God's written word; for their penning was brought about by special and immediate agency of the Holy Spirit, who incited the authors to the writing, suggesting to them thoughts and words which should be penned, and guarding them from every error in the writing — that is, the canonical books were *inspired* by the Holy Ghost to the authors, in both form and content'.[3]

(c) The Position of the Reformers

The legitimacy of the belief of the Puritan and Westminster divines that their understanding of the subject was a true interpretation of the Reformers, is a matter of importance. That they DID consider themselves to be continuing their teaching is beyond question. The whole subject is however confused by the desire of

[1] *The Westminster Assembly and Its Work* (O.U.P., New York), p. 161. Cf., 'No reader of the Puritan literature of the seventeenth century will fail to observe how hard it leans upon the great Reformed divines of the Continent — freely appropriating from them lines of argument, forms of expression, and points of view. While also, no doubt, freely adapting them to their own purposes. The consequence is that the sources of several sections of the Confession of Faith can with almost equal readiness be found in Ball or Du Buc, in Cartwright or Calvin, according as we choose to look near or far for them. There is scarcely a leading divine of the first three-quarters of a century of Reformed theology, who wrote at large on the Scriptures, from whom statements may not be drawn as to make it appear to be the immediate source of the Westminster sections.' B. Warfield, op. cit., ibid. Cf., also, 'Undoubtedly the English Puritans owed their heaviest debt to the theology, political theories, and principles of ecclesiastical polity that were based upon the continental reformers in Geneva, Zurich, and the Rhineland cities.' P. W. Dawley, *John Whitgift and the Reformation* (1955), pp. 133, 134.
[2] Quoted from Heppe, B. Warfield, *Westminster Assembly and its Work*, p. 166.
[3] Op. cit., p. 164.

opposing parties to claim the Reformers as their Fathers. Contradictory statements are consequently made under the supposed authority of Luther or Calvin. Each is made to speak the language of controversial necessity. The truth of this last observation can be seen from statements made by recent writers. Referring to Luther, A. L. Lilley says: 'No Christian doctor of the front rank ever disparaged the revelational role of the Scripture more consistently than the great reformer.'[1] On the other side, F. R. Barry, putting Luther and Calvin together, asserts, 'In their zeal for the newly discovered Scriptures . . . the Reformers allowed themselves to be intoxicated with a crude and fanatical bibliolatry.'[2] He goes on to maintain that their Bible worship has led to disastrous results; 'the authority of an infallible Scripture has proved to be more sterilizing in morals than the autocracy of an infallible pope.'

Here we have two writers — and their number could be multiplied[3] — attributing to the Reformers opposing doctrines. On the one hand there are those who believe that the Fathers of the Reformation rejected all external authority in the rediscovery of the freedom of the Spirit. On the other hand, there are those who stigmatize them because they substituted a new authority — an infallible Bible for an infallible Pope. They are thus supposed to be, at the same time, the creators of a new subjectivism and a new scholasticism. They are commended by some because they were 'liberal' in their attitude to the Bible; and they are condemned by others because they were 'bibliolaters'.

Of one fact, however, we may be certain, namely, that the Reformers rediscovered the doctrine of divine grace by which, through faith, the ungodly are justified. It was the experience of this new found truth which was the grounds of Luther's rejection of the authority of the Church. But while he did turn away from the Church as the umpire in the things of the soul, it is not true

---

[1] A. L. Lilley, *Religion and Revelation*, p. 79.
[2] F. R. Barry, *The Relevance of Christianity*, p. 24.
[3] Cf., e.g. Dr Schaff who declares that the Reformers did NOT believe in the theory of a literal inspiration and an inerrant Bible. (See Warfield, op. cit., p. 261.) On the other side, W. Herrmann regrets that they did. (See *Communion with God*, p. 40 f.) Brunner vacillates. He begins by claiming that his own position was that of the reformers. But in his *Revelation and Reason* he attributes the notion of verbal inspiration and Bible infallibility to the second generation reformers. But in his later *Dogmatics* (vol. 1) he allows that Luther held the view along with his other 'liberal' doctrine. The 'orthodox' doctrine is indeed the 'classic' one. The false idea of the words of Scripture as 'revelational' he sees already taking place within the New Testament itself, especially in the Pastorals. The passage 2 Timothy iii. 16. he quotes as illustrating this regrettable process.

that he thereby introduced a subjective regulative principle. It was his own personal experience of new life in Christ which gave birth to the Reformation and which became for Luther a fact of prime importance. As a reaction from the cold intellectual acceptance of certain credal propositions on the authority of the Church, it was inevitable that Luther should make the principle of justification by faith the standard by which all else was to be tested. So it came about that in his enthusiastic proclamation of the doctrine of 'sola fide' he should view with disfavour anything which seemed to call its truth in question. It was this fact, which, for example, made him refer to the Epistle of James as 'a perfect straw-epistle'.

It was also this fear of compromising the absoluteness of God's grace which led Luther to hurl his invectives against the place given to reason in the Roman system. Aquinas had made natural religion an essential preface to revealed, without which the latter could not be really understood. Not only was this, in the thinking of Luther, a failure to appreciate the true effects of the 'Fall', but it was a compromise of the fundamental Biblical principle, that a man has no merit to plead before God; not even that he is able to grasp Him by his unaided reason. Reason is, therefore, for Luther 'blind and dark'; it is 'contrary to faith', and so forth.[1] Yet Luther's strong words are to be understood as a vigorous repudiation of the native ability of man, either to find out God of himself, or to originate saving faith.[2]

It is considerations such as these which have led some to conclude that Luther abandoned all external authority, and that his 'repudiation' of reason, meant the enthronement of feelings. This is not, in fact, the case. It is certain he did emphasize, it may be did over-emphasize, the 'material' principle of the gospel, justification by faith. So vivid was the experience of it to him that he came to consider it to be the sum and substance of revelation. From this point of view Luther would have the whole Bible interpreted, according to the 'analogy of faith'. Every part of Scripture was to

---

[1] Much more, in language less choice, is collected by Martiain, e.g. 'You are to abandon your reason; knowing nothing at all, annihilate it completely or you will never enter heaven', 'Aristotle (is) the godless bulwark of the papists,' etc., etc. J. Martiain, *Three Reformers* (E.T.), p. 30 ff.

[2] Yet Luther in a passage in his *Table Talks*, has made it clear what is involved in his repudiation of reason. 'The natural wisdom of the human creature in matters of faith, until he be regenerate and born anew, is altogether darkness, knowing nothing at all in divine cases. But in a faithful person, regenerate and enlightened by the Holy Ghost, through the Word, it is a fair and glorious instrument, and work of God.' *Table Talks*, Hazlitt's translation, ccxciv.

be read in the light of this principle. The less vital sections got their validity here.

Setting out, therefore, from his own experience, Luther did strongly assert the 'material' principle, and from that stand-point did 'judge' the Scriptures,[1] but he also maintained the 'formal' principle, the exclusive authority of the word of God. 'Luther', observes Dorner, 'clearly discerned, and succeeded in exhibiting, in the most pregnant manner, *justification by faith in Christ*, and the *sole divine authority of the Holy Scriptures*, i.e. the *so-called material and formal sides of the Evangelical principle*, each in its independent worth and title, but both also in their inward inseparable connection.'[2]

While Luther spoke of the 'word of God' as the gospel of justification by faith, whether written or preached, it remains true that 'the identity of the Holy Scriptures with the Word of God is generally assumed by Luther and occasionally expressed in explicit language'.[3] In fact the opening words of his Table Talks run thus: 'That the Bible is God's word and book I prove thus . . . .'[4]

The position is less equivocal with Calvin. Although giving strong emphasis to the doctrine of the *testimonium Spiritus Sancti internum*, Calvin was even more emphatic than Luther concerning the 'formal' principle, the authority of the Scriptures. His main view on the point is found in the opening sections of his *Institutes of the Christian Religion*.[5] There, having shewn the necessity for Scripture to embody the revelation of God, he goes on to deal with its authority. Faith in Scripture as the Word of God is assured by the 'secret testimony of the Spirit'. The Scriptures are declared to be divinely inspired. Herein is the ground of their infallibility and authority.

[1] Yet Luther can say: 'We ought not to criticize, explain, or judge the Scriptures by our mere reason, but diligently, with prayer, meditate thereon, and seek their meaning,' *Table Talks*, iv.

[2] J. A. Dorner, *History of Protestant Theology*, vol. 1, p. 220 (words in italics are in italics in the original). Cf., 'During the preceding period,' writes K. R. Hagenback, referring to the period prior to 1700, 'Protestant theology had been accustomed to call the Sacred Scriptures themselves the Word of God; in the course of the present a distinction was made between the *word of God contained in the Holy Writ* and the Sacred Scriptures.' *Compendium of the History of Doctrine*, vol. 2, p. 406.

[3] G. P. Fisher, *History of Christian Doctrine*, p. 280. Cf. (on the same point), W. P. Patterson, *The Rule of Faith*, p. 405. M. Reu, *Luther and the Scriptures*, pp. 17, 24, 35, 55, 63, 92, etc. Julius Kostlin, *The Theology of Luther*, 2, p. 252 (tr. Charles E. Gray).

[4] *Table Talks*, ad. loc.

[5] *Institutes of the Christian Religion*, bk. 1, chs. vi to x.

In his work, *The Theology of Calvin*, Wilhelm Niesel, makes a statement which calls for comment. Niesel contends that Calvin did not accept either a 'literal inspiration' of Scripture or its 'inerrancy'. He writes: 'There would be no need to add to them (i.e. the arguments of a book by Peter Brunner) if recently the opinion had not been expressed that Calvin taught a literal inspiration of Holy Scripture. . . . We might point out that in the Scriptural exegesis of Calvin there is nothing to suggest a belief in literal inerrancy.'[1] This is, we believe, not a fair statement of the facts.

It may be replied, first of all, that there was no need to set out in any detail the idea of a 'literal interpretation' of the Bible, because there was none other considered, at the time, among the generality of Christians. It was only men like Castellio, the Humanist and Rationalist, against whom Calvin strove so hard to maintain the absolute authority of the Word, who denied it. At the same time it is not really exact to say that Calvin had nothing to teach about a 'literal inspiration' of the Bible, and to conclude, therefore, that he did not believe it. He speaks, for example, of Moses as the amanuensis, or secretary, of God; and he tells us that 'the Holy Spirit so governed the language of Paul that not a superfluous word escaped him'.

Niesel points out that in the chapter in the *Institutes* dealing with the Scriptures, Calvin has nothing to say about the 'method' of inspiration. This is to be admitted, since Niesel means that Calvin does not set out in detail a 'mechanical-dictation' theory. But it is enough for Calvin to insist upon inspiration as extending to the whole Bible; and on that there is little room for doubt.

At the same time, it may be observed, that Niesel notes that there are three places outside the *Institutes* where Calvin writes with definiteness on the subject of the inspiration of the Scriptures. One of these is a comment on 2 Tim. 3. 16, which, as a matter of fact, Niesel does not quote. The passage is given here because it is, we believe, of the greatest importance and does not confirm the dogmatic statement of Niesel.

'In order to uphold the authority of Scripture,' writes Calvin, 'he (i.e. the Apostle) declares that it is *divinely inspired*; for, if it be so, it is beyond controversy that men ought to receive it with reverence. This is a principle which distinguishes our religion from

[1] W. Niesel, *The Theology of Calvin* (tr. Harold Knight), p. 31.

all others, that we know God hath spoken to us, and are fully convinced that the prophets did not speak at their own suggestion, but that, being organs of the Holy Spirit, they only uttered what they had been commissioned from heaven to declare. Whoever then wishes to profit in the Scriptures, let him, first of all, lay down this as a settled point, that the Law and Prophets are not a doctrine delivered according to the will and pleasure of men, but *dictated* by the Holy Spirit.'[1]

Turning back to the *Institutes* we find Calvin saying, 'But since no daily responses are given from heaven, and the Scriptures are the only records in which God has been pleased to consign his truth to perpetual remembrance, the full authority which they ought to possess with the faithful is not recognized, unless they are believed to have come from heaven as directly as if God had been heard giving utterance to them.'[2] Quoting the first half of this passage only, Dr A. Mitchell Hunter of New College, Edinburgh, in his able and accurate study observes; 'The logical concomitant of such a view was the assertion of the inerrancy of Scripture . . . . For the assurance of faith, it was necessary to be able to trust the accuracy of every word of the record. The inerrancy of the letter was the corollary of its exclusive and inclusive inspiration.'[3]

That Calvin then did accept the view held generally by Christians of the period, that the Bible was authoritative and infallible, because its words were given by the Holy Ghost, may be regretted, but it must be allowed. True he did not go into detail regarding the method of the Spirit's action. His concern was, after all, with the fact of inspiration since it was necessary to the very existence of the Reformed faith to proclaim the sole divine authority of Scripture over against the claims of the Roman Church. The time for a full statement of the method of inspiration was not yet.

Warfield, we believe, has correctly stated the position, when he observes that 'The Reformers, though using the language conformable to, or even suggestive of, the theory of dictation, do not formally present that theory, as do the Systematists of the seventeenth century as the fixed ground-work of their doctrine of the

---

[1] *Calvin's Commentaries* (tr. W. Pringle, 1948), ad. loc. Cf., 'in the *dogmatic formulation* of the authority of the Bible he (Calvin) was already entirely under the sway of the orthodox view of literal divine inspiration,' E. Brunner, *Revelation and Reason*, p. 275.
[2] *Institutes*, vol. i, ch. vii, (1), p. 68.
[3] *The Teaching of Calvin* (2nd edition), p. 72.

Scripture'.[1] It will be seen therefore why the Puritans regarded themselves as the interpreters of the Reformers: and why they and the Westminster divines believed themselves to be merely formally stating the doctrine of revelation and the Scripture proclaimed by the great Protestant Fathers of the Church.

(d) A Statement on the Evangelicals

The Puritans certainly identified revelation and the Scriptures. They regarded the words of the Bible as given by the Holy Spirit and therefore infallible and inerrant.

This exactly expresses the understanding of revelation of the Evangelicals of the eighteenth century. For this reason Bishop J. C. Ryle can declare concerning such men as Grimshaw, Venn, Berridge, Harvey and others of their company that 'the spiritual reformers of the last century taught constantly *the sufficiency and supremacy of the Holy Scripture*. The Bible, whole and unmutilated, was their sole rule of faith and practice. They accepted all its statements without question or dispute. They knew nothing of any part of Scripture being uninspired. They never allowed that man has any 'verifying faculty' within him by which Scripture statements may be weighed, rejected or received. They never flinched from asserting that there can be no error in the Word of God; and that when we cannot understand or reconcile some parts of its contents, the fault is in the interpreter and not in the text. In all their preaching they were eminently men of one book. To that book they were content to pin their faith, and by it to stand or fall.'[2]

This brings us to the second task specified at the beginning of this section, the task, that is, of finding someone who can best express the teaching of the Evangelicals. A reading of Bishop Ryle's book just quoted, will show that the Evangelicals were not as avowedly Calvinistic as their Puritan forerunners. They tended to modify, in some measure, what were regarded as the harsher elements of that system. But, at the same time, many of them as convinced Churchmen loyal to the articles of their Church, found it impossible to go on to a full Arminian position.[3] We thus find them, on the one hand repudiating Calvinism, or more accurately, repudiating what was popularly regarded as Calvinism, namely a

---

[1] *The Westminster Assembly and Its Work*, p. 262.
[2] *The Christian Leaders of the Last Century* (1873), p. 26.
[3] Cf., 'The Evangelicalism which developed within the Church of England had more in it of Whitfield than of Wesley. . . .' G. Faber, *Oxford Apostles*, p. 85.

strict necessitarianism. On the other hand, it is equally evident that they were in general agreement with the Reformers. While they considered themselves to be uniting, what they believed to be the truth in the two rival systems of Calvinism and Arminianism, their leanings were certainly towards the former.

It is this consideration, as well as the almost universal acknowledgement of his scholarship, which has led us to select Charles Simeon as

(ii) *The Exponent of their View*

CHARLES SIMEON

It has been said that, what theologians divide preachers unite. There is some justification for this remark, as there is some illustration of it in the message of Charles Simeon. In the 'Preface' to the twenty-one volumes of his works — *Horae Homileticae* — Simeon refuses to be placed in any one party. The true system of the Scriptures, he is persuaded, is not the exclusive possession of either Calvinism or Arminianism. His own position is clear-cut. He 'takes his religion from the Bible and endeavours, as much as possible to speak as that speaks'.[1] The distinctions brought into such sharp opposition in the different systems of theology are in the Scriptures set side by side. The verses, for example, of John 5. 40 and 6. 44 are drawn into antagonism by various writers; but he will not think of the one as opposed to the other.[2] He will dwell with equal pleasure upon both. It is, he thinks, 'better to state these apparent opposite truths in the plain unsophisticated manner of the Scriptures than to enter into scholastic subtleties, that have been invented for the upholding of human systems.'[3]

Such a position, he is aware, will be deemed inconsistent. But he is content to 'rest the vindication of his conduct, simply on the authority and example of the Inspired Writers'.[4] Since God has not given or required the reconciliation of these antitheses, he will

[1] *Works* (*Horae Homileticae*) (3rd edition, 1838), 21 vols., vol. 1, Preface, p. xiv.
[2] Cf., 'Some imagine, that if our salvation, depends wholly on the free and sovereign grace of God, there can be no need for exertion on our part. Others, on the contrary, argue, that if our salvation lie to be effected by means of our own free endeavour, it cannot be dependent on Divine Grace. But these apparently opposite assertions are not made only in different and detached passages, but oftimes in the very same passage,' vol. 10, p. 33.
[3] Vol. 1, Preface, p. xv.
[4] Ibid., cf., 'The Author is no friend of systematizers in Theology, He has endeavoured to derive from the Scriptures alone his views of religion: and to them it is his wish to adhere, with scrupulous fidelity,' 1, Preface, p. xxiii.

not have them imposed. Experience unites what systems divide.
Thus, each knows himself a free moral agent, and, yet, every redeemed man testifies to the fact that he is saved by grace alone
through a faith which is not self-originated.

Simeon 'bitterly regrets that men will range themselves in con-
verting the Inspired Writings into friends and partisans of their
peculiar principles'.[1] Both Calvinists and Arminians are guilty of
attaching more weight to passages which lend colour to their
special views. Simeon believes that there is 'not a determined
votary of either system, if he had been in the company of St Paul,
whilst he was writing his different Epistles, would not have recommended him to alter one or other of his expressions'.[2]

Yet both Calvinists and Arminians are one upon their knees.
There the former acknowledges his responsibility and the latter
his dependence. It is this union of the two systems, evident
in the attitude of prayer, which Simeon wishes to express in his
expositions.[3]

He desires to avoid, too, what he calls 'an ultra-Evangelical
taste',[4] which would read into certain passages the doctrine of
salvation where such was foreign to the author's intention. Where
practical teaching is found, it is to be given in the conviction 'that
lessons of morality are, in their place, as useful and important as
the doctrines of grace'.[5] Simeon is anxious to seek out the plain
meaning of Scripture. He will not read into a passage that which is
not there. Exegesis must never become eisegesis. He remarks: 'We
must not be deterred from speaking of the principles of Christianity, because some despise them as *evangelical*; nor must we omit
the practical parts of our religion, because others discard them as
legal.'[6]

Although Simeon can repudiate certain 'refinements of Calvin
(which) have done harm in the Church',[7] he can still declare
emphatically, 'I am no Arminian.'[8] He speaks with much more
definiteness upon the 'evils of Arminianism'.[9] The fact is that

---

[1] Vol. 1, Preface, p. xxii.
[2] Op. cit., Preface, p. xxiii. Cf., vol. 15, p. 39; vol. 18, p. 436, 494 f.
[3] Cf., 'What both these individuals are upon their knees, it is the wish of the
Author to become in his writings. Hence it is that he expects to be alternatively
approved by both parties, and condemned by both,' op. cit., 1, Preface, p. xxiv.
[4] Op. cit., Preface, p. xxv.
[5] Op. cit., Preface, p. xxv. Cf., 'Some place all their piety in contending for
doctrine, in opposition to morals; and others, in exalting morals, to the disparagement of doctrine,' vol. 14, p. 518.
[6] Vol. 5, p. 65.   [7] Vol. 2, p. 202.   [8] Ibid.   [9] Vol. 18, pp. 493–9.

Simeon really represents the standpoint, in the period, of the Evangelical within the Established Church. Men of such outlook, as late as 1815 were dubbed 'Church-Methodists' by their opponents.[1] Methodists they undoubtedly were in their faith and fervour, but in doctrine they tended more to the side of Calvin. On this account they were more inclined to stress the formal aspect of faith, the objective Word, than those who emphasized the human response. These naturally accentuated the material aspect, the principle of faith. Both the Evangelical Churchman and the Methodist proper were agreed as to the need for the Word and the Spirit, but whereas the former was more anxious to stress the place of the Word, the latter was concerned with the activity of the Spirit. The experience and teaching of Charles Simeon and John Wesley abundantly confirm this observation. It is for this reason that the present and following sections have been entitled, respectively, 'Revelation in the Word through the Spirit,' and, 'Revelation by the Spirit through the Word.'

Charles Simeon can rightly be taken as typical of the doctrine of the Evangelical Churchman of his day. Details of his life do not concern us here, except to say that he was a convinced Churchman.[2] At the same time the sympathies of Simeon extended far beyond the bounds of his own communion. He was as catholic as he was evangelical. He thus represented a wider body of opinion than that of the 'Church-Methodists'. As the most profound scholar amongst them he was naturally regarded as their leader and spokesman. 'If you knew what Simeon's authority and influence were,' wrote Lord Macaulay to his sister, years after Macaulay had graduated from Cambridge in 1822, 'and how they extended from Cambridge to the most remote corners of England, you would allow that his real sway in the Church was far greater than that of any Primate.'[3]

Concerned as we are here with Simeon's general views on revelation, we purpose, as far as possible, to let him speak for himself.

(a) Natural Religion

Although Simeon was supremely a preacher and an expositor, he

---

[1] W. L. Mathieson, *English Church Reform (1815–1840)*, p. 11.

[2] Cf., Series of Sermons preached before the University of Cambridge on the Excellency of Liturgy, vol. 2, Nos. 191, 192, 193, 194. Also *The Churchman's Confession*, vol. 16, pp. 406–21.

[3] Sir G. O. Travelyan, *Life and Letters of Lord Macaulay*, one vol., ed. Silver Library, p. 50 n.

was, no less, a scholar and a theologian. Above all he was a 'Biblical theologian' whose theology may be described as the Theology of the Word of God. It was, as has been indicated, his avowed purpose to discover and declare the meaning and message of the Bible.

It is obvious, however, that no one can expound the Christian Scriptures without some reference to those beyond to whom its revelation has not come, since the books themselves contain such references. How Charles Simeon understood, what is termed, Natural Religion, cannot but be a matter of deep interest.

Beginning with his comments upon Romans, chapter 1, it will be seen that he strongly emphasized the Pauline declaration that the Gentiles are 'without excuse', although not possessing the 'oracles of God'. 'The Gentiles', he observes, 'have in every age had sufficient opportunities of attaining the knowledge of God.'[1] True, the heathen were ignorant of those items 'exclusively made known in the book of revelation', but, in the works of creation they had sufficient evidence of God's existence. Theirs was the possibility of building up an idea of God, and of tracing everything up to a 'First Cause'. God's self-existence and eternity they could have deduced from what their observation could have assured. The excellency of His works should have made them aware of God's power and godhead. Here were the possibilities for the heathen, but they remained possibilities only. They 'did not improve these possibilities aright' and, as a result, they entertained the 'most unworthy conceptions of the Deity'.[2]

By allowing passion to override reason, the heathen failed to observe the signature of God on the spacious universe. Thus were the Gentiles 'altogether ignorant of God and unconcerned about him. They did not regard the notices of him which were visible in all the works of his hands'.[3] Even the most erudite of the ancients were unable to decipher the writings of God upon ordered nature. 'The most learned philosophers could not absolutely determine whether there were a God, or, if there were, whether there were one or many.'[4] And as 'all the principles of the greatest philosophers were involved in doubt and uncertainty, so were they altogether destitute of any sanctifying influences'.[5]

[1] Vol. 15, p. 16.   [2] Vol. 15, p. 17.
[3] Vol. 15, p. 395.   [4] Vol. 13, p. 436.
[5] Vol. 14, p. 164.

Yet while the Gentiles could not read the indications of God in the stars, they could not banish altogether the intimations of Him in their own souls. They were not completely destitute of an inner witness, since 'there is even in the minds of heathens some idea of a superintending Providence'.[1] There are none so ignorant 'as not to acknowledge the existence of a Supreme Being'.[2] He assures us that nothing 'can be more clear, than that the most uncivilized savages have an idea of a Supreme Being, whom they conceive themselves to have offended and whom they wish to propitiate'.[3] The Gentiles, therefore, had light sufficient, but they allowed themselves to be blinded. They have involved themselves in 'wilful ignorance'. Having put out their own spiritual eyes, they are brought to a just judgement and condemnation.[4] It is the witness to God in every heathen heart which becomes the basis of God's dealings with them. 'Belshazzar of old knew little of God, but was judged in the light of what he knew.'[5]

There was a day when God 'winked at' the ignorance of men. But that day has now passed since the night of darkness has gone and the Day Star has arisen. God has given a sure word to which men must take heed. 'He no longer leaves men to indulge their own vain reasonings and empty speculations. He has now revealed his will, which he has made known, not as a deduction from uncertain premises, or as a recommendation of doubtful expediency, but with an authority which supersedes all reasoning, and a plainness that dispels all doubt.'[6]

Simeon seems to teach that it is only within the light of Revelation that natural religion has any significance. It is from this vantage point that the writing of God on the universe becomes clear. Natural religion, apparently, has no practical value for the natural man. Whether on this point Simeon is in line with Calvin, those who have followed the discussion between Brunner and Barth on 'Natural Religion' will be ready with their 'Ja' or their 'Nein'. At all events, Simeon states emphatically that, 'in reading the book of creation, we, by means of our superior advantages, are enabled to see much that was hidden from' the heathen.[7] We only

---

[1] Vol. 14, p. 591.   [2] Vol. 11, p. 325.   [3] Vol. 7, p. 304.
[4] Cf., 'We need only open our eyes and survey the visible creation to be assured of his eternal power and godhead. In this respect the most stupid heathens, in respect of neglecting the worship of him, are without excuse,' vol. 6, p. 126.
[5] Vol. 9, p. 504.   [6] Vol. 14, p. 468.   [7] Vol. 15, p. 19.

rightly read the book of creation in the light of revelation. Thus 'the most ignorant amongst us excels the greatest philosophers of Greece and Rome'.[1]

Whether Simeon regards a direct appeal to nature, in these days, as of value in creating a belief in God, is not easy to decide. He does say that 'the variety and beauty of the things existing in this terraquous globe, all so adapted to their respective offices and uses, and all subservient to one grand design, the glory of their Creator, evince that his wisdom and goodness are equal to his power'.[2] He uses the illustration of the watch,[3] borrowing it, perhaps from Paley, whose works we know he had read,[4] to convince his hearers of the need for a designer. 'In the works of creation', he declares, 'somewhat of God may be discerned.'[5] He thinks there are clear and convincing proofs of God shown in the world. 'It seems astonishing to those who have ever considered the evidences of Christianity,' he says, 'that anyone should hesitate to embrace it or to acknowledge any one of its fundamental truths'.[6]

All this, however, he realizes, the partisans of natural religion will be ready to hear. All this agrees with man's pride in his own reasoning capacities. There is a sense of satisfaction in being able to ascend the ladder of syllogistic constructions and to have reached so worthy a conclusion. But such a result has no practical value. It has no dynamic significance for the life. 'There are those ready to hear somewhat of God as manifested in creation. But of his manifestation in redemption they will not hear.'[7]

In the first sermon preached before his university in 1785 on, 'The Only True and Sufficient Grounds of Glorying,' Simeon asserts that there is a knowledge of God in which to glory. It is not, however, 'the knowledge that there IS a God; for this is common to the evil angels as well as the good. It is not a knowledge of God from the works of creation: for that comes as much under the observation of heathens as Christians. But it is a knowledge of God as revealed in the inspired writings.'[8]

It would therefore appear that it is only for the believing man that natural religion has any real value. Nature must be read from

---

[1] Vol. 15, ibid., cf., pp. 53, 54.
[2] Vol. 6, p. 126, cf., There is sufficient evidence of a Divine agency in the world 'as will be abundantly sufficient to remove all doubts upon the subject of God's existence', vol. 13 p. 226.
[3] Vol. 13, p. 226.   [4] Vol. 6, p. 484.   [5] Op. cit., p. 313.
[6] Vol.13, p. 567.   [7] Vol. 5, p. 234.   [8] Vol. 9, p. 106.

the standpoint of grace. This comes out in a sermon on the 'Christian's Delight in God'. 'In all the works of creation,' he there asserts, 'in all the dispensations of Providence, and in all the wonders of redemption, he sees the glory and excellency of his God.'[1] Yet while the material world, at most, displays 'the *natural* perfections of God', 'not even the angels in heaven can set forth his moral perfections.'[2] This disclosure of God, Christ alone can make and has made.

There are those who have not the ability to follow a chain of argument, who cannot see the cogency of the theistic proofs. But these are not thereby any the less certain of God. There are those 'incapable of entering into abstract views of the Divine perfections: but this representation of the Deity they are as capable of comprehending as the most learned upon earth can be: yea; he knows both the existence, and the omnipotence of the Deity, as much from inward experience, as he possibly can do from the visible creation; because he feels himself to be a living witness of them'.[3]

(b) Reason — Natural and Enlightened

Those who, in the era of Charles Simeon, made natural religion the only reality, and who rejected revelation as both unnecessary and impossible, regarded reason as the only organ by which the religion of nature can come to be known. For them reason was omnipotent. But such a high estimate of the value of reason was refused by Simeon. Although he considered the possession of a rational faculty to be that which raised man above the animal, it is, at the same time, so vitiated by sin that its power is nullified.

'The endowment of reason', says Simeon, 'elevates us far above other creatures. They have instinct: man the capacity to comprehend things of spiritual and eternal import, and an ability to know, to love, to enjoy and to glorify our God.'[4] Religion is therefore a possibility for man as distinguished from the animals. Reason, indeed, is the remnant of the divine in man. It is that which puts him in a category by himself. Rationality is of the very essence of personality, and as such can never be completely eradicated. 'As *rational* beings', he observes, 'we have yet a considerable portion of the Divine image upon us; but as *moral* agents we are very far

[1] Vol. 6, p. 461.
[3] Vol. 5, pp. 502, 503.
[2] Vol. 14, p. 141.
[4] Vol. 6, p. 283.

from original righteousness.'[1] This 'original gift of understanding is our Creator's gift.'[2] And as such it is 'certainly the richest endowment of the human mind'.[3] This means that man can be addressed as a being capable of rational response. Appeal can be made to him as a creature able to appreciate the reason for things. 'Man is a rational being: and though, prone to abuse his reason for his evil ways is capable of judging when sound argument is proposed for his consideration.'[4]

But reason is, however, not the sovereign power the deists conceive it to be. It is now a corrupted organ, and an impotent instrument. Man is totally depraved; vitiated, that is, in the totality of his personality. There is no part which is not touched and tainted by sin. By the 'Fall' all the constituents of man's psychological make-up have been stained and strained. This means that reason can never be entirely disinterested. It is never impartial. Man, in fact, is 'capable of becoming so warped by specious reasonings, and selfish considerations, as to become an agency of Satan'.[5]

It becomes consequently a truism for Simeon that reason is no longer an adequate agent for the apprehension of spiritual truth. This conclusion is inescapable when once its incompetence within its own sphere is seen and acknowledged. Reason, therefore, 'is by no means a certain guide, even in the things which come within its proper and legitimate sphere; it is too frequently biassed in its decisions, even when the person itself is unconscious of any undue influence upon his mind.'[6] Being then an imperfect instrument where it should have been sufficient it follows that reason cannot be adequate in a sphere outside its operations. This is the fallacy of those who style themselves 'rational Christians'.

The truth is that the 'natural man neither does nor can understand spiritual truths'.[7] In a sermon entitled, 'Divine Knowledge Most Desirable,' Simeon stresses the point, which is basic to his whole teaching, that 'Reason is very inadequate to guide our steps'.[8]

---

[1] Vol. 8, p. 144.   [2] Vol. 3, p. 493.
[3] Vol. 11, p. 221.   [4] Vol. 5, p. 470.
[5] Vol. 11, pp. 221, 222. Cf., 'Reason can never suggest motives sufficient to counteract the passions,' vol. 14, p. 61.
[6] Vol. 13, pp. 667, 668. Cf., 'Reason in those things that are *within* its sphere, is a useful, though not an infallible guide . . . beyond its sphere . . . it ceases to be a guide indeed' (vol. 16, p. 121).
[7] Vol. 13, p. 390.
[8] Vol. 7, p. 198. Cf., 'We must confess the insufficiency of reason for the understanding of the sublime truths of Christianity' (vol. 16, p. 238).

We are to be thankful for the light reason sheds upon our ways in the affairs of every day. But it is the first principle of spiritual understanding, according to Simeon, to recognize that in the realm of the spirit 'unenlightened reason is not competent'.[1] Failure to understand this fact is the beginning of error. It was because the deists were unaware of reason's inability that they ended up in the self-deception that they could of themselves know God. But let the proper sphere of reason be observed and all will be well. Simeon says; 'while we acknowledge with gratitude the powers of reason in the investigation of speculative or temporal nature, we must be very jealous of its conclusions in matters that are purely spiritual and practical. In whatever relates to God and the soul, its decisions are apt to be biassed by prejudices, or interest or passion; and it yields, or withholds, assent, not so much according to the weight of evidence adduced, as according to the dispositions which are called forth into exercise'.[2]

This means that divine knowledge is not the discovery of natural reason. In a sermon on the 'Way of Attaining Divine Knowledge', Simeon makes the point that 'The heart is the proper seat of divine knowledge: other knowledge is seated in the head: it is acquired by deep study, and by the force of intellect: nor in whatever degree it is attained, does it at all satisfy and renew the soul. But the truth of God enters the soul'.[3]

For those who would understand the things of God, the reason must become enlightened. The believing man, to be sure, is not given a new faculty for spiritual apprehension. 'A natural man has the same faculties and powers as the spiritual man: his understanding is capable of comprehending common objects, or to investigate the depths of human sciences. . . . A spiritual man has no advantage over him in these respects.'[4] The difference is, however, that the natural man 'does not comprehend or enjoy what is spiritual'.[5]

Yet there is a sense in which the spiritual man does possess another means of knowing. The natural man would have all his reasons clear, he would believe only what he can comprehend. But the spiritual man knows by faith. 'It is not to human learning or to strength of intellect that the discovery of Christ is

[1] Vol. 15, p. 91, cf., vol. 6, p. 265, vol. 10, p. 161, vol. 11, p. 408.
[2] Vol. 13, p. 511.   [3] Vol. 7, p. 10, also pp. 12, 17, 19.
[4] Vol. 14, p. 53.   [5] Ibid.

made, but to faith.'[1] All the learning in the world, Simeon declares, will not give a spiritual understanding, just as a knowledge of the bodily mechanism does not furnish us with any additional corporeal organs.[2]

Does this mean that reason has to be renounced? Is it to be repudiated as a thing of no worth? Simeon will not allow us to think so. True religion does not cripple reason. God has assured to his people, not a 'spirit of delusion', but 'of a sound mind'. The prodigal's return to his father's house, was, he observes, his first proof of his sanity.[3] In all that the gospel declares, he is sure, that 'reason also is no less on our side than revelation'.[4]

Reason and Revelation

What then is the relation of reason to revelation? This is a question dealt with by Simeon in a discourse entitled, 'Means of Attaining True Wisdom.' The main point is that it is reason's office to judge whether revelation is credible. 'The only use of reason as applied to revelation', he tells us, 'is to ascertain whether the revelation, purporting to be from heaven, be indeed of Divine authority, and what is the true import of that revelation in all its parts.'[5] This is no isolated remark, elsewhere there is the same idea: 'reason must judge whether there be sufficient evidence of its (revelation's) divine origin,'[6] and that once satisfied there its activity ends. That which revelation discloses is for faith to receive.[7] Reason can no longer question that which revelation has brought. It is not at liberty to reject that which it cannot fathom or repudiate that which it cannot reconcile. 'If it be thought, that to expect a rational being so to submit to the authority of revelation is to require a sacrifice that is unworthy of him, I answer, that THIS is the very way in which all human knowledge is acquired.'[8] The

---

[1] Vol. 7, p. 507. Cf., 'There is an essential distinction between divine and human knowledge, so is there a very great difference in the ways by which each of them is to be obtained, the one being attainable only by rational investigation, the other only by faith' (vol. 13, p. 245).

[2] Vol. 7, p. 507, cf., p. 609.   [3] Vol. 9, p. 180.

[4] Vol. 14, p. 580.   [5] Vol. 16, p. 121.

[6] Vol. 6, p. 439. Cf., vol. 16, p. 121.

[7] Vol. 6, p. 439 f. Cf., 'Reason will presume to sit in judgement upon the truth of God. But this is not its province. Its proper office is to judge whether the Scriptures are a revelation of God: but when that is ascertained, faith is then to apprehend whatever God has spoken: and the highest dictates of reason is, to submit ourselves to God with the simplicity and teachableness of a little child' (vol. 16, p. 358).

[8] Vol. 6, p. 439.

child must first accept on trust, although later he discovers that
what he accepted agrees with experience: 'so receiving the mysterious truths of God, we first take them on the authority of our
Divine Teacher; then, gradually, we find that they correspond with
our own experience, we see that they are precisely as they have
been presented to us.'[1]

Simeon however will not have it that there can be any ultimate
disharmony between reason and revelation. Paul spoke to Agrippa
the words of truth and soberness, and what he declared he regarded
as the very truth of God. But he spake with the conviction that
'unbiassed reason must approve of all that he taught'.[2]

This is a point Simeon labours to establish in a discourse before
his university, 'An Appeal to Men of Wisdom and Candour.'
'There is no part of religion (he is referring, of course, to the
Christian revelation) repugnant to reason, nor any part which
enlightened reason must not highly approve.'[3] The idea is more
strongly emphasized in an earlier section of the same sermon:
'though revealed religion is neither founded on human reason, nor
makes its appeal to it; yet it is perfectly consistent with reason and
approves itself to the judgement of everyone whose mind is enlightened by the Spirit of God.'[4]

Yet the highest knowledge of God that man possesses 'is always
negative'.[5] We have no positive knowledge of Him at all. We call
Him, Spirit, but we know as little what Spirit is now, as the day
we were born.[6]

The teaching of Simeon, under this heading, which has been
illustrated from his works, may, then, be briefly summarized. He
regards reason in its 'proper sphere' as uncertain, outside of that
sphere, in the realm of the spiritual, as useless. It can assure the
credibility of revelation, but it is helpless to secure its contents.
The ideas of religion are not contradictory of revelation, although
revelation is not discovered by reason. To gain true wisdom a man
must become 'a fool'. His final position is, that if we would have
divine knowledge we must have; 'First, a consciousness of the

[1] Ibid.
[2] Vol. 14, p. 580. Cf., 'The truth of God though elevated above reason, is in
perfect accordance with reason' (vol. 15, p. 252).
[3] Vol. 16, p. 230.
[4] Op. cit., p. 229. Cf., 'You do not condemn reason because some pervert it to
the support of error and assume to themselves the title *rational* Christians' (vol.
16, p. 422).
[5] Vol. 3, p. 373.   [6] Vol. 16, p. 194.

weakness and fallibility of our reason in the things relating to God: and, secondly, a willingness to submit our reason to the teachings of God's word and Spirit.'[1]

(c) Revelation and the Scriptures

Natural reason cannot find out God; this, then, is the burden of Simeon's message. Even the very wisest of the philosophers of Greece and Rome could not gain any real knowledge of God and of the things that make for religion. Of God's existence and essence they could speak only hesitatingly.[2] They had no confident verdict about the immortality of the Soul; what 'faint conceptions' they had, were mere matters of conjecture — 'of surmise or opinion only, not of knowledge'.[3] Such uncertain views could never become a creative creed; they were powerless to move the soul or change the life. They had no message for the sin-oppressed soul. 'Go even to the wisest philosophers of Greece and Rome', he bids us, 'and see how vain were their expedients for pacifying a guilty soul, or purifying a polluted soul.'[4]

The position is, then, that unless God comes forth in self-revelation there can be no knowledge of Him. Divine knowledge is not a discovery by man but a disclosure from God. 'We know nothing of God or his ways, any further than he sees fit to reveal himself to us.'[5] Simeon bases the necessity for revelation upon the fact of man's inability to come to any meaningful knowledge of God.[6] A redeemed understanding of Him must be a revealed understanding of Him. The saving truth of God must remain forever in the realm of impenetrable obscurity unless God draws aside the curtain and comes forth in self-disclosure upon the stage of human history. The necessity of revelation arises from the fact that 'no man could possibly know God's will, unless God should be pleased to communicate information respecting it from above'.[7] It is the assurance of Simeon that this required revelation has been made. There has been an unveiling of the divine plan and purpose: 'we are not left to the uncertain deductions of reason.'[8]

---

[1] Vol. 16, p. 121.   [2] Vol. 16, p. 194.
[3] Vol. 19, p. 11.   [4] Vol. 4, p. 561.
[5] Vol. 6, p. 94.
[6] Cf., 'Divine truth is manifestly beyond our comprehension; and we must receive it simply on the authority of God' (vol. 16, p. 194).
[7] Vol. 5, p. 149.   [8] Vol. 1, p. 1.

The Revelation Confirmed

This revelation, according to Simeon, has all the marks of authenticity. He thinks that there are good reasons for studying the evidences of our religion.[1] An understanding of the facts concerning the faith will deliver us from becoming an easy prey to scepticism. The infidel's effort to shake our faith will be vain and impotent if the reasons for our religion were taught from early youth.[2] If indeed the unbeliever were to give impartial consideration to these evidences he could not but acknowledge their cogency and see the truth of what they are adduced to approve. The tragedy is, however, that he cannot be thus impartial and consequently he rejects the truth on the pretence that proof is wanting. 'Infidels pretend that their doubts arise from want of evidence: but they in reality arise from an indisposition of heart to weigh with candour the evidence before them.'[3]

Miracles and prophecies Simeon regards as the supreme proofs of the truth of Christianity as the revealed religion. 'It has pleased God', he says, 'to give us every evidence of the truth of our religion, that the most scrupulous mind could desire. The proofs arising from prophecies and miracles, are such as carry irresistible conviction to every candid enquirer.'[4]

Prophecy, he believes to be the most satisfactory evidence of the truth of Christianity. This is not because of the mere number of things foretold, but because of their content. Prophecies are not the result of lucky guesses or of human insight. They are in fact contrary to all human expectations.[5] They are of such a nature that human wisdom could not have devised them nor human power accomplished them.[6] Yet in number the prophecies are not meagre. It is by reason of its 'fulness', 'minuteness' and 'consistency' that prophecy can be regarded as a 'sure word'.[7] Simeon boldly states that the 'declarations of the prophets were so numerous and minute that a history of our Lord might be compiled from them, fuller, in many respects, than is contained in the Evangelists'.[8]

---

[1] Vol. 3, p. 327.   [2] Ibid.
[3] Vol. 14, p. 221.   [4] Op. cit., p. 351.
[5] Vol. 8, pp. 247–8.   [6] Vol. 18, p. 487.
[7] Vol. 20, p. 323.

[8] Vol. 14, p. 221. Cf., 'Every minute circumstance relative to the Gospel has been foretold by one or other of the prophets; in so much, that, if we understood perfectly every part of the prophetic writings, we might extract from them as complete an account of the person and work and offices of Christ . . . as from the New Testament' (vol. 14, p. 189).

No man, he asserts, can remain an unbeliever concerning the truth of Christianity if he examines the prophecies with a candid mind.[1] The agreement of event with prophecy will induce the strongest conviction. Anyone who sees how prediction is followed by fulfilment, sometimes after the lapse of a period, when none of those who had heard the declaratory word were alive, and could not therefore have engineered events as a pious fraud, must be convinced of the truth of Christianity.[2] The observation of fulfilled prophecy cannot be lightly set aside. It is the divine attestation of the genuineness of the gospel. It sets the seal of God upon it. Simeon therefore urges the study of prophecy, among other reasons, for the sake of its evidential value. Even if 'intellectual amusement' were our only desire, he tells us, 'we can scarcely conceive a richer feast to the mind than a study of prophecy.'[3]

Prophecy is to be understood as the unfolding of the purpose of God.[4] It is consequently not of human devising. It 'springs not from man's conjectures but from a divine revelation. The prophets, so far from being the source of their own predictions, could not even understand them, any further than they were illuminated by that very Spirit by whose immediate agency they were inspired'.[5] It is God Who has predicted and fulfilled. Thus prophecy is a proof that 'Christianity must be of divine origin'.[6]

For all that, the value of the evidence of prophecy is in some sense limited. The ability to compare event with fulfilment is not with everyone. It is a hard and hazardous task. Simeon thinks therefore that the proof from miracles is more direct and conclusive. Christ's claim is vindicated by both prophecies and miracles. But the 'completion of prophecy was indeed a decisive proof of his Messiahship to those who could compare the prophecies with the events; but that was a long and arduous process; a work which a few were competent to undertake: whereas the working of miracles afforded a short, compendious, and irresistible evidence, to the eyes of all who beheld them'.[7]

Simeon defines miracles as 'works contrary to the common

---

[1] Vol. 20, p. 322.
[2] Vol. 14, p. 202, cf., p. 300.
[3] Vol. 20, p. 327.
[4] Vol. 3, p. 243.
[5] Vol. 14, p. 327. Cf., The prophets were instructed 'by the immediate inspiration of God' (vol. 8, p. 759, cf., vol. 20, pp. 148, 151).
[6] Ibid.
[7] Op. cit., p. 224.

course of nature, works which God alone is able to perform'.[1] He is
certain that the miracles of Christ have evidential value. Christ
Himself appealed to them in this way.[2] They are to be regarded as
testimonies to His divine mission.[3] They are intended for us to be
acted parables, vivid demonstrations of God's saving mercies.
They 'shadow forth the spiritual blessings which he came to
bestow'.[4]

The miracles of the gospel are to be taken then as God's more
dramatic authentication of His revelation since it is not possible to
suppose that He would permit the working of miracles to establish
falsehood.[5] It is noted that God did allow Pharoah's magicians to
imitate some of the miracles of Moses. This leads Simeon to
qualify, in some measure, the stress he has placed upon the evidence of miracles. 'I am not prepared to say', he writes, 'that a
miracle is of itself, independent of all its circumstances, a sufficient
proof that the person performing it comes from God.'[6] There are
impostures. There are those who can work wonders. But the
miracles of Jesus are beyond doubt not of this type. He is such an
One Who could only work that which is good.[7]

Since miracles have ceased they can be appealed to now only on
the basis of their record. 'We cannot work miracles in confirmation
of doctrine but we appeal to the miracles by which it was confirmed
in the days of Christ and of his apostles.'[8] The record of the
miracles he believes to be 'not one whit less satisfactory than
ocular demonstrations'.[9] This point is made on more than one
occasion. 'But when the miracles of our Lord were recorded by
persons who were eyewitnesses of the same, and these records
were speedily circulated amongst myriads who also had been spectators of them; and when in these writings an appeal is made to the
bitterest enemies of our Lord, who would have been glad to contradict these assertions of the Evangelists on the supposition that
they would have been disproved; these records come down to us
with an evidence not at all inferior to ocular demonstration: and if

[1] Vol. 14, p. 223.
[2] Op. cit., p. 181, also, p. 376. Cf., 'That the miracles that Jesus did, were
intended to convince the Jews of his Divine mission, and that they were sufficient for that end, is manifest from the appeal which he himself made to them
in this very view' (vol. 14, p. 224).
[3] Vol. 13, p. 492.
[4] Vol. 14, 181, cf., p. 291 and vol. 13, 368, also, p. 373.
[5] Vol. 14, p. 224.   [6] Vol. 13, p. 367.
[7] Op. cit., p. 368, cf., vol. 14, pp. 367, 368.
[8] Vol. 13, p. 466.   [9] Vol. 14, pp. 224, 225.

any man rejects the testimony which is thus sanctioned both by friends and enemies, he is wilfully blind, and would reject any other evidence that could be given him.'[1]

Yet there is a demonstration of the truth of Christianity which has come to us, but was not given to those who witnessed the miracles. This particular proof is the resurrection of our Lord from the dead. 'The divine authority of the Christian religion', he declares, 'was chiefly to be proved by the resurrection. Hence our Lord gave his Disciples the most unquestioned evidence of the resurrection during the space of forty days previous to his ascension into heaven.'[2]

Simeon makes mention of other proofs by which Christianity is authenticated. He declares that 'no species of evidence is wanting to confirm it'.[3] He refers to the doctrines and morality of the gospel as beyond anything the greatest philosophers could invent.[4] There is further a compelling harmony and unity in all that which has been revealed. Of the several references to the conversion of Paul, he says, 'It seems to have been intended by God as a strong evidence of the truth of our religion.'[5]

Simeon does not ignore the place of internal evidences. 'It may well be supposed', he says, 'that any revelation purporting to come from God, should in addition to all external evidences, have internal proofs also of its divine original.'[6] The fitness of the revelation for fallen men and the gospel which gives all the glory to God are such convincing evidences.[7]

Simeon divides religion into two kinds, the theoretical and the practical. 'In the term *theoretical*, I include', he says, 'everything that is necessary to prove the truth of Christianity: and under the term *practical*, whatever is required of those who embrace it. To understand the theoretical part is desirable: to perform the practical is necessary. The two kinds, however, are not necessarily united: the theoretical may exist where the practical is disregarded; and the practical may exist, where the theoretical is unknown. Thousands of pious souls have neither time nor talent for collating MSS, or for weighing the evidences that may be adduced in favour of particular hypotheses: and to say that these cannot be religious, because they are wanting in critical acumen, would be as

---

[1] Vol. 13, p. 66. [2] Op. cit., p. 162.
[3] Vol. 18, p. 487. [4] Vol. 15, pp. 471, 499.
[5] Vol. 1, pp. 315, 316. [6] Vol. 14, p. 352.
[7] Vol. 15, p. 83.

absurd as to say a man cannot be honest, because he has not sufficient knowledge of the laws to be a judge.'[1] The good results
which Christianity produces must indicate the validity of the
faith. With regard to this proof he comments, 'If this be not a
proper test of our religion, whereby shall the superior excellency
of Christ be known? If the Bible produce no better effects than the
Koran, I do not hesitate to say that it is no better than the Koran.'[2]

Both external and internal evidences are, then, to be given their
full weight. If this is done, Simeon is certain that the truth of
Christianity cannot be long denied. He thus concludes, 'The divine
authority of our religion is fully established. Its external evidences
demonstrate God to be the author; nor are the internal evidences
less convincing.'[3]

Revelation and Mystery

Simeon was well aware of the reiterated dictum of the deists
that, where mystery begins, religion ends.[4] He meets the contention in a manner reminiscent of Butler. He points to the presence of
mystery within our own being and without our own selves.[5] As far
as nature is concerned, "'Tis mystery all'. He therefore boldly
declares 'that Christianity is altogether a mystery'.[6] The central
truth of the gospel, Christ crucified, is the greatest mystery of all.[7]
Simeon will not have Christianity reduced to a set of rational
propositions. Its majesty lies in its mysteries. In a sermon on the
passage, Great is the mystery of godliness, he makes the comment,
'It has often been said by infidels, that, where mystery begins,
religion ends. But if this were true there would be no uniformity
or consistency in the works of God. All his works of both creation
and providence are full of mysteries: there is not any one substance of which we know *all* the properties, or any one event, for
which we can assign *all* the reasons. If there were nothing in
religion above the comprehension of man it would afford a strong
presumption that our religion was not from heaven: for why should
it be revealed if man could have devised it without revelation?'[8]

That Christianity contains mystery is, then, both natural and

[1] Vol. 9, pp. 5, 6.   [2] Ibid.
[3] Vol. 20, p. 250.   [4] Vol. 2, p. 105, also vol. 18, p. 250.
[5] Cf., 'On whatever side we look we are surrounded by mysteries; yea, we are
a mystery to ourselves. The works of creation, and providence, and redemption
are all mysterious' (vol. 15, p. 456).
[6] Vol. 2, p. 105.   [7] Vol. 18, p. 210.   [8] Op. cit., p. 504.

necessary. It follows from the fact that man's reason is unable to
reach the saving truths of the gospel and that the doctrines that are
to be most surely believed have been revealed by God. The presence of mystery in things which concern our redemption follows
from analogy with the things of creation.

The mystery which around us and within us lies has to be
accepted. Those within Christianity should be likewise accepted as
part of the divine order. 'There are many things revealed to us in
the Gospel which are contrary to any generally prevailing opinion
of mankind . . . . In order to understand them aright we must receive them simply on the authority of God; and conclude them to
be true, because he has revealed them.'[1]

Revelation within the Record

For Simeon, the revelation which God has so graciously given
and so certainly authenticated is contained within the Scriptures.
He regards the Bible, not as the permanent possibility of revelation,
but as its permanent actuality. Objectively, and in themselves,
they are the word of God. Although, as we shall see later, Simeon
makes much of the inner witness of the Spirit, he never, like
Maurice, thinks of the Bible becoming the 'word of God' in the
context of experience. Simeon, therefore, considers the revelation
and the record to be for all practical purposes one and the same.
God's early revelation to man was, he observes, 'merely oral,' but it
was preserved in a guarded tradition until it could be put in
writing. He considers the Mosaic era as of special significance
because God then 'for the first time vouchsafed to man a *written
record*'.[2] The continuation of the revelation in an oral tradition he
regarded as impracticable. 'If there were no written documents of
the things transmitted,' he says, 'we could not have been sure that
our information respecting them was correct; seeing that many
variations must inevitably happen in traditions handed down
through so many succeeding ages.'[3]

The result therefore for Simeon is that, because the Bible contains the revelation of God we are confined to it as providing the
source and limiting the scope of our knowledge of God. 'Of God
we know nothing, but from his word.'[4] This does not mean that
other books are utterly useless. They have their place; but their

---

[1] Vol. 14, pp. 165, 166.   [2] Vol. 15, p. 452.
[3] Vol. 14, p. 224.   [4] Vol. 6, p. 438.

value depends upon the measure of their accord with the Scriptures. In so far as they are borrowed rays from the Bible, they will be of help. 'From human writings', he observes, 'you may learn *something* of God, but from the Scriptures alone can you acquire such knowledge of him as it is your privilege and duty to possess.'[1] This means for Simeon that the Bible, *in toto*, is to be regarded as the Word of God. It is throughout an inspired volume, 'with nothing superfluous or defective,' and, consequently 'may be wholly and exclusively, called "the Word of God" '.[2]

For such a doctrine of Scripture certain assumptions are necessary and from it certain conclusions follow.

With regard to the first, a very strict view of inspiration must be held. In this connection Simeon had no hesitations. He consequently declares that the Bible is the Word of God written by men 'who wrote only what God by his Spirit dictated'.[3] The 'whole Scripture was as much written by the finger of God, as the laws were, which he inscribed on the two tables of stone, and delivered to his servant Moses'.[4] In a reference to the apostolic writings, he says that the Holy Spirit kept the apostles 'from error of every kind: so that which they have spoken must be regarded as the Word of God, no less than if their very words had been dictated from above, yea, in all that they revealed, they were kept from error of every kind and every degree'.[5]

It must not be supposed, however, that Simeon regarded the Biblical writers as passive instruments in the hands of God. He has no 'docetic' doctrine of inspiration. The activity of the writer was not lost in the action of God. Whilst the matter of the biblical writers was inspired of God, and in the manner of their expression 'they were preserved by the same Spirit from any mistake and error', they still 'express themselves in their own way'.[6]

Simeon's conception of revelation as contained within the divinely-inspired Scriptures leads to some very definite conclusions. They are, first of all, to be received as an unerring and infallible body of revealed truths.[7] As such they are to be believed implicitly.[8] Because the Scripture contains 'the *whole* revealed will

---

[1] Vol. 5, p. 35.   [2] Vol. 17, p. 497.   [3] Ibid.
[4] Ibid.   [5] Vol. 14, p. 216.   [6] Vol. 19, p. 72.
[7] Cf., vol. 3, pp. 172, 385; vol. 4, p. 7; vol. 8, p. 122; vol. 9, p. 341, etc. 'There is no reason for questioning the divine authority of the sacred oracles, for God is as immutable in his word, as he is in his nature' (vol. 15, p. 56).
[8] Vol. 3, p. 230, cf. The Scriptures must be 'received implicitly in whatever they declare and be obeyed in whatever they command' Sermon on Christ's

of God',[1] it must be taken as the one rule of faith and practice.[2] Simeon constantly refers to the Bible the words of Isaiah 12. 3. It is a 'well of salvation from which we are to draw water with joy'.[3] It is a 'sure directory'.[4] It is a 'kind of map, whereby we find our way through this tractless desert and arrive safely at our Father's house'.[5]

In a comment on the parable of the Rich Man and Lazarus he notes that the former in his anxiety for his brethren was reminded that they had the Scriptures. They are the guide to heaven wherein 'there is no instruction wanted, which is not contained in the sacred volume, and conveyed, too, in the most edifying manner. Its warnings are most solemn, its invitations most earnest, its expostulations most affectionate, its promises most enlarged'.[6]

In a sermon on Psalm 138. 2, he tells us that God honours His word above everything else, and 'magnifies it above all his name'. A little concerning God may be gathered from creation, but 'the mysterious transactions' which took place in the 'council-chamber of the Most High', are made known only here.[7]

The last sermon but one of the *Horae Homileticae* is entitled, 'The Perfection and Sanctity of the Holy Scriptures.' Here the point is made that the Mosaic dispensation ended with the injunction, 'ye shall not add unto the word which I command you, neither shall ye diminish ought from it.' In like manner the Christian dispensation is concluded with the solemn declaration that nothing is to be added to or taken from the things written in the book, not merely the book of Revelation itself, for 'as this book completes and closes the sacred Canon, I consider the warning as extending to the whole of the New Testament Scriptures'.[8] The Bible is the perfect revelation of God within which His glorious perfections and eternal purposes are set forth. 'It is at our peril to change or modify any part of that system which God has revealed in his word.'[9]

It need not be thought that God should have given specific rules for every possible case, for then 'the Scriptures would have been so voluminous, that a whole life of study would not be sufficient to

Appeal to the Scriptures, preached before the Society of Scripture Readers, Dublin, 1830.

[1] Vol. 3, p. 516 (cf., vol. 6, p. 152).   [2] Vol. 2, p. 334; vol. 3, p. 190.
[3] Vol. 6, p. 152; vol. 7, p. 560, etc.   [4] Vol. 6, pp. 304, 366.
[5] Vol. 8, p. 421.   [6] Vol. 12, p. 565.
[7] Vol. 6, p. 437.   [8] Vol. 21, p. 278.
[9] Vol. 21, p. 280.

make us acquainted with them'.[1] By supplying us with 'a few general principles, and embodying them in living examples, God has given us all the information we need'.[2]

The Reformers, he declares, stood for the authority of Scripture. But many at the present time instead of 'submitting to be taught of God' adopt their own sentiments. Simeon urges his hearers and readers 'to regard the Scriptures' with the veneration that is due to them.[3]

It will be clear from what has been said that Simeon makes the relation between Christ and the Scriptures to be an absolute one. 'The body of Scripture', he writes, 'is penetrated by a soul, which though invisible, really pervades every part; and that soul is Christ.'[4] Yet we are not to think of Christ as imprisoned within the pages of a book. Christ lives for us, in and through the Word. He observes, 'in ascribing our salvation to the knowledge of the Scriptures we do not derogate from the honour of Christ; since it is only by revealing his work and offices to us, and leading us to depend upon him, that they become effectual for this blessed end. But at the same time we must put an honour on the Scriptures to which no other book has the smallest claim. Other books may be the channels for conveying divine knowledge; but the Bible alone is the fountain from which it flows.'[5]

The Bible is, however, no mere record of past events. It is not simply a dated document, an account of transactions passed. 'The history of the Jews is not a mere record of times and persons far distant from us, but a display of the Divine procedure towards others, as a pledge of a similar procedure towards us.'[6] Any occasional declaration, any insignificant ordinance, any personal promise can come livingly into the present and be God's word for us. 'There is not a precept that is not binding upon us as on those to whom it was delivered: there is not a threatening, at which *we* have not cause to tremble; nor a promise, on which *we* are not warranted to rely if only we believe in Jesus Christ.'[7]

(d) The Scriptures and the Spirit

Although Charles Simeon regarded the Bible as a book of divinely communicated truths to be accepted and believed just

---

[1] Vol. 21, ibid.   [2] Op. cit., p. 279.   [3] Op. cit., p. 282.
[4] Vol. 16, p. 481.   [5] Vol. 19, p. 69.   [6] Vol. 6, p. 64.
[7] Vol. 17, p. 409.

because they were revealed, it is not to be concluded that he considered faith to be mere assent to these truths. He states emphatically that to believe in Christ is 'much more than a bare assent'.[1] If there were one point more than another emphasized by Simeon, it was this; mere speculative knowledge of the Scriptures is useless. The words are almost a refrain throughout the 2,526 sermons. The references given below, although by no means complete, will give some impression of how constantly the point was made.[2]

The acceptance of doctrine was not therefore sufficient of itself. Indeed Simeon repudiates such a view as mere 'notional' faith as of no value to the saving of the soul. 'The mere report, as contained in the written word, is not of *itself* sufficient to bring to a saving knowledge of these sublime truths: Christ must be revealed *in* us, as well as *to* us.'[3] It is, as a matter of fact, just here that Simeon finds the distinction between the so-called 'orthodox' and the Evangelical.[4] The former like to pass by the 'name of rational Christians'.[5] For Simeon, however, the true seat of religion is the heart not the head. It is not primarily the assent of the human mind but the activity of the Divine Spirit.

Simeon emphasizes again and again that without the inner working of the Spirit, the Bible is a 'dead letter'. 'Even the Scriptures themselves will be a "dead letter" and "a sealed book" unless the Spirit of God open the understanding to understand them.'[6]

Simeon consequently gives an important place to the work of the Spirit. No man is to imagine that faith in the Bible, as such, is of saving value. If the question is asked, Can such faith save him? The answer returned by Simeon is an unhesitating, No. This is brought out in an important passage in a sermon in volume 10; 'First, then, it is not the word that does good; but the Holy Ghost by the Word. If the word wrought anything, its operations would be uniform and universal, or, at least, in a much greater degree than it is now, and people would be benefited by it in proportion

---

[1] Vol. 13, p. 358.

[2] Vol. 4, p. 142; vol. 5, pp. 5, 7, 151, 312; vol. 6, p. 108, 'A speculative knowledge of the Gospel is possessed by many who have no personal interest in it, and no desire after its blessings . . . .'; vol. 6, pp. 176, 261, 448; vol. 7, p. 12; vol. 8, pp. 152, 445; vol. 9, p. 238; vol. 11, pp. 42, 60, 70, 149, 153, 344; vol. 12, p. 313; vol. 13, pp. 315, 447, 496, 540, 541, 568; vol. 14, pp. 350, 549; vol. 15, pp. 54, 242, etc., etc.

[3] Vol. 6, p. 94.

[4] Vol. 20, p. 524.

[5] Vol. 20, p. 146.

[6] Vol. 5, p. 373, also vol. 6, p. 309; vol. 7, p. 506; vol. 8, p. 30; esp. vol. 16, pp. 450–61, 477–81; vol. 17, p. 500; vol. 18, p. 319.

to the strength and clearness of the intellect . . . . Next, it is not the knowledge of the word that benefits, but the knowledge of Christ in the record. We might be able to repeat the whole Bible and perish at the last. Christ must be known by us; and that not speculatively but experimentally.'[1]

It is not, then, to be imagined by anyone that because God has revealed His secrets in the written word, 'that we need no further revelation of it to the soul.'[2] All need this divine influence to improve the revelation already given.[3] A mere critical study of the Bible cannot give spiritual understanding. Some may burn the midnight oil and labour all the day long to investigate the meaning of the letter of the Scripture, but such a knowledge may leave the person entirely ignorant of God.[4]

For Simeon then, a knowledge of God comes by the Word and the Spirit.[5] Anyone who has studied Simeon's works cannot fail to see that he made much of the place of the Spirit in the things of the soul. There is hardly a page in all the twenty-one volumes of the *Horae Homileticae* in which there is not some reference to the Holy Spirit. So abundant are these allusions that it comes as a surprise to learn of the criticism that 'Charles Simeon and his friends said little of the Paraclete'.[6] It is worthy of note that at the very time Irving was proclaiming that Pentecostal miracles were being revived in London, Simeon was giving his balanced discourses in St Mary's on 'The Offices of the Holy Spirit'.

It was Simeon's conviction that the Word without the Spirit was of no saving value. He illustrates his point like this: an object which is obscure may be made visible either by reflecting stronger light upon it, or by strengthening the organs of vision. God's methods of instructing us are analogous to these, 'in that he brings home with power to our souls the truths which we hear, and inclines our hearts to embrace them.' The telescope and the microscope, he observes, make no difference either to the organ or to the object of

[1] Vol. 10, pp. 284, 285. Cf., 'A man might commit to memory the whole Bible, and yet not understand one spiritual truth in it, if he trusted in his own spiritual powers, instead of looking up to God for the teaching of his Spirit' (vol. 7, p. 7).
[2] Vol. 5, p. 169.
[3] Vol. 5, p. 149, cf., vol. 21, pp. 232, 233.
[4] Vol. 6, p. 309, 374; vol. 7, p. 562, etc.
[5] Cf., 'In the Scriptures nothing is wanting. It is God's rod of strength to quicken and to sanctify . . . . Yet all that is wanting to render the word effectual is to get it applied to our hearts by the Spirit of God' (vol. 12, p. 565, cf., vol. 17, p. 506, etc., etc.).
[6] See H. C. G. Moule, *Charles Simeon*, p. 82.

vision. 'So there is no difference in the truths which are heard by different persons, or in the capacity of those by whom they are perceived: the difference is in the manner in which the truths are presented to the mind: and if we, by instruments of human contrivance, are able thus to bring to the sight of men things that are invisible to the naked eye, we may well suppose that God is able to bring home to the souls of men truths which the unassisted mind is unable to comprehend.'[1]

The Spirit and 'Enthusiasm'

By his continual insistence upon the necessity for the illumination of the Holy Spirit, Simeon had to guard his hearers and readers against the excesses of 'enthusiasm'. He was well aware of its evil, on the one hand, whilst, on the other hand, he realized how easy it was to go to the other extreme and so to repudiate any warmth and zeal in religion as to make it a cold rational affair. To this extreme, he believed, had gone those who styled themselves 'rational Christians'. 'A supreme delight in God is by many deemed enthusiasm, whereas the religion that exists in speculation, theory, and forms, is supposed to be exclusively entitled to the appellation of *Rational*.'[2]

To fall into the excesses of enthusiasm was the one fear of many throughout our period. To avoid this pitfall they seemed to find it necessary to reject altogether any doctrine of the inner working of the Spirit.[3] They limited His activity to the apostles in whom He worked miracles and to whom He communicated divine truths. Since this body of doctrine has now been given it was the business of the modern Christian to give it his assent and not to look for any extraordinary action of the Spirit. Consequently, as Simeon notes, any reference to the divine influence of the Spirit was considered as enthusiastic and absurd.[4] Any warmth in religion was therefore regarded with loathing. Any strong expression of faith or burning

---

[1] Vol. 10, p. 274.

[2] Vol. 4, p. 10.

[3] Cf., 'The error of modern times *within* the pale of faith is a spiritual error, as well as that without: I mean enthusiasm: So clearly is this such that we are continually suffering our jealousy and fear of it to keep our tempers back from that spirituality, to which belongs the kingdom of heaven', J. Miller, *The Divine Authority of the Holy Scripture*, p. 45.

[4] Cf., 'They believe that the Holy Ghost was given formerly to the Church for the working of miracles; but they will not believe that he is continued to the Church for the purpose of guiding, comforting and sanctifying the soul,' vol. 20, p. 405.

manifestation of devotion was written off as enthusiastic deceit.[1]

But however much those whose hearts have been strangely warmed are derided as deluded, Simeon is convinced that there is a real place for enthusiasm. Where earthly things are the objects of pursuit, he observes, the affections are not only approved but applauded, 'but when the soul is attracted by heavenly objects, the livelier emotions of the mind are deemed enthusiasm.'[2] This is for Simeon an impossible position. As he sees it, a religion without warmth is a religion without worth. It may be orthodox, but it cannot be operative. He therefore declares that 'Lukewarmness in religion is as odious to God as an utter neglect of it'.[3] There must be a true zeal like that for which Phineas was commended.[4]

The Sadducees of old 'ridiculed as enthusiasm' whatever opinion was contrary to theirs.[5] Even the joyous exuberances of the children singing their glad Hosannas was disapproved as the effusion of weak and uninformed minds. Those who would give vigorous voice to their faith and praise are regarded as likewise deficient. A religious zeal is however a necessity of true faith. Without it religion becomes a form without a life and worship an association without an inspiration, and Christian living a duty without a devotion. Of our Lord it was said, His zeal consumed Him, 'but remember', adds Simeon, 'it was *himself* it consumed, not others.'[6] Therefore, 'a man's own heart is the first sphere for the exercise of zeal.'[7]

Such an attitude, he believes, will not be understood by those who are strangers to all spiritual joys.[8]

While, however, Simeon insists on the place of the feelings in religion, he is far from giving sanction to the eccentricities and contentions of many who suppose themselves inspired of the Spirit. In a series of sermons on David dancing before the Lord, he says, 'I will not say that the body is not to participate in the emotions of the mind . . . . But there is a delicacy and refinement in Christian feelings, so the less they savour of the *animal* the better.'[9] Feelings are not therefore to be undervalued. Yet they are not to

---

[1] Cf., 'The world may represent us as enthusiastics because we believe that in the end all will be well,' vol. 5, p. 297. 'Some represent the preaching of God's anger upon sin as nothing better than gloomy enthusiasm,' vol. 5, p. 201. 'I cannot wonder that the world should cry out against the people of the Lord as enthusiastic and absurd . . . .' vol. 6, p. 37.

[2] Vol. 13, p. 68.   [3] Vol. 7, p. 250.   [4] Vol. 6, pp. 225–35.
[5] Vol. 11, p. 442.   [6] Vol. 3, p. 523.   [7] Vol. 14, p. 499.
[8] Vol. 11, p. 501.   [9] Vol. 3, p. 251.

be taken as the criteria whereby the existence of true religion is to be judged. If there were not more substantial evidences of piety than passing feelings the result would be perpetual uncertainty. He makes the point that it is 'not by vain conceits, or transient impressions that we judge, but by practical results .... Beware then how you substitute the reveries of enthusiasm for the holiness of the Gospel'.[1] The truth and the genuineness of our faith and profession are to be judged, not by occasional feelings but by our abiding taste, by a life redeemed and regulated by the word of God.[2]

For those who deny the influence of the Spirit, regarding such a doctrine as opening the way for all sorts of enthusiastic excess, Simeon retorts, 'It would be enthusiasm to tell men that their own reason is sufficient for every purpose of spiritual instruction.'[3]

Simeon did not wish to escape the opprobrious title of 'enthusiast' by denying the inner workings of the Spirit. The rational Christian might make the charge, but he could retort with a *Tu Quoque*. It would seem a far greater evidence of vain conceit to regard religion as the discovery of man's own unaided reason. He is ready to give place to the Spirit, and if he is derided as a poor enthusiast, he will accept it. He can point out, however, that the 'necessity of Divine Teaching, in order to a spiritual acquaintance with the truth of God, is by many denied, and all expectation of the Spirit's influence for this end is denied as enthusiasm'.[4] There are those who 'value themselves on the opposition they give to what they call enthusiasm',[5] but they are, in fact, really rejecting the true emphasis of the primitive and reformed Church.

If to insist upon the inner witness of the Spirit is the reason why so many would brand him an 'enthusiast', Simeon is content to be so branded. At the same time, he is aware that there is a claim to the witness of the Spirit which is false and fatal. 'There is such a thing as enthusiasm: and it is by no means uncommon for persons to mistake some feelings or conceit of their own for the sanctifying influences of the Spirit of God.'[6]

[1] Vol. 14, p. 38.
[2] Vol. 6, p. 479. Cf., vol. 3, pp. 518, 519; cf., also, 'Lay not too great a stress on some transient emotions: but judge yourselves by the most certain test of a willing and unreserved obedience' (vol. 1, pp. 413, 414).
[3] University Sermon, 'Means of Attaining True Wisdom,' vol. 16, p. 1.
[4] Vol. 6, p. 306.
[5] Vol. 7, p. 137.
[6] Vol. 1, p. 491.

This mistaken enthusiasm arises from two main errors. Firstly, it is false to suppose that because the Holy Spirit gave the early disciples powers to work miracles, therefore, His presence, in these days, will produce the same results. According to Simeon the miracles are finished. They have fulfilled their purpose in authenticating the gospel and in vindicating Christ's claim to be the Messiah. We have now the abiding testimony to these facts in the inspired records so that the need for continued miracles has passed. It is a fallacy into which some have fallen to conclude that the possession of the Spirit means the performance of extraordinary works. 'We willingly concede', he writes, 'that it would be enthusiastic and absurd in us to expect the miraculous influences which were vouchsafed to the early disciples.'[1]

A clear distinction must consequently be drawn between the miraculous activity of the Holy Spirit in the early Church and the illuminating action of the same Spirit in the present Church. In the one case the Holy Spirit came as an occasional visitant: in the other He comes as a continual resident. 'We are not to expect the miraculous aid of the Holy Spirit, but a gracious influence we may expect.'[2]

Then, secondly, trouble arises when the influence of the Spirit is made to, or better, perhaps, is thought to operate apart from the word. It may be ideally true to assert that God can act without the word. Taken in the abstract it may be right to say, 'It becomes not us to restrict God in the use of means.'[3] God may, if He see fit, speak directly to man by dreams and visions. He has done so in the past.[4] There is, however, no reliable evidence that He does so now. Simeon confesses that he is not partial to the claim to the activity and guidance of God's Spirit arising from such means. It can only lead, he thinks, to certain delusion.

There is no reason, Simeon teaches, why God should speak in this special way. He has given His word to the world, and all that is needed now is for the Spirit to illuminate that word. He thus

[1] Vol. 13, p. 84.
[2] Vol. 20, p. 569. Cf., 'To have the Spirit is not to have those miraculous powers, which were given in the apostolic age . . . but . . . those special influences of the Spirit, whereby men are enlightened and transformed into the divine image' (vol. 15, pp. 205, 206).
[3] Vol. 20, p. 37.
[4] Cf., vol. 1, p. 482; vol. 20, p. 37, cf., 'We can place no confidence in any special manifestations which are professedly derived from such sources. We may also say that nothing certain can be known from any direct impression of the Spirit of God upon the mind' (vol. 5, p. 482).

says emphatically, 'It is by the Scriptures that the Holy Spirit speaks to men.'[1] This for Simeon is the safeguard against all false enthusiasm. Let this be understood and all occasion for wild excesses and fantastic claims has been taken away. Of one thing we are to be sure, not only does the Spirit not speak contrary to the word, but He does not really speak apart from it. By other means He may indeed call attention to the word, but it is in and by the word only that the Spirit bring us to the knowledge of God.[2]

The conclusion is this: 'We are therefore to submit to the teaching of God's word and Spirit. To this advice it may be objected, that we promote an enthusiastic dependence on divine impulses . . . We should indeed promote enthusiasm, if we exhorted anyone to follow impulses that were independent of the written word: but if we recommend all persons to regulate their sentiments *solely* by the written word, and to rely on the influence of the Holy Spirit *no further than they accord with that*, then neither we, nor they, are in any danger of enthusiasm: because the sacred oracles are an unalterable standard to which every thought and action may be brought, and by which its quality may be infallibly determined.'[3]

It is a false enthusiasm, then, to go beyond what is written. Some have laid claim to a revelation of which even the apostles knew nothing. They have attributed to the influence of the Holy Spirit that which has been the very antithesis of His presence. They have sometimes credited to the Spirit of God actions which are the very work of the devil. 'A person of warm imagination and a confident mind can easily be wrought upon by that subtle spirit, so that he shall appear both to himself and others to be eminently distinguished by manifestations from God, whilst yet he is only under the influence of a Satanic delusion.'[4]

It is an evidence of a false enthusiasm to assert that God has communicated a truth in some special manner, by a dream, for example, or a vision, when that truth is already made known in the written oracles of God. What is so written is sufficient; and, since the canon of Scripture is now closed, there is no reason for, as there is no possibility of, such special information to be made known to select individuals. God has nothing further to add to His word.

[1] Vol. 21, p. 499.   [2] Vol. 20, p. 38.
[3] Vol. 16, p. 131.   [4] Vol. 5, p. 482.

'There are enthusiasts in the world' he writes, 'who will persuade themselves that they are God's people, because they have
had a revelation of it from heaven or a dream whereby it has been
made known to them . . . I will not say that God *may* not reveal
to man as he pleases: but I will say, that we have no reason to
expect that God will make known to us by revelation anything,
which without such a miraculous interpretation, may be easily and
safely deduced from his blessed word.'[1]

It is true enough that with some the inner witness of the Spirit
is more strongly realized than with others. Their experience is so
vivid that it might almost seem as if the Spirit of God acted directly.
So dramatic is His action, in some cases, that it appears to those to
whom it comes, as if the Holy Spirit brought a new and personal
revelation. Even in the case of one's own experience, one receives
an 'immediate impression', 'imparted in a more instantaneous
manner, and in a higher degree at some times than at others.'[2]
However true this may be, Simeon is quite sure that the Spirit's
testimony is not given without any reference to the Scriptures.

There is therefore a true and a false enthusiasm. In that which is
true Simeon will rejoice since therein lies that which completes
within the individual the revelation which God has given. It is by
the inner action of the Spirit that the outward revelation of the
word is realized. Thus a mere assent to objective doctrines is
inadequate. It may lead to 'orthodoxy' but it is not the true
'fiduciary' faith of the New Testament.

On the other hand, the claim to the leading of the Spirit apart
from the word results in a false enthusiasm. This is both a delusion
and a vain conceit.

This means that there must be certain criteria whereby the true
can be distinguished from the false. In one passage the special
characteristics of both are drawn together. 'I grant', he says, 'that
there are enthusiasts who pretend to such impulses and such
communications as the Scriptures do not warrant us to expect . . .
but we must not despise those manifestations which God does
vouchsafe to his people, because there are enthusiasts who profess
to have experienced more.'[3] 'We apprehend then' he goes on to
state later, 'that the genuine experience of communion with Christ

---

[1] Vol. 13, pp. 455, 456, cf., p. 494.
[2] Vol. 15, p. 284.
[3] Vol. 13, p. 167.

may be distinguished from enthusiastic pretentions to it, both by its rise, and its operations on the mind. Enthusiasts found their pretentions on some visions or dreams, or on the word of God coming in a peculiar manner to their minds.'[1] As a result they are elated to presumptuous confidence and spiritual delusion.[2]

It is of the greatest importance then, both for the individual and for the Church, to be able to clearly understand the nature of false enthusiasm. The difference between this and the true is worked out by Simeon under three headings. First, by 'what preceded it'. In the case of true enthusiasm there is a conviction of 'our lost estate'. Then, secondly, by 'what accompanies it'; it is the very essence of the true to inspire humility. Thirdly, by 'what follows it'. 'Manifestations of God to the soul always produce zeal in his service; victory over sin; and a longing for the enjoyment of him in heaven; but supineness, subjection to evil tempers, and a "forgetfulness" of the eternal world, generally characterize the self-deceiving professor.'[3]

Simeon has, then, a very definite doctrine of revelation. He finds it contained and confined within, what he constantly refers to as the 'oracles of God', or the 'inspired volume'. Yet complete as the word is in itself, it is not sufficient by itself. There must be, in addition to the objective revelation in the word, the subjective illumination of the Spirit. Mere assent to the doctrines of the objective revelation in the word is not the faith of the gospel, while a claimed impression of the Spirit, apart from the word, is only an enthusiastic conceit. Thus, for Simeon, revelation is to be found IN the word THROUGH the Spirit.

Two main criticisms have been directed against the doctrine of revelation just outlined. Some have felt that by confining revelation within the Bible there is a consequent detraction from the absolute and unique self-disclosure of God in Christ. Revelation, therefore, it is maintained in opposition, is not found in written words but in the Word absolutely, that is, in the living Person of Christ. It has been seen that in the case of the 'orthodox' there was a real danger of making revelation a matter of propositions and of missing the

---

[1] Vol. 13, ibid.

[2] Cf., 'Enthusiasts put their vain conceits in the place of the word and have presumed to call their own feelings or fancies by the sacred appellation of a promise,' Funeral Sermon for Hon. the Rev. Wm Bromley Cadogon, late St Giles, Reading, Jan. 29th, 1797.

[3] Vol. 15, p. 285.

divine Person of Christ. Simeon, however, it must be acknowledged, was at pains to stress the absoluteness and uniqueness of Christ. His theme was, as Dean Howson suggests, the pre-eminence of Christ. On the other hand, as we have seen, he was aware of the uselessness of a mere knowledge of the letter of Scripture. The Bible was, of course, for Simeon, objectively and fully the word of God, yet it was only as one encountered, through the illumination of the Spirit, the living Word within the written word that the divine revelation was completed within the soul. This is well brought out in a passage quoted earlier, but here repeated because of its relevance to the question; the words are a summary of his point of view. 'First, then,' he declares, 'it is not the word that does good; but the Holy Spirit by the Word . . . . Next, it is not the knowledge of the word that benefits, but the knowledge of Christ in the record. We might be able to repeat the whole Bible and perish at the last . . . .'[1] He sees Christ as the 'soul' of the Bible. Simeon would, we think, agree with the idea of revelation as the action of God within history. As he sees it God did act dramatically and revealingly in the history of Israel and in the events of Christ's life. But for Simeon these acts of God in history, of which we have the divinely inspired record become God's saving acts in individual experience by the action of the Holy Ghost in and through the word.

The other criticism, later directed against the view-point of Simeon was that he was ignorant of the newer understanding of biblical history. He lived at a period when what later came to be called 'higher criticism' was in its infancy; when, indeed, it was really operative amongst those outside the Church. Had Simeon lived later, would he have modified his position regarding the Scriptures? The question is, of course, purely a hypothetical one. But we think the answer would be emphatically, No. There is evidence throughout the twenty-one volumes of his works that he was not unacquainted with the direction in which things were moving. There are passages, indeed, in which he specifically rejects the criticism of Bible history, which, in his day, was mainly associated with deistic scepticism. He will not admit to the altering of the 'events' of the history to fit into preconceived philosophical principles. Event and interpretation belong together. If the interpretation is to be taken as valid then, too, the history must be

[1] Vol. 10, pp. 284, 285.

regarded as authentic. This seems to be the point of view taken by Simeon; and it does mean for him, as it did mean for all those who followed the same understanding of revelation, that the biblical events are divinely given and that no human reconstruction of them is admissible.

CHAPTER IX

THE DOCTRINE OF A LEADER

U nder this heading, 'The Doctrine of a Leader,' attention is to be directed to John Wesley's understanding of revelation. It is neither necessary nor fitting for us to enter upon any details of a life the influence of which is stamped indelibly upon the passing centuries. Account will be taken, therefore, of his character and career only in so far as they may illustrate and illuminate the subject with which we are concerned. Wesley's particular understanding of revelation may be placed under the caption

REVELATION BY THE SPIRIT AND THROUGH THE WORD

Stating it in this way it will be seen that Wesley's doctrine is in harmony with, and yet contrasts with that of Charles Simeon. Both Wesley and Simeon equated revelation with the Scriptures. They were agreed that the Bible alone contained the revelation of God. Yet, whereas Simeon put the emphasis upon the adequacy of the word used by the Spirit, Wesley placed it upon the action of the Spirit Who uses the word. Thus while they were alike in their estimate of the Scriptures, they differed in their emphasis upon the Spirit.

Coming then to Wesley's own statement of his position, it will be our first concern to refer to

(i) *The Source of Wesley's Faith*

A similar attitude to the Scriptures prevailed throughout the eighteenth century amongst those who have been described as 'orthodox Churchmen' as well as those designated Evangelicals. Although the Evangelicals gave expression to what has been called a 'Bible-religion' as distinct from the 'Church-religion' of the orthodox, the place given to the Scriptures was in each case the same.

John Wesley was, in his early life, a 'high Churchman' and as such was ordained to the ministry. Yet even before his conversion he is to be found proclaiming the sufficiency of the Scriptures and warning against adding to them.[1]

Such then was the understanding of the Bible to which Wesley was heir and to which he remained faithful. His opponents imagined, however, that by stressing the action of the Holy Spirit, he was somehow undermining the authority of the Bible. This is clearly indicated in his letter to the Rev. Mr Potter. In his criticism of Wesley, Potter had written: 'But the Scriptures are a complete and a sufficient rule. Therefore to what purpose could any further inspiration serve? All further inspiration is unnecessary: the supposed need of it is highly injurious to the written word. And the pretension thereto, (which must be either to explain, or to supply it) is a wicked presumption with which Satan hath filled their hearts to lie to the Holy Ghost.'[2]

Wesley replies that his teaching about the Holy Spirit is in no way detrimental to the Scriptures. Be the Scriptures, he says, ever so complete they will not save your soul. There must be, therefore, in addition to the revelation in the book, a revelation within the breast.

After the experience in Aldersgate Street, Wesley's attitude to the Bible did not change. What did change was his understanding of the action of the Spirit. It is to be observed that in the sermon to which reference has been made, 'On Corrupting the Word of God,' preached before that decisive day, there is no allusion to the Spirit of God. It is, perhaps, idle to discuss the source of this second emphasis. Allowance must necessarily be made for Wesley's earlier contact with the Moravians. It is well known that they spoke much about the 'witness within'. It may be that Wesley naturally borrowed their phraseology. But when every acknowledgement has been made, is it not more to the point to see Wesley's later expressions concerning the action of the Spirit as an interpretation of the experience which came to him on that momentous day when his heart was 'strangely warmed'?

(ii) *The Statement of Wesley's Teaching*
(a) *Reason and Revelation*

In his statement concerning the place of reason in life and re-

---

[1] 'On Corrupting the Word of God,' cxxx, vol. 11, p. 93 ff. (*The Works of the Rev. John Wesley*, edited by Joseph Benson, 15 vols., 1809.)
[2] Quoted by Wesley in his Letter to Rev. Mr Potter (sect. 17), vol. 13, p. 80.

ligion Wesley was aware of the contrary extremes of deism and mysticism abroad in his day.

Nothing, he believed, was so contradicted by the facts of experience as the Cartesian assumption that reason is equal in all men. Knowledge is obviously, in some measure, conditioned by geographical location. The condition of some people is such that 'to compare them with horses or any of our domestic animals would be doing them too much honour'.[1] The dispensations of God's grace, like His providence, have resulted in the light of civilization having come to some and not to others. The realities of experience give no justification to the deist's optimism. The fact of inequality follows from the operation of God's mysterious ruling and cannot be used as an objection against revelation. Pressed as an argument, it would tell with equal force against natural religion, and the result would be 'flat Atheism'. 'It would conclude, not only against the Christian Revelation, but against the Being of God.'[2] The inequalities of life are not its injustices, since the reason for them lies in the mysterious purposes of God. The sure fact is that times and seasons are in His hands.

But while the deist exalts reason to the throne as the absolute monarch, mysticism abases it to the dust and will not even recognize it as an unprofitable servant. 'Among them that despise and vilify reason, you may always expect to find those Enthusiasts, who suppose the dreams of their own imagination to be revelations from God.'[3]

The Golden Mean

Wesley seeks a *via media* between these two extremes. Reason must be neither overrated nor undervalued. 'So much easier is it to run from East to West, than to stop at the middle point!'[4] It is Wesley's purpose in the sermon from which quotation has been previously made to prove that we know in part.[5] The desire for knowledge is universal, but the possession of it is a different matter. There are limits beyond which none can go however much he may wish to do so.

With this premised Wesley goes on to specify these limits. He sees man as a half-blinded spectator in a universe of mystery. The

[1] 'The Imperfections of Human Knowledge,' lxxiv, ii, sect. 7, vol. 9, p. 318.
[2] Ibid., iii, sect. 2.
[3] 'The Case of Reason Considered,' lxxv, Intro., sect. 2, vol. 9, p. 324.
[4] Ibid, sect. 3.
[5] 'The Imperfections of Human Knowledge.'

depths of the earth, the bounds of the world, the distance of the stars, are all beyond his penetration.[1] The true 'esse' of things familiar is unknown. What is it that makes a metal to differ from a stone? or one metal from another? or gold from silver? or tin from lead? 'Are microscopic Animals, so called, *real* Animals or not?'[2] Do not these things 'elude our utmost diligence?'[3]

When from the sentient world we turn to the spiritual our knowledge is infinitely less. How can we grasp such high realities? Here, for example, we can raise questions concerning the soul but we cannot answer them, What is it? Where is it? Such problems as these none can solve. 'Here we are at a full stop.'[4] What about God's works of providence; 'It is a childish conceit to suppose chance governs the world.'[5] Yet when we come to contemplate the superintending activity of God what insoluble problems are on our hands. There is the fact of inequality arising from education and civilization. There is apparent partiality. Who can explain such mysteries as these? And then God Himself in the reality of His being and essence is beyond the discovery of human knowledge. 'How astonishingly little we know of God! How small a part of His nature do we know! of His essence and attributes!'[6] The deist talks glibly about knowing God through nature, when he hardly knows nature. ''Tis mystery all.'[7]

And man himself is a mystery. The ancients counselled us, 'Know thyself.' But who can understand the secrets of his own being? Here is a mechanism too intricate for us to trace out. Within our own being there are depths we can never plumb. 'How shall we comprehend the ever-blessed God, when we cannot comprehend ourselves?'[8]

While, however, knowledge is thus, partial and imperfect, Wesley, like Butler, will not 'vilify reason'. He will not go to the other extreme. He acknowledges with some shame his earlier attachment to Luther's *Commentary on the Epistle to the Galatians*,

---

[1] Cf., 'How small a part of this great work of God (i.e. creation) is man able to understand!' 'God's Approbation of His Works,' lx, Intro., sect. 2, vol. 9, p. 132. Again, 'As to the internal parts of the earth, even to this day, we scarcely have any knowledge of them,' op. cit., i, sect. 3.
[2] 'The Imperfection of Human Knowledge,' i, sect. 11, p. 314.
[3] Ibid.
[4] Op. cit., i, sect. 13, p. 315.
[5] Op. cit., i, sect. 1, p. 316.
[6] Op. cit., i, sect. 1, p. 309.
[7] Op. cit., i, sect. 11, p. 314.
[8] *Thoughts on Memory*, vol. 15, p. 389.

which he now finds 'deeply tinctured with mysticism throughout'.[1] Referring to Luther, Wesley adds, 'How does he (almost in the words of Tauler) decry *reason*, right or wrong, as the irreconcilable enemy of the Gospel of Christ! whereas, what is reason, (the Faculty, so called) but the power of apprehending, judging, and discovering? which power is no more to be condemned in the gross, than seeing, hearing or feeling.'[2]

Wesley deals with those who 'overvalue' reason. There are those who 'extol it to the skies', and consider it to be 'the highest gift of God'.[3] Such believe that this 'all-sufficient Director of all the children of men' can guide into all truth and lead into all virtue.[4] With these 'overraters' of reason, Wesley links 'men of eminently strong understanding, who because they know more than most men, suppose they can know all things'.[5] It is on this ground that they reject the Christian revelation and repudiate the Scriptures as the oracles of God.[6]

To these 'overraters' and 'applauders' of reason, Wesley has some decisive points to make. 'Reason', he urges, 'cannot produce faith.'[7] He tells us that he himself drew together from the ancients and moderns the strongest arguments for the existence and being of God, but they had not carried conviction to his heart. They had left him bewildered; and instead of creating faith, actually led to unbelief.[8] Hobbes was, without question, a man of strong understanding; 'But', asks Wesley, 'did it produce in him a full, a satisfactory conviction of an invisible world? Did it open his understanding to see

"Beyond the bounds of this diurnal sphere"?'[9]

To these questions Wesley returns an unhesitating, 'No!' Not only is reason helpless to produce faith, it is equally useless in creating hope, or love, or happiness. Such then being the inadequacy of reason there is no ground left for boasting in its supremacy.

This does not mean, however, that reason is therefore to be undervalued. It is a 'precious gift of God'.[10] For Wesley, as for the Cambridge Platonists, it is the candle of the Lord.[11] Wesley was, in

---

[1] *Journal*, June 15, 1741. [2] *Journal*, June 15, 1741.
[3] 'The Case of Reason Considered,' lxxv, Intro., sect. 3.
[4] Ibid. [5] Op. cit., sect. 4.
[6] Ibid. [7] Op. cit., ii, sect. 1.
[8] Op. cit., ii, sect. 2. [9] Op. cit., ii, sect. 4.
[10] Op. cit., ii, sect. 10.
[11] Ibid.

fact, reproached from two sides. Those who stressed 'faith' believed
he made too much of reason. In a passage in his *Journal* he refers
to those who demanded belief without solid reasons. They say of
him, 'Your carnal reason destroys you. You are for reason: I am for
faith.' Wesley answers, 'I am for both: for faith to perfect my
reason: that by the Spirit of God not putting out the eyes of my
understanding, but enlightening them more and more, I may be
ready to give a clear, scriptural answer to every man that asketh me
a reason of the hope that is in me.'[1]

On the other hand, those who stressed reason condemned
Wesley as irrational. In a letter to the Regius Professor of Divinity
at Cambridge, Wesley denies the charge. 'You go on: "It is a
fundamental principle of the Methodist school that all who come
into it must renounce their reason." ' 'Sir,' replies Wesley, 'are you
awake? Unless you are talking in your sleep, how can you utter so
gross an untruth? It is a fundamental principle with us that to
renounce reason is to renounce religion, that religion and reason go
hand in hand, and that all irrational religion is false religion.'[2]

The Sphere in which Reason Operates

It is within the sphere of revelation that reason operates. It is the
means whereby the truths of God are apprehended and assured.
Man's rationality is the 'point of contact' for the divine revelation.
This means that faith will be 'always consistent with reason'.[3] This
is the assumption of his *Earnest Appeal to Men of Reason and
Religion.* Anyone who departs from true and genuine reason,
Wesley asserts, departs from Christianity. He is willing, indeed, to
join with those 'desiring a religion founded on reason and every
way agreeable thereto'.[4]

If reason in this context means 'the nature of things' then we
may be assured that Christianity is in complete harmony with the
essential rationality of existence. The Christian man is therefore
the really rational man. On the other hand, if by reason is meant
'the faculty of reasoning, of inferring one thing from another',[5]
then he can still address himself to men of reason. It is 'those who
are styled mystic divines'[6] who would renounce the use of reason.

---

[1] *Journal*, Nov. 27, 1750 (Thurs.), (In 'Letter to an Old Friend').
[2] *Selected Letters of John Wesley*, edited by Frederick C. Gill, No. 126.
[3] 'The Case of Reason Considered,' ii, sect. 1.
[4] *An Earnest Appeal*, sect. 28, vol. 12, p. 11.
[5] Ibid.   [6] Op. cit., sect. 30.

But there is no authority for such renunciation in Holy Writ.[1]
After Christ, the apostle Paul was the strongest reasoner.

At the same time Wesley insists that reason must have its
πο̂υ στ̂ω. It must have material upon which to work. He accepts the
epistemology which holds that knowledge comes by the way of the
senses. 'For many years it has been allowed by sensible men, *Nihil
est in intellectu quod non prius in sensu* . . . . All the knowledge
which we naturally have, is originally derived from the senses.'[2]
There are no innate ideas. In his Remarks on Mr Locke's *Essay on
the Human Understanding* Wesley makes it clear that he agrees
with Locke's doctrine of the '*tabula rasa*'.

But if the human reason works upon data provided by the
human senses to give human knowledge, then, by analogy, it is
only a divinely enlightened reason working upon the material
provided by the 'spiritual', or as Wesley also calls them, the
'internal' senses, which give us spiritual knowledge. A 'new set of
senses (so to speak) is opened in our soul'.[3] Wesley illustrates his
point by what he calls a 'trite instance'.[4] It is only those who have
the sense of sight who can reason about colours, 'so you cannot
reason concerning spiritual things if you have no spiritual sight;
because all your ideas received by your outward senses are of a
different kind.'[5]

The external senses cannot provide the spiritual material upon
which the reason can operate. This material is furnished by the
internal senses only, and when so supplied there can be no limit
to the activity of reason. 'We therefore not only allow', says Wesley,
'but earnestly exhort all who seek after religion to use all their reason
which God hath given them in searching out the things of God.'[6]

It is in this context that Wesley repudiates Dodwell's *Christianity Not Founded on Argument*. It was maintained by Dodwell
that Christianity is contrary to reason. For Wesley nothing could
be further from the truth. It is the very glory of the gospel to
liberate and elevate man's natural faculties. Those whose minds
were darkened have been enlightened by the gospel. They have
new spiritual 'matter' upon which to work. Faith gives the new

[1] Ibid.
[2] 'On the Discoveries of Faith,' cxiv, Intro., sect. 1, vol. 10, p. Cf., no. 8
'Difference of Walking by Sight and Faith,' cxv, sect. 7, vol. 10, p. 381; O '3
Faith,' cxxiii, sect. 18. Vol. 11, p. 37.
[3] 'On Faith,' cxxiii, sect. 18, vol. 11, p. 37.
[4] *An Earnest Appeal*, sect. 34.
[5] Ibid.   [6] Op. cit., sect. 31.

spiritual content and the enlightened reason makes the new constructions. Reason consequently becomes the handmaiden of faith and the servant of revelation. 'God did not take away your understanding but enlightened and strengthened it.'[1] At the same time the understanding of faith is not the discovery of even the enlightened reason. God sheds His light into the native darkness of the mind, 'and we then see, not by a chain of *reasoning* but by a kind of *intuition*, by a direct view.'[2]

Reason in the Natural Man

The unenlightened reason of the natural man, however, is helpless within the spiritual sphere. 'For his soul is in a deep sleep. His spiritual senses are not awake: they discern neither spiritual good or evil. The eyes of his understanding are closed; they are sealed together, and see not. . . . Hence, having no inlets for knowledge of spiritual things, all the avenues of the soul are shut up, he is in gross, stupid ignorance of whatever he is most concerned to know. He is utterly ignorant of God, knowing nothing concerning him as he ought to know. He is a total stranger to its true, inward, spiritual teaching.'[3]

In a sermon, 'On the Education of Children,' he goes further and denies that there are any innate ideas of God at all: 'it does not appear, that man has naturally any more idea of God than any of the beasts of the field: he has no knowledge of God at all: neither is God in all his thoughts.'[4] Apart from early instruction, he elsewhere asserts, children 'would have no more knowledge of God than the beasts of the field, than the wild ass's colt. Such is natural religion! abstracted from traditional, and from the influences of God's Spirit'.[5] We are by nature, he tells us, 'ἄθεοι, Atheists in the world.'[6]

There are declarations of man's natural helplessness with which the most extreme Calvinist could not quarrel. In spite of his 'boasted reason' man has 'no pre-eminence over the goats'.[7] He is

[1] 'The General Spread of the Gospel,' lxviii, sect. 11, vol. 9, pp. 236, 237.
[2] 'The End of Christ's Coming,' lxviii, sect. 11, vol. 9, pp. 236, 237.
[3] 'Spirit of Bondage and Adoption,' ix, i, sect. i, vol. 9, p. 230. Cf., 'The Circumcision of the Heart,' xvii, Intro., sects. 2, 3, vol. 7, pp. 241, 242. 'The New Birth,' xxi, ii, sect. 4, vol. 7, p. 297, etc., etc.
[4] 'On the Education of Children,' c, sect. 5, vol. 10, p. 208.
[5] 'On Original Sin,' xx, ii, sect. 4, vol. 7, p. 284.
[6] 'On Dissipation,' lxxxiv, sect. 7, vol. 10, p. 3. Cf., 'On Original Sin.' ii, sect. 3.
[7] 'On Original Sin,' ii, sect. 9.

'totally corrupted'.[1] The original likeness to God has been destroyed. Man has 'lost both the knowledge and the love of God, without which the image of God could not subsist'.[2] Every single individual has 'totally lost, not only the favour, but likewise the image of God'.[3]

The result of all this is to make the natural man completely impotent. This is a point continually stressed. 'Our nature is altogether corrupt, in every power and faculty. And our will depraved equally with the rest, is wholly bent to indulge our natural corruption.'[4] We are 'so utterly dead, that "in me dwelleth no good thing", that I am inclined to all evil, and totally unable to quicken my own soul'.[5] 'No power by nature, and no merit in man'; this was the grand principle with which the Oxford friends set out, Wesley declares in his funeral sermon on the death of Whitfield.[6]

In spite of these uncompromising statements, however, Wesley insists that there are truths of natural religion which the heathen are required to believe. He makes this point, for instance, in a sermon on 'Salvation by Faith'. 'Now God requireth a heathen to believe', he says, 'that God is: that he is a rewarder of them that diligently seek him; and that he is to be sought by glorifying him as God, by giving him thanks for all things: and by a careful practice of moral virtue of justice, mercy, and truth towards his fellow-creatures. A Greek or Roman, therefore, yea, a Sythian or Indian, was without excuse if he did not believe this much: The Being and Attributes of God, a Future State of Rewards and Punishments, and the Obligatory Nature of Moral Virtue.'[7]

Notwithstanding this 'black-out' of man's reason by the light-quenching power of sin, Wesley believed that there remained in human nature that which could respond to God. He maintained that man *qua* man is *capax Dei*. In one sermon, for example, he

[1] Op. cit., ii, sect. 2, etc.
[2] 'The New Birth,' xxi, i, sect. 2, vol. 7, p. 294.
[3] 'The Heavenly Treasure in Earthen Vessels,' cxxv, Intro., sect. 2, vol. 11, p. 49.
[4] 'On Self-Denial,' li, i, sect. 3, vol. 8, p. 359.
[5] 'On the Discoveries of Faith,' cxiv, sect. 5, vol. 10, p. 382. Cf., 'On Working out our own Salvation,' xc, iii, sect. 2, vol. 10, p. 82, etc., etc.
[6] 'Funeral Sermon on the Death of Mr Whitfield,' Sunday, Nov. 18, 1770, lvi, iii, sect. 2, vol. 9, p. 13.
[7] 'Salvation by Faith,' i, i, sect. 1, vol. 7, p. 8. Cf., 'Some great truths, as the Being and Attributes of God, and the difference between moral Good and Evil, were known, in some measure, to the Heathen world, the traces of these are found in all nations.' 'On Working out Our Own Salvation,' xc, Intro., sect. i, vol. 10, p. 75.

refers on several occasions to man as 'a creature capable of God'.[1]
It is this capacity for God which calls forth God's response in self-
disclosure. Reason is so utterly incompetent that man can only
know God as God draws aside the curtain and comes forth to be
known in the apprehension of faith. Little of the visible world is
known to the natural reason; less of the invisible. But the 'Author
of both worlds' has given us more than could be discovered by
natural reason: 'without Revelation how little certainty of the
invisible things did the wisest of men obtain! The smallest
glimmerings of light which they had were merely conjectural. At
best they were only a faint, dim twilight, delivered from uncertain
traditions; and so obscured by heathen fables, that it was but one
degree better than utter darkness.'[2]

But God has met the crying need of the human heart. He has
made a sufficient revelation of Himself and set it forth in secure
form in the Oracles of God. Here are the data for the spiritual
senses, and material for the enlightened reason.

Enlightened Reason not Absolute

Yet the reason enlightened by the Holy Ghost does not assure
complete knowledge. Wesley stresses this in a sermon on 'Christian
Perfection'. Christians are not perfect in knowledge, 'they know,
with regard to the world to come, the general truths which God
hath revealed.'[3] They know they are loved of God, and they are
aware of the working of the Spirit in their hearts, and the duties
God requires of them. 'But innumerable are the things they know
not.'[4] It is beyond them to fathom the perfection of God, the inner
nature of the Trinity, the mystery of the Incarnation, the workings
of the divine providence. Christians cannot say when God having
'accomplished the number of the elect, will hasten his kingdom'.[5]
There is much concerning God, like His omnipresence, 'too vast to
be comprehended by the narrow limits of human understanding.'[6]

The Christian is not only not free from ignorance, he is also not
free from error.[7] However the Christian may rise in the scale of

---

[1] 'The Great Deliverance,' lxv, i, sects. 2, 5, iii, 6, 11, vol. 9, pp. 192, 193, 200,
202. Cf., 'The Deceitfulness of Man's Heart,' cxxiv, i, sect. 2, vol. 11, p. 42.
[2] 'On Faith,' cxxiii, sect. 15, vol. 11, p. 36.
[3] 'Christian Perfection,' xlii, i, sect. 1, vol. 8, p. 215.
[4] Op. cit., sect. 2, vol. 8, p. 215.
[5] Op. cit., sect. 2, vol. 8, p. 215I.
[6] 'God's Omnipotence,' xlvii, i, sect. 2, vol. 8, p. 304.
[7] 'Christian Perfection,' i, sect. 4.

spiritual experience he never becomes all-knowing. 'The highest perfection which man can attain, while the soul dwells in the body, does not exclude ignorance and error, and a thousand other infirmities.'[1] But this acknowledgement of the presence of ignorance and error does not mean that there is no confidence or certainty, since 'the children of God do not mistake, as to the things essential to salvation'.[2] This means that there can be difference of opinion in many things. None can claim to possess all the truth. In things essential knowledge is sure, but in things unessential to salvation Christians can and do err frequently.

There are even different interpretations of the Scripture among those who are, without doubt, 'born of God'. Such difference of opinion, however, is no proof, 'that they are not children of God on either side. But it is a proof that we are no more to expect any living man to be *infallible*, than to be omniscient.'[3]

It is impossible for all men to think alike. There are differences due to education and environment; to capacity and to country. Still 'though we cannot think alike, may we not love alike?'[4] Here, indeed, 'is the sum of Christian Perfection; it is all comprehended in that word, Love.'[5]

(b) Revelation and Scripture

For Wesley God's special revelation is equated with the Bible which he regards as the oracles of God.[6] 'I really believe the Bible to be the Word of God,' he says with evident emphasis.[7] 'According to the light *we* have, we cannot but believe the Scripture is of God; and, while we believe this, we dare not turn aside from it, to the right hand or to the left.'[8]

By implication and by declaration Wesley leaves no doubt concerning his acceptance of the Scriptures, in their entirety, as the Word of God. There was none so bound by the Bible as Wesley.

[1] 'On Perfection,' lxxxi, i, sect. 3, vol. 9, p. 399. Cf., 'The Catholic Spirit,' xli, i, sects. 3, 4, vol. 8, p. 202.
[2] 'Christian Perfection,' i, sect. 4.
[3] Op. cit., sect. 5.
[4] 'The Catholic Spirit,' xli, Intro., sect. 4, vol. 8, p. 200.
[5] 'On Perfection,' lxxxi, i, sect. 4, vol. 9, p. 300.
[6] Cf., e.g. 'On Laying the foundation Stone of the New Chapel, Ap. 21, 1777,' liv, ii, sect. 2, vol. 8, p. 399. 'The Mystery of Iniquity,' lxvi, sect. 31, vol. 9, p. 217. 'The Signs of the Times,' lxxi, ii, sect. 10, vol. 9, p. 275. 'On Obedience to Pastors,' cii, ii, sect. 7, vol. 10, p. 234. *An Earnest Appeal*, sects. 6, 13, 46. *Further Appeal*, sect. 10.
[7] 'On Dissipation,' lxxxiv, sect. 16, vol. 10, p. 7.
[8] *An Earnest Appeal*, sect. 27.

He speaks of it 'as the History of God'.¹ Within its pages is set down 'a clear, concise and perfect account' of God's divine ordering. To preach Christ is to be linked and limited to the written word. '*To preach Christ*, is To Preach what God hath revealed either in the Old or New Testament.'²

Adherence to the divine record, is, he declares, the essential Protestant position. 'The faith of the Protestants, in general, embraces only those truths necessary to salvation which are clearly revealed in the Oracles of God. Whatever is plainly declared in the Old and New Testament is the object of their faith. They believe neither more or less, than what is manifestly contained in and proveable by the Holy Scriptures.'³

In reference to our Lord's parable of Dives and Lazarus, Wesley asserts, on the authority of the Bible, that there is everlasting torment for the unrepentant. 'I warn you in his name,' he says, 'that the Scriptures are the real word of God.'⁴ Some, like the rich man, may demand a dramatic event to bring to a knowledge of God. Such a startling demonstration Wesley argues would be useless. Anyone wakened at night by what appeared the touch of a vanished hand and the sound of a voice that is still; awakened, that is, by one purporting to have come from beyond the grave, would, in the morning, dismiss the experience as a dream. Such happenings can have no faith-inspiring effect. The event would, possibly, leave no abiding influences. The Scripture, on the other hand, remains, 'That standing Revelation', it 'is the best means of rational conviction: far preferable to any of those extraordinary means which some imagine would be effectual. It is our wisdom therefore to avail ourselves of this; and to make a full use of it, so that it may be a lantern to our feet and a light in all our paths'.⁵

All through his ministry, Wesley emphasizes that his attitude to the Bible has not changed. He refers to the time when, at Oxford, four young men united together 'each one of them was *homo unius libri*, a man of one book'.⁶ It was, in fact, this allegiance to the Bible which made them the object of derision. 'They were constantly reproached for this very thing; some terming them in

---

¹ 'On Divine Providence,' lxxii, Intro., sect. 4, vol. 9, p. 279.
² 'The Law Established through Faith,' xxxvii, i, sect. 2, vol. 8, p. 149.
³ 'On Faith,' cx, i, sect. 8, vol. 10, p. 343.
⁴ 'Dives and Lazarus,' xlviii, iii, sect. 2, vol. 8, p. 321.
⁵ Op. cit., xlviii, iii, sect. 7, vol. 8, p. 322.
⁶ 'God's Vineyard,' cxi, i, sect. 1, vol. 10, p. 349.

derision *Bible-bigots*; others, *Bible-moths*: feeding, they said, upon the Bible as moths do on cloth.'[1] Even before the event in Aldersgate Street he declared his purpose to abide by the Scriptures alone. After a conversation with Peter Böhler, on the nature of saving faith, he records, 'The next morning I began the Greek Testament again, resolving to abide by the Law and the Testimony.'[2] The passing years only confirmed him in his position. He was unshaken in his belief in the Bible as the embodiment of God's revelation. 'I will speak for one,' he says, 'after having sought for truth, with some diligence, for half a century, I am, at this day, hardly sure of anything, but what I learn from the Bible. Nay, I positively affirm, I *know* nothing else for certain, that I would dare to stake my salvation upon it.'[3]

God, then, has given to man certain information about the way to heaven. 'He has written it down in a book.' Thus the cry of Wesley's soul is, 'O give me that Book! At any price give me the book of God.'[4]

Such a position accorded by Wesley to the Bible means that it is for him an inspired and infallible volume.

Wesley, as far as we know, does not specify the method of inspiration. He is, however, very definite about the fact. A short article is boldly entitled: '*A Clear and Concise Demonstration of the Divine Inspiration of the Holy Scriptures.*' Miracles, prophecies, the goodness of its doctrines and the moral character of its penmen, are 'the four grand and powerful arguments which strongly induce us to believe that the Bible must be of God'.[5] Wesley sets out, what he conceives to be the only possibilities about the origin of the Scriptures. The Bible must be, he contends, the invention of good men or angels, bad men or devils, or of God. Good men or angels would never have prefaced their own statements with, 'Thus saith the Lord.' Bad men or devils, on the other hand, would not have originated a book which commands duty and forbids sin, and which, indeed, condemns their soul to eternal perdition. Thus the only possibility remaining is that the

---

[1] Ibid.
[2] *Journal*, Thurs., March 23, 1738. Cf., Fri., June 22, 1739. 'Second Letter to the Author of The Enthusiasm of the Methodists and Papists Compared,' vol. 13, pp. 37–8.
[3] 'The Good Steward,' xlvi, ii, sect. 7, vol. 8 ,pp. 292, 293.
[4] Preface to the *Works of John Wesley* by Joseph Benson, vol. 1, p. iv.
[5] *A Clear and Concise Demonstration of the Divine Inspiration of the Holy Scriptures*, vol. 15, p. 351.

Bible must be of God. 'Therefore, I draw this conclusion', Wesley adds, 'That the Bible must be given by Divine Inspiration.'[1]

This inspired book is, consequently, infallible. Wesley makes this point uncompromisingly in a passage in his *Journal*. He tells how on reading 'Mr Jenyng's admired tract, on the "Internal Evidences of the Christian Revelation" ', he was at a loss to know the writer's theology, 'whether he is a Christian, deist, or atheist.' He continues: 'If he is a Christian, he betrays his own cause by averring, that, "all Scripture is NOT given by inspiration of God; but the writers of it were sometimes left to themselves, and consequently made mistakes." Nay, if there be any mistakes in the Bible,' retorts Wesley, 'there may well be a thousand. If there be one falsehood in that book, it did not come from the God of truth.'[2]

But highly as Wesley regarded the Bible he still did not conceive of the faith of the gospel as a mere assent to its truth. Faith is, he teaches, more correctly to be defined as 'fiduciary'.[3] As such it is 'abundantly more than assent to the truth of the Bible'.[4] The devils, in fact, believe all that is written in the Bible.[5]

It is just here that Wesley sees the difference between his own position and those styled the 'orthodox'. But 'a man may be orthodox in every point', he may be zealous in the defence of right opinions, he 'may be almost as orthodox as the devil', and yet have no true religion.[6] Wesley refers to a time when he was himself ignorant of the nature of saving faith. He had then fondly imagined that it meant no more than a 'Firm assent to all the propositions contained in the Old and New Testament'.[7] Such a concep-

---

[1] Op. cit., ibid. Cf., 'In matters of Religion I regard no writings but the inspired . . . . In every part I appeal to the Law and the Testimony, and value no authority but this.' A 'Letter to Rev. Mr Law,' vol. 13, p. 340.

[2] *Journal*, Wed., July 24, 1776.

[3] *An Earnest Appeal*, sects. 58, 59.

[4] 'Second Letter to Mr Church,' vi, sect. 5, vol. 12, p. 396.

[5] Ibid. Cf., 'The Almost Christian,' ii, iii, sect. 5, vol. 7, p. 26, 'Marks of the New Birth,' xviii, i, sect. 2, vol. 7, p. 255. 'It is not, as some have fondly conceived, a bare assent to the truth of the Bible, of the articles of our creed, or all that is contained in the Old and New Testament,' 'The Way to the Kingdom,' vii, ii, sect. 10, vol. 7, p. 100. See also, 'Salvation by Faith,' i, i, sect. 4, vol. 7, p. 9.

[6] 'The Way to the Kingdom,' vii, i, sect. 6, vol. 7, p. 92. Cf., 'A religion of Opinions or what is commonly called Orthodoxy . . . ,' 'On the Unity of the Divine Being,' cxvi, sect. 15, vol. 10, p. 404. Also '. . . right opinion, assent to one or ten thousand truths is not true religion'. 'On the Trinity,' lix, Intro., i, vol. 9, p. 123. Cf., further, 'Difference between Walking by Sight and Faith,' cxv, sect. 18, vol. 10, p. 397. 'The Danger of Riches,' xcii, ii, sect. 1, vol. 10, p. 109.

[7] *A Further Appeal*, 6, sect. 1, vol. 12, p. 122.

tion he came to see was false to the New Testament itself. Faith is a relationship with a living Person and not allegiance to a set of doctrines. Like Charles Simeon, Wesley sees the possibility of the Bible becoming 'a dead letter'. The sacred oracles, he says, 'are a mere *dead letter*, if they are "not mixed with faith in those that hear them." '[1] There is no magic in the words of Scripture as such. The power belongs, not to the volume, as a volume, but to the actuating Spirit. 'We know', he says, 'that there is no inherent power in the words that are spoken in prayer, (or) in the letter of the Scripture read.'[2]

On the other hand, this must not be taken to mean that Wesley, in any way, despised the very letter of Scripture. No one was at more pains than he to seek out the specific meaning of every word.[3] In a conversation with a woman in Birmingham who repudiated the need for sacraments, Wesley asked, 'Is the word of God your rule?' She replied, 'Yes; the word made flesh: but not the letter. I am in the Spirit.'[4] The notion was completely anathema to Wesley. He had little regard for those who thus loosed themselves from the divine revelation. Consequently, while he denounces mere assent to the words of Scripture, he stresses the need for those very words. 'I have declared again and again, that I make the word of God the rule of all my actions: and that I no more follow any "secret impulse" instead thereof, than I follow Mahomet or Confucius.'[5]

(c) Scripture and the Spirit

True Christianity is, then, no mere speculative belief; it is rather a 'feeling possession of God in the heart, wrought by the Holy Ghost'.[6] This was one of the most important emphases of Wesley. He insisted constantly upon the need for the inner operation of the Spirit of God. This was true heart religion in contrast with the rational religion of the orthodox. So strongly did Wesley feel on this point that he bluntly calls 'Anti-Christ' anyone who denies the inspiration of the Holy Spirit or who would limit his

[1] 'On the Discoveries of Faith,' cxiv, Intro., sect. 4, vol. 10, p. 381, cf., 'Marks of the New Birth,' xviii, i, sect. 5, vol. 7, p. 257. 'On Charity,' xcvi, ii, sect. 2, vol. 10, p. 161.
[2] 'The Means of Grace,' xvi, sect. 3, vol. 7, p. 225.
[3] Cf., *An Address to the Clergy*.
[4] *Journal*, Sat., March 24, 1753.
[5] *Answer to Mr Church's 'Remarks'*, sect. 5, vol. 12, p. 318. Quoted again in a Letter to the Bishop of London, sect. 5, vol. 12, p. 408.
[6] 'Free Grace,' lv, sect. 14, vol. 8, p. 413.

influence to the Apostles.[1] It was in this context that Wesley was induced to speak of the Montanists as the 'real, Scriptural Christians'.[2]

The correct question to put to anyone is not, Are you in agreement with the propositions of the Bible? or the doctrines of the Church? but rather, 'Hast thou the witness in thyself?'[3] In a number of passages he stresses that it is the Spirit's action that makes revelation inward and spiritual.[4]

Accordingly, he teaches, there is, in addition to the revelation of God in the Scriptures, need for a further revelation of Christ in our hearts. This demand for a dual unveiling of God he sets forth in a powerful sermon preached before his University.[5] Those who are under the influence of the Holy Spirit have 'the witness in themselves'. Such have little need, for what Wesley calls, a 'distant witness'.[6] While the manner of the Spirit's witness within cannot be understood, there is 'a revealing, unveiling, discovering to us' which can be 'known and felt'.[7] In addition to the 'outward call', there is besides, what Wesley refers to as an 'inward call, by (God's) Spirit applying his word'.[8]

In one of his discourses on the 'Law Established through Faith', Wesley declares that 'God by His word and His Spirit, is always with us'.[9] How far the two, the Word and the Spirit, associate, Wesley does not make clear. He is not as definite on this point as Charles Simeon. On the one hand, we find Wesley making a severe comment on Count Morsay, whom he regards as a thorough 'enthusiast'. He was guided 'in all his steps, not by the written word, but by his imagination, which he calls the Spirit'.[10] On the other hand, in a sermon on the 'Witness of the Spirit', he declares, 'The testimony of the Spirit, is an inward impression on the soul,

---

[1] 'Awake, Thou that Sleepest,' iii, iii, sect. 7, vol. 7, p. 39.
[2] *Journal*, Wed., Aug. 15, 1750. Cf., 'The Mystery of Iniquity,' lxvi, sect. 24, vol. 9, p. 213. 'The Witness of God's Counsels,' lxxiii, sect. 9, vol. 9, p. 297.
[3] 'Awake, Thou that Sleepest,' iii, ii, sect. 8, vol. 7, p. 35.
[4] Cf., 'The Privilege of the Children Born of God,' xix, iii, sect. 2, vol. 7, p. 277, 'On the Trinity,' lix, sect. 17, vol. 9, p. 131, 'Letter to Rev. Mr Potter,' vol. 13, p. 81, etc.
[5] 'The Circumcision of the Heart,' xvii, i, sect. 7, vol. 7, p. 245.
[6] *An Earnest Appeal*, sect. 61, vol. 12, p. 25.
[7] *Further Appeal*, sect. 6, vol. 12, p. 56.
[8] 'On Predestination,' lxii, sect. 12, vol. 9, p. 159.
[9] 'The Law Established through Faith,' xxxvii, i, sect. 6, vol. 8, p. 161.
[10] *Journal*, Tues., July 4, 1775. Cf., comment on the 'Life of Mr Morsay', Sat., July 4, 1778, 'he was a consummate enthusiast: not the word of God, but his own imaginations, which he took for divine inspirations, were the sole rule both of his words and actions.'

whereby the Spirit of God directly "witnesses to my spirit, that I am a child of God." [1] Twenty years later he repeats the point in almost identical words. There he speaks of the direct and immediate testimony of the Spirit. [2]

Such declarations as these, in which Wesley seemed to regard the Holy Ghost as acting apart from the Word gave apparent substance to the charge made against him that he was himself the real enthusiast. He certainly does appear to regard the Spirit's influence and inspiration as operative in a direct and immediate way. Putting the matter psychologically, it may be said that in this sense Wesley was an 'introvert'. We are, in fact, guilty of no anachronism in thus classifying him, for it may come as a surprise to some to find Wesley himself using the terms 'introversion' and 'extroversion', which Karl Jung has brought into such vogue. [3]

Wesley makes no apology for his insistence upon the inwardness of true religion. He therefore, for example, makes a spirited reply to Mr Shinstra who condemns his witness as fanaticism. According to Wesley Mr Shinstra would condemn true heart religion which is the working of the Spirit within. To repudiate inward feelings as his critic would, is to reduce religion to a dry, dead carcase. [4]

Wesley's constant references to the Spirit's influence, action and leading made him an easy target for those who, regarding themselves as correctly orthodox, dreaded anything that savoured of the zealous and the enthusiastic. Right from the moment when his heart was 'strangely warmed' John Wesley found himself a centre of controversy on the score of 'enthusiasm'. The news of his 'conversion' perplexed his relations and friends. It was received by his brother Samuel with a sense of bewilderment, not a little tinged with anger. He regarded John as having being smitten with a fatal attack of enthusiasm. He confesses fear of it, and adds, 'I heartily pray God to stop the progress of this lunacy . . . . What Jack means by his not being a Christian till last month I understand not.'

Straightaway his experience was written off as an excess of

---

[1] 'The Witness of the Spirit,' x, i, sect. 7, pp. 137, 138.
[2] 'The Witness of the Spirit,' xi, ii, sect. 2, vol. 7, p. 148.
[3] According to Wesley the words were used by the mystics. ' — the attending to the voice of Christ within you, is what they call, INTROVERSION. The turning of the eye of the mind from him to outward things they call, EXTROVERSION.' 'On Dissipation,' lxxxiv, sect. 21, vol. 10, p. 9.
[4] *Journal*, Mon. Aug. 12, 1771. Cf., Thurs., Aug. 24, 1780, Sun., Ap. 25, 1784, Thurs., May 13, 1784.

enthusiasm. Throughout the following years John Wesley found it necessary, again and again, to refute what he came to refer to as this 'thread-bare charge'.[1] His brilliant reply to Bishop Lavington shows how seriously he regarded the calumny. Lavington was a bishop of the typical Hanoverian style, 'fat, drowsy, contented, and as destitute of spiritual sense as a block of wood.' He looked upon the 'revival' with anger and terror, and released against Wesley a torrent of bitter accusations, each one of which Wesley patiently answered, with short, packed sentences, the best medium for his swift logic and lofty emotions. But Lavington was one only of a host who took up the cry. The mere appellation, 'Enthusiast', was considered sufficient reason in itself for discrediting Wesley and his message. Wesley, however, believed that he was only giving the rightful place and prominence to the operations of the Holy Spirit. He quotes extensively from the homilies of the Church to show how the emphasis upon the immediate inspiration of the Spirit is the official doctrine of the Church.[2]

What he has to say on this head is, he believes, common to all Christians in all ages. He confesses himself at a loss to understand how for so many years the charge of 'enthusiast' is trumped up. Its usage, he thinks, 'generally spares the objector the trouble of reasoning, and is a shorter and easier way of carrying his cause.'[3] Yet he only insists upon the need for the inner witness and revealing of the Spirit. The one who has no such emphasis is unable to refute the proposition from Scripture and antiquity: 'What then shall he do? Why, cry out, Enthusiasm! Enthusiasm! and the work is done.'[4] Those who oppose him 'have a cant word for the whole religion of the heart, They call it Enthusiasm'.[5] But it is, Wesley asserts, 'no enthusiasm to teach that the unction from the Holy One belongs to all Christians in all ages.'[6]

Thus what many would dismiss as mere enthusiasm, Wesley sees as the very essence of true Christianity. Scriptural Christianity, he says in a sermon with this title, is a supernatural work of the Spirit in the soul.[7] This is the 'extraordinary work' which men like Dr Gibson, the late Bishop of London, affirms to be 'no better than

---

[1] 'A Letter to the Rev. Mr Downes,' sect. 14, vol. 13, p. 97.
[2] Cf., *A Further Appeal*, i, sects. 24, 25, 26, etc.
[3] Op. cit ii, sect. 27.
[4] Ibid.
[5] Op. cit., ii, sect. 20.
[6] Op. cit., iv, sect. 14.
[7] 'Scriptural Christianity,' lv, iv, sect. 10, vol. 7, p. 60.

down right enthusiasm'.[1] Wesley, in justification for his emphasis, contrasts the attitude to religion brought about by his preaching and that which earlier prevailed. Some sixty years ago, he observes, 'People in general were wonderfully cool about that trifle, Religion.'[2] It is different now. To-day there is a zeal and an earnestness not unbecoming for such an important issue as the salvation of the soul. Only a warm religion is a worthy religion. It is by an emphasis such as this that Wesley maintains that Christ has been brought into human lives. God is no longer conceived as having emigrated from His world. He is dramatically alive therein. He is not 'an idol compounded of fragments of tradition and of frozen metaphysics'.[3] Wesley was a true iconoclast. He had indeed annihilated a multitude of shrines and brought God back into His temple. Thus the century which opened with a cold formalism ended with a warm faith. 'Our light looks like the evening of the world' such was the description of the moral and spiritual condition of the people given in the *Proposal for a National Reformation of Manners*, published in 1694. Under Wesley the light had flamed afresh. God, it seemed, had given to the country another chance.

The contrast, for example, between the theological atmosphere of Warburton and Wesley is immense. Warburton's theology has not been unfairly summarized by Leslie Stephen as 'a supernatural chief justice whose sentences were carried out in a non-rational world; a constitutional monarch who had signed a constitutional compact and retired from the active government of affairs'. Such was Warburton's 'God'. For Wesley it was, 'Immanuel', 'God with us'. The love of God shed abroad in the heart by the Holy Ghost.[4] 'True Christian zeal' is therefore, 'no other than the flame of love.'[5] Such a religion as this is not to be dismissed as a mere excess of enthusiasm.[6]

[1] 'On Laying the Foundation Stone of the New Chapel, City Rd., Ap. 21, 1777,' liv, Intro., sect. 3, vol. 10, p. 170.
[2] 'On Zeal,' xcvii, Intro., sect. 3, vol. 10, p. 170.
[3] Leslie Stephen, *History of English Thought, etc.*, vol. 2, p. 338.
[4] Cf., Enthusiasm is usually regarded as 'something evil: and this is plainly the sentiment of all those who call the Religion of the heart Enthusiasm'. 'Nature of Enthusiasm,' xxxix, sect. 10, vol. 8, p. 171.
[5] 'On Zeal,' xcvii, i, sect. 3, vol. 10, pp. 171, 172.
[6] Cf., True religion is often dismissed as enthusiasm 'a word just fitted for their purpose, because no man can tell either the meaning of it, or even the derivation. If it has any determinate sense, it means a species of religious madness. Hence, when you speak your experience, they immediately cry out "much religion hath made thee mad", and all that you experience, either of the invisible or of the

Wesley allows that there is a false enthusiasm and he is not slow to unmask this 'many-headed monster'.[1] It is his purpose in a sermon on Acts 26. 24 to make clear the dreadfulness of a false enthusiasm. He discusses the meaning of the term, and rejects the etymological derivation of it from ἐν θεῷ, as 'unnaturally forced'. He observes that the term, as now generally used has a bad connotation, and accepting this he goes on to contrast the 'enthusiast' with the 'rational Christian'. Enthusiasm is then described as 'a religious madness arising from some falsely imagined influence of God'.[2] Such are those who are deluded by the notion that they possess in a special manner God's grace and gifts when in fact they do not. They affect a personal infallibility and imagine 'that God dictates the very words they speak: and that, consequently, it is impossible they should speak anything amiss, either as to matter or manner of it'.[3]

Their real error lies in their disregard for the means which God has given for the perfecting of the saints. They rely on sudden impulses and give no attention to the united testimony of the people of God and the written word. 'One general end of enthusiasm', he says, 'is expecting the end without the means, and expecting knowledge, for instance, without searching the Scriptures, and consulting the children of God.'[4] 'God has written all the Scriptures on my heart', say some, 'therefore I have no need to read them.'[5] For Wesley this was lamentable folly.

This discussion of 'enthusiasm' in relation to Wesley, is, we believe, of importance as it indicates how great was his emphasis upon the subjective aspect of revelation. From what has been said previously it will be clear that few would have called Charles Simeon an 'enthusiast'. His emphasis was, as we have seen, upon the objective aspect of revelation. The contrast, then, which was earlier indicated, has, we think, been sustained. For Charles Simeon, revelation is in the Word through the Spirit; for John Wesley, revelation is by the Spirit through the Word.

Wesley certainly will be behind no one in his emphasis upon the activity of the Spirit. He is ready to insist that there is no work of

eternal world they suppose to be only the waking dreams of a heated imagination'. 'Difference of Walking by Sight and Faith,' cxv, sect. 19, vol. 10, p. 397.

[1] 'The Nature of Enthusiasm,' xxxix, sect. 32, vol. 8, p. 180.
[2] Op. cit., sect. 12, p. 171.
[3] Op. cit., sect. 19, p. 175.
[4] A Plain Account of Christian Perfection, Answer to Question, 33.
[5] Ibid., cf., 'Nature of Enthusiasm,' xxxix, sects. 22, 27, vol. 8, pp. 176, 178.

God except by the Spirit. Yet, there is, he maintains, no private revelation given to any man; there is no secret disclosure of special information. God saves and sanctifies, liberates and leads by His Spirit, but it is by His Spirit through the Word. This for Wesley is the full and final revelation of God to man.

CHAPTER X

THE NEED FOR A UNIFICATION

(i) *Objective and Subjective*

In the foregoing review of developments in the understanding of
Revelation from 1700 to 1860, several clear-cut and sometimes
mutually hostile doctrines have been shown to emerge. Broadly,
an opposition can be seen to have been introduced between the
objective and subjective views. The exclusive stress on the objective
aspect which characterized the 'orthodox' doctrine gave rise to a
sterile notion of revelation. Revealed religion was conceived as
either adding a few extra ideas to natural religion, or as a body of
disclosed truths to which assent had to be given. Those who thus
repudiated the subjective aspect were especially concerned to guard
the transcendence of God. He was viewed consequently as a Being
completely different from man; a Being nevertheless Who had
declared His existence and attributes by leaving sufficient evidence
of His power and godhead on the universe of His creating. It was
such accentuation of the divine transcendence which pushed the
orthodox apologists close to the deists whom they sought to oppose.

On the other side, the subjective doctrine, starting with an insistence upon the divine immanence, renounced and ridiculed the
objective aspect, and made revelation to be the unveiling within of
the ever-present God. Pantheism was consequently the perpetual
danger of this view; and the charge was in fact made, not without
justice, in some cases. It was this emphasis upon the subjective, at
first under the influence of Hegelianism and later under that of
Existentialism, which was destined to hold the field throughout the
following decades. For Hegel, God is the All-inclusive Absolute.
This meant, according to Hegel's teaching, that

> '*All are parts of one stupendous whole,*
> *Whose body nature is, and God the soul*'.

These two lines from Pope's *Essay on Man* admirably summarize
Hegelianism and show it to be a philosophy of sheer immanence.

From this there developed in the succeeding years a type of pantheistic doctrine which found voice and vogue in the so-called, *New Theology*, which had such eloquent advocacy in the writings of R. J. Campbell.

On the other hand, Kierkegaard, from an existentialist point of view, put an emphasis upon the idea of God as 'infinite Subject', and upon the individual in his subjective reality and actuality. Kierkegaard was, to be sure, exasperated with Hegel whom he harangues for failing to take account of the existing individual. As a traditional 'Herr Professor', he declares, Hegel has gone to the extreme of absentmindedness and actually forgotten his own existence, the real subject of thought. It is in this way that Hegel has obliterated the individual by submerging him in the Absolute. He has thus, according to Kierkegaard, given a false subjectivity which it is Kierkegaard's purpose to correct. Had Hegel been content to add to his massive work a footnote declaring it to be but a 'thought-experiment', he would have gone down into history as a great thinker.[1] The trouble is that he wanted his system to be taken seriously; to be actually accepted as truth. And yet it is precisely his system which does not take seriously, what is the most serious reality of all, the actual self, the single individual. For Hegel, then, the single individual is submerged in the uncharacterizable Whole, the so-called Absolute. It is Kierkegaard's business to bring about his re-emergence; to call the existing individual from the grave of death to which Hegel had assigned him. And Kierkegaard will do this, not by any denial of subjectivity, but by an assertion, of what he claims, is true subjectivity, for 'the passion for the infinite is precisely subjectivity . . . and thus subjectivity becomes truth'.[2] Yet, at the same time, Kierkegaard will not have God mixed up in

---

[1] Bretall, *A Kierkegaard Anthology*, p. 191.
[2] *Concluding Unscientific Postscript* (trs. Swenson and Lowrie), p. 181. Cf., 'the polemic against Hegel must not blind us to the great characteristic of the age which Kierkegaard shares with Hegel in philosophy and Schleiermacher in theology. All three are children of the Romantic revival and revolt against the Enlightenment. In their different ways all three are apostles of subjectivity. "The absolute is subject not substance," said the philosopher. "Religion is the intuition of the infinite, the feeling of absolute dependence," said the theologian. It remained for Kierkegaard to correct what he found false emphasis in both teachers. "The passion for the infinite is . . . subjectivity, and thus subjectivity becomes truth." Against Hegel he says, "Your absolute Subject has swallowed up the individual, and so has become indistinguishable from the absolute Object; subjectivity has vanished in a boundless objectivity." Against Schleiermacher we can imagine him saying, "Your subjectivity has not sufficiently allowed for the specific quality of the 'object' in Christianity, where it is present to faith as paradox. Hence its true analogy is not aesthetic feeling but an activity

man's subjectivity. There is an infinite distance between God and man. God is the Wholly Other. For Kierkegaard the fundamental error in Hegelianism was its emphasis upon 'Immanenz'. Hegel dared to assert an existing continuum between God and man in such a way as to make it possible for man to arrive at a knowledge of God by his own innate abilities. He was led to this error by conceiving of Christianity as but a development, albeit the highest, in the religious consciousness of the race.

For Kierkegaard this 'historicizing identity-philosophy' (which, it may be noted, received a theological emphasis by Schleiermacher) was the abandonment of true Christianity, which would be restored only by the proclamation of an absolute qualitative difference between the divine and the human. There is, therefore, Kierkegaard asserts, 'an endless yawning difference between God and man,'[1] so much so, that, 'if God exists, and consequently is distinguished by an infinite difference of quality from all that it means to be a man, then neither can I nor anybody else, by beginning with the assumption that He was man, arrive in all eternity at the conclusion, "therefore it was God." '[2]

It is this accentuation of the 'Otherness' of God which has been specially stressed by Barth and Brunner, to give rise to, what may be called, a *neue Sachlichkeit*. It is referred to here as a 'new objectivity' in the sense that revelation is not thought of by these writers as an upsurge of the divine either latent or lively within the human. Indeed it is asserted, more particularly by Barth, '*Finitum non est capax infiniti,*' therefore, revelation comes to man 'in an irrational way, from without'. Revelation comes within the divine-human encounter. But the initiative is with God; God confronts man. Revelation is, therefore, supremely an activity of God. Here we see a new insistence upon the idea of the divine transcendence, with the result that, while the Kierkegaardian 'absolute qualitative difference' between God and man is stressed, man is in no way *capax Dei*. The question could, therefore, be raised, Has not the other aspect of Kierkegaard's teaching, namely, that upon the uniqueness of the single individual, been somehow compromised? We merely raise the question here: it is not within our purpose to

---

combined with a passivity which together constitute a passion which is the highest energizing and supreme manifestation of subjectivity." ' James Brown, *Subject and Object in Modern Theology*, pp. 35, 36.
[1] *Training in Christianity*, p. 67.
[2] Op. cit., p. 31.

seek an answer. By declaring 'immanence' to be the presence in the world of transcendence, and by conceiving of revelation to be the intrusion of the divine into the human, there does appear with these writers a new sort of 'objectivity'; an 'objectivity' in the sense that revelation is altogether from without, although it is to be added, 'and from above.' It would appear that for Barth and Brunner, however, the notion of 'objectivity' is not much more than the repudiation of the idealistic identification of the human and the divine. In the last analysis, knowledge of God comes in the revelational encounter. The 'objectivity', then, of Barth and Brunner is really an emphasis on the 'otherness' of God. There does not seem to be any objectively existing revelation. It is this specific teaching which A. C. Knudson had in mind, when, in a review of Brunner's *The Divine-Human Encounter*, he referred to the 'chief scandal of present day theology' as 'irrationalism and mystery mongering'.[1] Although, therefore, Barth and Brunner do lay emphasis upon the idea of God as objectively existing as the Wholly Other, their view of revelation seems to be a continuation of the Kierkegaardian existential subjectivity.

These facts reveal how the two broadly opposing doctrines of revelation, which we have seen coming into vogue in the period from 1700 to 1860, remain. The divorce has persisted throughout the following years; sometimes the objective and sometimes the subjective aspect received exclusive accentuation. What seemed to be needed was a remarriage of the two, but the succeeding ages do not reveal any sufficient attempt being made to achieve an adequate union of the objective and subjective elements.

But not only did the period uncover this broad opposition between objective and subjective, but it revealed, as a consequence, other divorces which have only in the last decade come into sharp focus. The present period shows a revived interest in the question of revelation. This fact can be seen from the spate of books which have appeared in the last quarter-century with the word 'Revela-

[1] While we have ventured here to refer to Barth's and Brunner's emphasis on the 'otherness' of God as a 'new objective' insistence, it should be noted that in an earlier section a similarity was indicated between the doctrine of the Friends and this modern school. Cf., above, p. 72 (note). Cf., 'the conclusion must be stated that the theologian who has spent his life in an effort to free Christian theology from entanglement with mysticism and with philosophy has in his own theology developed a perspective which embodies a philosophical mysticism whose classic exponent is a philosopher who does not depend upon the New Testament.' Daniel Williams, 'Brunner and Barth on Philosophy,' *The Journal of Religion*, vol. xxvii, No. 4, p. 251, Oct. 1947.

tion' in their titles,[1] not to mention the numerous works with other titles in which the subject is discussed. It is however the antitheses indicated by or latent in the understanding of revelation from 1700 to 1860 which are now receiving serious attention. In the broad context of the opposition already noted, the opposition, that is, between the subjective and objective doctrines of revelation, there are further divorces to be observed between the mediate and the immediate; between the Scriptures and the Spirit; between the words and the Word. Here were initiated divisions and separations which the theology of revelation, since, has not been able success-fully to unify.

(ii) *The Mediate and the Immediate*

The objectivists tended to make revelation something altogether mediate. God Himself is not known: there are truths about Him set forth in propositions which are to receive our assent, but God Him-self is still afar off, secluded behind syllogisms. On the other hand, the subjectivists placed emphasis upon the immediate and direct knowledge of God. But in their statements, the mediatory nature of revelation was either denied, ignored, or obscured.

It seemed impossible in the period for these two opposing doc-trines to come to any sort of terms. There were those who main-tained that revelation is mediated and is therefore not direct, and there were those who claimed it to be direct and therefore not mediated.

At the present day, the neo-Thomists who advocate an exclusive 'propositionalist' doctrine of revelation, are opposed by the Bar-thians whose exclusive emphasis is upon what may be called an 'activist' view. A large section of Protestant theology insists that God's self-disclosure is in terms of saving acts; revelation consists of divine events. Those who proclaim this doctrine are critical of any conception of revelation in terms of doctrine. Some take an extreme position and maintain that revelation contains no doctrinal

---

[1] The following titles will illustrate the point: F. W. Camfield, *Revelation and the Holy Spirit; Revelation: A Symposium*, edited by John Baillie and Hugh Martin; Etienne Gilsôn, *Reason and Revelation in the Middle Ages*; H. Richard Niebuhr, *The Meaning of Revelation*; H. Wheeler Robinson, *Redemption and Revelation*; H. Wheeler Robinson, *Inspiration and Revelation in the Old Testa-ment*; Herbert Cunliffe-Jones, *The Authority of Biblical Revelation*; E. Brunner, *Revelation and Reason*; L. S. Thornton, *Revelation and the Modern World*; E. P. Dickie, *Revelation and Response*; E. Lewis, *A Philosophy of the Christian Revela-tion*; J. Y. Mackinnon, *The Protestant Doctrine of Revelation*; J. Baillie, *The Idea of Revelation in Recent Thought*.

element at all. Others believe the Biblical doctrinal statements to be inferences made by Christians under the influence of the Spirit — inferences, that is, made from the knowledge of God's saving acts in history. Dr William Temple, for example, says emphatically 'there is no such thing as revealed truth'.[1] He grants, however, that there are 'truths of revelation'. These, he goes on to say, are 'propositions which express the results of correct thinking concerning revelation'. But in all these views, however 'doctrine' is understood, it is insisted that revelation in the proper meaning of the term is to be conceived of in terms of divine activity.

The question here is not, as Barth seems to think, simply that between those who regard the divine Spirit as a *datum* or as a *dandum*. Let it be granted, as we think it must, that the divine Spirit is always *dandum*, for the Spirit of God is God in action. At the same time the Scriptures themselves declare that the 'word of God' given in former days is the 'word of God' for us. The God Who spoke in the circumstances of a prophet's or an apostle's life was not simply declaring His interest in the individual to whom He addressed His word. He was speaking to the prophet for the sake of the people; to one man for the sake of other men. God's purpose in declaring His word was to speak to human needs; it was not merely to correct, console or constrain a single individual. What was immediate to the prophet or the apostle were his own personality and environment. But he spoke God's word indirectly to his contemporaries and to those who would follow after. In this sense, therefore, revelation as a disclosure of God must be mediated, and yet, How is it possible for mediate experience of God to become immediate? How can past and distant information become present and dynamic instruction? The question may not be easy to answer, but the fact remains that it can and it does. 'In any appropriation of the dramatic saving events of the Bible I meet not a doctrine about God, not a special type of religious experience, although these are secondary products of the encounter, but I meet God himself.'[2]

The problems raised by an exclusively propositional doctrine of revelation on the one hand and by a completely dynamic one on the other are many and far-reaching. Those who maintain the former

---

[1] *Nature, Man and God*, p. 317. The whole chapter entitled, 'Revelation and its Mode,' (Lecture xii) is important.

[2] W. J. Wolf, *Man's Knowledge of God*, p. 83.

can be asked, Does not a revelation in terms of mere propositions tend to obscure the divine Person? Would not this mean that there would be no knowledge of God Himself but only knowledge about Him? Does such knowledge, it might be further asked, meet the needs of the human spirit? And must not 'faith', in this context, be defined in exclusively intellectualistic terms as purely assent to doctrine? On the other side, to those who maintain that revelation is to be understood as divine action, another set of questions arises. The first is: Is such a view in line with the general teaching of the Church throughout the ages? Does not a revelation in terms of divine action alone leave open the question where is an adequate objective authority to be found? Is not the purpose of revelation the disclosure of some knowledge of God as well as the bringing of the human individual into fellowship with God Himself?[1] Is it sufficient to define revelation as God's saving acts in history and to exclude its application to the biblical significance given to those events?[2] While those who advocate this view of revelation are right to reject the notion that saving faith is faith IN doctrine, May not the truth be faith THROUGH doctrine? These are but a few of the questions which can be raised on each side. The point we stress however is this: Is there any need for this opposition? Can revelation not be both propositional and dynamic at the same time? This is the problem with which the theology of revelation may have to be concerned for some time to come. The point has been made by E. G. Homrighausen when he writes: 'Whether the Christian revelation is only personal and not to some extent propositional is another question, for if God reveals Himself adequately, man's mind must be satisfied.'[3]

It was the writers of the period 1700 to 1860 who brought into opposition the propositional and dynamic views of revelation. The

[1] G. Ernest Wright in his book, *God Who Acts*, denies that the Bible contains any 'static, propositional' statements of doctrine. See, e.g. pp. 35, 36. But is not such a declaration as 'Hear, O Israel: the Lord our God IS one Lord' (Deut. 6. 4) a doctrinal, indeed a metaphysical statement? Cf., E. J. Young, *Thy Word is Truth* (1957), p. 224 f.

[2] Cf., 'In so far as there is revelation of God there is something timeless and of enduring validity; yet this timeless element is mediated through a historical moment and historical circumstances,' H. H. Rowley, *The Faith of Israel*, Intro., p. 21. Also, 'The Bible is throughout based upon the belief that God has unveiled to men something of his own character and will, and that he has spoken through men, in whose mouth he has put his own word,' ibid.

[3] E. G. Homrighausen (Princeton Theological Seminary) Review of Brunner's *The Divine-Human Encounter*, Theology Today, vol. 1, No. 1, April 1944, p. 135 f. Cf., *A Philosophy of the Christian Religion*, Ed. J. Carnell, p. 29. Even Emil

hostility we believe need not be allowed to continue. To deny the mediate in the interests of the immediate, or vice versa, appears to ignore the experience of a multitude of believing people who attest the fact that a revelation which is mediated does become immediately direct and creatively real in the living experience of Christian faith. In the truths revealed, as, for example, God as active, as incarnate, as redeeming, and so forth, there is somehow found an experience of God Himself. The remark of Louis Berkhof is justified by the facts. 'Special revelation', he writes, 'does not consist exclusively in word and doctrine, and does not merely address itself to the intellect. This is more clearly understood at present than it was formerly . . . . The view once prevalent, that revelation consists exclusively in a communication of doctrine, was clearly one-sided. At present, however, some go to the other extreme, equally one-sided, that revelation consists only in communication of power and life.'[1]

(iii) *The Scriptures and the Spirit*

Another aspect of the same general problem left by the discussion of revelation from 1700 to 1860 concerns the relation between the Scriptures and the Spirit. We have seen how the divorce was brought about and the opposition created in the period of our review. It was then asserted by some that all that was needed for faith was assent to the propositions of the Scriptures: the activity of the Spirit was restricted to those of the early Church, or more particularly to those whose commission it was to draw up the things which were to be most surely believed. There was no need for any further action of the Spirit immediately to inspire or illuminate. Men had reason which was adequate to weigh, impartially, the 'evidences of Christianity' and to see how superior were its ethics

Brunner allows the significant word to escape him that 'A Church . . . can do justice to her commission only when she recovers the unity of the *Logos* and the *Dynamis*, of the word and the act of God, which is the distinctive element in the Biblical revelation,' *Revelation and Reason*, p. 164.

[1] *Reformed Dogmatics*: Intro., Louis Berkhof, p. 144. Cf., 'We can understand that man may have some sense of God's majesty and power through Creation or through the processes of history, that he may have some inkling of God through his natural reason or through the sense of the sacred which is part of the human constitution; even so, "behold these are the outskirts of His ways, and how small a whisper do we hear of Him!" But all such knowledge of God is mediate and indirect . . . . The Christian as much as any other is a mediated revelation. We see God in Christ, the Mediator between God and man. Yet Christians have maintained as the very essence of their faith that Jesus Christ is in some sense God Himself incarnate. Thus the revelation of God in Christ is different in kind from every other revelation', N. Micklem, *What is Faith?* pp. 44–6.

and doctrines to all other systems, whether religious or philosophical. And being thus convinced, it was their business and duty to avow the truth of that which was so evidently of divine origin. Revelation is therefore in the context of this conception, a matter of *truth* only.

On the other hand, in the sections, in which the doctrines of revelation as indwelling light and revelation as immediate experience were reviewed, we saw, in the first case in its extreme form, in the second in a modified form, the emphasis upon the place of the Spirit. In the first of these two views revelation is understood as an intrusion into man of the divine Spirit, which is totally distinct from anything human. Revelation is consequently the residence within of an Alien Spirit. In the second view the human and the divine are merged and revelation is conceived to be the upsurge within man of his own essential divinity. It is the coming to authority within of the 'Spirit' which is always there. Whereas in the one case, revelation is thought of as the incoming of an Alien Spirit, in the other it is thought of as the emergence of a Resident Spirit. Both views, however, are concerned to teach that revelation is a matter of *Spirit* only.

In this way there was set up an antithesis between 'Spirit' and 'Truth'. It is this divorce which has proved troublesome in the present era. Here indeed is one of the problems created by the earlier age in which modern theology has become specially interested. The school of Barth and Brunner, for example, as has been shown throughout the foregoing pages, has revealed a tendency to emphasize the place of the Spirit. Barth makes the Bible a 'witness' to the activity of the Spirit. Like Brunner he denies that revelation has or can ever be given in the form of truth. He insists that the will of God can only be known in the present moment. Revelation is God confronting and challenging in the 'now'. It is not a belief in something He has spoken long ago. It is to this immediate and direct activity of the Spirit of God that the written Scriptures bear witness. They attest the possibility of revelation, whenever God chooses to use them in this way.[1] Revelation, therefore, cannot ever be anything written; it cannot consist of truth presented to the minds of men as a static or propositional *datum*.[2]

---

[1] *Church Dogmatics*, I, i, pp. 57 f., 125 f.
[2] *The Word of God and the Word of Man*, pp. 46, 56, etc. Cf., D. M. Baillie's, *God Was in Christ*, pp. 36–8. Baillie notes Barth's lack of interest either in the historical personality of Jesus or in His teaching. Neither is any revelation of God, but rather a 'veiling' of Him. Cf., also, pp. 51, 52.

Is there not, however, a need for, and a possibility of, rewedding these two views, and thus bringing into an acceptable unity the idea of revelation as 'Spirit' and the idea of revelation as 'truth'? A less one-sided relationship between the Scriptures and the Spirit needs to be thought out, a relationship, indeed, more akin to the historic Evangelical position. The Scriptures themselves on their side, give witness to the reality and actuality of the Spirit: they give the assurance that the Holy Spirit has come. And they proclaim further that the Spirit will verify to our understandings the truth of that which the Scriptures themselves declare. On the other side, the Spirit makes authentic to us the reality of the Christ Who has come. But it is through the record that we learn that He has come: it is from its pages we are taught the reality of the Incarnation, 'Emmanuel', 'God with us'. The Spirit gives witness to the truths which are already declared in the Scriptures. It is, as William Cowper suggestively states, when the Spirit breathes upon the Word that the truth comes to sight. A more intimate relationship would seem to be demanded between the Spirit and the Scriptures than the protagonists of these opposing views appear to permit.

There were those, as we have seen, who denied the inner activity of the Spirit and maintained Christian faith to be belief in the Scriptures, while, in opposition, there were those who proclaimed divine revelation to be the direct and immediate inspiration of God and who denied the need for the Scriptures, or who saw them merely as a witness to this idea of revelation. But a Scripture without the Spirit makes for a fruitless faith, while the Spirit without the Scriptures gives an undisciplined faith. The one makes for a dead orthodoxy, the other for an unrestrained enthusiasm. The first gives lifelessness to the Church, the second licence to the individual.[1] There is, we believe, need for a more perfect under-

---

[1] Cf., the statements by Bishop Martensen on this point. Martensen thinks that the 'older Protestantism' which gave 'prominence to salvation as solely and exclusively the reference and design of Scripture' tended to a too individualistic use of the Scripture. But as the Scripture contains much more than the individual needs to know for his own salvation, he believes that emphasis must be put on the place and purpose of the Scripture within the Church. But even there, he declares, the Holy Spirit acts by means of the Scripture. 'The necessity of Scripture is not *principally* for the individual, but for the Church; and its full import and design is stated rather in the assertion, that it contains all truth necessary for the preservation of the Church, and for its progressive development towards its final consummation. This again is to say, that by means of Holy Scripture, under the guidance of the Holy Spirit, the Church not only may be kept in purity of doctrine and true worship, but that in the whole course

standing of the relation between the Scripture and the Spirit. It is the necessity for this understanding which lies behind some remarks made by G. W. Bromiley concerning the Barthian theology. He asks: 'Ought we to think that the Bible is trustworthy merely because we can demonstrate its historical accuracy? Ought we to think it authoritative merely because we have come to know the truth of its message through the Holy Spirit, and irrespective of the historical reliability or otherwise? Ought we not to seek the authority of the Bible in the balanced relationship of a perfect form (the objective Word) and a perfect content (the Word applied subjectively by the Holy Ghost) — the form holding the content. the content not applied except in and through the form?'[1]

(iv) *The Words and the Word*

There is one further and final point to be made. The writers of the period 1700 to 1860 developed another antithesis which in recent days has become an issue of importance. The 'orthodox' and the 'evangelical' writers were agreed in their view of the Scriptures. To both, they were, *in toto*, the 'Word of God'. For those whom we have referred to earlier as the 'Coleridgeans' the term 'Word of God' was regarded as misapplied to the written word.[2] For

of her development there can be no new practice or law established, be it in relation to doctrine or to life, which she cannot abolish by means of the eternal principle of truth and life laid down in the Holy Scripture: moreover, that on the one hand, all critical and cleansing activity in the Church, and on the other hand, all building up, edifying and strengthening activity (taking this expression in its widest sense), must find its governing type for all times in the Holy Scriptures. Maintaining as we do that the Holy Ghost guides the Church into all the truth by means of the Scripture, we attribute to the Scripture perfect sufficiency and clearness (*sufficientia et perspicuitas*); in so far, that is, as the Church is given through Scripture the revelation of the Spirit concerning what is advisable or useful for *any particular time*, while Scripture itself must be looked upon for *all times*, much that it contains not being perfectly accomplished until the latter days. Experience, moreover, teaches that whenever a true reform has been accomplished in the Church, the word, *It was not so in the beginning*, has been spoken with telling power against a lifeless ecclesiasticism, because it has been spoken in the strength of the Holy Scripture. This holds good not only of the great Reformation of the sixteenth century, but of the many successive protests which have been made both in the Middle Ages and in modern times. For as the Church has, in every age, triumphed over that false *gnosis*, which resolves Christianity into merely human reason, by the Word of Scripture, this same word has been a safeguard against a barren orthodoxy, which has built up ecclesiasticism at the expense of Christianity; and it has continually led back to an illumination inseparable from edification, because the apostolic illumination is in its essence an enlightenment which leads on to salvation.' H. Martensen, *Christian Dogmatics*, pp. 405, 406.

[1] *The Evangelical Quarterly*, vol. xix, No. 2, April 1947, p. 136.

[2] Cf., e.g. 'the word of God which saveth and redeemeth the soul is not the word printed on Paper, but is the . . . ever-speaking Word, which is the Son

Coleridge and his followers there was some justification for their eagerness to reserve the title 'Word of God' exclusively for Christ Himself. It was, they believed, a necessary protest against the orthodox notion of revelation as a body of divinely communicated truths to which assent was to be given. An influential body of theological opinion in these days maintains the same position. The 'Word of God', it is proclaimed, is the living person of Christ. The 'Word of God' is a Person, and it is inappropriate if applied to the written Scripture, which is regarded as the record of revelation, of God's saving acts in history.

It is a question however whether this divorce between the Scriptures and the 'Word of God' to which it bears witness can be maintained in view of the testimony of the Scriptures themselves. The phrase, for example, 'Thus saith the Lord' or its equivalent, occurs nearly 4,000 times in the Old Testament alone. In the New Testament, too, there are several passages where the phrase the 'word of God' undoubtedly refers to the spoken or written word.[1] There are other places in the New Testament where a life-giving quality is attributed to the 'Word', but it is not altogether clear whether the reference is to the Incarnate or the Written Word.

In Philippians 2. 16, for example, there is the expression 'the word of life' (λόγος ζωῆς); the title is here evidently applied to the written word. But the same description is given in John 1 of Christ Himself (ὁ λογος . . . ἐν αὐτῷ ζωὴ ἦν, ii, 4). Thus are the Incarnate and Written Word so identified that we are not always sure to which reference is made: yet the same attribute of 'liveliness' is applied to each. The fundamental resemblance lies in the fact that both are a tangible expression of the invisible God. As the written or spoken word expresses, for the purpose of communicating to another, the invisible and inaccessible thought, so Jesus Christ as the Incarnate Word and the Scriptures as the Written Word, express and communicate knowledge of the invisible and inaccessible God. It is this life-giving attribute of the Bible which

of God'. W. Law, *The Way of Divine Knowledge*, p. 137 (see above, p. 160). 'More and more he (F. D. Maurice) had come to look upon all expressions implying that the letter of the Bible is the word of God as denials of the living "Word of God" of whom the Bible speaks,' *Life of F. D. Maurice*, by his son, vol. 2, p. 452 (see above, p. 187).

[1] See Matt. vii. 13; Luke viii. 21; Acts iv. 31, vi. 7, xii. 24, xiii. 5, xiii. 7, xiii. 44, xviii. 11, xix. 20; Rom. ix. 6; 2 Cor. iv. 2; 1 Thess. ii. 13; 1 Tim. iv. 5; 2 Tim. ii. 9; Titus ii. 5; Heb. xiii. 7; 1 John ii. 14, etc. The Scriptures are called also 'the oracles of God', Rom. iii. 2; 'the word of the Lord', Acts xiii. 48; 'the word of Christ,' Col. iii. 16; 'the word of truth', Eph. i. 13, etc.

indicates that there is a unique relation between it and Him Who is rightly called the 'living Word of God'.

In Hebrews 4. 12 there is the statement, 'For the word of God is living (ζῶν γαρ ὁ λογος τοῦ θεοῦ), and active, and sharper than any two-edged sword' (R.V.). Commentators are not agreed as to whether the reference is to the Incarnate or the Written Word. On the whole, it seems to suit the writer's thought better to take it to mean the written word. Yet the very next verse unites the Incarnate Word, Who searches human hearts, with the action of the written word.

In 1 Peter 1. 23, there is another of these passages in which it is difficult to decide whether the Incarnate or the Written Word is in view. Peter speaks of 'the word of God which liveth. . .', or literally, 'the word of God living' (λόγου ζῶντος θεοῦ). It is more probable that here the reference is to the written word in view of the quotation from Isaiah 40. 6–8. In all these passages the attribute of 'liveliness' is applied to the Written Word in the way in which it is applied to the Incarnate Word. This point gives the right to Dr J. K. Mozley to observe 'it is finally true that it (the Scripture) is the Word of God, just as it is finally true about Christ that He is the Word of God'.[1] Certainly the conclusion to be drawn from the data provided by the Scripture itself is, as H. R. Mackintosh says that 'the tie between the Word of God and the Bible is an absolutely vital tie'.[2] It is this relationship between Christ and the Scriptures which the writers of the period 1700 to 1860 seem to have been unable to discern.

There was another distinction introduced in the period 1700 to 1860 which has become of importance in recent discussions on the problems of revelation and its record. Writers of the school of Coleridge and Maurice spoke of the Scriptures, sometimes as 'becoming' and sometimes as 'containing' the word of God. The statements of Coleridge and Maurice and the others were made as a conscious repudiation of the notion that the Bible is a divinely communicated volume in which the human instrument was so obliterated as to leave no room for the human element. To Coleridge and Maurice who had learnt from Kant that man must not be used as a means to an end, this idea was repugnant. The 'Coleridgeans' were anxious to show that the Bible contained

---

[1] *The Christian Faith*, edited by W. R. Matthews, p. 85.
[2] Quoted from the section by H. R. Mackintosh, in Charles Gore, *The Doctrine of an Infallible Book*, p. 57.

human elements, and in so far as it did so, such elements, they declared, were necessarily fallible and in some cases, at least, were definitely erroneous.

It is well known that in these days writers are divided in the same understanding of the 'word of God' in relation to the Scriptures. There are those who take the 'Coleridgean' position and maintain, as did the writers of this school, that the Scripture becomes the word of God in the context of experience. Many recent writers are insistent that the Bible is not in itself, in its totality, the Word of God, but is the vehicle of the divine word. Something of this teaching can be illustrated by reference to C. H. Dodd's book, *The Authority of the Bible*. Dodd says that 'in the expression "the Word of God" lurks an equivocation',[1] and he goes on to assert it is a 'metaphorical expression'.[2] The Bible really mediates the 'Word of God' and therein lies its authority.[3] Ultimately it is that which 'finds' me most, reveals God best. That which arouses and commends itself to the awakened moral consciousness is more certainly the 'word of God'. 'The criterion lies within ourselves, in the response of our own spirit to the Spirit that utters itself in the Scriptures.'[4] This means, therefore that 'Nowhere is the truth given in such purely "objective" form that we can find a self-subsistent external authority'.[5]

On the other side theologians of such diverse views as E. J. Young and J. K. Mozley reject completely all ideas of the Bible as either 'containing' or 'becoming' the 'Word of God'. Mozley, to illustrate, regards the distinction between the Bible and the Word of God as valueless both from the 'apologetic' and the 'dogmatic' points of view. On the apologetic side, Mozley argues that the idea that the Bible 'contains' the Word of God, destroys its unity and leaves us with no answer to the question of the sceptic or the doubter. From whence comes the Bible? On the dogmatic side he finds the 'usefulness' of the Bible compromised. Many of those who maintain that the Scriptures merely 'contain' the Word of God are ready to admit that Jesus Christ is objectively and in Himself, the Word of God. But what is true of Christ, is true also, Mozley maintains, of the Scriptures. He writes: 'So it is with the Bible; its nature as the word of God, as the book in which the deeper tone of the one divine voice is heard through the many changing tones of

---

[1] *The Authority of the Bible*, p. 16.   [2] Ibid.
[3] P. 289.   [4] P. 296.   [5] P. 289.

the human voices, is not open to demonstration; but, in the Christian view of the Bible, it is finally true that it is the Word of God, just as it is finally true about Christ that He is the Word of God. In neither case would the substitution of the expression "contains" or some similar term be an adequate embodiment of Christian faith.'[1] The necessities of a sound theological system demand that the whole Bible should be so designated, he urges. 'Whatever place belongs to the Bible in Christian theology belongs to it as a whole. If in any sense at all the thought of the Word of God may be brought into connection with the Bible it will be fatal to the maintenance of that wholeness, if in the course of the development of the dogmatic scheme it were necessary to enquire whether allowance were being made for the possibility that at such and such a point reference to the Bible might be illegitimate, since in that particular context there was no certainty that the Bible was containing the Word of God.'[2]

The advocates of each of these opposing views will require answers to certain important questions from the other. Those who maintain that the Bible 'contains' the Word of God will demand of their opponents: What precisely is the significance of the word 'is', in the proposition, 'The Bible *is* the Word of God?' Can the 'contradictions' within the record be reconciled with the assertion that the Bible is throughout the 'Word of God'? Is the statement, it is further asked, true to experience? Can it be maintained, for example, that the list of names in the book of Numbers is as much the Word of God as the Epistle to the Romans? And in the Epistle to the Romans itself, are the last two chapters as 'divine' as the earlier sections? Is Joshua as important for the spiritual life as John? What is to be said about such passages as the *Pericope Adulterae* and the last verses of Mark's Gospel? If the Bible is the 'Word of God', does not this mean that its several injunctions are

---

The Christian Faith (edited by W. R. Matthews), p. 55.

[2] This carefully worded statement of Mozley needs to be pondered for it is an exact statement of the position. Were it the purpose in these pages to follow through the implications of what is being disclosed by our study, this is the conclusion which we would maintain. In spite of all the problems which beset the doctrine that the Bible *is* the Word of God, the designation more truly than any other expresses its precise nature. The more thoroughly the doctrine of Scripture is studied in its isagogic and practical contexts the more unhesitatingly may it be referred to as the Word of God. The assertion that the Bible merely 'contains' the Word of God or that it is a 'witness' to a possible revelation, when made, as it now is, to repudiate the proclamation that it is itself the Word of God, is not only misleading but is clearly false.

all equally binding? In this case, is not the word concerning women not praying with uncovered head of as permanent force as the moral requirements of the redeemed life?

On the other hand, those who insist that the Bible in its totality and essence is the Word of God ask of their opponents: If the Bible only becomes or contains the Word of God, When can we declare that it is so? Does not the assertion that the Bible 'becomes' the Word of God, mean that it becomes in us what it is not in itself? Does not this mean that truth is made by experience? Is there no objective standard of truth by which the varying claims to have heard the voice of God may be tested? Does not the subjective method which this view expounds make the ultimate authority in the things of the Spirit to be the individual's own conscience? Did not Jesus frequently refer to the Old Testament Scriptures as the 'Word of God' although He was aware of the difficulties for faith which were involved? Is not all that is required for the subjective appreciation of divine revelation, not a denial that the Bible is the Word of God, but a clear understanding of what is meant by the inner testimony of the Spirit?

These are certainly important questions asked by one side of the other. The question, however, arises as to whether there should not be a union of the two ideas in any final statement of the meaning and significance of the Bible. Martensen, at any rate, seems to think so, although he expressed preference for one statement as against the other. Martensen notes that those who maintain that the Bible 'contains' the Word of God are anxious to safeguard its human element; while those who state that it IS the Word of God emphasize its divineness. But there must be asserted, he observes, as in the Person of Christ, 'not only the union of the divine and human in Scripture, but at the same time the distinction between the two. The old proposition, *the Scripture is the Word of God*, expressed the union; the modern dictum, *the Scriptures contain the Word of God*, expresses the distinction. The first proposition is clearly preferable to the second which is vague and indistinct, and may be applied to many writings. The first, however, is untrue, if it be taken so to affirm the union, as to exclude all distinction of the divine and human elements in the Bible .... The opposite proposition, which does not venture to assert that scripture IS the word of God, but that it only CONTAINS the Word of God, considers only the distinction between the divine and human elements, and overlooks the all-pervading, obvious, and typical union of these in scripture, the sacred, all-pervading, apparent, and fundamental truth, which in unsullied clearness enwraps and even subdues the temporal and human narrowness.'[1]

Fruitful use has, more recently, been made of another distinction indicated by the 'Coleridgeans' between revelation and its record. The important truth marked out by the distinction is that there is a real and objective revelation in divine works and words prior to, and independent of, any written word. Revelation, in the present era, is said to be God's activity in human history and experience. The question, however, needs to be asked; Is it possible to abstract this activity from its historical circumstances? Professor C. R. North refers to what he calls 'the modern Marcionite attitude to the Old Testament'. The error in it, he then goes on to say, 'is that we unconsciously tend to lay the emphasis upon certain *ideas about* God, which we assume to be true, or untrue, independently of history. It is a concession we make, quite needlessly, to Lessing. We grant that the ideas have been mediated through history, and we are scrupulously careful, when we expound them, to place them in their historical setting. We fail to see that the historical circumstances are an integral part of the revelation. Instead, we are inclined to treat them as so much husk to the pure grain of truth. The historical occasion, once it is past, is more or less irrelevant except for the purposes of illustration. It has served its purpose as a matrix for the truth, and may now, without much loss, be ignored. In point of fact, the historical occasion is an essential element in the revelation.'[2]

If it is allowed that 'the historical occasion is an essential element in the revelation', then we should go further. The 'historical occasion' of the divine act, it is argued, is known to us only as it is recorded. Revelation then, it must be maintained, may be conceived as God's divine actions in history, but these 'actualities' of God in history are as if they had not been, apart from their preservation in records. This must mean, in the last analysis, that 'the line between revelation and its record is becoming thin, and that, in another true sense, the *record*, in the fulness of its contents, *is itself for us the revelation*'.[3]

---

[1] *Christian Dogmatics*, p. 403.
[2] C. R. North, *The Old Testament Interpretation of History*, p. 153.
[3] J. Orr, *Revelation and Inspiration*, p. 159.

In this connection it is of interest to observe how a number of writers, who are most anxious to avoid any identity of revelation with its record are found unwittingly to make it.[1] The question then is, should the idea of revelation be extended to include, not only the acts of God in history, but the history of those acts, and the interpretation and application of those divine activities as they are preserved for us? This is the conclusion which seems to be demanded. It certainly is true that as 'soon as we try to abstract the values from their concrete embodiment, we evacuate them of all reality and become sentimentalists. The spiritual must always be embodied to be known and faithfully served; the eternal must clothe itself in temporal form to enter effectually within our horizon.'[2]

CONCLUSION

The historical study of the subject of revelation which has been our theme has shown how certain periods in the history of the Church are marked by specific interest in special ideas. The period 1700 to 1860 was concerned with the problems of the divine self-disclosure. But in this closing section it has been shown how in the present period of revived interest in the doctrine of revelation, it is the problems which the earlier period left unsolved which are demanding attention. There has been, of course, no exhaustive attempt made here to solve these problems. The question has, however, been raised whether the opposing doctrines which then came into conflict, and which still persist, are ultimately hostile. It is suggested that the full truth concerning revelation may be somehow a synthesis of the views indicated and illustrated. God's self-disclosure, we believe, cannot be reduced to any neat formula.

Varied, and sometimes opposing, as were the doctrines of revelation between the years 1700 and 1860, the one belief common to all was that there was a revelation of God. This is the certainty which men still require. They would know that God has disclosed Him-

---

[1] Cf., e.g. Brunner, 'the written record is part of this revelation it is not the whole,' *Revelation and Reason*, p. 12. 'Holy Scripture therefore does not only speak of revelation, it is itself revelation,' op. cit., p. 21. Dodd, 'The Church . . . offers the Bible . . . as the authoritative record of the divine revelation in history,' *The Bible To-day*, p. 15. 'The Church offers this book as a revelation of God,' p. 12.

[2] H. Wheeler Robinson, *Redemption and Revelation*, p. xliv, cf., p. 186. Cf., 'The Bible contains the record, the interpretation and the literary reflection of His grace in history,' A. B. Bruce, *The Chief End of Revelation*, p. 280.

self, and that the revelation given is adequate to and available for the deepest needs of every man as a rational and spiritual being.[1] And, just because man is both, revelation will be both. What may, therefore, become divided by the necessities of theory can become united in the realities of experience.[2] Because man is 'spiritual', revelation must come as 'Spirit', and because he is 'rational', revelation must come as 'Truth'. This means that, as a final fact, revelation will be, not one to the exclusion of the other, but at the same time both. Revelation, that is, will be not 'Spirit' only, and, not 'Truth' only; but revelation will be, at once, 'Spirit and Truth'. The experience of the apostle Peter illustrates the point. For him faith was not belief in 'truths' based upon the occular demonstrations of 'signs and wonders': and for us, faith is not belief in 'truths' reared on the strength of historical evidences. Peter's confession was the result of a divine illumination; for us, likewise, there must be the inner witness of the Spirit. 'And yet it remains true that the revelation came to Peter as an inward witness to the Jesus whom he knew in the flesh, and it comes to us as a witness to the Jesus whom we know as an historical personality through the Gospel story.'[3] God's full and final self-disclosure is in the Christ declared to us in and through the pages of the New Testament and

---

[1] It should be pointed out, however, that it is to Greek thought, not to the Biblical writings, is due the definition of man as a rational animal. 'The classical view of man, comprised primarily of Platonic, Aristotelian, and Stoic conceptions of human nature . . . is to be understood primarily from the standpoint of the uniqueness of his rational faculties. What is unique in man is nous.' (Reinhold Niebuhr, *Human Nature*, p. 6). The Scripture, on the other hand, presents man as a sentient being whose chief end is to worship and glorify God. Latent, perhaps, in the Greek doctrine, which it was not possible for its philosophers, clearly to indicate, is the idea of man as a worshipping being, since it is rational creatures alone who are qualified for the high purpose which the Scripture presents. Yet the Biblical literature which reveals man as a worshipping creature, most certainly assumes that he is a rational creature. He is addressed as a responsible being called 'to reason together' with God. An exclusive Greek conception results in the view of man whose best powers are seen in the perception of rational connection to formal syllogisms and revelation is consequently considered to be merely a disclosure of truth in logical propositions. But when the truth in the Scholastic view and the truth of the Scripture view are united it will give an understanding of revelation as at the same time a communication and a communion. There will be information for the sake of fellowship. In a final synthesis therefore, our understanding of revelation must unite the ideas of Greece and Galilee.

[2] Cf., 'An antimony simultaneously admits the truth of two contradictory, logically incompatible, but ontologically equally necessary assertions. An antimony testifies to the existence of a mystery beyond which the human reason cannot penetrate. This msytery nevertheless is actualized and lived in religious experience. All fundamental dogmatic definitions are of this nature,' Sergius Bulgakov, *The Wisdom of God*, p. 116, note.

[3] D. M. Baillie, *God Was In Christ*.

made known to us by the Spirit. Herein is a revelation adequate and available to all as 'Spirit and Truth'.

The modern understanding of revelation, it is claimed, has, on the one hand, made impossible a doctrine of a verbally inspired Scripture. The books of the Bible can no longer be regarded as written down by 'private secretaries of the Holy Ghost' as John Donne, for example, maintained. On the other hand, the protagonists of the modern view contend that their 'activist' doctrine of revelation has made obsolete the older liberalism which was obsessed with problems of the text and authorship of the books of Scripture in an effort to upset the accepted doctrine of the Bible as the Word of God. This type of liberalism, it is now asserted, is no longer valid. It missed the point because, by concerning itself with questions of introduction, it failed to focus attention upon the content of the Scripture itself. It was thus blind to the significance of revelation which is to be regarded not as a word spoken long since or as a doctrine once and for all given, but as an event, a divine activity. By casting out the idea of Scripture as itself the Word of God the older liberalism lost all idea of any Word of God.

The newer liberalism claims to have retrieved the situation. Now 'the term "Word of God" has been reconceived. As a word in inter-personal relations is a means of personal self-disclosure, as speech is a revelation or disclosure of personal life, so the "Word of God" is understood by analogy as the whole process of divine self-disclosure. It was in this sense — so runs the claim — that the Word of God was originally used in the Bible. Barth has spoken of a threefold process of divine self-disclosure, (1) God encounters and speaks to man, (2) man speaks or proclaims God's Word, and (3) someone writes down the record of these events.[1] Thus the emphasis is taken from the written word, which becomes simply a written record of revelation, and is placed upon an event or experience in which God is alleged to reveal or disclose himself to man. What others have called religious experience is viewed as a "divine-human encounter." '[2]

Stressing the Kierkegaardian emphasis upon the autonomy of the single individual, there is to-day, under the influence of Martin Buber, importance placed upon the 'I-Thou' relationship of religious knowledge in contrast with the 'I-It' relationship of

[1] K. Barth, *The Doctrine of the Word of God*, p. 98 f.
[2] John A. Hutchinson, *Faith, Reason, Existence* (O.U.P., New York), p. 112.

scientific knowledge. More recently there has been a declared effort to explain revelation in still more personal terms. This is shown, for example, in William Nicholls' book entitled, *Revelation in Christ*. It is acknowledged, of course, that the writers of the more immediate past have succeeded 'in the shifting of the locus of revelation from literature to history, and from the propositional to the personal'.[1] At the present, a firmer declaration that Christ is the only proper 'locus' of revelation is being called for. In some quarters this view is linked with the idea of the Church as an extension of the Incarnation and with the conclusion drawn that there may be more knowledge of Christ still to be disclosed. It is in this way that the wheel has come full circle and the very effort to safeguard revelation as final in Christ is consequently jeopardized.

It is a matter of astonishment to find it being constantly asserted that the idea of revelation in Christ is the special discovery of recent years. Such claims can be made only by a total disregard of historical facts. It is true, of course, that the older orthodox apologists did obscure the Person of Christ and did conceive of revelation as the communication of doctrinal propositions. Brunner has some justification for his remark that the idea early arose in the Church under the influence of Greek philosophy that divine revelation was the communication of doctrinal truths which were otherwise inaccessible to human reason, and that faith consisted in holding these supernaturally revealed doctrines for truth.[2] Brunner is perhaps too confident about the earliness of the influence: but, however this may be, it is a fact that there did come a time when there was the influence with the results as stated for the idea of revelation. The preceding pages will have made clear, however, that it was among the orthodox anti-deistic apologists where this idea prevailed. And they were merely carrying on the scholastic tradition. But the same charge cannot be sustained against the Evangelicals. They certainly held to an exalted view of Scripture; but their high view of Scripture was coupled with the highest view of Christ's Person. The very exaltation of the Bible, in their case, far from detracting from Christ, worked rather the other way. The investigation of the works of Charles Simeon and John Wesley will have made it clear that their profound view of the Person of Christ was not the summary of ideas derived from their own personal

---

[1] William Nicholls, *Revelation in Christ* (S.C.M., 1957), p. 9.
[2] E. Brunner, *The Divine-Human Encounter*, p. 12.

encounter with God in Christ. Their conception of Christ was based upon the Scriptures through which the experience was mediated. To begin with the personal encounter seems to be in the last analysis a falling back upon the view of Schleiermacher which makes *Dogmatics* to be the summary of the pious feelings. It is such ideas which account for the contradictions inherent in the newer liberal approach.

In its reactions from the 'Jesus of History' cult of the older school the newer emphasis upon the 'super-historical' Christ makes the Scriptures even less vital for faith. The historical picture is, after all, of little value, since revelation does not belong to the Christ Who lived and taught and died. It is the Christ Who is outside the historic process, the exalted Christ, Who is revelation. The Synoptic gospels have to do with the historic human Jesus and, it is said, it matters little for faith how factually correct they are. John's gospel, on the other hand, is a construction of faith and is therefore not historical. We are thus informed that, 'Faith presupposes, as a matter of course, *a priori,* that the Jesus of history is not the same as the Christ of faith.'[1] Professing to renounce Schleiermacher's views (for who is a more violent critic of him than Brunner?) this newer liberalism ends up by adopting his attitude to the biblical basis for faith.

The older liberalism has shown how difficult it is to accept the highest view of our Lord's Person when once the foundations upon which it rests have been undermined. It is certainly not as a result of a personal encounter that we learn that the Word became flesh and that the Word was God. The 'becoming' flesh is, to be sure, an event indeed, the divinest event of all. But it is declared as a doctrine. The statement that the 'Word was God' is unquestionably a doctrinal statement.

This means as a final result that the proclamation Christ is revelation, or Revelation is in Christ throws us back upon Scripture. It is not any Christ Who is revelation. Those who say, Lo, here is Christ, or, Lo, there, are not to be believed unless the Christ Whom they declare is the Christ of the New Testament. It is not the Jesus of History or the Christ of Faith as if there were two distinct beings. The Christ Who is final revelation is not the Christ of subjective experience, nor the Christ of personal encounter, nor the Christ of Church declaration, except in so far as these are identical

[1] E. Brunner, *The Mediator* (E.T.), p. 184.

with the Christ set forth in Scripture. The Christ Who is revelation is the Biblical Christ; no more and no less. This is the Christ Who Himself authenticated this conclusion when 'beginning from Moses, and from all the prophets, he interpreted to them in all the Scriptures the things concerning himself'.[1]

[1] Lk. 24:27 (R.V.)

ALPHABETICAL LIST OF
BOOKS MENTIONED

Adventure, (Edited) B. H. Streeter, 52
Age of Reason, The, T. Paine, 128, 141
Aids to Reflection, S. T. Coleridge, 28, 30, 172–3
Alciphron, or, Minute Philosopher, Geo. Berkeley, 29, 152–4
Analogy, (New Edition), Joseph Butler, 21, 55, 77, 94, 98, 108, 111, 112
Analogy of Religion and Science, F. Nolan, 120, 121, 124, 125
Answer to Tindal, Leyland, 54, 91
Answer to Toland, P. Browne, 22, 76
Apologetics, A. B. Bruce, 54
Apology, (10th edition, 1841), R. Barclay, 68–9, 72, 73
Apology for the Bible, R. Watson, 128, 140n., 141–3
Aquinas, F. C. Copleston, 104
Authority of the Bible, The, C. H. Dodd, 279
Authority of the Biblical Revelation, H. Cunliffe-Jones, 270n.
Authority of the Scriptures, The, J. W. C. Wand, 192n.

Beginnings of Quakerism, The, W. C. Braithwaite, 66, 67, 70, 71
Bible To-day, The, C. H. Dodd, 283n.
Bibliography of British History, 1714–1789, Edited Pargellis and Madley, 50

Case of Reason, The, W. Law, 76, 113–16
Chain of Principles, A, John Arrowsmith, 202
Changing Background of Religion and Ethics, The, H. Weldon Carr, 7, 8
Charles Simeon, H. C. G. Moule, 235
Chief End of Revelation, The, A. B. Bruce, 193, 283n.
Christian Apologetics, Alan Richardson, 87, 89, 99, 108–9
Christian Apprehension of God, The, H. R. Mackintosh, 59, 85
Christian Doctrine of God, The, Emil Brunner, 190–1
Christian Doctrine of Man, The, H. Wheeler Robinson, 151
Christian Dogmatics, H. Martensen, 275n., 276n., 282
Christian Faith, The, Edited W. R. Matthews, 278, 280
Christian Faith, The, F. Schleiermacher, 166–71
Christian in Philosophy, The, J. V. Langmead Casserley, 54
Christian Leaders in the Last Century, J. C. Ryle, 212

Christian Philosophy, V. Knox, 162
Christian Thought since Kant, C. E. Moore, 51
Christian Understanding of Man, The, several authors, 81n., 134n.
Christian View of God and the World, J. Orr, 62, 102
Christianity as Old as Creation, (3rd edition), M. Tindal, 17, 47–51, 53, 114
Christianity Justified upon the Scripture Foundation, etc., H. Stebbing, 3n.
Christianity not Founded upon Argument, H. Dodwell, 23, 150, 154–7, 251
Christianity not Mysterious, (3rd edition), T. Toland, 22, 43–6, 76
Church Dogmatics, 1, i, 1, ii; K. Barth, 12n., 72, 73n., 105n., 106n., 160, 177, 274
Commentary on the Epistle to the Galatians, M. Luther, 248
Communion with God, W. Herrmann, 207n.
Compendium to the History of Doctrine, K. P. Hagenback, 209n.
Concluding Unscientific Postscript, S. Kierkegaard, 267
Confessions of an Enquiring Spirit, S. T. Coleridge, 173–4, 233n.
Contra Celsus, Origin, 99
Contra Faust., Manich., Augustine, 100
Contra Gentiles, T. Aquinas, 79
Credibility of the Christian Revelation from its Internal Evidences, Samuel Bradford, 3n.
Credo, K. Barth, 73n.
Critique of Practical Reason, I. Kant, 165
Critique of Pure Reason, I. Kant, 6, 165

de Carne Christi, Tertullian, 38
de Civ. Dei., Augustine, 100
Defence of Dr. Clarke's Evidences of Natural and Revealed Religion, H. Stebbing, 77, 91, 101
Defence of Revealed Religion, A, J. Conybeare, 22, 91, 92, 107
Defence of the Authority of the Scriptures, W. Whitaker, 201
Demonstration of True Religion, Bishop Burnet, 3n.
Descartes, P. J. Mahaffy, 20, 21
Development of English Theology in the Nineteenth Century from 1800 to 1860, V. Storr, 6, 35n., 76
de Veritate, Lord Herbert of Cherbury, 40
Diary (vol. 1), Crabb Robinson, 171
Dictionary of National Biography, vol. 6, 163
Die protestantische Theologie im 19 Jahrundert, K. Barth, 12
Dionysius the Areopagite on the Divine Names and the Mystical Theology, C. E. Rolt, 29n.
Discourses, John Smith, 32, 34, 68

Discourse Concerning the Unalterable Obligation of Natural and Revealed Religion and the Truth and Certainty of the Christian Religion, (9th edition), S. Clarke, 3n., 22, 89, 90, 96, 141

Discourse Concerning the Truth of the Christian Revelation, (2nd edition), Jortin, 129, 140–1

Discourse of Freethinking, A Collins, 17, 46–7, 62

Discourse of Metaphysics, Rene Descartes, 11

Discourse of Method, Rene Descartes, 19, 20

Divine Authority of the Scriptures Asserted, Thomas Goodwin, 199, 200

Divine Authority of the Scriptures Asserted from Adaptation to the Real State of Human Nature, (2nd edition), John Miller, 129n., 133–4

Divine Dialogues, H. More, 122

Divine-Human Encounter, The, Emil Brunner, 286

Divine Original and Incomparable Excellency of the Christian Revelation, Josiah Woodward, 3n.

Divine Original of the Scriptures, J. Owen, (*Works*, vol. xvi), 196, 197–9

Doctrine of an Infalliable Book, The, Charles Gore, 278.

Draw-net of the Kingdom of Heaven, etc., H. Denne, 63

Early Puritans, The, J. R. Mersden, 199n.

Ecclesiastical Polity, R. Hooker, 371

Education of the Human Race, Lessing, 11

Emil Brunner's Concept of Revelation, P. K. Jewett, 174, 191

Endeavour of Making the Principles of the Christian Religion . . . plaine and easie, An, Henry Palmer, 202

English and American Philosophy since 1800, A. K. Rogers, 188

English Church in the Nineteenth Century, The, J. H. Overton, 35n.

English Church Reform, 1810–1840, W. L. Mathieson, 215

English Divines, S. T. Coleridge, 173

English Religious Tradition, N. Sykes, 10

English Thought, 1850–1900, L. E. Elliott-Binns, 6

Enquiry into the Evidences of the Christian Revelation, An, H. Stebbing, 28, 96, 97, 100

Enthusiasm, R. Knox, 66

Enthusiasm of the Methodists and Papists Compared, Geo. Lavington, 26, 119

Essays, D. Hume, 100

Essays and Addresses on the Philosophy of Religion, F. von Hügel, 82

Essays and Reviews, several authors, 11, 79

Essay on Man, A. Pope, 266

Essay on Reason, An, A. Collins, 46

Essay on the Human Understanding, (New edition, 1894), J. Locke, 31, 42, 50, 251

Essay on the Nature and Immutability of Faith in Opposition to Sophistry and Scepticism, J. Beattie, 128

Essays on Several Important Subjects in Religion and Philosophy, J. Glanvill, 25, 26, 35, 37

Ethica, Spinoza, 171

Evangelical Quarterly, April 1947, 276

Evidence of the Christian Religion, A Collection of Works, Tracts and Essays on the Subject, 1812, 140, 146–8

Excursion, W. Wordsworth, 25

Existence and Analogy, E. L. Mascall, 104n.

Expository Times, Jan. 1953, 137n.

Exposition of the Old and New Testament, M. Henry, 200–1.

Fable of the Bees, B. Mandeville, 153

Faith of Israel, The, H. H. Rowley, 270n.

Faith of a Moralist, A. E. Taylor, 107

Faith, Reason, Existence, John A. Hutchinson, 285

Freedom and Authority in Religion, W. Y. Mullins, 88

Freedom and the Spirit, N. Berdyaev, 15n.

Free Thinking, Benjamin Ibbot, 3n.

Gangraena, Thomas Goodwin, 64

God and the Modern World, H. S. Box, 104

God in Christian Thought and Experience, W. R. Matthews, 86, 192

God Was In Christ, D. M. Baillie, 274n., 284

God Who Acts, The, G. Ernest Wright, 272n.

Grace and Personality, J. Oman, 36

Grace in the New Testament, J. Moffatt, 80

Gradual Revelation of the Gospel for the Time of Men's Apostasy, William Berriman, 3n.

Grounds and Reasons of The Christian Religion, A. Collins, 46

Hagiomastrix, or, Scourge of the Saints, Thomas Goodwin, 199

Hastings Bible Dictionary, 86

He Who Is, A Study in Traditional Theism, E. L. Mascall, 56, 104

History of Christian Doctrine, G. P. Fisher, 4n., 41, 209

History of Dogma, A. Harnack, 2n., 4n.

History of English Rationalism, A. W. Benn, 171n., 175

History of English Thought in the Eighteenth Century, (2 vols.), L. Stephen, 47, 158, 263

History of Ethics, H. Sidgwick, 32

History of Europe, H. A. L. Fisher, 87

History of the English Church, (vol. 7), Overton and Relton, 75.

History of the English Church, (vol. viii), F. W. Cornish, 162
History of the Evangelical Party in the Church of England, G. R. Balleine, 194n.
History of Philosophy, S. W. F. Hegel, 21, 23, 29
History of Philosophy, W. Windleband, 20, 21
History of Protestant Theology, J. A. Dorner, 209
History of the Puritans, Daniel Neal, 199
History of the Synoptic Tradition, R. Bultmann, 137n.
History of Western Philosophy, B. Russell, 19n.
Human Nature, Reinhold Niebuhr, 284n.

Idea of Revelation in Recent Thought, J. Baillie, 270n.
Idea of the Holy, R. Otto, 167
Illustrations of the Truth of the Christian Revelation, (2nd edition), Edward Maltby, 140n., 143–6
Influence of Darwin on Philosophy, J. Dewey, 7n.
Inspiration and Revelation in the Old Testament, H. Wheeler Robinson, 270n.
Institutes of the Christian Religion, (2 vols.), (Beveridge's translation), John Calvin, 86, 88, 194, 209, 210, 211
Institutes of Theology, T. Chalmers, 196
Internal Evidences for the Truth of Revealed Religion, Thomas Erskine, 163–4
Internal Evidences of the Christian Revelation, Soame Jenyng, 258
Interpretation of Religion, J. Baillie, 57
Introduction to Protestant Dogmatics, Lobstein, 24
Introduction to Reformed Dogmatics, A. Lecerf, 28, 165
Introduction to the Philosophy of Religion, J. Caird, 58n.
Introductory Preface to the Pentateuch, Geddes, 136

John Whitgift and the Reformation, P. W. Dawley, 206n.
Journal, George Fox, 67, 68, 73
Journal of Religion, Oct. 1947, 269n.
Justification of the Good, Vlad. Solovyof, 58n.

Kant, S. Körner, 166
Kierkegaard Anthology, A, Robert Bretall, 267
Letter to Dion, B. Mandeville, 153

Letter to the Deists, H. Prideaux, 76, 77
Life and Letters of John Cairns, Prof. MacEwan, 19
Life and Letters of Lord Macaulay, G. O. Traveylan, (1 vol., Silver Library), 215
Life of F. D. Maurice, (2 vols.), by his son, 23, 26, 158, 178, 181, 183, 187, 277n.

Life of Matthew Henry, J. B. Williams, 200
Life of Milton, D. Mason, 65
Light of Nature, Tucker, 25n.
Limits of Human Thought, H. L. Mansel, 61, 184
Lives of the Puritans, Benjamin Brook, 202
Luther and the Scriptures, M. Reu, 209n.

Man in Christ, A, James Stewart, 80
Man in Revolt, Emil Brunner, 179n., 81n., 134n.
Man's Knowledge of God, W. J. Wolf, 87, 271
Meaning of God in Human Experience, W. E. Hocking, 166
Meaning of History, N. Beryvaev, 36, 87
Meaning of Revelation, The, H. Richard Niebuhr, 270n.
Mediator, The, E. Brunner, 287
Meditations, Rene Descartes, 20
Meeting of Extremes in Contemporary Philosophy, B. Bosanquet, 82
Miracles and Christianity, J. Wendland, 101
Mission of the Comforter, Julius Hare, 178
Modern Introduction to Logic, I. M. Stebbing, 106
Monodology, Leibniz, (tr. R. Latta), 11
Moral and Religious Aphorisms, B. Whichote, 32
Mystic Way, The, Evelyn Underhill, 86

Natural History of Enthusiasm, Isaac Taylor, 65, 66, 88
Natural Obligation to Believe the Principles of Religion and Divine Revelation, John Leng, 3n.
Natural Religion Insufficient and Revealed Religion Necessary, Thomas Halyburton, 196
Natural Theology, W. Paley, 25, 83
Nature and Destiny of Man, R. Niebuhr, 87
Nature, Man and God, W. Temple, 58, 84, 190, 271
Nature of the Atonement, J. MacLeod, Campbell, 163

Of the Divine Things, Jacobi, 166
Old Testament Interpretation of History, The, C. R. North, 282
On Truth as it is Distinguished from Revelation, Probability, Possibility, and Falsehood, Lord Herbert of Cherbury, 40
Outlines of Christian Theology, W. N. Clarke, 84
Outlines of Cosmic Philosophy, Fiske, 8n.
Oracles of Reason, Charles Blount, 40, 53
Origin of Species, Charles Darwin, 7, 8
Our Faith, Emil Brunner, 191
Our Knowledge of God, J. Baillie, 24
Oxford Apostles, G. Faber, 212n.

Oxford Young Gentleman's Reply to Dodwell and Two Letters from Dr. Layland, published together with Christianity not Founded on Argument, 157

Person and Place of Jesus Christ, The, P. T. Forsyth, 95, 96, 192–3
Personal Idealism and Mysticism, W. R. Inge, 70
Philebus, Plato, 38
Philosophical Approach to Religion, The, E. S. Waterhouse, 41
Philosophical Fragments, S. Kierkegaard, 160n.
Philosophical Method, R. G. Collingwood, 57
Philosophy and Religion, Hastings Rashdall, 58n.
Philosophy of Religion, Emil Brunner, 61, 191, 255n.
Philosophy of Religion, G. Galloway, 107
Philosophy of the Christian Religion, E. J. Carnell, 272n.
Philosophy of the Christian Revelation, E. Lewis, 86, 270n.
Physical Basis of Life, T. H. Huxley, 10
Physico-Theology, W. Denham, 3n.
Plea for Religion and the Sacred Writings, Simpson, 128
Popular Evidences of Christianity Stated and Examined, T. W. Lancaster, 129n., 130–3
Preamble to Act of Parliament of Blasphemous and Exerable Opinions, Aug. 9th, 1650, Scobell's Collection of Acts and Ordinances, Part ii, 65
Pretended Difficulties in Natural Religion no Excuse for Infidelity, Brampton Gurdon, 3n.
Priestcraft in Perfection, A. Collins, 46
Primitive Christianity Revived, W. Penn, 73
Principal Cairns, John Cairns, 19
Principles and Connection of Natural and Revealed Religion, Distinctly Stated, A. A. Sykes, 22, 78, 92, 93, 97, 98
Principles of Knowledge, Rene Descartes, 20
Principles of Psychology, H. Spencer, 5
Problems in the Relations of God and Man, C. C. J. Webb, 14n., 149
Procedure, Extent and Limits of the Human Understanding, P. Browne, 28, 94, 102, 103
Proposal for a National Reformation of Manners, (1694), 263
Proslogion, Anselm, 57
Protestant Doctrine of Revelation, The, J. Y. MacKinnon, 270n.
Protestant Era, The, P. Tillick, 37, 86

Ranter's Bible, Gilbert Roulston, 64
Rational Religion and Christian Theology, C. E. Raven, 32n.
Reality of God, F. von Hügel, 24
Reasonableness of Christianity, J. Locke, 30, 41, 42

Reason and Revelation in the Middle Ages, E. Gilson, 270n.
Redemption and Revelation, H. Wheeler Robinson, 60, 87, 270n., 283n.
Reden, F. Schliermacher, (tr. Oman), 59
Reformed Dogmatics: Introduction, Louis Berkhof, 273
Relevance of Christianity, The, F. R. Barry, 207
Religio-medico, Thomas Browne, 31
Religion and Evolution, F. B. Jeavons, 58n.
Religion and Revelation, A. L. Lilley, 207
Religion, Philosophy and Psychical Research, C. D. Broad, 55
Religions of Authority and Religion of the Spirit, A. Sabatier, 24, 74
Religion within the Bounds of Pure Reason, I. Kant, 13, 174
Religious Enthusiasm, G. F. Nott, 120–3
Religious Liberalism in the Eighteenth Century, R. N. Stromberg, 157
Religious Thought in England, (3 vols.), J. Hunt, 2, 4n.
Remarks on the Internal Evidences for the Truth of Revealed Religion,
     Thomas Erskine, 27, 28, 217–20
Report of the Society for the Promotion of Christian Knowledge (1832), 118
Retreat from Christianity, J. V. Langmead Casserley, 79, 83
Revelation, A Symposium, edited by John Baillie and Hugh Martin,
     270n.
Revelation and the Holy Spirit, W. F. Camfield, 73n., 270n.
Revelation and Inspiration, J. Orr, 282
Revelation and Reason, Emil Brunner, 72n., 88, 160, 166, 170n., 191,
     207n., 211n., 270n., 273n., 283n., 359n., 373n.
Revelation and Response, E. P. Dickie, 270n.
Revelation and the Modern World, L. S. Thornton, 270n.
Revelation in Christ, William Nicholls, 287
Rule of Faith, The, W. P. Patterson, 209n.

Sacred Theory of the Earth, Bishop Burnet, 25n.
Scandal of Christianity, Emil Brunner, 134n.
*Scheme of Divine Revelation, Considered Principally in Connection with
     the Progress and Improvement of Human Society*, George Chandler,
     125–7
Scheme of Liberal Prophecy, A. Collins, 46
Scholastic View of Inspiration, H. Pope, Irish Theological Quarterly,
     July 1911 (Published by Professors in the Faculty of Theology,
     Maynooth College), 178n.
Scripture Light, the Most Sure Light, William Bridge, 203, 204
Selected Letters of John Wesley, F. Gill, 330
Self in the Dramas of History, The, R. Niebuhr, 53, 81
Sequel to What is Revelation, F. D. Maurice, 186
Sermons, John Tillotson, 38
Sermons, Joseph Butler, 111

Seven Enigmas, The, E. Du Bois Reymond, 8n.
Seventeenth Century Background, The, B. Willey, 24, 31, 34, 41, 43
Short and Easy Method with the Deists, C. Leslie, 76
Short History of Our Religion, D. C. Somervell, 196
Short History of the English People, J. R. Green, 196, 204
Short History of Western Philosophy in the Middle Ages, S. J. Curtis, 29n.
Short Treatise, A, John Ball, 203
Smoke on the Mountains, Joy Davidson, 169
Spirit of Prayer, W. Law, 158, 161n.
Spirit of Love, W. Law, 158
Spirit of Mediaeval Philosophy, E. Gilson, 56
Spiritual Refining, (2nd edition, 1658), A. Burgess, 202
Statesman's Manual, The, S. T. Coleridge, 174
Students' History of Philosophy, A. K. Rogers, 11
Studies in Mystical Religion, M. R. Jones, 65, 87n.
Studies in Tertullian and Augustine, B. B. Warfield, 85
Studies in Theology, James Denney, 101
Studies in Theology and Religion, A. M. Fairbairn, 9, 10
Subject and Object in Modern Theology, James Brown, 16, 267n., 268n.
Sufficiency of a Standing Revelation, O. Blacknell, 3n.
Supremacy of the Scripture, W. A. Shirley, 129, 133–5, 137–40

Table Talks, S. T. Coleridge, 172
Table Talks, M. Luther, 208n., 209n.
Teaching of Calvin, The, A. Mitchell Hunter, 211
Theological Essays, F. D. Maurice, 29, 183, 185, 186, 247
Theology of Calvin, The, W. Niesel, 210
Theology of Luther, The, Julius Kostlin, 209n.
Theology of the New Testament, R. Bultmann, (Vol. 1), 137n.
Theology To-day, April 1944, 272n.
Theory of Vision and Other Writings, G. Berkeley, 152
Three Essays in Religion, J. S. Mill, 55n.
Three Reformers, J. Martain, 208n.
Thy Word is Truth, E. J. Young, 272n.
Towards a Religious Philosophy, W. de Burgh, 51, 57
Training in Christianity, S. Kierkegaard, 160n., 268
Treatise Concerning the Principles of Human Knowledge, G. Berkeley, 152
Treatise upon the Authenticity of the Scriptures, A. Jacob Bryant, 129, 140n., 194, 195
True Foundation of Natural and Revealed Religion Asserted, Being a Reply to the Supplement of a Treatise, Entitled The Nature, Obligations, etc. of the Christian Sacraments, A. A. Sykes, 93

Truth and Consistency of the Divine Revelation: with some Remarks on the Contrary Extremes of Infidelity and Enthusiasm, J. Bidlake, 119–20

Truth, Inspiration, Authority and End of the Scriptures, Considered and Defended, James Williamson, 129n., 130, 136

Types of Christian Doctrine, H. R. Mackintosh, 167, 169, 226

Use and Necessity of Divine Revelation, John Rogers, 90, 91, 110, 111, 147, 148

Usefulness, Truth and Excellency of the Christian Religion, John Foster, 83, 107–8

Use of the Word Revelation in the New Testament (*F. D. Maurice*), *Present Day Papers on Prominent Questions of Theology*, Edited by the Bishop of Argyle, 182

Vanity of Dogmatizing, J. Glanville, 26, 36

Varieties of Religious Experience, W. James, 68

View of the Evidences of Christianity at the Close of the Pretended Age of Reason, E. Nares, 5, 129n., 136

Victory of Faith, The, Julius Hare, 30, 179–81

Way of Divine Knowledge, W. Law, 158–61, 277n.

Westminster Assembly and its Work, B. B. Warfield, 206, 212

Westminster Confession, 205

Westminster Confession of Faith, with Introduction and Notes, J. Macpherson, 205

What is Religion?, W. Bousset, 13n., 26, 29, 182, 184–6

What is Revelation?, F. D. Maurice, 245, 246, 247

What is the Faith?, N. Micklem, 273n.

Wisdom of God, The, Sergius Bulgakov, 284n.

Word as Truth, The: A Critical Examination of the Christian Doctrine of Revelation in the Writings of Thomas Aquinas and Karl Barth, Alan Fairweather, 190

Word of God and the Word of Man, K. Barth, 274

Works, Lord Bolingbroke, 25n.

Works, William Bridge (Twenty-two several books of Mr. Bridge . . . collected in two volumes), 203–4

Works, R. Hooker, 176

Works of Owen, (edited by W. H. Goold, 1853, vol. xvi), 197–9

Works, Horase Homileticae, (3rd edition, 1838), Twenty-one volumes, Charles Simeon, 213–44

Works, J. Swift, (1859, vol. 2), 47

Works, John Tillotson, 39, 76, 102

Works, (1809), Fifteen volumes, John Wesley, 26, 39, 119, 150, 246–65

ALPHABETICAL INDEX TO
WESLEY'S WORKS QUOTED

Sermons	Number	Volume	Reference
Almost Christian, The	ii	7	258n.
Awake Thou that Sleepest	iii	7	260
Case of Reason, Considered, The	lxxv	9	247, 249, 250
Catholic Spirit, The	xli	8	255
Charity, On	xcvi	10	259n.
Christian Perfection	xlii	8	254, 255
Circumcision of the Heart, The	xvii	7	252, 260
Corrupting the Word of God, On	cxxx	11	247
Danger of Richer, The	xcii	10	258n.
Deceitfulness of Man's Heart	cxxiv	11	254
Difference of Walking by Sight and Faith, The	cxv	10	251n., 258n., 264n.
Discoveries of Faith, On	cxiv	10	251n., 253, 259n.
Dissipation, On	lxxxiv	10	252, 255, 261n.
Dives and Lazarus	xlviii	8	256
Divine Providence, On	lxxii	9	256
Education of Children, On the	c	10	252
End of Christ's Coming	lxviii	9	252
Faith, On	cxxiii	11	251, 256
Free Grace	lv	8	259
Funeral Sermon on the Death of Mr. Whitfield	lvi	9	253
General Spread of the Gospel	lxviii	9	252
God's Approbation of His Works	lx	9	248n.
God's Omnipotence	xlvii	8	254
God's Vineyard	cxi	10	256, 257
Good Steward, The	xlvi	8	257
Great Deliverance, The	lxv	9	254
Heavenly Treasures in Earthen Vessels	cxxv	11	253
Imperfections of Human Knowledge, The	lxxiv	9	246, 248
Law Established through Faith	xxxvii	8	256, 260n.
Laying the Foundation Stone of the New Chapel, On	liv	8	255n., 262
Marks of the New Birth	xvii	7	258n., 259n.
Means of Grace, The	xci	7	259n.
Mystery of Iniquity, The	lxvi	9	255n., 260n.

Sermons	Number	Volume	Reference
Nature of Enthusiasm, The	xxxix	8	262n., 264
New Birth, The	xxi	7	252, 253
Obedience to Pastors, On	cii	10	255n.
Original Sin, On	xx	7	252, 253
Perfection, On	lxxxi	9	255
Predestination, On	lxii	9	260
Privilege of the Children Born of God, The	xix	7	260n.
Salvation by Faith	i	7	253, 258n.
Scriptural Christianity	lv	7	262
Self-denial, On	li	8	253
Signs of the Times, The	lxxi	10	255
Spirit of Bondage and Adoption	ix	9	252
Trinity, On the	lix	9	258n., 260n.
Unity of the Divine Being, On the	cxvi	10	258n.
Way to the Kingdom, The	vii	7	258n.
Witness of God's Counsels, The	lxxiii	9	260n.
Witness of the Spirit, The	x	7	261
Witness of the Spirit, The	xi	7	261
Working out our own Salvation, On	xc	10	253
Zeal, On	xcvii	10	262

Other Works of Wesley:

An Address to the Clergy, 259

Answer to Mr. Church's Remarks, 259

Clear and Concise Demonstration of the Divine Inspiration of the Holy Scriptures, 257, 258

Earnest Appeal to Men of Reason and Religion, An, 150, 250, 251, 255, 258, 260

Further Appeal, 255n., 258, 260, 262

Journal
    Thurs. March 23, 1738, 257
    Fri.   June   22, 1739, 257
    Mon.   June   15, 1741, 249
    Wed.   Aug.   15, 1750, 260
    Thurs. Nov.   27, 1750, 250
    Sat.   Mar.   24, 1753, 259
    Mon.   Aug.   12, 1771, 261, 346
    Tues.   July   4, 1775, 260
    Wed.   July   24, 1776, 258
    Sat.   July   4, 1778, 260n.
    Thurs. Aug.   24, 1780, 261
    Sun.   April   25, 1784, 261
    Thurs. May   13, 1784, 261

Letter to Rev. Mr. Downes, 262

Letter to Rev. Mr. Law, 13, 258

Letter to the Bishop of London, 259

Letter to the Regius Professor of Divinity at Cambridge, 250

Letter to the Rev. Mr. Potter, 246, 260n.

Plain Account of Christian Perfection, 264

Second Letter to Mr. Church, 258

Second Letter to the Author of the Enthusiasm of the Methodists and Papists Compared, 257

Thoughts on Memory, 248

PRINTED IN GREAT BRITAIN BY ROBERT MACLEHOSE AND CO. LTD
THE UNIVERSITY PRESS, GLASGOW

Theories of Revelation

AN HISTORICAL STUDY

1860–1960

H. D. McDONALD

B.A., B.D., PH.D. (LONDON)

Vice-Principal London Bible College
and
Lecturer in Historical Theology

PREFACE

The Introduction will have made sufficiently clear our particular motive and method in presenting what follows. We have, on the one hand, endeavoured to be fair in our exposition of all the views with which we are concerned, and, on the other hand, we have not been hesitant in criticizing what we consider defective and commending what we regard as adequate. Whether we have been successful in these two intentions it must be left with the reader to judge. Our own position we have made no attempt to disguise.

In a passage quoted by Pascal from a book by the Jesuit Garasse, which calls forth his scorn in his *Provincial Letters*, there occurs the statement that 'God, who is perfectly just in all His proceedings, has capacitated even frogs to enjoy their own croaking'. In this assurance we may at least take some comfort.

It only remains to add a word of thanks where it is due. First to my elder daughter, Oonagh A. McDonald, A.L.B.C., B.D., M.TH., for checking the proofs and compiling the Indexes; and then to Messrs George Allen and Unwin for the consideration shown by the members of the Staff with whom we have had to deal.

INTRODUCTION

The problem of Revelation continues to be the central issue in the modern theological scene. And it promises to remain so for a long time to come. There can be no more momentous subject for theological thinking and no more important one for theological debate than that which is enshrined in the question: Can we be sure of a real self-disclosure of God?

We have endeavoured in a previous volume to give an account of the way this issue first forced itself upon the Church.[1] It was indicated how two broadly opposed emphases emerged. On the one hand, there was with some, such a strong emphasis upon the objective aspect that revelation came to be regarded as a body of Divinely communicated truths stated in strict propositional fashion to which all that was needed was to give the appropriate mental acknowledgement. Once the required assent had been given then the individual was designated as 'one of the Faith', since he had returned the desired 'I do' to the question, Do you believe in the body of sacred truths of the Christian faith which to doubt means anathema? Such an understanding of revelation left it soulless. It was something without heart and spirit; and especially did it appear to be very much without the Holy Spirit of God. In 'such a cheap and agreeable way, in a half-hour and with a turn of the hand, to get the whole thing about eternity settled, in order to be thoroughly able to enjoy life'.[2] On the other hand, there were those who with resentment and ridicule regarded the idea of revelation as existing *ab extra* as the worst of all follies and the wickedest of all fancies. To such revelation was essentially and entirely subjective. God was to be sought and found, neither in the starry skies above nor in the sacred Scripture without, but in the mystic depths of a man's own soul. It is something deeply inward. Such an understanding of revelation, however, left it without any truth-content: and tended to substitute individual feelings for historical facts.

[1] H. D. McDonald, *Ideas of Revelation*, 1959.
[2] Soren Kierkegaard, *Attack on Christendom* (E.T. 1946), p. 151.

As the study developed several clear-cut ideas of Revelation were noted. There were, for example, the opposite positions demonstrated by the Deistic emphasis upon the supremacy of reason and the stress given by the Friends to the adequacy of the inner light: and there were the no less extreme antitheses exemplified by the Orthodox theorists and the Coleridgeans. The exaggerations to which these views gave expression, it was shown, were corrected, in some measure, by the teaching of Charles Simeon, on the one side, who in contending for the objective Word saw also the need for the inner action of the Spirit, and, on the other side, by John Wesley, who, while emphasizing the Spirit's work, did not fail to insist upon the need for the Word without. But even their views brought no permanent settlement: they could not, for example, take into account the difficulties which came about only at a later time.

Yet the ideas which thus came into sharp relief in this earlier period, are precisely those which, after a short time of hesitancy occasioned by the publication of Darwin's *Origin of Species*, were taken up again later with varying degrees of clarity and confusion. As, however, we seek to follow the discussion of the subject of Revelation throughout the century beginning 1860, it will not meet the situation to continue the same procedure and merely to collect quotations from authors who group themselves behind one or other of the ideas which were thus earlier brought into prominence. The careful reader of the following pages will himself become aware of the preference of each writer to whom we must refer. Another method of procedure is demanded to understand the nature of the conflict in the new era.

The century with which we are to be occupied is characterized by the presence of other influences which had an important bearing on the subject of Revelation. The controversies initiated by Darwin's evolutionism and the coming of the Higher Criticism focused attention upon the Scriptures and raised the question of their place in the scheme of revelation. The Bible, in fact, became the storm centre and the main problem of the period was to give a convincing statement of its significance. The problem concerned the relation between Revelation and the Bible. And since an influential body of opinion came to the conviction that the Scriptures could be no longer regarded as an objective infallible authority, the whole question of religious authority was opened for discussion. In fact, as time went on these two subjects—Revelation and Authority—became merged so that a discussion of the problem of Revelation has become one and the same with a discussion of the subject of Authority. Our penultimate chapter will show the truth of this observation: while in the last chapter we have sought to give a summary statement of 'Revelation and Authority', in which the final section will indicate what we conceive to be the results for the present time.

It should be made clear that throughout an effort has been made to let writers on each side in the controversies, especially those concerned with the subjects of Biblical inerrancy, inspiration and authority, speak for themselves, as far as practical, in their own words. But we have not hesitated at various places to give our own criticisms; as we have also sought to give, as far as we conceive it, a positive statement.

In taking such an attitude we have not been unmindful of the subtitle which announces our investigation as 'an historical study'. We would, however, plead that it is quite impossible to approach a subject without any presuppositions. This is specially so in theology where a man's convictions should be deep and meaningful. Even those who approach theology purely from the historical point of view will betray on numerous occasions their own religious understandings. One has for example only to peruse Adolf Harnack's *History of Dogma* to be convinced of the justice of this remark. The truth is that the man who says he is altogether objective in this study knows not of what he speaks. Even in the realm of science it is no longer a tenable view to conceive of the scientist as, so to speak, one who stands over against his data having no postulates. Indeed the whole scientific endeavour would be a fruitless proceeding if this were so. In fact, as A. F. Smethurst and C. A. Coulson have shown, the postulates of the scientific enquiry when consciously thought out are essentially ethical, if not positively religious.[1]

It will be observed, however, that in our case we have not only criticized negatively where we have felt it to be needed, but we have, especially when dealing with the three related subjects

[1] Cf. A. F. Smethurst, *Modern Science and Christian Belief*, 1955. C. A. Coulson, *Science and Christian Belief*, 1955.

referred to above, given a positive account of our own convictions. In this way, we think, we have sought to avoid giving a mere dry catalogue of facts, like those 'stamp collector' type of scientists to whom Lord Rutherford used to refer. They are of the kind who lose themselves in their finds and admire their collection just as would any contented philatelist.

It remains to be added that we have sought to cover in an adequate manner the literature of the whole period. Doubtless some reviewer will have knowledge of some article or book to which reference, in his judgement, should have been made. We can only say that we have not ourselves made reference to every single source that was before us, because such a contribution did not seem to us to be of decisive significance in the development of the discussion. Or, of course, which is not impossible, it may have been because the work was unknown to us!

One result of our study, it is hoped, will be that there will be a clearer understanding by all of the ideas of revelation. An historical background will provide a truer perspective for discussion. The tendency in the past has been for each side to conduct a sort of private monologue and to proclaim its views in hostile disregard of what the other side was seeking to say. What is required today, and what is possible, is that which is involved in the expressive word of recent days, dialogue. And we have made some attempt to bring this about by seeking out the understanding of revelation and by stating as clearly as we are able our own position for the sake of those who would understand us.

LONDON BIBLE COLLEGE

CONTENTS

page

INTRODUCTION   7

ONE
THE DIVISION OF THE PERIOD
The Starting Date of the Period—The Changing
Temper of the Period—The Distinguishing
Volumes of the Period   13

TWO
THE IDEAS WITHIN THE ERA
The Challenge of Materialism—The Reaction of
Idealism—The Protest from Pluralism—The
Influence of Historicism—The Category of
Geschichte   41

THREE
THE BATTLE OF THE STANDPOINTS
The Advent of Criticism—The Advance of
Criticism—The Attack on Criticism   99

FOUR
THE FOCUS OF THE CONFLICT
Christ and the Scriptures   137

FIVE
THE SCRIPTURES AND THE WORD
Revelation and the Scriptures—The Word of God
and the Scriptures   161

SIX
THE QUESTION OF BIBLICAL INERRANCY
The Renunciation of Inerrancy—The Assertion of
Inerrancy—Renewed Conflict over Inerrancy   196

SEVEN
THE DISCUSSION OF BIBLICAL
INSPIRATION
Inspiration: The Focus Within—Inspiration: The
Focus Without   218

EIGHT
THE PROBLEM OF BIBLICAL
AUTHORITY
The Authority of the Bible Based upon Experience
—The Authority of the Bible as Existing Apart
from Experience   288

NINE
REVELATION AND AUTHORITY
The Revelation of Authority—The Authority of
Revelation   347

INDEX

CHAPTER ONE

The Division of the Period

A. THE STARTING DATE OF THE PERIOD

History has been marked throughout by certain decisive events which have, as it were, become the occasion of marking off one era from another. Sometimes these events have appeared at the time to be almost accidental, and yet later ages have turned back to them as having been of radical significance. Other divisions in the history of human thought can be dated from the work and worth of some significant personality who has succeeded, for one reason or another, in stamping his signature upon the brow of the hurrying centuries. The presence of such a person has often been revealed in some special contribution or some shattering act which appears to the following generations to have altered the direction of history. It is in such periods that history can be read, in Walt Whitman's pregnant phrase, as the lengthened shadow of a man. But when some decisive event, which has in itself creative significance, and, the presence of some man who is believed to have made some important contribution, coincide, then that date can be marked off with more assurance as the start of a new era.

Writers have perceived, although they have not always made the reasons clear, that the year 1860 is one of those dates which can be taken as the commencement of another state and stage in the history of ideas. It will, of course, be understood that no division in history is clear-cut. It is a fact more clearly emphasized today than ever before that there are no breaks in history; that the past is not isolated from the present, and that the present is creative of the future. The realization of this fact will be sufficient to warn us against the tendency to make neat divisions of history. The views which in one period become dominant are those very tendencies which stirred in the under-growth of that which preceded. These are the creative under-tones which indicated the pattern of the dawning era. Yet the truth remains that each age does reveal its own special charac-teristics and these special features can be generally marked and indicated.

The year 1860 is one of these significant dates which termi-nated one era and commenced another. The contribution of event and personality united to mark it out in this special way. L. E. Elliott-Binns points out that the year 1860 witnessed two events which were to have particular importance for religion and theology. These were the repeal of the paper duty in that year and the beginnings of a national system of education.[1] These events, to be sure, were not immediately recognized as destined to have such far-reaching consequences. The repeal of the paper duty which lifted from the trade a crippling burden, made possible an immediate increase in literature. One of the immediate results of the relief was an astonishing development in the production of newspapers and periodicals. Never before in history was it so possible for ideas to be as widely dis-seminated. Theological and religious subjects were eagerly discussed and debated. Among the most influential of these new media was the recently founded *Fortnightly Review* which took up a hostile attitude to orthodox beliefs and secured for itself an aura of authority on religious and theological questions. As a result of these new publications the country was thrown into a welter of conflicting ideas, in which, for a quarter of a century, the religious interest was uppermost.

The press found a public ready to receive its comments for or against established religious institutions and orthodox beliefs. Indeed so evident was this interest that Aubrey Moore could declare in 1889 that 'No periodical is complete without an article in which Christianity is defended or attacked'.[2] Not only was the interest there, but the effort to extend education meant that there were more persons whose interest was to be aroused. It was beginning to be seen that no one class had any monopoly upon knowledge. It was the right of every individual to enter in and to possess the land. This awareness, allying itself with the

[1] L. E. Elliott-Binns, *English Thought, 1860–1900*, 1956, p. 5.
[2] Aubrey Moore, *Science and the Faith*, 1889, p. 113.

growing democratic spirit of the times, was making it evident
that every individual was significant, as such, and was entitled
to have his say.

There were other events, too, which the year 1860 was to
witness and which played their lesser part in making that date
important. But the two just mentioned, when reinforced by the
contribution made at that time to biological science, had the
effect of initiating a crop of new ideas and problems of a nature
different from any which had gone before.

Although it was in the preceding year that Darwin's *Origin of
Species* appeared, its full meaning, as far as theological views
were concerned, was to be more clearly seen in the following
year. By 1860 it was evident that the book was to have a
decisive influence in many realms. Ideas which had previously
been generally accepted were turned upside down. The story of
the reception given to Darwin's volume is generally known, and
certain aspects of its influence will engage us later. But we may
note, for the present, that it soon became evident that the new
biological evolutionism would affect the historic Christian view
of the uniqueness of man and the meaning of original sin. As the
fuller implications of the thesis were understood, the whole
question of revelation was given a new context. An apologetic
of a type not previously conceivable was required. There was,
to begin with, the serious question of the very possibility of any
revelation at all. 'The doctrine of evolution practically began its
reign with the theory of natural selection. It was crowned with
shouts of "Down with Christianity! Long live Materialism!" No
wonder if theologians were prejudiced against it.'[1] True
enough, the Darwinian hypothesis, as such, did not appear to
touch the fundamental question of Theism and the possibility of
revelation. It is, indeed, a fact that Darwin, in the closing
section of the first edition of his *Origin of Species* had given
reverent acknowledgement to the idea of a Creator, and had,
also, entered the claim that the conception of nature to which his
book gave exposition involved a far loftier conception of God's
wisdom and power than the orthodox doctrine of the appearance
of separate species by distinct acts of God.

The first and immediate result of Darwin's own view was to

---

[1] D. Matheson in Review of A. Barry's *Some Lights of Science on the Faith*, being
the Bampton Lectures for 1892, *Expository Times*, Vol. IV, 1892–3, p. 415.

raise the question of the validity of the early chapters of Genesis. Prior to Darwin, apart from certain thinkers to whom the notion of evolution was a mere philosophical presupposition without any scientific evidence, the accepted Christian view was that Genesis had recorded a factual account of the origin of organic life. The record had to be read as a literal account more particularly of man's beginning. With such a reading of the story the Darwinian hypothesis was in evident conflict. This impression was given further emphasis by the subsequent publication of Darwin's *Descent of Man*. The issue was clear-cut. If Darwin were right then the Genesis account was wrong, and vice versa. Either God was in at man's beginning or He was not.

But this narrower discussion was to be held up for some years and to become one of the issues in the conflict between the Higher Critics and their opponents. Beguiled, it appears, by Darwin's rather accommodating reference to a Creator, a contemporary edition of the *Saturday Review* assured its readers that the views set forth in the *Origin of Species* were not in the least 'hostile to the truths of Revelation'. Yet this was not the conviction which even Darwin himself was to retain for long. Doubts were creeping over him: and any faith he had in the Old Testament was being undermined. Having rejected the miracles of the Old Testament he goes on to declare that those of the New cannot be regarded as authentic. In a later period, as by a natural transition, he does not hesitate to avow his disbelief in any supernatural realm. 'For myself', he states uncompromisingly, 'I do not believe that there ever has been any revelation.'

What influence Herbert Spencer had upon Darwin in bringing about this result is not easy to estimate. But the fact is that the association of Spencer's *Synthetic Philosophy*, of which the 'First Principles' was the introduction, with the *Origin of Species*, served to call in question the whole idea of a revelation. Spencer took up the evolutionary principle and applied it in a thoroughgoing fashion to the wider issues and problems of life. This wider application of Darwin's distinctive principle of natural selection is what is called, 'Ultra-Darwinianism'.

At the beginning Darwinianism as such was thought to be a purely scientific view of a limited part of the cosmos—the organic. But the extension of the principle of continuity was an expression of the philosophical spirit as distinct from the specifically scientific. Darwin's principle, it came to be urged, was necessarily included in the wider Spencerian system, which sought to explain the universe in terms of an anti-Theistic naturalism. The consequences appeared inescapable. There was no supernatural; nothing, indeed, other than the natural. The organic evolutionism of Darwin, boldly asserted as the scientific view of the origin of species, was, then, declared to have made the teaching of Genesis unacceptable: and, in so far as it appeared to imply the universal action of natural causes, it cast doubts upon any supernatural element in Christianity. The cosmic evolution of Spencer completed the picture. It was in open conflict with the idea of revelation. It was a definite and hostile repudiation of a divinely-instituted religion. It was, in fact, a complete rejection of Theism.

Throughout the period the fortunes of theological studies were bound up, or connected either directly or indirectly with the problems raised by Darwin. It would not, indeed, be very wide of the mark to say that the whole era might be designated, The Era of the Rise and Decline of Darwinianism. At its appearance in 1859, the ideas contained in the *Origin of Species*, were seen to be opposed to accepted biological and theological views.

T. H. Huxley, looking back from a later period, was able to declare concerning the position in 1860, 'The supporters of Mr Darwin's views were numerically extremely insignificant. There is not the slightest doubt that if a general council of the Church scientific had been held at the time, we should have been condemned by an overwhelming majority'. But the situation was soon to change. Reinforced by T. H. Huxley and Herbert Spencer, the Darwinian thesis was not only to gain ground, but its fundamental idea was to be extended to include every realm of life and thought, and to be applied especially to religion and ethics. The day was not far distant when its triumph seemed overwhelming. As early, indeed, as the year 1863 Charles Kingsley wrote to F. D. Maurice to the effect that 'Darwin is conquering everywhere'.[1]

As is so often the case, however, the period of triumph began the period of decline. This is the one certain truth that the

[1] F. E. Kingsley, *Charles Kingsley*, 1877, Vol. II, p. 155.

Hegelian dialectic of history has taught us. A dominant idea gives birth to its opposite and initiates tension and conflict. Or, as it is put in the Marxian philosophy, every triumphant system contains within it the seeds of its own destruction. Whilst the idealistic application of the principle as in the case of Hegel or the materialistic application of it as in the case of Marx can be rejected, the broad truth which Hegel and Marx took as the fundamental basis of their opposing dialectic remains. Nowhere is this more clearly illustrated than in the case of the triumph and decline of Darwinianism. That later years have seen a modification, and even a repudiation, of many of Darwin's ideas there is not the slightest doubt. Exactly when the tide began to turn against Darwinianism it is not easy to say. At any rate, a few years after the beginning of the century such a book as George Paulin's, in which he attacks the basic principle of Darwin's thesis, received favourable reviews.[1] Paulin had been for years a staunch advocate of Darwinianism. But fuller investigation had led him to the conclusion that there was no substantial evidence for it. He points out that Darwin himself took the idea of natural selection for granted. Paulin's book is not in itself specially important. But the very fact that it should have been published by T. & T. Clark, and that it should have been commended by some reviewers who showed no particular sympathy with a non-evolutionary approach, can be taken as showing that there was some willingness to question the finality of Darwinianism. There is no doubt that this readiness to re-examine the evidence for Darwin's fundamental idea, without the presupposition that it must be right, had grown with the years.

Twenty years later scientists themselves were expressing openly their uncertainty about the whole Darwinian thesis. In the year 1921, to take but one such example, there appeared the volume *The Advancement of Science*. This book contains a series of addresses by the President of the British Association for the Advancement of Science and the Presidents of its constituent sections. With one voice they spoke against the Darwinian conclusion. Reference need be made only to the remarks with which Dr D. H. Scott, the botanist, closed his discourse. After

[1] George Paulin, *No Struggle for Existence: No Natural Selection*. A Critical Examination of the Fundamental Principles of the Darwinian Theory, 1908.

giving due acknowledgement to the work of Darwin, and according to him credit for the illumination which his theory of natural selection has brought, he adds: 'For the moment, at all events, the Darwinian period is past; we can no longer enjoy the comfortable assurance, which once satisfied so many of us, that the problem has been solved—all again is in the melting-pot. But now, in fact, a new generation has grown up that knows not Darwin.'

In this regard it is of interest to note that in the year 1959 a commemorative edition of the *Origin of Species* was published. There are some astonishing remarks in the Introduction written by W. R. Thompson, FRS. Thompson openly confesses grave doubts about the beneficent effects of Darwin's theory on scientific and public thinking. He maintains that personal convictions and simple possibilities have been presented without real proof. He personally regards the whole thesis as inconclusive, and declares that 'the long-continued investigations on heredity and variation have undermined the Darwinian position'.[1] The 'mutations' of the modern evolutionists are not 'adaptive'. They are, in fact, he contends, 'useless, detrimental, or lethal'. In this Introduction to the *Origin of Species* the whole stately ediface is brought to collapse. Thompson sees the world of clear-cut entities separated by gaps which the evolutionary theory cannot bridge. Fossils show 'a remarkable absence of the intermediates required by the theory'. Damaging, too, is his statement that 'modern palæontologists are obliged, just like their predecessors and like Darwin, to water down facts with subsidiary hypotheses which, however plausible, are in the nature of things unverifiable'.[2] Thompson is quite certain that the success of Darwinism was accompanied by a decline in scientific integrity. The whole is built, he maintains, upon 'fragile towers of hypotheses based on hypotheses, where fact and fiction intermingle in an inextricable confusion'.[3] The result of which is to bring about a decline of Christian faith and a consequent abandonment of belief in the supernatural.

This Introduction by Thompson is a remarkable pronouncement. The question which arises is just this: Does it signify the fall of Darwinianism? This is, perhaps, something which it is

---

[1] *Origin of Species*, 1859 (Everyman's Edition, 1959), Introduction, p. xii.
[2] *Op. cit.*, p. xix.   [3] *Op. cit.*, p. xxiv.

not for us to answer. But it does, at least, serve to strengthen the view which we have taken that the century which began with the publication of the *Origin of Species*, and ends with the appearance of this centenary edition, can be referred to as the period of the rise and decline of Darwinianism.

B. THE CHANGING TEMPER OF THE PERIOD

Along with the rise and the decline of Darwinianism there went, in keeping with its changing fortunes, what we may call, a prevailing public temper. Whether this mood was a cause or an effect of the changing estimations of the evolutionary theory is not easy to say. At all events the fact of this parallel of temper with theory is undoubted. So evident is this that the century which began in the year 1860 can be divided broadly into two periods following the rise and decline of Darwin's influence. There is the period of confident optimism and the period of disillusioning pessimism.

The overweening optimism arose out of a strange faith in the ability of science to cure all ills. The age of religion, which had been of service at a time when men were in the twilight, was now to be superseded by the age of science. But science was the final stage which would not only render religion impossible, but would reveal its own inherent greatness by providing a world fit for progressing man to live in. Hitherto science had been regarded as the concern of a select class who enjoyed its pursuit in isolation from the common people. It was now conceived to be the only gospel giving promise of an endless progress and assuring to men an earthly paradise.

This sort of optimistic evaluation of science can be seen, for example, in the statements made by two writers who became intoxicated with the new power which science had provided. W. K. Clifford (1845–79), while pouring forth a torrent of vehement indignation against Christianity, was compelled to find a substitute for religious faith in a reverent awe and devout worship of the marvellous world which had already come to such perfection from so unpromising a beginning. He felt himself animated by what he called a 'cosmic emotion'. Indeed, as Rudolf Metz remarks, 'the temple of this religion was for Clifford the proud edifice of science, and it was from science that he hoped that all further progress of the spirit of man would come'.[1]

Karl Pearson (1857–1936), in his *Grammar of Science*, which first appeared in 1892 (cheap edition, 1937), took up the position that science is really divine; and whatever is not of science is not of truth. Pearson, indeed, carried his laudation of the scientific spirit to the point of apotheosis. The mission of modern science is to serve the human spirit: and the genuine scientist is the only true saint.

William James gives exposition to this optimistic result of evolution. He sees it as 'a new sort of religion of Nature, which has entirely displaced Christianity from the thought of a large part of our generation'.[2] He contends that the 'idea of a general evolution lends itself to a doctrine of general amelioration and progress which fits the religious needs of the healthy-minded so well that it seems almost as if it might have been created for its use'. He sees evolutionism 'interpreted thus optimistically and embraced as a substitute for the religion' of Christianity by those who have been scientifically trained and by those who have developed an interest in its popular exposition, and who have, as a consequence, become 'inwardly dissatisfied with what seemed to them the harshness and irrationality of the orthodox Christian scheme'.[3] Philip Leon contrasts the temper of the most modern science with that which prevailed some sixty years ago. 'Then "Science" was, except in details practically synonymous with "Omniscience", and the universe of possibilities, which is to lay the field open to speculation, was limited in the extreme, "Science" dogmatically laying it down before hand that only a very few things were possible.' Science was supposed to have liberated man from his mediaeval prison-house of dogmatic theology. 'Now, on the other hand', Leon states by way of contrast, 'the sciences are felt to be lucky guesses in a universe in which anything is possible, while a priori dogmatic pronouncements as to impossibility are regarded with less and less favour: the omniscience of "Science" has been replaced by the multi-possibility of the universe.'[4]

[1] Rudolf Metz, *A Hundred Years of British Philosophy*, 1938, second impression, 1950, p. 127.
[2] William James, *The Varieties of Religious Experience*, 1902, sixteenth edition, 1909, p. 91.   [3] *Ibid.*, pp. 91, 92.
[4] Philip Leon, *Body, Mind and Spirit*, 1948, p. 21.

The second half of the nineteenth century was, then, to witness the proclamation of another gospel—which a later period was to find out was not another—a gospel in which man was promised an earthly Utopia, a paradise regained by the magic of science. Endless progress was confidently assured. And in a few decades the earlier superstitions of basic social moralities and believed supernatural realities would be swept away by being revealed as the pathetic follies and fallacies of a past unenlightened age. The Religion of Nature was destined to take the place of the old notion of the existence of a supersensual realm. So optimism reached its height as it was reinforced by the glory of an expanding empire and the triumphant extension of the influence of the Mother Country which was regarded as the guardian of international morality and the conscience of the world.

In such a context Christian faith had no easy task to maintain itself. The thought of the people was, by the very method of science, the value of which was becoming every day more evident, directed to the present, the terrestrial and the human. And there was enough here to occupy the thoughts, to usurp the talents and to fill the time of every educated man. One could be a man of one world only. The notion of another world was too problematical for occupied lives. Besides, the whole idea of religion was attended by one big haunting question-mark.

It was in this spirit of optimism that the nineteenth century drew to its close. And it reached its crescendo in the early part of the twentieth century, by becoming wedded to the confident humanism of the times.

Gradually, however, the rosy picture was to become upset by the presence of harsh and ugly facts which could not be explained away. At first, of course, there appeared clouds only the size of a man's hand. Soon these were to thicken and darken into the grim night of the First World War. Then the whole optimistic spirit was dissipated and lost in the abyss of disillusionment and despair. The result of the great conflict was to leave us with a country which heroes did not find to be what was promised. Darkness still covered the face of the land in the form of unemployment, frustration and the loss of hope in man's ability to rise to new heights on the stepping stones of the dead of the recent past.

There were, to be sure, brave souls who sought to console

their fellows. There were insistent voices urging humanity to take up the task again and regain the far-off optimism of former years. But on the whole these voices were lost in the din of uncertainty. It was felt that they were pathetically unaware of the fresh evidence of human sinfulness which an earlier effete optimism had never seriously faced. There were, therefore, other teachers who were not prepared to accept the gay picture of man's growing perfectibility through the enlightening influences of an expanding education and political compromise.

C. E. M. Joad, who lived through the earlier period of optimism and on into the later period of pessimism recalls his own reactions. Like many others, he had been captivated by the glowing picture of the brave new world which was to be built by human endeavours. He, as they, abandoned what he believed was the out-worn superstition of orthodox Christianity. Joad grew up in a world which was intoxicated with the optimistic belief in 'man as infinitely perfectible'. Spencer had given the assurance that 'the ultimate development of the ideal man, is certain—as certain as any conclusion in which we place the most implicit faith, for instance that all men die'. Progress is, he urged, no accident. It is necessary and inevitable. And because it is so, 'man must become perfect'.

J. Addington Symonds, the Victorian poet, sang of this new religion.

> These things shall be! A loftier race
>   Than ere the world hath known, shall rise
> With flame of freedom in their souls
>   And light of science [sic] in their eyes.
>
> They shall be gentle, brave and strong,
>   To spill no drop of blood, but dare
> All that may plant man's lordship firm
>   On earth and fire and sea and air.
>
> Nation with nation, land with land,
>   Unarmed shall live as comrades free;
> In every heart and brain shall throb
>   The pulse of one fraternity.

New arts shall bloom of loftier mould,
And mightier music thrill the skies,
And every lift shall be a song,
When all of earth shall be a paradise.

These words found their way into many of the hymn books
and were sung with religious fervour and faith. The sentiment
which was here given poetic expression was for many a burning
conviction. And C. E. M. Joad, like the rest, passionately
believed it was all true. He was, however, to find out it was not
so easy and so confident. Speaking generally, he observes, 'the
era which came abruptly to an end in 1914 was one of the most
confident and successful in the history of mankind'.[1] With the
passing of the prophetic hope of Spencer during the years
following, Joad, from his own experience, recounts the sense of
disillusionment. He became aware that he had fallen 'a victim
to a shallow optimism in regard to human nature'. In the
presence of the burdening reality of the 'ineradicable nature of
human sinfulness' he confesses, 'that the rationalistic–optimist
philosophy, by the light of which I had hitherto done my best to
live, came to seem intolerably trivial and superficial—a shallow-
rooted plant which, growing to maturity amid the lush
and leisured optimism of the nineteenth century, was quite
unfitted to withstand the bleaker winds that blow through
ours'.[2]

The glowing picture of man's perfectibility and adequacy was
also to receive a blow from the findings of the psychoanalyst-
psychologists. Freud, Adler and Jung, each in his own way, had
uncovered the unconscious and maintained that the hidden
depths of human life were a veritable jungle of repressed desires
which, if they were to find an outlet in society without purification, would make human life a hell. Here within man's being
was a chamber of horrors, a charnel-house of every possible evil.
Every man was no longer to be thought of as a possible gentleman who needed only to be taught good manners. He was an
abyss containing the frightening possibilities of incalculable evil.

It was no wonder that such being the revised view of man
that the existentialist doctrine should make an appeal. It was

---

[1] C. E. M. Joad, *The Recovery of Belief*, 1952, p. 47.
[2] *Ibid.*, p. 82.

inevitable that Kierkegaard should come to his own. And then, as if to take away the last shreds of optimism, there came the Second World War with its Belsen and its Hiroshima.

In the context of this waxing and waning optimism, ideas of revelation can be seen to emerge in general harmony with it. The broad outline of these views can be indicated here.

The first shock of Darwinianism, it may be observed, was to give immediate birth to naturalism. Any idea of a revelation was thought to be ruled out as being incompatible with the new scientific understanding of the origin of life. But for one reason or another naturalism did not long appeal. It is simply not natural for a man to be a consistent naturalist.

Thus, before many years had passed, the teleological argument was rehabilitated. Hitherto, beginning from what was virtually a Deistic emphasis upon the divine transcendence the argument was from design to the idea of an existent designer. Now the stress was put upon the divine immanence and the argument was to design. All nature was regarded as instinct with divine life. It was to be thought of as the unfolding of the indwelling spiritual ζωή. Thus was all history to be understood as the general unveiling of immanent divinity, and revelation to be conceived of as the totality of human history, which, in greater or lesser measure, discloses the divine indwelling. In this way the clear-cut distinction between natural and revealed religion was broken down. There was no single people and no special history which could be claimed as the specific sphere of the divine activity. All religions developed from one common origin. There were cruder religious ideas suited to the under-developed state of the religious instinct. But, as the *sensus numinis* grew, so too did religion; from the natural to the spiritual, from the tribal to the universal. And through all the human spirit was showing its awareness of the divine working itself out within the movements of history and the events of experience. God was there as the immanent reality, energizing and unifying.

Such an idea, however boldly proclaimed as it was by its advocates, did not meet the need. It was too general, too indefinite, too vague. It attempted to be rid of any idea of a 'special' revelation by making all history revelational. But the effort to obliterate the distinction between general and special revelation could not be maintained.[1] It failed altogether to take account of the fact that Christianity is connected 'with a real event in time and space, which, so it affirms, is the unique, final revelation for time and for eternity, and for the whole world'.[2]

The view of all history as revelatory of the divine immanence only was seen to be further defective because it provided no 'clear standard of discrimination'. 'Where all is equally revelation, who shall determine what is being said, and what, of all that is being said, is most important?'[3]

There is need of something more precise, more particular. How, for example, could account be taken of the otherwise unaccountable existence of Israel? Thus was the idea of revelation narrowed down to read as the divine acts in history. It is in certain transforming events, like the Exodus of Israel from Egypt, the significance of which had been appreciated by men with a genius for religion or by men who had experienced a certain illumination, that we are to see the divine revelation. Reading these events as God's 'actuality' in the history, man is made aware of the living God, or as G. E. Wright puts it as the title of his book, *The God Who Acts*. Since God's divinest act is in the Incarnation, it is in such terms that His 'special' unveiling is to be sought at its highest.

Yet there is a difficulty. Human history, after all, is just *human* history: it cannot be other than that. And humans, especially in a period which has lost its optimistic view of man, are not little pieces of divinity. Thus human history is but the record of man's sinfulness; of man's varying and false estimate of himself. God who is distinct from man, who is the 'Wholly Other', cannot be brought into the record. He cannot be imprisoned within such a chronicle. God is, therefore, outside it all. We shall consequently 'need to think through the category of revelation again'[4] in such a context. Obviously, the story which tells of God's work for man's salvation cannot be read according to the usual understanding of human history. It is supra-historical— *Heilsgeschichte*. Revelation is, therefore, God's inbreaking into human lives in the grace of redemption. God is, after all, *actus*

[1] Cf. Emil Brunner, *The Mediator* (E.T. 1934), Chapters I and II.
[2] *Ibid.*, p. 30.
[3] Edwin Lewis, *A Philosophy of the Christian Revelation*, British edition, 1948, p. 4.
[4] Karl Barth, *The Word of God and the Word of Man*, 1928, p. 250.

purus.[1] Man has no natural 'point of contact' with Him. The idea of revelation as having any propositional form is consequently anathema. Man has sinned away his rationality and cannot be appealed to as a creature of reason. It is in the Divine–Human Encounter, an encounter in which God as the living God is the sole actor, and, in which man, whose whole history is but the chronicle of his sinning, can do nothing but wait to be awakened to response by the very impact of the Divine revelation. In all these views any idea of revelation as a communication of truth is sternly repudiated. No less rejected is any conception of Scripture as in itself revelational.

C. THE DISTINGUISHING VOLUMES OF THE PERIOD

Coming now to a more precise division of the period of our investigation, we may note how certain volumes had the effect of marking off new stages in the discussion of our subject by initiating fresh conflicts and controversies. These distinguishing works may be set out as follows.

(1) 1860—'*Essays and Reviews*'

This volume, it will be observed, appeared a year after Darwin's *Origin of Species* and purported to be in some measure a rapprochment with the new biological hypothesis. The outburst of hostility which greeted its coming astonished its contributors. None of them, we cannot but feel, was more surprised by the blunt criticisms, than Frederick Temple. Temple who was at the time headmaster of Rugby School was later to become Archbishop of Canterbury. He took only ten hours to write the essay and we are assured that he had no idea that he was sharing in a sort of manifesto.[2] The fact is, the essay was only a rehash of a sermon he had already preached at Oxford.

The seven essays which comprise the volume have really no binding idea. They are a miscellaneous collection of varying value. Stanley, who like Hort, had refused to contribute to the symposium, is certainly right in his criticism of them as too negative. Morley has observed that with the exception of Mark

---

[1] Karl Barth, *Church Dogmatics*, 1, i (E.T. 1936), p. 44.
[2] E. G. Stanford, *Frederick Temple*, An Appreciation, 1906, p. 205.

Pattison's 'Tendencies of Religious Thought in England, 1860–1750', the rest 'was neither learned nor weighty'. The 'tone was not absolutely uniform', he continues, 'but it was as a whole mildly rationalistic'.[1] Benjamin Jowett's essay 'On the Interpretation of Scripture', although modified we are given to understand at the instigation of Tennyson, was especially offensive at the time because of his apparently low view of the Bible.

Not all of the Essays have relevance to our topic. Temple took as his subject a title which Lessing had given earlier to his treatise, *The Education of the World*. He compared the human race to a colossal man which went through the stages of childhood, youth and manhood. God's progressive education of the race was suited to each stage, first according to laws, then by examples and finally by principles. In the Bible, he concludes, must be found these principles by which grown man is to live. And should 'careful criticism' he asserts 'prove that there have been occasional interpolations and forgeries in that Book'[2] the result need not be unwelcomed. The teaching of the Bible remains unaffected by any changes in the idea of inspiration which present knowledge necessitates. True enough, its hold upon the mind of believers and its power to stir the depths of the spirit of man may be weakened at first. But in the long run these shall be 'immeasurably strengthened' 'by the clearing away any blunders which may have been fastened on it by human interpretation'.[3]

In Rowland Williams's Essay entitled 'A Review of Bunsen's Biblical Researches' there is a clear acceptance of a rather advanced German liberal criticism. Bunsen virtually denies the supernatural outright and confines revelation within the sphere of the natural. Williams, indeed, accords Bunsen (should later generations be wise enough to follow his lead) 'a foremost place among the champions of light and right'.[4] A layman, C. W. Goodwin, writes on the 'Mosaic Cosmogony'. There are, he states, two accounts of the creation in Genesis. The first professing to be a scientific presentation has been demonstrated as clearly out of harmony with recent scientific findings. The

---

[1] J. Morley, *Life of Gladstone* (in three volumes), 1911, Vol. 2—1859–1880, p. 125.

[2] *Essays and Reviews*, 1860, tenth edition, 1861, p. 47.

[3] *Op. cit.*, p. 48.   [4] *Op. cit.*, p. 93.

second account may be regarded as poetical. Benjamin Jowett in his Essay 'On the Interpretation of Scripture' argues 'that any true doctrine of inspiration must conform to all well-ascertained facts of history or of science'.[1] He then goes on, after he has repudiated the orthodox view of inspiration, to deal with the question of interpretation. His main contention may be summed up in his own canon under which all else he has to say can be subsumed. It is simply this: 'Interpret the Scripture like any other book'.[2]

It might well have been that this volume would have caused little excitement but for the notice given to it by the Positivist, Frederic Harrison, in an article in the October 1860 issue of the *Westminster Review*. Harrison entitled his article, 'Neo-Christianity', and contended that the position reached by the essayists was that of his own. Here were denied miracles, inspiration and the Mosaic history: and gone with this denial was the whole idea of Biblical revelation.

This notice given to the volume by Harrison caused a stir. Hostility was at once shown to it by the two great parties of the Church. In January 1861, Wilberforce, Bishop of Oxford, in an article in the *Quarterly Review*, bluntly stated that the ultimate conclusion of the Essays must be infidelity, if not atheism. Two main replies soon appeared seeking to refute the position advanced in the *Essays and Reviews*. The first called *Aids to Faith*, edited by William Thomson, Bishop of Gloucester and Bristol and afterwards Archbishop of York, followed the same pattern as the essays it sought to correct. The second volume, *Replies to Essays and Reviews* was edited by the redoubtable Samuel Wilberforce.

(2) 1862—'*The Pentateuch and the Book of Joshua Critically Examined' by J. W. Colenso*

In the previous year Colenso, who in 1853 had been consecrated Bishop of Natal, South Africa, had produced a *Commentary on Romans*. This book did not create the stir which he had apparently expected. But his critical analysis of the Pentateuch and Joshua occasioned alarm. He rejected the Mosaic authorship of the former and pronounced the Bible to be no infallible Book.

[1] *Essays and Reviews*, 1860, tenth edition, 1861, p. 348.
[2] *Op. cit.*, p. 377.

It is not to be identified with revelation. Following F. D. Maurice, by whom he was strongly influenced, he maintained that while the Bible is not itself the Word of God it can be said to 'contain' His Word.

Colenso, a skilled mathematician, made much sport of the figures in the early biblical books especially that of Numbers. Wilberforce, with his usual ready wit, explained that the real trouble was that the Mathematical Bishop was unable to forgive Moses for writing a Book of Numbers!

Yet Colenso, although he proclaimed an advanced liberal view of the Pentateuch insisted that these 'narratives by whomsoever written' still imparted 'revelations of the divine will and character'. None the less they 'cannot be regarded as historically true'.[1]

This volume caused bitter antagonism. For the first time a bishop's name was associated with what was regarded as open infidelity. Demand was made by the English bishops, with the famous Thirlwall dissenting, that Colenso should be excommunicated. The result was a schism in the South African Church which was not eventually healed until nearly another half century had passed.

(3) 1881—'The Old Testament in the Jewish Church', William Robertson Smith

'The lectures entitled The Old Testament in the Jewish Church, by W. Robertson Smith, may be taken as the sign of the beginning of a new era.'[2] It was Smith who really popularized Old Testament German criticism. He followed Ritschl in repudiating any supernatural character in the records of revelation as such.[3] Robertson Smith had already made himself the centre of a stormy controversy by his article 'Bible' in the first volume of the ninth edition of the Encyclopaedia Britannica. He gave wholehearted support to the Graf-Wellhausen critico-literary method and conclusion. A gradual and natural evolutionary development of Israel's religion was advanced.

The views expounded in the article 'Bible' resulted in Robertson Smith's removal from his professorial chair in

---

[1] J. W. Colenso, The Pentateuch and the Book of Joshua Critically Examined, 1862, p. 81.

[2] J. K. Mozley, Some Tendencies in British Theology, 1952, p. 14.

[3] L. E. Elliott-Binns, English Thought, 1860–1900, 1956, p. 73.

Aberdeen. But it has been contended that although he had to forfeit this position the result was that 'the Church was allowed to find room for methods of research and for views of inspiration more free from the errors of tradition, and more true to the facts of Scripture itself'.[1] It was in this way, it is claimed, that the Free Church of Scotland secured its freedom by the sacrifice of one man.[2] Upon his dismissal from the chair at Aberdeen, Smith became joint editor of the *Encyclopaedia Britannica*.

The volume entitled, *The Old Testament in the Jewish Church*, is, from one point of view, Robertson Smith's most influential work. Having lost his case before the Presbytery of Aberdeen, he made an appeal to the Scottish laity in the form of a series of popular lectures in which he introduced the idea of biblical criticism to large audiences in Edinburgh and Glasgow. These lectures were given a wider public in book form in 1881 and in the short space of fifteen months 6,500 were sold.

Smith constantly urged that the new criticism could be held consistently with the conception of Scripture expounded in the catechisms and confessions of his Church. This is a point he laboured especially in the first lecture.

The ideas which he advanced in his article 'Bible' were reiterated and elaborated in the lectures. The fundamental thesis is that the religious history of the Hebrew people is to be reconstituted and reinterpreted in terms of a gradual evolutionary development in which the prophets of Israel are to be seen as key figures marking the advance of theological understanding. The history itself may be conceived as a natural development involving no supernatural elements. Or it may be regarded as the method chosen by God for man's discovery of enlarging ideas of the character and conduct of Deity.

The utmost stress was placed upon the subjective idea of revelation. Revelation was to be understood as the direct witness of the Spirit to the individual soul. It was not to be identified with the words of the Bible. Revelation is God Himself coming forth in direct personal encounter with human lives. It is not the giving of objective truths about God. And least of all is it to be thought of as an inerrant catalogue of

---

[1] George Adam Smith, *The Life of Henry Drummond*, 1898, New York, p. 142.

[2] *Ibid.* Cf. 'Robertson Smith became "not only the protagonist, but the martyr of Biblical criticism." ' T. H. Darlow, *William Robertson Nicoll*, 1925, p. 39.

doctrinal propositions. At the same time note must be taken of
the historical nature of revelation. The historical process is
marked by certain purposeful interventions in which God has
disclosed Himself. The Bible is the record of this historical
revelation which has culminated in Christ. It is here we have
the account of God's gracious self-disclosure. But being a record
of men, especially illuminated though they may have been, the
Bible cannot but betray evidences of verbal and historical errors.
But these errors do not detract from its worth; for the Word of
God is not the Scripture, but is that into which we are introduced
by the Scripture and to which it is a witness.[1]

Although we are concerned at the present mainly with an
account of Robertson Smith's views, it may be, none the less,
relevant to point out that there were vast problems left unsolved
and difficulties left untouched. It was not made clear, for
example, how the historical nature of revelation could be upheld
when it was maintained, at the same time, that the history was
not itself reliable. Nor was it at all easy to see how an understanding of God's revelation could be gained by those who were
unlearned. Even the broadest outline of the historical events as
they were claimed to have taken place by the new criticism
cannot be seen in the Bible as we have it. It is only those who
have special techniques and specialized equipment who can
discover, by a thorough reconstruction of its history, meaning
and significance in the Bible. Further, Smith gave stress, on the
one hand, to the subjective idea of revelation as the action of the
Divine Spirit within, and, on the other hand, he did allow for an
objective historical account, but he failed altogether to show the
relation that may be supposed to exist between them. He was
emphatic enough in his rejection of the so-called propositional
and intellectualistic view of revelation, yet, when he desired to
prove a point, he quoted the Scripture in propositional form
which he seemed to regard as sufficient to silence objections.
These are but a few of the serious weaknesses in Smith's idea of
revelation.

It was inevitable that such a conception of the Bible should
initiate a new outburst of controversy. In fact, T. K. Cheyne sees
the 'modern period' begun with the name of W. Robertson

[1] Cf. T. M. Lindsay, 'Professor W. Robertson Smith's Doctrine of Scripture',
Expositor, fourth series, 1894, pp. 241–64.

Smith 'who from the first gave promise of becoming the most brilliant critic of the Old Testament in the English-speaking countries'.[1] Into the details of the ensuing conflict we need not enter.[2] Robert Rainey was one of Smith's most formidable opponents, He addressed the students of the English Presbyterian College, London, and contended that since Christianity is an historical religion based upon an historical revelation it need not fear the most rigorous historical criticism. He stoutly maintained the inerrancy of Scripture and warned against the eagerness manifested by some to accept the conclusions of criticism which were in conflict with tradition. Rainey confesses that there are, and, indeed, must be, obscure passages in the Bible but he will not allow that there are any 'minor inaccuracies' in the sacred volume.[3]

Alfred Cave, a conservative Congregational scholar, made a strong attack upon Smith's position in *The British and Foreign Evangelical Review*.[4] The *London Quarterly Review* sees the critical view gaining its measure of success because of the temporary ignorance of many and the scientific scepticism of others. But, since truth must triumph in the end, it is assured that the Newer Criticism is destined to pass away.[5]

The fact, however, is that Robertson Smith's subjective understanding of revelation has remained and is specially influential at the present day.[6]

(4) 'The Lux Mundi', edited by Charles Gore

'Few books in modern times', contends J. K. Mozley, 'have so clearly marked the presence of a new era and so deeply influenced its character as the volume of essays by a number of Oxford men

---

[1] T. K. Cheyne, *Founders of Old Testament Criticism*, 1893, p. 212.

[2] Cf. 'Smith, William Robertson', *Dictionary of National Biography*; also Sutherland Black and George W. Chrystal, *The Life of William Robertson Smith* 1912, pp. 179 ff.

[3] Robert Rainey, *The Bible and Criticism*, 1878, pp. 69–70.

[4] Cf. *op. cit.*, 'The Latest Phase of the Pentateuch Question', Vol. XXIX, 1880, pp. 248–67; also, *ibid.*, 'Professor Robertson Smith and the Pentateuch', pp. 593–621.

[5] Cf. *op. cit.*, 'The Newer Criticism on the Old Testament', 1882, p. 305.

[6] Cf., e.g. *Revelation, A Symposium*, (ed. John Baillie and H. Martin), 1937: esp. W. Temple, pp. 106–7, 114–15, 119–23; Gustaf Aulén, pp. 275–6; H. Richard Niebuhr, *The Meaning of Revelation*, 1941, pp. 143–54; Ernest A. Payne, H. Wheeler Robinson, 1946, 'The Principle of Authority in the Christian Religion', pp. 177–8.

which was published in the latter part of the year 1889 under the
title of *Lux Mundi*.'[1] The aim of the work is clearly stated as an
'attempt to put the Catholic faith into its right relation to
modern intellectual and moral problems'.[2] The writers, it is
averred, are no 'guessers at truth', but interpreters of the faith
they have received. Elliott-Binns contends that the '*Lux Mundi*,
when compared with *Essays and Reviews*, is remarkable for its
constructive spirit'.[3] This is, perhaps, a little generous. The
subtitle states *Lux Mundi* to be 'A Series of Studies in the
Religion of the Incarnation'. But some of the subjects have little
relation to this topic, yet it would be incorrect to say, as A. M.
Fairbairn does, that 'the Incarnation is the very thing the book
does not, in any more than the most nominal sense, either
discuss or construe'.[4]

There are three essays in the volume which are important for
their influence upon the understanding of revelation. J. R.
Illingworth and R. C. Moberly wrote on aspects of the Incarnation, while C. Gore, who edited the work, caused excitement by
his essay on 'The Holy Spirit and Inspiration'.

Illingworth stressed the idea of the divine immanence and sees
in the Higher Pantheism 'which is so common in the present
day',[5] the feeling for this neglected emphasis. The 'physical
immanence of God the Word in His creation can hardly be over-
stated' he says, 'as long as His moral transcendence of it is also
kept in view'.[6] He regards the Incarnation as the climax of the
evolutionary process; as the introduction of a 'new species into
the world'.[7] The world is instinct with the Word, thus all truth
is a disclosure of His life. Consequently 'all great teachers of
whatever kind are vehicles of revelation'.[8] Yet 'the Word did
not desert the rest of His creation to become incarnate',[9]
therefore, 'the discoveries of science' may be welcomed 'as
ultimately due to Divine revelation'.[10]

Moberley in his 'Incarnation as the Basis of Dogma' maintains that 'the claim of the Church to knowledge through the

---

[1] J. K. Mozley, *Some Tendencies in British Theology*, 1952, p. 17.

[2] *Lux Mundi*, 1889, third edition, 1890, Preface, p. vii.

[3] L. E. Elliott-Binns, *Religion in the Victorian Period*, 1936, p. 238.

[4] A. M. Fairbairn, *The Place of Christ in Modern Theology*, 1908, p. 451
(footnote).

[5] *Lux Mundi*, 1889, third edition, 1890, p. 191.

[6] *Op. cit.*, p. 192.   [7] *Op. cit.*, p. 207.

[8] *Op. cit.*, p. 198.   [9] *Op. cit.*, p. 212.   [10] *Op. cit.*, p. 213.

Incarnation can only be rationally met, and only really answered, when the claim itself, and its evidence, are seriously examined'.[1]

Gore, too, sees Christianity as 'the religion of the Incarnation'.[2] With reference to the understanding of revelation he quotes Lotze's remark that revelation is 'either contained in some divine act of historic occurrence, or continually repeated in men's hearts'.[3] Gore maintains that it is both. But the history as we have it is not the history which contains these divine acts. This history has undergone 'unconscious idealizing'.[4] True, 'Our Lord, in His use of the Old Testament, does indeed endorse with the utmost emphasis the Jewish view of their history',[5] but in such instances He speaks as a man subject to the limitations of human knowledge. Critical questions concerning the Old Testament cannot be foreclosed by quoting Christ as an authority in this sphere. The Davidic authorship of Psalm cx. cannot be maintained because He referred it to David. 'The Incarnation' states Gore with emphasis 'was a self-emptying of God to reveal Himself under conditions of human nature and from the human point of view'.[6] His knowledge was, therefore, a natural human knowledge. As Gore states elsewhere, 'He exhibits no miraculous knowledge of history or of nature, such as was not accessible to other men'.[7] The 'kenotic' doctrine which Gore alludes to here in his essay in the *Lux Mundi* he develops and defends in his later *Bampton Lectures* and his *Dissertations*. By means of his kenotic doctrine Gore feels himself able to maintain that our Lord, because of His limited human knowledge, accepted the revised and idealized history which He found in His Old Testament.

There is, however, a problem here that Gore, and for that matter others who have followed him, have failed to meet. The question which has to be seriously faced is just this: Is human knowledge limited because man is finite or because he is a sinner? The answer which seems to be too readily given is 'because he is a sinner'. But none of us does or can know what knowledge is open to even a perfect human being, much less to

---

[1] *Lux Mundi*, 1889, third edition, 1890, p. 218.
[2] *Op. cit.*, p. 329.   [3] *Op. cit.*, p. 338.
[4] *Op. cit.*, p. 353.   [5] *Op. cit.*, p. 358.
[6] *Lux Mundi*, p. 359.
[7] Charles Gore, *The Doctrine of an Infallible Book*, 1924, p. 25.

One who is God-man. At any rate, discussing this subject in another context, J. V. Langmead-Casserley has rightly observed that there are those who have taken 'copious draughts of the critical epistemology of Immanuel Kant and his successors' who really say 'that it is the finitude of man's being which restricts his rational powers' and 'that the trouble with human reasoning is not so much that man is a sinner as that he is finite'.[1]

Gore is emphatic that inspiration does not assure inerrancy. He seems to regard inspiration as illumination, differing in degree, perhaps, from that which is common to all believing men. But, he contends, this 'spiritual illumination, even in the highest degree' has no tendency 'to lift men out of their natural conditions of knowledge which belong to their time'.[2] He can admit that 'almost from the first inspiration was regarded as "verbal" ' and 'commonly identified with infallibility'. But this false and fatal view, he states, following Coleridge, the Christians learned from the Jews.[3]

The chief merit of the *Lux Mundi* essays, as they touch upon our subject, was the clarity with which they stated the position. It may have been true as Scott Holland, one of the contributors, later contended, that what they said was not new. They were just repeating what they had been saying for years and what everybody else was saying. They were taken aback by its being spoken of 'as a bomb'.[4] The volume was, however, vigorously attacked in Convocation by Archdeacon Denison and was dismissed with contempt by Canon Liddon. It was, however, because it was so well said, and said by men whose names were coming to the forefront, that the *Lux Mundi* became so influential. The ideas which were here being elaborated were in essential harmony with the prevailing tone and temper of Old Testament criticism.

(5) 1901—*Article on the 'Gospels' in the 'Encyclopaedia Biblica' by Paul W. Schmiedel*
     Translation into English of 'What is Christianity?' by Adolf Harnack

[1] J. V. Landmead-Casserley, *Graceful Reason*, 1955, p. 35.
[2] *Lux Mundi*, p. 254.
[3] Charles Gore, *The Doctrine of an Infallible Book*, 1924, p. 46.
[4] S. Paget, *Henry Scott Holland*, 1921, p. 281.

These two works may be taken as marking another stage in the development of ideas which were to react upon the understanding of revelation. As the century began to draw to its close the extreme critical theories of the Old Testament were being either abandoned or greatly modified. There was a toning down of certain exaggerated views. In some quarters averse to the critical procedure, it began almost to be felt that there was a return to the traditional position. It is, at any rate, a fact that the more outrageous theories were being repudiated by critics of a more conservative outlook.

But the publication of Schmiedel's article was to open another era of fresh conflict. Here radical criticism was applied to the New Testament, and a new type of 'liberal Christianity' made its appearance. There must be a getting back to the Jesus of history. And to find Him there must be a clear understanding of the relevance and value of the records which tell of Him. When we discover Him, the real Christ of the Galilean road, apart from any idealization of Him by the later Church, then we are at the heart of the Christian gospel. Then we will know what He, the Mightiest among the mighty, the Greatest religious genius, the Man among men, believed and felt and knew about the Father of all. This is indeed revelation. It is the discovery in the ideals and ideas of Christ that we are of infinite value to God whose love must at last enclose all in its embrace.

It is to such a view as this—to revelation as centred in the historic Jesus—that Harnack's, *What is Christianity?* gave vogue. The gospel records, even when stripped of their miraculous legends, are still 'weighty'. They are so because 'they give us information upon three important points: In the first place, they offer us a plain picture of Jesus' teaching, in regard both to its main features and to its individual application; in the second place, they tell us how his life issued in the service of his vocation; and in the third place, they describe to us the impression which he made upon his disciples, and which they transmitted'.[1]

Yet the gospel is no creed about Jesus. 'Jesus never spoke of any kind of "creed" ' except 'to do the will of God, in the certainty that He is the Father'.[2] Such a declaration, for example, as 'I am the Son of God', Harnack maintains, was not

---

[1] Adolf Harnack, *What is Christianity?* (E.T. 1901), p. 31.   [2] *Ibid.*, p. 147.

a word of Jesus Himself.[1] In one clear statement found in italics, he states 'The Gospel, as Jesus proclaimed it, has to do with the Father only and not with the Son'.[2]

The influence of such ideas was, we believe, profound. It set scholars out on the Quest for the Historical Jesus, although it must be acknowledged that the Jesus who was discovered was not very much like the Christ of general Christian faith.

Into the obvious weaknesses and the glaring contradictions of *What is Christianity?* we need not enter. It is sufficient to observe that the 'boldness with which Harnack shifted the centre of Christianity from Christology to the Divine Fatherhood, certainly the most indefensible characteristic of the book from the point of view of historical criticism, caused a storm of protest in every theological and philosophical camp in Germany'.[3] Not less in England did its translation, coming at the same time as Schmiedel's article, have the effect of moving the locus of revelation from God's 'actuality' in history, to the 'historic' Jesus. But the tragic fact which emerged was that the Christ presented to men had no sure historical reality. It was a Figure constructed by men with an excessive confidence in their own reason and 'finding the sanction of truth in the mind of the individual and being in consequence arbitrary and subjective'.[4]

(6) 1933—*English Translation of Karl Barth's 'Commentary on the Epistle to the Romans'*

This is, we think, the next and last of the distinguishing volumes in our period to which we need to make special reference. There were, of course, many other works of major importance, but it is, we believe, true to say of them all that the ideas which they elaborated can be subsumed under one general view or other. The famous volumes, the *Cambridge Theological Essays* (1905) and the *Cambridge Biblical Essays* (1909), important as they are in themselves, do not seem to us to mark a new stage in the understanding of revelation. And the same is true of other writings which appeared.

But Barth's *Romans* does seem to indicate the introduction into theological thought of the Kierkegaardian idea of

---

[1] Adolf Harnack, *What is Christianity?* (E.T. 1901), p. 145.   [2] *Ibid.*, p. 144.
[3] E. Digges La Touche, *The Person of Christ in Modern Thought*, 1912, p. 100.
[4] E. Troeltsch, Art. 'Enlightenment', *The New Schaff-Herzog Religious Encyclopædia*, IV, p. 141.

'encounter'. In the Preface to the second German edition, he states: 'if I have a system, it is limited to a recognition of what Kierkegaard called the "infinite qualitative distinction" between time and eternity, and to my regarding this as possessing negative as well as positive significance: "God is in heaven, and thou art on earth". The relation between such a God and such a man, and the relation between such a man and such a God, is for me the theme of the Bible and the essence of philosophy'.[1]

It is well known that Barth has of recent years urged that he no longer occupies the position that he held when his *Romans* was first published. We are convinced in spite of this protest that what he has to say by way of exposition of the first chapter of the epistle is precisely that which he has expounded at great length in his *Church Dogmatics*.[2]

He writes, for example, of the 'incomprehensible' nature of grace. 'Grace', he observes, 'is the gift of Christ, who exposes the gulf which separates God and man, and, by exposing it, bridges it.'[3] He sees men standing so out of relation to God, that it is only in and through God's act that there can be reconciliation. 'Their union with God is shattered so completely that they cannot even conceive of its restoration.'[4] In such statements as these we have already in Barth the teaching of the complete obliteration of the divine image in man. Thus, he goes on to assert his characteristic repudiation of natural theology. There is no possibility, in the least, of knowing anything about God unless and until He Himself breaks into our darkness and night in the revelation of personal encounter. Yet it must be made clear that in the encounter the whole initiative is with God. 'To those who have abandoned direct communication, the communication is made. To those willing to venture with God, He speaks. Those who take upon them the divine "No" shall themselves be borne by the greater divine "Yes".'[5] The wisdom of the natural man issues in the Night of Folly. His so-called

---

[1] Karl Barth, *Epistle to the Romans*, (E.T. 1933), p. 10.
[2] Cf. 'In view of a controlling tendency at the present time to speak of two Barths, an earlier and a later Barth, it should perhaps be said at the outset that his position on this particular matter has not changed materially since the appearance of his epoch-making commentary on Paul's letter to the *Romans*.' R. C. Johnson, *Authority in the Protestant Church*, 1959, p. 162. What Johnson states here concerning Barth's understanding of authority is true also of other issues as well.
[3] *The Epistle to the Romans*, p. 31. [4] *Op. cit.*, p. 37. [5] *Op. cit.*, p. 41.

natural knowledge of God is an illusion. What he knows is 'No-God', since the true God is not a God to be known; He is a God to make Himself known. He is 'other' than we are. 'We press ourselves into proximity with Him: and so, all unthinking, we make Him nigh unto ourselves.'[1] It is when we know that we can never know Him, when we renounce our sophistication and are in despair that there is the possibility of God disclosing Himself to us. We have to learn that 'God is He whom we do not know' and so discover that 'our ignorance is precisely the problem and the source of our knowledge'.[2] It is here that faith comes, faith not of ourselves, but a faith brought to birth in the revelation of God's grace in His divine inbreaking. Such, indeed, is revelation: while 'Faith is awe in the presence of the divine incognito'.[3]

Looking back through the years of the century, then, it will be clear that certain distinctive types of revelation can be seen to emerge. While it would be inaccurate to attribute a separate origin for each to the volumes which we have seen to mark new stages in the development of religious ideas, it is, we believe, correct to see in these works more than suggestions which were bound to give rise to clearly stated positions. In a broad and general sense, then, the ideas of revelation, which at least find their germ, or were given impetus, by the books specified, can be singled out as follows.

Beginning with *Essays and Reviews* we can see the idea of revelation as historical process gaining ground. Colenso gave vigour to the subjective emphasis which was earlier set forth with such warmth and spirit by F. D. Maurice. Robertson Smith gave effect to the notion of revelation as God's acts in history. The *Lux Mundi* school emphasized the idea of revelation as finalizing the evolutionary process in Divine incarnation. Schmiedel and Harnack turn attention to the Jesus of history and locate revelation in the Figure reconstructed from the records after they had eliminated from them what they felt and fancied were *post factum* idealizations of the Church. And, finally, Barth seeks to make men aware of the living God as present and active. There thus comes the idea of revelation as divine encounter.

---

[1] *The Epistle to the Romans*, p. 44.   [2] *Op. cit.*, p. 45.   [3] *Op. cit.*, p. 39.

CHAPTER TWO

The Ideas within the Era

The changing climate of opinion throughout the century which began with the year 1860 is such that it is not easy to follow the weather chart. There were, in fact, times when contrary winds appeared to be blowing and many voyagers were caught in the place where two seas met. Sometimes, as far as it concerns the ship of the faith, it seemed that the wind 'blew softly', while at other times it was 'tempestuous'. There were those who deluded by the gentle breeze set forth with sails set optimistically only to find themselves caught in the storm and either stranded or shipwrecked. There were others who thought that they had discovered 'a bay with a beach' believing it to be 'commodious to winter in'. Others, however, still pressed on and at length reached the satisfying security of the shore.

It is possible, we think, to set forth the ideas which, throughout the century, brought changes to the winds of opinion. We must not suppose that these occurred in strict chronological order. There were, indeed, times when certain views existed as it were side by side and do not seem to have come into conflict. There were other times when there were clashes of opinions: times when the ideas which make for unbelief and the ideas which make for faith were in open war. But even in those periods when one opinion seemed to be dominant, others were not absent. It is these facts which must be kept in mind throughout this chapter.

A. THE CHALLENGE OF MATERIALISM

It was, it appeared, the first result of the theory of evolution to make men feel that the key to the riddle of existence had been discovered by natural science. The whole enigma of the universe was about to be solved. In earlier days the presence of mystery had created the superstition of religion. But now, it was confidently asserted, there was nothing which science could not explain.

Many of those who had come to treat the world as a machine came to believe that it was only such. What was legitimate as a scientific method was set forth as a body of doctrine claiming to be the only truth about the universe. While it is a fact that the greater minds among those who became absorbed in the study of physical nature did not lose completely the sense of the more than natural, it is clear that the idea was entertained by a large number that science had given the lie to the existence of a supernatural. At the same time, as we noted in the previous chapter, the omnipotence of science was unquestioned. What A. Wood calls 'the movement of self-criticism' which in more recent times 'has revolutionized the scientific outlook and completely changed the relation of natural science with theology and philosophy'[1] had not come about. Science had not yet learned its limitations: nor had scientists as yet admitted the fact that it too worked by faith no less than did religion. It was believed by not a few that religion could have no place in the new scientific world. Religion, it was proclaimed, was finished. Now that the age of science had begun it was 'something unverified and unverifiable by the only methods which were generally regarded as rational and scientific'.[2]

The more the scientific method yielded results, the more thoroughly many came to disbelieve in the existence of anything other than the material. It was, of course, not easy to be absolutely certain that there was really nothing beyond the things which could be seen and felt, measured and mastered. In the nature of the case the scientific method could not be used to test the reality of the non-material. Since, then, there was no possibility of scientifically demonstrating spiritual realities it was better to say that one was uncertain of their existence. Consequently it was thought to be more honest to admit that you did not know whether there was anything beyond or above the mundane. And for this attitude of ignorance T. H. Huxley coined the term 'agnosticism'.

[1] A. Wood, *The Pursuit of Truth*, n.d., p. 19.
[2] C. C. J. Webb, *A Study of Religious Thought in England from 1850*, 1933, p. 7.

It was, then, a chill wind which blew in the years immediately following 1860. And with the winds of doubt and dogmatism there went, as F. W. H. Myers saw it, a 'very flood-tide of materialism and Agnosticism, the mechanical theory of the universe, the reduction of all spiritual facts to physiological phenomena. It was a time when, not the intellect only, but the moral ideas of men seemed to have passed into the camp of negation. We were all in the first flush of triumphant Darwinianism, when terrene evolution had explained so much that men hardly cared to look beyond. Among my own group (at Cambridge), W. K. Clifford was putting forth his series of triumphant proclamations of the nothingness of God, and the divinity of man. Swinburne had given passionate voice to the same conception. Frederic Harrison was still glorifying Humanity as the only 'Divine'. George Eliot strenuously rejected all prospect save in the mere terrene performance of duty to our human kin. And others maintained a significant silence, or fed with vague philosophizings an uncertain hope'.[1]

Nor did the challenge of materialism with its attendent agnosticism quickly pass: perhaps, indeed, it can never quite do so, for all men have not faith. At any rate, in the year 1894, we find F. H. Woods of Oxford in an article entitled, 'Hebrew Prophecy and Modern Criticism', maintaining 'Now the spirit of the age is on the whole against the supernatural. This feeling sometimes takes a form definitely hostile to religion; but leaving this out of the question, there are many who feel the claim which Christianity makes to supernaturalism, so far from being the main ground for believing it to be true, is rather a hindrance to accepting it'.[2]

At the beginning the challenge of materialism was felt by many friends of religion to be formidable. There were some who resorted to the pathetic refuge of belittling science. Others took to reconciling what was regarded as the results of science with religious faith in a way which did credit to neither. Others seemed to fall back on the theory of double truth or to find consolation in the distinction between knowledge of facts and

[1] F. W. H. Myers, quoted in *The Life of Bishop Moule*, Hartford and Macdonald, 1922, p. 34.
[2] F. H. Woods, 'Hebrew Prophecy and Modern Criticism', *Expository Times*, Vol. V, 1893–4, p. 257.

knowledge of values. There were, however, those who were ready to eliminate the supernatural altogether from Christianity and to present it as little more than a system of naturalistic ethics. It was felt by those who yielded to this compromise that any idea of a divine activity within the world which operated according to unchanging natural laws, any idea of miracle and of answers to prayer, that is, was an unnecessary burden, and a hindrance to the defence of religion.

It was only gradually that the philosophy of materialism revealed itself as having no satisfactory solution for the deeper problems of man's unquenchable spirit. It was easy enough, at least for a time, to maintain the system by ignoring any facts which appeared to conflict with it. But gradually it began to be seen that to dismiss from consideration whole areas of experience as illusory or incompatible was itself unscientific. In spite of the vehemence with which materialism was maintained and in spite of the evident value and the good results of the application of the scientific method, it was soon realized that the mere multiplication of luxuries could provide only fleeting benefits. The human spirit began to reassert itself. Man needed the promise of another realm as well as possessions in this. Tyndall in 1874, in his wearying volume, *Eirenicon*, had, according to von Hügel 'offered to religion the shells of the oyster', and 'retained for mathematics and Natural Science and for Agnosticism' 'all the succulent food of truth and reality'.[1] But on the whole, people were not so easily satisfied. They were not convinced that the requisite diet for their lives was to be found there. They wanted eggs not shells, and certainly not oyster shells. The idea of the spiritual came creeping back, and, as William James asserts, 'spiritualistic faith in all its forms deals with a world of *promise*, while materialism's sun sets in a sea of disappointment'.[2]

But meanwhile the problem for Christian faith was a real one. It may be said, in this context, to centre around the question of miracles.

(1) *Miracles: Maintaining their Possibility*

In his lectures, *The Miraculous Element in the Gospels*, A. B.

---

[1] F. von Hügel, *The Reality of God*, 1931, p. 196.
[2] William James, *Pragmatism*, 1916, p. 108.

Bruce observed that 'The apologist of the present time has an interest in minimizing the miraculousness of miracles, and making them appear as natural as possible'.[1] This fashion had, indeed, been already set by Baden Powell, who, in his contribution to *Essays and Reviews*, had virtually denied their possibility. He maintained that Revelation is not established by these 'alleged external attestations', since their evidence could only be 'physical', and God's moral government does not need such 'proofs'.[2] Powell, in fact, goes so far in his essay as to assert his acceptance of materialistic determinism.[3]

It may be noted, too, that what Higher Criticism there was in England prior to Robertson Smith's appearance, who was able to unite his criticism with belief in miracles, was decidedly anti-supernaturalistic in its basic assumptions. Those who were earlier influenced by the continental schools of radical criticism seemed willing to reject any historical evidence in which a supernatural element was implied. Continental criticism was wedded to naturalism, and was not far removed from infidelity.

Even Robertson Smith's avowal of belief in miracles did not satisfy all. They could not see how a history which was to be interpreted as a natural process could be admitted to contain supernatural intrusions. There was consequently effort made by a variety of writers to naturalize, to minimize, or to eliminate the miraculous. Matthew Arnold, for example, made a bold attempt to preserve Christianity while denying miracles. They were explained, or, perhaps it would be better to say, explained away, as being the result of obscure physical activity of which we are but partially acquainted.[4] Without going into any details concerning Arnold's doctrine, it will be obvious that he has not dispensed with the divine working, he merely pushed it back to the origination of the system. Such a theory is certainly not compatible with atheism, but it most definitely is with deism. If Arnold sought to naturalize the miracles there were others who sought to minimize them.[5] A number of writers were ready to maintain that miracles have no necessary place in the Christian

[1] A. B. Bruce, *The Miraculous Element in the Gospels*, 1886, p. 43.
[2] *Essays and Reviews*, 1860, tenth edition, 1861, p. 133.
[3] Cf. *Cambridge History of England Literature*, XII, p. 327.
[4] Cf. M. Arnold, *Literature and Dogma*, popular edition, 1900, Chapter V.
[5] Cf. J. R. Illingworth, *Personality Human and Divine*, 1894, p. 203 f. H. Drummond, *The New Evangelism*, 1899, pp. 107 ff.

scheme. They may consequently be explained as either the relic of primitive beliefs, as the tendency of unenlightened man to attribute to God what he has been unable to explain by natural laws, or to the equally human desire for following generations to associate mighty deeds with the great figures of the past. Others seemed to have no inhibitions in the slightest, and resolutely eliminated miracles altogether. In 1902, for example, there appeared the work entitled *Contentio Veritatis*, in which it was roundly stated that miracles 'are unmeaning'.[1] This book professes to be a philosophical defence of the Christian Faith, yet it is declared, concerning miracles, that to admit the possibility of such events 'is to destroy the canons upon which not only our ordinary reasoning about matters of science, but in particular our ordinary canons of historical criticism, are based'.[2]

Not all, by any means, were prepared to take this line. It seemed to others obvious that miracles were somehow associated with the Christian message, and the very fact of them was an essential demonstration of a supernatural realm. An explanation of them must therefore be sought. In the period there were three main apologetic works on miracles, three series of Bampton Lectures, in which the subject received special attention. While it is a fact that the position taken by each one of these lecturers was not acceptable to the others, yet a reference to the volumes themselves will reveal how the idea of miracles was regarded as in some way essential for Christianity. The apologetic for miracles can be subsumed under the point of view taken by these Bampton lecturers.

We must begin with J. B. Mozley. In 1865 he focused attention on the miracles, the reality of which he had no doubt. His method was to reject the idea of a universal law as conceived by those who would have a world enclosed in iron and the Diety in adamantine fetters.[3] Mozley defends miracles by accepting Hume's theory of causation. Law is not, so to speak, something embedded in the constitution of the universe: it is really 'the perception of harmony and relation in nature'. The order of nature, to which the term law is given, is the observation only

---

[1] *Contentio Veritatis*, 1902, p. 88.

[2] *Contentio Veritatis*, p. 53. Cf. Aubrey Moore's statement to Reading Church Congress of 1883: a miraculous intervention is 'as fatal to theology as to science'. Cf. also his *Science and the Faith*, 1889, p. 225.

[3] J. B. Mozley, *Eight Lectures on Miracles*, Bampton Lectures, 1865, 1865, p. 59.

of sequence which begets the expectation of its continuance in the future. Mozley sees philosophy as having 'loosened the connection of the order of nature with the ground of reason, befriending, in exact proportion as it has done this, the principle of miracles'.[1] The argument against miracles on the score of law is, then, he says, 'answered by saying that we know nothing in nature of law in the sense in which it prevents miracles'.[2] Not only are the miracles not made impossible because incompatible with law, but, no less, are they not to be thought of as 'against experience; because we expect facts *like* to those of our experience; and miracles are *unlike* ones'.[3] Mozley contends that the general order of nature is not really disrupted by these miraculous interventions. The sense of sequence and harmony is not lost by these occasional intrusions. He concludes that 'it is not in the sense of harmony and system that the order of nature is opposed to the miraculous at all'.[4] The perfectly designed machine does not lose its perfection by being 'interrupted designedly for some purpose'. Indeed an injurious interruption of the relations of the human body does not make less wonderful our bodily structure. 'What', he therefore asserts, '*is* disturbed by a miracle is the mechanical expectation of recurrence, from which, and not from the *system* and arrangement in nature, the notion of immutability proceeds.'[5]

This defence of miracles is certainly a bold one. Mozley has taken up the weapons which Hume had used against their reality and used them instead to assure their certainty. It was, at the time, an original approach; although, at the present we are more familiar with the notion of science as an observation of the behaviour of phenomena, than, as it was mainly conceived to be then, a reading of the inner necessities of noumena. Huxley was impressed by Mozley's arguments and admitted the abstract possibility of miracles. Mozley was not, however, able clearly to establish that these unusual occurrences have necessarily a divine origin. Mozley's onslaught on the order of nature met with strenuous opposition from the author of *Supernatural Religion*.[6] A. B. Bruce rejects the validity of Mozley's thesis and while he

---

[1] J. B. Mozley, *Eight Lectures on Miracles*, Bampton Lectures, 1865, 1865, p. 49.
[2] *Ibid.*, p. 49.   [3] *Ibid.*, p. 50.
[4] *Ibid.*, p. 55.   [5] *Ibid.*, p. 56.
[6] Cf. *Supernatural Religion*, 1874, p. 59 f.

admits it to be 'as ingenious as it is bold' contends that 'it belongs to that class of arguments which silence rather than convince'.[1] He describes it as an 'eccentric attempt to confound unbelief by an assault on the natural order of which it makes an idol'.[2]

R. W. Church in a review of Mozley's lectures, however, took the opportunity of stating that 'The way in which the subject of Miracles has been treated, and the place which they have in our discussions, will remain a characteristic feature of both the religious and philosophical tendencies of thought amongst us'.[3]

While Mozley defended miracles, then, by an attack upon the idea of natural law, C. A. Row rejected Mozley's method and sought justification for the miraculous in man's freedom to act in an ordered universe. This is the presupposition of his Bampton Lectures of 1877. It is right to point out that Row had already given an intimation of his idea in his earlier work, *The Supernatural in the New Testament, Possible, Credible, and Historical* (1875). In this volume Row argued that man's freedom to act in a world ruled by law is a genuine fact. In this we have evidence for, as well as an illustration of, God's right and ability to act within His own world: and to act in special ways for special purposes. Man's freedom is not annulled by order, neither is order nullified by man's freedom. So, too, is it with God.

This is the idea which comes out in his lectures of 1877 whenever he touches upon the subject of miracles. Quite evidently, 'The conception of a miracle involves neither a suspension of the forces, nor the violation of the laws of nature'.[4] Man of his own free agency, he argues again, can modify the order of nature by imparting to its forces.[5] 'If man can change the direction of the forces of the universe, combine them, and neutralize one by the superior energy of another in such a way as to effectuate the results of purpose, without suspending them, much more must God be able to do the same for the effectuation of His purposes;

---

[1] A. B. Bruce, *The Miraculous Element in the Gospel*, 1886, p. 46.

[2] *Ibid.*, p. 48.

[3] Cf. R. W. Church, *Occasional Papers*, 1897, Vol. 2, p. 82 f. (Reprinted from *The Times*, June 5th, 1866.)

[4] C. A. Row, *Christian Evidences Viewed in Relation to Modern Thought*, being the Bampton Lectures for 1877, 1877, pp. 54–5.

[5] *Ibid.*, p. 61 f.

since His ability to effectuate the results of purpose without
suspending the action of existing force, or introducing a new
one, must be so much the greater as He is mightier and wiser'.[1]

This refusal of Row to define a miracle as in any way a
violation of the laws of nature was an important emphasis.
Christian apologists had too often needlessly embarrassed their
arguments by accepting Hume's definition.[2] It was far wiser to
insist that since man can bring about results which would not
otherwise have come about except by his interference, so was it
possible for God. A miracle is not, then, as Newman Smyth had
correctly insisted, 'a sudden blow struck in the face of nature,
but a use of nature, according to its inner capacities, by higher
powers'.[3] Row's stress upon man's free agency in an ordered
universe has been given much attention in recent years as having
an important bearing upon the whole argument for the possibility of miracles. Earlier H. L. Mansel, in his essay on miracles
in *Aids to Faith*, had shown awareness of its relevancy. Recent
writers such as C. S. Lewis in his *Miracles, A Preliminary Study*
and H. H. Farmer, in his discussion of the subject in his *World
and God*, make effective use of the same idea of man's ability to
initiate new results by his free activity without either suspending
or destroying the order of nature.

Frederick Temple, in his Bampton Lectures of 1884, makes
much of the concept of religious development as he had done in
his contribution to *Essays and Reviews*. He maintains that there
is really no final contradiction between the idea of evolution and
that of revelation. He deals in one lecture with the 'Apparent
Conflict between Religion and the Doctrine of Evolution',[4] and
in another with the 'Apparent Collision between Religion and
the Doctrine of Evolution'.[5] He concludes that 'we cannot find
that Science, in teaching Evolution, has yet asserted anything
that is inconsistent with Revelation, unless we assume that
Revelation was intended not to teach spiritual truth only, but

[1] C. A. Row, *Christian Evidences Viewed in Relation to Modern Thought*, being
the Bampton Lectures for 1877, 1877, p. 63.
[2] Cf. *Hume's Enquiries* (ed. L. A. Selbie-Bigge), 1951, pp. 105 ff.
[3] Cf. Newman Smyth, *Old Faiths in a New Light*, 1879, revised edition, 1891,
Chapter 1; J. Wendland, *Miracles and Christianity* (trans. H. R. Mackintosh, 1910),
Chapter 1; H. H. Farmer, *The World and God*, 1935, pp. 148 ff.
[4] Frederick Temple, *The Relations between Religion and Science*, being the
Bampton Lectures for 1884, 1884, Chapter IV.   [5] *Ibid.*, Chapter VI.

physical truth also'.[1] Temple finds religion to be a deep
necessity of the human soul and says that 'it is in knowledge of
God that man finds himself divine'.[2]

It is, however, on the subject of revelation and miracles that
the discussion is centred. And it is just here that we find the
lecturer, from one point of view apparently looking back to an
older apologetic, and, from another point of view, making
statements which are characteristically modern. In his defence
of miracles Temple falls back upon the hypothesis that they are
an effect due to the action of some higher law. This idea seems
to have had a wide appeal. It was used earlier by C. Babbage in
the *Ninth Bridgewater Treatise*. It was also the position
maintained by C. H. Curteis in the Boyle Lectures of the same
year as Temple's Bampton Lectures. Curteis contended that a
miracle is to be explained 'as a point of intersection between
some vast outer circle of God's ways and the smaller inner circle
to which we ourselves are better accustomed'.[3] Almoni Peloni,
likewise, sees miracles as due to the operation of a higher law.
He asks how some scientists can pronounce miracles to be impossible 'when even they themselves possess and wield a power
by which the ordinary course of nature is constantly modified'?[4]

Temple, however, was not ready to maintain that in every
case the higher law was itself an unknown physical one. He does,
indeed, say that certain miracles of healing, for example, can be
so explained. He regards a miracle as in some sense a 'break of
uniformity', and, he declares that 'Revelation has no interest in
denying' that 'the intervention which has apparently disturbed
the sequence of phenomena is, after all, that of a higher physical
law as yet unknown'.[5] Applying this canon, Temple can state
that such events as, for example, the Resurrection of our Lord
and the general resurrection, need not be considered miracles in
the scientific sense. At the moment the higher law, so to speak,
is not made active. At the time of the resurrection of Christ this

---

[1] Frederick Temple, *The Relations between Religion and Science*, being the
Bampton Lectures for 1884, 1884, Chapter IV, p. 188; cf. pp. 123, 220.

[2] *Ibid.*, p. 65.

[3] C. H. Curteis, *The Scientific Obstacles to Christian Belief*, Boyle Lectures, 1884,
1885, p. 76.

[4] Almoni Peloni, 'Miracles: The Problem Stated', *The Expositor*, second series,
Vol. IV, 1882, p. 240. Cf. 'Miracles: The Problem Solved', *The Expositor*, second
series, Vol. VI, 1883, p. 161 f.

[5] Frederick Temple, *The Relations between Religion and Science*, 1884, p. 195.

higher natural physical law operated, and at the time of the
general resurrection it will operate again. Meanwhile the
Divine will, we must suppose, acts to counteract these laws and
to render them dormant. On this hypothesis much of what we
have been in the habit of calling miracles are but 'the natural
issue of physical laws always at work'.[1] The impression that one
receives from some of Temple's arguments is that the miracles
appear to be the natural results of the permitted operations of
natural law.[2] If this is so, then a comment of Delitzsch can be
understood: 'it is a most disheartening sign of the times' he once
observed, 'that even such as in theory acknowledge the miracles,
in practice really reckon on naturalistic assumptions'.[3]

At the same time Temple does give supremacy to the Moral
Law and finds for some of the miracles an instance of the
assertion of that law in human affairs. In this way he is able to
put stress on the spiritual value of the miracles. He seems to
draw a sharp distinction between the moral and the scientific
understanding of a miracle. This point is constantly made. He
says, to quote but one reference, that 'it must therefore be always
remembered that Revelation is not bound by the scientific
definition of a miracle, and that if all the miraculous events
recorded in the Bible happened exactly as they were told, and if
Science were one day able to show that they could be accounted
for by natural causes working at the time in each case, this would
not in any way effect their character, as regards the Revelation
which they were worked to prove or of which they form a part.
Revelation uses these events for its own purposes'.[4]

It would seem from these words that Temple could regard a
miracle as the religious reading of a natural event. It is certainly
a correct thing to emphasize that miracles were performed for a
religious purpose. This, indeed, is one of the points which has
been given special stress today. Thus Wendland, for example,
contends that the Scriptures make clear 'that no miracles are ever
experienced by unbelievers'.[5] He goes on to urge that it is in the
context of religious experience that their independent, unique

[1] Frederick Temple, *The Relations between Religion and Science*, 1884, p. 197.
[2] Cf. A. B. Bruce, *The Miraculous Element in the Gospels*, 1886, p. 51.
[3] F. Delitzsch, 'The Deep Gulf between the Old Theology and the New. A Last Confession', *The Expositor*, third series, Vol. IX, 1889, pp. 54.
[4] *The Relations between Religion and Science*, 1884, pp. 195–6.
[5] J. Wendland (E.T. 1910), p. 3.

and real significance is to be found. This point is made with particular effectiveness by H. H. Farmer. He premises that 'Miracles being fundamentally a religious category and not a scientific or philosophical one, the proper place to begin is within the sphere of living religion itself'.[1] The very first thing to be considered, he maintains, is 'what is the significance of miracle for religion'. Justification for this way of regarding a miracle he finds in the etymology of the word 'miracle' itself which fixes attention upon the profound feeling response, akin to wonder and awe, which the event evokes. The 'mirabile' in the 'miraculum' has significance for the religious life as such. It is for this reason that Farmer can contend that 'a miraculous event always enters the religious man's experience as a *revelation* of God'.[2] The awareness of God as living is the decisive fact in the miraculous event.

Farmer argues with cogency in favour of the assimilation of the idea of a miracle with the idea of revelation.[3] He makes the point that 'a miracle for the religious mind is pre-eminently an event in which God is apprehended as entering succouringly into the situation'.[4] This insistence on the religious understanding of a miracle will mean, as, indeed, Farmer declares, that what is a miracle for one, is not for another. He is in agreement with Hunzinger that 'Only those who believe through the miracle can believe in the miracle'.

That there is valuable truth in this subjective emphasis there need be no doubt. The New Testament gives us warrant for stressing the religious significance of the event designated a miracle. The miracle is no arbitrary act of God, no stunning and silencing wonder. A miracle is a sign, a wonder wrought to express some spiritual reality. In a sense as Erasmus once remarked, 'the doings of Jesus are parables'.

Yet it must be made clear that it is not enough to regard a miracle as an event from which we simply gain the impression that God is working. There must be, in addition, the cognitive assurance of the metaphysical actuality of the event. A mere emotional impression is no satisfactory understanding of a miracle. There must be objective reality of the power displayed as well as subjective valuation of a spiritual disclosure.

---

[1] H. H. Farmer, *The World and God*, 1935, p. 108.
[2] *Ibid.*, p. 109.   [3] *Ibid.*, p.111 f.   [4] *Ibid.*, p. 116.

It is the error of the Ritschlian theology that miracles are given a completely subjective significance. A miracle is nothing more than a subjective impression.

Ritschl himself left the question of miracles in obscurity. His whole theology, it seems, begins with the Kantian stress upon the authority for religion of the moral proof and the impossibility of our knowing anything about noumena. Ritschl draws a sharp distinction between the practical and the religious view of the world. He desired to exempt religion altogether from the criticism of science by insisting that religion relates only to the category of value. Theology is altogether divorced from metaphysics. In the first edition of his *Justification and Reconciliation* he went so far as to set religious and theoretical knowledge in opposition. Although the antagonism is smoothed over in the third edition of the same work it is still asserted that the two are distinct functions which, even when applied to the same object, do not even partially coincide, but go wholly asunder.

It is this clear-cut distinction which lies behind his treatment of miracles. The idea of a metaphysical miracle is looked upon with disfavour as being incompatible with the modern scientific view of the world. But the religious idea of a miracle is still allowed since any event or experience which gives an immediate impression of God's presence and power is so designated. A miracle is therefore, not a scientific concept, but altogether a religious one. Ritschl states in the first sketch of his *Dogmatic* (1853) that a 'miracle has its truth, not for science, but for religious experience'. Later modifications and expositions do not alter this essential position.

How far Temple was influenced by this view is hard to say. But it is certain that some of his period were. There are, for example, a couple of articles entitled, 'God in Nature and History, Contributions towards a true Theory of Revelation' in which P. Thomson makes, what we cannot but call, this Ritschlian distinction. 'The physical or scientific interpretation of natural phenomena' he declares, 'is quite independent of their religious interpretation; they are of different spheres, and their propositions therefore can never come into collision'.[1]

---

[1] P. Thomson, 'God in Nature and History, Contributions towards a true Theory of Revelation', *The Expositor*, second series, Vol. I, 1885, p. 179; cf. also p. 250.

Ritschl's followers certainly saw that amid the ambiguity of their master's scheme it was clear that he regarded a miracle as the religious name for any event which might evoke a kindling impression of God's help, but, as an event which, none the less, did not require to be brought into relation with the scientific doctrine of the unbroken connection of natural law. It became a dictum, therefore, with those who took their cue from Ritschl, that faith was not concerned with the acceptance of special miraculous incidents. Harnack and Herrmann, for example, carried through the Ritschlian presuppositions. Harnack is emphatic that the 'historian cannot regard a miracle as a sure given historical event'. He goes on to assert that 'Every individual miracle remains historically quite doubtful, and a summation of things doubtful never leads to certainty'. He will grant that a historian may be convinced that Jesus did extraordinary things, which may be referred to, as in the strict sense miraculous. Such a conviction, however, derives from the unique impression he has obtained of His person which leads him to credit to Him supernatural power. Harnack is emphatic that 'This conclusion itself belongs to the province of religious faith'.[1]

Herrmann declares that the question of the trustworthiness of the miracle narratives of the gospels is, for the present-day theology, a matter of indifference. As the most thorough exponent of the Ritschlian theology, he defines a miracle as 'Any event in which we clearly perceive the impinging of God upon our lives'.[2] Such miracles cannot be made 'intelligible' to others, and they need no 'defence'. They lie in the realm of faith and have no real connection with the natural order, the province of scientific knowledge. In no sense can it be said that God breaks through the natural order. 'Our faith can only recognize miracle when in an event within our experience we recognize the impact upon our life of a power not ourselves'.[3]

Such statements as these could be paralleled in the thought of Sabatier. He, too, insists upon the religious understanding of a miracle; but he does not seem to regard it as metaphysically factual. He certainly divorces it from the world of scientific

---

[1] Adolf Harnack, *History of Dogma* (in seven volumes, E.T. 1902), Vol. I, p. 65 note.
[2] W. Herrmann, *Systematic Theology* (E.T. 1927), p. 83. [3] *Ibid.*, p. 85.

knowledge. 'The affirmation of piety is essentially different from scientific explanation,' he says, 'it places us in the subjective and moral order of life, which no more depends on the order of science than the scientific order depends on piety. There cannot be conflict between the two orders, because they move on different planes and never meet. Science, which knows its limits, cannot forbid the act of confidence and adoration of piety. Piety, in its turn, conscious of its proper nature, will not encroach on science; its affirmations can neither enrich, impoverish, nor embarrass science, for they bear on different points and answer different ends'.[1]

It is in the context of this understanding of the separate and distinct realms of science and religion that Sabatier treats of the idea of miracle. It is for Sabatier, as it is for all who take the exclusively subjective point of view, the religious reading of any event. The event may, of course, be in itself extraordinary but it still belongs to the realm of nature. It is piety which sees in the event some revelation of God. This is the conception which was given persuasive exposition by Schleiermacher. He sees 'Nature as the Vestibule of the Living Temple' as he puts it in his second *Discourse*, and religion produced 'chiefly where the living contact of man with the world fashions itself as feeling'. The prophet is the one who is the most sensitive to the actings of the Divine Force and the one who is able to make a living communication of its presence to others. Such a man needs no mediator for himself, he is rather a mediator for many. In the events which others pass by, he, seer that he is, stops, and feels the upsurgings of divine life.

The ideas of all these writers had become familiar to British readers and their views had a profound influence. With the passing of the years there was a growing tendency to press and stress the subjective understanding of miracles. But by so doing there was an evident danger that miracles would lose their sense of uniqueness. It is, of course, perfectly true, as W. N. Whitehead has said, that 'Every event on its finer side introduces God into the world'.[2] The Christian believer will have no doubt about that. He cannot think otherwise since he believes in

[1] A. Sabatier, *Outlines of a Philosophy of Religion*, third edition, 1906, p. 79.
[2] W. N. Whitehead, *Religion in the Making*, Lowell Lectures, 1926, 1926, pp. 155–6.

the immanence of God. But a miracle is not, however, a mere religious reading of every event. It is a religious reading of an event which is itself unique, and which would still be so however read. In other words, the objective reality of the event as resulting from God's act must be maintained. A miraculous event is not just an awareness of that general providential regard of God for His creation. There will be occasions, no doubt, when the man of faith will become strangely stirred as he contemplates the beauty of the natural order and the bounty of the divine provision. 'Yet the religious man would not spontaneously call such a revelation of God to him at such a moment a miracle; nor would he use the term of those orderly processes of nature which he apprehends as wonderful manifestations of the bounty and steadfastness and creative power of God. Reference is, indeed, sometimes made to the "miracles of nature", and we are bidden wonderingly to discern the miracles of God in the most humdrum familiarities of life, the growth of a plant, the pattern of a snowflake. We are far from suggesting that such phrases are improper, still less the sentiments they express; yet such a usage of the term miracle can hardly be taken as spontaneous and typical. There is an element of philosophic theorizing, perhaps even at times of self-conscious attitudinizing, in it. That this is so, is shown by the fact that if such a line of thought be consistently carried through, it ends in the view that everything is a miracle, and the term is evacuated of any distinctive meaning at all, except the quite jejune one that there is, despite all our knowledge, a residuum of the mysterious in every event. If there is one thing quite certain in this connection it is that the word miracle on the religious man's lips indicates something distinctive which is *not* applicable, even after reflection, to all events indiscriminately. In other words, the more generalized the awareness of God's goodness and succour, the less the word miracle is applicable.'[1]

(2) *Miracles: Indicating their Purpose*

It is impossible to mark the precise time when the transition was made from regarding miracles as compelling evidences for Christianity to the idea of them as having an intimate association with it. The usual line taken by the older apologists was to argue

[1] H. H. Farmer, *The World and God*, 1935, pp. 118–9.

that miracles (and prophecy) were to be taken as evidential adjuncts to revealed doctrines. It was in this way that the cause of Christianity was maintained against the deists.[1] And the method was continued into the first part of the second half of the nineteenth century. Bishop Butler had given the most polished exposition of the thesis that miracles and prophecy were the 'two direct and fundamental proofs' of the Christian revelation. All other evidences were to be viewed in the light of these two. Such, too, was the position urged by Paley. But the emphasis was to be changed.

W. E. Gladstone, in his edition of Butler's *Works*, expressed his awareness of the revised understanding of miracles in relation to revelation. He adds a footnote to the words just quoted: 'After the discussion of the last century and a half, Butler would perhaps have somewhat altered what he has written respecting the twin office of miracle and prophecy as evidences of revealed religion'.[2] Another writer a few years later contends that Paley's view of miracles gives them a sort of mechanical efficacy. 'Every divine revelation must be replete with miracles and with wisdom. A revelation without miracles cannot be proved to be divine; without consummate wisdom it is proved not to be divine. But we must advance further. The wisdom and the miracle are both of the very essence of revelation. In regarding miracles as only external buttresses of faith, Paley falls into the same mistake as to rest in the *opus operatum* of a sacrament.'[3]

In his characteristic manner P. T. Forsyth, writing in the *London Quarterly Review* for July 1909 on the subject 'Evidential Value of Miracles', contends that as evidences they can have little appeal. He quotes the saying 'Miracles, which were once the foundation of Apologetic, became in time its crutch; and now they have become its crux'. He even goes so far as to evince some sympathy with a remark of Rousseau who declared, 'Get rid of your miracles, and the world will fall at Christ's feet'. Yet Forsyth, who argues elsewhere against the tendency which some reveal to proclaim an undogmatic and toned-down

---

[1] Cf. H. D. McDonald, *Ideas of Revelation*, 1959, p. 98 f.

[2] Joseph Butler, *The Works of Joseph Butler* (ed. W. E. Gladstone), Oxford, 1896, pp. 302–3.

[3] *Expository Times*, Vols. I and II, 1889–91, I, p. 9.

Christianity, has no intention of getting rid of miracles. He is acutely aware of their difficulty for the modern mind. He thinks that the day has passed when they can be adduced as proofs of revelation. It is his conviction that now they embarrass faith, they do not support it, if used as external evidences.

Such statements as these could be continued but enough has been recorded to show how definite was the change in the understanding of the purpose of miracles.

It is certainly a question of fundamental importance to ask how miracles are related to revelation. Are they evidences or media? It was agreed by all theists that miracles, in some way, make God better known. 'They may communicate to men a knowledge of God's character and purposes higher in degree, if not different in kind from, that derived from the ordinary course of nature.'[1]

The so-called Evidential School of apologists had all along maintained that revelation was the communication to men of doctrinal truths which were authenticated by miraculous proofs. This was the view, general in the previous century and a half, which was brilliantly maintained by Mozley in his Bampton Lectures. Even to the present day writers of repute may be found who maintain this evidential regard for miracles. Christianity, contends a recent apologist, 'is under a special obligation to produce miraculous evidence of the truth of its claims. The Founder of Christianity, wiser than some of His modern followers, clearly recognized this obligation.'[2]

At the same time, we may not be far wrong in contending that J. B. Mozley was the last great exponent of the evidential idea of miracles. The first of his famous lectures is entitled, 'Miracles Necessary for a Revelation'. He regards revelation as the communication of truths otherwise undiscoverable by the human reason. This 'supernatural scheme for man's salvation' is not established 'without the evidence of miracle'. After what he calls a 'prefatory note', he states that 'There is one great necessary purpose, then, which divines assign to miracles, viz. the proof of a revelation. And certainly, if it is the will of God to give a revelation, there are plain and obvious reasons for asserting that miracles are necessary as the guarantee and

[1] A. B. Bruce, *The Miraculous Eelement in the Gospels*, 1886, p. 284.
[2] Charles Harris, *Pro Fide*, fourth edition, 1930, pp. 417–18.

voucher for that revelation. A revelation is, properly speaking, such only by virtue of telling us something which we could not know without it. But how do we know that that communication of what is undiscoverable by human reason is true? Our reason cannot prove of it, for it is by the very supposition beyond our reason. There must be, then, some note or sign to certify to it and distinguish it as a true communication from God, which note can be nothing else than a miracle'.[1]

Neither commendation nor criticism of this evidential regard for miracles needs to be made here. There is, without doubt, something to be said for and against the procedure. It may well be that the reaction has been too violent and that there is real need to reconsider the question.

But the evidential understanding of miracles could not be well maintained in the climate of opinion which prevailed in the last half of the nineteenth century. For one thing, the early apologetic view had begun from the standpoint of the divine transcendence. God was conceived of as standing outside and intruding, on occasional times and in special ways, to direct men's attention to the truths He had seemed fit to reveal. This emphasis upon the divine transcendence has been replaced by one upon the divine immanence with the result that a new appreciation of miracles was inescapable. For another reason, it was a period of stirring individualism, in which men were jealously aware of their liberty as single individuals, consequently anything in the nature of coercion of belief was resented. It was considered by believers and unbelievers alike that to adduce miracles as evidences of revelation is to seek to tyrannize men into faith. Emerson had given blunt repudiation of the idea of a faith resting upon the external attestation of miracles. To seek to convert a man by an appeal to such evidence is, he says, a profanation of the soul.

In a chapter entitled 'Signs as a Vehicle of Revelation', Wescott argued that faith is not born of the inescapable proof of compelling signs. It comes through the warm eagerness of the responding heart and does not really require such evidential appendages.[2] There was also a tendency to reject the apologetic

---

[1] J. B. Mozley, *op. cit.*, pp. 6–7.

[2] B. F. Wescott, *The Gospel of Life*, 1892, Chapter VII. Cf. '. . . absolute loyalty of God as recognized and known in the individual conscience must prevail over

view of miracles because of the apparent difficulty felt in giving any clear and convincing account of them in the light of the scientific understanding of the universe then prevailing. There could be no miracle possible, it was supposed, in a world controlled by unbreakable laws. There was consequently, in some quarters, a readiness to disparage the physical and natural and to emphasize the moral miracles of Christianity.

This emphasis on the moral miracles was a complete reaction from the supreme place given to the natural miracles by the Evidential writers. 'Even in the case of apologists of too well-balanced judgement to be guilty of totally neglecting the argument from miracles, the influence of reaction is apparent in a marked preference for other lines of argument. Thus the favourite theme for some time past has been the *moral* miracles of Christianity, the very title implying a disparaging reference to the physical miracles which form the basis of so much elaborate reasoning in older apologetic treatises.'[1]

C. A. Row, for example, in his Bampton Lectures of 1877 appears to take this position. He gives little significance to the evidential value of miracles. 'The proof of Christianity', he says, 'has been hitherto based on what is called its miraculous attestation. Miracles have been placed in the forefront of the Christian argument, and other evidences have occupied in it a very subordinate position.'[2] But it is the moral evidences, he contends, which should occupy the first place. It is these which decisively attest Christianity to be a divine revelation. The difficulties which have recently been brought to light concerning miracles make it clear that they 'should no longer occupy the van of our evidential position'.[3] The earlier apologists, he points out, were content to recommend Christianity on the strength of its attestation by miracles. This method is no longer either possible or valid. 'One feels a difficulty in believing', he urges, 'that if Paley's argument had been placed before a Father of the second or third century, it would have commended itself

every external sign . . . and no array of external "miracles" can justify us in referring to Him, as authoritative for our direction, any act or word which our moral constitution made in His image forces us to regard as immoral'. *Op. cit.*, pp. 215–16.
  [1] A. B. Bruce, *The Miraculous Element in the Gospels*, 1886, p. 294.
  [2] C. A. Row, *Christian Evidences Viewed in Relation to Modern Thought*, 1877, p. 25.   [3] *Ibid.*, p. 36.

to him as an efficient mode of persuading an unbeliever to embrace the Christian faith.'[1]

This repudiation of miracles, as having any real value for faith, was taken up by many succeeding writers. One more recent illustration of the desire to set Christian faith free from what is held to be the burden of miracles comes in the *Contentio Veritatis*. This work was hailed by one reviewer as 'a new *Lux Mundi*', which, it was declared 'will do for the beginning of the Twentieth Century what *Lux Mundi* did for the end of the Nineteenth'.[2] The volume is composed of seven essays contributed by six Oxford tutors. Among the names are Rashdall and Inge, whose scholastic stature grew with the years. The whole work from beginning to end is really concerned with the miraculous. The possibility of miracles is allowed by all the writers. But each one is acutely aware of the strength of scientific criticism. Yet for all the desire to admit the reality of the miraculous there is hesitancy. Rashdall, for example, contends that, while certain miracles may be due to the introduction of some unsuspected law, our knowledge of the ways of nature make it quite impossible to admit others as genuine. He instances the reference in Joshua to the 'stopping of the sun', and adds that 'The raising of the saints out of the tomb in their bodies, and some of what are called the "nature-miracles", may surely, with tolerable confidence, be placed in this class'.

There are two passages which may be quoted from this volume which give the viewpoint of all the contributors, 'The time is past', it is declared, 'when Christianity could be presented as a revelation attested by miracles, depending on these for the main evidence of its truth'.[3] In another passage illustration is made of the thesis with reference to the Incarnation. 'We should not now expect, a priori,' it is affirmed, 'that the Incarnate *Logos* would be born without a human father, that He would suspend His own laws during His sojourn on earth, or that He would resuscitate His earthly body, and remove it to the sky, nor do we see that those events, however well proved, are of any value as evidences of His divinity.'[4]

[1] C. A. Row, *Christian Evidences Viewed in Relation to Modern Thought*, 1877, p. 32.
[2] *Expository Times*, Vol. XIII, 1901–2, p. 343; cf. J. B. Mozley, *Some Tendencies in British Theology*, 1952, p. 27.
[3] *Contentio Veritatis*, 1902, p. 144. [4] *Op. cit.*, p. 88.

It would seem that writers who follow this method, while allowing for the possibility of miracles, were prepared to divorce them altogether from the essential Christian message. There were others, however, who were not committed to this conclusion. They preferred to see the miracles as having their place in the whole context of Christ's life and work, and as taking their part as media of revelation. Frederick Temple, for example, argued against the possibility of separating or eliminating the miraculous element from the history. In the Old Testament, indeed, 'the miraculous element in it occupied comparatively so small a place, and was so rarely, if ever, contemporaneous, that it might be left out'. In the New Testament, it is, he contends, otherwise. Here the 'miracles are embedded in, are indeed intertwined with, the narrative. Many of our Lord's most characteristic sayings are so associated with narratives of miracles that the two cannot be torn apart'.[1] Later, rejecting the evidential value of miracles, he states, 'to us they are, if accepted at all, accepted as a part of the revelation itself'.[2]

This idea of miracles as an integral part of the whole Christian story was given strong emphasis throughout the following years. They were more and more connected with God's redemptive purpose for the world and were regarded as occasioned by man's sin and disorder. They were held to be worked, as Leibniz had urged long before, not 'in order to supply the wants of Nature, but those of grace'. Thus what we may call a redemptive explanation was given to them.

One of the most sensitive and suggestive expositions of this idea will be found in a volume by Theodore Christlieb translated into English in 1874. Christlieb, the professor of theology at Bonn, accepted the Biblical miracles with conviction. Having urged, first of all, that miracles are not to be thought of as suspending the laws of nature, he goes on to argue that the internal aim of miracles is a redemptive one. They are not 'an unnatural breach of Nature, but a supernatural interruption of the unnatural'. They are needed for the redemption and consummation of the world. 'We can now recognize in the condition of the world as vitiated by sin, not only the possibility, but also

---

[1] Frederick Temple, *The Relations between Religion and Science*, 1884, p. 153.
[2] *Ibid.*, p. 203.

the *necessity of miracles*,[1] he asserts. It is in the moral condition
of the world after the entrance of sin that the reason for miracles
is to be found. 'We, too, are well aware of a rent in the world
and a disturbance of its original laws, not caused, however, by
God, but by man; not *provoked* by miracles, but rather *remedied*
by them. Our opponents say that the world would go to ruin if
God through His interference were to violate the order of
nature. To this we reply, that, on the contrary, since sin has
entered the world, it would immediately go to ruin if left to
itself, and therefore it only exists to this day because God in
every age has graciously interfered in its self-inflicted disorder.'[2]

This point is much stressed. Again and again Christlieb
argues that 'sin has made a "rent" in the world; but miracles
only enter in for the removal of the already existing disturbance'.[3] He notes that in the Bible the miracles are often called
signs, but he insists that they 'are always signs of the divine
intention which aims at the salvation of the world'.[4] They can be
understood only in this connection with the history of redemption. Christlieb sees the whole life of Christ as the supreme
miracle. 'The entire *history of miracles*', he adds, 'is grouped
around this central miracle, and stands in internal connection with
it, either as a prophecy or as an echo of that which is begun in Him.'[5]

A. B. Bruce likewise relates the miracles of the gospel to the
redemptive purpose of Christ. 'The simplest and most satisfactory view to take of these miracles,' he states, 'is to regard
them as the forthflowing of that love which, according to
prophetic oracles, was the chief Messianic charism.'[6] This view
may not indeed be obviously applicable to all the miracles. Bruce
specifies the nature-miracles in this connection, but he is
emphatic that the healing-miracles must be so understood. The
healing-miracles certainly indicate our Lord's concern for human
ills. But Christianity is more than a religion of Humanity: it is

---

[1] Theodore Christlieb, *Modern Doubt and Christian Belief*, 1874, p. 312.
[2] *Ibid.*, p. 312.   [3] *Ibid.*, p. 314.
[4] *Ibid.*, p. 315.   [5] *Ibid.*, p. 320.
[6] A. B. Bruce, *The Miraculous Element in the Gospels*, 1886, p. 258. Cf. 'Christ's
miraculous deeds were all useful, morally significant, beneficent works, rising
naturally out of His vocation as Saviour, performed in the course of His ministry
in the pursuit of His high calling, and just as naturally lying in His way, as
unmiraculous healings lie in the way of the ordinary physician'. A. B. Bruce, *The
Chief End of Revelation*, fifth edition, 1896, pp. 168–9. The whole chapter entitled,
'The Function of Miracle in Revelation' is important.

essentially a religion of Redemption. In this context the miracles are to be seen as 'parables' of Christ as the great spiritual Healer of man's sin-shattered and morally defeated lives. 'He healed their diseases that they might think of their sins and seek deliverance from them. In this point of view the whole healing ministry was one grand parable of Redemption. Jesus dealt with the physical effect, the evil of which all could appreciate, to advertise Himself as one prepared to deal with the spiritual cause, to the evil of which many were insensible. He healed disease with an unsparing hand that the presence of the Spiritual Physician might be the better known, and to proclaim a plenteous redemption.'[1]

In contrast, then, with those who had no useful place for miracles, this view brings them into the very heart of the divine purpose of God's revelation. Following writers, more aware perhaps of the difficulty which Hort saw in such an emphasis as early as 1859, continued to stress the connection between the miracles and redemption, but, at the same time, they seemed to be more ready to recognize their evidential value.[2] Thus, to take one later example, Marcus Dods insists that above all else miracles give expression to the mercy of God. 'What, then, was our Lord's purpose in performing miracles?' he asks. 'The answer is', he replies, 'He performed them not to convince people that He was the Messiah, the messenger and representative of God, but because He had that understanding of God's love and that perfect fellowship with God which made Him the Messiah. . . . But just because the primary purpose of the miracles was to give expression of God's mercy and not to prove our Lord's Messiahship, on this very account they can be appealed to as evidence that Jesus was the Messiah. The poet writes because he is a poet, and not for the purpose of convincing the world that he is a poet. And yet this writing does convince the world that he is a poet.'[3]

---

[1] A. B. Bruce, *The Miraculous Element in the Gospels*, 1886, p. 309.

[2] Cf. L. E. Elliott-Binns, *English Thought, 1860–1900*, 1956, p. 57.

[3] Marcus Dods, *The Bible: Its Origin and Nature*, 1905, pp. 225–7. Cf. 'There is no claim that Jesus Christ made, there is no truth that Jesus Christ taught that is not bound up with His signs. If we leave His signs out of sight, we must leave Him out of sight. . . . In short, we find not that miracles prove doctrine, but that *miracles are doctrine*'. A. A. Brockington, 'Miracles as Signs', *The Expository Times*, Vol. XVII, 1905–6, p. 495.

In reaction, then, from the earlier readiness to discard miracles, the later period was to see them as an integral part of the Christian revelation. The day when men professing allegiance to the Christian faith and saying at the same time in the blunt words of Matthew Arnold, 'miracles do not happen', had passed. Strauss had 'explained' miracles (away) as the legendary creations of a later generation. Renan in his *Life of Jesus* had maintained that they were thaumaturgical activities of Jesus into which He was occasionally forced by circumstances, but which He performed only after prayer, and with a sort of bad humour, and with a rebuke to those who demanded them on account of their carnal desires. The newer emphasis made much of the Redeemer and the miracles were related to His redemptive purpose.

There was one other question which arose in connection with our Lord's miracles which had interest and importance for Christology. The discussion centred on the way by which Christ performed His miracles. Had He resident within Himself a natural faculty of miracle-working power or was He by reason of His nearness to God the vehicle of a divine ἐξουσια και δυναμις? Many able writers took the view that the former position harmonizes best with a right understanding of Christ's Person. In this context the supreme miracle is Christ Himself; all His words and works are divine wonders. And what are termed miracles are outflashings of His divine Person. The whole of Christianity rests upon a supernatural basis and the gospel story unveils a supernatural Person, not only when what are called miracles are being wrought, but all the record through. Christianity is itself supernatural, it was urged. The question is, then, 'not about isolated "miracles", but about the whole conception of Christianity—what it is, and whether the supernatural does not enter into the very essence of it? It is the general question of a supernatural or non-supernatural conception of the universe. Is there a supernatural Being—God? Is there a supernatural government of the world? Is there a supernatural relation of God to man, so that God and man may have communion with one another? Is there a supernatural Revelation? Has that Revelation culminated in a supernatural Person— Christ? Is there a supernatural work in the souls of men? Is there a supernatural Reedmption? Is there a supernatural hereafter?

It is these larger questions that have to be settled first, and then the question of particular miracles will fall into its proper place'.[1]

Others, wishing to give due regard to the human conditions of our Lord's life on earth, maintained that life in its divine aspect was depotentiated by subjection to 'kenosis', and in its human aspect it was a life lived in dependence on and faith in God His Father. He, too, like those He is not ashamed to call His brethren, had to walk by faith. And the more assurance He received that He was the Father's Elect One, the more did His confidence of success in His beneficient ministry of love increase.

This kenosis view was given impetus by Charles Gore. Gore quite unhesitatingly asserted that Christ's knowledge was limited by its human conditions.[2] Consonant with this he maintained that 'His powerful works, no less than His humiliations, are in the Gospels attributed to His manhood'.[3] He is able to quote Wescott in support of his view. 'His greatest works' Wescott comments 'during His earthly life were wrought by the help of the Father through the energy of a humanity enabled to do all things in fellowship with God.'[4]

The human character of our Lord's miracles is one of special emphasis of recent years. Whether it is 'one particularly fruitful insight that has been gained in the modern world in the interpretation of the Gospel story', as D. M. Baillie suggests,[5] is something about which opinions will necessarily differ.

It is certainly true that the idea has come into special vogue in later years. Leonard Hodgson in a chapter on 'Miracles' has stated quite categorically that Christ performed His miracle-signs, not through any exercise of inherent divine energy, but by virtue of His perfect manhood. 'The miracles of Christ are worked through "faith". That "faith" was born of knowledge that certain things were necessary for Him to fulfil His mission.'[6]

---

[1] J. Orr, *The Christian View of God and the World*, Kerr Lectures, 1890–1, pp. 10–11.

[2] Cf. C. Gore, 'The Consciousness of Our Lord in His Moral Life' in *Dissertations on Subjects connected with the Incarnation*, 1895; cf. H. R. Mackintosh, *The Person of Christ*, second edition, reprint, 1937, p. 397 f.

[3] C. Gore, *Dissertations*, etc., p. 140 f.

[4] B. F. Wescott, *Epistle to the Hebrews*, 1889, 'Additional Notes on ii.10: The τελέωσις of Christ', p. 66.

[5] D. M. Baillie, *God Was In Christ*, 1947, p. 13.

[6] Leonard Hodgson, *And Was Made Man*, 1928, p. 140.

In an earlier passage he put his position with uncompromising clarity. We are to think, he says, 'of the powers exercised by Christ as being powers open to manhood where manhood is found in its perfection'.[1]

The same idea is advocated in challenging form by D. S. Carins in his persuasive volume, *The Faith that Rebels*, which appeared in the same year—1928—as Hodgson's work. Cairns can accept neither the Modernist notion of miracles as 'anomalies' in a world subject to absolute uniformity,[2] nor the 'portent theory'[3] of the traditionalists. He cannot regard our Lord's miracles as signs of 'some inherent and unconditional Divine energy'. Having examined the miracles of Christ, he concludes, 'The Gospel theory of the "miracles" of Jesus is that they are the answers of God to the prayers of the Ideal Son, the Man who is the supreme instance, in history, of Faith, Hope, and Love; and they say with unambiguous plainness that the ideal Man invited His disciples to similar enterprises of faith, encouraging them to believe that in proportion to their faith would be the manifestation of God's order, the revelation of man's life as God meant it to be'.[4] That this is a suggestive and inspiring view none can doubt. And it will come as a rebuke to us men of little faith. Some will, however, feel that all has not been said here. To refer the miracles to Christ's humanity, perfect though it was, seems to admit to a Nestorian view of Christ's Person. What He did, He surely did as the One Christ; as the God-Man.

The point which can be emphasized following the discussions of the past years is that 'Christ and His works are all of a piece, and he who has apprehended Christ, or rather been apprehended by Him, will not seek to reduce the self-manifestation of the Saviour to the measure of humanity. . . . To prove the miracles one by one is as impossible as to disprove them in the same way, but they unite with the Person and the words of Jesus into one divine whole through which God reveals His very heart to man'.[5]

---

[1] Leonard Hodgson, *And Was Made Man*, 1928, p. 133.
[2] D. S. Cairns, *The Faith that Rebels*, 1928, p. 34.
[3] *Ibid.*, p. 73; cf. Chapter I, 'The Rival Theories of Miracles—Traditional and Modernist'.
[4] *Ibid.*, p. 85.
[5] James Denney, *Studies in Theology*, 1894, p. 208.

The ultimate fact, as far as we can see it, seems to be, that it is the one who has experienced a miracle who will be the more ready to believe in miracles.[1] What Hamann says is certainly cogent, 'Miracles cannot even be believed without a miracle'. He who has experienced in his own heart the power of Christ to forgive and redeem will have no doubt that miraculous power is the most certain of all things possessed by Him who was God manifested in the flesh.

B. THE REACTION OF IDEALISM

The history of ideas, whether religious or philosophical, it has been noted, is characterized by reaction. This fact, and the results which flow from it for the understanding of revelation in the previous period, have been investigated and illustrated in an earlier volume.[2] There the main oscillation was seen to be between what was termed the rational and the mystical. First there was emphasis upon reason with the consequence that the theology of the era was abstract. God was viewed as a mere transcendental Object whose existence had to be proved by discursive reasoning. But soon reaction set in[3] and a type of philosophical mysticism developed. God was sought, not above but below, not without but within. He was not detached from the human consciousness. God is the Eternal Spirit, occupying the innermost shrine of man's spirit to be discovered by an intuitive awareness. Emphasis is placed here upon the 'kinship' between God and man; upon the divinity of man and upon the humanity of God.[4]

The new era, in a broad sense, followed the same pattern, except that the rationalism with which it started tended towards agnosticism, whereas the rationalism of the old tended towards deism. The middle of the nineteenth century initiated the modern world view which at the beginning was essentially antisupernaturalistic. The religious reading of the world had given place to the scientific. A. M. Fairbairn points out the main feature of the new Weltanschauung. 'Its characteristic is Naturalism, the expulsion from thought, not merely of the supernatural, but of

[1] Cf. P. T. Forsyth, *The Principle of Authority*, 1913, second edition, 1952, p. 153.
[2] H. D. McDonald, *Ideas of Revelation*, 1959.
[3] Cf. C. C. J. Webb, *Problems in the Relation of God and Man*, 1911, pp. 69, 73.
[4] H. D. McDonald, *op. cit.*, pp. 14–15.

the ideal, of the transcendental and spiritual, and a return to a nature sensuously interpreted. This Naturalism is so marked as to constitute the differentiating element of our intellectual movement. The thought of the Christian centuries, even when it has been least Christian, has still been penetrated by the ideal and theistic elements. Theism has been, as it were, its common basis.'[1] Deism, it may be observed, although it moved away from Christ, did not discard God. By relieving Him of the care of the universe it doubtlessly gave Him little to do. Still God was necessary for thought, and the fact of His being an essential postulate to account for the beginning of the world.

Darwin's theory altered all this. The new account of the origins of human life and thought to which his researches had appeared to give scientific justification made naturalism seem to be the only apparent logical conclusion. It therefore became the fashion to declare, not simply as the deists had done, that there was no special revelation, but to assert doubt about any existing God and the possibility of any revelation at all. The progress of science, it was confidently asserted, had rendered all such belief invalid. Thus T. H. Huxley in his 'Lecture on the Physical Basis of Life' maintained that 'the extension of the province of what is called matter and causation' means 'the concomitant gradual banishment from the region of human thought of what is called spirit and spontaneity'.

As, however, the years of the second half of the nineteenth century passed, a change can be discerned in the theological and philosophical atmosphere. In the earlier period the reaction was broadly from naturalism to idealism in philosophy. And Philosophical idealism always tends towards mysticism in religion. 'The challenge of Darwinism', says Spinks, 'drove the churches into various theological camps. The High Churchman retired to a castle of transcendence-and-mysticism. The Broad Church party set out to rationalize the records of the Old Testament; and educated lay men, while not ceasing to regard themselves as Christian, ceased to regard themselves as members of organized churches. All this was in keeping with the general change in theology which went by the name of immanentism.'[2]

[1] A. M. Fairbairn, *Studies in Theology and Religion*, 1910, p. 80.

[2] G. S. Spinks with E. L. Allen and James Parkes, *Religion in Britain since 1900*, 1952, p. 20; cf. C. C. J. Webb, *Religion and the Thought of Today*, 1926, pp. 36 ff.

It is certainly clear that with the passing of the years the trend towards naturalism which is usually connected with the laws of physical evolution became less pronounced. It was becoming evident to thoughtful and religiously inclined men that the moral history of man could not be resolved into a natural history. In the sphere of theology there was a new stress given to the idea of the divine immanence. The half truth in Pantheism which the orthodox apologists of the former period in their combat with deism overlooked, was being given serious recognition. The deistic habit of thought which made man's relation to the universe external and artificial was being supplemented by a more intimate connection of God with the world. It was this change, as we have seen, which brought about the altered attitude to the question of miracles in the scheme of divine revelation. 'Darwinianism', declared Aubrey Moore, writing on 'The Christian Doctrine of God', 'under the guise of a foe, did the work of a friend. It has conferred upon philosophy and religion an inestimable benefit, by showing us that we choose between two alternatives. Either God is everywhere present in nature or He is nowhere. He cannot be here and not here.'

Religious mysticism and philosophical idealism—the emotional and the rational side of the one approach to reality—are, then, the characteristic features of the reaction to the earlier naturalism. Mysticism, it is true, during the greater part of the century had been suspect. The excesses of the Enthusiasts of the previous period had not been forgotten.[1] Mysticism was, too, regarded as hazy and dangerous. Indeed, as late as 1888, Aubrey Moore is able to awaken caution by writing of 'the dangerous haze of mysticism'.[2] The revived interest in mysticism owes something to a renewed appreciation of the sense of wonder which became evident in general literature which was itself a part of the reaction from the naturalistic estimation of the world in which all was explicable. It is of interest therefore to observe that Watts-Dunton's novel, *Aylwin*, which did much to stimulate interest in mysticism generally, appeared in 1898 just a year before Dean Inge delivered his famous Bampton Lectures entitled *Christian Mysticism*.

---

[1] H. D. McDonald, *Ideas of Revelation*, 1959, Chapter IV.
[2] Aubrey Moore, *Science and the Faith*, 1888, p. 56.

The mysticism, however, which emerged at this period was characterized by a certain depth of understanding which brings it into favourable contrast with that of the previous age. 'A measure of reasonableness', observed G. P. Fisher, 'is conceded to the Mysticism which, in the past ages, in varied forms, has made much of the inward, living presence of God in the devout soul.'[1] Some evidence of this intelligent appreciation of mysticism may be seen in a number of volumes of permanent value which appeared around the same time. At the turn of the century George Tyrrell made an important contribution to the subject. In 1898 came his *Hard Sayings*, and in 1901 the two volumes entitled, *The Faith of the Millions*, which, according to von Hügel are 'full of insight into mysticism'.[2] Inge's *Studies in English Mystics* appeared in 1906 and Rufus Jones produced his suggestive *Studies in Mystical Religion* in 1909. In the same year von Hügel's profound work, *The Mystical Element of Religion*, was added to the list. In 1917–18 Inge gave the Gifford Lectures on *The Philosophy of Plotinus*. And in 1924 Franz Pfeiffer's edition of the works of Meister Eckhart were translated into English 'with some omissions and additions' by C. de B. Evans; a second edition of these two volumes was called for in 1947. Note, too, must be taken of Evelyn Underhill's several contributions, of which, *The Mystic Way* (1913), is, we consider, the most important.

There are two volumes, however, in which philosophic idealism, which is the other side of mysticism, is the more obviously exhibited. There is Robert Flint's work, *On Theological, Biblical and Other Subjects* (1905). Flint is opposed to Ritschl's expulsion of metaphysics from theology and of his criticism of mysticism. He insists upon the necessity of metaphysics and on the value for mysticism in religion. Flint acknowledges that mysticism has had its shortcomings, but he contends that 'it has often been of great service, and carries with it a large fund of truth, which the theologian of no period can afford to neglect'. Dean Inge, likewise, in his *Personal Idealism and Mysticism* (1907), speaks out against the Ritschlian school, especially as represented by Herrmann and Harnack. Flint had remarked that he was 'inclined to think that there has been too

[1] G. P. Fisher, *History of Christian Doctrine*, 1902, p. 545.
[2] F. von Hügel, *The Mystical Element in Religion*, 1909, Vol. I, Pref. p. xv.

much mysticism in the Catholic and too little in the Protestant Church' and with this verdict, however much some might be ready to question it, Inge was in the fullest sympathy.

Just a cursory reference needs to be made to the philosophic idealism of the period which expressed in rational form the mystical reaction from naturalism. The view derives from Hegel and may with equal propriety be called neo-Hegelianism. While J. H. Stirling's book, *The Secret of Hegel* may be taken as the starting point of the new Idealistic movement in British thought, John Caird may be singled out as giving the most effective emphasis to the idealistic view. 'The religious aspect of neo-Hegelianism is nowhere presented with more lucidity and more attractively than in the pages of the eminent theologian John Caird.'[1] It is a question whether Caird's doctrine is essentially pantheistic. W. Preston Warren in his *Pantheism in Neo-Hegelian Thought* (1933) quotes extensively from his works and concludes that he is correctly to be described as a pantheist. At any rate, there is, we think, no doubt about John Caird's idealism. His brother Edward states that 'Christianity and Idealism were the two poles of my brother's thinking, and the latter seemed to him the necessary means for interpreting the former'. In his Memoir prefixed to John's Gifford Lectures, Edward, however, notes that there are respects in which certain of Hegel's ideas are repudiated. He observes that Hegel is seldom quoted, but he still grants that his brother was profoundly influenced by him. Passing beyond, what appeared to him to be the limitation of Kant's epistemology, Edward Caird goes on to remark that his brother's 'thought turned more and more to the Hegelian development of this principle and its application to theology. He was interested in Hegel mainly for two reasons: first, by the thoroughness with which he carries out the idealistic principle, and, secondly, by the strong grasp of ethical and religious experience which is perhaps Hegel's greatest characteristic'.[2] He adds later, 'He was drawn to Hegel, therefore, most of all, because he seemed to find at the basis of all Hegel's speculation a close and living perception of the facts of the moral and religious life'.[3] John Caird was then one of the

---

[1] Hiralal Halder, *Neo-Hegelianism*, 1927, p. 135.
[2] John Caird, *The Fundamental Ideas of Christianity*, 1899, Vol. I, p. lxxiv.
[3] *Ibid.*, p. lxxv.

most eloquent advocates of a sort of spiritual idealism which was characteristic of the period and which regarded revelation in terms of the apprehension of the divine immanence. His brother Edward in his own Gifford Lectures on *The Evolution of Religion* (1893) gives weighty exposition to the same fundamental view: 'the unity of God and man' and 'the self-revelation of God in humanity'. Yet while it is true that there is no simple identification of God with the world in this type of idealism—the stress was upon immanence and manifestation—there were others like Bradley in his *Appearance and Reality* (1893) who has a world of ideas without God.

Without continuing further we may note something of the strength of the movement by a remark of Quiller-Couch concerning its chief centre, Oxford. 'The young tenants of the Home of Movements, turning from Mill and Mansel to Kant and Hegel, pursued the evasive Absolute far into the night.' On the other hand something of the popular preaching of the pantheistic outcome of the idea can be seen in R. J. Campbell's *New Theology*, in which we have, as has been stated, immanentism 'run mad'.

C. THE PROTEST FROM PLURALISM

Pluralism is a distinctive philosophical doctrine which stands in opposition to every 'block-universe' theory whether materialistic or idealistic. In pluralism the claims of the Many are upheld against that of the One. 'Pluralism', says William James, 'lets things exist in the each-form or distributively. Monism thinks that the all-form or collective-unity form is the only form that is rational.'[1] The idea is, of course, not an altogether new one. Throughout the history of philosophy there have been occasions, when under one label or another, the reality of the particular has been maintained against the tyranny of the One. This may be seen in the case of the mediaeval nominalists such as Duns Scotus and William of Occam, who against the realistic philosophy of the scholastic Churchmen generally, sought to emphasize that particular things are real.

The classical type, as well as the fountain-head of modern pluralism is, however, Leibniz, whose *Monadology* is a vigorous

[1] William James, *A Pluralistic Universe*, edition, 1916, p. 324.

repudiation of Spinoza's monism. Leibniz, it is worth noting, did not regard particulars as having independent existences. All simple existing substances are ultimately derived from the one supreme and necessary substance, the ultimate Monad. Unlike the modern advocates of pluralism, Leibniz does not regard God as merely *primus inter pares*. It is characteristic of the pluralism of more recent times that in stressing the autonomy and freedom of finite centres of existence it has found it necessary to limit God by the existence of such beings. There have therefore been a number of writers, who in their effort to safeguard the existence of particulars, have advocated the idea of a finite God. God is regarded, in William James's famous phrase as 'one of the eaches'. A popular statement of the idea of a finite God can be found in H. G. Wells's *God the Invisible King*;[1] while a more religious exposition of the view, if the term 'religious' is not too narrowly defined, is that found in Henry Jones's *A Faith that Enquires*.

More to the point of our study is the fact that pluralism came into vogue towards the end of the nineteenth century in conscious opposition to the prevailing idealism of F. H. Bradley, Bernard Bosanquet and especially that of T. H. Green.[2] The most consistent exponent of the doctrine was the American philosopher G. H. Howison (1834–1916). He was 'impressed by the danger which monism threatens to the integrity of ethical freedom, and it is to save these that he sets out to develop, on a Kantian basis, an idealistic pluralism'.[3] He sees a 'universal world of Spirits, every one of whom is free—that is, independently self-active, self-moved from within and none operated either directly or indirectly from without by any other'. He speaks of an 'Eternal Republic', and declares that God is One among the Many. 'He is if they are, they are if He is; but the relation is freely mutual, and He only exists as *primus inter pares*, in a circle eternal and indissoluble.'[4]

William James gained a public for the pluralistic philosophy in his Hibbert Lectures of 1909. He rejects the 'all-form' of

---

[1] Cf. 'The Doctrine of a Finite God in War-time', R. H. Dotterer, *Hibbert Journal*, Vol. XVI, No. 3, April 1918, p. 428; also *Pluralism and the Problems of Religion*, New York, 1915.

[2] Cf. William James, *op. cit.*, p. 6 f.

[3] A. K. Rogers, *British and American Philosophy since 1800*, 1923, p. 303.

[4] G. H. Howison, *The Limits of Evolution*, 1901, pp. 328–9.

absolutism and contends for the 'each-form', a distributive form of reality, as 'logically as acceptable and empirically as probable'.[1]

The influence of pluralism was many-sided. In politics it manifested itself in the form of a sturdy individualism. In the field of practical ethics it tended to humanism. The human individual, the reality of which was assured by pluralism, became the centre of the picture. Thus W. K. Clifford, influenced by the conclusion to be drawn from evolution that man had made a great move forward and was, indeed, being made the measure of all things, writes in the closing section of his work, *Cosmic Emotion:* 'Those who can read the signs of the times read in them that the kingdom of Man has come.'

One important aspect of pluralism was the regard it created for the real individual. It is interesting to observe how in this period what is known as Personalism came to the fore. Personalism may be defined as the psychological counterpart of pluralism. More particularly, personalism gave focus to the single individual as a moral and spiritual entity. The beginning of this emphasis can be seen already in a work by John Grote who held the chair of moral philosophy at Cambridge from 1855 to 1866. Personalism is anticipated in his volume, *A Treatise on the Moral Ideals* (1876).

It is, however, to Hermann Lotze that we can trace the first of the creative influences in the direction of a spiritual personalism. He began a reaction from the prevailing Hegelian idealism in which man's personality was lost in a devouring Whole. T. H. Green, in fact, testifies to the influence of Lotze, who, he says, made him dissatisfied with Hegel. The important place he gave to the idea of the Divine Personality rescued Haldane from the materialism to which he had turned after the abandonment of his early faith.[2]

It is through his huge work, *Microcosmos*, which was translated into English in 1887, that his ideas became known. As far as we are concerned, his teaching can be best summed up in a few words from his work on the *Philosophy of Religion*. His message is that ' "self-consciousness" is a spiritual phenomenon'.[3]

---

[1] William James, *op. cit.*, p. 34.

[2] Cf. L. E. Elliott-Binns, *English Thought, 1860–1900*, 1956, p. 69; see Hastings Rashdall's remark on Lotze, in *Contentio Veritatis*, 1902, p. 43.

[3] Hermann Lotze, *Philosophy of Religion*, trans. G. T. Ladd, 1887, p. 55 f.

Lotze has, of course, much to say about the ultimate unity of all in God, but he insists upon the reality of the individual. It is true that throughout his works 'there is an opposition to idealism, yet a rejection of materialism; the reality of the individual is asserted, yet the unity of all in the universal spirit is maintained'.[1] A. E. Garvie notes the inconsistency in his teaching concerning the basic unity and adds, 'To very many he will seem rather to emphasize individuality at the expense of unity. He does not care at all for the immanent development of the Absolute Idea; his enthusiasm he reserves for the beatitude of finite spirits. To him the world-aim is not the progressive realization of an ideal rational or ethical, but the self-realization of personal existences'.[2]

This was the point to be emphasized in different ways by a number of personal idealists, such as the brothers, Andrew Seth Pringle-Pattison and John Seth, W. R. Sorley and Hastings Rashdall, and by Theistic philosophers of religion such as James Ward, C. C. J. Webb, A. E. Taylor and William Temple.

All these writers, it may be said, reserved their enthusiasm 'for the beatitude of finite spirits'. A. S. Pringle-Pattison's successive works show a gradual movement away from Hegel. In his *Hegelianism and Personality* (1887) and his later *Man's Place in the Cosmos and Other Essays* (1887), this growing dissatisfaction may be noted. W. R. Sorley, especially in his Gifford Lectures of 1914–15, stresses the factuality of the individual whom he regards supremely as a bearer of value. It is in this way, indeed, that he argues for the objectivity of value. 'It is therefore in the existent, the individual, that value is found, not in the general or universal. Now the individual is always unique. . . . As value belongs to the existent or individual, and as the individual is unique, we tend to think of uniqueness as essential to value.'[3]

James Ward refuses the term pluralism as descriptive of his position because he was emphatic upon the need for an ultimate One as the ground of the Many. Pluralism, he observes, 'assumes that the whole world is made up of individuals, each

---

[1] A. E. Garvie, 'Hermann Lotze', *The Expository Times*, Vol. IV, 1892–3, p. 540.
[2] *Ibid.*, p. 541.
[3] W. R. Sorley, *Moral Value and the Idea of God*, 1918, third edition, 1935, p. 113.

distinguished by its characteristic behaviour'.[1] And it further assumes, he states later, 'that there exists an indefinite variety of selves, some indefinitely higher, some indefinitely lower than ourselves. But even the highest, if there be a highest, will, it is assumed, be only *primus inter pares*, one among the many, and not an absolute reality including them all'.[2] It may be said to be Ward's purpose to retain the first characteristic of pluralism, that the world is made up of separate individuals, and to deny the second, that there is no absolute unity to include them all. He maintains that there is need of the One as the ultimate source and the ultimate end of the Many. His final position is, then, a pluralism supplemented by Theism. But Ward does not rob the individual of having independent worth.

Another effort to do justice to the free, moral and independent reality of personality from several points of view can be found in the volume, *Personal Idealism* (1902) to which a number of Oxford men contributed. Here is to be found, brought together in one work all pointing to the same conclusion, the voluntaristic psychology of G. F. Stout, the Berkeleian theism of Hastings Rashdall, the Pragmatism of F. C. S. Schiller, and H. Sturt, and the spiritualistic idealism of Boyce Gibson, who translated and made popular the ideas of Rudolf Euchen.[3]

The question may be asked, What bearing had these ideas on the understanding of revelation? In all its forms and phases it gave emphasis to the inward aspect. It accentuated the subjective appreciation of revelation. More particularly in personalism, in which man is seen as a spiritual entity, it was to give point to the idea of man's religious development, to the growth of his religious consciousness and its advancing discovery of divine truths. As a consequence there was a tendency to regard the great prophets as supremely outstanding examples of religious geniuses, pioneers in the realm of the spiritual. While, in regard to the subject of Biblical inspiration, place was given to the human bearers of revelation. The human, it was argued, was not to be overridden in the interests of the divine. The emphasis upon the freedom of the human spirit was thought by some indeed to reinforce the growing denial of Biblical inerrancy, since, it was urged, to preserve the writers from all error would

---

[1] James Ward, *The Realm of Ends*, 1911, third edition, 1920, p. 51.   [2] *Ibid.*, p. 52.
[3] Cf. C. A. Richardson, *Spiritual Pluralism and Recent Philosophy*, 1919.

be inconsistent with man's true nature as a free being. The human errors in the Bible, of course, it was allowed, were no rejection of its essential message, which, too, was often regarded from man's point of view, as teaching the intrinsic value of every individual.

Along with pluralism there went empiricism. And in the realm of religion this was to turn attention to religious experience. The psychological approach to religion became, therefore, a olive issue. Important, in this context, are the Gifford Lectures of 1901-2 by William James, *The Varieties of Religious Experience*. 'His arguments reinforced the current tendency to look for guidance in religion less to authority and more to experience. . . . Increasingly the Bible was read as the record of a growing religious experience and Christian doctrine was assessed, as by Schleiermacher, in accordance with its reflection in the "religious consciousness".'[1]

The result of all this was clearly seen in the state of affairs which could be observed in the religious situation. The foundation of faith was changed from that of dogmatic inspiration to that of current experience. Theology was placed at the mercy of psychology with rather precarious consequences. Belief was, in fact, put under the authority of the laws of thought and incurred the bane of an alarming subjectivism: or, more tragic still, it was sometimes debased by an unhealthy preoccupation with inner states and sympathies, processes and problems, and lost vital contact with that reality behind and beyond these and the authority over them.

D. THE INFLUENCE OF HISTORICISM

The opening years of the nineteenth century witnessed a remarkable revival of the historical spirit. It is, indeed, in its appreciation of historicism that we have its distinctive feature. Looking back over the years of the nineteenth century, V. F. Storr contends that it is in its feeling for history that we have 'the most marked characteristic of the intellectual development of the last hundred years'.[2] The previous age, by contrast, had no real

[1] G. S. Spinks with E. L. Allen and James Parkes, *Religion in Britain since 1900*, 1952, pp. 52-3.

[2] H. V. Storr, *Development of English Theology in the Nineteenth Century*, 1913, p. 1; cf. his *Development and Divine Purpose*, 1906, pp. 210 ff.

or clear understanding of history. Continuing the Enlightenment's repudiation of the historical in the interests of the rational the writers of the eighteenth century showed a complete indifference to its significance. 'The ideas then prevalent of an ideal primitive society and of a social contract which was the result of deliberate action, were "the negation of history".'[1] History was conceived of as static. That age, according to Leslie Stephen, failed through lack of historical imagination.[2] And its apologists were able to keep apart in their thought a natural and a supernatural view of the world by simply separating them in time. 'They combined, that is', Stephen says, 'Hume's view of the eighteenth century with Wesley's view of the first.'[3]

Attention has been given elsewhere to some of the influences which shaped the direction of historicism in the period prior to 1860. A reference was made to the importance of Leibniz who expounded the idea of continuity in his doctrine of the graduation of the monads, as well as stressing, at the same time, the conception of connection and union, albeit in an artificial manner, in his principle of pre-existing harmony. Lessing, taking these fundamental principles, saw in them the key to the understanding of history. In this way, it is said, he brought about 'a deeper sense of the meaning of the historical'.[4]

After the middle of the nineteenth century the revived historical spirit wedded itself to the idea of evolution. As a result it became the fashion to seek an explanation of all things in heaven and on earth, in theology no less than in biology, by the application of the historical method. Historicism, in fact, became a sort of magic wand by which, at last, the riddle of the universe was about to be solved.

History and development were conceived to be synonymous terms, and, it was supposed, to trace out development was to state history. In this way mystery was expunged and the truth laid bare. So it was thought; but it was wrongly thought. L. E. Elliott-Binns points out that 'The new scientific influence, however, was not without its drawbacks, for it led to the

---

[1] L. E. Elliott-Binns, *Religion in the Victorian Era*, 1936, second edition, 1946, p. 172.

[2] Leslie Stephen, *History of English Thought in the Eighteenth Century*, second edition, 1881, Vol. I, p. 192; cf. p. 378.

[3] *Op. cit.*, Vol. II, pp. 414–5.

[4] A. K. Rogers, *A Students' History of Philosophy*, new revised edition, p. 410.

extension of the idea of "evolution" to departments of knowledge to which strictly speaking it did not apply. The crude transference of the hypothesis to the conduct of human affairs, for example, did much harm, for "evolution" in history is a very different thing from "evolution" in Nature, since the human element takes a conscious part, exhibiting will and purpose. Furthermore, the notion began to prevail that to have traced out the development of an idea or an institution was fully to have accounted for it'.[1]

For the first part of the story, it may be noted that immediately after Darwin, historicism, uniting with the doctrine of biological evolutionism, gave the notion of a mechanical development of all life and thought. Haeckel regarded the 'scientific' right to account for life by a purely mechanical process as 'the inestimable value' of Darwin's contribution. Historical occurrences, it was urged, were to be explained as the product of natural laws. The creative causes of all such events must be sought in man's physical environment. As a consequence history was said to be based on anthropogeography. Several writers looked to the social environment as providing the answer to the riddle of existence. While Spencer, Comte and writers of like mind, developed the notion of society as itself a sort of higher organism, which, like other living things, is subject to biological laws and will eventually come to perfection in the struggle for existence by natural selection and heredity.

Not for long, however, did the view that all existences are the result of the operation of natural laws survive. There was too much missing from the account. 'Evolution in its Darwinian form—the only form ever heard of by many—has been used as the foundation of a materialism which does not, like the old law of gravitation, require even the Great Mathematician. It manages everything by the ingenious process of spreading sufficiently small changes over sufficiently long time. This way of begging the cause piecemeal of so vast and wonderful a phenomenon as the world grows less and less convincing, especially as it cannot move a step without admitting a goal regarding every detail as directed towards it.'[2]

Under the pitiless assaults of James Ward, *Naturalism and Agnosticism*, Frazer, *Philosophy of Theism* and Kennedy, *Natural*

---

[1] L. E. Elliott-Binns, *English Thought, 1860–1900*, 1956, p. 93.
[2] John Oman, *The Problems of Faith and Freedom*, 1906, pp. 199–200.

Theology and Modern Thought, the materialistic tendency of historicism, in the immediate post-Darwinian period, was vastly weakened.

The fact is that it was not from the notion of biological evolution 'but from the less ostentatious advances in the field of history that faith received its greatest blow'.[1] It was, indeed, the strong historical sense which developed throughout the earlier period which formed the climate of opinion in which the idea of biological evolution was but a natural result.

As time went on, historicism was wooed by idealism. Materialism weakened by the attacks made upon it was compelled to accept the divorce. This marriage of the historic spirit with idealism was given philosophical dress by Hegel. History was exalted by the union. It was no longer conceived to be a mere chronicle of successive events, but as C. C. J. Webb puts it, as 'the actual unfolding of the nature of mind or spirit'.[2] In such a context, revelation ceased to be regarded as something coming from without, but as the progressive unfolding of the immanent principle of divine life.

But apart from the results deriving from historicism in its union, first with materialism, and then with idealism, it had significant consequences on its own account. It gave strength to a tendency and vogue to a method.

The idea of evolution produced an interest in the study of comparative religion which was to become a characteristic feature of the second half of the nineteenth century.[3] The new awareness of history inspired a desire to trace the growth and development of religion from its early beginnings in animism, or magic, or ancestor worship, or whatever idea appeared the most reasonable to the individual writer. This tracing out of the gradual evolution of religion is considered by F. S. Marvin to be 'among the greatest of the conquests of the nineteenth century'.[4] Hastings Rashdall insists that 'To underestimate the importance of the great historical Religions and their creators has been the besetting sin of technical religious Philosophy'.[5]

---

[1] W. B. Glover, *Evangelical Nonconformity and the Higher Criticism in the Nineteenth Century*, 1954, p. 13.
[2] C. C. J. Webb, *History of Philosophy*, 1915, p. 224 f.
[3] Cf. S. A. Cook in the *Encylopædia of Religion and Ethics*, Vol. X, pp. 664 ff.
[4] Quoted in *The Century of Progress*, F. S. Marvin, 1919, p. 217.
[5] Hastings Rashdall, *Philosophy and Religion*, 1909, p. 149.

By this study of comparative religion, it was claimed, a clearer conception was to be gained of the phenomenon of religion. It was seen to be a necessity of human life; whether instinctive or acquired, was not, however, quite clear. In a variety of forms it manifested itself, but shows throughout a gradual, and virtually a straight-line development from its early beginnings.

The particular interest was in the study of origins. A vast literature dealing with such titles as the Origin, the Growth, the Evolution of Religion appeared. But besides this interest in religion generally there was particular account given of special religions. Direction was given to this phase of the study by Robertson Smith in his work, *The Religion of the Semites*, and it was he, we are told, who 'opened out a new field of research or rather he opened it out in a new manner'.[1]

This attention to the study of comparative religion caused much disquiet. Rashdall might assure that 'because we recognize a measure of truth in all the historical Religions, it does not follow that we can recognize an equal amount of truth in them all'.[2] Elliott-Binns contends that had the 'ultra-orthodox souls' as he calls them, 'been better acquainted with the Logos theology they might have been saved from much needless heart-burning'.[3] But there were those who were acquainted with the Logos doctrine, and with the use made of it by F. D. Maurice in his Boyle Lectures of 1846 in his discourses on *The Religions of the World*, who felt that there was something suspicious about the result brought about by the application of the historical method to religion.

Questions began to arise in the hearts of not a few who were concerned with Christian faith and the mission of the Church. Was Christianity to be regarded, after all, merely as a special expression of man's religious spirit? Was it the latest phase in the evolutionary process and perhaps not therefore the last and the best? Point was given to these doubts by the outspoken scepticism of a number of critical writers on comparative religion. Advocates might protest that by such study a clearer view of the element of divine revelation in these other religions

---

[1] W. Robertson Smith, *The Religion of the Semites*, 1907, third edition, Pref. p. xxix.

[2] Hastings Rashdall, *Philosophy and Religion*, 1909, p. 149.

[3] L. E. Elliott-Binns, *English Thought, 1860–1900*, 1956, p. 208.

can be discovered, and thereby the superior revelation in Christianity could be seen. But so long as the study was continued in the context of the historical method with its essentially critical and apparently destructive spirit doubts could not but persist. Fears could not be allayed so easily since historicists seemed to be attempting to 'gather apologetic figs from sceptical thistles' as Harnack once charged Friedrich Loofs about the latter's somewhat analogous endeavours in theology.[1]

Time revealed that it had to be made clear and certain that the unique in Christianity is not the mere greater clarity of ideas obscure in other religions. Christianity is not just the best of a class. It is what it is, not by its *continuum* with other religions, but by its *peculium*. It confronts other creeds; it does not prolong them. Its distinctiveness lies not in what it shares with other beliefs but in how it separates from them. 'It is not under the control of natural religion, of general spiritual truths enacted in some parliament of religions. Such rationalism is the worst Erastianism. Christianity is not the dominant partner in the world's religion, the *doyen* of equal faiths.'[2] The fact is as R. E. Speer has remarked, 'Calvary closes the issue of comparative religion'.[3]

Not only did the feeling for history give strength to a tendency but it also gave vogue to a method. The historical method became one of the major factors in the theological reconstructions of the period.

The feeling for history was a very real thing during the later years of the nineteenth century. Interest was taken in the subject for its own sake and a serious attempt was made to discover the actual happenings of the past. Impetus was given to the movement by the establishment in 1866 of *The English Historical Review* with Creighton as editor. Some years later Lord Acton, who in 1895 succeeded Seeley as Regius Professor of Modern

---

[1] Quoted D. M. Baillie, *God Was In Christ*, 1947, p. 23; cf. F. Loofs, *What is the Truth about Jesus Christ?* 1913, p. 122.

[2] P. T. Forsyth, *The Principle of Authority*, 1913, second edition, 1952, p. 77.

[3] Cf. 'Christianity holds no brief whatever for false gods. The modern vague idea, which has even infected a good deal of our missionary work, that there is much truth in all religions and that the task is to bring out and strengthen this indigenous approach to God rather than preach the gospel of Jesus Christ, is no part of the authentic Christian tradition'. L. W. Grensted, *Psychology and God*, 1930, p. 60.

History at Cambridge, was responsible for planning the *Cambridge Modern History* series.

It was characteristic of the new school of historians to pay attention to facts. And in thus following the dictum of Ranke there was a tendency to concentrate on the study of details. The older school of historians were considered to have been deficient in critical ability and consequently permitted to pass for facts what an enlightened scrutiny would have shown to have been fancy. They were unable to distinguish what was genuine from what was fiction: and they could not observe the later accretions which like rust on iron had gathered round the original event. The new school, by contrast, set out to expose all that was fictitious. They thus subjected past statements, stories and statistics to a serious scrutiny. Much that was hitherto accepted without question was, as a result, cast aside as worthless. In the eyes of those who regarded such a method as an iconoclastic excess the whole procedure appeared to be destructive.

Criticism which expressed itself in minute analysis and showed itself ready to cast aside much which the earlier age had taken as fact may, then, be regarded as the chief characteristic of the historical method. Storr who lived through some of this period of changing outlook well remarked, 'The Spirit of the age is pre-eminently historical; and because it is that, it is also critical'.[1]

The application of the historical method to the Old Testament was immediate and was, at first, used as a synonym for the 'Higher Criticism'. The conflict which ensued will concern us in the following chapters, but, as was inevitable, it was not possible for the method to be restricted to the Old Testament. By the turn of the century the New Testament was also set in the context of historical development. Quest was made for 'the Jesus of History'. The result was the 'Liberal Protestant' reconstruction in which the Gospel Figure was said to have been rescued from the debris of dogma under which the later Church had submerged Him. The Jesus, coloured and characterized by an excess of enthusiasm, was set forth, recaptured from the traditions of Church and creed. We need not refer here to the many 'reconstructions' which were presented for acceptance, some dull, some daring, and some dangerous, as they were.

---

[1] V. F. Storr, *Development and Divine Purpose*, 1906, p. 211.

A general account of the result of the application of the historical method, however, is required since it will be helpful in understanding the more recent position. To begin with, emphasis was put upon the teaching of Jesus and the impression He made upon His first disciples. He is to be seen supremely as One who rose out of humanity and who is Himself a great and good human. It was Paul who inserted into the story the leaven of the Pharisee, and became the arch-corruptor of the Gospel of Jesus. Then, too, confusion was worse confounded, when the Gnostic poison, which seduced even St John, got wedded to the story of the Peasant of Galilee. Historicism was recovering the truth and presenting us with the significance of Jesus by providing us with the 'clue' to the history. It has rescued from the confusion and misfortune His real message which can be found amidst the rudiments of St Mark's Gospel, and which has its formal statement in the Epistle of James. The rest of the New Testament can be written off as a speculative excrescent and a blind-alley for the true purpose of Christ. In such a reconstruction Harnack was to take the lead. But, as George Tyrrell remarks, 'The Christ that Harnack sees looking back through nineteen centuries of Catholic darkness, is only the reflection of a Liberal Protestant face, seen at the bottom of a deep well'.[1]

It was not, however, so easy to scrap the rest of the New Testament. The less the historical method was vitiated by presuppositions the more difficult it became to write off what remained outside a 'reduced' gospel, as of no account.

So a compromise must be found, which it was hoped would satisfy all who have a regard for Jesus. Two types of Christianity are then stated to exist side by side in the primitive Church. Some there are who followed Christ and others who worshipped Him. Those who have a care for the facts of history, it was maintained, will consider Jesus as the first Christian, and will seek to imitate Him. Others there were, and these for the most part those who were healed and helped by Him, who worshipped Him. This is an understandable extravagance, to which later the great-hearted Paul sought to give theological justification. Those who belong to the imitation school claim to stand so close to the sound realism of the simple truth that they can afford to be tolerant of those who worship Christ as God. The hope was

[1] George Tyrrell, *Christianity at the Cross-roads*, 1909, p. 44.

expressed that both sides should live together in the same
Church, with equal rights, common charity and mutual respect.
Although the historical method has made the Christ of the
Epistles a mere creation of the Church's faith there is no reason
to rob the simple believer of the consolation and comfort which
the creation gives. After all, if it has value to him and if it works,
what more need be said?

This tendency to admit such a value in the Christ of faith was
important. It reinforced the growing suspicion concerning the
validity of the results of the application of the historical method
which was producing so many conflicting and competing
Figures all claiming to be the real 'Jesus of History'. Besides,
the whole idea of 'history' was itself under review. There began
to appear a crop of volumes claiming to present its 'meaning',
or to give its 'clue', or to indicate its 'significance', and so forth.
There was, in fact, a repudiation of historicism. That the movement did give full justice to the essential humanity of Jesus is to
be granted as its permanent good result. But its total rejection
of the Christ of faith as essential to the authentic gospel was
both false and fatal. It was bound not to survive. 'Theological
thought', rightly observes D. M. Baillie, 'has largely left
behind the movement which we symbolize by the phrase "the
Jesus of history".'[1] The modern reconstruction which can say
with it, 'No more docetism', can say *against* it, 'No more
historicism'.

E.　THE CATEGORY OF GESCHICHTE

'No more historicism', such has become the modern cry for many.
Herein lies the contrast between the older liberalism and the
new modernism, or, as some would prefer to call it, the 'neo-
orthodox' position.[2] 'Neo-orthodoxy', contends W. M. Morton,
'differs from scholastic and fundamentalistic conservatism in its
free and symbolic use of the Bible, and its impressionistic
interpretation of orthodox doctrines; from radical Protestantism
in its profound distrust of natural science and natural theology
as possible paths to deliverance; from liberal Protestantism, in

---

[1] D. M. Baillie, *God Was In Christ*, 1947, p. 9.
[2] Cf. E. J. Carnell, *The Theology of Reinhold Niebuhr*, revised edition, 1960,
Chapter I.

its sharp opposition to every theology based on human experience, even if the experience be "religious" and "Christian".'[1]

The main emphasis of this new theological reconstruction is the place it gives to the Christ of Faith and its disregard for the Jesus of History. The Jesus of history has little or no significance, it is claimed, since Christian faith does not rise out of any appreciation of the historic Jesus. The Jesus of history has, indeed, relatively no importance: what really matters is the interpreted Jesus, the Christ of faith. It will be seen, then, how opposed and opposite, are the two views, the Jesus-of-History cult and what we may call the newer 'Geschichte' cult.

With the Dialectical theologians, for the most part Continentals, and, therefore, less compromising than the British, the pendulum swing has gone its full length. The repudiation of the 'historical Jesus' is complete.

In this country, years before the appearance of Barth and Brunner, one of its greatest theological thinkers, said many of the corrective things that they have been saying of recent years, but, at the same time avoiding the exaggerations which weaken their position. Barth has given us to understand that he knew nothing of P. T. Forsyth's work before he had developed his own ideas. But Forsyth had made many of the points which are now stated to be characteristic of the Dialectical theology.

Those acquainted with the special stresses of the Crisis theologians will recognize at once the parallels in the thought. Forsyth insists upon the 'otherness' of God in a manner characteristic of Barth. 'God is God by His difference, even more than by His unity with us', he says.[2] Forsyth's whole theology is built upon this fact: and it was a position more difficult for Forsyth to defend, living in the period when there was emphasis put upon the idea of monistic continuity and affinity, than for Barth. Forsyth's world was not congenial to such a doctrine. Forsyth, too, makes much of the point that faith is not natural to the natural man. In the divine–human encounter it is created. 'The Gospel must *create* the power to believe it' he says in almost 'Barthian' language. 'Revelation here is so radical that in the

---

[1] W. M. Horton, *Christian Theology: An Ecumenical Approach*, 1955, first British edition, 1956, p. 32.

[2] P. T. Forsyth, *The Principle of Authority*, 1913, second edition, 1952, p. 151.

same act there must be Regeneration. The calling voice of a holy God to us sinners is such a judging, crushing voice that it becomes effectual only as a new-creating word.'[1] Such parallels and echoes as these could be multiplied, but it is not our particular interest to find them.

With reference to our special subject we are to note that in contrast with the earlier view which repudiates the Christ of faith in the interests of the Jesus of history, and the recent view which repudiates the Jesus of history in the interests of the Christ of faith, can be placed Forsyth who seeks to do justice to both.

(a) Forsyth's 'Geschichte' view a necessity for the full reality of revelation in Christ. In an important passage Forsyth discusses (as indeed Barth does later) the meaning of Lessing's famous dictum: 'The accidental truths of history can never become proof for the necessary truths of reason.' To get at Lessing's 'real meaning', Forsyth draws a distinction 'between history in the great sense and history in the small, between history as a tissue of great ideas and powers and history as a mass of empirical events, between history as divined and history as proved'.[2] To designate these two types of history, Forsyth uses two German words which Wobbermin had already applied with the same effect. There is *Geschichte* and there is *Historie*. '*Historie* is history as it may be settled by the methods of historical science, where our results, like those of all science, are but relative, and either highly or poorly probable. *Geschichte* on the other hand is a larger thing, out of which *Historie* has to sift, but which may embody or convey ideas greater than the critical residuum retains power to express.'[3]

How Forsyth applies this distinction to Lessing's dictum we need not pause to indicate. But what it is important to observe is that Forsyth will not discard *Historie* for the sake of *Geschichte* nor will he allow that *Geschichte* can be ultimately divorced from Historie. The revelation was not complete in the historical Jesus. It had to be continued and completed in the apostolic word. 'The apostolic interpretation is an integral part of the revelationary fact, process, and purpose, a real, though

---

[1] P. T. Forsyth, *The Principle of Authority*, 1913, second edition, 1952, p. 119.
[2] *Ibid.*, p. 112; cf. K. Barth, *Church Dogmatics*, I, i, p. 166, iii, pp. 112–13.
[3] *Ibid.*, pp. 112–13.

posthumous, part of Christ's own continued teaching.'[1] It is in the Jesus of *Historie* and the Christ of *Geschichte* that we have the full disclosure of God; not in the one as against the other, but in the one as permeated by and as necessary to the other. Revelation 'is not simply the critical residue of the Synoptics, but their totality—the whole apostolic burthen of the New Testament, pervading the Synoptics themselves. The only fact ever offered by the Church is the total New Testament fact, where the synoptic figure of the Lord is self-interpreted by the same Lord acting as the Spirit. The New Testament revelation is the person of Christ in its whole and universal action, and not the character of Christ in its biographical aspect'.[2] Forsyth points out that the criticism which has abolished the apostolic interpretation has gone on to abolish Christ's historic reality.[3] Evidence of this fact was abundant all around him in the variety of contemporary 'Lives of Jesus', all claiming to portray the Jesus of History. But Forsyth will not permit the synoptic facts to be torn away nor the apostolic interpretation to be discarded. 'We have no access to the fact but through them. If they are final for the historic fact, they are no less final for its central interpretation.'[4]

Forsyth's final position can, then, best be put in one significant sentence: 'The great fact' he urges 'is the historic phenomenon, Jesus, *plus* its "meta-historic" Word'.[5] Forsyth, therefore, so to speak, puts *Historie* and *Geschichte* side by side, and maintains that they belong together in the totality of revelation. With the 'Barthians' it is otherwise.

(b) With the Crisis theologians the category Geschichte is used for the repudiation of the historical Jesus. In contrast with Forsyth their position might be stated as seeking the locale of revelation in the 'meta-historical' Word *minus* the historical phenomenon, Jesus. They do not merely subject the Jesus of history to the Christ of faith, but actually glory in the repudiation of the historical—in the sense of *Historie*—altogether. The recorded events of the gospels are not history in the sense of actual historical happenings. The gospel 'events' fall within the realm of Geschichte, to denote that which is above history. Thus is

---

[1] P. T. Forsyth, *The Principle of Authority*, 1913, second edition, 1952, p. 133.
[2] *Ibid.*, p. 130.   [3] *Ibid.*, p. 135.
[5] *Ibid.*, p. 115.   [4] *Ibid.*

repudiated any literal reading of, for example, the 'Fall'. The account of which is to be understood as a type, a parable, a myth. It is essentially *Urgeschichte*, supra-temporal and supra-historical. It belongs to the realm of *Heilsgeschichte*.

Something of the application of this idea to the understanding of the gospel can be seen in Brunner's *Mediator*. Brunner shows no particular interest in the 'historic' figure of the Synoptics. Forsyth made the point, following Kierkegaard, that the current interest in the 'personality' of Jesus was a decidedly wrong beginning. It focused attention upon the human history, the human Figure, and the human circumstances. But the locale of revelation was in the divine drama, in the supernatural happenings, and not in the reconstructed human personality of Jesus. Brunner presses this point. The Jesus of history has no significance for faith. 'Faith presupposes, as a matter of course, *a priori*, that the Jesus of history is not the same as the Christ of faith.'[1] Faith is not the least concerned with the Jesus presented by critical investigation. In fact the most radical biblical criticism, of which Brunner is an ardent adherent, does not affect the issue in the slightest. It may well be, indeed, that the Synoptic gospels do less than justice to the stark literal humanness of Jesus. The fact, not for Brunner in any way disturbing, is that any genuine picture of the historical Jesus cannot be salvaged from the records. But this is a matter of no great moment since 'Christian faith does not arise out of the picture of the historical Jesus, but out of the testimony to Jesus'.

Barth is even more emphatic in his rejection of the 'Jesus-cult'. He vigorously repudiates any attempt to reconstruct a picture of the 'personality' of Jesus. He takes delight in stressing that the historic Figure is not revelation but a hiding of the Divine. Herein God is veiled rather than revealed. His human personality, he declares, was not very attractive, nothing convincing or winning. The Word became 'flesh'; but the 'flesh' assumed, Barth declares, well knowing that he is not taking the orthodox position, was 'fallen' human nature.[2] As such it cannot be the sphere of revelation. Revelation belongs rather to the realm of *Heilsgeschichte* which hovers over and acts within the otherwise unknowable and undiscoverable 'historical' Jesus. The

[1] Emil Brunner, *The Mediator* (E.T. 1934), p. 184.
[2] Karl Barth, *Church Dogmatics* (E.T. 1956), I, ii, p. 151 f.

resurrection can be taken as an example which will make clear
the significance of Barth's idea. The resurrection is 'true', not in
the sense of recoverable history, but as *Geschichte*. It need not
be thought of as following chronologically Christ's death.[1] It belongs to the realm of the supra-temporal and the supra-historical.[2]

The neo-orthodox, then, sharply oppose the liberal attempt to
build theology on human experience, even if designated as
'religious' and 'Christian' experience. Emphasis is placed, in
contrast, upon the transcendence of God and His difference from
man. He is the 'Wholly Other' and there is no natural unity—so
especially Barth—between God and man. Special revelation is
located in the Word of God, God the Son. But it is not 'Christ
after the flesh, the Christ who is tractable to historical and
critical enquiry, but the Christ after the Spirit is the subject of
revelation'.[3]

Into the implications of all this we need not enter here. It
could be shown that for all their emphasis upon objective
revelation, Brunner and Barth have really returned to the
Kierkegaardian subjectivity—a subjectivity which in their
respective criticisms of Schleiermacher they have professed to
renounce.[4] And, further, by eliminating the historical Jesus from
account they can entertain the most radical critical conclusions
regarding the records, but they appear to be left with a Christ
who remains, only because He has the value of God for man,
since He is who He is by the Church's valuation and interpretation of Him. In the end it appears that we have a Christ who has
the 'value' of God for us. It is when I am 'convinced in my

[1] Cf. Karl Barth, *Church Dogmatics*, I, ii, p. 147 f.; IV, i, pp. 331 ff.; IV, ii,
pp. 118–22.
[2] Cf. E. J. Young, *The Study of Old Testament Theology Today*, 1958, pp. 13–31.
[3] F. W. Camfield, *Revelation and the Holy Spirit*, 1934, p. 64. The whole passage
could have been quoted as it gives the essential position of the Dialectical theology.
'. . . historical criticism of the records (of the New Testament) for the purpose of
discovering the actual human Jesus and reconstructing the events of his life, do not
touch the nerve of revelation. For the New Testament witness is that not in him
treated from the historical point of view does revelation lie. Not the Christ after the
flesh, the Christ who is tractable to historical and critical enquiry, but the Christ
after the Spirit is the subject of revelation'. F. W. Camfield, *Revelation and the
Holy Spirit*, 1934, p. 64. Cf. 'The new doctrine seems to say "Jesus of Nazareth was
truly a human historical person; but his history and personality do not matter in the
revelation of the Word of God".' D. D. Williams, *What Present Day Theologians
are Saying*, New York, 1959, p. 129.
[4] Cf. H. D. McDonald, *Ideas of Revelation*, 1959, p. 269.

conscience' of 'Christ as the truth' that I can believe in the
Scripture testimony to Christ.[1] Here Ritschl has come back to
his own, edged himself in at the back door having been rather
violently flung out at the front. This riddance from reckoning of
the Jesus of history does injustice, not only to the facts, but much
more to the necessities of the faith. It is the whole Christ of the
New Testament, as Forsyth had so clearly insisted, who is the
source and the object of faith. Faith presupposes, as a matter of
course, a priori, that the Jesus of history is the same as the Christ
of faith. The position of the neo-orthodox is all very one-sided
and is the result of a reaction from the Jesus-of-History cult. It
is right in its emphasis upon the necessity of the New Testament
interpretation of the Christ Figure, but it is false in its repudiation of the historical Jesus. 'It is not the mere picture of the
Jesus of history, constructed by historical science, that lays hold
of us for our salvation, but the whole Christian story, with both
its historical and its supra-historical elements, which is the
substance of the original kerygma'.[2]

(c) The lack of interest in the historical Figure of the
gospels finds its completest expression in the 'Form-Geschichte'
school which blends in an extraordinary way theological
dogmatism and historical scepticism.

The chief advocates of this view take their stand against
'liberalism' in theology. Here we have a radicalism which
professes to be both 'confessional' and 'biblicist'; but it is a
radicalism, nevertheless, which has no place for the Synoptic
account of Jesus. Modern radical Protestantism, it seems to us,
sets out from the neo-orthodox conclusion and develops a
'reconstructionist' theory which is reactionary indeed. Its
advocates seem to be agreed that their position is an 'advance'
on that of Barth and Brunner. But agreement among themselves
is more difficult to come by. Not only is it insistently denied that
finality can be claimed for their constructions, but special delight
is expressed by exponents over disagreements among themselves. Paul Tillich writes of the 'many theological disputes' he
has had with his 'great friend' Niebuhr.[3] Niebuhr maintains that

[1] E. Brunner, Christian Doctrine of God, Dogmatics, I, 1950, p. 110.
[2] D. M. Baillie, God Was In Christ, 1948, pp. 51–2.
[3] Paul Tillich, 'Reinhold Niebuhr's Doctrine of Knowledge', Reinhold Niebuhr, His Religious, Social, and Political Thought (ed. Charles W. Kegley and Robert W. Bretall), 1956, p. 43.

an indebtedness to Greek intellectualism was necessary so that Christianity might convincingly adapt itself to prevailing views. This was a missionary requisite. Tillich denies the legitimacy of this type of intellectualism and insists, in opposition, that Greek thought was not in fact rationalistic but 'mystical', a claim which would put Greek thought in harmony with his own 'mystical' position. Brunner states that the label 'neo-orthodox' is unfortunate and really inapplicable to Niebuhr 'since in all the world there is nothing more unorthodox than the spiritual volcano Reinhold Niebuhr'.[1]

Bultmann, the new monarch in the theological arena, seems to be viewed with a little suspicion by the Dialectical theologians. Brunner, at all events, charges that he 'thins out the Gospel too much'.[2] Bultmann, certainly the most thorough exponent of the 'Formgeschichte' theory, openly rejects the factuality of the gospel records. They are legend-tinted and altogether fragmentary. This 'Strauss of the twentieth century', as he has been called, declares that his is convinced 'that we can know almost nothing concerning the life and personality of Jesus, since the early Christian sources show no interest in either, are, moreover fragmentary and often legendary; and other sources about Jesus do not exist'.[3] This lack of possible knowledge concerning the life and personality of Jesus is not a matter for regret. The earlier Jesus-of-history cult focused attention on the records and gave too much authority to the 'reconstructionist' critic.

Bultmann, then, dogmatically excludes any interest in the personality of Jesus. But the reason, he adds, is not merely because of the absence of any sure information which would compel him to make virtue out of necessity. For him the truth is that Christian faith is not concerned with an historical Figure at all, but with the Christ of dogma, the interpreted Jesus. Those whose interest is in the personality of Jesus are told that 'the

---

[1] Emil Brunner, 'Some Remarks on Reinhold Niebuhr's Work as a Christian Thinker', *op. cit.* above, pp. 28–9.

[2] H. D. McDonald, 'The Conflict Over Special Revelation', *Christianity Today*, Vol. V, No. 8, January 16, 1961; cf. the remark of Tillich '. . . R. Bultmann's bold programme of a "demythologization of the New Testament" aroused a storm in all theological camps and the slumber of Barthianism . . .' Paul Tillich, *Systematic Theology*, Vol. II, 1957, p. 102.

[3] Rudolf Bultmann, *Jesus and the Word* (E.T. New York, 1958), p. 8; cf. p. 13.

situation is depressing or destructive'. For Bultmann the Jesus of history in so far as the account can be stripped from its later colouring by the Church's faith and dogma, is of no account. As far, indeed, as we are allowed any glimpse of the real Jesus we see a none-too-compelling Figure; virtually, in fact, an ignorant Gallilean peasant. But we are hastily assured that this need not be a cause for alarm: what matters is the Jesus of faith.

The task of theology today, for the newer school of radical Protestants, is not to be content with the neo-orthodox, super-historical Christ but to reconstruct the whole by 'demytholo-gizing' the 'myths'. It is consequently urged, for example by Niebuhr, that such ideas as the Trinity are mere symbolic expressions, quite meaningless if read literally. Since it would be absurd to assert that the finite can be infinite, we are told that Jesus was not really, literally divine. Only in a 'gnostic, symbolic' sense can it be said that He died and rose again.

The upshot of this line of thought is that we are left with a new humanism in which revelation seems to be nothing other than the unveiling to man of the ultimate divinity of his own being. We are back again to Schleiermacher's subjectivism and to Ritschl's value judgement epistemology.

In Paul Tillich this strange combination of Schleiermacher and Ritschl meets. Tillich contends that the 'biblical picture of Christ' is not an historical presentation.[1] 'The search for the historical Jesus was an attempt to discover a minimum of reliable facts about the man Jesus of Nazareth, in order to provide a safe foundation for the Christian faith. This attempt' Tillich adds, 'was a failure.'[2] The character reconstructed is no certain historical reality. The picture possesses, at most, a faint possibility.[3]

It is in this context of ideas that the concept revelation is to be understood. 'Revelation is the manifestation of what concerns us ultimately'[4] it is declared. Everything is a bearer to man of such a revelation when it seizes him as a 'miracle' and as 'ecstasy', thereby inducing an 'elevation of heart'. Of this reality Christianity is the profoundest 'symbol'. 'A Christianity which

---

[1] Cf. Paul Tillich, *Systematic Theology*, Vol. II, 1957, pp. 101 ff.
[2] *Ibid.*, Vol. II, p. 105.
[3] Cf. Paul Tillich, *The Interpretation of History*, 1936, p. 260; cf. p. 165.
[4] *Systematic Theology*, Vol. I, 1951, p. 110.

does not assert that Jesus of Nazareth is sacrificed to Jesus as the Christ is just one more religion among many religions', he says. But this too is 'symbol'; indeed, 'tis 'symbol' all. The 'symbol' Son of Man is to be regarded as the symbol of the original unity between God and man. In fact 'The whole picture given by Tillich of Jesus becoming "the Christ" is one of the gradual divination of a man. A divination which occurred fully in him and which must occur to some extent in all if they are to have what Tillich calls "eternal life", that is to enjoy a union with the Ground of their being or God'.[1] Jesus, it seems, was the first who just happened to unite the estranged conditions of existence, He is thus the picture of that 'new being' which all can attain. The development of the 'divinity' in Christ is what, in its measure, the process should be in ours if we are to be united with that Ground of our being which is for us a matter of 'ultimate concern'. Man must become 'grasped by the ultimate power' which is the Ground of his being, Tillich asserts; and when this happens there is a 'miracle'.[2] But a 'miracle' however is not quite what we might suppose; it must be defined in the context of Tillich's ontology. There is no supra-natural interference by Being-Itself in nature. Such an idea would mean that 'God would be split within himself' and as a house divided against itself it would result in collapse of the very concept of God. God, as the Ground of being, would be at odds with the structure of being, therefore this 'bad connotation of a supra-natural interference' must be abandoned. A miracle is not supernatural in the sense of a Divine intrusion, it is rather the result of a group of elements in reality itself being brought into relationship with a group of elements in the mind of man, in such a way that the rational elements in the mind are neither destroyed nor removed.[3] Ultimately, as in Schleiermacher, miracles are limited to personal subjective experiences.

It seems to us that the whole strange thesis which Tillich elaborates in the two volumes of his *Systematic Theology* as well as in his other several writings is best summarized in a sermon which he preached on the 'Holy Spirit' at the Rockefeller Chapel

[1] R. Allan Killen, *The Ontological Theology of Paul Tillich*, 1956, p. 167.
[2] Cf. Paul Tillich, *The Protestant Era*, 1948, p. 88.
[3] Cf. R. Allan Killen, *op. cit.*, p. 69; cf. also *The Theology of Paul Tillich* (ed. Charles W. Kegley and Robert W. Bretall), 1956.

at the University of Chicago. Referring to his topic as a 'neglected subject' Tillich proceeds to advance ideas about the Holy Spirit which have little resemblance to the orthodox Christian doctrine. He maintains that the Spirit of God is virtually another way of asserting the immanence of God. True, God is always near and far, but He becomes the 'absent God' to us if our awareness of Him should become shallow, or habitual or familiar. But the divine Spirit is really God everywhere, not bound to Christianity or any one of its Churches; he works 'in every human situation'. This means for Tillich that 'spiritual experience' is a reality for everyone, it is 'as real as the air we breathe'. 'For this is what Divine Spirit means; God present in our spirit', he says. 'Spirit is not a mysterious substance, it is not a part of God. It is God Himself . . . present in communities and personalities, grasping them, inspiring them, transforming them.'[1] In such an account Tillich reveals how much he has reacted from the Barthian emphasis on transcendence and has returned to the Schleiermacherian immanence and mysticism.

Tillich is as insistent as any follower of Schleiermacher or Coleridge or Maurice could be that revelation is something inward. And he is as scathing in his repudiation of a 'book religion' and a 'verbal revelation'. 'Probably nothing has contributed more to the misrepresentation of the Biblical doctrine of the Word than the identification of the Word with the Bible', he says.[2] When once the Bible is called the Word of God theological confusion results; a dictation theory of inspiration, dishonesty in dealing with the biblical text and a 'monophysitic' dogma of infallibility of a book.[3]

Basic to all these ideas which have reacted against the Jesus-of-history cults is the assertion that faith has nothing to do with the historical Figure which, as a matter of fact, cannot be drawn from the gospel records. The 'Christ-event' is the creation of the Church.[4] British writers, not, it must be admitted, with the same devastating thoroughness as in Bultmann or Dibelius, have also contended for the Christ of faith as the true locale of revelation. 'It seems, then', says R. H. Lightfoot at the

[1] Cf. Report of Sermon, by Dave Meade, *The Chicago Daily News*, Monday, January 16, 1961.
[2] Paul Tillich, *Systematic Theology*, Vol. I, 1951, pp. 158–9.
[3] *Ibid.*, p. 158.
[4] John Knox, *Jesus, Lord and Christ*, 1958, pp. 63 ff., 145 f.

conclusion of his Bampton Lectures, 'that the form of the earthly no less than the heavenly Christ is for the most part hidden from us. For all the inestimable value of the Gospels, they yield us little more than a whisper of his voice; we trace in them but the outskirts of his ways. Only when we see him hereafter in his fulness shall we know him also as he was on earth. And perhaps the more we ponder the matter, the more clearly we shall understand the reason for it, and therefore shall not wish it otherwise. For probably we are as little prepared for the one as for the other.'[1]

This, as we should expect from R. H. Lightfoot, is a spiritually sensitive statement of the case. Yet the strange fact is that even he seems to give more credit to the records and more appreciation of the 'historical Figure' than his fundamental thesis would seem to permit. John Knox, in like manner, talks of the 'importance of the "Quest" for the historical Jesus' as an 'indispensable theological task', yet how it can be important and why it should be undertaken we just cannot make out.[2]

Bultmann, Tillich and Niebuhr, having renounced the thesis that divine revelation contains truths, are left without any rational basis for theology. This in a lesser way is also true of their more moderate supporters. It is not very evident to us why Tillich especially, whose position is a sort of Christianized Neoplatonism, speculative after the fashion of Johannes Scotus Erigena[3] and mystical after the style of Dionysius, can be so dogmatic about the Christian faith when its central Figure is no historical reality.

Revelation it seems to us must come as truth as well as act. And most certainly the knowledge of God which is discovered by experience is not a knowledge which could have arisen in experience. Man's encounter with God comes by way of the truth communicated to God's chosen prophets and apostles. The acts of God and the word of God are not two separable realities.

[1] R. H. Lightfoot, *History and Interpretation in the Gospels*, Bampton Lectures 1934, 1935, p. 225. Cf. 'As a figure calculated to inspire men to heroic acts of self-sacrifice, it may be doubted whether the figure of Jesus, if detached from what Christians have believed about Him, is adequate'. Edwyn Bevan, quoted by D. M. Baillie, *God Was In Christ*, 1948, p. 38; cf. Edwyn Bevan, *Christianity*, 1932, p. 239 f.

[2] John Knox, *Jesus, Lord and Christ*, 1958, p. 240.

[3] Cf. Richard Kroner, *Speculation and Revelation in the Age of Christian Philosophy*, 1959, p. 146 (footnote).

God's acts are known only as they are interpreted by His word, and by His word we are brought into saving contact with His acts. With the neo-orthodox, and more particularly with the modern school of radical Protestantism, the pendulum swing, as Donald Baillie points out, has gone too far. There is an essential place for the Jesus of history in the creation, as well as in the upbuilding of faith. It is altogether impossible to dispense with the Jesus of history completely, needful as it was to insist that we do not really know Christ if that knowledge is limited to the synoptic picture. It is a fact that 'The Jesus of history Himself can tell us that the Jesus of history is not enough'.[1] But it is also true as Nathan Söderbloom says, that 'If you wish to have Christ, you must take history with him'.[2]

Radical Protestantism, it seems to us, has no objective Word of God, with the result that it flounders in the abyss of irrationalism and subjectivism.

---

[1] D. M. Baillie, *God Was In Christ*, 1948, p. 42; cf. H. R. Mackintosh, 'Christ and Historical Research', *The Doctrine of the Person of Christ*, 1912, pp. 310 ff.

[2] Nathan Söderbloom, *The Nature of Revelation*, E.T. 1933, p. 171.

CHAPTER THREE

The Battle of the Standpoints

One of the most distinctive features of the last quarter of the nineteenth century as it concerns the subject of revelation was the conflict over what became so well known as the 'Higher Criticism'. It was regarded by its opponents as a novel brand of scepticism, and by its advocates as the truly scientific approach to an understanding of the Bible. Higher Criticism became at the time the centre of discussion and the focus of debate. It was the one vital topic which drew forth a flood of letters, pamphlets, articles and books. The press was inundated with calls upon its space for expressions of opinions for and against this new method of dealing with the Scriptures, and the new verdict which was being passed upon its contents.

'It is a paper war', it was declared in a contemporary issue of the *Expository Times*, 'As no theological controversy ever before, it is being fought out in the periodical press'.[1] An examination of such periodicals as, for example, *The British Quarterly Review*, *The British Weekly*, *The British and Foreign Evangelical Review*, and *The Contemporary Review*, will give some impression of the seriousness of the debate.

The Church was in a state of turmoil; forces were arrayed in opposition. It was indeed 'a paper war', a battle was being waged for the Bible. The issues at stake concerned an understanding of its historicity, its inspiration, its accuracy, its authority, and its interpretation. That these were considered the real problems may be gathered from the debate between Alfred Cave, on the one side, and, on the other side, T. K. Cheyne and S. R. Driver. In an issue of the *Contemporary Review*, Cave wrote an article entitled, 'The Old Testament and its Critics'[2] and he

[1] *Expository Times*, Vol. III, 1891–2, p. 292.
[2] Cf. *op. cit.*, No. lvii, 1890, pp. 537–51.

followed this in the next year with another on, 'Canon Driver on the Book of the Law',[1] in which a severe attack was made on Driver's, *Introduction to the Literature of the Old Testament*. Driver replied in the February issue of 1892, under the caption, 'Principal Cave on the Hexateuch'.[2] Already in 1890 Cave had shown his hostility to the higher criticism in an address on 'The Old Testament and the Higher Criticism', given to the Manchester Conference of the Evangelical Alliance. This address appeared in print in the December issue of *Evangelical Christendom*,[3] and was later expanded and produced in a pamphlet form with the title, *The Battle of the Standpoints*, which has been taken as the heading of the present chapter.[4] That this may be regarded as a fairly accurate account of the conflict the later part of this chapter and the one following will make evident. Each side certainly had its presuppositions, the critics no less than their opponents, although it must be confessed that the critics of the time believed themselves to be without any. Each side from its own standpoint attacked the other, and it is this conflict which demands our attention. Meanwhile, however, we must note how the issue of the higher criticism took the first place in this particular period.

In the first year of the appearance of the *Expository Times*, it is observed in one issue that 'In some circles in England the discussion of the Higher (or Historical) Criticism of the Old Testament has, since the publication of *Lux Mundi*, and Canon Liddon's St Paul's sermon on the other side, reached a tolerably acute stage'.[5] A little later F. H. Woods in an article entitled, 'A Critical Examination of Genesis i to vi' begins with the observation that 'One of the most remarkable features of Biblical study is the attention which is being increasingly paid to what is called "the higher criticism" '.[6] In a long review of Driver's *An Introduction to the Literature of the Old Testament*, A. K. S. Kennedy noted the 'daily increasing attention which is being paid by all sections of the Church to the questions of Old Testament criticism'. The higher criticism was, then, the big

---

[1] Cf. *Expository Times*, Vol. III, No. lx, 1891, pp. 892–910.
[2] Cf. *op. cit.*, No. lxi, 1892, pp. 262–78.
[3] Cf. *Evangelical Christendom*, Vol. XXXI, 1890, pp. 370–7.
[4] Alfred Cave, *The Battle of the Standpoints*, 1890.
[5] *Expository Times*, Vols. I and II, 1889–91, i, p. 146.
[6] *Op. cit.*, 1889–91, ii, p. 102.

issue of the closing years of the nineteenth century. The main storm-centre was, of course, the Old Testament. It was not, as we have already noted, until the beginning of the new century that critical opinions concerning the New Testament were given any serious place in the Church.

In the present chapter the main problem remains of bringing some sort of order into the bewildering amount of literature which is before us in periodicals and pamphlets, in letters and books. We are not intending a full scale history of the conflict over higher criticism—that would take a volume on its own account—but we must give some attention to it as it was finally concerned with the question of the way God has revealed Himself and how this revelation is known to us.

A. THE ADVENT OF CRITICISM

Our summary can best begin with a reference to the contention of C. J. Ellicott, Bishop of Gloucester and Bristol. He dates the beginning of criticism in the English Church with the publication of the *Lux Mundi*. Before then it stood outside the main stream of 'the Catholic faith', and was generally associated with German scepticism in which the tendency was more and more to disintegrate the inspired records. 'The pedigree is certainly not satisfactory', he remarks.[1] Ellicott's pin-pointing of the publication of the *Lux Mundi* as the start of the higher criticism conflict is broadly true. It may, however, be more properly stated that the period began with the appearance of Robertson Smith's lectures, *The Old Testament in the Jewish Church*. The truth in Ellicott's remark is that before the date of the *Lux Mundi* anyone advocating a critical position was soon made to feel, by the strength of the opposition to it, that it had no general support either of the scholar or the ordinary Christian.

Taking, then, the date 1880 as marking out a new stage in the controversy, the period prior to that may be called, as in our title to this section, the advent of criticism.

At the beginning the term 'higher criticism' was used as a synonym for historical criticism, but, as time went on, as we shall see, higher criticism was stated to be other than historical

[1] C. J. Ellicott, 'The Teaching of Our Lord as to the Authority of the Old Testament', *Expository Times*, Vol. III, 1891–2, p. 158.

criticism and was identified more particularly with literary criticism. The first occurrence of the designation 'the historical method' seems to come in Joseph Priestley's *History of the Corruptions of Christianity*, 1782, in the Preface of which Priestley maintains that the historical method 'will be found to be one of the most satisfactory modes of argumentation'. The term 'higher criticism' was used as early as 1787 in the Preface of J. G. Eichhorn's *Einleitung in das Alte Testament*. Eichhorn is referred to by T. K. Cheyne as 'the founder of the modern Old Testament Criticism'.[1]

In England, the higher criticism did not make any significant headway prior to 1880. Alfred Cave, writing in this very year in *The British and Foreign Evangelical Review*, was certainly correct in stating that the overwhelming weight of current Biblical scholarship, both in the British Isles and America, supported the traditional Mosaic authorship of the Pentateuch.[2] Yet even before this date there were those who afterwards were to attain positions of authority in the Church who did express critical opinions. There was, for example, Edmund Law (1703–87), who became Bishop of Carlisle in 1768. In his *Considerations on the State of the World with Regard to the Theory of Religion*, Law argued that the Scriptures must be approached 'with the same freedom that we do, and find we must do, every other book we desire to understand'.[3]

In 1825 there appeared an English edition by an anonymous translator of Schleiermacher's *Essay on the Gospel of St Luke*. It was subsequently revealed that Connop Thirlwall (1791–1873), later to become Bishop of St David's, was responsible for the work. Bishop Perowne, making special reference to this production, contends that the volume marks 'an epoch in the history of English theology'. An attack, he notes, is made upon verbal inspiration, and the 'historical method' is used to establish 'critical' conclusions. Account has already been given of the critical presuppositions of *Essays and Reviews* and of the reception given to Colenso's work. Concerning the latter it was estimated by William Boyce, a Wesleyan minister who wrote

[1] T. K. Cheyne, *Founders of Old Testament Criticism*, 1893, p. 13.

[2] Alfred Cave, 'Professor Robertson Smith on the Pentateuch', Vol. xxix, 1880, p. 597.

[3] Edmund Law, *Considerations on the State of the World with Regard to the Theory of Religion*, 1745, sixth edition, 1774, p. 71, cf. p. 264.

decades later, that 300 replies were forthcoming, although, he adds, 'few of them dealt with the critical bearings of the questions at stake'.[1] Boyce urges preference for Colenso's work to that of the Germans because he at least wrote in 'plain English!' The verdict given in Colenso's favour by the Lord Chancellor, Lord Westbury, February 4, 1864, declared among other items that it was not penal for a clergyman of the Established Church to assert that the Bible is not inspired in all its parts. This judgement was claimed by later critics to constitute the charter of free enquiry into the origin and composition of the Scriptures in the Church of England and to secure for it the liberty of biblical criticism.[2]

Two other names, both Congregationalists, need to be mentioned. First chronologically comes Samuel Davidson, who became lecturer in Manchester Independent College in 1842. For the opinions he expressed in the revised tenth edition of *Horne's Introduction to the Critical Study and Knowledge of the Holy Scriptures* (1856) Davidson lost his position at the College in 1857.[3] Not only had Davidson denied the Mosaic authorship of the Pentateuch but he had compromised the traditional view of inspiration by admitting a strong element of German naturalistic criticism.[4] He had propounded a 'lower' view of inspiration than that held by the Church at large. A review of *Horne's Introduction* was given in the *Wesleyan Methodist Magazine* for 1856. The theory of inspiration which Davidson had suggested could not be permitted since it admitted the 'perilous experiment' of 'distinguishing the human and the Divine' 'in the Record which is "given by inspiration of God" '. The 'whole speculation', it was declared, was 'quite modern' and had no justification whatever in the Scripture itself.[5] The action of the College committee in dismissing Davidson was generally approved and strongly supported.[6] Indeed, Watkins in his Bampton Lectures goes so far as to suggest that the more

[1] William Boyce, *The Higher Criticism and the Bible*, 1881, p. 129 f.

[2] Cf. J. Estlin Carpenter, *The Bible in the Nineteenth Century*, 1903, pp. 38 ff.

[3] Cf. *The Autobiography and Diary of Samuel Davidson*, edited by his daughter, 1899, pp. 35–70.

[4] Cf. *British and Foreign Evangelical Review*, Vol. VII, 1858, pp. 470–1.

[5] Cf. *Wesleyan Methodist Magazine*, Vol. LXXXIX, 1856, p. 116.

[6] Cf. John Kelly, *An Examination of the Facts, Statements, and Explanations of Rev Dr S. Davidson*, relative to the second volume of the tenth edition of *Horne's Introduction*, etc., Liverpool, 1857.

extreme critical opinions which Davidson expressed in his later work, *An Introduction to the Old Testament, Critical, Historical, and Theological* (three volumes, 1862–63), were due to his resentment at his expulsion from his professorship. Davidson certainly advanced further towards a more and more liberal attitude towards the great central message of the faith. As time went on he drew away from its essential truths. He came to regard Christianity as little more than an ethical code although he retained a vague belief in God as a sort of good-natured Father.[1]

The other name is that of Archibald Duff, who became lecturer in the Airdale College, Bradford, in 1878. Duff, who had received part of his education in Germany, had evidently imbibed a fair measure of its critical views. This is clear from his inaugral address in 1878 in which he suggested his belief that the earlier parts of the Old Testament could not have been prior to 800 BC. He also doubted whether even the prophets had arrived at the conception of pure monotheism.[2]

It has been stated that the famous trio of the Cambridge school—Lightfoot, Hort and Wescott—are to be reckoned amongst the critics. Their interest was, of course, in the New Testament, but they were by no means critics of the radical type. Their whole approach was conservative. Indeed Wescott declared his own position, which was broadly that of the other two, in a paper entitled 'Critical Scepticism' read before the Church Congress at Brighton in October 1874. He maintained that the claim of those who pursue criticism that they are merely being impartial is to be gravely doubted. Concerning the records of our Lord's life, he says, 'fantastic scepticism is not consistent with their truth'.[3] Sceptical criticism, he states, fails to recognize the nature of the problems discussed. He adds several further charges against the 'sceptical' position implicit in 'criticism' which may be best put in his own words: '(1) Sceptical critics fail to take account of the culminative and total

---

[1] Cf. *British Quarterly Review*, Vol. LXXXV, 1882, pp. 521–6. Cf. *Autobiography and Diary of Samuel Davidson*, 1899, pp. 334–5. Cf. H. W. Watkins, *Modern Criticism and the Fourth Gospel*, Bampton Lectures, 1890, 1890, pp. 284 ff.; also *Dr Davidson, his Heresies, Contradictions, and Plagerisms*, by Two Graduates, 1857.

[2] Archibald Duff, *The Use of the Old Testament in the Study of the Rise of our Doctrines*, 1878, p. 12 f.

[3] Cf. *Expositor*, first series, Vol. I, 1875, p. 215.

force of the direct evidence in favour of the facts alleged. (2) They criticize special documents without regard to the general belief which the documents express. (3) Of these documents they criticize special parts without regard to the relation in which the parts stand to the entire book. (4) They isolate the documentary evidence from the testimony of the living body'.[1]

The period, then, prior to 1880 we may regard as one of the preparation of the stage for the appearance of the real protagonists of criticism.

B. THE ADVANCE OF CRITICISM

The 'modern period' of biblical criticism has been dated from the year 1880, the year of Robertson Smith's lectures on the *Old Testament in the Jewish Church*. Two names already prominent were to take the lead in establishing it in these isles. They were T. K. Cheyne in England and A. B. Davidson in Scotland. O. C. Whitehouse in a review of Cheyne's *Founders of Old Testament Criticism* associates Davidson with Cheyne as having 'the honour of being the real "Bahnbrecher" of our modern British Old Testament research by the work contributed by each during the eventful decades 1870–1880'.[2]

Back in the year 1867 Cheyne, then but twenty-eight years old, was given charge of the Biblical department of the newly created *Academy*. At that period he was the acknowledged disciple of the leading German rationalistic critics. And as such he had little influence in this country; indeed, in the earlier period there was very little serious attention paid to the Old Testament.[3] In the year 1880 Cheyne underwent some sort of spiritual experience, which affected, at least for a time, his attitude to the Scriptures. He came to see that certain of the radical views of the German sceptics if carried to their conclusion would be destructive of real religious faith. He did not abandon, by any means, his main critical ideas, but his change in spiritual orientation was noted, and as a consequence his works were more readily received. In fact the impression was given in some over zealous reviews of his *Isaiah* (1880–1) that he had altered

[1] *Expositor*, *ibid.*, pp. 215–16.
[2] *The Thinker*, Vol. IV, 1893, p. 280.
[3] Cf. W. Robertson Nicoll, 'Professor Cheyne', *Expositor*, third series, Vol. IX, 1889, pp. 61–2.

his critical views. This is evident, for example, in two issues of the *British Quarterly Review*, as well as two of the *Expositor*.[1] The truth is, however, that Cheyne reverted to his earlier radical tendencies and in his later criticism put forth ideas which were fruitless as well as fanciful.

Yet Cheyne has been given the reputation of being the chief initiator of higher criticism in England. 'Though he had predecessors', says A. S. Peake, 'it is to Cheyne that the distinction belongs of initiating with adequate scholarship the critical movement in his native country'.[2] Up to 1880, Peake notes elsewhere, Cheyne was dominated by rationalism. And he makes reference to his confession 'that his too exclusive devotion to criticism was injurious to his spiritual life'.[3] By the influence of 'one obscure student' at Oxford 'Johannine religion' asserted 'its supremacy over criticism and speculation'.[4] This changed tone and temper which began to appear in his works has been noted. Yet it is certain that he soon became fascinated again by criticism and speculation and showed a readiness to accept the most audacious views of the Old Testament books. Peake, indeed, remarks with commendable mildness that 'Perhaps he has a tendency in criticism to lay stress on minute indications of date, and to give too much play to imagination'.[5]

A. B. Davidson has been hailed by this same Cheyne as the chief advocate of criticism beyond the border. Cheyne, in fact, is emphatic that 'no one has done more to "found" criticism, at least in Scotland, than this eminent teacher'.[6] Robertson Smith had been one of Davidson's students, and it was not until after the storm caused by Smith's views that Davidson came out in the open defence of criticism. Earlier, indeed, Davidson had given very definite hints of his sympathy with it; and because of his avowed allegiance to the main evangelical doctrines he was able to express this sympathy in the pages of the *British and Foreign Evangelical Review*.[7]

[1] Cf. *British Quarterly Review*, No. lxxii, 1880, p. 544; lxxiii, 1881, pp. 518–20. *Expositor*, first series, Vol. XI, 1880, pp. 399–400; second series, Vol. I, 1885, p. 237.

[2] 'Cheyne, Thomas Kelly', *Dictionary of National Biography, ad. loc.*

[3] A. S. Peake, 'Thomas Kelly Cheyne', *Expository Times*, Vol. VI, 1894–5, p. 441.   [4] *Ibid.*   [5] *Ibid.*, p. 443.

[6] T. K. Cheyne, *Founders of Old Testament Criticism*, 1893, p. 225.

[7] Cf. *British and Foreign Evangelical Review*, No. xxi, 1872, pp. 618–19; No. xxviii, 1879, pp. 337–67.

At the same time, S. D. F. Salmond, while he acknowledges that Davidson 'was the first to teach in any proper and continuous way in Scotland the methods of Higher Criticism'[1] also stresses that 'The self-restraint which is natural to him has been one of the best notes of his criticism'.[2] 'He had a better appreciation than is often possessed by critics', Salmond continues, 'of the limits which are imposed upon Old Testament science, by the comparative scantiness of the Old Testament literature'.[3] Davidson's hesitancy in giving strong statement to the critical ideas disappointed those who wished for this emphasis. Thus A. B. Bruce in an article in the October 1896 issue of the *Biblical World* says, 'Dr Davidson has rather disappointed his admirers even in the region of criticism. He has not kept his place in the van of the movement which he created. He has rather lagged behind or stood on one side, while the company of the prophets marched on, wondering what had possessed them'. The *Expository Times* makes reference to Bruce's remarks and asks, '*Are* they prophets that march past?' True Bruce fortifies his judgement with the opinion of Cheyne. 'But is it not possible that there are those whom Professor Cheyne would call prophets of Old Testament criticism, while Professor Davidson would not; and is it not possible that Professor Davidson would be right? . . . Is it possible that both Professor Bruce and Professor Cheyne have placed him (i.e. Arndt from whose tract, *The Place of Ezekiel in Old Testament Prophecy*, Davidson dissents) among the prophets? Is their judgement better than his? For is it not, after all, a matter of position? Again and again Dr Cheyne publicly declared himself in advance of his colleague Dr Driver. He may be also in advance of Dr Davidson, and Professor Bruce may be forward at his side. Whereupon it were just as easy and just as reasonable for Dr Davidson and Dr Driver to say that *they* were in the midst of the prophets, and that their distinguished colleagues had moved somewhere out of line'.[4]

There is no doubt but that in the eyes of some critics Davidson had failed to keep pace. The fact is, however, that he was not

---

[1] S. D. F. Salmond, 'A. B. Davidson, D.D., LLD,' *Expository Times*, Vol. VIII 1896–7, p. 445.
[2] *Ibid.*   [3] *Ibid.*
[4] *Expository Times*, Vol. VIII, 1896–7, pp. 102–3.

happy about the growing tendency to excessive analysis which certain of them displayed. He apparently came to feel that such criticism in the hands of some uninhibited critics would issue in lamentable absurdities. He is to be found, as a consequence, protesting against the minute dissection of the Old Testament books. In a notice in the *Critical Review* (Vol. II, p. 31), concerning Cornhill's *Einleitung* he observes: 'The criticism of the Pentateuch is a great historical drama, which needs to be put upon the stage with appropriate scenery and circumstances. When performed by a company of puppets called J.E.D.P., with all their little ones down to J^1 and PP, it loses its impressiveness. It will not be strange if some spectactors mistake the nature of the performance and go home with the impression that they have been witnessing a farce'.

(1) *Hindrances to Advance*

For the first half-dozen years or so after 1880, higher criticism did not make any rapid progress in this country. The reasons, were, on the one hand, its pedigree, and, on the other hand, the object of the critical investigation.

(i) The Source of the Critical View.

Higher criticism, it is well known, was born in Germany and came to maturity amongst a company in which rather outspoken sceptical pronouncements were being made concerning the Bible and even the Lord of whom it spoke. The pedigree certainly was not considered satisfactory. The term 'Germanism' was in vogue at the time to designate the rationalistic Hegelianism of much German theology.[1] And it was used at the beginning of the conflict as a synonym for higher criticism as such. Thus in a review of William L. Alexander's *Christ and Christianity* (1854), the *British and Foreign Evangelical Review* refers to the invasion of Christian evidences 'by transcendental modes of thinking, and by a destructive criticism imported from Germany'.[2] The same journal, fifteen years later, reviewed Samuel Davidson's *An Introduction to the Study of the New Testament* (1868) and makes mention of German intellectualism which 'soars away through thin air'.[3] The truth is that for long,

---

[1] Cf. Ernest A. Payne, *Studies in History and Religion*, 1942, pp. 239–40.
[2] *British and Foreign Evangelical Review*, Vol. III, 1854, p. 683.
[3] *Op. cit.*, Vol. XVII, 1869, pp. 502–15.

and it must be admitted not without reason, higher criticism and 'German rationalism' were regarded as one and the same.[1]

A. H. Sayce, then Professor of Assyriology at Oxford, did not feel it was an injustice to speak of 'the exaggerated scepticism of the so-called "Higher Criticism" ', although by so characterizing it he irritated S. R. Driver.[2] In a passage in his book, *The Higher Criticism and the Monuments*, he remarks that 'a good deal of historical criticism which has been passed on the Old Testament is criticism which seems to imagine the compiler of the Book of Judges or the Books of Kings was a German scholar surrounded by volumes of his library, and writing in awe of his reviewers'.[3] Once again Driver did not like the insinuation. Thus in a review of Sayce's book in the *Contemporary Review* of March 1895 he took exception to Sayce's use of the designation 'higher criticism'. Driver was however ready to accept some of Sayce's conclusions but he contended that what Sayce credited to the 'higher critic' should rather be spoken of the 'hypercritic'.

Not only professors but preachers felt bound to associate criticism and German scepticism. J. D. Jones refers to his famous predecessor, Ossian Davies, at Richmond Hill, Bournemouth, who often 'spoke rather scornfully of the men who cut up the Bible with "German scissors" '.[4] The renowned Baptist preacher, C. H. Spurgeon, who cannot be brushed aside as an obscurantist, also comments upon the 'German poison'.[5]

Born, then, in an atmosphere of German rationalism and scepticism, it is not difficult to understand how the higher criticism came to be regarded as its product. How, it could be asked, can a fountain bring forth at the same time sweet water and bitter? Thirlwall had, indeed, earlier rebuked a Bampton lecturer for denouncing the theology of a people whose language he did not know. And it is said that two persons only knew German at Oxford at the time Pusey began his study of the language there between the years 1880–2. But what had been

---

[1] Cf. Leslie B. Peake, *Arthur Samuel Peake, A Memoir*, 1930, p. 113.

[2] A. H. Sayce, 'The Fourteenth Chapter of Genesis', *Expository Times*, Vol. IV, 1892–3, p. 14. See S. R. Driver's reply, *ibid*, p. 95, and Sayce's answer, p. 118.

[3] A. H. Sayce, *The Higher Criticism and the Monuments*, 1895, fifth edition, p. 15; cf. 'The arrogance of tone adopted at times by the "higher criticism" has been productive of nothing but mischief', *op. cit.*, p. 5.

[4] J. D. Jones, *Three Score Years and Ten*, 1940, p. 71.

[5] Cf. *The Sword and the Trowel*, 1891, p. 87.

imported in English dress, however, did not inspire general confidence: there was enough to hand to make it appear that higher criticism and unbelief went together.

(ii) The Object of the Critical Enquiry.

'The real battle is over the Old Testament', wrote W. R. Nicoll in 1887.[1] And so it was. Yet the Old Testament was an integral part of the Christian Bible. And it was this which was being subjected to the critics' analysis. Throughout the history of the Church, the Old Testament, no less than the New, had been accepted as a divine revelation. In fact successive confessions and creeds had stated that Book to be an unerring and inspired record. It was the conviction of Christians through the ages that the Holy Spirit's inspiration, of which all the Scripture is a product, was not limited to the men who wrote. It was held that the sacred volumes themselves contained the words of God.

It was, then, this Book which was the object of the critical enquiry. And there was the allied question of Christ's authority. The very Old Testament which some critics gave the impression of handling lightly and dissecting freely was the Old Testament which He read and quoted. In and through its pages He found His Messiahship authenticated and His Mission vindicated. What was to be said about our Lord's authority in relation to the Old Testament. This was the issue which was to become central in the discussion.

In a comment in the *Expository Times* concerning the 'great controversy raised by the *Lux Mundi*' it was remarked, 'the real subject of dispute has been the limitation of Christ's human knowledge—a subject with which it is doubtful' the writer himself thinks, 'if the criticism of the Old Testament has anything to do'.[2] But there was no reason for this doubt. How indeed could it be otherwise? George Adam Smith, in a work in which he made a strong plea for the recognition of the higher criticism, states in the same breath the high regard our Lord had for the Old Testament. 'Above all, He fed His own soul with its contents, and in the great crises of His own life sustained Himself upon it as upon the living and sovereign Word

---

[1] W. Robertson Nicoll, 'The Coming Battle', *The British Weekly*, Vol. II, 1887, p. 225.

[2] *Expository Times*, Vols. I and II, 1889–90, i, p. 242.

of God.'[1] If He so accepted the Old Testament Scriptures, and there was no doubt that He did, then the question pressed, Was He altogether ignorant of the 'true' nature of their history and compilation? And, further, How far is that acceptance of the Old Testament, as He found it, a warrant for those who follow Him to receive it in the same way? These and other questions, as we shall see, and as later editions of the *Expository Times* came to recognize, had to be faced. Cheyne in fact openly asserted that it was the idea of our Lord's absolute authority in the whole domain of Old Testament studies which stood in the way of 'critical progress'. The real issue, he notes, is a theological one and concerns the amount of knowledge that Christ in the days of His flesh may be said to possess.[2]

(2) *Reorientation for Advance*

It will be clear from what has been observed that if the higher criticism were to advance it must needs be toned down in certain important respects. The British critic must rid himself, and openly profess that he has done so, of the taint of German scepticism. Only thus will the critical reconstruction of the Old Testament gain any wide acceptance.

(i) To begin with, a more acceptable colouring, so to say, had to be given to the historical method.

At the first, we noted earlier, historical criticism and higher criticism were virtually regarded as one and the same. And by their application of the method German critics were constantly found making statements concerning the Old Testament of a radical and revolutionary nature. The impression was given, not without reason, that the Old Testament was the result of the stringing together of stories which in themselves were rather fanciful and fabulous, but which religious men of genius and insight were to take up and use to teach certain great spiritual truths which they had discovered. Historical criticism had consequently appeared to be in the hands of such investigators

---

[1] G. A. Smith, *Modern Criticism and the Preaching of the Old Testament*, Layman Beecher Lectures, Yale, 1899 (New York, 1901), p. 11. Cf. '... the Old Testament Canon is credited in addition by an authority of which the New Testament is devoid. This is the authority of Jesus Christ Himself. . . . What was indispensable for the Redeemer must always be indispensable for the redeemed', *op. cit.*, pp. 10–11.

[2] T. K. Cheyne, *Aids to the Devout Study of Criticism*, 1892, p. 392. Cf. S. R. Driver, *Introduction to the Literature of the Old Testament*, 1891, seventh edition, 1898, Preface, p. xii f.

the very destruction of history. The very term seemed to be a misnomer. Higher criticism, thus identified with historical criticism, was considered to have torn from the pages of the Old Testament the historical reality of men whose presence was found and felt in subsequent periods.

In this country, too, there was at the beginning a tendency to give rigorous application to the historical method. George Adam Smith is therefore able to state that the criticism of the Old Testament is mainly 'historical'.[1] And as a result of the 'unsparing criticism' and the 'industrious research' of recent years many of the figures which appear in the early records were virtually eliminated from history. Allowing, for example, to the patriarchs the smallest 'substratum of actual personal history', G. A. Smith asks us, 'But who wants to be sure of more? Who needs to be sure of more?' The fact is many did: They wondered, if being left with so little, were they really assured of even this 'substratum'. If so much were gone, why was anything left? George Adam Smith was able to console his readers with the information that there was a reaction of late in favour of admitting the historical personality of Abraham. While A. M. Fairbairn, no friend it may be admitted of the critics, pronounced with emphasis his own belief in the 'real historical personality of Moses', and maintained that 'everything distinctive' in the history of Israel, 'runs back into him'. This historical significance of Moses, he insisted, can be accepted 'in face of the most recent criticism'.[2]

We will not, then, be surprised to read A. H. Sayce charging the critic with treating the biblical history 'unfairly'.[3] He begins, Sayce argued, 'with certain fixed ideas and presuppositions, which have made him deny the historical character or early date of all statements and documents which run counter to them'.[4]

There was no doubt much justification for the strong opposition to the higher criticism for its pronouncements upon the historicity of the Old Testament. History was being read as a natural development, and into that picture the Old Testament was made to fit. No catena of quotations are needed to show how

[1] Cf. G. A. Smith, *Modern Criticism and the Preaching of the Old Testament*, New York, 1901, p. 46 f.

[2] A. M. Fairbairn, *The City of God*, 1897, p. 110.

[3] A. H. Sayce, 'Biblical Archaeology and the Higher Criticism', *Expository Times*, Vol. III, 1891-2, p. 15.   [4] *Ibid.*

this 'naturalistic' view was a fundamental one in much earlier criticism. 'The Old Testament as now interpreted', observed J. Estlin Carpenter, 'tells the story of the rise and growth of a religion.'[1] And the tendency was to explain this rise and growth very much in naturalistic terms. Critics, with a certain 'naturalistic' bias, have continued this stress. Thus as late as 1932, S. A. Cook declares, 'In the Old Testament some fundamental religious ideas not unique in themselves, were uniquely shaped by Israel'.[2]

But it was not long before the radical denials of historical criticism were repudiated, and the admission of a more than natural element was being allowed.

Historical criticism tended more and more to be understood in terms which granted a larger area of historical facts which were later interpreted for the nation of Israel in a religious sense. Importance was attached to this 'tendency' view of the Old Testament accounts; the regard, that is, more for the religious valuation than the historical actuality of an event. H. Wheeler Robinson, in his most influential book, observed, 'the ancient writer felt free to mould the traditions of the past into an illustration of the convictions of the present'.[3] A. F. Kirkpatrick had earlier remarked that 'The prophets were the historians of Israel (a footnote reminds us that the Books of Joshua, Judges, Samuel and Kings are classed in the Jewish Canon as "the former prophets"). They regarded the history of the nation from a religious standpoint. They traced the direct control of Jehovah over the fortunes of His people, in mercy and judgement. It was their function to record and interpret the lessons of the past for the warning and encouragement of the present and future'.[4] Driver had laid down as a dictum that 'None of the historians of the Bible claim supernatural enlightenment for the *materials* of their narrative'.[5] In a paper entitled 'The Claims of Criticism upon the Clergy and Laity', read at the

---

[1] J. Estlin Carpenter, *The Bible in the Nineteenth Century*, 1903, p. 463.

[2] S. A. Cook, *The Place of the Old Testament in Modern Research*, 1932, p. 28.

[3] H. Wheeler Robinson, *The Religious Ideas of the Old Testament*, 1913, seventh impression, 1947, p. 4.

[4] A. F. Kirkpatrick, *The Doctrine of the Prophets*, the Warburtonian Lectures, 1886–90, third edition, 1901, p. 14.

[5] S. R. Driver, *Introduction to the Literature of the Old Testament*, 1891, seventh edition, 1898, Preface, p. x.

Church Congress at Northampton in October 1902, Kirkpatrick emphasized this natural aspect of Israel's story. God's revelation, he declared, was a gradual one 'affected to a large extent by the action of ordinary forces, developed in ways which we should call natural rather than supernatural'.[1]

This rather forbidding statement was somewhat modified by Wheeler Robinson. He appears to stress the importance of historical criticism and tells us that the religious ideas of the Old Testament are in a sense a product of its evolving history. 'Underneath the conventional form of the Old Testament literature', he states, 'critical scholarship has taught us to recognize successive strata that have built up the mountain peaks of faith and vision, each with its own fossil survivals from the past.'[2] He admits that the 'critical view of the Old Testament seems to many to exclude the reality of revelation by surrendering the history to purely naturalistic, or, at any rate, purely human factors'.[3] But he will not allow that this is so, for he claims the critical arrangement 'yields a view of the history of Israel which is natural without being naturalistic'.[4] 'The issue is not', he affirms, 'as to the presence here or there of a "supernatural" element amid "natural" conditions. The distinction, so used, is a legacy from the categories of the eighteenth century. We gain a much deeper insight into the divine activity, when we conceive the evolution of the nation's life as both natural and supernatural throughout, and not a mosaic of both.'[5] It is to Wheeler Robinson's merit to give greater emphasis to the supernatural aspect, even if, as we believe, it is not adequately related to the Old Testament account, for he tends to equate the supernatural with the prophets' religious reading of 'natural' happenings. In a later essay, he stresses the intimate connection between the natural and the supernatural within events in a more suggestive way, although, even here, we would like to have seen a greater emphasis put upon the result of God's impact upon the 'prophet's own consciousness and outlook' as yielding a permanent divine self-disclosure.[6]

[1] S. R. Driver and A. F. Kirkpatrick, *The Higher Criticism*, 1911, p. 11.
[2] H. Wheeler Robinson, *The Religious Ideas of the Old Testament*, 1913, seventh impression, 1947, p. 2.   [3] *Ibid.*, p. 216.   [4] *Ibid.*, p. 6.   [5] *Ibid.*, p. 25.
[6] H. Wheeler Robinson, 'The Philosophy of Revelation', in *Record and Revelation*, 1938. *Essays on the Old Testament* by members of the Society for Old Testament Studies (ed. H. Wheeler Robinson), pp. 315–16.

There was, however, a certain measure of dissatisfaction expressed by one and another, concerning the historical method. This can be seen in a remark of Driver's: 'I readily allow', he says, 'that there are some critics who combine with their literary criticism of the Old Testament an *historical* criticism which appears to me to be unreasonable and extreme'.[1] He, therefore, seeks to distinguish between the two.[2]

In a chapter entitled 'The Methods of Higher Criticism', T. H. Robinson draws the distinction, upon which Peake had so much insisted, between 'higher' and 'historical' criticism. Higher criticism is described as the study of the structure of any particular book or collection of books. Historical criticism deals with 'the historicity or otherwise of any narrative that may be involved'.[3] It is an 'attempt to reconstruct the history from the conflicting material at our disposal'.[4] The whole purpose, then, of all genuine Old Testament study, it is declared, 'is to discover the process by which God led Israel to higher truth'.[5] More and more, in this way, some of the outrageous statements of certain historical critics, to whom the Old Testament was merely 'idealized' history, could be discounted as not the necessary results of higher criticism. Much which the historical critic brushed aside as folk lore and legend was treated in a more factual way by the higher critic and in this respect it appeared to be less 'destructive'.

(ii) There was indeed a growing willingness to assert the *religious* value of the Old Testament, and to insist, at the same time, that the purpose of criticism was not to rob the Church of the Old Testament but to gain for it an enriched understanding. There was an evident disarming flavour about the very title T. K. Cheyne chose for his book which he entitled, *Aids to the Devout Study of Criticism*. And at the beginning of it he urges that 'true criticism must be constructive'.[6] This theme was reiterated by writer after writer. Carpenter, although he maintains that the Bible must be interpreted 'in the light of historical

---

[1] S. R. Driver, *Introduction to the Literature of the Old Testament*, 1891, Preface, p. xviii.

[2] Cf. S. R. Driver and A. F. Kirkpatrick, *The Higher Criticism*, 1911, Preface.

[3] T. H. Robinson, 'The Methods of Higher Criticism', *The People and the Book* by members of the Society for Old Testament Studies (ed. A. S. Peake), 1925, p. 154.

[4] *Ibid.*, p. 174.   [5] *Ibid.*, p. 175.

[6] T. K. Cheyne, *Aids to the Devout Study of Criticism*, 1892, p. 15.

imagination' (although some could not help feeling that the emphasis might be put on the word 'imagination' rather than 'historical'),[1] still insists that 'the true value of the Bible has been enhanced'.[2] It 'supplies the noblest witness which we have to the reality of divine things'.[3] Driver, also, in a lecture on 'The Old Testament in the Light of Today', given at the Jubilee of New College, Hampstead, Wednesday, November 7, 1900, spoke much of the 'new light' criticism has brought. Beyond the 'idealized' history, he says, there may be realized those abiding truths which lie beyond the range of criticism.[4] And H. E. Ryle, speaking at the Church Congress at Folkestone in 1892 on the 'Holy Scripture and Criticism' made the point that there can be no real quarrel between criticism and the Bible. The real conflict is between the 'progress of truth' and the sluggish inability of some minds to keep pace with it.

With assurances of this nature the higher criticism made rapid advance. George Adam Smith, before the turn of the century, contended that the battle was won. Peake's, *A Guide to Biblical Study*, and a popular and unscientific account of the higher criticism by an American, I. Gibson entitled, *Reasons for the Higher Criticism of the Hexateuch*, did much to accelerate the progress. Thus before the century ended it was declared that the Churches had 'passed from opposition to acquiescence'.[5] While a comment on W. H. Green the author of *The Higher Criticism and the Pentateuch*, refers to him 'as the one scholar who rejects the results of criticism'.[6] Although this remark is certainly exaggerated it serves to indicate its spread. The influence of the higher criticism, says a reviewer of H. T. Knight's *Criticism and the Old Testament,* had already penetrated to 'the country clergyman'. 'Now', he continues, 'however, he (i.e. the country clergyman) seems to be awake all over the country. One evidence of this is the meetings of the Church Congress, another the letters in the newspapers, a third the books on Higher Criticism that are written and read so numerously.'[7]

---

[1] J. Estlin Carpenter, *The Bible in the Nineteenth Century*, 1903, p. 511.
[2] *Ibid.*, p. 453.   [3] *Ibid.*, p. 512.
[4] Cf. S. R. Driver, 'Essay in The Higher Criticism', 1911, reprinted from the *Expositor*, January 1901, p. 27 f.
[5] *Expository Times*, Vol. VIII, 1896–7, p. 196.
[6] *Op. cit.*, Vol. VII, 1895–6, p. 227.
[7] *Op. cit.*, Vol. XVIII, 1906–7, p. 279.

Higher criticism seemed to be so well established that it was possible for Peake to talk of its 'assured results'. As time went on, however, these began to appear less secure. Thus in the volume *The People and the Book*, J. E. McFadyen has things to say to those who had supposed that all was settled. Allowing that there is a certain agreement on the broad outline, he adds, that on details 'there is at the moment practically no unanimity anywhere'.[1] No sooner is a position 'established' than it is challenged and critics professing to use the same methods arrive at widely different conclusions. McFadyen does not admit that this 'kaleidoscopic confusion' discredits the use of the method,[2] but he does quote Herrmann to the effect that today the Pentateuchal problem is more open than ever and that the era of purely literary criticism, which was believed to be as good as closed, is far from anything of the kind.

More recently the same point is made with sharpness by H. H. Rowley. 'Many of the conclusions that seemed most sure', he writes, 'have been challenged, and there is now a greater variety of view on many questions than has been known for a long time.'[3] This statement needs to be well pondered by those parsons and school-teachers who are teaching with an assured dogmatism theories they learned in their training colleges years ago. Rowley maintains that 'In general, it may be said, that there is a tendency towards more conservative views on many questions than were common at the opening of our period'.[4] This conservatism, he agrees, is the fruit of the critical method. And he believes it to be, therefore, 'both other and firmer than the old conservatism, just because it is critically, not dogmatically based'.[5]

It was, perhaps, inevitable that criticism should find itself in this position. Many of the ideas from which it sprang seem to be no longer tenable. The whole environment of thought has changed, and gone with it are the optimism and confidence displayed by the earlier advocates of the critical method. Besides, the claim that criticism was giving a Bible more readily under-

---

[1] J. E. McFadyen, 'The Present Position of Old Testament Criticism', *The People and the Book* by members of the Society for Old Testament Studies (ed. A. S. Peake), 1925, p. 183.   [2] *Ibid.*, p. 184. Cf. p. 194 f.

[3] H. H. Rowley, *The Old Testament and Modern Study* by members of the Society for Old Testament Studies, 1951, Preface, p. xvi.

[4] *Ibid.*, p. xvii.   [5] *Ibid.*, p. xviii.

stood has not been fulfilled. The reconstructions suggested have been so many and so intricate that the ordinary person has not been able to follow. Indeed, it was boldly stated by J. Estlin Carpenter that the Bible which must be interpreted in the light of historical imagination means that 'modern study has not made it an easy book for the casual reader'.[1] Herbert Danby has observed that 'There has been a lessening of interest in the Old Testament since the beginning of the present century. Old controversies have died down, and indifference has taken their place. A defensive, almost a diffident, attitude is considered fitting to him who today would put forward the Old Testament's claim to be a usable and even a useful item in the Christian's spiritual armoury'.[2] How much this indifferent attitude derives from the uncertainty concerning the Old Testament due to the higher criticism is not easy to assess. But it is without doubt that the influence in this direction is not small.[3]

C. THE ATTACK ON CRITICISM

There has always been a readiness among critics to dismiss as obscurantists those who refuse to credit their views. They could not believe it possible for any to be thoroughly acquainted with and aware of their arguments in favour of the critical position and honestly to reject their validity. But the sheer fact is that some did, and more do. It was too confidently claimed that scholarship was always on the critics' side. Emil Reich, who for many years, he tells us, 'fully believed in the "scientific character" of Higher Criticism' recalls something of its ' "scientific" spell'.[4] He observed with some justification that 'By far the majority of the public bow to Higher Criticism out of a vague yet strong

---

[1] J. Estlin Carpenter, *The Bible in the Nineteenth Century*, 1903, p. 511.

[2] Herbert Danby, 'The Old Testament', *The Study of Theology* (ed. H. E. Kirk), 1939, p. 189.

[3] Cf. 'Foremost among the influences causing unbelief was that of modern Biblical Criticism', W. B. Selbie, paper on 'Difficulties of Belief' read at the Congregational Union, Glasgow, 1902.

Referring to A. J. Balfour's address at the Centenary of the British and Foreign Bible Society in the Mansion House, London, March 6, 1903, in which Balfour speaks of the critical view of Scripture which chills enthusiasm and damps ardour, the *British Weekly*, March 13, 1903, adds: 'Mr Balfour must surely know that many of the Higher Critics have ceased to be believers'.

[4] Emil Reich, *The Failure of the Higher Criticism*, 1905, Preface, p. v.

feeling of awe caused by the alleged character of that Criticism. People really do think that Higher Criticism is part of the undoubted scientific progress in which we moderns glory'.[1]

The attack on criticism was long and sustained. It will be already realized how vehemently opposed to higher criticism was A. H. Sayce. He was, of course, not chiefly an Old Testament scholar, but an Assyriologist. In his book, *The Early History of the Hebrews*, however, he gives a fairly competent summary of the critical reconstruction. He then contends, on the basis of archaeology and other data, that the correct reading of the history of the Hebrews is in conflict with that reconstruction. To choose the one, he argues, is to reject the other. The critical method of writing, or, as he thinks, of rewriting Israel's history, is, he declares, 'worthless'. In an article in the *Expository Times*, he asserts that 'the term "higher criticism" is an unfortunate one. It has the appearance of pretentiousness, and it is to be feared that in some cases it has led to the unconscious assumption of a tone of superiority on the part of its confessors and their followers'.[2] Sayce argues that 'The conclusions of the "higher criticism" were supported by an assumption and a tendency'. The assumption was that writing was unknown at the time of the Exodus; and the tendency 'was the extreme scepticism with which the earlier periods of secular history were regarded'.[3] Ellicott, too, from the point of view of our Lord's authority took exception to the critical methods and conclusions.[4] Under the title, 'Is the Old Testament Authentic?', J. Elder Cumming of Glasgow contributed a series of articles to the *Expository Times* in which he sought to meet certain stated results of criticism. The 'authors of the New Criticism' he says, 'have claimed to have invalidated the entire historical accuracy of the earlier portions of the history of Israel, as well as the still earlier history which the Old Testament embodies'.[5] This claim Cumming will not grant. He cannot admit an opposition between the priestly and the prophetic elements in Israel, and

---

[1] Emil Reich, *The Failure of the Higher Criticism*, 1905, pp. 72-3.

[2] *Expository Times*, Vol. III, 1891-2, p. 15.

[3] *Op. cit.*, p. 17.

[4] *Op. cit.*, Vol. III, 1891-2, pp. 157 f., 235 f., 359 f., 457 f., 538 f.; Vol. IV, 1893-4, pp. 169 f., 362 f., 450 f.

[5] *Op.cit.*, Vol. VI, 1894-5, p. 61; cf. pp. 166, 308 f., 421 f. Vol. VII, 1895-6, p. 38 f.

consequently duplicate documents reflecting these separate outlooks. He cogently repudiates the idea that the discovery of the book in the Temple in the reign of Josiah in 620 BC was, as Cheyne and a number of other critics maintained, its first appearance. It was, he insists, not the original authorship of Deuteronomy that is here recounted, but the discovery of that lost book.

These references are taken from substantial articles attacking criticism. But there were besides, on platform and in pamphlet, much more of a popular kind most of which was ranting rather than relevant. Many, not understanding criticism, fell upon the critic. As a consequence action was often substituted for argument: zeal was mistaken for knowledge. What was lacking in information was made up for in perspiration. The loud voice, the thumped pulpit, the poorly written booklet were thought by many a sufficient answer to the patient and scholarly work of the Old Testament critic. Some imagined it to be enough to surround the term 'critic' with a distasteful odour. It can therefore be understood why the careful critic impatiently dismissed some of his opponents as obscurantists.

But this was not the whole story. There were critics of criticism as painstaking as those who took the other view. Some of these works can still be examined with profit; and they must be by anyone who seeks to give any sort of true account of the battle of the standpoints.

We will refer first in chronological order to some major works. One of the most scholarly opponents of criticism was Professor James Robertson of Glasgow. In his Baird Lectures he sought to establish that the prophets are not earlier than the law. Then in his later Croall Lectures of 1893–4 on *The Poetry and Religion of the Psalms,* he rejected the position of those who sought a later date for the Psalms. Robertson, therefore, endeavoured to restore the traditional order of Law, Psalms and Prophets. He was convinced that we do possess pre-exilic psalms and he sees no valid arguments which hinder David from being a psalmist. Driver takes Robertson to task in a contemporary issue of the *Critical Review* and urged that his conclusions are out of touch with even those of 'moderate criticism'. Commenting on Driver's notice of Robertson's work the *Expository Times* remarked that the Glasgow professor 'seems to be the only opponent of the Higher Criticism whom the critics now consider worthy of reply'.[1]

In 1894 the formidable volume entitled, *Lex Mosaica, or The Law of Moses and the Higher Criticism* appeared. This is a work by a number of scholars well acquainted with the critical arguments. The Introduction was written by the Bishop of Bath and Wells: and among the contributors are men of such reputation as George Rawlinson, who was at one time Camden Professor of Ancient History at Oxford; F. Watson, Lecturer of Theology and Fellow of St John's College, Cambridge; Henry Wace, Principal of King's College, London; Stanley Leathes, Professor of Hebrew in the same place. The Preface of this considerable tome refers to the 'Sporadic efforts' that 'have been already made by responsible writers to show that the new position is either untenable or fraught with greater difficulties than the traditional view'. The writers show thorough competence in dealing with their subject. In every case the critical view is given fair statement. It is noted in one place that the concern is not for those critics who deny the supernatural. It is for 'those who admit a revelation from God in the sense in which the term is ordinarily understood'.[2] Lias in his essay on 'The Times of Samuel and Saul' urges that no one need repudiate criticism as such. There is a good and a bad criticism. Much criticism, however, is destructive. Lias comes out strongly against the historical criticism of Robertson Smith. 'The history, we are told, has been re-written at a later period, and these details have been introduced, some say with a purpose, and others under a mistaken impression. Anyhow, the history, in the opinion of the critics, has been falsified, or at the least revised, under the influence of a dominating idea. But this is not to study documents "in the light of history", it is to study them in the light of historical speculation.'[3] It is not, of course, possible, nor is it quite to our purpose, to summarize in any detail this massive volume. Throughout its pages all the works then available of the leading critics, German, British and American, come into review. There are abundant references to Wellhausen, Keil, Briggs, Robertson Smith, Driver, Cheyne, and so on. The writers are convinced about the importance of their task. They

[1] *Expository Times*, Vol. X, 1898–9, p. 242.
[2] *Lex Mosaica*, 1894, p. 77.   [3] *Op. cit.*, p. 207.

feel that the critical ideas are inconsistent with a true understanding of Scripture; it is declared 'that the view put forward
by the new school of criticism is inconsistent alike with the
language of the prophets and the facts of history'.[1] The critical
theory, it is stated, 'has already involved grave questions
respecting the limits of our Lord's authority and knowledge, and
it must entail not less grave questions respecting the authority
and the inspiration of the Apostles and Evangelists'.[2] The
writers claim to have subjected the issue of criticism 'to a fresh
and thorough historical investigation'. And they conclude that
as a result the critical theory is unacceptable. They find nothing
to compel the conclusion that this ancient book, any more than
any other ancient historical record, was 'composed like a
tessellated pavement, in which several unknown sources are
dovetailed into one another, sometimes in the most minute
pieces'.[3] Any other nation would have found the process difficult,
'but it would be tenfold more difficult in the case of the Jews,
one of whose chief characteristics, at once their strength and
their danger, is their intense tenacity, and who were always, for
good or for harm, "a stiff-necked people" '.[4]

Her Majesty's Printers, Eyre and Spottiswoode, in 1894,
published a book by W. L. Baxter called *Sanctuary and Sacrifice,
A Reply to Wellhausen*. The first of the two parts into which the
book is divided consists of a series of four contributions to *The
Thinker* magazine for November and December 1893, and for
March and April 1894. Baxter really limits himself to an
examination of Wellhausen's *Prolegomena to the History of
Israel* in this volume of his of over 500 pages. 'We have not
sought', Baxter declares, 'to weigh the *theological value* of
Wellhausen's conclusions; our exclusive occupation has been in
*assailing the truth, and the warrantableness of the definite positions,
which he successively propounds.*'[5] He believed that the errors
which he has revealed in the pages of the 'most admired
champion' of the Higher Criticism will show how fragile the
whole critical thesis is.

Baxter's book cannot honestly be said to have had any great
effect. It was limited to one individual whom the British critic

---

[1] *Lex Mosaica*, p. 612.
[2] *Op. cit.*, p. 611.   [3] *Op. cit.*, p. 617.   [4] *Op. cit.*, p. 618.
[5] W. L. Baxter, *Sanctuary and Sacrifice*, 1896, p. 505 (italics in original).

could plead did not represent their more believing approach. At any rate Wellhausen was not stirred to reply: this may, of course, have been because a much more formidable attack was about to be issued against him by Hommel, Professor of Assyriology at Munich, and he, we are told, was 'a foeman worthy of any critic's steel'. It is, however, much more likely that Wellhausen did not deem it necessary to reply to Baxter. Yet A. S. Peake does rally to Wellhausen's defence. In a long and detailed review of *Sanctuary and Sacrifice*, he asserts that 'Wellhausen's contribution is relevant to the state of criticism at the time'.[1] It seems that Baxter was assailing a position which was already out of date. Yet there is a remark made by Baxter which hints that he was expecting some such 'defence'. Baxter refers to 'A recent volume, with a notable affectation of "Lux", was fain, on this topic, to execute a somewhat helpless retreat into "Flux". But there may be times', he adds, 'when "Flux" is treason'.[2] Peake maintains that Baxter's arguments will make no difference to others, as, is to be expected, they have made no difference to him. Baxter comes back to the attack upon Peake's criticisms in a later issue of the *Expository Times*.[3]

John Smith calls his book in which he attacks criticism, *The Integrity of Scripture*. There is a subtitle describing it as 'Plain Reasons for Rejecting the Critical Hypothesis'. Smith had been for a year a class-fellow of Robertson Smith at Aberdeen. The book is really a series of discourses given to the congregation of Broughton Place Church, Edinburgh, and the Preface states that 'They are not to be considered as a discussion from a purely critical standpoint, though it is believed that they expose the fundamental logical fallacies pervading the critical method'. The titles of the chapters show that Smith knew how to make his points. He was well aware of the issues involved in the 'new construction'. He is also convinced that 'The standpoint of the prophets is the reverse of what modern criticism avers'.[4] They do not speak, he argues, to a people slowly emerging from polytheism to monotheism. He objects to the reduction of the authentic history of the Old Testament to the barest minimum

[1] *Expository Times*, Vol. VII, 1895–6, p. 401; cf. pp. 400–5.
[2] W. L. Baxter, *Sanctuary and Sacrifice*, 1896, p. 505.
[3] *Expository Times*, Vol. VII, 1895–6, p. 505 f. But the battle of words continued, cf., e.g. Peake's reply, *ibid.*, pp. 559 ff.
[4] John Smith, *The Integrity of Scripture*, 1902, p. 57.

as evidenced by his namesake, Robertson Smith and George Adam Smith. He shows the difficulties in the disintegrating process and the embarrassing results.

There are, he contends, 'no external standards outside the sacred writings by which to judge of their date and authorship'.[1] He will not allow that it was the imagination working on 'the *tabula rasa* of the wilderness', quoting Wellhausen's phrase, which reared the hierarchical system pictured in Exodus. 'Where the Higher Critics, in our judgement', he says, 'have gone astray is, in supposing, against tradition and the strongest internal evidences, that, with whatever differences, Jewish sacred history followed the same course of natural development; and in applying methods, suitable enough in dealing with common human fact and growth of legend, to a totally different situation, the incoming of a true revelation of God, and its creative influence on the life and institutions of the people.'[2] The critical reconstruction of Scripture he regards as inadequate and improbable. The result is an hypothesis built upon hypotheses. 'Thus pulled down and built up, the Old Testament is a book out of which the very soul of revelation has gone.'[3] Smith's book breathes the very atmosphere of devotion. He was, as one reviewer states, 'absorbed in the religion of the Bible'. 'The critics have their minds on its science, Dr Smith has his on its religion.' 'And in these days', the same writer adds, 'when so many preachers of the religion of the Bible are spending their time on its science, we rejoice exceedingly in the whole-hearted devotion to what is first and last in Bible study.'[4]

A year after Smith's work came Thomas Whitelaw's *Old Testament Critics, An Enquiry into the Character, Effect, and Validity of their Teaching*. This volume is marked by an adequate scholarship. The author was well acquainted with the main teachers and theories of criticism. It is, however, not his intention 'to vindicate the traditional theory of the origin and structure of the Old Testament or to undertake the removal of such difficulties in connection therewith as are usually felt by honest doubters or anxious seekers after truth'.[5] It will be his

[1] John Smith, *The Integrity of Scripture*, 1902, p. 117.   [2] *Ibid.*, pp. 131-2.
[3] *Ibid.*, p. 163.
[4] *Expository Times*, Vol. XIII, 1901-2, p. 472.
[5] Thomas Whitelaw, *Old Testament Critics*, 1903, Introduction, p. xiii.

endeavour to present the doctrines of the critics 'in as colourless
a light as possible, with no exaggeration in either one direction
or other'.[1] Whitelaw restricts his enquiry to four main topics:
The Manufacture of the Hexateuch, The Colouring of the
History Books, The Extrusion of David from the Psalter, and
The Disintegration of the Prophets. In part two of the volume
he deals with 'The Indemnity of the Critics, or The Cost of the
Higher Criticism (to be paid by the Christian People)'. He
notes what the 'advanced' German critics have surrendered and
what the 'believing critic' questions. In the third part of the
book, Whitelaw institutes a 'criticism of the critics'. He quotes
the words of Dr Mead: 'The right to criticize a critic's theories,
is as sacred as the right of the critic to propound them'.[2]

Whitelaw questions what he regards as certain critical presuppositions. It is maintained that the Bible was subject to the
usual processes of composition and should be approached as any
other book. Having said that and done that then the critic goes
on to insist that the Bible is no ordinary book. Sanday remarks,
'Let us by all means study the Bible, if we will, like any other
book, but do not let us beg the question that it is wholly like any
other book'.[3] It is to be approached critically like any other
volume, but as John Ker asks, 'Is this possible?'[4] There is a
spiritual and moral element in the Bible which are absent from
all other books. It is indeed itself the critic, judging our thoughts
and uncovering our need.

Certain 'improbabilities of criticism' as Whitelaw calls them[5],
are considered, as, for example, the complete disappearance
from the world's and the Church's knowledge of all the great
men the critics have discovered to have been authors and
redactors of the principal parts of the Hebrew Scriptures.
Cornhill has identified twenty-six hands at work in the production of the Hexateuch. But 'the alphabetical gentlemen who
have been ticketed J,E,D,P,R,&c', have passed into oblivion.[6]
The pros and cons of the documentary hypothesis are intelli-
gently discussed.[7] Whitelaw cannot accept the contention that

[1] Thomas Whitelaw, *Old Testament Critics*, 1903, p. 1.
[2] *Ibid.*, p. 169.
[3] W. Sanday, *Inspiration*, Bampton Lectures, 1893, third edition, 1908, p. 2.
[4] John Ker, *Thoughts for Life and Heart*, n.d., p. 89.
[5] Thomas Whitelaw, *Old Testament Critics*, 1903, pp. 192 ff.
[6] *Ibid.*, p. 205.   [7] *Ibid.*, pp. 212 ff.

there are no Davidic psalms.[1] Concluding with the three criteria of 'immediate luminousness, philosophic reasonableness, and moral helpfulness', which William James has set forth in his recent Gifford Lectures,[2] Whitelaw maintains that the critical theory examined in the light of these tests is found wanting.

It will be expected that a reference should be made to James Orr's Bross Prize volume, *The Problem of the Old Testament*, which was published in 1906. No justice can possibly be done to its contents here. It is a work of accurate scholarship and profound knowledge of the subject.[3] Orr gives due respect to those critics who are 'convinced upholders of supernatural revelation'.[4] He understands that there is a right higher criticism which is 'simply the careful scrutiny, on the principles which are customary to apply to all literature, of the actual phenomena of the Bible, with a view to deduce from these such conclusions as may be warranted regarding age, authorship, mode of composition, sources, etc., of the different books'.[5] But he then goes on to bring weighty arguments against the critical presuppositions. These he regards in general as the ideas of the natural development of Israel's religion and the equation of revelation with a mere providential guidance of history. Having attacked these necessary assumptions, Orr then deals with the superstructure which has been reared upon such foundations. He concludes his book with a reference to the culmination of the progressive revelation of the Old Testament in the Christ of the New. It is He who clasps the two into one: and in His light the Old Testament finds its significance. He calls for, what is now seen to have been needed, a deeper understanding of the connection of the Old Testament with the New. It is this connection, he declares, which gives to the critical problems their keenest interest. 'The tendency of late', he maintains, writing at the beginning of the century, 'has been to make too light of this connection. The storm of criticism which, in the last decades, assailed the Old Testament, was fondly thought by

---

[1] Thomas Whitelaw, *Old Testament Critics*, 1903, p. 307.

[2] Cf. William James, *Varieties of Religious Experience*, 1902, sixteenth edition, p. 18.

[3] Cf. 'Dr Orr's work is of a very different quality from the screaming invective of an Emil Reich', *Expository Times*, Vol. XVII, 1905–6, p. 320.

[4] James Orr, *The Problem of the Old Testament*, 1906, seventh impression, 1909, p. 8.   [5] *Ibid.*, p. 9.

many to leave intact the New Testament. What mattered it about Abraham and Moses, so long as Jesus and His Gospel remained? This delusion is passing away. The fact is becoming apparent to the dullest which has long been evident to unbiased observers, that much of the radical criticism of the Old Testament proceeded on principles, and was conducted by methods, which had only to be applied with like thoroughness to the New Testament to work like havoc. The fundamental ideas of God and His revelation which underlay that criticism could not, as we set out by affirming, lead up to a doctrine of the Incarnation, but only to a negation of it.'[1]

In addition to these larger works there were others of lesser proportions emanating from the learned which attacked criticism. Of the more important of these volumes of slender dimensions a passing reference need only be made here.

The volumes of the Bible Students' Library were designed to meet the critical challenge. R. B. Girdlestone in the first book in the series set forth the results of his own 'studies in Old Testament criticism'. He assures his readers that neither the increasing knowledge of Old Testament Hebrew, nor the discoveries of some old manuscripts have tended to shake men's faith in the trustworthiness of the Sacred Books, but rather is it because 'the critics have been influenced by a growing disinclination to regard the Bible as *unique*'.[2] He believes that the traditional view of the Old Testament 'fits fairly with the facts all round'. He has sought throughout his discussion to be 'rational and reverential'.[3] Critics, he claims, do not pay enough attention to what the author of an Old Testament book 'says of himself'. He admits that both sides in the controversy have not been blameless. 'We have been afraid', he says, 'of allowing textual corruption, late editorial work, the use of ordinary materials, and human ways of putting things. We have confused inspiration with omnipotence, and have forgotten that the Sacred Truth is committed to earthen vessels. We have minimized inconsistencies and refused to face difficulties. We have imported modern science into ancient books, and have sought to shut up those questions of age and authorship which

[1] James Orr, *The Problem of the Old Testament*, 1906, 1909, p. 477.
[2] R. B. Girdlestone, *The Foundations of the Bible*, 1890, fourth edition, revised, 1892, Preface, p. v.   [3] *Ibid.*, p. 193.

God in His providence has left open.'[1] Yet the Bible is falsely regarded if it is thought of as an ordinary book. It is not an ordinary Book, since it is the result of the action of the Spirit of God, who restrained and impelled its writers. It was produced by inspired men: and this reality no critic can dare to neglect. Things human and divine are woven throughout. We have natural phenomena and national polity and history from a Divine point of view, and we must throw all the side-lights we can on the physics and metaphysics, on the history and biography, of Scripture.[2] These books of Scripture are evidently on the side of truth and righteousness. They bear the marks of fidelity and reveal themselves to be of God.

Leathes, who had already given the Bampton Lectures on the subject 'The Religion of Christ', dealt with *The Law and the Prophets* in the second volume and refused the critical conclusions. Lias, who with the other two contributed to the *Lex Mosaica*, wrote in the third book in the series on *Principles of Criticism*. The *Church Times* describes this work, though small of compass, to be an 'admirable . . . exposition of the ingenious puzzles which German criticism has been weaving under the guise of truth'. Lias, who had been a Hulsean lecturer, in this work enforced some of the points he makes in the *Lex Mosaica*.

In 1900, at the invitation of W. Robertson Nicoll, D. S. Margoliouth produced in a book a series of articles he had contributed to the *Expositor* for the same year. Margoliouth was at the time the Laudian Professor of Arabic in Oxford, and this work is punctuated with discussions of Arabic and Hebrew words and passages. His purpose is to show the genuineness of the Christian revelation in the Bible and exhibit its superiority and supremacy. In Chapter VII, the only one which did not appear in the *Expositor*, he deals with 'The Principles of Criticism'. A 'sound argument' he urges, 'is one in which the major premise claims assent on all occasions, whether the particular consequence deduced gives pain or pleasure to him who deduces it'.[3] It is his idea that certain facts have thrown the

---

[1] R. B. Girdlestone, *The Foundations of the Bible*, 1890, fourth edition, revised, 1892, p. 196.

[2] *Ibid.*, pp. 196–7.

[3] D. S. Margoliouth, *Lines of Defence of the Biblical Revelation*, 1900, p. 277.

major premise of criticism into confusion. To face these facts would be to discredit 'the *whole* of the Higher Criticism'. He charges the critic with evading these disconcerting facts rather than acknowledge that they have made the colossal error which they have.

A passing reference was made earlier to Emil Reich's *The Failure of the 'Higher Criticism' of the Bible.*[1] Of the five chapters in it the first two appeared in the *Contemporary Review* for February and April 1905. Reich was an historian of some repute. It is, however, impossible to credit him with having fulfilled his intention in this volume. 'It is intended', he declared, 'not only to destroy the "scientific" spell of "Higher Criticism", but also to construct the right method of comprehending the Bible.'[2] The most enthusiastic supporter of his position must allow that he has not carried out his promise. A reading of the book will reveal, however, that he was in touch with an extensive literature in French and German as well as English. Reich maintained that it was impossible to separate between historical and literary criticism. And as a consequence he insists that to 'deny or question the received authorship, text, and dates of the books of the Bible, i.e. the Higher Critics, do thereby declare that the Bible is a forgery'.[3] To deny Abraham is, he contends, to deny Jesus. His conclusion is: 'Higher Criticism stands condemned by history fully as much as by true religion. It is neither true nor helpful. It is the distortion of historical truth as well as the desecration of true religion'.[4]

In his *Bible Under Trial: Apologetic Papers in View of Present-Day Assaults on Holy Scripture*, James Orr gives a popular exposition of critical conclusions and his attack upon them. The volume is marked by Orr's usual accurate scholarship. He shows, and he has Cheyne for his support, how indebted criticism is to Deism.[5] He feels that criticism 'is for the present so settled on its lees in its confidence in its immoveable results that little anyone can say will make any impression on it'.[6] Orr, however,

---

[1] Cf. p. 118 and see p. 126 (footnote).
[2] Emil Riech, *The Failure of the Higher Criticism*, 1905, Preface, p. vi.
[3] *Ibid.*, p. 82.   [4] *Ibid.*, p. 193.
[5] Cf. James Orr, *The Bible Under Trial*, 1907, p. 16; see T. K. Cheyne, *The Founders of Criticism*, 1893, pp. 1–2 and H. D. McDonald, *Ideas of Revelation*, 1959, Ch. iii.
[6] James Orr, *The Bible Under Trial*, p. 54.

is quite convinced that neither is the confidence justified nor are the results secure. 'No argument', he observes, 'is more frequently employed to silence objection to modern critical theories than the alleged agreement of competent scholars as to the main results of their criticism.'[1] Orr, however, contends that these 'settled results' are advertised rather than actual. He is certain that the new view which reconstructs the Old Testament record 'not only inverts the Bible's own account of Israel's history and institutions; it cancels that history in large part altogether, and proposes for acceptance another'.[2] It 'lifts off its hinges the history of worship and literature in Israel as hitherto accepted' as Delitzsch remarked concerning Wellhausen's theory. Orr will not grant that the Old Testament history can be resolved into myths.

He points out how naturally the ideas undergirding Old Testament criticism are passed on into the New Testament. He can quote N. Schmidt's *The Prophet of Nazareth* in this connection. Schmidt boldly affirmed that 'The movement could not stop at the Old Testament'.[3] Applying the so-called 'historical-religious' method to the gospels, What view of Jesus results? We are left with a sketchy Picture of a Humanitarian Jesus who, by reason of His good deeds, was supplied with supernatural qualities by His enthusiastic followers. Against such a naturalistic conception, the natural result of the critical doctrine continued into the New Testament, Christian faith and experience are in flat contradiction. Dealing with the 'Opposition of Science', Orr declares 'that neither Christianity nor the Bible are in the slightest danger from the results that genuine science has succeeded in establishing'.[4] He warns, however, against trying to read the Bible as a textbook on modern science. It was not within its purpose to anticipate recent astronomical discoveries.

In two of his volumes, Robert Anderson dealt with Higher Criticism from the point of view of a legal expert. His *The Bible and Modern Criticism* carries a Preface by Bishop Moule of Durham, and was noted in *The Times* as 'A vigorous criticism of the methods of the "Higher Critics" '. His *Pseudo-Criticism*,

---

[1] James Orr, *The Bible Under Trial*, p. 73.   [2] *Ibid.*, p. 97.
[3] *Ibid.*, p. 150; cf. N. Schmidt, *The Prophet of Nazareth*, 1905, p. 29.
[4] *Ibid.*, p. 200.

or *The Higher Criticism and its Counterfeit,* was, according to *The English Churchman,* 'a masterpiece of apologetics'.

In his *Daniel in the Critics' Den,* Anderson makes a spirited attack on Farrar and Driver. He had earlier made a 'Reply to Dean Farrar's *Book of Daniel*' in the *Blackwood Magazine* and this volume contains that 'Reply' as well as an examination of Driver's *Book of Daniel* in the Cambridge Bible series. Anderson cogently argues for the historicity of Daniel and he cannot justify in any degree Farrar's statement regarding it as an 'avowed fiction'.[1] It is not as the Dean openly contended an 'idle legend abounding in "violent errors" of the grossest kind'.[2] The higher criticism is, according to Anderson, 'a rationalistic "crusade" ' which seeks 'to account for the Bible on naturalistic principles'.[3]

If Robert Anderson seeks to rehabilitate Daniel as an historical reality in Israel's story, the same desire is shown for Jonah by L. T. Townsend. In his book, *The Story of Jonah in the Light of Modern Criticism* (1897), he writes with conviction regarding the literal truthfulness of the account. There is a compelling logic in his approach.

In 1896 J. Cynddlyan Jones delivered the Davies Lectures on 'The Mosaic Theology'. These were published under the title *Primeval Revelation.* They are really a consideration of the first eight chapters of Genesis. Jones tells us that he examined the critical hypothesis and also the traditional view and having 'once and again wavered in my decision', he says, 'he dipped finally on the traditional side'. It must be confessed, however, that Jones introduced certain 'liberal' views into his allegiance to the traditional idea. He maintained for example, that Moses wrote the fragments which have gone into the composition of the Pentateuch during the period of the wilderness wanderings and that these were later cemented into a whole.

Henry Harris in 1890 produced his book, *The Old Testament Scriptures*—a work of a sound scholar and a clear thinker. He endeavoured to allay the rising fears over the outcome of the critical procedure. He maintained that there was much in the Old Testament beyond the ability of criticism to touch.

---

[1] Robert Anderson, *Daniel in the Critics' Den,* n.d., fourth edition, p. 7; cf. F. W. Farrar, *The Book of Daniel,* 1901, p. 43.
[2] *Ibid.*; cf. F. W. Farrar, *The Book of Daniel,* p. 119.   [3] *Ibid.,* p. 11.

The following year Clement Clemance wrote on *How to Treat the Bible*. He had no desire either to bless or to ban higher criticism, but he sought to guide puzzled readers to find a meaning in the Scriptures for themselves. James Lindsay about the same time, writing on *The Significance of the Old Testament for Modern Theology*, after a summary account of the criticism of the previous fifty years, concludes with the assurance that the Bible still possesses a spiritual significance for 'the wise reader'.

Other writers were even more anxious to stress the continual usefulness and value of the Bible even allowing for the acceptance of certain critical ideas. J. B. Snell in his *Gain or Loss?*—a series of five lectures given at Brixton Independent Chapel on the topic 'Recent Biblical Criticism' concludes that, in spite of all that has been said about the Bible it is still with us and still speaks to us: and if it is not God's word, it is very like it! R. L. Ottley in his Bampton Lectures of 1897 on *Aspects of the Old Testament* entered the field of Old Testament study, not as an authority himself but, he says, as one who has made himself acquainted with what was going on in this sphere. His intention in these lectures is to relieve the stress on faith which recent criticism has introduced, and to make people, especially teachers and students, appreciate the religious significance and value of the Bible itself.

We shall conclude this account of the battle of the standpoints with a reference to two volumes, one at the end of the last century and one of recent date, in which it will be noted how from different approaches the same conclusion is reached.

The first volume is that of Adolph Saphir, *The Divine Unity of Scripture*. Saphir originated in Germany and had a thorough training in German philosophy and literature. As a youth he had been attracted by Hegelianism as well as the prevalent materialism. He had also been a Jew but was converted to Christianity, so that here too he had an advantage. Saphir had a thorough grasp of the critical thesis.[1] The book to which we refer comprises a series of lectures delivered in Kensington at the close of the year 1888 and the beginning of 1889. The date

[1] Cf. 'He (Saphir) goes to the facts himself with as much knowledge and discernment as the ablest, and he fairly states the things he has himself honestly come by. If there are any persons who have been shaken through the incredible answers of hurried orthodoxy, let him seek this book. It is clear, considerate, and convincing', *The Expository Times*, Vol. V, 1893-4, p. 46.

is important since it was right in the midst of an era when all the stress was on the diversity of the Bible, and it was viewed, for the most part, as a collection of heterogeneous fragments.

Saphir's approach is that of a strictly conservative evangelical. He saw, as few in his day saw, the need to pay attention to the unity of the Bible. He says, 'notwithstanding all the complex and manifold character of the Old Testament revelation, which was unfolded very slowly "at sundry times, and in diverse manners", and in which there were a great many elements combined, that appear to us at first sight not to be spiritual but rather ephemeral—notwithstanding all this, there was great simplicity and great unity'.[1] He refers, for example, to the idea of the divine 'election' into God's 'covenant' mercy as constituting a fundamental principle of that divine unity.[2]

Saphir stresses also that the history of Israel is 'theological' history.[3] It is history written in the prophetic spirit, the object of which is to show God's will to us and His purposes concerning the human race, what man is to think of God, and what life it is that God requires of man.[4] He will, however, insist that it is genuine history which is being recorded. The Greeks and Romans as they advanced sought to discard their early history. It was otherwise with Israel. Old Testament history, unlike ancient history generally, is as Niebuhr remarked, free from all 'national patriotic falsehood'. It is unadorned, sober and severe. In the Bible ideas and facts unite to make it the history of redemption. 'Ideas without facts make up a philosophy. Facts without ideas make up a history.' But 'all Scripture facts are full of ideas'.[5] The history of the Bible cannot however be understood in any 'natural' way. The difficulty in accepting its history is not due to lack of evidence for its historical and geographical accuracy. 'The difficulty lies in this, that the things which are spiritual—and, above all, God Himself—can only be the object of faith; and this whole Bible history is a history in which God is the great agent, and Israel only responding to His agency, and afterwards the Church only responding to His agency.'[6]

Saphir contends, without any reserve, for the human element in the Bible. It is 'the Word of God', he says, 'and yet an

---

[1] Adolph Saphir, *The Divine Unity of Scripture*, 1892, p. 244.
[2] *Ibid.*, cf. pp. 250 ff. [3] *Ibid.*, p. 303.
[4] *Ibid.*, p. 241. [5] *Ibid.*, p. 201. [6] *Ibid.*, p. 210.

intensely human book, written by men and for men, and breathing everywhere the atmosphere of human life and human emotions'.[1] He notes nevertheless that Christ never spoke 'of the ideas of Scripture, of the teaching of Scripture, of the promises of Scripture, of this or that in Scripture, of "the divine element" in the Scripture, as our moderns would say, or of the Word of God contained in the Scripture'.[2] He simply spoke of 'the Scripture'. He therefore rejects the need for and the possibility of any verifying faculty for judging of the disclosures within the Bible. Saphir is however concerned throughout to maintain the unity of the Scripture. Its truths are not put before us 'in a systematic and methodical form, so that doctrine succeeds doctrine, and that the facts and the promises are arranged for our learning'.[3] The 'harmonious irregularities' found in nature are seen likewise in the Bible. Yet it is 'the golden history of election and grace'. It has its divine unity which brings it into organic union with the New Testament so that the Old Testament must be in some measure Christologically interpreted.

No one has done more within recent years to give the fullest recognition to the history and theology of the Old Testament than H. H. Rowley. His later books seem to show a greater tendency to stress the deep spiritual realities of Israel's story. This is seen, for example, in his suggestive volume, *The Faith of Israel*. Our reference here, for the second volume to which we desired to draw attention to conclude this chapter, is to his *Unity of the Bible*. Rowley begins by remarking that when he started his own theological studies such a topic as the unity of the Bible would have been viewed with suspicion, as evidence of 'an out-of-date obscurantist'. It was a day when the antithesis between the legal and the prophetic books was over-emphasized and when the predictive element in prophecy was minimized and Messianic prophecy largely explained away. The prophets were for the most part regarded as preachers of righteousness and moral reformers rather than as men who in any sense pointed onward to our Lord.

The New Testament robbed of its essential message was severed from the Old, and exclusive emphasis was placed upon the diversity of the Bible. This was, as we have seen, the actual

---

[1] Adolph Saphir, *The Divine Unity of Scripture*, pp. 1–2.
[2] *Ibid.*, p. 48.   [3] *Ibid.*, p. 34.

situation in which Saphir found himself and which makes his book all the more significant and suggestive. It is the purpose of Rowley, while urging that due recognition should be given to the diversity in the Bible, to stress the fact of its fundamental unity: 'the diversity of the Bible must be recognized fully and clearly', he says, 'even though we see a more profoundly significant unity running through it all'.[1] This regard for the unity of the Bible is, he notes, a recent thing. But it is, he urges, a real fact.[2] Rowley sees the unity not as 'static' but as 'dynamic'.[3] Israel's history is 'no automatic spiritual growth': God is active within its history. 'To study the Bible simply as a human story, and to treat men's beliefs about God without asking what validity they have, is sometimes thought to be the scientific study of the Bible. This tacitly assumes that there was no validity in their beliefs, since if there was validity, and if men were genuinely moved by God, the story cannot be fully under-stood while ignoring the supremely important factors in it. . . . But it is just as dogmatic to suppose that God is not a vital factor in human affairs as to suppose that He is.'[4]

The human element in the Bible is to be recognized because 'Divine inspiration came through the organ of men's person-ality'.[5] Yet for all that it possesses a divine authority. Rowley, too, like Saphir, lays hold of the ideas of the divine election of Israel into covenant relationship with God as the fact which gives to the Old Testament its fundamental unity. Here is the 'thread that runs all through the Old Testament at least from the time of Moses, and that gives unity to its thought. The principle of election is carried back, indeed, far beyond Moses in the Bible. But here it takes a new, and richly significant, form. God chooses Israel in unmerited grace, and not because of her worth; and having chosen her, He claims her for Himself by what He does for her'.[6] Rowley concludes with the observation that 'A historical sense is essential for all satisfying study of this Book, but along with that sense there must go a perception of the continuing thread that runs through all, and that makes this library also a Book'.[7]

[1] H. H. Rowley, *The Unity of the Bible*, 1953, second impression, 1955, p. 3.
[2] *Ibid.*; cf. references quoted by Rowley on p. 29.   [3] *Ibid.*, p. 7.
[4] *Ibid.*, p. 9.   [5] *Ibid.*, p. 15.
[6] *Ibid.*, pp. 26–7; cf. H. H. Rowley, *The Biblical Doctrine of Election*, 1950.
[7] *Ibid.*, p. 29.

Here, then, we have two books separated by over half a century both stressing the need to see the unity in the Bible. But the standpoint from which each writer begins differs. Saphir's position is traditionally conservative having no compromise with higher criticism. Rowley, on the other hand, begins from the critical position, although many of the more recent conclusions of the critics are much more moderate than those claimed as assured results at the end of the last century. Yet both Saphir and Rowley come out with the same emphasis upon the need to recognize a fundamental unity in the diversity of Scripture: and they both see that unity in the same basic facts. The future outlook may therefore be regarded as promising.

CHAPTER FOUR

The Focus of the Conflict

The Battle of the Standpoints, it will be clear from the last chapter, brought the Bible, in a new way, into the storm centre of controversy. Questions at once arose regarding its origin, its purpose, its authority and the like. But, perhaps, the most fundamental issue brought to the fore concerned the relationship of our Lord to the subject of Old Testament criticism. As we have noted, the new theory had played havoc with many traditional views. Yet the one undoubted fact stood out clearly: the same Old Testament which appeared to many to be roughly handled by many moderns, was the same Book from which Christ quoted with a certain ring of authority and in the spirit of which He lived, and moved and had His being. What, therefore, was to be thought of His relationship to those Scriptures? This was the most urgent question which had emerged from the heated discussions concerning Biblical criticism. In this connection, as we shall see in more particular detail later, one of the 'much discussed references', as it was alluded to by one writer of the period, was the authorship of Psalm cx.[1] This aspect of the controversy flared up as a result of an article by W. E. Gladstone in *The Record* of January 8, 1892. The controversy centred around the subject: 'Has modern criticism the right to question whether Psalm cx was written by David or not?' This problem, however, soon opened out into the larger one, or, perhaps, it might be more correct to say, that it was an instance of a wider issue—an issue which involved the whole question of the extent of our Lord's knowledge.

This is a point made in a notice of H. C. Powell's book, *The Principle of the Incarnation*. 'It was the discovery', the observer

[1] Buchanan Blake, *Expository Times*, Vol. III, 1891–2, p. 519.

states, 'that the 110th Psalm was *not* written by David' which 'opened the whole question of our Lord's personality, producing the great theological controversy of our generation'.[1] Thus had the problem been raised, but soon it became evident that even if it were conclusively proved that David *did* write the psalm the controversy would not have been settled. The issue concerning our Lord's knowledge would have remained.

Although it is a fact that the question came to prominence in connection with criticism, it is probable that it could not have been evaded in view of the emphasis which Gore had given to the doctrine of 'Kenosis' in his *Lux Mundi* essay. By the year 1891 it was observed, 'The controversy raised by the *Lux Mundi* has nearly spent itself'. The question was asked, 'What has it brought us?' Our writer answers his own query with the assurance, 'no real gain to the cause either of the science of theology or the cause of true religion'. Yet there was something which did remain to become the point of theological debate for some years as the letters in contemporary issues of *The Spectator* (Nos. 3222–5) and *The Record* (Nos. 7556–64) show. 'The real subject of dispute' the writer just quoted adds, 'has been the limitation of Christ's human knowledge.'[2] Although doubt is expressed by him as to whether the criticism of the Old Testament has anything to do with such a subject, it is quite evident that numbers on both sides were satisfied that it had. While those who thought it had not were compelled, at any rate, to show why it had not, and in so doing they committed themselves to a positive statement concerning our Lord's knowledge.

A. CHRIST AND THE SCRIPTURES

Looking back at the host of letters and articles which appeared in the general and religious press over the period of the last ten years of the century, one becomes aware of how important were the subjects of Christ's attitude to the Old Testament and the wider question of the area of His knowledge. It is not easy to convey to the modern reader, unfamiliar with this literature, in addition to the larger works which have remained as general

---

[1] *Expository Times*, Vol. VIII, 1896–7, p. 174.
[2] *Op. cit.*, Vols. I and II, 1889–91, i, p. 242.

reading, how vast and vital the subject was. The issue was deeply felt. Those who sought to accord to Christ the high place He had occupied in orthodox faith could not but believe that His deity and uniqueness were being jeopardized and compromised. Those who believed in an infallible Bible regarded such statements of Christ as 'And Moses wrote', and, 'And David said', as sufficient attestation and warrant of the truth. They were able to point out that it was only in the interests of a preconceived theory that the critic had to set about weakening the force of Christ's authority. It was out of regard for their acclaimed scientific method that the critic had in some way to restrict the sphere of our Lord's knowledge. It was, they felt, a case of special pleading.

The 'devout' critics, on the other hand, while at pains to state their belief in the deity of Christ, yet maintained that the authority of Christ could not be adduced to foreclose the right of criticism. It did not belong to His purpose either to validate or to correct current ideas of Old Testament authorship and dates. Some argued that He could not do so even if He had desired since such knowledge lay outside the religious purpose for which He came. Others preferred to urge that He did not really bother Himself about such general notions on these matters, but rather accepted them, and without involving Himself in irrelevancies sought to get men to face the deeper issues of faith and destiny.

Seeking now to reduce the material of the conflict to some sort of order we shall bring quotations to show that it resolved itself, in the main, into two clear-cut oppositions. There were those, the critics generally, who maintained that Christ's knowledge, in the days of His flesh, was relative, whereas their opponents were emphatic that it was absolute.

(1) *Christ's Knowledge as Relative*

We are concerned here, it should be stated, with what Cheyne would call the 'devout' critic. There were radical theorists like T. H. Green, J. Warschauer, P. Gardner, whose views lie outside our particular interest.

Leaving then out of account these rationalist constructions, we are to see how the moderate critic sought to explain our Lord's quotation of certain Old Testament passages and the wider question of His knowledge.

A beginning may be made with a reference to W. Sanday's volume, *The Oracles of God* (1891). Sanday recognized what he calls 'the change of front as to the nature of God's revelation of Himself in the Bible respectively in the Old Testament, or more accurately, as to the nature of the methods by which the revelation has been conveyed'. Sanday cannot be regarded either as a vigorous opponent of criticism or as an ardent advocate of the traditional view. Actually his interest lay elsewhere than in the sphere of biblical criticism. But he sought to assess the position as he saw it in his day. He draws attention to the way that Christ's authority has been used in the controversy. Sanday regarded reference to that authority as authenticating the Mosaic authorship of the Pentateuch or the Davidic authorship of the Psalms to be a mistake. He regrets that the controversy respecting criticism of the Old Testament should have taken this 'unfortunate turn'. The question which has to be faced, however—the question which is now inescapable is, he sees, that of our Lord's knowledge and authority. Of the enormous correspondence which in recent months has appeared on the subject—he is writing in 1891—two different solutions only are, he thinks, possible. The one is that Christ accommodated His language to the current opinions of the Jews of His day regarding the Old Testament Scriptures. The second suggestion, which Sanday in this volume favours, is that His knowledge was limited by His incarnation experience on such subjects.

It is the first view, however, the 'Accommodationist'[1] which seems to have been followed by Gore in his Bampton Lectures of 1891 on *The Incarnation of the Son of God*. Gore, it is right to point out, defends our Lord's infallibility as a teacher as well as

---

[1] The accommodationist theory was not, of course, specially devised at this time to meet the needs of critical conclusions. The Fathers had spoken of a certain 'economy' (δικνομια), or 'condescension' (συγκαταβασις), or 'accommodation' (συμπεριφορά) as characteristic of God's revelations, but they were careful to distinguish it from all forms of 'hypocrisy' (υπόκρισις) in which, for one reason or another, truth was concealed; and from 'dissimulation' (dissimulatio) which to attain its ends stoops to tolerate error (cf. ,e.g. Cyril of Alex., Thesaur., Assert. xxxiv, t. 5; Theodoret, Dial. 11, t. iv; Tertullian, Avd. Marcion, Book IV, c. 36). Spinoza seems to have been the first to use the 'accommodationist' idea in a manner characteristic of later biblical critical scholars (cf. Tractatus Theol. Polit., cap. ii, circ. fin.). See also the discussion by William Lee, *Inspiration of Holy Scripture*, 1854, fourth edition, 1865, pp. 63 ff.

the impeccability of His character.[1] At the same time he
emphatically maintains the limitation of His knowledge in His
incarnated life.[2] He elaborates in this way the kenosis theory
which he had advocated earlier in his *Lux Mundi* essay, and
applies it to the realm of Biblical theory. Whatever our Lord
teaches He did with 'plenary authority'; although, speaking
continually under the limitations of a properly human consciousness He never yielded Himself up to fallible human reasonings.[3]
Gore pays special attention to what he calls 'the argument from
Psalm cx'. He has already contended that it was not part of
Christ's purpose to bind us 'to the acceptance of the Jewish
tradition in regard to the Old Testament'.[4] The declaration
'Moses wrote of me' does not tie us to the Mosaic authorship as
a whole; nor does the reference to Jonah's three days' sojourn in
the belly of the great fish authenticate the story 'as simple
history'. About the psalm itself, he is sure, that by referring it to
David our Lord never intended to support Jewish tradition with
an infallible guarantee. He will allow that our Lord's argument
does in some way depend upon David's personal authorship of
the psalm, but 'there are reasons which draw us back from
accepting the conclusion that He in fact meant to teach us the
authorship of a psalm'.[5] Gore believed that there is evidence of
'accommodation' in our Lord's teaching. He accepted ordinary
assumptions in order to cross-examine His critics or to check
His seekers. In this way He desires them to face the real
questions which on their own assumptions should have been
faced. He was not, therefore, either proving or disproving,
affirming or denying, these ordinary assumptions; He was
merely using them for a higher and diviner end.

Somewhat akin to this statement of Gore's is that of S. R.
Driver's. Driver was apparently upset by the suggestion that the
authority of Christ forbade the full application to the Old
Testament of critical methods. In the Preface of his *Introduction
to the Literature of the Old Testament* (1891), he says: 'It is
objected, however, that some of the conclusions of critics
respecting the Old Testament are incompatible with the
authority of our blessed Lord, and that in loyalty to Him we are

[1] C. Gore, *The Incarnation of the Son of God*, 1891, p. 154.
[2] *Ibid.*, pp. 147 ff.   [3] *Ibid.*, p. 199.
[4] *Ibid.*, p. 195.   [5] *Ibid.*, p. 197.

precluded from accepting them'.[1] Driver was himself convinced
that it is not so. It was not Christ's purpose to pronounce upon
critical conclusions, he declares. Questions of authorship and
date of this or that writing were never, it appears, submitted to
Him, or, if they were, there is no record of what His views were.
He accepted the prophetic significance of the Old Testament and
its spiritual lessons. Judging from a footnote reference to Psalm
cx, it seems that Driver was satisfied with Gore's explanation
of the limitation of our Lord's knowledge. And he finds support
for this elsewhere.[2] Driver insists that since Christ's aim was a
religious one it was no part of that aim to give a verdict upon
the authorship and date of the different parts of the Old Testament. He accepted, as the basis of His teaching, the opinions
current at the time. 'In no single instance' says Driver, 'so far
as we are aware, did He anticipate the results of scientific
inquiry or historical research.'[3] Driver's neat expression of the
position backed by the authority of his own name tended to
silence those who might otherwise have sought to raise a
protest. Many were overawed, and succumbed to the suggestion
that to think other was to fail to keep abreast of the modern
advancing scientific study of the Old Testament.

T. K. Cheyne openly acknowledged that the principle which
stands in the way of 'critical progress' is a theological one.
'Jesus Christ, being the "teacher come from God" and even "the
Son of God", cannot be liable to error.'[4] He asks whether it was
necessary that the Messiah should at that period have a clear
intuition as to the date and authorship of the Psalms. Cheyne
dated Psalm cx as 'post-Exilic', but he allows that this conclusion is still exposed to much criticism from those who claim
Christ's authority for its Davidic authorship. Cheyne argues
that in the discourse of Matt. xxii. 41–3, Christ's purpose was
merely to get the Pharisees to see that no mere son of David
or King of Israel could fulfil the highest prophecies respecting
the bringing in of Divine salvation. The question of the

---

[1] S. R. Driver, *Introduction to the Literature of the Old Testament,* 1891, seventh
edition, 1898, Preface, p. xii.
[2] Cf. Bishop Moorhouse, *The Teaching of Christ,* 1891, Sermons I and II; A.
Plummer, 'The Advance of Christ in σοφιά', *The Expositor,* p. 891; W. S. Swayne,
'An Enquiry into the Nature of our Lord's Knowledge as Man', *op. cit.*
[3] S. R. Driver, *Introduction to the Literature of the Old Testament,* Preface, p. xii.
[4] T. K. Cheyne, *Aids to the Devout Study of Criticism,* 1892, p. 392.

authorship of the psalm was beside the point. 'Our Lord made no declaration of His own belief or knowledge.'[1] He may, indeed, have accepted 'the current ideas of the schools'. At any rate so ignorant are we of the 'inner life of Jesus Christ' that we cannot pronounce with certainty concerning His attitude on questions of criticism.

Cheyne joins issue with an able writer in the *Church Times* (December 11, 1891) who in a review of Gore's lectures expressed the doubt whether critical scholars 'have done justice to the difficulty which now exists of verifying traditions about the original authorship of poems handed down through successive generations amongst the members of musical guilds, and liable from time to time to such modifications as we see exemplified in Psalms xiv and liii'. Cheyne weakly replies that if such psalms did exist in pre-exilic days they would have had to be modified or 'even recast' to adapt them to post-exilic use. Psalm cx he cannot conceive to have existed in any form 'either as Davidic or even pre-exilic'.[2]

What may be regarded as a less question-begging statement of the accommodationist theory is that advanced by Buchanan Blake. Blake argued that 'The Law', 'The Prophets' and 'The Psalms' were the three recognized divisions of the Old Testament. By referring the 'Law' to Moses, and the 'Psalms' to David, Christ was merely using a recognized and familiar formula. The question of authorship, or, indeed, of the substantial truth of a particular passage was not in mind. 'In an *argumentum ad hominen* He used a recognized book in a recognized interpretation. He asks men, who were putting captious questions to Him, to reconcile their own beliefs.'[3]

Here and there among the abundant correspondence it is evident that there were those who found no difficulty in accepting the accommodationist solution. A typical statement occurs in an issue of the *Expository Times* for the year 1900. It comes in the form of a short article by Herbert W. Horwill.

---

[1] T. K. Cheyne, *Aids to the Devout Study of Criticism*, 1892, p. 393.

[2] *Ibid.*, p. 394. G. H. Rouse in his *Old Testament Criticism in New Testament Light*, 1905, upholds against Driver the Davidic authorship of Psalm cx on the basis of Christ's authority. The words of Mark xii. 35-7 he suggests settles the matter, since, he argues, the pronoun 'himself' appears twice in the passage and should be emphasized.

[3] *Expository Times*, Vol. III, 1891-2, p. 519.

Horwill begins with the observation that 'There are many biblical students who would accept the newer views respecting the date and authorship of the books of the Old Testament but for one difficulty—the apparent sanction given by our Lord to the older position'. They refuse, out of a high regard for His person, to accept either His ignorance due to limitation or that He accommodated His teaching to current views. The writer himself takes the accommodationist position. He supports his argument by reference to the narrative of Luke xi. 19, and the story of the man born blind in John ix. Horwill contends that the latter passage proves that the disciples believed in transmigration but that our Lord did not correct their mistaken view. In fact, His reply, he says, 'must be understood as sanctioning the doctrine of metapsychosis' if it be contended that He did not accommodate His views to current belief. He concludes that 'those who refuse to allow the possibility of our Lord's reference to Old Testament authorship being accommodation to the critical position of the time must be prepared to accept, on the same authority, the contemporary belief in *exorcism and transmigration*'.[1]

It need hardly be pointed out that the evidences here for the accommodationist theory are very insecurely based. There is little convincing proof that the Jews held to a belief in transmigration and there is not the slightest evidence that the disciples, even at this early period of their association with Christ, accepted such a notion.

In spite of the care with which the theory was propounded and the apparent eagerness with which the use of the word 'accommodate' was avoided, there was still, in many minds, something suspect about the whole procedure. It did not seem right somehow to credit Him who came as the Truth, with unreadiness, on any pretence, to correct a known error. It was, of course, clearly stated by some that in accommodating His language to current ideas our Lord was not sanctioning any error which would have had any real religious significance or repercussions.

But if it is a harmless thing to accept the Mosaic authorship of the Pentateuch or the Davidic authorship of Psalm cx, then, the question must have arisen in many minds, Why all the fuss about

---

[1] Herbert W. Horwill, 'Christ and the Old Testament', *Expository Times*, Vol. XI, 1899–1900, p. 477.

the results of criticism? Were not the critics telling their readers that at last the key to the true understanding of the Scriptures had been discovered? How then could it be supposed that our Lord interpreted them rightly if He did not openly interpret them as the new analysis and the historical method demanded? These are but a few of the thoughts which must have arisen in many hearts. And the fact is that the accommodationist view, however important were the names attached to it, did not appear to capture general consent.

There seemed to many minds more reason in the 'limitationist' view. 'I should be loath to believe', Sanday acknowledged, 'that our Lord accommodated His language to current notions, knowing them to be false. I prefer to think, as it has been happily worded, that "He condescended not to know".'[1]

It appeared therefore to many that the idea of a limited knowledge in the incarnate Lord, which restricted the area of His knowledge, was more reverent and a truer induction from the facts. 'If our Lord had not Himself declared', states one, 'that there was one subject of which He was ignorant, few of us would have found it difficult to ascribe to Him omniscience. That declaration being there, one subject being unmistakable beyond His ken, other items may be found to go along with it.'[2] The one subject upon which our Lord was said to be ignorant regarded the time of His second coming. On the basis of this many were ready to argue that this lack of knowledge was to be extended to include such items as the authorship and dates of the Old Testament. In the eighth of his articles on 'Hebrew Prophecy and Modern Criticism', F. H. Woods of Oxford rejected the accommodationist view and concluded, 'The most natural alternative is to suppose that our Lord's knowledge on these points was really limited by the conditions of the times in which He lived'. The supposition of ignorance, he thinks, cannot be rejected on the grounds of Christian doctrine or reverence. He contends, however, that a devout agnosticism is the only wise conclusion: 'to confess honestly that the union of an omniscient Godhead and a limited humanity in one Person absolutely transcends our human faculties; and that we therefore cannot say a priori what limitations to the one nature or the other, from

[1] W. Sanday, The Oracles of God, etc., 1891, fourth edition, 1892, p. 111.
[2] Cf. Expository Times, Vol. VIII, 1896–7, p. 148.

one point of view, that union necessarily involved'.[1] Attention need not be focused upon the Apollinarian flavour of this conclusion of Woods, but the theologically minded will look askance at the thought of a limitation of either the one nature or the other.

Two series of Bampton Lectures of the period show concern for the subject of our Lord's knowledge and its relation to biblical criticism. We have referred to Sanday's volume, *The Oracles of God.* In his later lectures on *Inspiration*, Sanday seeks to explain the nature of the restriction of that knowledge to which his earlier work had made reference. He asserts that it is not inconsistent with Christian belief to suppose that our Lord with the assumption of human flesh and a human mind should also have assumed the natural workings of such a mind, even in its limitations.[2] In order to make his position clear, Sanday now speaks of what he calls 'a neutral zone' in our Lord's knowledge. 'Is there not', he asks, 'what we may call a *neutral zone* among our Lord's sayings? Sayings, I mean, in which He takes up ideas and expressions current at the time and uses them without endorsing them.'[3] It is in this way that he seeks to explain the reference by Christ to Psalm cx (Matt. xxii. 45). 'It is not criticism or exegesis that were at issue', he says.[4] The true method of these might well be left to later discovery. In the quotation, 'the Pharisees were taken on their own ground: and the fallacy of their conclusion was shown on their own premises. All that we need say is that our Lord refrained from correcting these premises. They fell within His "neutral zone" '.[5]

There appears to be a change of view here. A reading over the passage just quoted from his *Inspiration* seems to link him with the accommodationist view. The suggestion of a change of view was early noted; but Sanday denies it. In a letter discounting the idea he states that the word 'refraining' which he had used must not be wrongly pressed. We are not to 'regard this refraining as merely the suppression *at the moment* of something which it was (so to speak) on His lips to say, but did not say. Imagine that it goes much further back, and was implied in the limitations which

[1] *Expository Times*, Vol. VI, 1894–5, p. 371.
[2] W. Sanday, *Inspiration*, 1893, seventh impression, 1911, p. 415.
[3] *Ibid.*, p. 419.   [4] *Ibid.*, p. 420.   [5] *Ibid.*

He assumed when He became man. The one great *condescension* included all other smaller condescensions'.[1]

Three years later R. L. Ottley gave his Bampton Lectures on *The Doctrine of the Incarnation* (1896). In the closing section of this scholarly tome Ottley concerns himself with the problem of our Lord's knowledge. He has a number of references to the early Fathers, drawn mainly from A. B. Bruce's *Humiliation of Christ*. A typical quotation is one from Athanasius: 'In the Godhead there cannot be ignorance; but ignorance is proper to the flesh'.[2] Ottley states his own belief that 'Our Lord in His human nature possessed an *infallible knowledge*, so far as was required by the conditions and purpose of His incarnation'.[3] Outside of this necessity, however, Ottley seems to admit a certain area of which He could not pronounce because He did not know. He adopts an 'altruistic' view, to borrow a word earlier used by J. A. Clapperton,[4] and states that the limitation of our Lord's knowledge, whatever was its degree, was a fact resulting from *love*. Yet while he insists that Christ's knowledge was limited, He was Himself neither deceived nor could He mislead others. Our Lord, he states, though Divine, did not teach positively on all subjects which He incidently touched. 'It is admitted that He never teaches positively on points of science; analogy makes it equally probable that He never taught as to the authorship of different books of Scripture or their mode of composition.'[5] There is, he says, nothing to suggest that He possessed 'modern critical knowledge', or, indeed, 'that He intended to finally endorse the traditional views of His country-men in regard to the nature of their Scriptures'.[6] In a footnote Ottley draws attention to Sanday's 'law of parsimony'[7] which according to the earlier Bampton lecturer underlies revelation. Having assured so much and set out to explain so much Ottley falls back upon the limitation of our own knowledge concerning the Person of Christ. The reality of our own ignorance should make us hesitate to form clear-cut theories about Him who is so beyond us all. 'We may well shrink from constructing any

[1] Cf. *Expository Times*, Vol. V, 1893–4, p. 229.
[2] R. L. Ottley, *The Doctrine of the Incarnation*, 1896, third edition, 1904, p. 622; cf. Athanasius, Orat. c. Arian, iii, 27–8. [3] *Ibid.*, p. 623.
[4] Cf. *Expository Times*, Vol. V, 1893–4, p. 277.
[5] R. L. Ottley, *The Doctrine of the Incarnation*, p. 625. [6] *Ibid.*
[7] Cf. W. Sanday, *Inspiration*, p. 417 f.

general theory as to our Lord's human knowledge. We are too apt to discuss and dispute where we should wonder and adore.'[1] It is not very clear, however, how this last observation is to be related to his own general theory of our Lord's knowledge.

Despite his association with Driver, A. F. Kirkpatrick, too, seems to prefer the limitationist theory. He states, 'In condescending to become incarnate as a Jew at a particular epoch in a particular country, our Lord necessarily accepted the conditions and limitations of time and place'.[2]

Among a vast literature it will be found that those who took the critics' side were either accommodationists or limitationists. But there were others who sought to develop their own original line. H. C. Powell, for example, in his book *The Principle of the Incarnation*—a work which in its way is as able as either Gore's or Ottley's—sought to explain the position by what we may think of as two non-communicating centres of activity in Christ. The thesis worked out by Powell was suggested by an article which another writer had supplied to an earlier edition of *The Church Quarterly Review*. Powell claims that as far as he was concerned the idea was entirely his own and that he had not borrowed the *Review* article. For Powell divine knowledge or omniscience differs radically and structurally from that which arises out of the human consciousness. The difference is not simply one of degree, but fundamentally one of character. The knowledge which Christ has as a man, a knowledge, so to speak, derived from the structure of human consciousness, was necessarily limited. Thus, as man, Jesus could be ignorant of that which He knew most intimately as God. As he persuasively develops his theory, Powell takes account of the other prevailing views and shows them to be less tenable than they seemed.

Under the caption 'Christ's Knowledge, Was it Limited or Unlimited? A Solution in Altruism', J. A. Clapperton, to whom we made reference in our comments on Ottley, maintains that any limitation of our Lord's knowledge was due to His voluntary act. He illustrates his thesis by drawing attention to the distinction known to us all between knowledge present in the

---

[1] R. L. Ottley, *The Doctrine of the Incarnation*, p. 625.

[2] A. F. Kirkpatrick, 'The Inevitability and Legitimacy of Criticism' in *The Higher Criticism*, S. R. Driver and A. F. Kirkpatrick, 1911, p. 27; cf. A. B. Davidson, *Biblical and Literary Essays*, 1903, Chapter VII.

memory and knowledge at the moment in use. Christ, he states then, 'knew all things as we may be said to know everything that we can recall at a moment's notice. But . . . *He voluntarily declined to take advantage of the power and joy that the facing of every truth would naturally bring Him. In His personal trials He chose to be ignorant'.*[1] In reference to His own affairs He employed 'limited knowledge'. But for the sake of others He drew 'upon His omniscience'. For our sakes He would see to it that divine truth and fulness stamped His utterance, but for His own life and His own sake, He, like us, had to learn to 'cope with difficulty and darkness'. Clapperton applies this to Christ's use and knowledge of the Old Testament. When He used the Old Testament for the sake of its spiritual truth for others 'we cannot understand Him to speak with merely human wisdom as far as the lessons taught are concerned'. But as far as authorship and readings are concerned these were questions of no great moment in comparison with the messages He had to convey. Such ideas were 'so utterly out of touch with the moral and spiritual interest of those around Him, that He could scarcely concern Himself with the accuracy or inaccuracy of the traditions involved'.[2]

An interesting comment is made by W. C. Shearer of the United College, Bradford, on Mark xiii. 31–2, which was the passage adduced by the kenoticists as evidence of the limitation of our Lord's knowledge. Shearer points out that the verses are often taken as proof of Christ's ignorance. 'And the inference is drawn', he continues, 'If ignorant *then*, how much more in regard to the authorship and dates of the books of the Old Testament!'[3] Shearer contends that in interpreting the passage in this way the premise is wrong and the conclusion consequently false. After analysing the verses he states that it 'was not intended to be an acknowledgement of ignorance, in a special instance, on the part of our Lord; but was simply a devout ascription to His Father of an omniscience which transcended the conditions of time. What was known to the Son, in His temporal and relative condition, as an event occupying a considerable space of time, can be viewed by the Father as a day, an hour, a moment, an instant of time. It was a prompting of the same devout and

---

[1] *Expository Times*, Vol. V, 1893–4, p. 277.   [2] *Op. cit.*, p. 278.
[3] *Op. cit.*, Vol. IV, 1892–3, p. 554.

reverential feeling in the Lord's mind, as that to which He gave expression when He said, "Why callest thou me good? One is good, God". Our Lord no more denied His own goodness in the latter, than He asserted His ignorance in the former'.[1]

Before we turn to deal with the other position it is worthwhile to note that as time went on the discussion concerning our Lord's knowledge became divorced from the more immediate issue of His relation to critical questions about the Old Testament Scriptures. The problem became abstracted from its historical origins and was developed along the lines of a Christological interest as such. In this way kenotic doctrines of Christ's Person came into vogue, each with its own peculiarity, such as that of A. M. Fairbairn's, H. R. Mackintosh's, P. T. Forsyth's and others. At the present day kenoticism finds support in the writings of Vincent Taylor.

(2) Christ's Knowledge as Absolute

As was to be expected the idea that Christ accommodated Himself to popular notions or that He was ignorant about biblical facts came in for a lot of criticism. An immense amount of discussion took place, and, in many cases, it must be acknowledged, those who felt that they were upholding the honour of Christ and the Bible, plunged into the controversy with little reason and less result. Many of the letters and pamphlets and articles which are to hand were both furious and feeble. Too often the character of the individual critic was made the object of attack, and the impression was created, that those claiming to defend orthodoxy fulfilled the logical fallacy which in popular parlance has been put, when you cannot kick the ball, kick the man. But it would be altogether wrong, however, to conclude from the multiplicity of attempted replies which turned out to be hopeless irrelevancies, that this was the whole story. Some apologists for criticism, understandably impatient as they were with what was produced by way of answer, sought to win their case by dubbing all who could not readily accept their latest views as obscurantists. But all were not so. There were men, no less concerned for truth, who genuinely felt that the absoluteness of Christ was being undermined if His complete knowledge were

---

[1] *Expository Times*, Vol. IV, 1892–3, p. 555.

denied. And they made a better showing of their cases than is sometimes known or allowed.

C. C. J. Ellicott was no obscurantist, but a careful student of Scripture. A series of articles from his pen appeared in the *Expository Times* between the years 1891–3 under the title 'The Teaching of our Lord as to the Authority of the Old Testament'. He shows in these contributions that he had a grasp of the recent critical theories and his exposition of them is clear. For what he calls the 'traditional view' he asserts that, in contrast with the new theories, it 'can with every appearance of probability, claim the authority of our Lord and Master Jesus Christ'.[1] He deals also with the question, Was the kenosis 'of such a kind that His knowledge in regard to the authorship and composition of the Books of the Old Testament . . . (was) no greater than that of the masters of Israel at His own time?'[2] He makes an extended reply and concludes with reasons that Christ's knowledge was not so restricted. It is impossible, he insists, to draw inferences from our human nature and transfer them to Him.[3] Allowance must be made in His case for the supernatural endowment of the Holy Ghost which fitted Him for His Messianic office. As a consequence of the union of the two natures in the one Person, it is impossible that He who quoted the Scriptures so frequently should know less about their composition than the critics of our times. In this connection the *Lux Mundi* comes in for Ellicott's severest treatment.

In reference to Psalm cx, Ellicott maintained that by the evidence David was necessarily the author. He asks, Could such a 'metrical fabrication claiming to be a psalm of David and an oracle of God, and challenging attention by setting forth a doctrine so unfamiliar as the Messiah's everlasting priesthood have crept into the jealously guarded Scripture, three or four centuries after the date of Ezra's Bible, and remained there undetected?'[4] Ellicott quotes Liddon's statement 'If it be obvious that certain theories of the Old Testament must ultimately conflict with our Lord's unerring authority, a Christian will pause before he commits himself to these theories'.[5] He realizes that 'those who have deliberately crossed the Rubicon' will be

---

[1] *Expository Times*, Vol. III, 1891–2, p. 458.
[2] *Op. cit.*, p. 539.   [3] *Op. cit.*, p. 544.
[4] *Op. cit.*, Vol. IV, 1892–3, p. 368.   [5] *Op. cit.*, p. 456.

unmoved by these considerations. But he thinks that the critical views are at one with the growing minimizing of the supernatural, but whether as a cause or an effect he does not say. He sees the loss of spiritual authority and the increase of spiritual paralysis to be the result. 'This downward drift and ultimate issue may easily be traced out . . . the temptation to believe in a possible ignorance on the part of our Lord, becomes in many minds irresistible, and the way is paved for a belief in the possibility, not only of this ignorance, but even of our hope in Him, here and hereafter, being found to be vain and illusory.'[1] The final question to be faced is 'With whom have we to do, here and hereafter; a fallible or the infallible Christ?'

In a series of articles in the same journal between the years 1894 and 1896, J. Elder Cumming asks, 'Is the Old Testament Authentic?' In a section of one of these articles Cumming discusses the relation of Christ to the Old Testament. He is emphatic that Christ could and did teach with absolute authority. He was not lacking in the knowledge concerning the authorship of the Old Testament or its several parts. 'He, in His divine person, knew what the truth was about these holy writings.'[2] We can be absolutely assured that whatever He taught was true, whether that truth was about the resurrection from the dead or about the Scriptures. As a teacher He can be relied upon implicitly. True He 'emptied Himself', and in this sense the words of Mark xiii. 32, are to be understood. 'But there is a whole hemisphere surely between such a statement and the idea that what He *did* teach on any subject, He taught without knowing!'[3] 'We, therefore, have no doubt' he says again, 'that it lay in the power of Jesus Christ to settle all disputed questions regarding the authority or the meaning, or the truthfulness of the Old Testament Scriptures.' He quotes Cheyne's comment on our Lord's reference to Jonah. 'Jesus interpreted the story as an instructive parable' declared Cheyne. 'And then he adds' continues Cumming, 'Even if He did, with His wonderful spiritual tact, so interpret it, we cannot be sure' (*Expositor*, March 1892). 'Has it come to this' retorts Cumming, 'that our Lord relied, in interpreting the Scriptures, on "His TACT"? "His spiritual tact!" "His wonderful spiritual tact"!'[4]

---

[1] *Expository Times*, Vol. IV, 1892–3, p. 458.
[2] *Op. cit.*, Vol. VII, 1895–6, p. 39.   [3] *Op. cit.*   [4] *Op. cit.*

The *Expository Times* gave hospitality also to Thomas Whitelaw to deal with the same subject in a further series of articles under the title 'Could Jesus Err?' Whitelaw took the opportunity to answer Paul Schwartzkopff of Wernigerode, whose brochure, *The Prophecies of Jesus Christ relating to the Death, Resurrection, and Second Coming, and their Fulfilment*, had, he states, just been translated into English.[1] Schwartzkopff had credited Jesus with a good deal of error, especially concerning the Second Coming. Whitelaw, in opposition, maintains that Jesus could not have been guilty of intellectual error and that this being so, His ascription to Moses of the Pentateuch and Psalm cx to David must authenticate these. The 'higher critics of today claim to have reversed the judgement of those who stood more than 2,000 years closer to the Psalms of David than we do'.[2] Schwartzkopff had rejected Kenoticism maintaining that it inevitably leads to a denial either of the true humanity or the Godhead of our Lord. A God depotentiated of omnipotence, omniscience and omnipresence, if such were conceived possible would, as Beidermann says, be a mythological and gnostical god —no real god at all. Schwartzkopff, however, denies outright the ascription to Christ of Godhead (Gottheit), and allows to Him merely godlikeness (Gottlichkeit). He is a God-filled man, and as such the possibility of error remains as an inseparable part of His teaching. Whitelaw attacks the view and shows the disastrous theological and soteriological consequences which must follow.

The writers to whom we have referred showed in their articles that they found it impossible to let go their belief in the absolute infallibility of Christ's knowledge. To do so would have been tantamount to denying His uniqueness even on the plane of the human. But apart from such articles there were several books which sought to establish the same conclusion.

In a massive volume of over 700 pages published by T. & T. Clark entitled *Is Christ Infallible and the Bible True?* Hugh McIntosh covers the whole field of contemporary thought and deals trenchantly with any theory which would limit the infallibility of either Christ or the Scriptures. McIntosh's book, into the bargain, is an elaborate exposition of numerous

[1] *Expository Times*, Vol. VIII, 1896–7, p. 299; but cf. p. 524.
[2] *Op. cit.*, p. 301; cf. p. 365.

Christological doctrines which, to borrow a word from T. P. Forsyth, had the effect of merely 'Boswellizing' the Figure of the Gospel.

It is impossible to convey any idea of the fulness of the treatment of the subject in this detailed work. McIntosh raises the serious issue whether Christ is to be regarded as an infallible teacher.[1] And if not so considered, then, What ground have we for certainty? May He not, indeed, be mistaken concerning the very possibility and method of salvation? He poses the question 'If not infallible, can He be Divine?' On the other hand, should His infallibility be admitted, then, according to McIntosh, it must be taken seriously. He is ready to admit to the reality of 'kenosis', as a Bible revelation and a profound fact,[2] but he denies that this provides any ground for questioning Christ's infallibility as a teacher. 'While holding as fully as any, and more fully than most, the veritable humanity, and the mental and moral development of Christ, and the reality of the Kenosis revealed in the Scriptures, we utterly repudiate the dangerous and antiscriptural inferences drawn therefrom, limitative, and ultimately subversive of the Divine authority and infallibility of His teaching.'[3] McIntosh believes that Mark xiii, 32 gives no basis for the idea of our Lord's nescience, but boldly argues that the reverse is the case.[4] Having, then, in books i and ii concluded that there is nothing to tell against Christ's infallibility but rather that His infallibility ·is overwhelmingly ·established, McIntosh goes on to relate this conclusion to the Scriptures. He has stated in the concluding section of book ii that if Christ erred as the Word of God He may have erred as to His being the Son of God.[5] It is this conclusion that he has now to apply to the Scriptures. They are substantiated and authenticated by Christ's authority.

McIntosh does not, it ought to be pointed out, contend for 'absolute inerrancy in every trivial detail and possible aspect', but he does argue that 'there is no possibility of making it appear that Christ did not teach at least the truthfulness, trustworthiness, and the Divine authority of Scripture'.[6] He ends this long discussion with the answer to the question of the title, Is Christ

---

[1] Hugh McIntosh, *Is Christ Infallible and the Bible True?*, third edition, 1902, pp. 277 ff.   [2] *Ibid.*, pp. 238 ff.   [3] *Ibid.*, p. 238.
[4] *Ibid.*, p. 232.   [5] *Ibid.*, p. 261.   [7] *Ibid.*, p. 550.

infallible and the Bible true? with these words: 'the Bible, is true, because Christ is infallible: and He who is "The Truth" and the faithful and true Witness declares it to be true. The Bible, then, is the Word of God—true, trustworthy, and of Divine authority, and the Divine rule of faith and life; or the Bible is the Word of God, of infallible truth and Divine authority, *in all it teaches*, and the Divine rule of faith and life'.[1]

Another volume along the same lines is John Urquhart's *The Inspiration and Accuracy of the Holy Scriptures*. In the second of the books which comprise this composite work, Urquhart shows that he is thoroughly acquainted with the whole field of German rational criticism. The views of Eichhorn, Paulus, Astruc, Strauss, Vatke, Kayser, Kuenen have all been mastered as well as those of English critics. Urquhart deals with the doctrine of kenosis and examined the usage of the word κενοω and maintains that it does not mean the emptying of nature (cf. Jer. xiv. 2; September).[2] He is certain that our Lord was not reduced to a state of ignorance by His becoming flesh. And, he argues, therefore in His use and reference to the Old Testament He has given them their endorsement.[3]

In 1903 there appeared, condensed into one volume, *The Divine Rule of Faith and Practice*, three books by William Goode, which were first published in 1841. Goode was a Cambridge Scholar and has been Dean of Ripon. The work did not, of course, touch the special problems of the new period, but it was apparently felt that its appearance at such a time of unrest would give confidence to those who were through criticism losing faith in the Bible as the Word of God. Goode showed the place of the Bible in the early Church and maintained that it was the sole and sufficient rule of faith and practice. He concluded with a chapter in which it is asserted that the Church of England recognizes the Bible only as its authority and acclaims it as the Word of God without equivocation. A typical statement is a quotation from Dean Mowell's *Catechism*; 'the Christian religion is to be learnt from no other source than from the heavenly word of God Himself, which He hath delivered to us in the Holy Scriptures'. And another comes from Jewell's

---

[1] Hugh McIntosh, *Is Christ Infallible and the Bible True?* 1902, p. 664.
[2] John Urquhart, *The Inspiration and Accuracy of the Holy Scriptures*, 1895, p. 74.
[3] *Ibid.*, pp. 73 ff.

Apology: 'the very sure and infallible rule whereby may be tried whether the Church do swerve or err and whereunto all ecclesiatical doctrine ought to be called to account'.[1]

A work by H. D. Brown, at one time a barrister, and no mean scholar, who became pastor of the Harcourt Street Baptist Church, Dublin, should be given a passing reference. The substance of the book published under the title *Christ or Critics?* or, *God's Witness to His Word*, was a series of articles contributed to *The Sword and the Trowel*. Brown speaks of Christ's 'subservience' to the Scriptures. He raises the question, 'Was our Divine Lord's Knowledge Limited?'[2] He marshals the evidence of New Testament passages to prove that He knew Himself and showed Himself to be possessed of a unique understanding. The accommodationist theory he finds specially distasteful. 'Jesus', he retorts, was 'no Jesuit'. He did not simply accommodate Himself 'to the generally-accepted traditional and popular, albeit somewhat legendary and historically-false, views of the Jews, in order to evade unnecessary discussion and to avoid awakening continual hostility and prejudice'.[3] The idea of a limitation of our Lord's knowledge is also unacceptable. Thus, he says, 'while "Accommodationists" rob us of Christ's integrity, "Limitationists" would unintentionally but surely undermine His Godhead'.[4]

Our Lord's Use of His Bible by H. E. Fox, the honorary secretary of the Church Missionary Society, may be a slender volume, but it is closely reasoned. While acknowledging the 'reverent tone of many of the leaders' of criticism in England, Fox refuses their conclusion that the Bible is a 'literary patchwork'. In the case of the neo-criticism, the disciple is above his Master, and there are those 'to whom the Great Master seems to be a person less well informed about His own sacred literature, and the religious history of His own nation, than any callow divinity student of these days'.[5]

Fox cannot believe that if the story of His nation as given in the Bible had been only the legendary lore of an illiterate race, He would have failed to drop some hint to that effect. Parts of

[1] William Goode, *The Divine Rule of Faith and Practice*, edited by his daughter, Anne E. Metcalf, 1903, p. 314.
[2] H. D. Brown, *God's Witness to His Word*, 1905, second edition, p. 127.
[3] *Ibid.*, p. 133.   [4] *Ibid.*, p. 143.
[5] H. E. Fox, *Our Lord's Use of His Bible*, 1905, p. 23.

the Old Testament, for example, the Book of Deuteronomy, most roughly handled by the critics, were the parts to which He appealed the most. On Psalm cx he says, 'If the new criticism is right in saying that David had nothing to do with this Psalm, and that the Psalm had nothing to do with the Messiah, then the whole of our Lord's argument falls to the ground'.[1] Fox has a well written chapter on the kenosis theory. He believes, however, that it does not support the idea of a limitation of our Lord's knowledge. The whole passage is hortatory. He quotes from Dr Stubbs's recent *Visitation Charges* (p. 151) to the effect that kenosis should not be used as the keynote of a theory with which it has so little to do; or as the decisive proof of a doctrine which if it were intended to be taught, could not safely be left to an isolated text.[2] Christ, he says, did not accommodate Himself to other men's mistakes. It is essential for faith that He be absolutely trustworthy. 'The Saviour who cannot be trusted absolutely cannot be trusted at all.'[3] Fox shows some fatal consequences of accepting the kenosis doctrine: and he is emphatic that in emptying Himself Christ did not become void of 'the knowledge that He once possessed', which would mean His teaching 'His disciples to receive as genuine and authoritative Scriptures which in fact were neither'.[4] Neo-criticism fosters doubt, and, concludes Fox, 'to foster doubt is a strange way to preserve faith'.[5]

Beginning, then, with the conviction that Christ's knowledge is absolute, these writers felt themselves bound to the highest view of Scripture, which, they believed, He has validated. Their attitude was well stated by Bishop Moule: 'the Christian student sees the most impressive characteristic of the Holy Scriptures in the fact of the attitude towards them taken by Jesus Christ'.[6]

As time went on the discussion concerning our Lord's relation to the Old Testament seemed to be less bound up with the attempt to justify or to repudiate criticism as such. It became more concerned with wider issues as, for example, the way the Old Testament entered into the development of our Lord's Messianic consciousness, and how far the term, Son of Man,

---

[1] H. E. Fox, *Our Lord's Use of His Bible*, 1905, p. 47.
[2] *Ibid.*, pp. 73–4.   [3] *Ibid.*, pp. 79–80.
[4] *Ibid.*, p. 78.   [5] *Ibid.*, p. 92.
[6] H. C. G. Moule, *Christian Doctrine*, 1889, p. 5.

which He took as His own special designation for Himself, was to be understood against its Old Testament usages. At the same time there is evidence here and there, more particularly in the earlier part of the present century before the complete divorce between Christ's attitude to the Scriptures and the right of criticism came about, of allegiance being given by one and another to either the accommodationist or the limitationist view.

An illustration of the first comes in an essay by V. Storr. Storr writes of 'the grave problem of the authority of our Lord in regard to His references to the Old Testament'.[1] He notes the hostility to Biblical criticism springing from belief in our Lord's authority and he allows that 'He clearly regarded the Scripture as being of Divine origin'. Storr confesses the dilemma to be a serious one. But for him Christ's authority is essentially 'moral and spiritual'. He then asks, 'Does that authority suffer if we think of Him as sharing the current Jewish opinion about the Old Testament?'[2] The Jews, he maintains, believed in the Davidic authorship of Psalm cx: scholars say the psalm was much later. Jesus accepted the popular notion. 'Is His spiritual authority really lessened if we hold that David did not write the Psalm?'[3] Storr then goes on to answer these questions with the 'No' already implied in their formation.

While Storr favours the accommodationist hypothesis as the explanation of our Lord's references to the Old Testament, A. H. McNeile, in an essay of his on 'Our Lord's Use of the Old Testament' seems to accept the limitationist alternative. In 'emptying Himself' Christ became truly man, truly human. The 'one thing that was not at all essential', he states, 'was a superhuman omniscience, and that we believe He continuously and consciously held in abeyance. It was part of the divine self-sacrifice to refuse to know, as man, anything which He could learn by human methods'.[4] His 'precocity' exhibited when speaking with the doctors in the temple was not, like ours, clouded by sin. Facts however relating to the literature and history of the Old Testament '*He could not because He would* not

---

[1] V. F. Storr, 'The Bible and Its Value', *Liberal Evangelicalism: An Interpretation*, by members of the Church of England, p. 96.

[2] *Ibid.*, p. 97.   [3] *Ibid.*

[4] A. H. McNeile, 'Our Lord's Use of the Old Testament' in *Cambridge Critical Essays*, Essays on Some Biblical Questions of the Day (ed. H. B. Swete), 1909, p. 249.

know'.[1] Traditional ideas about the Scriptures which were the 'intellectual standpoint of His day and country' He accepted because it would not become Him to be otherwise than really human for our sakes. *'And He could not because He would not* know otherwise, for us men and for our salvation.'[2]

The stress on the absoluteness of our Lord's knowledge, on the other hand, was also stated and applied with equal seriousness. This can be seen, for example, to permeate such a book as James Orr's *The Bible Under Trial*, which concludes with the declaration, 'But so long as Christ, in His self-attesting power, commands the allegiance of believing hearts, the Bible, which contains the priceless treasure of God's Word regarding Him, will remain in undiminished honour'.[3]

To balance the words of Storr from his essay in *Liberal Evangelicalism*, it seems proper to refer also to *Evangelicalism*. In a lengthy essay in this volume, T. C. Hammond writes of 'The Fiat of Authority'. Christ, he argues, taught with authority which 'could not have been of any external character, because our Lord never received an ecclesiastical imprimatur'.[4] His was the authority of truth, of God. Hammond maintains that 'Our Lord establishes once and for all the possibility of a perfectly human thought exhibiting absolute harmony with the Divine purpose: He set His seal to that sacred code which ages treasured as presenting the mind of God to man. Therefore alike the Sacred Scripture and He Who is the Subject of its eternal message are called the Word of God'.[5]

Of more recent days Evangelical scholars can be found referring to our Lord's ascription of Psalm cx as a sufficient authentication of its Davidic authorship.[6] Exception to the procedure continues to follow the line now axiomatic to those convinced of the validity of the critical position. Gabriel Hebert,

---

[1] A. H. McNeile, 'Our Lord's Use of the Old Testament' in *Cambridge Critical Essays*, Essays on Some Biblical Questions of the Day (ed. H. B. Swete), 1909, p. 250 (italics in original).   [2] *Ibid.* (italics in original).

[3] James Orr, *The Bible Under Trial*, 1907, second edition, p. 307. But see his observations on this point in his *Revelation and Inspiration*, 1910, p. 150 f.

[4] T. C. Hammond, 'The Fiat of Authority' in *Evangelicalism*, essays by members of the Fellowship of Evangelical Churchmen (ed. J. Russell Howden), 1925, p. 195.

[5] *Ibid.*, pp. 185–6.

[6] Cf. *The New Bible Commentary* (ed. Davidson, E. F. Kevan, A. Stibbs), notes on Psalms, Matt., Mark, Lk., *ad. loc.* Cf. R. V. G. Tasker, *Our Lord's Use of the Old Testament*, 1953, pp. 17 ff.

to take a typical example, asserts that 'we must not invoke our Lord's authority to decide a question He was not answering'.[1] This statement is a clear case of *petitio principii*, and leaves the question where it was. The fact is that the subject of our Lord's attitude to the Old Testament is for all Christians a vital one. For evangelicals it is decisive. It is maintained, for example, by J. I. Packer, with no uncertain emphasis, that Christ 'never opposed His personal authority to that of the Old Testament'.[2] He accepted its authority without question and submitted to it without demure.[3]

---

[1] Gabriel Hebert, *Fundamentalism and the Church of God*, 1957, p. 69.

[2] J. I. Packer, *'Fundamentalism' and the Word of God*, 1958, p. 55.

[3] Cf. R. V. G. Tasker, *The Old Testament in the New Testament*, 1953, Chapters 1 and 2; cf. 'The testimony of our Lord to the Old Testament and His claims to divinity are, it would seem, more closely associated than many in our day are prepared to acknowledge. I would therefore urge in conclusion that, while we should welcome all the light archaeological, linguistic and textual studies can throw upon the Old Testament, nevertheless, as Christians, we are bound to look at that unique literature primarily through the eyes of Him who claimed to be the light of the world, our Lord and Saviour' (*ibid.*, p. 19). See also J. W. Wenham, *Our Lord's View of the Old Testament*, 1953: 'To Him (i.e. Jesus), what the Scripture said, God said' (*ibid.*, p. 8). 'The total impression is that the mind of Christ is saturated with the Old Testament and that, as He speaks, there flows out perfectly naturally a complete range of uses varying from direct verbal quotation to an unconscious utilization of scraps of Old Testament phraseology. There is no trace of artificial quotation of Scripture as a matter of pious habit, but His mind is so steeped in both the words and principles of Scripture that quotation and allusion spring to His lips naturally and appositely in all sorts of different circumstances' (*ibid.*, p. 27). Cf. also F. F. Bruce, *The Christian Approach to the Old Testament*, 1955: 'To approach the Old Testament in the light of Christ's fulfilment of all its parts is to approach it aright; *this* is the Christian approach to the Old Testament' (*ibid.*, p. 20).

CHAPTER FIVE

The Scriptures and the Word

The discussion concerning Christ's relation to the Scriptures
leads on to a review of the allied problem, which came to light,
of how revelation was to be brought into connection with the
Scriptures. It had been the prevailing view that revelation and
the Bible were for all practical purposes to be equated. Deriving
from the great Reformers, Protestant theology had stated a
complete identification of Scripture with the Word of God.[1] The
truth of God had been given and that truth was conserved and
preserved in the Bible. But with the inerrancy and the infallibility of Scripture believed to be undermined, it was necessary
to raise the question of the 'locus' of revelation.

A. REVELATION AND THE SCRIPTURES

There was, to begin, a sharpening of the divorce between
revelation and Scripture, and, as we shall see more particularly
later, revelation came to be identified with, for example, the
spiritual experience or insight of the prophets or with the
recognition by them of God's redeeming acts in history, and so
forth. It is, however, the idea of revelation as divine activity
which is the characteristic note of the modern era. The view that
revelation was given in propositions, that it was in any sense a
communication of supernatural knowledge, was vehemently
repudiated. So, too, of course, was, in a measure, the earlier
reactionist idea which interpreted revelation in terms of the
subjective appreciation of the religious genius. Revelation was
not to be understood as the mere stimulation of the numinous

---

[1] Cf. R. Preus, *The Interpretation of Scripture*, A Study in the Theology of the
Seventeenth Century Dogmaticians, 1955, Chapter 2.

feelings.[1] Emphasis came to be placed upon what H. Wheeler Robinson called the 'actuality' of God in history.[2] John Baillie in his American series of Bampton Lectures, contends that the 'recovery of this fundamental insight', as he regards it, 'is the first thing we notice as running broadly through all the recent discussions, marking them off from the formulations of earlier periods'.[3]

The tendency has been of late to urge that revelation is an entirely personal, subject to subject, affair. This view has been given vogue by a number of writers who in other respects greatly differ. William Temple, it is well known, laid special stress upon the notion of revelation as a divine self-disclosure. A typical quotation can be taken from his rightly famous Bampton Lectures. 'What is offered to man's apprehension', he says, 'in any specific revelation is not truth concerning God but the living God Himself'.[4] This view elaborated in Chapter XII of his *Nature, Man and God*, is given emphasis in his earlier essay in the symposium *Revelation*. Here he makes the point that Personality is the nature of ultimate reality. Revelation must, therefore, be understood as a divine self-disclosure. 'The belief in Divine Personality and the belief in specific revelation go together: each necessitates the other.'[5] Such statements as these could be multiplied and others of similar import could be added from a host of other writers. But Temple, we think, did not limit revelation to the divine activity of God in history, to the meeting of event and interpretation, as other, and especially earlier writers seemed to do. The more recent tendency is to state revelation in terms entirely personal. The watchword of the modern era might then be put like this: revelation is personal encounter not propositional disclosure. An illustration of this shift of emphasis can be seen, for example, in William Nicholls's book, *Revelation in Christ*. Nicholls allows that the writers of the more immediate past have succeeded 'in the shifting of the locus of revelation from literature to history and from the

---

[1] Cf. Kitell's, *Theological Dictionary of the New Testament*, word, καλύπτω, *ad. loc.*

[2] H. Wheeler Robinson, *Redemption and Revelation*, 1942, Chapters IX and X; cf. 'The actuality of the Biblical history is vital to the process of revelation'. C. H. Dodd, *The Authority of the Bible*, 1928, Preface, p. xi.

[3] John Baillie, *The Idea of Revelation in Recent Thought*, 1956, p. 29.

[4] William Temple, *Nature, Man and God*, 1947, p. 322.

[5] William Temple in *Revelation* (ed. J. Baillie and Hugh Martin), 1937, p. 95.

propositional to the personal'.[1] But a firmer declaration that Christ
is the proper 'locus' of revelation is called for at the present
time. This is, of course, a very proper and needful insistence.

It is doubtful, however, if there is anything specifically
original in the idea. It might, indeed, be convincingly demonstrated that this was the fundamental faith of the Church from
the first. Brunner has some justification for his remark that the
idea early arose in the Church under the influence of Greek
philosophy that revelation was a communication of doctrinal
truths which were otherwise inaccessible to human reason.[2]
Although Brunner may be a little too confident about the earliness of the influence, it remains a fact that whenever the Church
lost touch with the essential Biblical view of God in His gracious
self-disclosure and trusted in mere philosophical wisdom and
institutional authority, the true idea of revelation became
obscured. It may be ungrudgingly acknowledged as one of the
gains of the recent many-sided discussion of the subject of
revelation that the essential personal note has been brought into
its rightful place. In this sense point may be given to the claim
that in emphasizing revelation as personal in Christ the modern
era has made great gains. Perhaps it would be more correct to
say it has recaptured an essential element which had been
virtually lost during the period of controversy between the
deists and their opponents. Yet as early as 1881, A. B. Bruce
gives stress to the personal nature of revelation in words which
could well have been written by some influential modern writer
on the same subject. Bruce asks what the idea of revelation
connotes. He is emphatic that it does not mean causing a sacred
book to be written for the religious instruction of mankind. The
term, he declares, 'signifies God manifesting Himself in the
history of the world in a supernatural manner and for a special
purpose. Manifesting *Himself*; for the proper subject of
revelation is God. The Revealer is also the Revealed. This is the
recognition in the words of the Westminster Confession: 'It
pleased the Lord to reveal Himself . . .'' '.[1]

[1] William Nicholls, *Revelation in Christ*, 1957, p. 9.

[2] Cf. Emil Brunner, *The Divine–Human Encounter* (E.T. 1944), p. 12.

[3] A. B. Bruce, *The Chief End of Revelation*, 1881, pp. 57–8; cf. Emil Brunner,
Revelation and Reason (E.T. 1944), p. 8. The essays by Karl Barth, William
Temple and A. Aulen in *Revelation* (ed. J. Baillie and H. Martin), 1937. H. Richard
Niebuhr, *The Meaning of Revelation*, New York, 1941, pp. 143–54.

Three broad views of revelation affecting the subject of this section can, we think, be discerned in the period. Revelation is first stated to be located in man's growing enlightenment, then in the divine events of history, and finally in the living personality of Christ. The question then arises: What is the relation of revelation so conceived to the Bible?

(a) The Bible gives an account of man's developing religious experience. This was, of course, an extreme and radical view which failed altogether to commend itself in any general way to those who desired to remain within the sphere of acceptable Christian faith. It had, however, its enthusiastic advocates— Unitarians for the most part—who took delight in pointing out the 'humanness' of the biblical record. Yet in spite of its manifold 'imperfections' it was granted that the Bible 'supplies the noblest continuous witness which we know to the reality of divine things'.[1]

The most elaborate exponent of the idea was that of Martineau whose book *The Seat of Authority in Religion* was hailed at the time as 'for the present the most notable contribution to recent literature'.[2] Martineau rejected outright both Church and Bible as possessing external authority. His 'Messianic mythology', as S. D. F. Salmond called it, is 'an elaborate assault upon historical Christianity', on both the Christian doctrine of our Lord's Person and the Protestant basis of faith.[3] Martineau is at pains to show his disregard for the idea of Scripture as being either the vessel or the vehicle of revelation. Whatever revelation there is must be sought within; there it must be 'given'. It is not something discovered by man who of himself labours to peep behind the folds of the invisible world to seek God who coldly awaits there for the seeking man to arrive and find out the secret. The 'one condition that the desired Revelation must fulfil is plainly this', says Martineau, 'it must be *immediate*, living God and living man, Spirit present with spirit; knowing Him, indeed, but rather "being known of Him" '.[4] But the Spirit is everywhere and in all. The centre of man's personal

---

[1] J. Estlin Carpenter, *The Bible in the Nineteenth Century*, 1903, p. 512.

[2] *Expository Times*, Vols. I and II, 1889–91, i, p. 192.

[3] S. D. F. Salmond, 'Dr Martineau's "Messianic Mythology" ', *Expository Times*, Vols. I and II, 1889–91, ii, p. 125.

[4] James Martineau, *The Seat of Authority in Religion*, third edition, revised, 1891, p. 305.

life is enfolded by it, and 'though it ever speaks it cannot be spoken of; though it shines everywhere it can be looked at nowhere; and because presupposed as reality it evades criticism as a phenomenon'.[1] Revelation is essentially personal. Like the modern Tillich, whose views have a strange similarity to those of Martineau, he sees revelation as a sort of 'ecstasy' and he quotes Philo in this connection. In the nature of the case it cannot therefore be communicated from mind to mind for it is not a 'datum'.

It is no wonder that Martineau's volume called forth hostility from all quarters. William Sanday records how he felt compelled to yield to the request of the editor of the *Expository Times* and give his impressions of *The Seat of Authority in Religion*. He focused his attention upon Martineau's critical assumptions which were vulnerable because so many of them were fatuous. His exegesis, too, left much to be desired. Sanday may be thought a little unkind in his statement regarding the volume as a whole: 'I honestly do not think it an important book. It is not a book which needs to be read. To speak quite frankly, it is in my opinion a book which would be better left unread'. Sanday, indeed, calls it 'a dangerous book'.[2] It was regarded as having a 'greater success than it deserves'.[3] The volume appeared to many capable observers to suffer from wrong assumptions. It is not true, it was urged against its assertion, that Protestantism points conclusively 'to a field of divine revelation, discoverable only by the telescope, halfway towards the horizon of history'.[4]

The very radicalness of such a view of the relation between revelation and the Bible was its defeat. Its critical presuppositions were proved false and its tone and temper out of harmony with even the most 'advanced' of the 'devout' critics.

(b) A much more acceptable position was therefore sought by others who either felt the impact or accepted the conclusions of criticism. It was desired to accord to the Bible a more vital place in the process of revelation. It would be, we think, a fairly accurate generalization to say that during the early part of the period the Bible was regarded as having the sole power of

---

[1] James Martineau, *The Seat of Authority in Religion*, third edition, revised, 1891, pp. 305–6.

[2] *Expository Times*, Vols. I and II, 1889–91, i, p. 284.

[3] *Op. cit.*, ii, p. 2.   [4] Cf. *op. cit.*, i, p. 193.

conveying revelation to man by awakening him to his need through the stimulation of his religious consciousness. Later, under the impact of criticism, when the doctrine of the Bible's inerrancy was in a large measure abandoned, the Scriptures came to be regarded as containing the record of God's revelatory acts in history.

As early as 1854, William Lee, Archdeacon of Dublin, in his weighty volume, *The Inspiration of Holy Scripture*, noted the difference between the new view, of which he considers Schleiermacher the fountain-head, and what he believes to be the historic doctrine of the Church.[1] The teaching of Schleiermacher, we have shown elsewhere, is the background of what Coleridge and Maurice had to say about the relation between revelation and the Bible.[2] It is their views which provide the clue for the modern understanding of revelation and its connection with Scripture. Maurice especially, whom A. C. Hebert speaks of as 'that seer and prophet of the future whose importance has never yet been recognized',[3] has been, in this context, specially influenced. It is of interest, therefore, in this connection, taking but one example, to observe the use made of Maurice by John Baillie in his own positive statements on the subject in his book, *The Idea of Revelation in Recent Thought*.

The view as it was developed by later writers is that revelation consists of a series of divine acts in which God enters into redeeming contact with human lives. Of these encounters the Bible is the record. The position was given precise statement by W. Robertson Smith. S. D. F. Salmond, giving an account of Smith's teaching on the death of the latter, declares, 'Revelation was to him not a communication of so much truth, but the entrance of God Himself into history and into man's life, the direct personal message of God's love to men. The Bible he held to be the record of this personal revelation of God'.[4]

Such a statement of the position has found vogue and favour. Writer after writer desires us to understand that the Bible is not

[1] William Lee, *The Inspiration of Holy Scripture*, 1854, fourth edition, 1865, p. 21; cf. J. D. Morrell, *The Philosophy of Religion*, pp. 143–4.
[2] Cf. H. D. McDonald, *Ideas of Revelation*, 1959, pp. 166 ff.
[3] A. C. Hebert, *The Function of the Church in the Modern World*, 1936, p. 108.
[4] S. D. F. Salmond, 'Professor William Robertson Smith', *Expository Times*, Vol. V, 1893–4, p. 361; cf. H. Wheeler Robinson, *Inspiration and Revelation in the Old Testament*, 1953, p. 281.

itself the revelation. However ideas about the Bible as such may
have fluctuated, the one point of agreement amongst all those
who reject inerrancy and infallibility is that the Scriptures are
not to be equated with God's self-disclosure. Revelation is
essentially personal whereas the Bible is a form of words and as
such can only tell of revelation. Thus, to give a few illustrations
of this insistence, A. B. Bruce writes, 'The Bible contains the
record, the interpretation and the literary reflection of His
(God's) grace in history'.[1] A. S. Peake argued that we have so
identified revelation with its record that it is now possible only
with great difficulty to recognize that in the strict sense of the
term, revelation lies behind the Bible.[2] He argues further for the
necessity to keep a clear distinction between the Bible as a
record and the revelation to which it witnesses. He is prepared
to grant that without the record we would be in a 'bad way'. 'The
facts themselves and their interpretation are presented to us with
far greater certainty and fulness in Scripture than they can be in
institutions. Moreover, as experience abundantly proves, Scripture is among the most valuable means of grace... We must
accordingly hold fast to the conclusion that it would have been an
irreparable loss if the revelation had not been fixed in a written
form.'[3]

The very title of the volume edited by H. Wheeler Robinson
in 1938, *Record and Revelation* is indicative of the same outlook.[4]

[1] A. B. Bruce, *The Chief End of Revelation*, 1881, p. 280.
[2] A. S. Peake, *The Bible, Its Origin, Its Meaning, Its Abiding Value*, 1913, fifth
edition, p. 290.   [3] *Ibid.*, p. 295.
[4] The position had been given popular and rather exaggerated emphasis by R. F.
Horton in his volume *Revelation and the Bible*, 1892. Horton, it may be noted,
however, had not come to regard revelation as personal and activist. He defines
revelation as 'a truth or truths received from God into the minds of men, not by the
ordinary methods of enquiry, such as observation and reasoning, but by a direct
operation of the Holy Spirit' (second edition, p. 4). Not all in the Bible is, however,
apparently revealed truth or truths. It is that which commends itself by 'direct
manifestations of the Spirit to the Christian consciousness' which may be declared
as revealed truth, as the word of God. The idea therefore 'of a revelation confined to
the Sacred Writings cannot be said to be the idea of those Sacred Writings themselves' (p. 16). He opens his volume however with the remark 'It is proof of the
revelation contained in the Bible that large numbers of Christian men cannot divest
themselves of the idea that everything in the Bible is revelation' (p. 2). Cf. This
idea of Horton's with a remark of Brunner's: 'We are not required to believe the
Scriptures because they are Scriptures; but because Christ, whom I am convinced
in my *conscience* (italics ours) is the Truth, meets me in the Scriptures—therefore
I believe' (Emil Brunner, *The Christian Doctrine of God, Dogmatics*, Vol. I, p. 110,
(E.T. 1950)).

A recent emphatic declaration, which could be paralleled from a hundred volumes, reiterates the same view: 'the Bible is not revelation, but the record of it'.[1] According to E. P. Dickie, it is the modern recognition of the Bible as 'the *record* of the most profound religious experiences leading up to and culminating in Jesus Christ' that we see its 'true nature'.[2]

(c) Those who have sought to lay stress upon the personal nature of revelation and especially those who have been influenced by Barth and Brunner, in regarding Christ as the 'Word of God' and the locus of revelation, have been eager to accentuate the distinction between revelation and the Scripture. These writers have been at pains to make two things clear. First, to deny, as Barth repeatedly does, that revelation is 'a static sum of revealed propositions'. Any such notion is declared anathema. Brunner in his *Revelation and Reason* reiterates the thesis that 'Divine revelation is not a book or a doctrine'.[3] Here we have what G. S. Hendry regards as 'a commonplace of modern theology' namely, 'that the Biblical revelation is not a system of abstract propositional truths, but, both in form and substance, a history of the acts of God'.[4] The second point these writers are anxious to guard against, to quote Barth again, is 'the freezing of the connection between Scripture and revelation'. The idea that revelation has to do with a communication of truth is usually attributed to the intellectualization of the Reformers' doctrine and as an illustration of the ever-recurring tendency to scholasticism.

Having then the idea of revelation as a divine self-disclosure of the 'Word of God' it remains to be noted that in this context the Bible is usually spoken of as a 'witness' to the actuality and the possibility of revelation. John Baillie, for example, sees the position of the Bible as that of John the Baptist: it, like him, is

---

[1] C. B. Moss, *The Christian Faith*, 1943, p. 211.

[2] E. P. Dickie, *Revelation and Response*, 1938, p. 129.

[3] E. Brunner, *Revelation and Reason* (E.T. 1946), 8; cf. p. 53. Cf. E. Brunner, *Dogmatics*, Vol. I (E.T. 1950), p. 53. K. Barth, *Church Dogmatic*, 1, i (E.T. 1936), p. 162 f. Nathaniel Micklem, *Ultimate Questions*, 1955, p. 55. F. W. Camfield, *Revelation and the Holy Spirit*, 1934, pp. 27 ff. and Chapter 2. H. Cunliffe Jones, *The Authority of Biblical Revelation*, 1946, Chapter II, etc. W. H. Morton, *Christian Theology*, An Ecumenical Approach, 1955, p. 46. *Liberal Theology* (ed. Roberts and Vandusen), 1942, p. 231.

[4] G. S. Hendry, 'The Dogmatic Form of Barth's Theology', *Theology Today*, Vol. XIII, 1956, 3, pp. 312 ff.

not the Light, but is to bear witness to the Light. Brunner[1] regards the Scripture as human testimony to revelation. True, he does not consider every part of the record as having the same witness value. Some parts of it do not 'point' to the inbreaking of God into human experience in the same decisive way. Some parts but 'stammer' out His name. Other passages, such as II Peter ii. 4, fall outside the 'rim' and have no witness value.[2]

The constantly reiterated statement that revelation is always communion and that it is never communication has, it should be noted, come in for increasing questioning of late. The Barthian activist view, of course, is an understandable repudiation of the exclusive emphasis upon the propositional notion which dominated a certain type of theological thinking of an earlier period. Many, however, have gone to an extreme position and deny that there is any doctrinal element at all in revelation. Some permit statements of biblical truths as inferences made by Christians under the influence of the Spirit; inferences which are based upon the knowledge of God's saving acts in history. William Temple, argued that 'there is no such thing as revealed truth'.[3] There are, he will allow, 'truths of revelation' which are 'propositions which express the results of correct thinking concerning revelation'.

A. E. Wright, in like manner, denies that the Bible contains, what he refers to as 'static, propositional' statements of doctrine. 'Does the Bible contain a *system* of doctrine?' he asks. His answer is: 'Certainly none of its writers was primarily concerned with the presentation of such a scheme. Consequently, we must say that static, propositional systems are those which the Church itself erects by inference from the Biblical writings'.[4] Emphatic declarations of this nature are constantly being made. But it is of interest to observe that those who are the most insistent that revelation is always in acts, never in propositions, find themselves unable to maintain their own thesis with any consistency. This is true even of Brunner and Barth. Brunner, to take him as an example, urges that 'A Church . . . can do

---

[1] John Baillie, *The Idea of Revelation in Recent Thought*, 1956, p. 125.

[2] E. Brunner, *Revelation and Reason* (E.T. 1938), pp. 15–17, 48, etc. E. Brunner, *The Philosophy of Religion*, 1937, p. 153 f; cf. H. D. McDonald, *Ideas of Revelation*, 1959, p. 191.

[3] William Temple, *Nature, Man and God*, 1947, p. 317.

[4] A. Ernest Wright, *The God Who Acts*, 1952, p. 35.

justice to her commission only when she recovers the unity of the *Logos* and the *Dynamis*, of the word and the act of God, which is the distinctive element in Biblical revelation'.[1] A. G. Hebert in a chapter on 'The Biblical Idea of Revelation', makes the significant observation that in the Scriptures there is throughout a 'double conception of Revelation, as the revelation of God Himself, and of truths concerning Him'.[2] We have ourselves argued elsewhere that since man is a 'spiritual' and 'rational' being revelation must come to meet the whole man. Because man is 'spiritual' it must come to him as 'Spirit', and because he is 'rational' it must come to him as 'truth'.[3] It has been our contention that the divorce between the activist and the propositionalist ideas of revelation is ultimately invalid. 'Whether the Christian revelation is only personal and not to some extent propositional is another question', states E. G. Homrighausen in a review of Brunner's *Divine–Human Encounter*, 'for if God reveals Himself adequately, man's mind must be satisfied'.[4] Undoubtedly, as Louis Berkhof readily admits, 'The view, once prevalent, that revelation consists exclusively in a communication of doctrine, was clearly one-sided. At present, however', he continues, 'some go to the other extreme, equally one-sided, that revelation consists in communication of power and life'.[5]

It seems to becoming clearer as the subject becomes more and more discussed that 'The modern view makes an unnecessary cleavage between the personal and the propositional in revelation'.[6] The two are complementary, not contradictory. True,

---

[1] Emil Brunner, *Revelation and Reason* (E.T. 1946), p. 164; cf. 'Revelation is a concept that both *relates* religious knowledge to the more ordinary forms of knowledge and *distinguishes* it *from* them' (W. H. Morton, *Christian Theology, An Ecumenical Approach*, 1955, p. 41).

[2] A. G. Hebert, *The Authority of the Old Testament*, 1947, p. 80.

[3] H. D. McDonald, *Ideas of Revelation*, 1959, p. 274.

[4] E. G. Homrighausen, *Theology Today*, Vol. I, No. i, April 1944, pp. 153 ff. Cf. E. J. Carnell, *A Philosophy of the Christian Religion*, 1952, p. 29.

[5] Louis Berkhof, *Reformed Dogmatics*, Introductory Volume, 1932, p. 144. Cf. 'The Bible does contain much objective propositional truth. The central truths of the Bible are literally correct; for example, God is love and was in Christ reconciling the world unto Himself. Therefore Barth's contention that the Bible becomes the Word of God *only* for faith is too deeply tinged with subjectivism to speak the full truth'. Nels F. S. Ferré, *Christ and the Christian*, 1958, p. 37.

[6] Francis I. Andersen, *The Westminster Theological Journal*, Vol. XXII, No. 2, May 1960, p. 127.

information is not God: but it seems certainly impossible to
know God personally apart from the information. 'To belittle
propositions because they are impersonal is to destroy human
relations by despising their normal medium. The bliss of being
loved is different from the words of love-making, but the
"proposition", "I love you", is a welcome, nay, an indispensable
means of the consummation of love in actuality. . . . But in
modern theology we have a Lover-God who makes no
declarations!'[1]

The idea that God can be known 'personally' apart from ideas,
or at any rate apart from 'images' is given a specific and unique
denial by Austin Farrer. Farrer agrees, to be sure, that the
modern view of revelation in and by divine events alone is more
satisfying than the theory of dictated propositions.[2] He is quite
ready to admit, what, we suppose, all Christians do really
maintain, that the primary revelation is Jesus Christ Himself.
Farrer, however, is insistent that 'the events by themselves are
not revelation'.[3] He therefore concludes that it is in the interplay
of image and event where we have the locus of revelation. His
thesis is, then, that 'the events without the images would be no
revelation at all, and the images without the events would
remain shadows on the clouds'.[4] Farrer opens Lecture IV with a
statement of the conclusion to which his enquiry has so far led.
It is a significant declaration; 'We have concluded', he says, 'that
divine truth is supernaturally communicated to men in an act of
inspired thinking which falls into the shape of certain images'.[5]

Farrer raises the question consequent upon his teaching:
'Does God feed His saints with nothing but figures of speech?'

---

[1] Francis I. Andersen, *The Westminster Theological Journal*, Vol. XXII, No. 2,
May 1960, p. 127. Cf. 'For love is self-affirmation as well as self-impartation; it
must be first self-affirmation in order that it may become self-imparting love'.
Newman Smyth, *Christian Ethics*, 1896, p. 328.

[2] Austin Farrer, *The Glass of Vision*, 1948, pp. 36 ff.; cf. also his chapter
'Revelation' in *Faith and Logic* (ed. Basil Mitchell).

[3] *Ibid.*, p. 43.   [4] *Ibid.*

[5] *Ibid.*, p. 57. An interesting comparison could be drawn between Farrer and
the teaching of Dionysius the Areopagite. Dionysius has the same idea of 'images',
but perhaps he fails to stress the need for 'event' as does Farrer. 'Revelation'
according to Dionysius, 'itself does not convey any knowledge of God that could
be expressed in speculative terms. Revelation veils as well as reveals. It is for this
reason that figurative speech, metaphor, image, and parable abound throughout
the Bible'. Richard Kroner, *Speculation and Revelation in the Age of Christian
Philosophy*, 1959, p. 134.

He insists that the 'images' will not be understood without the prior action of, what he calls 'supernatural life' in the soul.[1] Without this 'revealed truth is dumb to us'. He adds, however, that it is absurd to suggest that the supernatural action we exercise is the adequate real counterpart of the divine truth we believe. At this point, we believe John Baillie has misinterpreted Farrer.[2] As far as we can see, all that Farrer is saying in his own way is what orthodox faith has always stressed, namely, there must be for the subjective realization of saving truth, the inner witness of the Holy Spirit. It might, in fact, although Farrer might not concur, be contended that Farrer is using the term 'image' for what others refer to as 'proposition'. And if the term were substituted for Farrar's 'image' in the quotation at the end of the paragraph above then we have a clear enough statement of what conservative theology demands. God does not feed His saints on propositions and yet it is through propositions, in some sense, that they are fed.

In order to complete the story it remains to be pointed out that conservative evangelicals, as will be expected, maintain what they regard to be two important facts in their statement on the subject of revelation.

They insist that God's revelation consists of revealed truths. There must be a propositional, that is, a verbal aspect to it. It is regarded as a fallacy to reserve the idea of revelation for divine acts and to deny the reality of divine words. The position is clearly and unequivocably argued by J. I. Packer in his closely reasoned defence of the conservative evangelical case. 'God reveals Himself to men', he declares, 'both by exercising power for them and by teaching truth to them. The two activities are not antithetical, but complementary. Indeed, the Biblical position is that the mighty acts of God are not revelation to man at all, except in so far as they are accompanied by words to explain them.'[3] The same insistence is found to underlie the various essays to which a number of British conservative evangelical scholars have contributed to the volume *Revelation and the Bible*. In his essay on 'Contemporary Ideas of Revelation', R. A. Finlayson rejects the antithesis created by the modern school of

---

[1] Austin Farrer, *The Glass of Vision*, p. 59.
[2] John Baillie, *The Idea of Revelation in Recent Thought*, 1956, p. 39 f.
[3] J. I. Packer, *'Fundamentalism' and the Word of God*, 1958, p. 92.

theology, both neo-liberal and neo-orthodox, between revelation as encounter and revelation as communication. He urges
that 'our encounter with God rests upon the mediation of His
truth to chosen prophets and apostles. In virtue of the divine
inspiration that communication is for us completely trustworthy,
introducing us to the living and true God'.[1]

The other major antithesis, namely that between revelation
and Scripture, is also being strongly challenged. Brunner,
Barth, Baillie and numerous others, as we have indicated,
sharpened the divorce between them. Yet these very writers
themselves, it will be discovered, have found it hard to avoid the
identification which they so strenuously deny. One cannot read
very far in the writings of any one of them before one comes
upon a passage in which the identity of revelation with the
record is unwittingly made. Brunner who has been so strong in
his denial of the legitimacy of equating revelation with Scripture
can say: 'Holy Scripture therefore does not only speak of
revelation; it is itself the revelation'.[2] C. H. Dodd, in the same
manner, urges on one page that the Church offers the Bible 'as
the authoritative record of the divine revelation',[3] yet on
another page states in categorical fashion, 'The Church offers
this book as a revelation of God'.[4]

---

[1] *Revelation and the Bible* (ed. Carl F. H. Henry), 1958, p. 228. Carl Henry,
himself, argues in his massive volume, *Christian Personal Ethics*, 1957, that the
dialectical existential ethics by rejecting propositional revelation altogether has
denied a rational basis for theology and ethics. The message of the Bible, he insists,
'centres in the disclosure to mankind of a transcendent supernatural reality. Jesus,
in the tradition of the Hebrew prophets, upholds unconditional imperatives which
are transcendent to individual experience, objectively confronting man as divinely
authoritative. He asserts principles which have not arisen *in* human experience but
which are to be received as universally trustworthy and dependable guides for life.
They reflect ethical realities external to human experience' (p. 138). George F.
Thomas is quoted as urging that abandonment of ethical propositions discloses a
'nominalistic tendency to stress the particular at the expense of the universal aspect
or moral situations', and the result 'leads . . . perilously close to the abyss of
irrationalism'. *Ibid.*; cf. George F. Thomas, *Christian Ethics and Moral Philosophy*,
p. 386. The position from a Christian point of view might be simply put like this:
revelation is essentially redemptive and redemption is essentially ethical. The
ethical can only come in terms of ethical imperatives so that revelation must involve
essential ethical propositions. The same argument can be used to insist upon the
truth-content of revelation. '*Intellectual* evaluation and assent are indispensable
elements in significant moral decision. Moral decision which is wrenched from man
in the absence of rational criteria is deficient' (p. 139).
[2] Emil Brunner, *Revelation and Reason* (E.T. 1946), p. 21.
[3] C. H. Dodd, *The Bible Today*, 1946, p. 15.　　　[4] *Ibid.*, p. 12.

There is an apparent growing sensitiveness to the rightness of the modern cleavage between revelation and its record. This is seen, for example, in Lionel Thornton's important book, *Revelation and the Modern World*. Thornton's thesis seems to be that God's self-manifestation is bound up with the minutiae of contemporary life. It is virtually impossible to abstract the essence of revelation from the sacred literature in which it is enshrined.[1] They stand together. Thornton declares that the writers of the Bible 'wove the garments in which the theophany is clothed, apart from which it cannot be manifested'.[2] Without this dress it would disappear as surely as in the modern scientific romance 'the invisible man' was no longer seen when he took off his clothes. Thornton, therefore, stresses that 'Scripture as a whole is the Whole with which Revelation is to be identified'.[3] As the onion which cannot be peeled it must be accepted as it is. It must not be supposed, however, that Thornton in rejecting what he calls the Liberal Experiment, is committed to what he refers to as 'the opposite error of bibliolatry or "fundamentalism" '.[4] Revelation has identity with the vessel, but there is a real distinction at the same time between the two. He will admit that there are 'imperfections of the earthen vessel in which the divine treasure is conveyed', but even so, these 'are themselves integral to the very nature of revelation itself'.[5] Although there is much in Thornton's thesis commendable and much which is questionable, its significance in our present context lies in its expression of obvious dissatisfaction with the neo-orthodox complete separation between revelation and the record.

The necessity for a more intimate relationship between God's self-disclosure and the Scriptures we ourselves have argued in the closing section of our *Ideas of Revelation*.[6] Acknowledgement was there given to the truth which the distinction seeks to maintain. There is a real and objective revelation in divine works and words, prior to and independent of, any written record. The

---

[1] L. E. Thornton, *Revelation and the Modern World*, 1950, p. 16.
[2] *Ibid.*, p. 53.   [3] *Ibid.*, p. 130.   [4] *Ibid.*
[5] *Ibid.*, p. 132. Cf. 'While we must accept the Bible as an earthen vessel with flaws and limitations which are part of the living manifestation of God's word in and through men, we must beware of magnifying these flaws so as to obscure the great supernatural fact to which the Bible testifies.' H. Cunliffe-Jones, *The Authority of the Biblical Revelation*, 1946, second impression, 1948, p. 117.
[6] H. D. McDonald, *Ideas of Revelation*, 1959, p. 282.

central aspect of revelation, so to say, is God's saving deeds in history, but these divine acts come necessarily in an historical context and, as C. R. North remarks, 'the historical occasion is an essential element in the revelation'.[1] It is, however, only as the 'historical occasion' of the divine act is recorded that it can be known to us. Revelation, to be sure, may be thought of as God's acts in history, but these 'actualities' of God in history would remain in the limbo of forgotten things if they were not preserved in record. In the last analysis, then, revelation must be taken to include, not merely the acts of God in history, but the history of these acts, and their interpretation and application to the concrete realities of human experience.[2] It is beyond question that as 'soon as we try to abstract the values from their concrete embodiment, we evacuate them of all reality and become sentimentalists. The spiritual must always be embodied to be known and faithfully served; the eternal must clothe itself in temporal form to enter effectually within our horizon'.[3]

James Orr, defending the evangelical assimulation of revelation with the record—and this is the second important fact conservative scholars desire to maintain—postulates that 'if a revelation has been given by God, it is reasonable to expect that provision will be made for the *preservation* of the knowledge of the revelation *in some permanent and authoritative form*'.[4] He argues that the recorders of revelation must be men who stand in a special intimate connection with the original act of self-disclosure and that they must be men who possess in an eminent degree the Spirit of the revelation. The revelation, he then urges, includes, 'not only direct acts and communications, but *the whole divinely-guided history* of the people of Israel, and in the New Testament, *the apostolic action* in the founding of the Church'.[5] As for the recorders themselves they must be given a special inspiration for the right use of their materials and a special illumination to see into the meaning of history. All must

---

[1] C. R. North, *The Old Testament Interpretation of History*, 1946, p. 153.

[2] Cf. 'Christianity in an historical religion is a particularly technical sense that the term possesses—it presents us with religious doctrines which are at the same time historical events or historical interpretations.' H. Butterfield, *Christianity and History*, 1950, p. 3.

[3] H. Wheeler Robinson, *Redemption and Revelation*, 1942, p. xliv; cf. p. 186.

[4] James Orr, *Revelation and Inspiration*, 1910, reprint, 1952, p. 155.

[5] *Ibid.*, p. 157.

be taken into account, not the divine side merely, but no less the human reception of the revelation and the actings of the human spirit under its influence, and in response to it. What is ultimately required in a book which is to be an adequate record of divine revelation is 'not only the record of what may be called its *external* historical course, but the record of its *internal* history in the life and experience of souls that have grasped their meaning, and felt their power'.[1]

Having in the Bible, Orr concludes, a record which fulfills all the required criteria, it becomes God's complete word. Beyond it there is no need to travel to discover God's whole will for our salvation. Consequently, he contends, this being the position and the purpose of the Scripture, 'the line between revelation and record is becoming very thin, and that, in another true sense, *the record*, in the fulness of its contents, *is itself for us the revelation*'.[2]

B. THE WORD OF GOD AND THE SCRIPTURES

From what has gone before, the reader will not be surprised to discover that a sharp antithesis was also set up throughout our period between what was regarded as the Word of God and the Scriptures. The distinction was already to hand, it should be noted, popularized more especially by S. T. Coleridge and F. D. Maurice who reacted vigorously against the orthodox apologists who, in their polemic against the Deists, had maintained revelation to be a body of divinely communicated truths unerringly given in the Bible. Attention had been focused, by way of opposition, on the inward and the subjective. Protest was raised against what was regarded as 'book worship' in Protestantism; and the important dictum was laid down by Coleridge that it is when the Bible 'finds me' that it authenticates its authority as a witness to the Word of God. This principle of Coleridge has been used with effect by many in the present period who have continued to distinguish between the Word of God and the Scripture in which it is contained or through which it is discovered.[3]

---

[1] James Orr, *Revelation and Inspiration*, p. 158.

[2] *Ibid.*, p. 159 (italics in original in each case).

[3] Coleridge's phrase is constantly quoted as a statement of the position of many modern writers: cf., e.g. the two writers, Alfred Peel and R. H. Lightfoot in *The Interpretation of the Bible* (ed. C. W. Dugmore), 1944, pp. 60 and 90.

Before the full effect of criticism had been felt, a large body of religious opinion was committed to the cleavage between the Word of God and the Bible. The number was greatly increased with the coming of the higher criticism. The vital and intended result of criticism was to give attention to the 'humanness' of the Bible. It was to be treated as any other book would be. So constantly reiterated was this point that some came to regard the Scripture as a very imperfect vessel whatever might be the treasure it was claimed to contain. It was false, it was declared, to speak of such a collection of books, compiled over a vast period from a multiplicity of documents of varying degrees of reliability, as the Word of God.

In the immediate post-Darwinian period, the Bible was thought of by many as giving a highly interesting account of man's progressive discovery of God. In the early days of criticism the tendency was, at first, to take the same line and to see the Bible as more or less a valuable record of vital religious experience. 'Thus the view of the Bible having the term "religious experience" for its key-word came to be widely accepted'.[1] Here, also, the historic identification of the Word of God with the Scriptures was rejected. The Word of God, the claim went, was a term to be reserved for the creative religious experience of all prophetic men in general and of the great men of the Bible in particular.

As more and more Christ was specified as the locus of revelation, it was maintained that He and He alone was properly to be designated the Word of God. In this the theologians of crisis have come to insist upon the idea for which the earlier Coleridgean school had contended.[2] The title belongs to

[1] A. G. Hebert, *The Authority of the Old Testament*, 1947, p. 33; cf. J. M. Graham, ' "After Fifty Years" Revelation and the Bible', *Expository Times*, Vol. I, 1938–9, pp. 537–40.

[2] B. E. Meland makes the interesting observation that whereas the feeling–experience derives from Schleiermacher the attention focused upon the Person of Christ is due to Ritschl. It was, he states, the reaction against rationalism which led theologians like Schleiermacher and philosophers like Coleridge to extend the appeal to religious experience. 'Ritschlian theology, while it continued the emphasis upon feeling and experience which had characterized the thought of Schleiermacher, narrowed the appeal to a specific object within the Christian tradition. The object was the *person* of the historic Jesus. Accordingly the appeal to Christ, or more particularly, the appeal to the immediate experience of the person of Christ, replaced the appeal to experience, based upon the "sense of dependence".' N. H. Wieman and B. E. Meland, *American Philosophies of Religion*, 1936, p. 42.

Christ alone.[1] Barth, it is well known, has put great emphasis
upon this point. Revelation, he argues, is the '*Deus dixit*', the
'one Word of God within which there can be neither a more or
less'.[2] He maintained the two-way equation; 'God's Word is
God's Son' and 'God's Son is God's Word'.[3] The constant note
of much writing on the subject of revelation is that we must
beware of imprisoning the Word of God within the covers of a
book.[4] And fearful warnings are issued against 'bibliolatory',
and against making, as the seventeenth century teachers are
said to have done, 'absolute surrender' to a 'paper pope'.
Brunner charges those whom he designates 'fundamentalists'
with being 'in bondage to the Biblical text' and thereby making
'the Bible an idol and me its slave'. More recently Nels
F. S. Ferré in America has been eloquent in repudiating the
identification of God's Word in revelation with the Bible. He
regards the desire to make such an equation as an illustration of
Vaihinger's law of the tendency to substitute the means for the
end. Thus the book comes to be considered perfect and its words
inerrant. 'Fearful human beings, claiming a liberating Gospel,
barricade themselves behind a book. God's good means is thus
defiled through perversion. The false use becomes demoniac and
destructive, and faith flees. Relaxed love and spontaneous
creativity cease.'[5] Many would, of course, be ready to join issue
with Ferré about the rightness of his charge and they would
certainly wish to question the correctness of his conclusion
regarding the dire consequences of regarding the Bible as
'perfect' and the complete container of the Word of God. But,

[1] Cf. 'The word of God which saveth and redeemeth the soul is not the word
printed on paper, but is the . . . ever-speaking Word, which is the Son of God.'
W. Law, *The Way of Divine Knowledge*, p. 137. 'More and more he (F. D. Maurice)
had come to look upon all expressions implying that the letter of the Bible is the
word of God as denials of the living "Word of God" of Whom the Bible speaks.'
Life of F. D. Maurice, by his son, Vol. 2, p. 452.
[2] Karl Barth, *Church Dogmatics* (E.T. 1936), 1, i, p. 164.
[3] *Ibid.*, p. 156; cf. William Nicholls, *Revelation in Christ*, 1957, Chapter II.
[4] Cf. 'But if the Bible is called the Word of God, theological confusion is almost
unavoidable. Such consequences as the dictation theory of inspiration, dishonesty in
dealing with the biblical text, a "monophysitic" dogma of the infallibility of a book,
etc., follow from such an identification. Probably nothing has contributed more to
the misinterpretation of all biblical doctrine of the Word than the identification of
the Word with the Bible.' Paul Tillich, *Systematic Theology*, Vol. I, 1951, pp. 158–9.
[5] Nels F. S. Ferré, *The Christian Understanding of God*, 1951, p. 179. See Chapter
VII in that volume entitled, 'The Work of God in Revelation'.

be this as it may, it is a fact that the statement of an antithesis
between the Word of God and the Bible became characteristic of
the period. The result of this divorce has been a certain amount
of hesitancy and doubt about the way the Bible itself is to be
conceived. And as a consequence, as H. Cunliffe-Jones justly
observes, 'for many reasons, the Christian Church is uncertain
at the present time, how to treat the Bible as the Word of
God'.[1]

In the main, however, it has become usual for those who, for
whatever their reasons, accept the antithesis, to refer to the
Bible as 'containing' or as 'speaking of', or as 'witnessing to',
or as 'becoming' the Word of God. There is general agreement
that it is not to be identified with the Word of God. Some of
those who have adopted this understanding of the relation of the
Word of God to the Scriptures have claimed the Reformers as
their Fathers. But such a claim is unquestionably biased. Albert
Peel asserts that the Reformers would have some criticisms to
offer to those who speak today of the Bible as the Word of God.[2]
He suggests that they drew a distinction between the Word of
God and the Scriptures which convey or becomes it. It is not
easy, we think, taking an objective view of the data, to get
support for such a contention in the teaching of the Fathers of the
Reformation. That Calvin equated the Word of God with the
Bible is a certain fact. In the case of Luther, pre-eminently a
preacher and little of a systematic theologian, there is less
exactness and consistency of statement in this connection. Yet he
opens his *Table Talks* with the words 'That the Bible is God's
word and book I prove thus . . .'. G. B. Fisher correctly
assesses the situation when he declares that 'the identity of the
Holy Scriptures with the Word of God is generally assumed by
Luther and occasionally expressed in explicit language'.[3]
Recently the same position has been confidently maintained
by Robert Preus who contends that the Lutheran reformers

[1] H. Cunliffe-Jones, *The Authority of the Biblical Revelation*, 1946, second
impression, 1948, p. 132.
[2] Albert Peel, 'The Bible and the Book', *The Interpretation of the Bible* (ed. C. W.
Dugmore), 1944, p. 67; cf. pp. 52, 66 and 68. Cf. E. P. Dickie, *Revelation and
Response*, 1938, p. 130.
[3] G. B. Fisher, *History of Christian Doctrine*, 1896, edition, 1922, p. 280. Cf.
W. P. Paterson, *The Rule of Faith*, 1932, p. 405. M. Reu, *Luther and the Scriptures*,
1944, pp. 17, 24, 35, 55, 63, 92, etc.

accepted the complete identity of Scripture with the Word of God.[1] While at an earlier date K. R. Hagenbach affirmed that 'During the preceding period', he is referring to the time prior to 1700, 'Protestant theology had been accustomed to call the Sacred Scriptures themselves the Word of God; in the course of the present a distinction was made between the *word of God contained in Holy Writ* and the Sacred Scriptures'.[2]

Whether, however, the Reformers are called upon to justify the distinction between the Word of God and the Scriptures, or not, the fact remains that many in our period have preferred to regard the Bible as 'containing' that Word. To think of Scripture itself as the Word of God, it has been argued of late by J. K. S. Reid, is to compromise the sovereignty of God and the result must be that 'God's word is petrified in a dead record'.[3] It is not very clear from Reid, it may be remarked in passing, why God's sovereignty is not rather revealed in His use of the Scripture as the source of His life-giving power in the personal experience of redemption. It is, at any rate, worthy of notice that it is the written word which in several passages in the New Testament is referred to as 'the Word of God'.[4]

The first advocates of the higher criticism implied in their manifold writings their satisfaction with the disassociation of the idea of the Word of God from the Scriptures. The concept of the Bible as that which 'contains' the Word of God, was, for example, argued for strongly by F. W. Farrar. Farrar, in fact, goes so far as to contend that it is the doctrine of the Church of England that 'Scripture *contains* the Word of God'.[5] And he maintains that 'To assert that the phrase "Scripture containeth" (*complectitur*) instead of "is" (*est*) the Word of God is only *an accident* of the formularies of the English Church is the reverse of the fact'.[6] Farrar says that 'The Bible as a whole may be spoken of as the word of God, because it *contains* words and passages of God to the human soul; but it is not in its whole

[1] Robert Preus, *The Inspiration of Scripture*, A Study in the Theology of the Seventeenth Century Lutheran Dogmaticians, 1955, Chapter 2.
[2] H. R. Hagenbach, *Compendium of the History of Doctrine*, 1880, Vol. 2, p. 406.
[3] J. K. S. Reid, *The Authority of Scripture*, 1957, p. 279.
[4] Cf. H. D. McDonald, *Ideas of Revelation*, 1959, pp. 277–8. Cf. W. M. Horton, *Christian Theology*, An Ecumenical Approach, 1955, pp. 65 ff.
[5] F. W. Farrar, *The Bible, Its Meaning and Supremacy*, 1897, p. 136.
[6] *Ibid.*, pp. 136, 137.

extent, and throughout, identical with the Word of God'.[1] Farrar endeavours to destroy the proposition by which the Puritan writer, Thomas Cartwright, in his *Treatise of the Christian Religion* (1616) had sought to demonstrate the thesis that the books of the Bible may be 'discerned to be the word of God'.

A popular exposition of the idea that the Bible can at most be said to *contain* the word of God only was given by R. F. Horton. Horton tells in his *Autobiography* how he was compelled to reject the idea of 'the verbal infallibility of the Bible',[2] and as a consequence set out on a 'quest to find the sure foundation'.[3] Of one fact alone could he be sure, he acknowledges, namely, that faith must be centred in Christ and the Christian experience. He had hoped to clarify the position regarding the relation of the Bible to revelation, but he boldly states that his book, *Revelation and the Bible*, 'pretends to be nothing more than a series of tentative suggestions'.[4] He, however, maintains, not merely as a suggestion but as an assured fact, that to speak of some parts of the Bible—his instance in this particular is the Book of Ecclesiastes—'as the Word of God is an impiety'.[5] Earlier he had contended that 'Nothing could be further from the truth to describe Psalm LXXXIII, for example, as the Word of God; it is by its very form the word of men, of men, too, who have not entered very deeply into the counsels of God'.[6] Statements of

---

[1] F. W. Farrar, *The Bible, Its Meaning and Supremacy*, 1897, p. 131; note heading of chapter 'The Bible contains the Word of God'.

[2] R. F. Horton, *Autobiography*, 1918, p. 144.   [3] *Ibid.*, p. 100.

[4] R. F. Horton, *Revelation and the Bible*, 1892, second edition, Preface, p. viii.

[5] *Ibid.*, p. 204.

[6] *Ibid.*, 1888, pp. 188–9. Even a more explicit statement will be found in his *Verbum Dei*, 1893: 'The unthinking dogma of orthodoxy that the Bible as such is the Word of God . . .' (p. 107) is a typical declaration. Cf. His *Inspiration and the Bible*, 1888, Preface, p. 10. Yet note Horton's strange words in his *Verbum Dei*, 'The Bible itself is in so unique and peculiar a sense the Word of God . . .' (p. 155).

In the volume *Inspiration, A Clerical Symposium*, 1884 (ed. F. W. Farrar), there is an explanatory subtitle in the form of a question to which the eleven contributors sought an answer: 'In what sense, and within what limits, is the Bible to be regarded as the Word of God?' Three of those who wrote on the subject, S. Leathes, John Cairns, and G. W. Oliver, contended that the phrase 'the Word of God' is applicable to the Bible as a whole, and they emphatically rejected the idea that the Bible 'contains' the Word of God (see esp. pp. 23 ff.). Other writers who find a place in the company of the historic orthodox Christian Churches (there are writers in the volume who do not stand in this association; there is, e.g. a Jew, a Swedenborgian, and a Unitarian), contend for the idea that the Bible *contains* the Word of God. Here E. White and F. W. Farrar are the two most important.

this nature, which could be paralleled from other sources, were, to say the least, disconcerting to those who had been taught to regard the Bible in itself as the Word of God. Horton's position was a popular rehash of Robertson Smith's doctrine,[1] although stated in a rough and crude manner. 'The Word of God authenticates itself' the slogan ran: and it does so through those parts of the book which the enlightened Christian consciousness can appreciate. Taking their cue from the Coleridgeans, these writers maintained that the Scriptures become the Word of God in the context of experience. It is not to be regarded in itself, in its totality, as the Word of God: it is the vehicle of the divine activity, the witness to revelation.[2]

C. H. Dodd gave refined exposition to the thesis. 'In the expression "the Word of God" ', he says, 'lurks an equivocation'.[3] It is a 'metaphorical expression'.[4] He sees the Bible as the 'seminal' word, but not the final word. It mediates the 'Word of God' and herein lies its authority.[5] Dodd's position appears to be, concerning the Bible, that those parts of it which 'find' me most, reveal God best. Whatever commends itself to the aroused moral consciousness within the seeking individual is to be designated the 'Word of God'. 'The criterion' contends Dodd, 'lies within ourselves, in the response of our own spirit

---

[1] Cf. T. M. Lindsay, 'Professor W. Robertson Smith's Doctrine of Scripture', *Expositor*, fourth series, Vol. X, 1894, pp. 241–64; see also Smith's own *Answer to the Form of Libel*, 1878, pp. 18–44.

[2] The importance of the new emphasis is reflected in the differences introduced into the Articles of Faith of the English Presbyterian Church about this time. In 1888, after three years of study the appointed committee proposed the draft form of the new creed which was recommended as an interpretation of the old Westminster Confession. The article on Scripture was put No. 18 instead of at the beginning as in the case of the Westminster symbol. In place of the term 'Word of God' that of 'Revelation' was proposed. More significant, instead of the emphatic declaration that the Bible 'is' the Word of God came the suggestion that it should read (as in the Shorter Catechism) 'is contained in'. The alterations were vigorously challenged and emendations suggested. After an extended period allowed for consideration and discussion a compromise was reached and was adopted by the Synod of 1890. In the adopted articles the one on Scripture comes as the nineteenth. The phrase 'is contained in', which was regarded as recent and inadequate by the conservative opposition was omitted. But they were unsuccessful in gaining the admission of the Westminster declaration that the Bible 'is' the Word of God. The article as it now stands, and subscription to which was required by the Synod of 1892, reads: 'This Revelation has been, so far as needful, committed to writing by men inspired of the Holy Spirit, in the Scriptures of the Old and New Testaments, which are to be devoutly studied by all as God's written Word or Message to mankind'.

[3] C. H. Dodd, *The Authority of the Bible*, 1928, p. 16.   [4] *Ibid.*   [5] *Ibid.*, p. 289.

to the Spirit that utters itself in the Scriptures.'[1] This means that a subjective valuation of what is to be understood as the Word of God is proclaimed. It is, indeed, emphatically declared that 'Nowhere is the truth given in such purely "objective" form that we can find a self-subsistent external authority'.[2]

On the lips of the more radical critics any reference to the Bible as the objective Word of God was specially abhorrent. The more advanced became the critic, the more was the gospel conceived to be a message *about* God, not a message of God, and certainly not a message from God.

Dialectical theology, we have seen, has reserved the title the Word of God for Christ alone. W. M. Horton in his essay in the symposium *Revelation*, believes it to be one of the distinctive results of the modern discussion of the subject that this antithesis should be maintained. He says, 'We are not likely again to identify God's eternal Word with the Book which contains the record of its revealing'.[3] Actually in the same volume Sergius Bulgakoff does seek to give significance to the Scripture as itself the Word of God; but he, of course, does not stand in the same tradition as the other writers. The rest, in spite of their deep differences (for the difference between Barth and Temple, for example, is great) are at one in repudiating the idea that the concept 'Word of God' can be properly applied to the Bible.

By its failure to give any significant meaning to the historic description of the Scriptures as the written word of God, the older liberalism stands condemned. It was, as T. H. Manson observes, so 'vitiated by its dogmatic presuppositions' that it could not deal adequately with 'the history of Biblical religion'.[4] The romantic and evolutionary ideas which undergirded it were insecure. Manson is perfectly right to speak of 'The failure of Liberalism to interpret the Bible as the Word of God'.[5] The only

[1] C. H. Dodd, *The Authority of the Bible*, 1928, p. 296.   [2] *Ibid.*, p. 289.
[3] *Revelation* (ed. John Baillie and Hugh Martin), 1937, p. 264.
[4] *The Interpretation of the Bible* (ed. C. W. Dugdale), 1944, p. 102.
[5] Cf. Title of T. H. Manson's essay, *op, cit.* Cf. C. J. Cadoux, 'Dr T. W. Manson's Attack on Liberalism', *Congregational Quarterly*, Vol. 24, 1926, pp. 25 ff. Although not actually using the word Cadoux seems to regard Manson's attack as a betrayal. Cf. The remarks of Nathanial Micklem: he tells that when earlier in his experience he wrote his Liberal appreciation of Christ 'it brought no protest from any responsible person in the Free Churches, while later writings, in which I have appeared to be swinging towards orthodoxy, have been widely represented as a kind of treason!' *What is the Faith?*, 1936, Preface, p. 12.

way open, he believes, is to retrace our steps to where Liberalism went off the track; and, having reached that point, we must go forward, not backward.[1] Courage, he adds, is needed to believe that God has spoken.[2]

Manson has the older Liberalism in view in his castigation. But many are beginning to think that perhaps the same thing could be said about neo-liberalism. Here, too, there is an inadequate understanding of the way the Scripture is related to the Word of God.

In the period of the high-tide of criticism there was evident disquiet and dissatisfaction with the growing tendency to refer to the Scripture as 'containing' the Word of God. In an earlier footnote, attention was called to the opposition within the Presbyterian Church of England to the proposed change in its Articles of Faith, from the emphatic declaration that the Bible 'is' the Word of God to that of the Word of God 'is contained in' the Scriptures. Scholars of the stature of James Orr and Robert Rainy saw no difficulty in speaking of the Bible in the terms of the Westminster Catechism. They were as clear as anyone else that there is a human element in the inspired record, but they could not, on that account, admit the distinction which was sought by the critics.[3]

As will be expected the preachers of the conservative evangelical school who had already rejected the critical method could not give their assent to the new slogan. History and tradition they knew were on their side. And they could not but feel that the present critical phase would pass. There did not seem to be sufficient reason to make concessions to what was considered an ephemeral mood. It was his uncompromising insistence that the Bible was to be regarded in its totality as the Word of God which was in part the cause of Spurgeon's involvement in what became known as the 'Downgrade' controversy.[4] Spurgeon, indeed, criticized Alfred Cave for compromising in a

---

[1] *The Interpretation of the Bible* (ed. C. W. Dugdale), 1944, p. 101.

[2] *Op. cit.*, p. 107.

[3] Cf. 'If we would speak in the language of Scripture faith, we must hold that it is better to say, "The Bible is true, because we have found it to be the Word of God", than to say, with Coleridge, "The Bible is the Word of God because we have found it to be true".' James Bannerman, *Inspiration*, The Infallible Truth and Divine Authority of the Holy Scriptures, 1865. Cf. S. T. Coleridge, *The Confessions of an Inquiring Spirit*, p. 73.

[4] Cf. esp. *The Sword and the Trowel* for the years 1887–90. W. Y. Fullerton, *C. H. Spurgeon, A Biography*, 1920, pp. 296–301. J. C. Carlyle, *C. H. Spurgeon, An*

measure the traditional view of the Bible in the latter's Congregational Union Lectures of 1888. Cave took as his subject *The Inspiration of the Old Testament Inductively Considered*, and courageously attacked the Graf-Wellhausen theory, and sought to restore the traditional view. The critics' verdict on Cave's attempt was naturally unfavourable and Cave himself was written off as an ignoramus. A reviewer in the *Spectator* maintained that he omitted from evidence items in his sources which seem to conflict with his view.[1] W. G. Elmslie contended that Cave's treatment would be ineffective in allaying suspicion about the Old Testament. Spurgeon, however, felt compelled to disassociate himself from Cave's defence because Cave had conceded that Genesis gave evidence of being a composite document. Such an admission Spurgeon considered unnecessary; at any rate, it compromised the genuine historicity and accuracy of the account. Cave had attempted to prop up faith in the Bible as the Word of God. Spurgeon retorted that no such props are needed by those whose judgement is not perverted by critical unbelief.[2]

As it fell to R. F. Horton to give a popular exposition of the view of the Bible as 'containing' the Word of God, so it was another eminent Congregationalist divine who sought to give popular statement to the view that the Bible 'is' the Word of God. Thus Joseph Parker of the City Temple opens his book, *None Like It*, with a chapter entitled 'The Word of God'. He refers to those who 'regard it as not *being* but as *containing* the Word of God'.[3] Such claim, he goes on to say, 'that humble and obedient souls may find "the Word of God" in the Bible'. Parker takes exception to the assertion that Jesus Christ alone is the Word of God. When did He make that claim? he asks.[4] Parker does, of course, believe that Jesus Christ is the Word of God; indeed, 'not only the Word of God, he is God the Word'.[5] He sees a parallel between Christ and the Scripture. 'I am disposed to think that the very process by which the Bible is

Interpretative Biography, 1933, p. 245. A. C. Underwood, *A History of the English Baptists*, 1947, pp. 229–32. Sir James Marchant, *Dr John Clifford*, 1924, pp. 27, 29, 81, 155 f.

  [1] *Spectator*, Vol. LXI, 1888, p. 1330.
  [2] *British and Foreign Evangelical Review*, Vol. XXXI, 1882, pp. 205–38. *The Sword and the Trowel*, 1891, p. 246.
  [3] *None Like It*, 1893, p. 15.   [4] *Op. cit.*, p. 21.   [5] *Op. cit.*, p. 22.

turned from *being* the Word of God into *containing* the Word of
God might for the self same reason and without loss of one
degree of cogency be employed in an attack upon the deity of
Jesus Christ.'[1] The book of Ecclesiastes with all its materialism,
its sensuousness and its pessimism, can be described as the Word
of God because it is part of the unified whole without which the
Scripture would not be complete. Parker stresses that he has no
scruples about speaking of the Bible as the Word of God.[2] 'If I
may not say that the Bible is the Word of God because the
infidel will at once draw my attention to a hard verse', he says,
'neither will I tell him prayer is answered, because he will at
once tell me that many a prayer for safety has been followed by a
shipwreck, and many a prayer for recovery has been followed by
bereavement.'[3] Parker's book was written as he says 'from the
standpoint of a preacher'.[4] He therefore appends a chapter
addressed '*Ad Clerum*'. But this has not added anything very
substantial to the rest. It must, indeed, be acknowledged in all
honesty that Parker's efforts had little effect. The critic, if ever
he bothered himself to read it, would not have been impressed.
There are to be sure Parker's brilliant epigrams and powerful
and pointed sentences. But in the main there was more assertion
than argument. Yet, it is right, for anyone seeking to give an
account of the conflict, to make reference to this popular defence
of the orthodox position that the Bible *is* the Word of God, as we
have alluded earlier to R. F. Horton's popular statement of the
opposing view that the Bible *contains* the Word of God.
Horton's attempt it should be added was no more weighty than
that of Parker's.

In more recent years increasing evidence of a desire to give
to the Bible the title 'the Word of God' is to be observed.
Theologians who cannot be claimed as belonging to 'Fundamentalism' are expressing dissatisfaction with the antithesis
between the record and the word of God in the record. A new
emphasis, as we noted earlier, is being placed upon the unity of
the Bible. And it is this fact which seems to hinder us from
isolating some parts as more 'divine' than others. Thus J. W. C.
Wand argues that 'the title, Word of God, if it is to be used at
all, as we hold it must, applies to the whole Bible and not to mere

---

[1] *None Like It*, 1893; cf. Chapter IV.
[2] *Op. cit.*; cf. p. 44 f.   [3] *Op. cit.*, p. 148.   [4] *Op. cit.*, p. 197.

parts of it, however supreme their value may be'. It is impossible, he argues, to distinguish some short sentence out of the whole as having a divine character above the rest. 'The Word of God', he concludes, 'is heard both in the events themselves and in the record of them.'[1]

By reason of this prevailing unity in its variety, it is being felt, that the Bible must be accepted as a whole. Throughout it there is to be heard the notes of one Divine music. In this connection, J. K. Mozley writes his conviction about the Bible, 'its nature as the Word of God, as the book in which the deeper tone of the one divine voice is heard through the many changing tones of the human voices, is not open to demonstration, but, in the Christian view of the Bible, it is finally true that it is the word of God, just as it is finally true about Christ that He is the Word of God. In neither case would the substitution of the expression "contains" or some similar term be an adequate embodiment of Christian faith'.[2]

L. S. Thornton is voicing the conviction of a growing number, in spite of outspoken protests on the other side, that the Bible can be rightly assessed only as it receives the designation 'the word of God'. Thornton's own particular explanation of the position of the Bible in religious experience and the relation between the human and the divine element in it, appear to satsify neither side in the controversy. He has critics to the right of him and critics to the left. He does, however, compel the assent of an increasing number, we appear warranted in claiming, by his assertion that 'It is not enough to say that the Word of God is contained *in* the Scripture. We must insist once more that the Scripture *is* the Word of God'.[3]

Reflecting upon the literature over the last half century one becomes aware of a move from both sides to urge the legitimate use of each formula. Whether each side can be satisfied with the precise meaning involved by the other party is another matter. Our own observation is that those who would normally refer to the Bible as 'containing' the Word of God, seem ready to speak of it as being the Word of God on that account. On the other side, those whose faith is expressed in the dictum that the Bible 'is'

[1] J. W. C. Wand, *The Authority of the Scriptures*, 1949, p. 83.
[2] *The Christian Faith* (ed. W. R. Matthews), 1944, p. 55.
[3] L. S. Thornton, *Revelation and the Modern World*, 1950, p. 130.

the Word of God, because it is in all its parts accounted so, can maintain that it must 'become' the Word of God in experience.

At an early date A. S. Peake referred to the dispute between those who say that the Bible 'is' the Word of God and those who say it 'contains' it. He gives his own understanding of the reasons for the controversy. Those who plump for the first do so because of a belief, contends Peake, 'that from the beginning to the end the Bible was dictated by the Holy Spirit Himself to selected men who acted as His amanuensis. Nothing in it had a human origin, the book was wholly divine in all its parts'.[1] Under the impact of critical assessment this 'high-sounding theory' broke down. There was so much crude morality, low spirituality and defective theology discoverable in it that such an exalted view of its origin could no longer be entertained. A book so evidently human could not be called the Word of God. Thus the formula was coined, the Bible is not the Word of God but it can be said to *contain* it. Peake rather optimistically regarded this state in the discussion as passed. He maintains that the 'antithesis is unreal, the distinction concentrates on a false issue'.[2] In the old conception, the Bible was regarded mainly as a compendium of doctrines and ethics. No longer can it be so conceived, he states, in this fashion. Nor, indeed, do we think of it as a book in which a clear-cut dichotomy can be seen between the divine and the human in it. It is impossible to say at what point God is speaking and at what it is only man's voice that can be heard. There are in the Bible words of God to man, authenticating themselves as such by their own intrinsic quality. The ideas, which were at first part of the human consciousness, were later framed in speech and recorded. On the other hand there are in the Bible words of men to God, words prompted by the Holy Ghost. There is, then, in the Bible the intermingling of the human and the divine. But it must be stated, both from the immediate and the wider context of Peake's teaching, that the 'human' element appears to be very human indeed. At any rate, he seems to suggest that the Bible is entitled to the designation 'the Word of God' because it is the record of God's coming into human life in an intense and human way.[3]

---

[1] A. S. Peake, *The Bible, Its Origin, Its Significance, Its Abiding Worth*, 1913, pp. 398–9.   [2] *Ibid.*, p. 399.
[3] *Ibid.*; cf. p. 400. Cf. also his book, *The Nature of Scripture*, 1922.

Conservative writers could no doubt have retorted that Peake has given a very false account of their position. But be this as it may, one fact is certain, writers on the other side could not have been happy about the way he explained the Bible as that which *is* the Word of God. They will have seen here a rather compromising illustration of 'accommodation'. For them the Bible *is* the Word of God because here the Word of God is verbally expressed; and expressed in words given by the inspiration of God. Peake, on the other hand, can say, 'The inspiration we find in the Bible is that of supreme religious genius'.[1] On this showing those who were maintaining that the Bible *is* the Word of God could not but feel doubt about the rightness of Peake's designation of it as such in the light of his general approach. It is not, we think, unfair to say, that by the drift of all his teaching Peake's sympathies must be, in the long run, with those who think of the Bible as 'containing' the Word of God merely.

Cunliffe-Jones, to take an example from a living author, approaching the subject as one who accepts the critical conclusions, is strong in his insistence upon the idea that the Bible is the Word of God. In a chapter of his entitled 'The Bible as the Word of God',[2] he is willing to grant that the title should be applied to it in a primary as well as a derivative sense. It is the Word of God in the first sense because, he argues, it is from the Bible we gain our knowledge of Jesus Christ, the revelation of the prophets and the apostles and the content of preaching. The Bible is to be treated as the Word of God because it is the supreme witness we have to the Gospel of God. At the same time, he goes on to contend, the Bible 'becomes' the Word of God in experience. Both formulae are to be retained. The Bible *is* the Word of God because it is a standing witness to the gospel, and yet it must become the Word of God 'in a special way' as 'a living power in our hearts'.[3]

From the conservative side, in more recent years, acknowledgement will be found of the right to admit the formula that the Bible 'contains' the Word of God. But this concession is granted only, it must be immediately added, on the strength of the

[1] A.S. Peake, *The Bible, Its Origin, Its Significance, Its Abiding Worth*, 1913, p. 402.
[2] H. Cunliffe-Jones, *The Authority of the Biblical Revelation*, 1946, second impression, 1948, Chapter XII.   [3] *Ibid.*, p. 133.

conviction that the whole Bible *is* the Word of God. The position is stated with commendable clarity by J. I. Packer. Packer readily allows that there is a sense in which it is correct to refer to the Bible as 'containing' the Word of God. He asserts the identity of Scripture and the Word of God. 'The Bible' is then 'a written document declaring a message'. It is 'the inspired volume as a literary product, a verbal expression of thought'.[1] In this sense 'the Bible' and 'Scripture' are synonymous: 'it will thus be correct to call the Bible the Word of God, and to affirm that what it says, God says'. If the Bible should be thought of simply as a printed book, then according to Packer, 'it will not be wrong to say that the Bible *contains* the Word of God, in the same sense in which any other book *contains* the pronouncements of its author'.[2] Packer is, however, not too happy about the admission of the concept 'contains'. It would, he thinks, be better to avoid it 'since Liberal theologians have been in the habit of using this formula to insinuate that part of what the Bible contains is no part of the Word of God'.[3] He adds, therefore, the declaration: 'When we call the Bible the Word of God, we mean, or should mean, that its message constitutes a single utterance of which God is the author'.[4]

The hesitancy expressed by Packer concerning the formula the Bible *contains* the Word of God is not shared by all who accept his fundamental position. What Packer would have us avoid, others of the same school of thought boldly assert.

In an article in the *Evangelical Quarterly* in 1949 there is an interesting statement of the confusion which follows when

[1] J. I. Packer, *'Fundamentalism' and the Word of God*, 1958, p. 88.
[2] *Ibid.* Cf. The New Curriculum, Second and Third Articles on New Teaching Material in Preparation for the Presbyterian Church, U.S. ii 'Revelation', *The Presbyterian Journal*, Vol. XIX, No. 47, March 22, 1961. iii 'The Bible and Church as Witnesses and Instruments of Revelation', *Ibid.*, Vol. XX, No. 48, March 29, 1961.   [3] *Ibid.*, pp. 88–9.
[4] *Ibid.*, p. 89. Packer's position is understandable as an answer to H. G. Hebert's outspoken volume *Fundamentalism and the Church of God*, 1957. Hebert really adopts the formula that the Bible 'contains' the Word of God. He speaks of 'the study of the Word of God in the Bible'. He appears to limit the designation to Christ. He then makes a slashing attack upon what he calls 'fundamentalism' which has an 'evil sense' and as such 'is a grave menace to the Church of God'. Hebert does little to allay suspicion about the use of the designation of the Word of God as applied to the Bible by adherents of the liberal school. Packer's volume, *'Fundamentalism' and the Word of God*, 1958, is a vigorous reply and must be evaluated in this context.

revelation is identified with inspiration. Although the writer of the article is a Frenchman he would have most of his readers, we believe, on his side. Underlying all the subjects of the Ecumenical agenda, its debates on the Sacraments, the Ministry, the Church, and so forth, is, the writer contends, the fundamental question of the exact rôle of the Holy Spirit. It is the place of the Holy Spirit in revelation and inspiration which needs clarification. The testimony of the Spirit in experience is not to be confused with the Quaker idea of the 'inner word', even when that experience is 'evangelical'. It is in the Scripture that the Holy Spirit speaks. It is maintained that 'Revelation and Inspiration constitute eternal acts of God. In other words, the Word of God is always actual in the two senses of the word. It is always an *act* of God, never a theory about God; and this act is always *present*, never bound to the age of the document which transmits it'.[1] Developing this proposition it is stated that the Bible is, for the reader, the Word of God, and also 'that He speaks *to me today* through Jeremiah, St John and St Paul, in vivifying their testimony by that of His Holy Spirit'.[2] It is then concluded: 'The whole Bible is *in itself* Word of God, but *for each of us* it only becomes Word of God in a living fashion where the Holy Spirit brings conviction of it'.[3] The Bible *is* the Word of God *for faith*, it is declared. Bucer's parallel between the Bible and the Word of God and the Church visible and the Body of Christ is then upheld. The Bible, like the visible Church, is the garment with which it is clothed in order to take a place in visible reality. The Church as the 'sign' of the invisible Church is holy but to faith only. So is it with the Bible; it *is* the Word of God but only to faith. In spite of its human defects, its faults of style, its errors in name, and so on, it is still to be believed in as divine. Yet all its words are God's words, even those texts which the Holy Spirit may not as yet have 'inspired' for us. It is impossible to sort out in the Bible the Word of God from the human word.

In an earlier part of this section we made reference to Farrar's contention that the formula, that the Bible *contains* the Word of God, is the specific teaching of the Church of England. It will,

[1] Jean de Saussure, *The Evangelical Quarterly*, Vol. XXI, No. 1, January 1949, p. 22.　　　　　　　　　　[2] *Ibid.*, p. 23 (italics in original).
[3] *Ibid.*, p. 24 (italics in original).

therefore, be of interest to bring this assertion into contrast with the conviction of another writer of the same communion. W. H. Griffith Thomas, sometime Principal of Wycliffe Hall, Oxford, while openly acknowledging his readiness to accept the thesis that the Bible *contains* the Word of God, is none the less emphatic that it is the intended and consistent teaching of the Church of England that the Bible is the Word of God. The Anglican Church quite plainly urges that God Himself is the Source of Authority; but it states, according to number vi of the Thirty-nine Articles, that the seat of authority is to be found in the Word of God recorded in the Bible.[1] Griffith Thomas remarks upon 'the emphasis placed in recent years' on the 'human element' in the Scriptures. He has no scruples in admitting the 'traces of the idiosyncrasies of various writers'. Too much, however, he thinks, can be made of them. 'Inspiration', he then declares, 'means such a union of the Divine and human elements that the result is guaranteed to us as the thought of God for the life of man.'[2] But the two cannot really be separated and distinguished. It is not a case of the Divine *and* the human, but, more accurately 'the Divine *through* the human'.

Griffith Thomas has a comment to make upon Coleridge's dictum that it is that in the Bible which 'finds' us which is of the Holy Ghost. He grants that, in contrast with uncanonical literature, the Bible does reveal its inspiration by 'finding' us more thoroughly than any other book. He adds, however, that Coleridge's view is inadequate 'unless this effect is understood to arise out of the supernatural revelation objectively contained in the Scripture'.[3] The Bible, not only 'finds' us, but as James Denney, contends, by its truth it creates and transforms.[4] The two formulae, the Bible 'contains' the Word of God and the Bible 'is' the word of God are acceptable to Griffith Thomas. Both are true, he says, if held together. Either taken alone is liable to misunderstanding. To say the Bible 'is' the Word of God only is to lose sight of the fact that it contains words of men also. And some of the words of men it records are not true in themselves, though the record that they were spoken is true. On the other hand, to limit belief to the phrase that the Bible

---

[1] W. H. Griffith Thomas, *The Principles of Theology*, An Introduction to the Thirty-nine Articles, 1930, second edition, p. 117.
[2] *Ibid.*, p. 118.   [3] *Ibid.*, p. 119.   [4] *Ibid.*

'contains' the Word of God, leads us to the entirely impossible position of having to discriminate between what is God's word and what is man's. It is, therefore, concluded, that the 'Bible *is* the Word of God in the sense that it conveys to us an accurate record of everything God intended man to know in connection with His will. The Bible *contains* the Word of God in the sense that in it is enshrined the Word of God which is revealed to us for our redemption'.[1] Although Griffith Thomas stresses the fact of the union of the Divine and the human, he can still say that it is the presence of the Divine element 'that constitutes the Bible, the Word of God'.[2]

We have given our own conviction on this matter elsewhere. In any final statement of the meaning and the significance of the Bible, it was contended, there certainly must be an acceptable union of the two ideas. Perhaps, as yet, the antithesis has not been resolved in a manner with which both sides can agree. It may well be that this will be one of the permanent results which will emerge from the discussion. Our own view was declared. In spite of the problems which beset the declaration that the Bible *is* the Word of God, this, we believe, designates more clearly and truly than any other its precise nature. The assertion that the Bible merely *contains* the Word of God, or that it is a *witness* to a possible revelation when made, as it sometimes is, to repudiate the proclamation that it is in itself the Word of God, is not only misleading, but certainly false.[3] Allusion was made to the words of Bishop Martensen, whose *Christian Dogmatics* was translated into English in 1866, as being for the present and for ourselves, at any rate, a happy conclusion to the matter. Those who use the formula, the Bible *contains* the Word of God, as Martensen allows, are anxious to safeguard the human element, while those who say the Bible *is* the Word of God seek to maintain its divineness. Both ideas, as in the Person of our Lord, must be asserted: 'not only the union of the divine and human in Scripture, but at the same time the distinction between the two. The old proposition, *the Scripture is the Word of God*, expresses the union; the modern dictum, *the Scripture contains*

---

[1] James Denney, Article 'The Authority of Christ', *Dictionary of Christ and the Gospels* (ed. Hastings), ad. loc.

[2] W. H. Griffith Thomas, *The Principles of Theology*, p. 118.

[3] H. D. McDonald, *Ideas of Revelation*, 1959, p. 280 (note); cf. pp. 276–83.

the Word of God, expresses the distinction. The first proposition is clearly preferable to the second, which is vague and indistinct, and may be applied to many writings. The first, however, is untrue, if it be taken so to affirm the union, as to exclude all distinction of the divine and human elements in the Bible. . . . The opposite proposition, which does not venture to assert that Scripture *is* the word of God, but that it only *contains* the Word of God, considers only the distinction between the divine and human elements, and overlooks the all-pervading, obvious, and typical union of these in Scripture, the sacred, all-pervading apparent, and fundamental truth, which in unsullied clearness enwraps and even subdues the temporal and human narrowness'.[1]

All, we think, will wish to concur with the declaration of T. H. Robinson, on behalf of most, 'if not all' the contributors to the volume *The Old Testament and Modern Study*. Whatever be their individual explanation of the assertion, each writer, we are told 'would regard the Old Testament as the very word of God, ranking second only to the person of Christ Himself. It is, therefore, rational to assume that it is in some way or other valid for all generations of mankind and for all types of humanity . . . the Old Testament is a God-given book, produced by divine inspiration . . . according to the principle that God works always through human agents, and that without eclipsing their personality'.[2]

The Old Testament is a God-given book indeed; and, of course, the New Testament no less. For all men this Bible of both Testaments is objectively the Word of God whether they are awakened to it, found by it, or not. But to the faith-awakened it has *become* such; for to them the Scripture has spoken as the Word of God through the Spirit.[3]

---

[1] H. Martensen, *Christian Dogmatics*, 1866, p. 403. Cf. H. D. McDonald, *Ideas of Revelation*, pp. 281–2.

[2] *The Old Testament and Modern Study* (ed. H. H. Rowley), 1951, pp. 347–50.

[3] Reflecting upon the discussion of this section as it relates to the subject of the Scriptures and the Word of God, we find ourselves driven to the conclusion that much misunderstanding has been due to an extraordinary instance of the logical fallacy of 'false conversion' or of '*A dicto secundum quid ad dictum simpliciter*', for which both sides are in varying degree responsible. The declaration that the Bible is the Word of God has often been defended in such a way as to suggest that its simple converse is also to be regarded as true. On the other hand, those who oppose are often found contending against this very converse which they have tacitly

THE SCRIPTURES AND THE WORD

assumed, and which careful writers (of the opposition) would have repudiated. To say that the Bible is the Word of God is one thing, but to maintain that the Word of God is the Bible, is another matter, and is, indeed, altogether false. It is theologically correct to say that Jesus Christ is God, but it is obviously very theologically incorrect to convert the proposition simply and to declare that God is Jesus Christ. The failure to grasp this distinction is at the bottom of much of the inability to come to grips with the fundamental issue.

An interesting illustration of this confusion will be found in a provocative little volume by Albert Ervine, which carries a commendation by C. F. D'Arcy, Archbishop of Armagh and Primate of All Ireland. Ervine's argument, in which he strongly repudiates the designation the Word of God as applicable to the Scriptures, seems to us to proceed on the assumption that all who make the assertion would have to defend the converse; and judging from the favourable reviews given by acknowledged conservative leaders, for example G. Campbell Morgan among others, it is evident that they failed to see the implications of Ervine's position (Albert Ervine, *Bible Studies*, 1935, pp. 9–15). Ervine indeed falls back upon the idea that the Bible 'contains' the Word of God (p. 27 f.), but his last chapter seems to undermine his own thesis since in his presentation of Christ he simply draws together the biblical statements regarding Him and leaves us wondering as to what view of Christ these may be said to 'contain' (cf. also his pamphlet, *Divine Words and Human Symbols*, n.d., in which he gives a synopsis of his views and a repudiation of the idea of verbal inspiration which he assumes is inherent in the designation of the Bible as the Word of God).

There has been throughout the discussion a too-easy acceptance or rejection of the term. The manifoldness of the idea 'the Word of God' has not been given rightful assessment. While we would not concur in every statement of an article by David W. Hay (Professor of Systematic Theology, Knox College, Toronto), yet we do agree with him when he says that 'The habit of referring to the Bible as the Word of God has disguised the fact that the expression has a multiplicity of uses in Scripture' (David W. Hay, 'The Expression "Word of God" in Scripture', *The Canadian Journal of Theology*, Vol. II, No. 3, July 1956, p. 135). 'Men want to have', he says later in the same article, 'a simple notion of the Word and think they can achieve it by a simple identification of the Word with the Bible' (p. 141).

CHAPTER SIX

The Question of Biblical Inerrancy

The second half of the nineteenth century witnessed a change within the Church in its valuation of the Bible. Prior to the year 1860, the idea of an infallibly inerrant Scripture was the prevailing view. What has been stated as the characteristic estimation of the Bible throughout an earlier era could with equal exactness be referred to the years down to the middle of the nineteen hundreds. Apart from the Quakers, 'The doctrine of unerring literal inspiration was almost everywhere held in the strictest form'.[1] Such indeed was the view of the Bible before the change of Zeitgeist brought about by the appearance of Darwin's evolutionism. The orthodox apologists in their polemic against the Deists moved on the assumption of a Bible at once verbally infallible and inerrant. There may be truth in Leslie Stephen's contention that the downfall of the Deists was due to the inherent weakness of their theories rather than to the superior logical acumen of their opponents.[2] There was certainly a climate of opinion in favour of the orthodox apologists. The Bible was by general consent regarded as an inspired book, which, as such, must be inerrant and infallible.

And apart from the dogmatisms of the orthodox in this respect, had not this high estimate of the Bible been demonstrated by the preaching of Wesley as creatively effective in the experiences of thousands? It was Wesley who had vindicated the reality of the Bible's inspiration, and he, too, had maintained its inerrant infallibility. To say that the Bible is *not* inspired, he

---

[1] *The English Church in the Eighteenth Century*, Abbey and Overton, Vol. I, 1887, second edition, p. 243.

[2] Leslie Stephen, *History of English Thought in the Eighteenth Century*, 1881, Vol. I, p. 90; cf. pp. 169–72.

had contended, would be tantamount to admitting error in the sacred volume. Thus he declared, 'if there be any mistakes in the Bible, there may well be a thousand. If there be one falsehood in that book, it did not come from the God of truth'.[1]

Such, then, was the position. It fell to the Deists, if they were to gain their end, to demonstrate the falsity of such an estimation. The burden of proof lay with them. The Deists endeavoured to secure their particular purpose by seeking to reveal series of inconsistencies in the Bible itself. It was not too difficult for their opponents to show the inconsistencies in their allegation of inconsistencies; and, at the same time, to offer some explanation of these supposed contradictions. As far as Christians generally were concerned the issue was clear-cut. Either the Bible is to be dismissed altogether as a tissue of errors and deceits, or it is to be accepted *in toto* as a verbally inspired and inerrant Book. There was no middle path. The question really resolved itself into whether there is an authentic special revelation of God or not. It was the purpose of the Deists to disprove the general belief that there was such, and they consequently set themselves to destroy faith in a trustworthy Bible. Their attack was not directed specifically to the question of whether there is a verbatim revelation, but to the larger issue of the existence of a special revelation. It was, therefore, consistent for their opponents not to focus their attention on the existence of alleged minor discrepancies, but to take their stand upon the general reality, certainty and trustworthiness of the special revelation of the Bible as a whole.

The Deists really lost their case by overstating it. They supposed that by indicating, what they jubilantly proclaimed as 'errors' in the record, the whole notion of a special revelation had been shown to be false. Their opponents had merely to stake their case upon the substantial truth of the Scripture. And having demonstrated this fact, the general belief in its inerrancy remained unshaken. Besides, even if difficulties could not all be solved and inconsistencies all be reconciled, it did not follow that the Bible was anything other than what Christian faith claimed it to be. Had not Butler, after all, made it clear that there were things in nature which could not be understood? And, by

---

[1] John Wesley, *Journal*, Wednesday, July 24, 1776. Cf. H. D. McDonald, *Ideas of Revelation*, 1959, pp. 255–9.

analogy, was it not reasonable to suppose that there must be much in revelation beyond our comprehension?

In a period in which faith in the Bible as an inerrant Book was general such a reply had point. Inability to resolve all alleged contradictions was not to be taken as evidence that they were ultimately real. An answer would be forthcoming: the assurance was, someday we will understand. Meanwhile, patience, not panic, was the becoming attitude for the devout. The general trustworthiness of the Bible had been demonstrated against the Deists and the divinity of its truths had been convincingly sustained.

A. THE RENOUNCIATION OF INERRANCY

But this situation was to change after 1860. The *Origin of Species* became the 'bible' of the new age, and it seemed, to some at any rate, to be regarded as inerrant and infallible as the Scriptures it was held to replace. There was a conflict, everyone was made aware, between Genesis and Darwin, between the Bible and the *Origin of Species*. The general esteem of the Bible was undermined. It was Darwin that the common people were to hear gladly, since in doing so, they were assured, that they were no longer common people, but informed and modern and open-minded. And who really wanted to be other? No longer was it possible for scientifically instructed men to believe in an inerrant Bible. Darwin had brought such a notion to collapse. The recommendation to wait in faith for further light or to accept it that unresolved difficulties must be allowed in revelation, as well as in nature, was received with impatience.

It was for this reason that certain important works in defence of the Bible failed to satisfy. Perhaps the ablest in this regard was Henry Rogers's Congregational Union Lectures of 1873 entitled *The Superhuman Origin of the Bible Inferred from Itself*. In lecture ix, Rogers discoursed 'On Certain analogies between the Bible and "The Constitution of Nature" '. It was a formidable oration. In it Rogers declares that 'If the Bible be from the same source (i.e. as the constitution of nature), it is in analogy with this that he (i.e. man 'the minister and interpreter of nature', Bacon), is summoned to similar functions here. The Bible has its difficulties and mysteries, as nature has; and it requires, just as nature does, prolonged thought and effort to penetrate or decipher them'.[1] The 'errors' of which men are so often aware, are, like the *idola* of Bacon, within the mind, to be dispelled only by a determined effort. Useful as Rogers's book was it did not suit the new situation. This was clearly seen by Marcus Dods who pointed out that it was more of an apology for Christianity itself than for the Bible.[2] The *British Quarterly Review*, while giving the volume a favourable review, likewise observed that it did nothing to rehabilitate the plenary inspiration, scientific accuracy and eternal trustworthiness of the Scripture.[3] It was the contention of the *British and Foreign Evangelical Review* that Rogers's argument was merely a restatement of Butler's, which in the new context 'altogether fails to understand and meet in a scientific way the speculative (and critical) difficulties which are advanced against the thesis Mr Rogers defends'.[4]

A defence of the same kind was made by G. W. Olver. He, too, urged that it was not for the Christian believer to profess that he could iron out all the problems and harmonize all the statements in the Bible since neither he nor anyone else 'can solve all difficulties and harmonize all facts of Nature'.[5] But the contention was no more valid by being made by Olver than by Rogers.

The plain fact is that the idea of an inerrant Bible was being discarded. The view had prevailed that the Bible was one book, a unity which stood or fell as a whole. This situation seemed no longer possible. The unity of the Bible had to be disrupted to fit into an evolutionary context. The vigorous application of the historical method cast doubt upon the factuality of the record, as well as did the increasing uncertainty as to the genuineness of the miraculous element in the account. All this added up to an open acknowledgement, it was claimed, that the Bible was no longer to be regarded as an inerrant volume. As a result the way was prepared for the easier acceptance of the higher criticism. The regrettable delay, as it was referred to by some writers, in

[1] Henry Rogers, *The Superhuman Origin of the Bible inferred from Itself*, 1873, New York, 1875, p. 385.
[2] Marcus Dods, *The Expositor*, fourth series, Vol. VIII, 1893, p. 158.
[3] *The British Quarterly Review*, Vol. LIX, 1874, pp. 585–9, *ibid.*
[4] *The British and Foreign Evangelical Review*, Vol. XXIII, 1874, pp. 582–4, *ibid.*
[5] *Inspiration*, A Clerical Symposium (ed. F. W. Farrar), 1884, p. 134.

yielding to the claims of the new criticism was not a result of its contradicting the doctrine of inerrancy. This doctrine was being renounced on other grounds.[1] It had become the fashion to make reference to the 'errors' in the Bible and it was held to be an evidence of honest biblical scholarship to admit their existence. It might be argued that the progress of criticism was facilitated because of the prior weakening of belief in an inerrant Bible. It was the difficulties found by many in the acceptance of an unerring literal inspiration which in part accounts for the readiness with which the critical assumptions were accepted. Rigorous research into the origin of religion revealed, it was argued, the unauthentic nature of the biblical claim.[2]

The *Essays and Reviews* were influential in this direction. Its writers expressed openly their sympathy with the naturalistic approach to the Bible. Their attitude with regard to biblical criticism was on the whole conservative. But the loose views on the inspiration of the Bible presupposed in their contributions led to a denial, either openly or implicitly, of the central doctrines of the Church's faith. R. Williams expressed rather radical views concerning the atonement and resurrection,[3] while Baden Powell showed evident disregard for miracles.[4] B. Jowett virtually denied the doctrine of original sin and the personality of the Holy Spirit.[5]

It was thus observed by many that a lessening of the idea of verbal inspiration must necessarily weaken faith in an inerrant Bible. The *British and Foreign Evangelical Review* condemned the *Essays* on this score.[6] This periodical, it may be noted in passing, had already defended inerrancy against Samuel Davidson. In a review of his new edition of Horne's *Introduction* it asks, 'If the Biblical writers were liable to error in one

---

[1] But cf. 'Until criticism made it impossible for us any longer to identify infallibility with literal inerrancy, it was a delusive and non-existent infallibility that was ascribed to the Bible'. Marcus Dods, *The Bible, Its Origin and Nature*, 1905, pp. 138–9. Also Biblical Criticism destroyed 'the theory of the infallibility and inerrancy of Scripture'. A. S. Peake, *The Bible: Its Origin, Its Significance, Its Abiding Worth*, 1913, fifth edition, p. 310. Cf. B. J. Snell, *Gain or Loss?* 1896, p. 20.

[2] Cf. W. Robertson Nicholl, 'The Coming Battle', *British Weekly*, 11, 1887, p. 225.

[3] Cf. *Essays and Reviews*, pp. 80–1.

[4] *Op. cit.*, pp. 133–4.   [5] *Op. cit.*, pp. 358–9.

[6] *British and Foreign Evangelical Review*, 'The Oxford Essayists—Their Relation to Christianity and to Strauss and Baur', Vol. X, 1861, pp. 407–30.

particular, what guarantee have we that they were not equally fallible in another?'[1]

Such statements, however, did not stay the tide. General opinion was running against the idea of an inerrant Scripture. It may be acknowledged that the higher criticism would have made necessary modifications in the religious attitude to the Bible. But such modifications would have been, perhaps, less decisive, less acceptable and less conclusive had the doctrine of inerrancy not been previously so seriously questioned. The abandonment of the traditional view of inerrancy was, then, a cause of the acceptance of the higher criticism, not a result. The reason for the wholesale rejection of the historical idea of inerrancy is therefore to be found in the climate of opinion. The period which began with Darwin's *Origin of Species* was of a different spirit from that which had gone before.

Gore's famous essay in the *Lux Mundi* did much to induce Churchmen to settle for an errant Bible. Gore there made clear his repudiation of what he later gave as a title for his little volume *The Doctrine of an Infallible Book*. Even more cogent and captivating for its thesis was the contribution of A. B. Bruce who, in association with three American scholars, C. A. Briggs, L. J. Evans and H. P. Smith, produced the volume, *Inspiration and Inerrancy*. Bruce, writing in the Introduction, maintains that a true doctrine of Scripture does not involve such an idea as inerrancy. He declares openly and unequivocally against it.[2] So it was that inerrancy was boldly repudiated.

Something of the strength of the rejection of an inerrant Bible can be seen in statements made by acknowledged leaders of religious opinion. Alexander Raleigh, who at any rate as late as the year 1875 believed higher criticism to be merely a form of infidelity, could declare in 1868, when Chairman of the Congregational Union, that there were 'errors and mistakes' in the Bible.[3] R. W. Dale, too, in 1873 made the same

---

[1] *British and Foreign Evangelical Review*, 'The New Edition of Horne's Introduction', Vol. VI, 1857, p. 404; cf. 'The Book of Genesis', Vol. IX, 1860, p. 533, and 'Inspiration', Vol. XVI, 1867, pp. 537–56.

[2] A. B. Bruce and C. A. Briggs, *Inspiration and Inerrancy*, 1891, pp. 32 ff. Cf. 'Nothing could be more fitted to mislead us as to the nature of Inspiration than to lay emphasis on the supervision necessary to insure perfect harmony'. p. 32, A. B. Bruce in Introduction.

[3] Mary Raleigh, *Alexander Raleigh: Records of his Life*, 1881, pp. 143 f. and 283 f.

admission.[1] Nothing, indeed, is so extraordinary in this respect, as the reversal of the earlier estimation of the Bible. The earlier apologists had with fairly general consistency stood by an inerrant Scripture. Those who followed the year 1860 contended that such a notion was impossible to sustain and they believed the idea an unnecessary burden. Christian faith did not depend upon a verbally infallible Book. Thus John Clifford, for example, admonishes preachers to avoid such 'surface' questions as the 'apparent discrepancies of Scripture'.[2] He asks elsewhere, 'Are there errors in the Bible?' He has no hesitation with the answer. 'It is not God's way', he avers, 'to give us an absolutely inerrant Bible and He has not done it.'[3] 'It would be an unspeakable convenience if the theory of total Biblical inerrancy were according to the facts',[4] he says. But it is not so, Clifford maintains. He then seeks to answer what he regards as the three defences of an inerrant Bible.[5]

R. F. Horton was even more outspoken. As a writer Horton showed himself to possess few inhibitions. He was scathing in his repudiation of what he calls 'the cast-iron theory of inspiration'. Although Horton's book, to which reference is now being made, bears the title *Inspiration and the Bible*, the major portion of it is devoted to an elaborate statement of the ways the new criticism has contradicted the old view of the Bible and thus justifies the total rejection of inerrancy. The evidence of inconsistencies he finds everywhere; in Paul's interpretation of the Old Testament, in the Book of Acts and the Epistles, between the Gospels, in the accounts of the ascension. Commenting on Gal. iii. 20, he tells us that the verse has been given some 430 different interpretations and, according to his own belief, not one of them satisfactory. Here Paul has been guilty of the grossest obscurity. 'Such want of lucidity it may be less dangerous to charge upon St Paul than on the Spirit of God.'[6] As far as Horton is concerned, the Old Testament abounds in errors. The result of his treatment is to make the whole Bible appear little more than a fallible

---

[1] R. W. Dale, 'The Old Testament and the New', *Congregationalist*, ii, 1873, pp. 321-2.
[2] Sir James Marchant, *Dr John Clifford*, 1924, pp. 41-2.
[3] John Clifford, *The Inspiration and the Authority of the Bible*, 1889, third edition, 1899, p. 49.   [4] *Ibid.*, p. 42.   [5] Cf. Chapter V, *ibid.*
[6] R. F. Horton, *Inspiration and the Bible*, 1888, pp. 49-50; cf. pp. 36-78 and 144-75.

record in which evidences of human mistakes are everywhere revealed.

G. P. Mains attributes the false idea of inerrancy and infallibility of the Bible to the Reformers. 'There need be no misunderstanding of the fact,' he says, 'that, so far as the Bible is concerned, the Reformation left the Church as a part of its inheritance the conviction of an infallible Book.'[1] In the brief compass of seven pages, having quoted Marcus Dods for support, Mains dismisses the whole subject with the assurance 'that Christian scholarship has been forced to abandon the hypothesis of Scriptural inerrancy'.[2] In a conclusive manner W. L. Knox summarizes the general attitude to the Bible when he writes, 'The scientific development of the last century has rendered untenable the whole conception of the Bible as a verbally inspired book, to which we can appeal with absolute certainty for infallible guidance in all matters of faith and conduct'.[3]

B. THE ASSERTION OF INERRANCY

While Gore, Bruce, Clifford and Horton and many others were declaring themselves against the doctrine of an infallible and inerrant Bible, the traditionalists, as they came to be called, were insistent that it was only an infallible and inerrant Bible which could be used as God clearly intended the Bible to be used. Only such a Book, it was their contention, could give 'absolute certainty for infallible guidance in all matters of faith and conduct'. In maintaining this position they considered themselves to be remaining true to the historic Christian faith and to the more recent Confessions. Infallibility and inerrancy were terms used to indicate the Church's faith in the divine origin and the absolute truthfulness and trustworthiness of its Scriptures.

During the nineteenth century the description of the Holy Scriptures as 'the infallible truth' came into vogue to express repudiation of the growing proclamation of its errancy, although, it may be noted, the expression was already used in the Westminster Confession. The traditionalists, by adhering to

---

[1] G. P. Mains, *Divine Inspiration*, 1915, p. 81. [2] *Ibid.*, p. 109.
[3] W. L. Knox, *Essays Catholic and Critical*, 1926, third edition, 1931, p. 99.

the words—infallible and inerrant—felt they were giving validity to the Scriptures as an objective authority. Christianity was, after all, an historical religion based on an historical revelation and it is in the Bible alone that that revelation is to be found. If no sure appeal could be made to the record, then the serious question arose, What ground is there for certain faith?

It was, of course, replied that the traditionalists were wrong in asserting that the Bible was authoritative in itself when what was actually authoritative was the revelation to which it was a witness or a record. But this was precisely the question at issue. As far as the traditionalists could see there was no existent or evident revelation apart from the Bible. No one could say, 'Lo, it is here', or, 'Lo, it is there'. The only revelation known is the Bible revelation; consequently, if that revelation is punctuated with errors, then there is no certainty left in divine things, since there is really no 'infallible truth'. The only alternatives to such an understanding of the Scriptures were for the adherents of inerrancy and infallibility impossible. There were those, it appears, quite ready to renounce the Protestant and Reformed faith and fall back upon the authority of the Church. Others, however, sought to emphasize the ultimacy of religious experience, only to find themselves bogged in the quagmire of subjectivism. As far as the traditionalists were concerned, they saw the traditional valuation of the Bible by the Church openly repudiated within the Church itself, wounded, indeed, as they declared, in the house of its friends. But most tragic of all, in their view, was the way the Bible, as God's direct message to men, was being snatched from the hands of the common man to be acclaimed as a book fit only for the researches of the scholar. No longer was it for the wayfaring man, who was unequipped with critical techniques to reconstruct it according to the new pattern and detect its manifold mistakes.

Joseph Parker had no hesitation in pointing out the tragic religious consequences of making the Bible 'a priest's book'. And he asks, 'Have we to await a communication from Tübingen, or a telegram from Oxford, before we can read the Bible?'[1] John Kennedy charged the critics with assuming for themselves the

---

[1] Joseph Parker, *None Like It*, 1893, pp. 73 ff. Cf. ' "Theology in Transition" and the Bible in "Suspense" ', *Wesleyan Methodist Magazine*, Vol. CXVI, 1893, pp. 714–15.

infallibility they deny to the Bible. They pronounced *ex cathedra* on the dates and the unreliability of the documents of Scripture with an assurance and certainty no whit less than their opponents whom they condemned for their dogmatism.[1]

It is because the traditionalists held firmly to the practical identity of the revelation with its record that the arguments of the 'errorists' had such little effect. It was not, of course, difficult to trap them by urging that they were ensnared in the net of the circular argument. The charge went like this: inerrancy is no self-evidencing truth. The traditionalists' doctrine of it is based on their 'cast-iron theory' of inspiration. Their logic then is; the Bible must be inerrant because it is verbally inspired, and it is verbally inspired because it is inerrant.[2]

To such a charge the great preachers, at any rate, were unconcerned to reply. But if they did not, and perhaps as some will think, could not, they were able to stress that belief in an infallible and inerrant Bible was productive of the greatest practical and theological good. They were deeply concerned with the possible ill results for the cause of the Evangelical faith that the idea of a Bible fraught with 'errors and mistakes' would have. Liddon, Parker, Spurgeon, Moule, Ryle were a few of those who maintained a firm belief in the inerrancy of the Bible and the infallibility of its truth. It was, indeed, Spurgeon's constant insistence that a Bible with mistakes is a Bible without a message. And it was the open descent from the position taken by Clifford on this point which was in part the cause of the controversy which finally led to his withdrawal from the Baptist Union.

J. C. Ryle, in a passage in which he is stating the view of the Bible held in an earlier period by such Christian leaders as Grimshaw, Venn, Berridge, Harvey and others of their company, is really giving expression to the position occupied by himself and those of like evangelical spirit. The 'spiritual reformers of the last century', he writes, 'taught constantly *the sufficiency and supremacy of the Holy Scriptures*. The Bible, whole

[1] Cf. John Kennedy, *Old Testament and the Rights of the Unlearned, Being a Plea for the Rights and Powers of Non-experts in the Study of Holy Scriptures*, 1897.

[2] Cf. How Paul Tillich for his own purpose contends for 'the circular character of systematic theology' and adds 'theologians should not be afraid to admit this circle. It is not a shortcoming'. Paul Tillich, *Systematic Theology*, Vol. I, 1950, p. 135.

and unmutilated, was their sole rule of faith and practice. They accepted all its statements without question and dispute. They knew nothing of any part of Scripture being uninspired. They never allowed that man has any "verifying faculty" within him by which Scripture statements may be weighed, rejected or received. They never flinched from asserting that there can be *no error* in the Word of God; and that when they cannot understand or reconcile some parts of its contents, the fault is in the interpreter and not in the text. In all their preaching they were eminently men of one book. To that book they were content to pin their faith, and by it to stand or fall.'[1] Like their Puritan forefathers, the Evangelicals of the following centuries continued strenuously to maintain that the words of the Bible, because given by the Holy Spirit, constitute the whole volume infallible and inerrant.

In a powerful chapter in his *Old Paths*, Ryle contends that as an inspired book the Bible reveals an 'extraordinary accuracy' in facts and statements.[2] He does not, apparently, actually use the term 'inerrant', but certainly the idea is maintained throughout. Among a fairly generous number of footnotes, all intended to sustain the accuracy of the Bible record, he quotes with approval from Bishop Wordsworth on *Inspiration*: 'We affirm that the Bible is the Word of God, and that it is not marred with human infirmities . . .'.[3] He faces the question that may be raised, 'Have the writers made no mistakes?' Ryle argues that talk about 'grave discrepancies' in the Biblical record is 'grossly exaggerated'. And he contends that 'in many cases they are only apparent, and disappear under the touch of common sense. Even in the hardest of them we should remember, in common fairness, that circumstances are very likely kept back from us which entirely reconcile everything, if only we knew them'.[4]

The thinking evangelical of the time, and they were not all as John Oman seemed to think, 'encased in the jointless armour of obscurantism hard enough to turn the edge of any fact',[5] saw that the liberal dilemma was a real one. The devout critics strove to maintain some sort of objectivity and givenness for the revelation in the Bible so as to escape the pitfalls of a complete

---

[1] J. C. Ryle, *The Christian Leader of the Last Century*, 1873, p. 26.
[2] J. C. Ryle, *Old Paths*, 1897, new and improved edition, p. 10.
[3] *Ibid.*, p. 20 (footnote). Cf. C. Wordsworth, *Inspiration of the Holy Scriptures*, 1861, p. 11.   [4] *Ibid.*, p. 27.
[5] John Oman, *Grace and Personality*, 1919, second edition, revised, p. 9.

subjectivism. They sought on the one hand to retain the idea of an errant Bible, and, on the other hand, to neutralize the effects of such an idea by insisting that the same Bible was still the only authority for faith and doctrine. They did not succeed in showing how the Bible could be acclaimed as the judge of human errors, when, at the same time, man appointed himself as a judge of the 'errors' of the Bible. The Bible was commended as a true witness, while it was being condemned as containing falsehood. Spurgeon and Parker, and the others mentioned above, were keenly aware of the liberal difficulty. And it is this awareness which lies behind their clear-cut alternative: let us have either a Bible which we can keep as entirely trustworthy or let us admit it to be a book with 'errors and mistakes' and honestly discard it as not being of decisive authority for faith and doctrine.

If the protagonists of inerrancy were unable to match argument with argument, they could, at least, appeal to the results which the loss of faith in an infallible Bible had brought about. On all sides there was floundering, uncertainty and hesitancy. Horton's was no exceptional case. He was typical of numbers of clergy and ministers who, like him, could no longer base their faith 'on the foundation of Biblical infallibility', and as a result had to set out on the quest to find the sure foundation.[1] After a time of search, however, Horton could only report his discovery of 'a series of tentative suggestions'. Meanwhile, without a sure resting-place themselves, how, asked their opponents, were they supposed to bring certainty to others? With the great evangelical preachers of the day it was otherwise. They, as Spurgeon urged, had their authority. They were expounders of an infallible truth, propagators of the sure Word of God.

Further, those who stood for an infallible Bible were able to point to the religious and spiritual results that a Bible so understood and proclaimed secured. As a lion let loose, as Spurgeon contended, the Bible could maintain itself from all the assaults of its enemies. Parker appealed to the power of the Bible to convert, to comfort and sustain. He will not let the critics rob him of it until they have something more to offer than 'a series of tentative suggestions'.[2]

[1] R. F. Horton, *An Autobiography*, 1918, p. 100.
[2] Joseph Parker, *None Like It*, 1893, p. 244.

C. RENEWED CONFLICT OVER INERRANCY

For over a period of years now there seem to be evidences of a reawakening of faith. The cloud may be only the size of a man's hand, but those who know the spiritual weather-chart appear to be confident that there is a reviving interest in spiritual things throughout the land. Coming with this reviving interest is a new emphasis upon the Bible as infallible truth. It is not our business here to discuss whether this new emphasis is a cause or consequence of this reawakening. Of the fact there cannot be the slightest doubt. In opposition to this association comes evidence of a renewal of insistence that the doctrine of inerrancy and infallibility is no integral part of genuine Christian faith.

Throughout the years intervening between the time when inerrancy was generally renounced and the present period which is witnessing a new stress on what the concept is meant to convey, the position of both the liberal and the conservative evangelical Christian remained unaltered. There was on the whole, however, no serious conflict, because, not only were other interests uppermost, but evangelicals were in the backwood as far as convincing Biblical scholarship was concerned. They had, of course, their preachers such as J. H. Jowett, F. B. Meyer, J. Stuart Holden, W. Campbell Morgan, and others of lesser breed, who were committed to faith in the Bible as absolutely and altogether trustworthy. None of these would have allowed that there are 'errors and mistakes' in the Bible.

But as far back as 1924 Charles Gore gave voice to his concern about the possibility of a return to the idea of an infallible Bible. None had fought so strenuously against such a view, but he seems to express doubts about the finality and decisiveness of the victory which was claimed. He certainly regretted the evidence of 'a revival today of the position that faith in Christianity, as really the divinely-given gospel for the world, is bound up with the old-fashioned belief in the Bible as the infallible book'.[1] During recent years the very thing Gore sought so much to restrain has come to pass. The phenomenal growth of the Inter-Varsity Fellowship groups in colleges and universities is some indication of the strength of the movement in which the idea of an infallible Bible is fundamental. The

[1] C. Gore, *The Doctrine of an Infallible Book*, 1924, p. 7.

campaigns throughout the country of the evangelist, Dr Billy Graham, with his assertion, 'the Bible says', has also been another factor creating the modern re-emphasis upon the Bible as an altogether trustworthy book. Of no less importance is the influence of the revived interest in Puritan studies which has become a characteristic of our times.

We may be saying too much in asserting that at the present time A. G. Hebert seems to have taken on the rôle which Gore had earlier assumed, namely, that of urging upon the Church that Christian faith is not to be tied to the idea of an inerrant and infallible Bible.[1] In his volume *The Authority of the Old Testament*, Hebert appears as the true successor of the author of *The Doctrine of an Infallible Book*.[2] And incidently Hebert gives his allegiance, as did Gore, to the High Church group in the Anglican communion. Hebert shows his concern, too, for the apparent revival of the 'old-fashioned belief' in a verbally infallible Bible. It is consequently his aim to divorce the growing interest in Christian faith from the idea of literal biblical inerrancy. He therefore makes an attack upon those whom he refers to as 'Fundamentalists',[3] who, in holding to 'verbal inspiration' are said to be guilty of a 'materialistic conception of inspiration'.[4] They declare that the Bible is consequently 'free from error' and therefore 'inerrant'. He adduces a number of 'duplicate' and 'inconsistent' accounts designed to show that the 'doctrine of the Inerrancy of the Bible must be then regarded as, at least in reference to material fact, extremely vulnerable'.[5] He charges the Fundamentalist 'with asserting something that no previous age has understood in anything like the modern sense' in proclaiming literal inerrancy.[6] He declares that the New

---

[1] Cf. C. H. Dodd, *The Authority of the Bible*, 1928, p. 353. William Temple, *Nature, Man and God*, 1949, pp. 351 ff. John Baillie, *The Idea of Revelation in Recent Thought*, 1956, pp. 111 ff.

[2] Cf. C. Gore, *Reconstruction of Belief*, 1921, etc., new edition in one volume, 1926, reprint, 1945, pp. 621 f. and 864 f. It is of interest to note how Gore, as does Hebert, makes use of the 'mystical' and 'allegorical' sense of Scripture. Cf. pp. 884 ff.

[3] Cf. A. G. Hebert, *Fundamentalism and the Church of God*, 1957, Chapter I. J. I. Packer, *'Fundamentalism' and the Word of God*, 1958, Chapter I. Douglas Johnson, *The Christian Graduate*, March 1955. Correspondence in *The Times* on 'Fundamentalism', August 1955; cf. esp. letter by J. R. W. Stott, 25 August 1955. See also Robert Abba, *The Nature and Authority of the Bible*, 1958, pp. 63–5. J. K. S. Reid, *The Authority of the Bible*, 1957, pp. 158–64.

[4] A. G. Hebert, *The Authority of the Old Testament*, 1947, p. 25; cf. pp. 93–100.

[5] *Ibid.*, p. 31.   [6] *Ibid.*, p. 98.

Testament writers inherited from the Jews the idea of inspiration as involving inerrancy, but while they did not criticize it, they did *not* accept it.[1] The apostolic writers assumed the inerrancy of the Old Testament 'but did not take over unadulterated the rabbinic notion of Inspiration'.[2] In truth, the doctrine of verbal inerrancy is not after all an 'old-fashioned belief' but something quite new to Fundamentalists' circles, something different from the idea of 'theological and religious inerrancy'. This materialistic inerrancy, Hebert asserts, 'has been a potent cause of modern unbelief'.[3]

Armed with these assurances, Hebert, in a later volume sets himself to make a more pointed attack upon the position regarding Scripture advocated by the Inter-Varsity Fellowship of Christian Unions in general[4] and by *The New Bible Commentary* in particular.[5] The Bible, according to Hebert, is the record of God's saving purpose in history and its 'truth' is therefore limited to this theological reality. This saving purpose has been consummated in the person of Christ; and it is through the 'words of men' that this 'Word of God' becomes known to us. 'It is', he then declares, 'in this larger context that we need to study the words Inerrancy and Infallibility'.[6] Because these words are 'negative' they are pronounced to be 'troublesome and unsatisfactory' 'like the word "sinless" applied to our Lord'.[7] Hebert is committed to the allegorical method of interpretation and he can consequently refer to the Bible as 'true history' in so far as it 'truly relates the working in history of God's Purpose of salvation'.[8] The 'rigid theory of factual inerrancy' is then stated to be 'too narrow'[9] because it 'seems to

---

[1] A. G. Hebert, *The Authority of the Old Testament*, 1947, p. 235. But cf. the following, 'The Church from the outset accepted the old Jewish Scriptures and regarded them, just as the Jewish Church had done, as the verbally inspired teaching of God'. W. L. Knox, *Essays Catholic and Critical* (ed. E. G. Selwyn), 1926, third edition, 1931, p. 98. Then C. Gore, 'Nothing, I think, is less justified on the whole than to represent our Lord as accepting current Jewish interpretations on the meaning of inspiration, however true it is that it returned in great measure upon the Church in later days'. *Reconstruction of Belief*, p. 377. It will be remembered that Gore who now cannot think of our Lord as accommodating himself to current ideas of inspiration, earlier argued that He did in connection with biblical dates and authorship.

[2] *Ibid.*, p. 236.   [3] *Ibid.*, p. 307.
[4] A. G. Hebert, *Fundamentalism and the Church of God*, 1957, p. 10.
[5] *Ibid.*, p. 84 f.   [6] *Ibid.*, p. 42.   [7] *Ibid.*
[8] *Ibid.*, p. 43.   [9] *Ibid.*, cf. pp. 55–6 and 148.

allow for a satisfactory account of the story of Adam and Eve'.[1] Hebert can go so far with regard to the Old Testament, at any rate, as to say that taken by itself it contains errors 'not in small matters of literal fact, but in matters of faith and morals'.[2] He admits it is a 'paradox' to assert 'the Book of God's Truth' contains 'error'. But 'a deeper consideration of the word "truth" and "error" will solve the problem, since', he assures us, 'the "error" is not of the absolute sort'.[3]

Having made his case in this manner, Hebert seeks to apply his results to *The New Bible Commentary*, which was published by the Inter-Varsity Fellowship in 1953.[4] He endeavours to show that the writers of the volume have not been able to interpret the Bible in a manner consistent with their declared faith. Packer, he observes, uses the 'rigid word "infallibility"', whereas Bromiley 'avoids it'. Hebert then accuses the Fundamentalists with upsetting the ecumenical cause. They demand as the Ground of Unity, not merely the Gospel of God, but the gospel *plus* the Inerrancy of the Bible and the necessity of a particular kind of conversion.[5]

Such accusations have not been left unanswered by the conservative evangelicals. J. I. Packer, for example, attacks Hebert head on. Attention is here called to this reply because it is certainly as scholarly as the work it opposes. He points out that, historically, the Church had always taken the position that the Bible, because inerrant, was there to correct tradition and reason.[6] He denies that faith in it as 'the infallible word' is 'a form of idolatry'.[7] He sees the understanding and evaluation of the Bible as the 'crucial issue' of the present day. The opponents of Fundamentalism, basing themselves on the presuppositions and conclusions of nineteenth-century critical Bible study, believe it to be necessary to assert that statements are definitely erroneous. They 'cannot accept the axiom that whatever

---

[1] A. G. Hebert, *Fundamentalism and the Church of God*, 1957; p. 43.

[2] *Ibid.*, p. 46. Cf. 'We are led to question the traditional belief, because it seems plain that the Bible contains inconsistencies and contradictions, not only on points of historical fact but in matters of 'faith and morals', which can be reconciled with belief in its inerrancy or infallibility only by doing violence to intellectual honesty.' John Burnaby, *Is the Bible Inspired?* 1940, Vol. 9 in the Colet Series of Modern Christian Thought and Teaching (ed. W. R. Matthews), pp. 112–13.

[3] *Ibid.*, p. 55.   [4] *Ibid.*, pp. 84 ff.   [5] *Ibid.*, p. 123; cf. p. 125.

[6] J. I. Packer, '*Fundamentalism*' and the Word of God, 1958, p. 48.

[7] *Ibid.*, p. 62.

Scripture is found to assert is part of the word of God; for untruths cannot be God's word. Hence they think it impossible to take seriously the "Jewish" conception of the nature of God-given Scripture which Christ and the Bible teach. Instead, they say, we must use our Christian wits to discern beneath the fallible words of fallible men the eternal truth of God'.[1] Packer boldly maintains that 'Evangelicals are accustomed to speak of the Word of God as *infallible* and *inerrant*'.[2] But this does not mean the infallibility and inerrancy of every interpretation put upon the Scripture, nor does it imply that the writers of the Bible did not use modes of speech about the natural order and human experience as were current in their day, and the language that was common to themselves and their contemporaries.[3] Hebert is in error, he insists, in crediting to the Evangelicals a rigid theory of factual inerrancy of the Bible which excludes any symbolic mode of interpretation.[4] It is simply not true, Packer contends, that the inerrancy of the Word of God commits its adherents to a literalistic type of exegesis.[5] Packer draws attention to the analogy used by Hebert between the divine and the human in Christ, and the divine and the human in the Bible.[6] And he replies that the analogy 'can be only a limited one'.[7] It is right enough to point to the union of the divine and the human in both, but if the analogy is pressed it is contrary to the conclusion Hebert desires. The human nature of our Lord was free from sin 'so Scripture, though a truly human product, is truly free from error. If the critics believe that Scripture, as a human book, errs, they ought, by the force of their own analogy, to believe also that Christ, as man, sinned'.[8]

The conflict concerning inerrancy and infallibility has thus become once again a live issue. Hebert, like Gore before him, does not appear to apprehend the ideas which the Church throughout the ages sought to convey by these words. Nor is he

[1] J. I. Packer, *'Fundamentalism' and the Word of God*, 1958, p. 72.

[2] *Ibid.*, p. 94. Cf. '. . . the idea of Biblical inspiration which defines it as the "dictation of the Holy Ghost" and makes it incompatible with any error in the writings so inspired . . . (is) the traditional belief of Christendom'. John Burnaby, *Is the Bible Inspired?* 1949, p. 111.

[3] *Ibid.*, p. 96.   [4] *Ibid.*, pp. 98–9.   [5] *Ibid.*, p. 99.

[6] Cf. *'Fundamentalism' and the Word of God*, pp. 82 ff. A. G. Hebert, *Fundamentalism and the Church of God*, pp. 73 ff., esp. pp. 77–8. H. D. McDonald, *Ideas of Revelation*, 1959, pp. 153 ff.

[7] J. I. Packer, *'Fundamentalism' and the Word of God*, p. 83.   [8] *Ibid.*

always consistent in his criticisms. He, for example, builds his case upon the 'materialistic view of inspiration' which he credits to his opponents and yet acknowledges that the 'dictation-theory' is repudiated by all conservative evangelical leaders.[1] But all along he is virtually crediting them with this notion. Packer, on the other hand, has on several occasions assumed the position he is out to prove.

It would be quite wrong, however, to regard the whole thing as a mere strife about words. The issue is a real and deep one. Yet there was a question about the use of the words inerrancy and infallibility. Hebert sought for what he calls the 'positives to describe the inspiration of Scripture'. Having made reference to the Biblical passage II Tim. iii, 16 and II Peter i. 21, he adds, 'The positives of Inerrancy and Infallibility might be "true and faithful witness to the Truth of God" '.[2] Packer, too, would not contend for the mere terms. They 'are not essential for stating the evangelical view'.[3] He goes on to expound his position like this: ' "Infallibility" denotes the quality of never deceiving or misleading, and so means "wholly trustworthy and reliable"; "inerrant" means "wholly true". Scripture is termed infallible and inerrant to express the conviction that all its teaching is the utterance of God "who cannot lie", whose word, once spoken, abides for ever, and that therefore it may be trusted implicitly'.[4]

It would, of course, be idle to pretend that in the end Hebert and Packer are saying the same thing. The simple fact is that

---

[1] A. G. Hebert, *Fundamentalism and the Church of God*, p. 56.

[2] *Ibid.*, p. 42.

[3] J. I. Packer, *'Fundamentalism' and the Word of God*, p. 95.

[4] *Ibid.*, p. 95. Cf. E. J. Young takes up a statement of C. A. Briggs who argued that the Bible's infallibility is limited to matters of faith and practice. (Cf. C. A. Briggs, *The Bible, The Church, The Reason*, 1892, pp. 93–4.) Young asks, Where does 'faith' end and historical details begin? What, in other words, are the precise limits of 'faith' in the first chapter of Genesis? What are the matters of 'faith' herein revealed concerning which we may say the Bible is infallible? And more than that, we may ask, who is to tell us what is and what is not a matter of faith? E. J. Young, *Thy Word is Truth*, 1957, pp. 101–2. Young contends that the word, 'infallibility' applied to the Bible means that the Scripture possesses an indefectible authority (p. 113). He rejects the *a priori* approach to the question of Inerrancy and Infallibility (p. 114). He contends, to take the example of the parallel passages in the gospels, that by 'Inerrancy' it is not meant that each account should be in exactly the same words, but that each writer told the truth, recorded matters accurately, has given us a true picture of what transpired (p. 136). The quotations from the Old Testament in the New reveal that there was 'no mechanical parrot-like repetition' (p. 161). The human writers acted as responsible agents. And, he

Hebert divorces the revelation of God's saving purpose from the Scripture and credits the 'positives of inspiration' to the former. His words quoted above do not mean exactly what they say. Hebert, we think, does not intend us to infer that the positives of Inerrancy and Infallibility apply to the Bible as a witness to revelation, but, as his whole thesis seeks to prove, to the revelation itself. Packer, on the other hand, wishes us to conclude that what the words signify belong to the Bible as the written Scripture.

The whole question needs the most careful rethinking. The wholesale repudiation of inerrancy in the days before and following the coming of the higher criticism may well be revealed as having been too hasty. In discarding the word something of real and permanent significance may have been lost which modern theologians are seeking if haply they might find.

Geoffrey W. Bromiley, well known as the editor of the translation of Karl Barth's *Church Dogmatics*, has drawn attention to an interesting fact. He has shown how the Lutheran and Reformed dogmaticians of the seventeenth century are in line with the main teaching of the Reformers themselves respecting their doctrine of Scripture. But he observes withal 'certain shifts of emphasis, slight in themselves but serious in their historical consequences'.[1] These dogmaticians tended to return to the patristic overwhelming of the human author by the divine thus giving rise to ambiguous words and phrases in relation to inspiration, as, for example, 'dicto' and 'assistants and amenuenses'. The result is 'a tendency to press to an unnecessary extreme the intrinsically true doctrine of verbal

contends, it is precisely here that 'we begin to understand the true nature of verbal inspiration and also inerrancy' (p. 161). Young is sure that the original autographs of Scripture are without error and it is the purpose of scholarship to restore them. If we assert that the autographs of Scripture contain error, we are saying that God is guilty of having told us something that is not true. It may be a matter which we ourselves would call minor, but in this case a minor error is no less an error than a major one. . . . If God has communicated wrong information even in so-called unimportant matters, He is not a trustworthy God. It is therefore the question of Biblical theism which is at stake. . . . If, as a matter of fact, the revelation of God is not free of error, the message of Christianity must ever remain in doubt' (pp. 165–6); cf. Chapters 5 and 6 on 'What is Inerrancy?' and Chapter 7 'Are there Errors in the Bible?'

[1] Geoffrey W. Bromiley, 'Church Doctrine of Inspiration', *Revelation and the Bible* (ed. Carl F. H. Henry), 1958, p. 213.

inspiration'. Bromiley then specifies the third shift of emphasis which brought about an important consequence as 'a tendency to give a false importance to the doctrine of inerrancy, as if the inspiration of Scripture were finally suspended upon the ability to prove it correct in every detail. To be sure, inspiration is itself the basis of inerrancy, and there is no obligation to prove the latter. But in face of attacks upon the inerrancy of the Bible, whether by those who do not regard it as essential to inspiration or by those who deny both, it is only too easy to reverse the true relationship and to come to think of inerrancy as the basis of inspiration'.[1] There are other developments due to the high-lighting of certain aspects of the Reformers' doctrine noted by Bromiley which do not concern us here. But he goes on through the brilliant period of the eighteenth century rationalism to show how the Christian apologist took a false step in seeking to answer Lessing and Herder by trying 'to defend inspiration in terms of inerrancy' and thus 'to commit it to inevitable relativization'. It was Herder who initiated the intensive research of the modern period with its more or less sustained polemic against inerrancy and therefore upon the special revelation of the Bible. By reducing inspiration to the aesthetic level and uniting it with the idea of the inward testimony of the Spirit, he opened the way for that complete subjectivism of which Schleiermacher was the father and liberal Protestantism the off-spring. And before the flood the orthodox seemed helpless. They could erect no staying barrier. The truth is that the 'attack on the historical reliability of the Bible was damaging just because orthodoxy no longer had a full confidence in the witness of the Spirit but must find for it rationalistic support by a reversal of the relationship between inspiration and inerrancy, suspending the former on the latter'.[2] As Bromiley sees it, the real need is to go back to the Reformers 'and through them to the Bible and its self-witness by which all our views of inspiration must be tested, corrected, strengthened, and empowered'. Such a method is not by any means to weaken inspiration, nor yet is it to compromise

---

[1] Geoffrey W. Bromiley, 'Church Doctrine of Inspiration', *Revelation and the Bible* (ed. Carl F. H. Henry), 1958. Cf. 'The Reformers not infrequently speak about the Bible in ways to suggest its literal inaccuracy. But this verbal inspiration is a *consequence* of their view that God is the author of Scripture, not the *basis* of it'. Paul L. Lehmann, 'The Reformers' Use of the Bible', *Theology Today*, Vol. 3, p. 339.   [2] *Ibid.*, p. 216.

with any distortions and dilutions of the truth. The prophetic and apostolic word comes as the word of divine wisdom not to exalt man's mind, but to summon all the rationalism of man to repentance and renewal. The Bible comes with God's saving message to man. 'The inspiration of Scripture is genuinely the work of the sovereign Spirit, whose operations cannot finally be subjected to human analysis, repudiation or control, but who remains the internal Master of that which he himself has given, guaranteeing its authenticity, and declaring its message with quickening and compelling power.'[1] With such a note we may conclude this section since it seems to us that to such a conclusion we are being driven by our reflection upon the subject of the Bible's significance and by our observation of the hesitancies and uncertainties which afflicted an earlier period in which the 'humanness' of the Bible, if the paradox be permitted, was virtually defied.

The immediate result of the breakdown of belief in 'literal inerrancy and infallibility', to take up the story again, was to open up for prolonged discussion the allied subjects of the inspiration and the authority of the Bible. 'Criticism compels us to revise our doctrine of the inspiration of Scripture', declared A. F. Kirkpatrick in October 1902 at Northampton, in a paper on 'Modern Criticism and its Influence on Theology', read at the Church Congress. 'We must not ascribe' he goes on to maintain, 'an equal value and authority to every part of the Old Testament. We must no longer talk of its infallibility and inerrancy. We must distinguish its temporal, imperfect elements. Our Lord Himself taught us to do so. While we hold fast to the belief that the Old Testament contains the record— the divinely-shaped record—of God's revelation of Himself to Israel, we seem forced to admit that the record was not given and has not been preserved in such forms as we might antecedently have expected as has generally been believed.'

In a reference to the cognate subject in an issue of the *Expository Times* for the year 1892, in a notice of Marshall Randles's book, *The Design and Use of Holy Scripture* comes the statement: It is 'the great controversy of today—The Authority of Scripture. We have barely entered upon it yet. So the signs

[1] Geoffrey W. Bromiley, 'Church Doctrine of Inspiration', *Revelation and the Bible* (ed. Carl F. H. Henry), 1958, p. 117.

demand to be read. And it threatens to assume proportions we never dreamt of. The Authority of Scripture—of how much Authority? and who have this Authority?'[1] The inspiration and the authority of the Scriptures, then, were the topics which became the centre of theological debate and which to this day continue to be issues of major importance. Volume after volume has appeared bearing such a title as The Inspiration and Authority of the Bible, or with the more restricted one of, The Authority of the Bible, and the like.

It is our purpose in the next two chapters to treat these two topics separately and to draw together something of what has been said respecting them.

---

[1] *Expository Times*, Vol. IV, 1892–3, p. 43.

CHAPTER SEVEN

The Discussion of Biblical Inspiration

The whole period following the general repudiation of inerrancy and the introduction of the higher criticism has been marked by an attack on the 'mechanical' theory of inspiration. It is just, however, to point out that this was a view of inspiration credited to the traditionalists generally rather than actually taught by them. The traditionalists have been consistent in contending for a doctrine of verbal inspiration but it was not the main view that this necessarily involved a mechanical process.[1] The term 'mechanical' would denote a process, but it was agreed that little could be stated in this respect. By the term 'verbal', on the other hand, emphasis was placed, not on the process, but on the result. The idea intended by the traditionalists in their use of the concept was to insist that the words of the Bible are the direct

---

[1] Cf. 'It ought to be unnecessary to protest again against the habit of representing the advocates of "verbal inspiration" as teaching that the mode of inspiration is dictation.' B. Warfield, *The Inspiration and Authority of the Bible*, 1893, reprint, 1948, p. 173 (note). 'When for instance we find that anything partaking of the character of Verbal Inspiration, is charged with turning the sacred penmen into "human ventriloquists" and "automaton poets", the result being nothing less than to "petrify the whole body of Holy Writ, with all its harmoniousness and symmetrical graduations"; all we need to say in reply is that whatever force such objections may have against the theory of Inspiration which represents the writers as mere *machines*, possessed of no power of choice in the selection and use of words they used, they do not at all bear on the view of Inspiration which we have shown as taught in Scripture, and which is in perfect harmony with the manifestation of individual peculiarities'. D. Fraser, *The Inspiration of the Bible*, 1874, pp. 62–3. The 'dictation theory' is 'repudiated by all the conservative evangelical leaders, because it leaves no room for the individuality of the human writers'. A. G. Hebert, *Fundamentalism and the Church of God*, 1957, p. 56.

'We do indeed believe . . . that the Holy Spirit spoke through the human authors so directly that their words were in a real sense His words, but we do not imagine that the process was a mechanical one'. J. R. W. Stott, Statement at Oxford Conference of Evangelical Churchmen, 1960. Cf. Letter in the *Baptist Times*, by V. Perry, November 10, 1960.

result of holy men of God being moved by the Holy Ghost. Inspiration relates to the words which have been given: it does not primarily describe what took place in the psychological nature or the spiritual experience of God's chosen men.

Opposition to the 'mechanical' theory, and because of its identification with verbal inspiration the consequent repudiation of the latter, became characteristic. Although his language may be more vehement than most, F. W. Farrar gives typical expression of this antagonism. He does not mince words. He allows that Paul shared in the Jewish ideas of inspiration as verbal and as demanding 'absolute infallibility'.[1] He then seeks to discredit the idea in which the apostle shared. Paul is made to set forth doctrines to be believed on a foundation which cannot be shared. 'To say that every word and sentence and letter of Scripture is divine and supernatural', says Farrar, 'is a mechanical and useless shibboleth, nay, more, a human idol, and (constructively, at least) a dreadful blasphemy'. It is a superstitious and fetish-worshipping dogma, 'not only unintelligible, but profoundly dangerous'. It 'has for many ages filled the world with misery and ruin' and 'has done more than any other dogma to corrupt the whole of exegesis with dishonest causistry, and to shake to its centre the religious faith of thousands, alike of the most ignorant and of the most cultivated in many centuries, and most of all in our own'.[2] This is certainly strong language indeed, but it is more eloquent than convincing. It is doubtful, to put it mildly, if any considerable fact could be adduced to support Farrar's contention. It seems besides to overstep the bounds of enthusiasm to credit the apostle Paul with being implicated in such a dreadful blasphemy which has filled the world with so much ruin!

The position being as it was, however, a reconsideration of the idea of inspiration became imperative. The general situation demanded it. And from a particular point of view, as Alan Richardson states, 'The rise of Biblical scholarship made necessary a new doctrine of the inspiration of Holy Scripture'.[3] This necessity arose, Richardson adds, because it was found

---

[1] F. W. Farrar, *The Life and Work of St Paul*, 1880, Vol. I, p. 49; cf. p. 341.

[2] F. W. Farrar, *Inspiration, A Clerical Symposium* (ed. F. W. Farrar), 1888, second edition, p. 219; cf. p. 241.

[3] Alan Richardson, *A Preface to Bible-Study*, 1943, second impression, 1944, p. 33.

'impossible to continue to hold to the "dictation" theory'.[1] We can perhaps say that it was Charles Gore's essay in the *Lux Mundi* which sparked off the conflicts.[2] The essay which he contributed to the volume under the title 'The Holy Spirit and Inspiration' was, at the time, described as 'broad'. Every race has its great interpreters who have had a 'divine inspiration' which was at the same time 'natural'. The Jews, however, had an inspiration which was 'supernatural', since they were a people specially chosen to teach the world of God's relation to men. This is the 'point of view' of the Bible. Here lies the inspiration of its prophets, psalmists and historians. The writers of the Bible were 'inspired' because they saw what God was about, but such 'inspiration' neither enabled them 'to dispense with the ordinary means' nor did it carry with it a guarantee of accuracy.

Driver sought to allay fears that criticism would banish all ideas of an inspired Bible and leave us with a book altogether human. 'Criticism in the hands of Christian scholars', he stated in the Preface to *The Introduction to the Literature of the Old Testament*, 'does not banish or destroy the inspiration of the Old Testament; it presupposes it; it seeks only to determine the conditions under which it operates and the literary form through which it manifests itself.'[3]

But withal the question was urgent and pressing. Where does inspiration lie? Is it to be found in the words which the Bible contains, or in the religious experience which the Bible attests, or in the creative message which the Bible conveys? The traditional answer, with which we are not concerned at the moment, of course, affirmed the first.

A. INSPIRATION—THE FOCUS WITHIN

Immediately following the upheaval brought about by criticism, there was a tendency to maintain the view that the locale of inspiration was particularly the experiences of religious geniuses. Contemporary thought, on the other hand, seems to regard inspiration as the redemptive message of the Bible as

---

[1] Alan Richardson, *A Preface to Bible-Study*, 1943, second impression, 1944, p. 33.
[2] Cf. *Expository Times*, Vols. I and II, 1889–91, i, p. 121.
[3] S. R. Driver, *Introduction to the Literature of the Old Testament*, 1891, Preface, p. xiii.

that message is realized within the responding individual. These two ways of stating inspiration are not exactly successive or clear-cut. They overlap at many points.

It was certainly a direct result of criticism to shift attention from the words of the Bible to the men to whom we owe its existence. A. E. Garvie set himself to 'correct' 'the prevalent error of viewing the Bible as primarily an inspired book', and to do so he emphasized the fact that revelation is historical. He then stresses the idea of Providence and appears to equate inspiration with the prophetic interpretation of Israel's history as the sphere of God's selective activity. Yet the 'personal' aspect of inspiration is to be noted in which 'God by His indwelling and inworking Spirit made the men fit and worthy to be His messengers'. 'How interesting', he adds, 'the Bible is because the Divine Author of the revelation disguises Himself in the dress of the human authors of the writings.'[1]

John Clifford expounds as well as any other the idea of inspiration which was to emerge in the context of the new Biblical criticism. It is his contention that the question of inspiration should not be made fundamental.[2] Experience, he urges, gives the key to the understanding of the idea of inspiration. We have known 'inspired men' whose presence quickened emotion, stirred the conscience and strengthened the will. And Biblical inspiration 'was of men' and the Bible is a 'report' of the experiences of God-inspired men'.[3] Thus, as a man rightly uses the Bible so he will discover its inspiration. It is wrong to come to the Bible, with the mind made up regarding the method of inspiration.[4] One must accept what one finds. He however expresses the hope that 'the unhappy, inadequate, and misleading words "verbal inspiration" ' should be got rid of. Inspiration appears to be in Clifford's treatment a matter of degree. He writes on 'Present Day Inspiration' and states that 'the last Word of God has not been spoken'.[5] He talks eloquently

[1] A. E. Garvie, 'The Value of the Old Testament', *Expository Times*, Vol. XLVIII, 1936–7, p. 376. Cf. 'The Synthesis of History, Experience and Reason, in the Knowledge of God', *op. cit.*, Vol. XLIII, 1931–2, pp. 103 ff.

[2] Cf. 'The question of the nature and effect of Inspiration is not fundamental to the Christian argument'. R. Rainy, *Critical Review*, Vol. I, p. 11.

[3] John Clifford, *The Inspiration and Authority of the Bible*, 1888, third edition, 1899, p. 18.

[4] *Ibid.*, pp. 34 ff.   [5] *Ibid.*, p. 232.

of the inspired life and adds, 'Inspired personalities inspire'. He therefore closes his book with the hope that all the Lord's people be, not readers or teachers, but 'prophets'.

Inspiration was then to find the focus within. Those who saw God's acts in history, who read the account from the religious point of view, were indeed inspired to see and to read in this way. 'It is not their *words* that are inspired—as one might say perhaps of "automatic writing"—it is the *men* who are inspired.'[1] And the men were inspired because they had what A. F. Kirkpatrick refers to as the 'religious eye'. Being in possession of this 'incomparable eye', to use a phrase preferred by Angus M. Mackay, the men of the Bible were able, as others were not, to see God active and to feel God present.

Religious genius and religious experience; such were the two operative words in the earlier statement of inspiration. R. Brook, for example, finds in the two words we have singled out the central truth about inspiration. Inspiration, he tells us, is the exercise of a profound religious instinct which some possess since there are those 'in whom this religious sense exists in a highly developed form, who have a special genius for religion, as others have for art of music'.[2] Marcus Dods likewise comes near to the same position. The fundamental problem is to rightly adjust the Divine and the human elements. The 'mechanical theory' is declared to be 'heathen' and 'Jewish'. But Paul did not accept it, nor can we, because it suggests that 'the Spirit of God inserts or puts into the mind of the inspired man a truth, as it were ready-made, and not in any necessary connection with the previous contents of the inspired mind or its moral action'.[3] Dods rejects also the 'essential dynamic theory' in which it is declared that accuracy is secured in all matters of conduct and doctrine, but need not be thought to extend to non-essential details and subsidiary particulars. In this case, the 'discrepancies' discovered in the science or the history cannot disturb. ('Perhaps they can be explained, perhaps they cannot, who cares a straw whether they can or no?' Coleridge.) Dods, however, rejects this on many accounts.[4] And having done so he leaves himself with less

[1] C. H. Dodd, *The Authority of the Bible*, 1928, p. 30 (italics in original).

[2] R. Brook, *Foundations*, A Statement of Christian Belief in Terms of Modern Thought, by Seven Oxford men (ed. B. H. Streeter), 1912, p. 52.

[3] Marcus Dods, *The Bible, Its Origin and Nature*, 1913, p. 117.

[4] *Ibid.*, pp. 122 ff.

than half a dozen pages to seek a 'positive' statement. This amounts to the assertion that inspiration has to do with the men, not with the words they have given. Its presence is seen in their perception of revelation. Those whom the Scriptures designate 'inspired' are so because they 'are distinguished above their fellow-Christians by a special readiness and capacity to perceive the meaning of Christ as the revelation of God and to make known what they see'.[1] Inspiration relates to character and godliness of life. 'The inspired man might not see the facts of history more clearly than the uninspired; but he saw God in history where the uninspired only saw human passions.'[2] In the last, inspiration is really the spiritual gift possessed by men of special godliness and character who could see what it is not given to others to behold.

A statement of the same import comes in Angus M. Mackay's *The Churchman's Introduction to the Old Testament* (1901). In the opening chapter on the subject of Inspiration he appears to regard it in the same general manner. 'Inspiration does not guarantee him who possesses it against all error', he writes, 'Here also an analogy may help us. When we say that Shakespeare surpassed all other men in *poetic* inspiration, what do we mean? Not that in dealing with disputed historical questions he was infallible, but that he had an incomparable eye for the *poetic* and *dramatic* elements in history. His genius did not make him an authority upon botany or astronomy, but only inspired him to turn flowers and stars to the very highest *poetic* uses conceivable. So the prophets were inspired in matters pertaining to God; they had a genius for religion.'

A. S. Peake hesitates to attribute inspiration to religious genius, but in the end he seems ready for the admission. 'What the inspiration of the Bible is,' he contends, 'we can assert only from the investigation of the Bible itself.'[3] It is reluctance to admit errors in the Bible which is responsible for the rigorous mechanical theory. But since these have been discovered by criticism, a 'more flexible theory' is demanded. 'The history (of Israel) as a whole', he maintains, 'is in truth inspired, when we look at it, that is to say, as an element in the development of our

---

[1] Marcus Dods, *The Bible, Its Origin and Nature*, 1913, p. 124.
[2] *Ibid.*, p. 125.
[3] A. S. Peake, *The Bible, Its Origin, Significance and Abiding Worth*, 1913, p. 29.

race.'¹ To supress the human in personality would be entirely
out of harmony with the Spirit of God.² In a chapter on 'The
Nature and Mechanism of Inspiration'³ he claims that the 'old-
fashioned' doctrine of inspiration is now 'happily fast dis-
appearing'. Peake's whole endeavour is to show how the Holy
Spirit inspired the men. The inspired man is the 'possessed' man.
This leads him to discuss, in a manner followed later by J.
Burnaby,⁴ the action of the Spirit in the lives of men in the Old
and New Testaments. It was Paul's merit, he declares, to stress
the activity of the Spirit in the lives of ordinary Christians;
'the Church was in danger of overrating the value of the
abnormal phenomena'.⁵ The Spirit, however, does seek as
instruments those who have the qualifications. 'He desires the
religious genius rather than the physical subject.'⁶ Yet this does
not reduce inspiration, he asserts, to a higher form of religious
genius, although a few pages later he writes, 'The inspiration
we find in the Bible is that of supreme religious genius, often
combined, it is true, with a superb gift of expression, but still
having its value rather in the fact that it is religious, than that
it is great literature'.⁷

Urging that 'the hearty recognition of the human element is
incompatible with a belief in verbal inspiration' Peake goes on
to refer inspiration to the men behind the Bible. It is they who
were inspired because they were religiously sensitive to the
movements of God in history. In them the divine and the human
so combined that the significance of what they were aware 'was
the joint product action of the Divine and human factors; that no
boundary line should be drawn between the two; that its primary
purpose is not to divulge doctrines or lay down moral principles
but to bring us into contact with God Himself and disclose His
action in revelation and redemption; that whatever errors be
recognized and uncertainties remain we have enough and far
more than enough for all our religious and moral needs'.⁸

Prior to the appearance of the *Lux Mundi* certain rather loose
views of inspiration can be noted. The idea of Samuel Davidson,
for example, gave particular offence. Strong objection was taken

¹ A. S. Peake, *The Bible, Its Origin, Significance and Abiding Worth*, 1913, p. 254
² *Ibid.*, p. 352.   ³ *Ibid.*, Chapter XIX.
⁴ J. Burnaby, *Is the Bible Inspired?* 1949.
⁵ A. S. Peake, *op. cit.*, p. 390.   ⁶ *Ibid.*, p. 395.
⁷ *Ibid.*, pp. 402-3.   ⁸ *Ibid.*, p. 407.

to his stress upon 'degrees of inspiration'.[1] Colenso, too, it may be observed, although he nowhere expressed denial of the doctrine of inspiration, shows by some of his critical conclusions that he was opposed to any verbal theory.[2]

In 1884 there appeared the Symposium on *Inspiration* to which eleven writers contributed. F. W. Farrar, the originator and editor of the volume, himself contributed a chapter and gave a sort of summary of the views of the other writers. Farrar notes that S. Leathes, John Cairns and G. W. Olver 'appear to maintain the current view of the Bible as being throughout supernaturally infallible and inspired'.[3] The first of the trio, an Anglican, contended that the Bible as a whole is to be designated the Word of God and is therefore fully inspired. He does, however, stress that this does not necessitate any 'mechanical' theory.[4] At the same time he states, 'If the Bible is the Word of God at all, it must be so in such a sense as that we may trust its most important and crucial utterances to the very letter. Supposing the exact words to have been accurately ascertained, there seems to be no limit to which we may not trust and rely upon them to the very letter. If words are the vehicles of thought, then the more exact the thought the more accurate the words must be, unless they are to misrepresent and not do justice to it'.[5] To this view, the Presbyterian, Cairns, gives his fullest assent and in his own essay acknowledges his heavy debt to Leathes. Olver, too, writing as a Methodist, is in general agreement, although he declined to propound any specific theory of inspiration. He has none, he avers, except that which can be expressed in the words, 'Men spake from God, being moved by the Holy Spirit'. 'I accept the fact', he declares, 'and do not profess to explain the manner. The fact furnishes all the authority that the state of the case renders necessary. The result is a message from God. It is more. It is the one and only message so credited to the human race as "*the* Word of God".'[6]

Such a statement was too conservative for the other writers. An Independent, E. White and an Anglican, F. W. Farrar, took

---

[1] Cf. *The Wesleyan Magazine*, Vol. LXXIX, 1856, p. 116; Vol. LXXX, 1857, pp. 1118–20. See also J. Allanson Picton in *The Autobiography and Diary of William Davidson* (edited by his daughter), 1899, pp. 57–9.

[2] Cf. *British and Foreign Evangelical Review*, Vol. XII, 1863, p. 891.

[3] *Inspiration*, A Clerical Symposium (ed. F. W. Farrar), 1884, p. 207.

[4] *Ibid.*, p. 43.   [5] *Ibid.*, 44–5.   [6] *Ibid.*, p. 128.

a fairly extreme 'liberal' position. Edward White sees the Bible, not as a whole, but as a heterogeneous collection, and he argues that each separate contribution is a result of a 'divine personal instruction of men of old', to grasp as they were able the movements of the divine purpose. His view of inspiration he grants is 'exceedingly different from that of the ecclesiastical Canonists'.[1] He believes that a first step in coming to an understanding of inspiration sufficient to meet the modern situation is 'resolutely to fling aside the post-Nicene theory of the inspiration of "the Bible" as a whole; to resolve this Bible into its elements; and to regulate our view of each of these component parts by the writer's own testimony concerning the degree in which he was "moved by the Holy Ghost" '.[2]

F. W. Farrar states that his own views 'coincide in great measure with those of the Rev. E. White'.[3] The ideas which Farrar elaborated in more detail later are already expressed here. He strongly objects to the position taken up by Leathes and the other two and argues that it is wrong to say that the Bible *is* the Word of God: it only *contains* it. Verbal inspiration is repudiated and degress of inspiration according to the type of writing is maintained. As a book to inspire the value of the Bible is acknowledged, but it is a corrupting form of 'dishonest casuistry' to regard the Bible as a communication to men and for men of infallible divine truths.

In 1888, R. F. Horton, in line with his recent acceptance of the results of Biblical criticism, produced his *Inspiration of the Bible*. In 1884, Horton confesses he had never read a book on criticism. He had, indeed, heard Kuenen lecture at Oxford on 'Israel', and he had, he tells us, a vague awareness of the destructive criticism of the New Testament by the Tübingen school. It was, however, the publication of the Revised New Testament which stirred his interest and resulted in his wholehearted capitulation to literary and historical criticism.[4] In 1887 he began a series of lectures designed to introduce the new teaching to his congregation at Hampstead and the *Inspiration of the Bible* is the result.

Horton's conversion to criticism was, however, too recent for the task he undertook. He had not had time to reflect and he

---

[1] *Inspiration,* A Clerical Symposium (ed. F. W. Farrar), 1884, p. 148.
[2] *Ibid.,* p. 154.   [3] *Ibid.,* p. 219.
[4] R. F. Horton, *An Autobiography,* 1918, p. 85.

failed to see the real issues. He had no constructive statement to give. Horton attacked with all the logic at his command and the light which he now supposed himself to have received, 'the cast-iron theory of inspiration'. His apparent purpose was to show that the Bible contained numerous errors and inconsistencies in order to make the 'mechanical' theory impossible to square with the alleged facts. But having done so Horton had nothing convincing to put in its place. In his later *Revelation and the Bible* (1892) he adds the note on 'Attempt at Reconstruction', but all that he could give was, as it was observed earlier, a 'series of tentative suggestions'. The earlier book, however, is characterized by the absence of any serious effort to offer even these. Horton rather naïvely remarks in his *Autobiography* that he had no thought of discrediting the Bible by his onslaught on the prevailing idea of inspiration. Indeed he imagined himself 'defending it from the assaults of Infidelity, which acquired all their force from an erroneous conception of what the inspiration of the Bible was'.[1]

It was the alleged errors in the Bible which led so many to declare against verbal inspiration. The *British Quarterly Review* of the year 1873, in an article on 'G. H. Augustus von Ewald' urged that what it referred to as the 'scribe theory' of inspiration, was no longer tenable in the light of the results gained by textual criticism. Ewald had maintained that the people of Israel, as God's selected nation, were 'inspired', and although he did not commit himself openly to the conclusion, he appeared to suggest that the Bible, as the record of the dealing of Israel with God, partook of inspiration in a derivative sense only.[2]

The focus on inner experience as the sphere of inspiration came specially to vogue after the appearance of Gore's *Lux Mundi* essay. So strong, indeed, did this insistence become that at a much later period, C. H. Dodd could use the emphasis to deny the possibility of verbal inspiration which he identified with the 'dictation' theory. 'Whatever such a process of "dictation" may be', he declares, 'it is naturally impossible to say, since *ex hypothesi* no living man has experience of it.'[3]

[1] R. F. Horton, *An Autobiography*, 1918, p. 85.

[2] *British Quarterly Review*, Vol. LVII, 1873, pp. 170-3. Cf. Heinrich Ewald's *Revelation and its Record* (E.T. 1884), where the same idea is elaborated, but there is actually no discussion of inspiration; but cf. pp. 270-99.

[3] C. H. Dodd, *The Authority of the Bible*, 1928, p. 35.

Gore did more than any other to revise the idea of inspiration. Elsewhere he reiterates in a more dogmatic manner the ideas of inspiration of his *Lux Mundi* essay. In one of the volumes which make up the trio published under the title *Reconstruction of Belief*, he acknowledges that belief in inspiration is the 'belief of the Christian Church' which 'has its ground in the inspiration of the Old Testament which they inherited from the Jews'.[1] But it was, he maintains, the prophets who were inspired, and the Bible comprises 'the books of inspired men'.[2] Gore argues against 'literal accuracy' and contends, as does Hebert later, that the notion of verbal inspiration has 'a very large place' among the 'root causes of present-day unsettlement in matters of religion'.[3]

Many were the efforts made to reconstruct the doctrine of inspiration in the new context. One of the most important of these was that made by W. T. Davidson, Classical Professor at the Richmond Methodist Theological College. In a paper read at the London Wesleyan Ministers' Meeting, March 16, 1891, and entitled 'Inspiration and Biblical Criticism', Davidson raised the question: 'How far is the doctrine of Inspiration and the Divine Authority of Holy Scripture affected by the modern Biblical Criticism?' He refers to the articles on the Bible in the ninth edition of the *Encyclopaedia Brittannica* and the fact that the *Lux Mundi* has reached its eleventh edition mainly because of Gore's essay on 'Inspiration' as evidence of the need to reconsider the question. He suggests that the 'ecclesiastical doctrine of Inspiration' which has become the common property of the orthodox, needs to be modified to meet the present situation. It is no longer possible to begin, as the earlier theologians did, with a statement of Inspiration and on that basis to assert the infallibility of the Scripture. 'The doctrine of Inspiration is the very last thing we come to in a time of searching inquiry and unsettlement of foundations.' There are other questions to be faced first; for example, the genuineness, the authenticity and so forth, of the several books. But if we do not begin with inspiration and infallibility where then rests the authority of the Bible? Neither on the authority of the Church

---

[1] C Gore, *Reconstruction of Belief*, 1921–4, new edition in one volume 1926, reprint, 1945, p. 875.
[2] *Ibid.*, p. 888.   [3] *Ibid.*, p. 874.

nor yet in the Coleridgean dictum that what *finds me* in the Bible is true. It is in the experience of Jesus Christ that its authority is revealed and its 'inspiration' ultimately discovered. In a later article Davidson defends his position, maintaining that no 'preconceived doctrine of "inspiration", or any theories concerning what "revelation" ought to contain, or how far the records of the Scriptures must agree in detail must be held *a priori*'.[1]

Under a similar title, J. J. Stewart Perowne discussed the doctrine of inspiration.[2] Making reference to the Revisers' translation of II Tim. iii. 15–17, he sees the Scriptures as 'being full of the breath of God'. Yet it is not possible to define exactly the nature of the inspiration any more than we can define life itself. Possessing divine life the Scripture reveals its presence in its power and effect. Perowne, however, goes into some detail concerning the process of inspiration. 'Now I think we cannot too clearly or too firmly grasp the principle laid down by St Paul', he says. 'By inspiration we are to understand that influence of the Spirit of God upon the writers of the Old Testament, by which they were empowered to teach such spiritual truths, and in such a measure as was necessary for the religious welfare of those whom they addressed. Inspiration does not imply that the writers were lifted altogether above the level of their contemporaries in matters of plainly secular import. They do not antedate the science of the nineteenth century. Marvellous as is their historical accuracy, it does not imply supernatural infusion of knowledge on subjects lying within their own observation. They were the faithful witnesses and recorders of the things they themselves had seen and heard.'[3]

We have made reference a few pages back to A. F. Kirkpatrick's statement concerning the 'religious eye' possessed by those who saw God in the events of Israel's national life. The idea comes in his volume, *The Divine Library of the Old Testament: Its Origin, Preservation, Inspiration and Permanent Value* (1891). Concerning our present subject his thesis is that the essential nature of inspiration is to be seen as the purification of

[1] W. T. Davidson, *London Quarterly Review*, Vol. XCIII, 1900, pp. 1–24; cf. p. 13 f.
[2] J. J. Stewart Perowne, *Expository Times*, Vols. I and II, 1889–91, ii, pp. 54 ff.
[3] *Ibid.*, p. 55.

the primitive traditions by the Biblical recorders and their adaptation to religious purposes. These inspired men were able to show that it was God in His actions of grace who ruled history and was in it. Inspiration did not guarantee immunity from errors in matters of fact, science, or history, and most certainly it did not exclude imperfection, relativity and accommodation.

Two series of Bampton Lectures in the early years of the eighteen-nineties gave attention to the topic of inspiration. The first of these by A. Barry in 1892 was not dealing specifically with the question, yet he does feel it necessary to say something regarding it. In one of the lectures on 'Criticism and the Holy Scriptures', he begins by maintaining the legitimacy of criticism. He believes that in the midst of the diversity of the Bible there is discoverable by 'faith' a 'subjective unity'. This may be denied by criticism but Christians have a sure faith 'in a Supreme Inspiration—whether of origination or selection it matters not —which has guided and overruled all these varieties of age and authorship to one Divine Purpose'.[1] Barry admits that criticism has given 'some shock to the old unquestioning faith, which holds it to be above all human judgement, and is content to listen to every sentence as a complete Word of God'.[2] He contends however that we have learned, as a result of the recent discussion, that 'in grace, as in nature, the Divine Inspiration expresses itself in methods different from what we should have *a priori* expected'.[3]

Barry raises the question of the distinctive and essential character of the Scripture which justifies the Christian claim to it as the supreme authority. The enquiry, he suggests, resolves itself into that concerning inspiration. He doubts the correctness of speaking about 'an inspired Book'. It is its authors who were inspired. 'For inspiration is the action of the Spirit of God upon the living spirits of men.'[4] He adds, however, that inspiration must be thought of as extending to a choice of words 'though not (in) its usual sense of dictation, in which we can speak of "verbal inspiration" '.[5]

Barry is clearly anxious, in spite of this last admission, to

[1] A. Barry, *Some Lights of Science on the Faith*, Bampton Lectures, 1892, p. 265.
[2] *Ibid.*, p. 268.   [3] *Ibid.*, pp. 271–2.
[4] *Ibid.*, p. 282–3.   [5] *Ibid.*

insist that inspiration refers to the men who wrote, not to what and how they wrote. To speak of an inspired book is to obscure the important truth, that the writers of the Holy Scriptures were not mechanical instruments through whom the Holy Spirit wrought. He expresses unhappiness about 'The Inspiration of the Bible'. He would have us draw a distinction between revelation and inspiration and refer to the Scripture as itself a unique revelation of God, whereas inspiration is to be 'viewed as the power by which the writers of Scripture were quickened to understand and to declare' the revelation.[1] He illustrates his idea from the experience of teaching. 'Revelation to others is for us comparatively easy: inspiration of others infinitely difficult.' To present, illustrate and enforce the truth we know is within the experience of many, but to inspire the minds of learners, to stimulate intelligence, to give insight, even to awaken interest is far from being an easy thing. This means for Barry, as he boldly declares, that inspiration is subjective and as such must vary in form and degree.[2] So difficult is it for us to understand inspiration in respect of ourselves that it becomes obviously impossible to comprehend the process by which God has moved men's minds. Contrasting the theory of 'mechanical' inspiration with the 'dynamical' and the special inspiration of the writers of Scripture with the general inspiration of Christian believers, may, he says, be useful in its way. But they are ultimately a mere matter of speculation: 'The one all-important thing for us is to know whether we have in Holy Scripture a real Revelation of Truth; how it was given, through what forms or measure of Inspiration, is one of the secrets of God'.[3]

In the following year W. Sanday discussed the whole subject of Inspiration from an historical and reconstructionist point of view. The main ideas were already stated in his volume, *The Oracles of God*. He there bluntly maintained with reference to the Bible that 'its text is not infallible; its grammar is not infallible; its science is not infallible; and there is grave doubt whether its history is altogether infallible'.[4] In the last of his later Bampton Lectures, having traced in a manner which he

---

[1] A. Barry, *Some Lights of Science on the Faith*, Bampton Lectures, 1892, p. 284.
[2] *Ibid.*, p. 289.   [3] *Ibid.*, p. 290.
[4] W. Sanday, *The Oracles of God*, Nine Lectures on the Nature and Extent of Biblical Inspiration and the Special Significance of the Old Testament Scriptures at the Present Time, 1892, fourth edition, p. 36.

appears to regard as satisfactory the origin and early history of the doctrine of Biblical inspiration, he turns to compare what he calls the 'traditional' view with the 'inductive or critical'. He allows that the 'Inspiration implied by both is real and no fiction, a direct objective action of the Divine upon the human'.[1] The danger in the 'traditional' doctrine, he thinks, is that it might easily slide into a dead and mechanical notion. In contrast with it, the 'deductive' method seeks to understand inspiration 'by examining the consciousness of the Biblical writers', to learn from them what they have to say of their own inspiration.[2] At times these prophetic men arrived at the truth through the inspiration of devout meditation and reflection, and at times they were vividly aware of a special divine *afflatus*. They were not men 'dictated' to, but men 'inspired'. The divine revelation 'came through human *media*; and from time to time we are reminded that the *media* are human'.[3]

We have already noted Farrar's harsh condemnation of the 'mechanical' theory of inspiration. In his book, *The Bible, Its Meaning and Supremacy*, he returns to his aversion. He associates the two words 'verbal' and 'dictation' and contends that they suggest 'an untrue and unscriptural hypothesis', and he later remarks on the 'dangerous results of the "supernatural dictation" theory'.[4] Farrar seems to take a very broad view of inspiration. It is apparently not specifically limited to the writers of Scripture; they are rather an instance of that influence which the Spirit of God exercises upon all men. They were, to be sure, more responsive and co-operative. As all great literature awakens a response in the sensitive soul, so the Bible 'speaks directly and unmistakably to our inmost hearts and consciences. We shall hear it each according to our capacity and our power to receive it, and we shall hear it all the more surely in exact proportion to the measure in which we have arrived at "truth in the inward parts" '.[5]

The lectures of T. George Rooke, the late President of Rawdon Baptist College, on the subject of Inspiration were published posthumously in 1893 'edited by two of his students'.

---

[1] W. Sanday, *Inspiration*, Bampton Lectures, 1893, third edition, 1908, p. 399.
[2] *Ibid.*, p. 402. [3] *Ibid.*, p. 423.
[4] F. W. Farrar, *The Bible, Its Meaning and Supremacy*, 1897, Chapters VII and XII. [5] *Ibid.*, p. 132.

They are the work of a scholar who made a serious attempt to understand his subject. Rooke is convinced that we should cease to talk of the Bible as an 'inspired Book' and reject such phrases as the 'Inspiration of the Holy Scriptures'.[1] He makes a study of the Biblical passages in which the idea connoted by the word inspiration comes up. Concerning II Tim. iii. 16, he says that it 'is impossible to show that the passage means anything more than this: "Every writing which breathes a divine spirit is also profitable for teaching, for conviction, for correction, for training, which (begins and ends) in righteousness" '.[2] Other passages, however, make it clear that the prophets spoke as the result of a Divine 'afflatus'. Rooke regards the idea of inspiration as but another name for genius to be inadequate, although, he adds, that it 'does not so much lower our thoughts of a Divine origin and authority in Scripture, as it raises our conceptions of a Divine origin and authority in things which we have been, perhaps, accustomed to regard as triumphs of unaided human wisdom and strength'.[3]

Gathering together the results of his investigation of the Scripture passages, Rooke then gives his definition of inspiration as 'the preparation of a man's heart or mind, or both, by the Holy Spirit, in view of some task for which God would use that man'.[4] He states that the 'theological term Inspiration' ought to mean 'the inward spiritual preparation of a man to know and feel what God chooses to communicate of His Divine thought and will'.[5]

Rooke, however, believed that the term 'inspiration' should be banished from theological textbooks[6] since the terms inspiration and revelation are to be regarded as correlatives, and the latter term should be retained as less question-begging. Because inspiration means the special preparation of a heart and mind by the Holy Spirit then many kinds of inspiration can be supposed. Rooke classified the theories of inspiration. He allows that the 'mechanical' view to which he refers first, 'does explain

---

[1] T. George Rooke, *Inspiration and Other Lectures*, 1893, p. 131.
[2] *Ibid.*, p. 119.　　　　[3] *Ibid.*, p. 125.
[4] *Ibid.*, p. 131.　　　　[5] *Ibid.*
[6] *Ibid.*, p. 133. Cf. 'But the best of all courses for the student will be to settle with himself once and for all never to use the word, 'Inspiration' unless he means "the inward (or suggestive) preparation of the human heart or mind by the Holy Spirit" ' (p. 134).

better than any other the origin and character of certain parts of Scripture'.[1] But there are objections to it which reveal it as 'positively harmful'. The 'dynamical, or assistance or direction theory' is also found wanting; so, too, is the 'illumination or mystical' view. Rooke then comes to his own 'Comprehensive theory' or as he prefers to call it, the 'Theory of Sufficient Knowledge or Gracious Purpose'. Although no book has yet been written to expound the theory, it is held, he states, by Farrar and is substantially the idea propounded by Martensen and Dorner. The ideas can be properly referred to as 'plenary' because it is 'full' in the sense that God's revelation is progressive, and inspiration and revelation are to be identified. Because inspiration is the preparation of heart and mind of man by the Holy Spirit to receive His revelation then the term is applicable to every part. He grants that the view is not 'absolutely satisfactory', but it is 'more helpful' than other views and it solves problems for which they have no answer; for example, the moral difficulties in the Bible and the like difficulties. Rooke tests out each theory of inspiration with reference to the various types of literature in the Bible itself and finds the idea of 'Sufficient Knowledge' or 'Gracious Purpose' as answering best the difficulties involved. He raises certain problems which the concept of inspiration brings to the fore, such as the character of the inspired men and of their records.

Rooke makes a special point of the analogy between 'the Living and the Written Word'. He regards the letter of Scripture as corresponding to 'the fleshly and material aspect of our Lord's humanity' and its 'matter' as corresponding to 'the human soul and spirit of our Lord'. The parallel is truly a strange one, but Rooke carries it through in thorough fashion. The flesh of Christ cannot be forever pervaded by His Deity. It was an indispensable vehicle of His real humanity to which Divinity has been inseparably conjoined. Rooke draws the conclusion that 'the Divine character of Scripture dwells inseparably, not in its letter and outward form as above described, but in the matter and spirit; we can think away the letter and distinguish it from the spirit, and perceive how incomparatively unimportant the mere vehicle of Divine revelation is'.[2] Yet the Bible is to be

[1] T. George Rooke, *Inspiration and Other Lectures*, 1893, p. 149.
[2] *Ibid.*, pp. 178–9.

cherished as the disciples cherish their Master's material form and 'this attitude of ours towards the book is not Bibliolatry' nor is it inconsistent with whatever defects there may be in it. Rooke maintains, indeed, the possible existence of 'physical blemishes' in our Lord's earthly life. His members could well have been defective, as some of the Christian Fathers seem to have thought, without detracting from the reality and power of His divinity. The presence of deformities in Christ, if they were proved to exist, would not cancel out belief in His divinity. 'Why then', he asks, 'should anyone allege in regard to the Bible that it cannot be Divine in its matter unless it is also faultless in its literary form according to the ever-shifting standards of human taste, human logic, or human conceptions of perfection in science, in history, in philosophy, and even in morality?'[1]

As the nineteenth century drew to its close, all that had been said concerning the Bible's inspiration was summed up in an article by J. E. M'Quot. The rise of textual criticism, M'Quot contended, had made it impossible to maintain the infallibility of any existing document and so the discovery of discrepancies and inaccuracies in minor matters of fact, as well as characteristic varieties of style, necessitated a modification of the old mechanical theory of inspiration.[2] If inspiration can be regarded, he argues, as consistent with varieties of form and style among the sacred writers, then it is but an easy step to admit still freer use by the Divine Spirit of the literary methods of the times. M'Quot contended then for the mythological and legendary nature of certain parts of the Old Testament, particularly the early chapters of Genesis. The superior quality of the Old Testament, however, 'the divine purity and loftiness' of its prophecy and the 'infinite deeper and more spiritual' nature of its poetry, in contrast with heathen oracles and other kinds of literature, is what is meant by Inspiration. M'Quot notes that although the new understanding of it means that 'the lines of external evidence are weakened', yet we still can 'cling the more closely to the self-evidencing realities of the spiritual life'.[3] In this way religion will, as a result, become more experimental

[1] T. George Rooke, *Inspiration and Other Lectures,* 1893, p. 179.
[2] J. E. M'Quot, 'Divine Revelation in the Light of the Old Testament Criticism', *Expository Times,* Vol. XII, 1900–1, pp. 488–9.   [3] *Ibid.,* p. 494.

and inductive; more an affair of the heart, and thus the Bible will remain 'our one supreme and unerring authority'.

In spite of all that had been said, by the turn of the century the whole idea of inspiration had become suspect, due in part to the unsatisfactory account given of it by the new apologists. The optimistic mood, which prevailed as the twentieth century opened, preferred to see inspiration, if the word must still be used, as a specific instance of the spirit which was making humanity great. Besides, the literature of the New Testament which was being brought under criticism and discussion was centred upon the various sources, either known or unknown, which its several writers employed. The New Testament was considered to be as much the result of a patchwork process as the Old had ever been. It was all very natural and very human, and, as a consequence, the idea of inspiration seemed to be eliminated, or, at least, it became something very remote and vague. Thus, when in 1910 James Orr wrote his commanding volume, *Revelation and Inspiration*, the comment was made in the *Expository Times* to the effect that it was 'a courageous thing—for all the popular writing on revelation and inspiration at the present seem to be in the way of denying the existence of both'.[1] During the optimistic years before the First World War there was little thought for the idea of inspiration, while throughout the pessimistic years of that upheaval there was little time for a discussion of such a subject. The few contributions there were seemed bent upon stating inspiration in as 'natural' a way as possible.

In 1909 the Cambridge University Press published a book by T. H. Sprott in which an effort was made to give meaning to the idea of inspiration in the light of the modern criticism and its results.[2] Sprott includes a 'Table of dates and authorship' taken from J. E. McFadyen's *Old Testament Criticism and the Christian Church* in which these aspects of the critical reconstruction are set forth. In the Table will be noted such conclusions, for example, as these: 'Traditions, war-ballads, and other songs, 1200–1000 BC'; 'Deuteronomy, 621 BC'; 'Deutero-Isaiah, 540 BC'; 'Priestly Code (Leviticus, etc.) 500–450 BC'; 'Pentateuch in practically its present form, before 400 BC'; 'Daniel, 167 BC'.

---

[1] *Expository Times*, Vol. XXI, 1909–10, p. 373.
[2] T. H. Sprott, *Modern Study of the Old Testament and Inspiration*, 1909, Chapters I and II.

Sprott having expressed the conviction that he has given a 'substantially accurate view of the modern critical position' then asks, 'Can the writers of that literature have been the subject of a Divine inspiration?'[1] He regards the notion of the Bible being 'verbally inspired' as totally unacceptable. The Scripture itself, he contends, does not make such a claim, 'Neither does the authoritative teaching of the Catholic Church involve this theory, or furnish any definition'.[1] Having quoted some remarks of F. D. Maurice concerning the prayers, hymns and confessions of the Psalms, Sprott remarks that 'The phenomena, then, of the Biblical literature, as disclosed to careful study, refute the *a priori* notion of Divine dictation'.[2] Sprott then goes on to elaborate his theory of inspiration as the energizing of the faculties of the contributors to the Scripture. Prophecy is to be regarded as 'inspired preaching'. The conclusion of the matter is this: 'By Inspiration I understand the quickening and heightening of man's apprehensive powers by the Spirit of God, whereby he is enabled to apprehend the Divine revelation and become an interpreter of it to his fellows. Inspiration is not the direct communication of knowledge to the human mind: it is power of insight, so that he perceives the Divine meaning in Nature or Conscience or History, which though always there and always appealing, had been before unperceived'.[3]

In his volume, *The Inspiration and Authority of Holy Scripture*, J. M. Gibson, as P. T. Forsyth states in the Introduction to the work, sought to mediate 'between the world of modern knowledge on the one hand and the world of traditional religion on the other'.[4] Gibson declares for the general view of inspiration which we have seen stated by one and another in the preceding pages. He seeks, however, to exercise caution and to avoid extremes. But he confesses that he received much help from 'the work of the more spiritual critics' and gained, as a result, 'a conviction of the inspiration and authority of the sacred Scriptures far stronger and more satisfying than I had in the old days'.[5]

Following the statement in the *Expository Times* noted above

---

[1] T. H. Sprott, *Modern Study of the Old Testament and Inspiration*, 1909, p. 36.
[2] *Ibid.*, p. 42.   [3] *Ibid.*, pp. 55–6.
[4] J. Munro Gibson, *The Inspiration and Authority of Holy Scripture*, 1908, p. x.
[5] *Ibid.*, pp. 8–9.

238 THEORIES OF REVELATION

in reference to Orr's book, it is instructive to examine the teaching of inspiration which appeared now and again throughout the following years.

In his *Inspiration and Prophecy* (1910), G. C. Joyce, a contributor to the *Encyclopaedia of Religion and Ethics*, applied psychology for the first time in an effort to explain the phenomenon of prophetic inspiration. Joyce conceives of inspiration as the communication of new truths. 'Recognizing and accepting the reality and authority of the revelation enshrined in the Bible', he declares, 'I am convinced that the fullest and freest inquiry into the various modes of Inspiration, so far from weakening faith, cannot but serve to increase our reverence for the work of the Holy Spirit among men.' Joyce regards inspiration as an abnormal, indeed, as a supernormal, activity of the mind, consequently it cannot be accounted for by the laws of text-book psychology. It is to 'Psychical Research' we must turn since it has shown the 'existence in man of faculties extending beyond the limitation of normal consciousness'. Prophetic inspiration is then an abnormal psychical occurrence. This does not mean that its reality is in any way lessened because its method is so to be understood. As telepathy is the work of one man on another, so prophecy is the work of God. The modes of inspiration change according to man's growing experience but what is given in any mode tends to take the position of a dictum after the analogy of all human custom and experience. The phrase, 'Thus saith the Lord', is frequent in Amos, for example. It was begun for the prophet in some 'substratum of mystical hearing' but in the process of time, the phrase acquired 'in some measure a conventional use'. Succeeding prophets did not have the same experience of 'mystical hearing' as it would be too much to suppose that every time any one of the prophets took the words upon his lips he did so in virtue of some physical experience in the way of audition.

In *The Higher Criticism* of which Driver and Kirkpatrick were, the joint authors, there is reference to the subject of inspiration. Kirkpatrick insists upon his right to call the Old Testament inspired, but he will 'not venture to define' its 'nature and limits'.[1] Driver scorns the idea of verbal inspiration and contends that the process of inspiration did not assure freedom

[1] Driver and Kirkpatrick, *The Higher Criticism*, 1911, p. 12.

from 'imperfection, error, and mistake in matters of fact'. He, however, describes inspiration as 'a Divine *afflatus* which, without superseding or repressing the human faculties, but rather using them as its instruments, and so conferring upon Scripture its remarkable manifoldness and variety, enabling holy men of old to apprehend, and declare in different degrees, and in accordance with the needs and circumstances of particular ages or occasions, the mind and purpose of God'.[1] The prophets show their inspiration, it is declared, 'in the spirit with which they breath into the narrative and in their interpretation of history; they show how a providential purpose overrules it; and bring out the spiritual and moral lessons implicit in it'.[2] He speaks of the 'Divinely quickened intuition' of the 'thinkers and seers of Israel' which enabled them gradually to elevate and purify their conception of God and to discern Him more clearly as history moved on and their own spiritual perceptions were enlarged.

G. P. Mains in his *Divine Inspiration* (1915), sees the Bible as leading up to God in contrast with the old view which regarded the Bible as brought down from God. The Bible 'finds' us and in doing so reveals its inspiration. The reality of its inspiration lies in its spiritual appeal.

A title now familiar comes once again from the pen of G. D. Barry. In his work, *The Inspiration and Authority of Holy Scripture* (1918), he points out that the central word in which belief in the paramount authority of the Bible is expressed occurs once only in the New Testament. In the passage in II Tim. iii. he maintains that the Apostle is simply giving a definition which 'Inspired Scripture' may be rightly expected to fulfil. It is not stated which books, in his judgement, are to be designated 'inspired Scripture' and which are not. But he has another declaration in which he tells us the originating source, which gave birth to the books of Scripture. 'Men spake from God, being moved by the Holy Ghost.' Here is the key to the deeper meaning of inspiration. Barry is, however, careful to insist that when influenced and taught by the Spirit their human powers were not suspended. Each exercised his own freedom under authority, expressing himself in his own characteristic way. The inspired writer absorbs into himself what has been communicated to him from God and then gives it out in his own

[1] Driver and Kirkpatrick, *The Higher Criticism*, 1911, pp. 53–4. [2] *Ibid.*, p. 56.

language. 'The supernatural fertilises and does not annihilate the natural'—the individuality of the author, saturated, we might say, by the revelation, is still there in fullest expression.

In the year 1921, a comment appeared in the *Expository Times* declaring that, 'Now the doctrine of the inspiration of the Bible has been so severely handled of late that we can scarcely be sure if there is a doctrine left, and for the most part we have lost interest in it'.[1]

Within a few years, however, as if by way of protest against this comment, statements on the subject began to appear anew. True enough, for some time there were no formal treatises on the subject, but rather chapter treatment of it in the wider context of the significance and authority of the Bible itself. But the stress seems to be shifted from the idea of the Bible as a record of the religious experience of inspired men to an emphasis upon the Bible as a medium through which God speaks. This is not to say that the idea of the Bible as evincing 'degrees of inspiration' according to its power to awaken in us a genuine religious experience of God was discarded. This is by no means the case. The pragmatic test of inspiration still remained and the apologists were still concerned to show the validity of the religious experience, which the inspirational message of the Bible evoked.

To be aware of the Bible as that through which God speaks is to be aware of its inspiration, such was the view gradually emerging. This idea did not come out clearly for some time but it is more than hinted at in some remarks on the subject by E. A. Knox in his last charge as Bishop of Manchester, written, as he says, for those who seek to honour God with their minds as well as heart and soul.[2] A chapter on Inspiration in their volume *The Old Testament and Today*, by J. A. Chapman and L. D. Weatherhead, indicates the same movement of ideas. While Chapman himself in one of *The Fellowship of the Kingdom* pamphlets continues to stress the idea of the inspiration of the Bible as the gripping message which it speaks.[3]

Thistleton Mark, whose book is dedicated to Charles Gore and carries a brief forward by Hewlett Johnson, Dean of

---

[1] *Expository Times*, Vol. XXXIII, 1921-2, p. 5.
[2] E. A. Knox, *On What Authority?* 1922, chapter on Inspiration.
[3] Cf. J. A. Chapman, *The Bible and Inspiration*, 1929.

Manchester, seems to look back rather than forward in his scattered remarks on the subject. 'It is a gain, not a loss,' he says, 'to give up the comparatively recent doctrine of the word-for-word infallibility of the Scriptures, in order to win back our hold upon the abiding reality of their Inspiration.'[1] It is men of 'spiritual insight', he then declares, who have it in them to read more deeply the meaning and tendency of events. He grants that inspiration, though 'real' is 'not easy to define'. An 'inspired man', however, 'sees more history, and writes profounder history, than an inspired man'.[2] Paul is, at the same time, both 'human and inspired'.[3]

In his *Approach to the Old Testament*, J. E. McFadyen in a spirit akin to his earlier *Introduction to the Old Testament*, and *The Use of the Old Testament in the Light of Modern Knowledge*, begins with an attack upon 'verbal inspiration' which is equated with a mechanical process and regarded as excluding all human activity on the part of the writers. McFadyen's attack amounts to a play with Hebrew letters. Having indicated the possibility of variant translations occasioned by unpointed Hebrew and noting the different line taken in some passages by the Greek Septuagint translators, he asks, 'Which of the Hebrew texts is inspired, ours or theirs?'[4] Following this, he asks the same question concerning the differing accounts of parallel events in the gospels. After referring to the 'moral difficulties' in the Old Testament, he says, 'vastly too much has been made of them',[5] although he has himself been making quite an issue of them. The main purpose of his book is to meet the 'Conservative defence' of the Bible's inspiration and infallibility. He attacks four books, Martin Kegel's *Away from Wellhausen*, Thomas Jollie Smith's *Studies in Criticism and Revelation*, H. D. Woolley's *The Modernist Bible and How it was Compiled*, and W. H. Fitchett's *Where the Higher Criticism Fails*. These last three are selected, he states in a footnote, 'not because of their importance, but because of their representative quality: they are thoroughly typical of the conservative position'.[6] This section of the book is entertaining enough and doubtlessly McFadyen makes his

---

[1] Thistleton Mark, *The Appeal of the Bible Today*, 1925, p. 7.
[2] *Ibid.*, pp. 59–60. [3] *Ibid.*, p. 124.
[4] J. E. McFadyen, *The Approach to the Old Testament*, 1926, p. 25.
[5] *Ibid.*, p. 51. [6] *Ibid.*, p. 104 (footnote).

points with effect, except that few would have thought of these names as the first ones in the conservative camp.

Referring to Deut. viii. with its solemn warnings he says, 'Whatever be its date, it "finds" us, and for the purposes of religion as distinct from historical and literary criticism, that is all that matters'.[1] What he has to say on this passage is, we suspect, what he could say about the whole. It is what 'finds me' that reveals its inspiration by being inspirational.

T. H. Binley, in his volume on *Inspiration*, sees the phenomenon of the Bible as a particular instance of inspiration in general. He traces the idea of its infallibility to the Reformers' attack upon the infallibility of the Church and their substitution instead of the infallibility of a book. Inspiration is defined as 'that quality which stirs the divinest thing in us, which touches those chords in our inmost self which thrills to the Divine Breath'. A much 'broader' view of inspiration was taken by Snell of the Church Missionary Society in his slender volume *Inspiration*. This small word was intended especially for Indian pastors and its appearance caused concern amongst conservative Churchmen. Snell was ready to admit a fairly generous number of 'errors' in the record while the 'idealistic' view of history is allowed. To 'conceive of Scriptural prophecy as anticipated history is an inadequate conception', he says. So bluntly stated were Snell's 'liberal views' that it was hard to recognize any significant doctrine of inspiration at all in what he had to say.

It was the purpose of W. M. Grant in his *The Bible of Jesus Christ* (1927), to prove that Jesus did not teach any mechanical theory of inspiration. He showed a certain freedom of attitude in regard to the Old Testament so that by attributing Psalm cx to David He is not 'throwing His shield over the Davidic authorship of the Psalm'. Grant insists that the 'all or nothing' view of inspiration must be repudiated, and he contends that our Lord adopted an attitude towards the Old Testament of 'authority, superiority, and reserve'.

R. H. Malden's Cathedral Lectures for 1935 were published under the title *The Inspiration of the Bible*. Malden thinks that agnostics and fundamentalists are hindered from a careful study of the sacred volume because they assume that its value, inspiration and truth are bound up with the idea of a 'literal

[1] J. E. McFadyen, *The Approach to the Old Testament*, 1926, p. 98.

verbal accuracy'. It is Malden's set purpose to disabuse them of such a false notion. He investigates the Biblical use of the word 'inspiration' and concludes that the inspiration which possessed the men of the Scripture is authenticated within present religious experience.

A 'little book of quite distinctive character and excellence';[1] such was the enthusiastic description given to Alan Richardson's *A Preface to Bible-Study*. Richardson sees the question, What is inspiration? forced upon the Church by the rise of biblical criticism. The reply given at first was that inspiration of the Bible does not differ in *kind* but merely in *degree* from that possessed by other religious literature. It is, however, in contrast with this other literature that the merit of the Bible shines forth clear and uneclipsed. 'The Bible thus comes to be looked upon as the record of progressive deepening of man's religious experience and of the evolution of man's knowledge of God.'[2] To assert that the Bible is inspired was to assert that it was the record of the religious experience of inspired men. The inspiration of the Bible was, then, a matter of degree to be measured by the level of truth which it contained and by its power to awaken in man a genuine religious experience of God.

This theory of inspiration, widely accepted as it was by scholars, Richardson declares, did not satisfy the ordinary Christian believer: 'It was instinctively felt to be too thin'.[3] It was, indeed, based upon presuppositions no longer unquestionable. To begin with, it placed too strong an emphasis upon religious experience, and however valid such may be it is no sufficient basis for vital faith: 'we want God, not the experience of God: we want truth, not a true theory which explains the universe or life, but truth to live by, to serve and to obey'.[4] The deep question which this earlier view did not answer was, Is there a word from God? Furthermore, the idea of evolution which undergirded the whole thesis has today lost its magic and its appeal. The Bible, therefore, is no longer valid for us if it be the mere purveyor to us of richer religious experiences than in any other book. 'The question which our generation asks is not

---

[1] *Expository Times*, Vol. LIV, 1942-3, p. 309.
[2] Alan Richardson, *A Preface to Bible-Study*, 1943, second impression, 1944, p. 34.
[3] *Expository Times*, Vol. LIV, 1942-3, p. 309.
[4] Alan Richardson, *A Preface to Bible-Study*, p. 36.

where the highest human wisdom about God can be found, but whether there is any place in which God Himself speaks to us.'[1] It is not even what religious geniuses have to say about God which is of interest to us, but what God has to say to us. And we have become aware that the Bible is a book through which God speaks. This means that inspiration is not a proposition to which we give assent, but it is the recognition that we have in the Bible a message 'sent into the world with my name and address on it'.[2] 'Unless' therefore 'I find in the Bible God's word for me, I may be convinced that the Bible is supreme among books as a work of religion or morality or anything else, but I shall not know that it is inspired in the way in which the Christian Church has always understood the doctrine of inspiration and the authority of Holy Scripture.'[3] It is in the context of the Christian doctrine of salvation that both the inspiration and the authority find their meaning. God reveals His purpose to save men through Christ, that is the message of which the Bible is 'our only first-hand record'. Here we have the source-book of saving knowledge, the only witness to what God has done for us men and our salvation. 'Its uniqueness lies not in any special miraculous method of dictation by which it was received, nor yet in any exalted state of religious experience to which its writers attained, but in its testimony to the great things that God had done.'[4] Richardson's position is, we believe, substantially the same as that elaborated in N. H. Snaith in his Peake Memorial Lecture for 1956. Snaith's title is the *Inspiration and Authority of the Bible*, and in it he gives it as his view that both are revealed by the fidelity of the Bible to the essential idea of God as Saviour: 'The work of God the Saviour runs through the whole', he declares, and 'the Bible is all concerned with what God has done'.

It was the purpose of H. Wheeler Robinson in several of his studies to investigate the psychology of inspiration. This is, indeed, the particular end he had in view in his *Inspiration and Revelation in the Old Testament*. The prophet is to be seen as the main vehicle of the divine revelation. Revelation has 'a transcendent source', but it is only as it comes into contact with

---

[1] Alan Richardson, *A Preface to Bible-Study*, p. 37.
[2] *Ibid.*, p. 38.   [3] *Ibid.*, p. 40.
[4] *Ibid.*, p. 41. Cf. his *Christian Apologetics*, 1947, Chapter IX.

experience that it becomes possible of scientific study. 'The primary question to be answered', he says, 'is, how did the prophet himself become convinced that Yahweh was speaking to him and through him?'[1] Robinson contends that it was a fundamental belief of the Hebrews that human personality was open to invasion by some external energy or spirit. This 'invasive energy', they supposed, could take possession of the organs of the body and use any one of them 'in quasi-independence of its owner'.[2] Some of the essentials of revelation are, he asserts, 'forcibly expressed through the Hebrew psychology of inspiration in spite of what seems to us its crudity and its obvious ignorance of the true facts of physiology'.[3] Revelation begins with God and accordingly the prophet had no difficulty in believing himself to be instrumental of the divine activity. Although the ancients believed in a 'quasi-magical power' the modern psychological parallel 'is seen in artistic creation and/or scientific discovery'.[4] An important difference between aesthetic and intellectual inspiration and that experienced by the prophets is, however, to be admitted. The latter recognized the presence of a divine Person and it is this which gives to prophecy 'a peculiar and intense note of authority'.[5]

Robinson refers to what he calls 'the intuitional character of prophecy'. The term although suspect to every student of psychology and ethics and philosophy, in no way weakens but really proves the validity of the phenomenon of prophecy. It serves 'to bring out the ultimate *immediacy* of personal judgement which we have found to belong to prophecy, from its first reception by the prophets down to our own response to the record of it. Intuition is not taken here to beg the question of validity, but simply to mark that subjective feature of prophecy, and indeed of all religion, which we have again and again found to be present'.[6] The 'value-judgement' of the prophet is the ultimate psychological reality and in making it 'the prophet feels himself divinely directed to exercise his own judgement on all the medley of thought and feeling which is his'.[7] In this 'value-judgement' the total personality is involved.

[1] H. Wheeler Robinson, *Inspiration and Revelation in the Old Testament*, 1946, p. 178.

[2] *Ibid.*, pp. 181–2.   [3] *Ibid.*, p. 191.   [4] *Ibid.*, p. 192.
[5] *Ibid.*, p. 194.   [6] *Ibid.*   [7] *Ibid.*, pp. 194–5.

In his earlier contribution to *Record and Revelation*, a more precise account even is given of the divine communication as caught up in the prophet's consciousness. The divine consciousness, he there argues, is always associated with the character and historical conditions of the recipient. There is no escape from this human condition and mediation. Whatever God reveals, he declares, is revealed as part of the prophet's own consciousness and outlook. However the prophet might draw an absolute line between the divine oracle and his own reaction to it, we most certainly cannot. The 'event' which he was led to interpret as divinely controlled might mean something else to other eyes, 'there was nothing inevitable in its interpretation'. But, he contends, if God takes up a man's thought, words and deeds into the orbit of revelation, the result is not a partnership capable of analysis, but a blended unity.[1]

Much use is made by Robinson of his concept of 'intuitional judgement'. By means of it the Jewish and the Christian canon were formed. Some words are quoted from Origen to show that 'the appeal to an intuitional value-judgement is no device of yesterday invented by Coleridge when he said, "Whatever *finds* me bears witness for itself that it proceeded from a Holy Spirit" '.[2] Great stress is laid on the authority of religious experience. He argues elsewhere against the notion of a closed canon on the score that such a formal list of books is based upon the attribution to the prophet of an abnormal psychology which is made the test of inspiration. Deeper criteria must be found in which account must be taken of 'the life of the people in and through whose experience God is revealed'.[3] The Protestant cannot be satisfied with the definiteness of the Roman Church, 'he must base his own recognition of that unique quality on the intrinsic work and ministry of the books themselves, as witnessed by his own experience to their message under the guidance of the Holy Spirit'.[4] It is emphasized that this idea does

[1] H. Wheeler Robinson, *Record and Revelation*, 1938, pp. 315–6.

[2] H. Wheeler Robinson, *Inspiration and Revelation in the Old Testament*, p. 196.

[3] H. Wheeler Robinson, 'Canonicity and Inspiration', *Expository Times*, Vol. XLVII, 1935–6, p. 119. Cf. 'The Theology of the Old Testament' in *Record and Revelation*; also 'The Bible as the Word of God' in *The Bible and its Ancient and English Versions*, 1940.

[4] Cf. 'Canonicity and Inspiration', *ibid*. In our Ideas of Revelation we have noted how Brunner, like the Quaker Barclay, sees no conclusive reason to accept the idea of a 'filled-canon'. The scripture is given a 'second place' and the emphasis is on the

not make revelation merely subjective nor yet does it destroy the idea of canonicity.

H. Cunliffe-Jones joins issue here, it may be observed, with Wheeler Robinson. He contends that there is something wrong with the interpretation which allows such uncertainty concerning the canon. The authority of the Biblical writings depends upon something more than their being the finest expression of religious experience interpenetrated with the divine. Cunliffe-Jones contends for a closed canon and for the Bible as still the standard and rule of our faith and not merely the manifestation of it.[1] He refers to the question whether inspiration is something to be taken for granted *before* we study the Bible in detail and therefore as governing that study or whether it is something whose nature is strictly dependent upon an inductive study of what the contents of the Bible actually are. He maintains that a belief in inspiration is something which the Christian theologian brings with him and in this connection the summary of the position at the close of James Orr's *Revelation and Inspiration* is pronounced as still satisfactory.[2]

A. G. Hebert refuses 'to identify Inspiration with the personal insight of each writer'.[3] He prefers to attribute it 'to the Canon as a whole' and in so doing acknowledges that he is 'laying a great weight on the Canon, and asserting a providential guidance in the formation' of it.[4] Such a conclusion follows, he argues, when right emphasis is put upon the idea of God's activity in history through which men become aware of His saving purpose. 'The apprehension by men of God's revelation has been partial and imperfect; yet through His imperfect human instruments His word has been spoken. The Scripture, too, is inspired, and is imperfect; inspired because it is divine, and imperfect because it is also human.'[5] Hebert indeed insists upon the correctness of the distinction made by 'Conservative' writers between revelation and inspiration, but he thinks that the 'literal theory of inspiration' in which an identity is made

---

subjective. Cf. H. D. McDonald, *Ideas of Revelation*, 1959, p. 72. R. Barclay, *Apology*, tenth edition, 1841, p. 86. E. Brunner, *Revelation and Reason* (E.T. 1946), p. 132.
[1] H. Cunliffe-Jones, *The Authority of the Biblical Revelation*, 1946, second impression, 1948, p. 78.　　　　[2] *Ibid.*, p. 115.
[3] A. G. Hebert, *The Authority of the Old Testament*, 1947, p. 106.
[4] *Ibid.*　　　　[5] *Ibid.*, p. 104.

between inerrancy and inspiration ends with the unacceptable doctrine of an infallible book. On the other hand, to treat inspiration psychologically as denoting the religious experience of inspired individuals is to admit 'degrees of inspiration', and this, for Hebert is inadmissible in view of the facts. 'Yet it is obvious that there are degrees of *something*, not indeed of Inspiration, if Inspiration is co-extensive with Canonicity; but degrees of revelation, or of prophecy.'[1]

Hebert, of course, repudiates the notion of 'mechanical' inspiration as deriving, he states in a later volume, from 'pagan sources'.[2] He readily admits however, that such a 'dictation-theory' is 'repudiated by all the conservative evangelical leaders, because it leaves no room for the individuality of the human writers'.[3] It is not very clear from Hebert's two books in what precise way inspiration is to be regarded. It refers to the Canon as a whole, that we learn. But does it belong to the guidance of God by which the Church collected the separate books which make up the Bible into a whole, or to the message which is unfolded through the whole of God's saving acts and in the totality of which He speaks?[4] The word 'Church' which figures in the title of the second of his books seems to indicate that Hebert would stress the Church's part in the formation of the Canon.

The 'old view' of inspiration in which the writers were regarded as more or less unconscious instruments in the hands of God is rejected by J. W. C. Wand. According to him the inspiration of the Bible is revealed in a particular and general way: in particular passages which 'arrest the attention and stick in the memory',[5] and in the whole anthology which creates the effect of being a communication from another world—'a breath from heaven'. Wand asks the question, Where does inspiration lie, in the words or the total thought? 'It would probably be true to say', he replies, 'that the traditional answer would affirm the first, while our contemporary answer would be more likely to affirm the second.'[6] Wand finds difficulties in each view. The

[1] A. G. Hebert, *The Authority of the Old Testament*, 1947, p. 101; cf. esp. pp. 71–2.
[2] A. G. Hebert, *Fundamentalism and the Church of God*, 1957, p. 57.
[3] *Ibid.*, p. 56.
[4] Cf. A. G. Hebert, *The Authority of the Old Testament*, pp. 70 ff.
[5] J. W. C. Wand, *The Authority of the Scriptures*, 1949, p. 54.
[6] *Ibid.*, p. 55; cf. p. 60.

traditional doctrine, he thinks, tends to make every word an organ of divine revelation and to conceive of inspiration as equally distributed in every word. The inspiration of the Bible, he then declares, is the substance of which the inspiration of Virgil and Shakespeare and Goethe is the shadow. It is the merit of the 'modern view' to have shifted the 'onus of inspiration' from the book to the writer. 'We do not call a writer inspired because he has written an inspired book, but we call a book inspired because it was written by an inspired writer.'[1] Factual accuracy is no guarantee of inspiration. Acknowledging that his view of inspiration may be disappointing to some, he asserts, 'The sacred writers enjoyed no gift of infallibility'.[2]

Is the Bible Inspired? is the title-question which J. Burnaby gives to his volume in which he considers the subject. At the beginning the familiar comment is made to the effect that the assured results of criticism have rendered the traditional doctrine of inspiration impossible, and this in spite of the acknowledgement that the 'old view' was grounded in the Church's faith from the first. Burnaby discusses the idea of inspiration in pagan literature and then goes on to seek the 'marks of prophetic inspiration'.[3] The subject of the Spirit's action in the Bible is then assessed and it is contended that the 'influence of the Holy Spirit upon the soul of man is therefore rightly to be understood by analogy with the influence of person on person'.[4] Inspiration presupposes election so that 'inspired men of God are thus necessarily an élite', although they are not to be regarded as a 'moral autocracy'.[5] Their authority is not absolute since they seek to persuade not to impose. From this 'general theory' of inspiration Burnaby comes to the question of his title.

Essentially inspiration consists in the power to *see* the things, which are of God. But the general theory of inspiration to which

[1] J. W. C. Wand, *The Authority of the Scriptures*, 1949, p. 60.   [2] *Ibid.*; cf. p. 102.
[3] John Burnaby, *Is the Bible Inspired?* 1949, The Colet Library of Modern Christian Thought and Teaching (gen. ed. W. R. Matthews), pp. 53 ff.
[4] *Ibid.*, p. 80.
[5] *Ibid.*, p. 88. Cf. 'This phenomenon (inspiration) is not confined to Biblical characters, nor is the controlling power always good; it may quite well be evil. Hence it is hardly possible to speak of the Bible as inspired in any literal sense of the word. . . . Its inspiration lies wholly in the extent to which the things it says compel the assent of our conscience and our minds'. S. H. Hooke, *What is the Bible?* 1948, p. 69.

the major part of his book is devoted, 'cannot provide us with any tenable doctrine of inspiration of the Bible, unless their inspiration be found predictable of the Bible as *a coherent whole, an organic unity*'.[1] The Bible is inspired, it then appears, because it demonstrates the principle of election carried to its highest pitch. The Bible is to be held as inspired 'since it begins with the stirring of men's hearts by the Holy Ghost'.[2] Its inspiration is revealed in its message of God's saving acts which runs right through it and of which it is the record. Inspiration does not lie in any part of either the Old or the New Testament, but in the whole.[3] Men are inspired because they saw and responded to certain events as God's acts. It has nothing to do with inerrancy and infallibility. The Bible is inspired in a unique way, because it contains the interpretation which 'inspired men' gave to certain events in which they had been enabled to, and in which they enable us, to see the story of God's salvation.

In 1951 the important volume entitled *Biblical Authority for Today*, appeared, edited by Alan Richardson and W. Schweitzer. The 'tentative character of the document' was indicated in the Introduction.[4] Writers representing the several Churches contributed, and, although the main purpose is to indicate the nature of biblical authority, there are to be found statements regarding the inspiration of the Bible. Georges Floroosky, for example, maintains that the Scriptures are 'inspired' and 'are the Word of God'. He is, however, unable to say what inspiration is. There 'is a mystery therein', he says. Holy men of God heard the word of the Lord, but how they could articulate it in words of their own dialect is beyond understanding? 'Yet, even in their human transmission it was the voice of God.' The mystery and the miracle of the Bible lies in the fact that here is the Word of God in human idiom. The Scripture transmits and preserves in human words the Word of God.[5] In the same volume, Vinjamuri E. Devadutt states, 'The Bible is an inspired record of revelation. When we say it is inspired we mean that the people who share

---

[1] John Burnaby, *Is the Bible Inspired?* 1949, The Colet Library of Modern Christian Thought and Teaching (gen. ed. W. R. Matthews), p. 94 (italics in original).   [2] *Ibid.*, p. 95.   [3] *Ibid.*, p. 109.
[4] *Biblical Authority for Today* (ed. A. Richardson and W. Schweitzer), 1951, A World Council of Churches Symposium on 'The Biblical Authority for the Churches' Social and Political Message', p. 8.
[5] *Op. cit.*, p. 172.

in its writing were under the guidance of the Spirit of God. Inspiration is not verbal communication, making of the writer merely a pen for the Divine Spirit. Inspiration is that which moves and guides. It is such an inspiration of the Divine Spirit which enables the writers of the Bible to see God's activity'.[1] Clarance Tucker Craig, in his essay, likewise repudiates verbal inspiration. It is not to be found in a communication of truths nor yet is it a mere supervision of the Holy Spirit for their right formation. The 'word in book-form' like the Word incarnate constitutes the union of the two elements, the divine and the human. The 'essence of the Bible is divine, and the form human', it is declared. Inspiration is chiefly related to the essence, yet it is a matter of degrees.[2] The subject is also touched upon by W. L. Knox, who contends that the gift of the Holy Spirit does not imply that the writers of Scripture 'wrote with explicit consciousness of anything but ordinary human motives, or that they were divinely delivered from the possibility of human error'.[3] He does, however, allow that the Bible possesses an inspiration different from that which is to be found in the greatest monuments of human literature.[4]

One of the most voluminous writers on the Bible, especially on the Old Testament, in recent years, is H. H. Rowley. He has made a massive contribution, in which, we believe, it would be true to say that there can be detected a growing appreciativeness of the permanent spiritual significance of the Scriptures as a whole. In several of his books he makes passing references to the subject of inspiration, and in a couple of them he has sought to deal with it in more detail.

It seems to us that his general position is somewhat akin to that of H. Wheeler Robinson to whom he readily acknowledges his debt. Thus, having made the comment to the effect that 'Revelation is fundamentally the divine-unfolding, while inspiration lies in the use of human personality for the declaration of the message', he refers his readers, in a footnote, to Robinson's *Inspiration and Revelation in the Old Testament*.[5] In the main, Rowley regards the Bible as a record of profound religious

---

[1] *Biblical Authority for Today* (ed. A. Richardson and W. Schweitzer), 1951, A World Council of Churches Symposium on 'The Biblical Authority for the Churches' Social and Political Message', p. 71.   [2] *Op. cit.*, p. 23.
[3] *Op. cit.*, p. 102.   [4] *Op. cit.*
[5] H. H. Rowley, *The Faith of Israel*, 1956, p. 21 and footnote references.

experiences. Like other writers in the same general context he is anxious to maintain the essential human element in the sacred records. 'Few today', he states, 'regard it (i.e. the Old Testament) as a purely superhuman book, whose words bear none of the marks of the spirit of its human authors, but perfectly and exactly reflect the *ipsissima verba* of the inspiring God.'[1] The point is reiterated in a later volume in which it is declared that 'The divine inspiration came through the organ of man's personality. Though they were men who were consecrated to God and sensitive to His Spirit, they were nevertheless imperfect men, with false presuppositions and with limited outlook'.[2]

Rowley allows, too, for degrees of inspiration. 'There have been some,' he writes, 'and alas! there are still some, who regard the whole Bible as on a flat level of inspiration and authority and who make no differentiation whatever in this respect between the Old and New Testaments.'[3] He argues convincingly elsewhere for what he calls the 'dynamic unity' of the Bible, but, he insists, nevertheless, that this admission does not permit the conclusion 'that the whole Bible is on a flat level in inspiration and authority'.[4]

These references come from volumes in which Rowley does not have it as his purpose to expound the idea of inspiration. In two other books, however, he does seek to give a fuller account of his view. We shall follow what he has to say in the earlier of these two since there is no important deviation from his main thesis to be observed in his later *The Authority of the Bible*.[5]

A characteristic note is struck when Rowley asks the question in a chapter entitled 'The Prophets of the Old Testament', 'From whence did the prophets get their inspiration?'[6] A little further on the answer is given, 'it was ever from their experience of God that they found their inspiration'.[7] In an earlier chapter Rowley writes specifically on 'The Inspiration of the Bible'. The 'older view', which maintained that the divine origin of the

---

[1] *The Recovery of the Old Testament*, 1945, p. 25.
[2] *The Unity of the Bible*, 1953, p. 15.
[3] *The Recovery of the Old Testament*, p. 13.   [4] *The Unity of the Bible*, p. 14.
[5] Cf. *The Authority of the Bible*, 1950, pp. 5 ff.
[6] *The Relevance of the Bible*, 1944, p. 73. Cf. H. H. Rowley, 'The Inspiration of the Old Testament', *Congregational Quarterly*, Vol. 18, April 1940, pp. 164–77.
[7] *Op. cit.*, p. 74.

Bible guaranteed it against all error, is naturally set aside. The difficulties in it are regarded as needing 'little demonstration'. Rowley, however, proceeds to indicate certain disagreements and discrepancies in the records. The writers of the Bible were, he declares, 'real men, responsible for their writings as we are for ours'.[1] This leads him to urge that, since revelation was mediated through human personalities, it must partake of the characteristics of these personalities. 'Were the writers of the Old Testament helpless instruments in the hand of God, completely controlled by Him, the revelation would be independent of their personality, but if they were imperfect and fallible, then their imperfections and infallibilities could not but affect the revelation.'[2]

Rowley, however, expresses dissatisfaction with the view that the inspiration of the Bible is due to the writers' 'own reflection and skill and penetrating insight' by which they saw the heart of God and recorded what they saw. Men of serious spirit and clear judgement they were undoubtedly, but the notion that it was even the insight of such men, which was the source of their inspiration and authority is pronounced 'inadequate'. The prophets, indeed, made no such claim that it was a result of their own wisdom and insight that they came with their 'Thus saith the Lord' message. What they saw of God's purposes was the result of God's grace. They were not themselves the originators, but the organs, of the divine word, human though they remained and enfolded in their imperfections as was the divine word. 'The errors and the imperfections we find in no sense challenge the foundation of our faith, for that rests, not on our view of inspiration, but on a living experience of the grace of God in Jesus Christ.'[3]

Rowley refers to 'the process of inspiration'. He reiterates that, 'It was not a case of the writer's hand being supernaturally controlled to write words that came to him wholly from without'.[4] He sees the Old Testament, not as giving exact records of history, inerrant in every detail, or as authoritative revelations of the future, or even as wholly trustworthy revelations of God. It is rather a record of the experiences and thoughts of men who

---

[1] *The Relevance of the Bible*, p. 25.
[2] *Op. cit.* Cf. *The Faith of Israel*, 1957, pp. 39 and 86.
[3] *Op. cit.*, p. 36.   [4] *Op. cit.*, p. 42.

reached out after God, and responded to God's reaching after them.[1]

The question comes, Is the New Testament to be regarded in the same light? Rowley thinks that it is. The idea of inspiration is fundamentally the same in the New Testament as in the Old. There is no verbal infallibility: indeed, there are here, too, inaccuracies, and reflections of the ideas and expectations of the fallible authors. The case of the New Testament is as that of the Old; each of its writers was, as Paul, 'charged with a divinely given message, but that for the form in which it was delivered he was himself responsible. He was the ambassador, not the postman'.[2] In the last, however, it is Christ who is the test of the truth and the measure of the inspiration of the Old Testament, as He is of the New. Inspiration does not elevate the letter to a place of final and unchallenged authority. The Church itself is 'the vehicle of inspiration', and consequently has, Rowley contends, an authority beside the Bible. Yet neither is an ultimate authority since both go back to Christ and derive both their inspiration and authority from Him; 'For God is Spirit, and through Spirit He speaks His final Word to us'.[3]

Two books stating similar conclusions appeared in successive years. Reference has been already made to J. K. S. Reid's *The Authority of Scripture* (1957). Reid approaches the subject from the historical point of view and seeks to state the Reformers' understanding of the matter. His conclusion is in general agreement with that of Raymond Abba's. Abba has remarks to make on the subject of inspiration, which bring him into the context of ideas with which we have been concerned. He speaks of the 'dynamic' nature of the Bible's inspiration, and contends that it 'has to do with its content rather than with its evolution'.[4] He firmly rejects the doctrine of verbal inspiration and quotes from a review of Warfield's *Inspiration and Authority of the Bible* by McIntyre the statement that the notion of plenary inspiration is 'a patent *petitio principii*'.[5] Abba is particularly anxious to insist that inspiration in no way and in no sense

---

[1] *The Relevance of the Bible*, p. 43.
[2] *Op. cit.*, p. 47.   [3] *Op. cit.*, p. 51.
[4] Raymond Abba, *The Nature and Authority of the Bible*, 1958, p. 108; cf. p. 103.
[5] *Ibid.*, p. 108. Cf. Review of Warfield, *The Reformed Theological Review*, Vol. IX, No. 2, p. 20.

curtailed the human bearers of revelation,[1] and he quotes several writers to support him.[2] Abba contends that the inspiration of the Bible is something 'felt'. 'It is through an experience of the spiritual power of the Bible' that the term inspiration 'first comes to have real meaning'.[3] Coleridge's words about the Bible finding the soul are quoted and herein is indicated the position occupied by this writer. This dictum of Coleridge's we have in fact seen stated again and again by writer after writer with whom we have been concerned in this section. It is here we have the setting for and find the key to these views of inspiration which have their focus within.[4]

The main purpose of these reconstructionist views of inspiration, it was acknowledged, was to seek a theory which would allow for the 'errors and discrepancies' which, it was urged, must be allowed in the sacred volume since its writers, whatever the degree of their dedication, were still imperfect men. At first the emphasis was put upon the view of inspiration as the penetrating insights of religious geniuses, whose thoughts about God have been preserved in the pages of the Bible. The religious genius, even in his own realm, any more than any other genius in his, is not infallible. And when he comes to make observations which fall outside his particular sphere he must be less so. In the recording of these insights there was no special act of God keeping the writer from added mistakes.

[1] The idea of man as a 'deficient instrument' in the process of inspiration was a Scholastic, not a Reformed doctrine. It was the position taken up by Aquinas. Cf. 'In the case of Prophetic Revelation, the prophet's mind is moved by the Holy Ghost in the same way as a deficient instrument is used by the principal agent.' H. Pope, A.P., of the Collegio Angelico, Rome; 'Article on the Scholastic View of Inspiration', *The Irish Theological Quarterly*, July 1911. Produced by the Professors in the Faculty of Theology, Maynooth, St Patrick's College.

[2] Raymond Abba, *The Nature and Authority of the Bible*, p. 108. Cf. T. H. Robinson, *Prophecy and the Prophets*, 1923, p. 20; H. H. Rowley, *The Relevance of the Bible*, 1944, p. 47; J. W. C. Wand, *The Authority of the Scriptures*, 1949, p. 16; James Orr, *The Faith of a Modern Christian*, 1909, p. 16; H. B. Swete, *The Holy Spirit in the New Testament*, 1909, p. 339.

[3] *Ibid.*, p. 103. Cf. J. Strachan, 'Inspiration', *Encyclopaedia of Religion and Ethics*, Vol. VII, p. 347.

[4] Cf. 'This subjective theory of inspiration (of which Schleiermacher is the father) soon found its way into this country, and although not indigenous, may now be said almost to be naturalized. We are indebted to Coleridge, more than any other, for the importation of it first, and for the currency afterwards among ourselves, of forms of expression and thought in connection with inspiration unfamiliar to British theology, and deriving from Germany.' James Bannerman, *Inspiration*, etc., 1865, p. 144. Cf. H. D. McDonald, *Ideas of Revelation*, 1959, Chapter VII.

The idea, it was noted, did not continue to satisfy. It had the result of putting the Bible apart and remote from the experiences of ordinary persons, who felt that they had no gift of religious genius and no special spiritual faculty as such. It was in this way that the claim made by many that they were giving back the Bible to everyman in a fresh and fascinating light, and in a context they could understand, was nullified.

A change of emphasis is therefore to be observed. Inspiration came to be less and less identified with the insights of religious geniuses and began to be identified more and more with the inner illumination of the Spirit of God. The Bible was then conceived to be the record of these revelations which this divine illumination assured to chosen men. Often reference was made to the Biblical teaching concerning the believers' illumination by the Holy Spirit as being an illustration of this concept of inspiration. Such an action by the Spirit, it was stressed, did not involve infallibility. In the case of those to whom we owe the Bible the process was the same, only, of course, much more intense; but even here there was no guarantee of infallibility.

It is certainly true that there is an illumination of every man by the Spirit of God. But there is also a vast and vital difference between the illuminated Christian and the inspired prophet or apostle. In the former case the Holy Spirit works to give a vivid apprehension of truth already revealed: in the latter case there is a communication of truth altogether new. It is not a question of mere difference of degree, but a difference of kind. There is a subjectiveness in the view of inspiration reviewed above which makes uncertain any sure objective standard of truth and duty. Wescott warns against failure to appreciate this objective necessity: 'if we regard inspiration only subjectively', he observes, 'we lose all sense of a fresh and living connection of the prophet with God. He remains indeed a man, but he is nothing more. He appears only to develop naturally a germ of truth which lies within him, and to draw no new supplies of grace and wisdom from without. There is no reunion of the divine and human in the soul on which a Church may rest its faith'.[1] No canons were given by which varying degrees of reliability of the record could be adjudged. In the end, the Illumination theory of inspiration seems to regard as inspired

[1] B. F. Wescott, *Introduction to the Study of the Gospels*, 1882, p. 32.

that which inspires. That which commends itself to the individual reason or conscience or moral sense is of the Holy Spirit. In this way the single individual becomes the judge of truth, and man the measure of things. Such a doctrine of inspiration has its origin in Schleiermacherian and Coleridgean subjectivism and is based on a pragmatist epistemology.

Others sought to illustrate the relation between the divine and the human in the Bible by reference to the two natures in Christ.[1] By separating the human from the divine they felt themselves able to regard the Biblical history and *Wissenschaft* as subject to the defects of human imperfections. Those who emphasize the humanity of Christ in such starkness as do Barth and Brunner can easily view the Bible, on its human side, as a very imperfect vessel in which the divine treasure is carried. The crib in which the divine Christ lay, was set there by human hands and was crude and rough and inadequate in itself. From Him who was within it has gained its glory and got its significance.

But the parallel is not rightly drawn. It was, indeed, the error of the mechanical dictation view to adopt an Apollinarian attitude with regard to the agents of divine revelation. Its advocates saw the human element, as it were, 'reduced' and the deficiency made up by the presence of the Spirit: only in this way, it was believed, could the Bible be secured from all error. This Alexandrian approach, in which exclusive emphasis was placed upon God's activity, secured the divineness of the Bible, but at the sacrifice of the obvious fact of its humanness. 'The human side of the record of Scripture, certainly, cannot be ignored. There is not, nor could be, in Divine inspiration any suppression of human genius, faculty, or individuality. Limitations in the instrument condition receptivity for the message. The treasure is in earthen vessels (II Cor. iv. 7). But the Divine moulds the human to its ends, and in the result God's strength is perfected in human weakness (II Cor. xii. 9).'[2]

---

[1] This is not really a modern illustration. Compare the remark made by James Bannerman in his *Inspiration*, etc., 1865. 'There is a remarkable parallel often noticed in connection with this controversy, between the case of the union of the divine and the human natures in the one person of Christ, and the case of inspiration' (p. 465). Cf. J. I. Packer, *'Fundamentalism' and the Word of God*, 1958, pp. 82 ff.

[2] James Orr, *The Faith of a Modern Christian*, 1910, p. 16.

The opposing view, with which we have been concerned, like Nestorius, set the human and the divine in juxtaposition, and introduced an unwarranted cleavage between the two. But having done so, its protagonists did not consistently apply their thesis. The divine is severed from the human so that the 'errors and mistakes' in the Bible might be allowed for, but, Does this hold in the case of Christ with whom the Scripture is brought into this analogy? The fact is, a very opposite conclusion from that desired would follow if the parallel between the two natures in Christ and the divine and the human in the Bible is to stand.

B. INSPIRATION—THE FOCUS WITHOUT

It will have been noted how consistently, and at times vehemently, the idea of a verbally inspired Bible was repudiated. The focus was within. Believing that verbal inspiration was one and the same thing with a mechanical process it was not difficult to show the considerable strain such a doctrine put upon faith. Under the pressure of a sustained attack the idea of a mechanical process of inspiration was made to look raffish. Since verbal inspiration was consistently equated with it, that too, fell into disfavour throughout the last half of the nineteenth century. To continue to assert the doctrine of verbal inspiration was due, it was maintained, to inability to meet squarely the new situation in which the Church found itself and the altered view of the Bible which honest criticism necessitated. Conservative writers, it was thought, continued to serve up the dish as a sort of spiritual réchauffé, but to men aware of the new situation, it was no longer digestible or palatable; it had lost its flavour and relish. The new day demanded a new diet.

The charge persists. 'Nowadays we call this traditional view the theory of verbal inspiration, or fundamentalism', says Alan Richardson. 'It is still met with amongst those who have not had the opportunity of sympathetically understanding the achievements of modern Biblical scholarship, and amongst those few better-educated Christians who confuse the doctrine of the Spirit in our hearts with the theory of verbal inspiration. From the second to the eighteenth century the theory was generally accepted'.[1]

[1] Alan Richardson, *A Preface to Bible-Study*, 1943, p. 25. In the 1950 edition of

It was asserted early in our period that all competent writers had become convinced that inspiration could no longer be referred to the words of Scripture. British scholars to a man, it was declared, were unable to take up the gauntlet thrown down by the opponents of inerrancy and infallibility.[1] W. R. Nicholl in a letter to James Denney under date, August 7, 1894, declared that 'the only *respectable* defenders of verbal inspiration' are 'the Princeton school of Green and Warfield'.[2]

The situation, however, is not altogether as these statements seem to suggest. It is not a fact that there were no capable writers able to defend the traditional cause, and that the victory was complete for those who had renounced the notion of a verbally inspired Bible. By no means all had fallen in line behind Coleridge. There were those who persisted, in spite of the reiterated charge of obscurantist, to urge that any theory of revelation and inspiration which limited it to thoughts and ideas is inadequate to the facts and to the necessities of the case. Such writers were not satisfied with the thesis that God had no regard for the language in which the biblical writers clothed their thoughts and embodied their ideas. Inspiration, if such there be, must penetrate words as well as thoughts, it must find its living medium in language. Inspired thought there may be, but it has no permanent significance unless it is finalized in words capable of and adequate to its transmission. Wescott was quite sure that this must be so. 'The slightest consideration', he says, 'will show that words are as essential to intellectual processes as they are to mutual intercourse. . . . Thoughts are wedded to words as necessarily as soul is to body.'[3]

There were several writers, as we shall see, who could gain nothing from their allegiance to the traditional doctrine, who were thoroughly convinced of its truth. To talk of inspired men, they maintained, was less than half the truth. What was

Chambers's Encyclopaedia, Richardson defined 'Fundamentalism' as 'the theory of biblical inspiration which regards words of the Bible as divinely dictated'. *Ad. loc.*, cf. J. I. Packer, *'Fundamentalism' and the Word of God*, 1958, pp. 10 ff.

[1] Cf. 'The Pentateuch Controversy', *London Quarterly Review*, Vol. LXXIII, 1890, pp. 290–1.

[2] T. H. Darlow, *William Robertson Nicholl*, 1925, p. 341.

[3] B. F. Wescott, *Introduction to the Study of the Gospels*, 1882, p. 40. Cf. D. Fraser, 'Because the Mechanical Theory of Verbal Inspiration is manifestly incorrect, it does not, however, follow that no authority attaches to the *words* of Scripture'. *The Inspiration of the Bible*, 1874, p. 72.

required, they felt, was an inspired Bible. Their opponents limited inspiration to the men who gave us the Bible, but in order to understand what was meant by 'inspired' men, they investigated the meaning of the term itself as it occurs in the Bible. They attached a significance to the very word. They quote the words of Scripture to sustain their view that inspiration does not spread to its words and in this way proclaim their belief that the words were only the individual's own unaided human statement of the position. Such an idea seemed to be, not only the elimination of all certainty, but the destruction of the very idea of inspiration which was being maintained.

The doctrine of verbal inspiration was, as we have seen, criticized on the score that it was essentially mechanical. But that identification, it has been shown, was not acceptable to or accepted by traditional writers.[1] In fact, as James Orr points out, 'The phrase "verbal inspiration" is one to which so great ambiguity attaches that it is now very commonly avoided by careful writers'.[2] Lee prefers the term 'plenary', and James Bannerman 'dynamical', although he, too, refers frequently to plenary inspiration.[3] Both Hodge and Warfield, although they are not prepared to discard the term 'verbal', yet insist that it must be carefully explained. 'There is more excuse' they say, 'for this misrepresentation because of the extremely mechanical conceptions of inspiration maintained by many former advocates of the term "verbal". The view, however, we repudiate as earnestly as any of those who object to the language in question.'[4]

[1] B. F. Wescott, *Introduction to the Study of the Gospels*, 1882, p. 40.
[2] James Orr, *Revelation and Inspiration*, 1910, reprint, 1952, p. 209.
[3] James Bannerman, *Inspiration*, etc., 1865, pp. 312 ff.
[4] Cf. James Orr, *Revelation and Inspiration*, p. 209. Cf. A. A. Hodge and B. B. Warfield, Article 'Inspiration', *Presbyterian Review*, April 1881, p. 233. Cf. also B. B. Warfield, *The Inspiration and Authority of the Bible*, reprint, 1948, p. 105. Cf. 'we would take exception to the principle . . . that there is nothing which can claim the authority of Verbal Inspiration, save words immediately dictated by the Spirit, and in regard to the uttering of which the inspired writers were mere machines. . . . We have no sympathy with that theory of Verbal Inspiration'. D. Fraser, *Inspiration*, 1874, pp. 70–1. Fraser is not too happy about the use of the word 'plenary' used as a substitute for 'verbal'. 'Different degrees of importance in the truths revealed must not be confounded with different degrees of Inspiration'. he writes. 'From this it follows that the phrase "Plenary Inspiration" as employed to some writers, is inaccurate, and calculated to mislead. The qualifying adjective *plenary* tends to obscure, rather than to throw light upon the subject. It lends countenance to the erroneous notion that there are *different degrees* of Inspiration.

By insisting upon the idea of verbal inspiration the purpose was to emphasize, against the Insight Theory, that inspiration is not a natural process: and, on the other hand, to insist against the Illumination Theory that inspiration is not a partial process. Not a part of the Bible, but the Bible in all its parts is to be regarded as the Word of God. By contending that the Bible was verbally inspired interest was centred, not on the method, but the result. The idea was that the Holy Spirit so bore along the writers of the Scriptures that their words are to be regarded as in a very real sense His words. Peake had stated that the new theory of Inspiration sought to give 'hearty recognition to the human element'. The traditional writers replied that they did not obscure the human element, but they were anxious to give hearty recognition to the divine element. It was, then, the specific purpose of the writers we are now to review to contend for the objectivity of inspiration. Here, in contrast with the Insight or Illumination view, the focus was without. The Bible itself is regarded as an inspired Book.

Before the date from which our investigation commenced, there appeared two important volumes in which it was closely argued that inspiration has only valid significance if it relates to the words of Scripture. In 1830 came Robert Haldane's *The Verbal Inspiration of the Scriptures Established*, and twenty-four years later William Lee's *Inspiration of the Holy Scripture*. Lee's work has remained as a classic, and within a few years after our period it had reached its fourth edition. 'The Bible presents to us,' he premises, 'in whatever light we regard it, two distinct elements: the Divine and the Human.'[1] There is, he argues, a divinely given revelation and there is a conveyance of that revelation in human language by the men specially chosen for

All Inspiration is plenary, that is, full and complete, or it is no inspiration at all. We are free to acknowledge great and striking diversities in the mode or process of Inspiration, and also different degrees of importance in the truths revealed; but as to their inspired authority, they are all on a level. All are true and their Inspiration by the Spirit is the guarantee of their truthfulness' (*op. cit.*, pp. 65–6).

Cf. '. . . unfortunately, the view of Verbal Inspiration has so often been associated with dictation, that as soon as it is mentioned, it is in many quarters at once branded "mechanical", and that hard word is made to do duty for argument—indeed, it is thought there is no need for arguing with us or considering our belief. We repudiate as strongly as any the idea of "mechanical" in this connection . . .'. A. McCaig, *The Grand Old Book*, Being Lectures on Inspiration and the Higher Criticism, 1894, second edition, p. 168.

[1] William Lee, *Inspiration of the Holy Scripture*, 1854, fourth edition, 1865, p. 18.

the purpose. There has been, he notes, a tendency to accentuate the divine element at the expense of the human and to end up in a 'docetic view' of inspiration, to quote the later words of Dorner. On the other hand, of recent years, the human side has been over-stressed. This has been done by those who have 'changed the formula "The Bible *is* the Word of God", into "The Bible *contains* the Word of God", and by all, who like Daniel Wilson,[1] argue for "degrees of inspiration", as well as by those who follow Schleiermacher in regarding the Bible "as having the sole power of conveying a Revelation to man by awakening and elevating his religious consciousness" '.[1]

Lee lays down two conditions which need to be satisfied in any true doctrine of inspiration. First of all due emphasis must be given to the human element in Scripture. The writers of Scripture did not resign both body and mind to God in a passive manner.[2] They were God's penmen, not His pens. A purely mechanical theory fails to do justice to the human element. Lee contends for a 'dynamical' view in which, he declares, 'the divine and human elements, mutually interpenetrating and combined, form one vital, organic whole: not mechanically, still less ideally, but as it has been termed, *dynamically* united'.[3] The second condition to be satisfied is the necessity of drawing a distinction between revelation and inspiration. Revelation is a direct communication from God to man of a knowledge, which is otherwise beyond man's natural sagacity or reason to acquire or discover. Inspiration is the 'actuating energy of the Holy Ghost, in whatever degree or manner it may have been exercised, guided by which the human agents chosen by God have *officially* proclaimed His will by word of mouth, or have committed to writing the several portions of the Bible'.[4]

Lee carries through the discussion of these two conditions. 'The human element', he insists, 'instead of being supressed, becomes an integral part of the agency employed: moulded, it is true, and guided, and brought into action, by the co-operation of the Spirit; but not the less really, on that account, participating in the result produced.'[5] He argues that the 'dynamical' theory,

[1] William Lee, *Inspiration of the Holy Scripture*, 1854, fourth edition, 1865, p. 20 Cf. Daniel Wilson, *Evidences of Christianity*, 1828.
[2] *Ibid.*, p. 21.   [3] *Ibid.*, p. 26
[4] *Ibid.*, pp. 27–8.   [5] *Ibid.*, p. 146.

however, is not sufficient to account for all the phenomena which the Bible presents. It satisfies the first condition mentioned. We must, therefore, he continues, seek for a second principle to meet the demands of the second condition. Here he returns to a discussion of the relation between revelation and inspiration, and suggests that there are instances of divine communications not having been committed to writing for some time after they were received, in some cases, indeed, only after the lapse of several years. In such instances, it must be granted, the Holy Spirit acted 'to bring the original communication before the mind of the sacred writer, in its primitive perfection, and to enable him to record it with infallible accuracy'.[1] By using the distinction between revelation and inspiration, Lee can argue further that what some regard as errors or imperfections in the Bible as God's revelation are nothing of the kind. They are indeed 'nothing more than historical details which have been inserted as simple matters of fact in the Scripture narrative, under the guidance of its Divine Author'.[2] Lee maintains that the impartation of the Holy Spirit to the Apostles was for the purpose of rendering them, in their official teaching, infallible organs of the Truth.[3] In their case the influence of the Spirit was 'absolute, unique, and *specifically* different from those preventing and assisting graces of the Holy Ghost which have been the gift of Christ to His Church'.[4] The Scripture, it is concluded, is the result of this absolute, unique, and specifically different movement of the Spirit in the experiences of God's chosen vehicles for the perpetuation of revelation in written form.

It is not possible in short compass to do justice to the massive volume of nigh on 600 pages in which James Bannerman, Professor of Theology at New College, Edinburgh, states and defends his high view of inspiration. There is evidence that this book profoundly influenced such giants in theology as James Orr and A. H. Strong. Bannerman maintained that the difference between an inspired and an uninspired Bible is the same as that between a divine and a human faith.[5] He sets down the proposition 'that inspiration in its results comprehends these two

---

[1] William Lee, *Inspiration of the Holy Scripture*, 1854, fourth edition, 1865, p. 149.   [2] *Ibid.*, p. 150.   [3] *Ibid.*, p. 242.
[4] *Ibid.*
[5] James Bannerman, *The Infallible Truth and Divine Inspiration of the Holy Scriptures*, 1865, pp. 96 ff.

ideas—namely, the *infallible truth* and the *divine authority* of everything which the inspired man asserts or sanctions as true'.[1] Having argued that an inspired Bible gives faith an objective basis and a sure ground, he goes on to insist that faith without such a foundation stands in the wisdom of men.

Bannerman refers to the two propositions which, when taken together, exhibit, he says 'the substance of the immemorial and all but universal doctrine of the Church of Christ in regard to the inspired Scriptures'.[2] In the first place, the Scriptures contain a communication of truth from God supernaturally given to man: and in the second place, they contain that truth supernaturally transferred to human language, and therefore free from all mixture or addition of error.[3] Revelation has reference to the first of these processes and inspiration to the second. The mode of revelation is, he contends, inexplicable. It is, however, essentially objective and is finally co-extensive with the Scripture. Inspiration he conceives of as a supernatural power of God, which enables the prophet unerringly and without failure to transfer the revelation given to him to permanent written form.[4] This means that inspiration is itself supernatural[5] and finally inexplicable as to its mode.[6] Bannerman joins issue with the subjective idea of revelation advocated by Coleridge, Maurice, Arnold, Hare, Morell, MacNaughton and others. They reject verbal inspiration and yet retain the term for that which is hardly anything more than a mere sharpened insight or an increased illumination. Bannerman, however, sees that the term verbal inspiration can be misunderstood, since it may be equated with the idea of a mechanical process and thus 'open to the objection of being inconsistent with the free exercise of the faculties of the writers according to their ordinary laws'.[7] It is for this reason he prefers the term 'dynamical', but he is still sure that the words of Scripture are really words which the Holy Spirit has given. Bannerman is convinced that the Scripture itself establishes that inspiration is supernatural and plenary. He therefore proceeds to an investigation of both Testaments. At the end of a long and thorough research, he concludes that the

[1] James Bannerman, *The Infallible Truth and Divine Inspiration of the Holy Scriptures*, 1865, p. 94 (italics in original).
[2] *Ibid.*, p. 149.   [3] *Ibid.*, pp. 149–50.
[4] *Ibid.*, p. 214.   [5] *Ibid.*; cf. pp. 218 ff.   [6] *Ibid.*; cf. pp. 243 ff.
[7] *Ibid.*, p. 246.

Bible is a product of a two-fold authorship—God's and man's. It is of God and it is by man. And in neither case is there a deficiency. Here all the human is divine and all the divine is human.[1] 'The supernatural and the natural, each in its peculiarity and entireness—the divine and human, both in their fulness and freedom—the objection from without, and the subjection from within—must be combined to make up a Bible such as we actually have it. The divine idea coming down from God, and true as it came from Him, must meet with the human idea fresh from the heart of man, and purified from its imperfections; and the two must become one in order to constitute the inspired Scripture.'[2]

Placed beside the substantial tome of Bannerman's, the work by Donald Fraser constitutes a slender volume, but it is, none the less, marked by deep thought and sincere conviction. The substance of what he has to say, had already been delivered as lectures to the students of Airdale College, of which Fraser was President and theological Tutor. Fraser boldly asserts verbal inspiration, but he is careful to distinguish what he means by this from any mechanical notion.[3] Inspiration is not to be confused with genius since the inspiration of Scripture belongs essentially to 'the economy of grace'.[4] Fraser maintains that the important issue in connection with inspiration is not to determine its mode or manner, but rather, 'With what authority does it invest the truth revealed, and what moral obligation does that truth, in consequence, lay upon us?' In other words, 'What has an inspired record that any other truthful record has not?'[5] He is, however, emphatic that, as regards the mode, the idiosyncrasies of each writer are manifest. The human is certainly there.[6] The question is then, Where is the evidence of the divine? In the direction of the minds of the writers of the choice of those words to convey the truth to subsequent generations. Fraser insists upon this. 'The *words*', he says, 'as they exist in the record, reveal to us the mind of the Spirit, and come with His seal as to their truthfulness.'[7] As he sees it, the words of Scripture are God's words, however mysterious the mode of their giving must

[1] James Bannerman, *The Infallible Truth and Divine Inspiration of the Holy Scriptures*, 1865, pp. 96 ff.; cf. pp. 418 ff.   [2] *Ibid.*, pp. 449–50.
[3] D. Fraser, *Inspiration of the Bible*, 1874; cf. pp. 54 f., 62 f. and 72 f.
[4] *Ibid.*, p. 37.   [5] *Ibid.*, p. 39.   [6] *Ibid.*, p. 53.
[7] *Ibid.*, p. 46.

remain. Fraser refers to what unsatisfactory conclusions a denial of this must inevitably lead. He then deals with objections to his position on the score that anything partaking of the character of verbal inspiration means the turning of the writers of the Bible into human ventriloquists and automaton poets. The objection holds only if the idea of verbal inspiration be identified with a mechanical process; and this Fraser denies. 'Because the Mechanical theory of Verbal Inspiration is manifestly incorrect, it does not, however, follow that no authority attaches to the *words* of Scripture.'[1] Fraser rejects the idea of degrees of inspiration and concluded that the Bible is inspired 'not in special portions merely, but in its entirety'.[2]

One of the strongest statements of the traditional view of inspiration comes in the Carey Lectures of 1884 by Robert Watts, Professor of Systematic Theology at the Assembly's College, Belfast. Watts, one of the contributors to the *Lex Mosaica*, among his several volumes had already written one on *The Newer Criticism and the Analogy of Faith* (1882), which is referred to in a subtitle as '*A Reply to the Lectures of W. Robertson Smith on the Old Testament and the Jewish Church*'. In the Carey Lectures, he first set about establishing the Bible to be the Protestant rule of faith. 'To serve us as a rule of faith and life', he then argues, 'the Scriptures must be infallible, and to be infallible they must be the Word of God, and to be the Word of God they must be Divinely Inspired'.[3] The question of inspiration is then discussed. The Bible is θεόπνευστος, 'God-breathed'. Watts contends that the inspiration extends to the language employed. He is not too happy about the adequacy of the epithet 'plenary'—'it is best to employ the term Verbal Inspiration', he avers, 'which properly understood expressed the doctrine of Scripture on this subject'.[4] Christ's support is claimed for this view. The apostles, it will be agreed, were inspired preachers, but, if inspired as preachers, 'how much more so as writers'.[5] New Testament passages, such as Matt. v. 17–18; John x. 33–36; II Tim. iii. 16, etc. are adduced as proof of the inspiration of the Old Testament Scriptures. Watts meets objections to the doctrine of verbal inspiration. It is not to be

---

[1] D. Fraser, *Inspiration of the Bible*, 1874, p. 72.   [2] *Ibid.*, p. 86.
[3] Robert Watts, *The Rule of Faith and the Doctrine of Inspiration*, 1885, p. 90.
[4] *Ibid.*, p. 97.   [5] *Ibid.*, p. 135.

equated with dictation, he asserts. Commenting on the term 'verbal inspiration' he observes, 'By the opponents of the theory, it is very commonly understood to teach that the Holy Spirit dictated to the inspired speaker or writer the words he was to employ. This is an idea entertained by no intelligent advocate of the doctrine in the present day.'[1] In this connection he pronounces Coleridge's statement in his *Confessions of an Inquiring Spirit* to the effect that the writers of Scripture in the view of the advocates of verbal inspiration were 'successively transformed into automaton compositors' as unjustified. The sacred writers, he adds, were not 'pens' but 'penmen'.[2] Watts pays special attention to the argument concerning the free quotation of the Old Testament by the New Testament writers. He sees this, not as a disproof of his conclusion, but as evidence of the sovereignty of the inspiring Spirit. In his last lecture he stresses, in defence of the 'Westminster Standards' against the criticism of William Lee that faith in Scripture as the Word of God must necessarily find its authentication by the inner witness of the Spirit. The Scripture is the instrument of the Spirit, Watts argues.[3] 'In substance and in form, then,' he concludes, 'the Bible is Divine. The Spirit of God has determined its matter and fashioned its mould.'[4] It is consequently the Word of God, 'a Divinely determined record, whose contents have been selected by the Holy Ghost, and recorded "not in the words which man's wisdom teacheth, but in words which the Holy Ghost teacheth" '.[5]

One of the most controversial books of the period dealing with the subject of inspiration was Alfred Cave's *The Inspiration of the Old Testament Inductively Considered*. This volume of just on 500 pages by the Principal of Hackney College constitutes the Seventh Congregational Union Lectures. Cave refers to the importance of the theme, as shown by a historical survey, in the Introductory Lecture. He points to the 'indefiniteness, if not disrepute, into which the Doctrine of Inspiration has fallen in many quarters'.[6] He notes how as a result of the heat and passion of Coleridge's attack upon the doctrine of mechanical

---

[1] Robert Watts, *The Rule of Faith and the Doctrine of Inspiration*, 1885, pp. 166–7.
[2] *Ibid.*, p. 172.   [3] *Ibid.*, p. 267.
[4] *Ibid.*, p. 270.   [5] *Ibid.*, p. 273.
[6] Alfred Cave, *The Inspiration of the Old Testament Inductively Considered*, 1888, second edition, p. 12.

inspiration, 'A great vagueness' 'has fallen of late upon all deliberate statements concerning inspiration. Men know what theory they disbelieve; they do not know how to express their belief in a theory.'[1]

Cave discusses his subject under two headings. He seeks first to gather the data for, and then, to elaborate a doctrine of, inspiration. His inquiry is to follow the inductive, as distinct from the dogmatic, method.[2] Three lectures are given to a consideration of the Book of Genesis. The subject of the Law, its authorship and divine origin, takes up two more, while the divine origin of prophecy is the burden of lecture seven. Throughout Cave shows himself a convinced and hearty believer in the supernatural. Revelation is no mere human discovery: there is a real divine self-disclosure. The Law and the Prophets alike, not only in the revelation which they give, but no less in the records of their revelation, reveal a supernatural origin. Inspiration, indeed, is involved in revelation. 'As the Inspiration of Moses is the pledge of the Inspiration of the Books of Moses, so the Inspiration of the prophets is the guarantee of the Inspiration of the Books of the Prophets.'[3] The prophets were inspired organs of divine revelation and when such inspired men committed their communication from heaven to writings 'the literary product was an inspired product'.

Having disposed of the Law and the Prophets with the assurance that they are inspired in regard to both the revelation and the record, Cave turns to deal with the third section of the Bible, the Graphia or Hagiographia. In contrast with the prophets who present us with a record of a progressive revelation, from Moses to Malachi, the Holy Writings *present us with a record*, not of revelation, but *of the assimulation of revelation*.[4] In the Graphia, we have a mirror of life in God. Here is portrayed religion, not revelation. Cave compares the Psalms with Isaiah. Both are exalted poetry: but whereas the Psalter is lyric, Isaiah is didactic. The Psalter depicts subjective experience: Isaiah describes objective revelation: 'If Isaiah details experience, it is in order to emphasize revelation; if the Psalter dwells upon revelation, it is to accentuate experience'.[5]

[1] Alfred Cave, *The Inspiration of the Old Testament Inductively Considered*, 1888, second edition, p. 12.   [2] *Ibid.*; cf. pp. 17 ff.
[3] *Ibid.*, p. 439.   [4] *Ibid.*, p. 455 (italics in original).   [5] *Ibid.*

Reviewing what his study of the data has revealed, Cave emphasizes first of all that there can be no doubt about the human element in the Old Testament. This, indeed, has been taken for granted throughout his inquiry.[1] But 'the question of questions', as he puts it, 'which has engrossed us from the first has been, whether human causes suffice to explain the existence of the Old Testament'.[2] Cave contends that the inductive inquiry has made it abundantly clear that a supernatural cause is required for the Old Testament. It could never have been produced without divine assistance. Moses and the Prophets and the saints who wrote its several parts were 'fellow-workers with Deity'. This brings him to discuss the different kinds of inspiration. There is an inspiration, a co-operation of God with men which sustains life (cf. Gen. vi. 3). There is, also, an inspiration, as illustrated in the case of Bezaleel, which imparts excellence of intellect (cf. Ex. xxiv. 1–5). A special gift of ethnic prophecy was bestowed on Balaam (cf. Num. xxiv. 2). Believers, too, are subjects of divine inspiration, and there is, besides, an inspiration which blends masses of individuals who possess the Christian consciousness into one great organism.[3] He then asks is it possible to find the differentia which may distinguish the Inspiration which resulted in the Old Testament from other varieties of inspiration. Several kinds of inspiration are to be observed: first the Hagiographic type or the co-operation of the divine with man which issued in the assimulation of revelation.[4] This type of inspiration underlies every book in the Old Testament.[5] Prophetic inspiration enabled the prophets to be the media of revelation;[6] while, what he calls Transcriptive inspiration worked upon the authors so that, in co-operation with the Holy Spirit, they were led to preserve the communication they had received in written form. In this two processes can be observed: first, the inspired act of committal to writing, and second, the superintendence which imparted adequacy and faithfulness.[7] Cave adds a note on Canonical inspiration which is defined as 'that co-operation of the Holy Ghost which prompted the formation of the Canon'.[8] The sum

---

[1] Alfred Cave, *The Inspiration of the Old Testament Inductively Considered*, 1888, second edition, p. 12; cf. p. 457.   [2] *Ibid.*

[3] *Ibid.*; cf. pp. 460 ff.   [4] *Ibid.*, pp. 462 ff.   [5] *Ibid.*; cf. p. 477.

[6] *Ibid.*; cf. pp. 477 ff.   [7] *Ibid.*, p. 478.   [8] *Ibid.*, p. 495.

of the matter is this: 'Inspiration is a co-operation of the Holy
Ghost with the spirit of man, guaranteeing reliableness of the
record'.[1] Cave adds that inspiration assures the substantial truth
of the record: this is the result to which the inductive inquiry
leads. 'That the record is absolutely devoid of mistakes we do
not know; the record is a human record of the Divine; but that
the record is substantially true, is veracious, trustworthy, and
historical, our whole inquiry has shown. It has also shown the
need of the greatest caution before errors are attributed to the
Old Testament.'[2]

As was to be expected, Cave's book was vigorously attacked.
His hostility to the new criticism was well known. He had
already revealed his opposition to the Graf-Wellhausen hypothesis and had bravely sought to demolish the arguments by
which Robertson Smith sought to make it acceptable in Britain.[3]
In the changing and challenging situation in which Cave found
himself, he could not hope for mercy from his opponents. And he
certainly did not get it. In their estimation he was fighting a
losing battle, and in spite of his reputation for scholarship, was
defending an obscurantist position. His thesis was ridiculed and
riddled. A recent writer states bluntly and unsympathetically
that Cave's work 'is a travesty on scholarship'.[4]

Weaknesses in Cave's position cannot be denied. It was
charged against him by a writer in the *Spectator* that his treatment of the critics was unfair. There is no doubt about his
knowledge of them, but it was contended that he quoted only
such statements as suited his purpose.[5] It was naturally
declared that his effort merely revealed the inability of
traditionalists to come to grips with the real issues and to admit
the humanness of the record and cease to talk about an inspired
Bible.[6] There was, however, evident enthusiasm by others

[1] Alfred Cave, *The Inspiration of the Old Testament Inductively Considered*, 1888,
second edition, p. 12.   [2] *Ibid.*, p. 496.
[3] Cf. Alfred Cave, 'The latest Phase of the Pentateuch Question', *British and
Foreign Evangelical Review*, Vol. XXIX, 1880, pp. 248–67; 'Professor Robertson
Smith and the Pentateuch', *ibid.*, pp. 593–621.
[4] Willis B. Glover, *Evangelical Nonconformity and the Higher Criticism in the
Nineteenth Century*, 1954, p. 189; cf. p. 190, etc.
[5] Cf. 'The Inspiration of the Old Testament', *Spectator*, Vol. LXI, 1888, p. 1330.
[6] Cf. Review of Cave's *Inspiration of the Old Testament*, Academy, Vol.
XXXVI, 1889, p. 252; cf. *London Quarterly Review*, Vol. LXXIII, 1890,
pp. 270–1.

because of Cave's boldness, on the one hand, in admitting the legitimacy of criticism, and, on the other hand, because, acquainted though he was with the Graf-Wellhausen theory, he rejected its validity and sought to reconstruct a view of Scripture in the context of biblical criticism more akin to the traditionalist position.[1]

Only a passing reference needs to be made to Francis F. Sharr's Fernly Lectures delivered in Nottingham, July 31, 1891, on the subject *The Inspiration of the Holy Scriptures*. Although this lecture comes some months after the one by W. T. Davidson, to which reference has already been made, it is significant for the reason that Sharr maintained the traditional doctrine of Scripture. A review of Sharr's statement is given in an edition of the *London Quarterly Review* for 1892.[2] This periodical had become less conservative with the years and consequently Sharr's view, in which the inerrancy of the Bible was defended, was not too enthusiastically received.

He 'has the ability to make even that which we now consider the extreme of conservatism seem not only the most reasonable, but the only possible position';[3] such is the statement made concerning James Macgreggor's *Revelation and the Record*. Macgreggor, sometime Professor of Systematic Theology in New College, Edinburgh, was nothing if not an exact scholar.

It was Macgreggor's conviction that the supernaturalism of the Bible's inspiration and the divinity of its authorship are one and the same reality. 'We will avoid', he says, 'as ambiguous the expression "verbal inspiration", and will proceed simply on the view that inspiration of a scripture means authorship of the (written) *word*. About any other kind of "verbal" inspiration— e.g. of the printer's ink?—we will not inquire. Nor will we inquire whether there can be any "literal" inspiration which is not "verbal".'[4]

Revelation, Macgreggor makes quite clear, is a different thing from its record. And he admits the possibility that though the revelation be divine, the record might be merely human. Indeed,

[1] *Congregational Review*, 11, 1888, p. 1058; *ibid*. n.s.l, 1889, p. 89, etc.

[2] *London Quarterly Review*, Vol. LXXVII, 1892, pp. 358–9.

[3] *Expository Times*, Vol. V, 1893–4, p. 85.

[4] James Macgreggor, *The Revelation and the Record*, 1893, p. 79 (italics in original).

it might be conceivable as an 'ideal possibility' that there should have been no record at all. But it is not in fact so. Macgreggor then seeks to justify his thesis of the divineness of the Bible's authorship. This leads him to deal with the question of whether there are errors and mistakes in the Scriptures. There can be no evasion at this point, he declares. But he contends that to suppose that infallibility has reference only to mysterious doctrines, and not to plain facts, *is* a form of evasion. 'Nor is there escape in merely harping on misconstructions of the doctrine of inspiration, as if it had meant that the printer's ink is infallible, or that the inspiration is in the "letter" *as distinct* from the spirit, while in fact *it is the spirit in the letter.* These are not ways of real escape from the difficulty, but may be ways of concealing, from ourselves or others, *denial of the fact of divine* inspiration.'[1]

Macgreggor repudiates the assertion of Rothe that emphasis upon the divinity of Scripture means an undervaluation of its humanity. Analogy with the Person of Christ is made, but the analogy must be consistently applied. The doctrine of a mechanical inspiration is also anathema to Macgreggor. The notion that the human is overborne by or submerged in Deity is 'a heathenish conception'. The Christian view of inspiration is something other than this. The mechanical view must be 'not only repelled as false, but revolted from as profane'. 'The imputation of that conception', adds Macgreggor, 'to Christians by whom it is repudiated is a shameful calumny.'[2]

Phrases such as the human authors of the Scriptures being 'pens of God, flutes of the Holy Spirit' have been used. But such statements, Macgreggor contends, do not mean that inspiration makes men to be merely passive organs of divine utterances. They are employed simply to describe the 'complete possession and use of the producing human writer's faculties by the Deity inspiring the Scripture produced'.[3] Of course the exact process is a 'mystery' and we have to accept the mystery unless we reject the fact. Inspiration had the effect upon, for example, the writer's judgement and memory. And it issued in an inspired utterance. These are two facts which Macgreggor strives to maintain. 'The divine possession is not a supersession, but the contrary', he says. 'What it involves is, not effacement or suspension of a creature's

[1] James Macgreggor, *The Revelation and the Record*, 1893, pp. 89–90.
[2] *Ibid.*, p. 95.   [3] *Ibid.*, p. 96.

free individuality (II Cor. iii. 17), but a completed fulness of God-given freedom for the individual. A pen*man* cannot be *merely* a man. But a man whom God employs as penman may be a *man-pen* of God ("Rabbi" Duncan). His being *God's* pen ensures his being completely free in all the writing; for, "where the Spirit of the Lord is, there is liberty". He is in full exercise of his own distinctive human individualities; for it is *this individual* man that is employed. A human flute of the divine Spirit is a man whose whole distinctive individuality is, *because employed* divinely, therefore most vividly alive and free; as were the dry bones in Ezekiel's valley when the Spirit breathed upon them (cf. Gen. ii. 7) to make them a great *army* (of *machines?*).'[1]

Macgreggor goes out of his way to state his belief in verbal inspiration. There is, in fact, he thinks, no other which has significance and permanent reality. 'Those who imagine', he writes, 'that there can be an inspiration of a Scripture that is *not* a "verbal" inspiration may have some notion of divine "ideas" floating in the air, like "songs without words", when men are talking like Moses and Elias on the Mount of Transfiguration. The world's greatest master of wisdom in song has a stricter conception of the relation of ideas of a Scripture to its words. To his apprehension—as in Justin Martyr's experience—so long as the ideas are only in the air—while "the poet's eye, in a frenzy rolling, doth glance from heaven to earth, from earth to heaven" they are but "airy nothings", as of "imagination bodying forth the forms of things unknown". That which fixes them *(Americanism)* [*sic*] "turns them to shape", "gives them local habitation and a name", so that (cp. John xiv. 22–4) we may apprehend them and they abide with us, is "the poet's *pen*".'[2]

The title, *The Grand Old Book*, put by Archibald McCaig to his volume of lectures given to the students of Pastor's (now Spurgeon's) College, of which he was the Principal was, perhaps, unfortunate. It might be supposed by some, not aware of the facts, that the author was a ranter or obscurantist. But McCaig was by no means either of these. By qualifying the title with the epexegetical addition, 'Lectures on Inspiration and the

---

[1] James Macgreggor, *The Revelation and the Record*, 1893, p. 96 (italics in original). Cf. A footnote to this passage which states: 'It is the *Scripture* that is inspired: the human writer is *employed* in producing it' (p. 96, footnote).

[2] *Ibid.*, pp. 109–10 (italics in original).

Higher Criticism', McCaig gave a better statement of his purpose. 'I have specially considered the views of the Critics as set forth in the writings of the representatives of the school in this country', he writes in the Preface to the first edition. 'Dr W. Robertson Smith, Dr Driver, Dr Cheyne, and Dr Horton, for although the last-named has produced no work specifically on the Higher Criticism, yet just as the before-mentioned trio have popularized the critical theories among students, so Dr Horton has endeavoured to familiarize the "common people" with the results of these theories.'[1]

McCaig conceived authority and inspiration to be one and the same reality. In the first four chapters Christ's authority is asserted against the critics as establishing the 'plenary and verbal' inspiration of the Old Testament, and their consequent veracity and accuracy. Several chapters follow in which the use of the Old Testament by the apostolic writers is claimed to yield the same result. 'We do not wish to twist the Scriptures to agree with our doctrine, but we hold the doctrine because, from repeated examination, we believe the Scriptures teach it.'[2] The fact of inspiration is patent all through the Bible,[3] and, he maintains 'we have not only the fact of the Inspiration of the *men* thus declared, but also the fact of *the Inspiration of the Book* indicated'.[4] It is not that holy men *thought* as they were moved by the Spirit, but they *spake*: not only were the *ideas* Spirit-given, but the verbal expression was under the direction of the Spirit.[5]

McCaig argues that, not only is the fact of inspiration everywhere evident in the Bible, but that there is also a clear account given of its form. The forms were, indeed, many and varied; by vision and dream and so forth: 'but in all these varied forms it was God who spake; it was a Divine message that reached the heart of the inspired man'.[6] The essence throughout was the same, so that the whole Book is the voice of God to us. 'No theory of Inspiration', he then premises, 'can be complete which does not take account of all the facts.' McCaig enumerates certain theories which he considers inadequate precisely in this respect. There is the Naturalistic or Ordinary view in which

---

[1] A. McCaig, *The Grand Old Book, Being Lecturers on Inspiration and the Higher Criticism*, 1894, second edition, Preface, p. vi.
[2] *Ibid.*, p. 2. Cf. chapter on 'Inspiration' in his *Doctrinal Brevities*, 1923.
[3] *Ibid.*; cf. p. 139.   [4] *Ibid.*, p. 140 (italics in original).
[5] *Ibid.*, p. 158 (italics in original).   [6] *Ibid.*, p. 163.

inspiration of the sacred writers is thought to differ only in degree from the inspiration of genius. In the Intermittent, or, as Farrar prefers to call it, the Illumination theory, reference is made to degrees of inspiration with the result that the individual finds it difficult, if not impossible, to decide which portions were perfectly, and which imperfectly, inspired. The Partial or Essential theory is also set aside because it confines inspiration to matters of doctrine and morality, and above all, matters of faith. A distinction is drawn between the Bible and the Word of God 'contained' in it. McCaig argues that doctrine, morality and matters of faith are so embedded in the historical, biographical and descriptive parts of Scripture that one cannot consistently attribute inspiration to the one element and deny it to the other.

In more detail McCaig protests against the Mechanical or Organic, sometimes called the Dictation theory. It is certainly right in declaring that inspiration is verbal, but it does not sufficiently recognize the human element.[1] He calls his own view, the Dynamical, or, as it is often called, Plenary—the more exact term, he then declares, is Plenary and Verbal.[2] It is plenary because 'full', and 'if the Inspiration is really "full", it must extend to the *words*, and so be also *verbal*'.[3] Under the possession of the Divine *Afflatus*, the speaker and writer retain the full and free use of their faculties. The man is not a machine, but a God-controlled man.[4] But inspiration relates essentially to the final product. 'There is', he states, 'no doctrine of Scripture but what is built upon *words*.'[5]

In part two of his volume, McCaig seeks to defend his doctrine from criticism. He meets such objections as, for example, the 'Alleged Impossibility of a Book Revelation',[6] and the immorality of the Old Testament,[7] as well as the assertion of incorrect historical and scientific statements,[8] and discrepancies and contradictions.[9] A discussion of variations in the quotations from the Old Testament in the New, and Paul's 'so-called disclaimer of inspiration' comes in Chapter XV. McCaig urges

[1] A. McCaig, *The Grand Old Book, Being Lectures on Inspiration and the Higher Criticism*, 1894, second edition, p. 165. McCaig returns again and again to a denial that verbal inspiration is mechanical. Cf. pp. 167–8, 170, etc.

[2] *Ibid.*, p. 166.   [3] *Ibid.* (italics in original).

[4] *Ibid.*, p. 170.   [5] *Ibid.*, p. 184.   [6] *Ibid.*; cf. pp. 187 ff.

[7] *Ibid.*; cf. pp. 204 ff.   [8] *Ibid.*; cf. pp. 225 ff.   [9] *Ibid.*; cf. pp. 246 ff.

that 'The same Spirit which inspired the Old Testament inspired the writers of the New to quote the Old in the way they have quoted it'.[1] McCaig is sure that the admission of various readings in Manuscripts, and possible errors in transmission do not affect the position. He is not in the least 'opposed to legitimate criticism'. Indeed he welcomes it.[2] But he contends that 'while we speak of the inspiration of the original, we are not speaking of something which is hopelessly lost, and forever out of reach'.[3] God may well have permitted the loss of the original autographs lest, as in the case of the brazen serpent in Israel, idolatry might have resulted: 'if these manuscripts had been in existence, they would have been elevated into a kind of Christian Palladium; and as every supposed relic of the Saviour has been worshipped, so there would have been in reality what our opponents are fond of attributing to us—Bibliolatry'.[4] McCaig regards belief in verbal inspiration to have been the faith of the Church from the first, and he considers himself, and those who maintain the same position as himself, to be in the apostolic succession. The doctrine of the Plenary and Verbal inspiration of Scripture, he adds, in conclusion, is 'the doctrine upon which this College (of which he is the Principal) was founded and glories in proclaiming' and 'the doctrine fought for by our honoured Founder and President'.[5]

John Urquhart in his volume of 576 pages not only maintains, as was noted earlier, the inerrancy of Scripture, but contends that verbal inspiration has always been the presupposition and doctrine of the Church. 'Let men say what they will about "the absurdity" of Verbal Inspiration, no one can deny that every creed of Christendom had been hammered out upon that anvil.'[6] By its words is the Scripture really judged. It is the working hypothesis of all Christian teaching, that it is the words of the Bible which convey with intention and precision the mind of God. 'In other words,' he says, 'to use a well-known phrase, the common basis of study, teaching, and argument has been belief in the "Verbal Inspiration" of the Bible.'[7]

---

[1] A. McCaig, *The Grand Old Book*, Being Lectures on Inspiration and the Higher Criticism, 1894, second edition, p. 301.
[2] *Ibid.*; cf. p. 304.   [3] *Ibid.*, p. 308.
[4] *Ibid.*, p. 309.   [5] *Ibid.*, p. 322.
[6] John Urquhart, *The Inspiration and Accuracy of the Holy Scriptures*, 1895, p. 18.
[7] *Ibid.*, p. 19.

A view of inspiration in general agreement with this is stated by J. C. Ryle in the first chapter of his *Old Paths*. Ryle insists that inspiration to have any meaning must be verbal, and he, too, at the same time refuses to admit that this is the same as conceiving of it as mechanical.[1]

The name of Frederick Watson has already cropped up as one of the contributors to the *Lex Mosaica*. In his later years, Watson became interested in the subject of inspiration and his thoughts regarding it, found in manuscript form, were published after his death. There is evidence that Watson moved away from the strong conservative position he took up in his essay to the *Lex Mosaica*.[2] This may be, as has been suggested, because as theological lecturer in St John's College, Cambridge, he associated with such men as Jeremie, Selwyn, Swainson and Lightfoot, and their influence 'was congenial to Watson's temper and led him quietly towards the calm and cautious Churchmanship by which Cambridge has been privileged to influence a large number of English Churchmen'.[3]

In the book itself Watson does certainly show more sympathy with the higher criticism. Yet he contends 'that the Higher Criticism has nothing to say on matters of faith, and such the Inspiration of the Bible is'.[4] He bluntly asserts that 'Unbelief is the main element in a very large number of critical results'.[5] Watson is sure that the Bible is an inspired Book. He does not therefore limit inspiration to the writers. As an inspired book it is the Word of God.[6] And its inspiration is unique and distinctive. 'The Bible differs from all other books, in the character and degree of its Inspiration. It is the supreme manifestation of Divine inspiration embodied in human words.'[7] Watson finds proofs for this inspiration in the Bible itself, in, for example, its doctrine of sin, the harmony, purity and permanence of its teaching as well as the history of its chosen people and the reality of its prophecy. He makes a special point of the human

[1] J. C. Ryle, *Old Paths*, 1897, Ch. 1

[2] But note the following comment: 'This essay on Inspiration is not what could be called advanced, but it is in line with moderate criticism and the ripest scholarship of our day'. *Expository Times*, Vol. XVIII, 1906–7, p. 118.

[3] A. Caldecott in *Introduction to Inspiration*, p. v.

[4] Frederick Watson, *Inspiration*, 1906, p. 2.

[5] *Ibid.*   [6] *Ibid.*; cf. pp. 3 f., 16 f., etc.

[7] *Ibid.*, p. 17.

element in the Scripture.[1] It is in its nature like a sacrament. 'It has its outward and visible part, as well as its inward and spiritual grace.'[2]

The composition of the Books of the Bible is in very truth a work of man.[3] Concerning the psalms, for example, he remarks upon their expressions of human feelings, and their longings of the human spirit after God. 'But what an unreal and Docetic character', he adds, 'it gives these expressions of human desires and eagerness, if we regard them as "dictated" by the Holy Spirit.'[4] This means, as Watson insists, 'that the Bible though thoroughly Divine, is thoroughly human also'.[5]

On the human side imperfections are to be allowed. Mistakes in details may be permitted. Docetism, he remarks, destroys our holy faith, so we must beware of introducing it into the Bible. 'Those who believe that our Lord was true man, and therefore weak man, should not stagger at the Bible's true humanity or at the imperfections which its humanity involves.'[6]

Watson admits degrees of inspiration; and he is not prepared to apply the term infallibility to the Bible as such, since 'infallibility, does not allow of degrees. He contends for what he calls 'practical efficiency' rather than for 'actual perfection' as the best term to describe its authority.[7] Those who have faith in Christ will not, he thinks, stumble at this admission. It is, indeed, this belief which makes sure that the Bible is the Word of God. 'Believing in one Lord Jesus Christ, Word of God, Son of God, Son of Man', he concludes, 'it becomes not impossible for us to believe that God and man have co-operated in the making of the Bible. We feel ourselves in no way compelled to admit that it is not the Word of God, when it is proved to us by unmistakable signs that it is the word of man.'[8]

A brief reference may be made to William Kelly's *Inspiration of the Scriptures*. Well known as one of the leaders of the Brethren Movement, his position will be anticipated. He argues resolutely for the full inspiration and verbal accuracy of the Bible as a 'God-inspired' volume. 'It is not a question of *man's* spirit, but of God's, who is beyond doubt able to secure the

---

[1] Frederick Watson, *Inspiration*, 1906, p. 2; cf. pp. 148 ff.
[2] *Ibid.*, p. 149; cf. p. 189.   [3] *Ibid.*; cf. p. 152 f.
[4] *Ibid.*, p. 167; cf. p. 176.   [5] *Ibid.*, p. 189.
[6] *Ibid.*, pp. 190–1.   [7] *Ibid.*; cf. pp. 20 f., 189 f.
[8] *Ibid.*, p. 248.

truth absolutely, as the Lord and the apostles and prophets everywhere assume and assert.'[1] A true plenary doctrine of inspiration does not allow for degrees, and consequently the idea is excluded of man being left to himself to set forth the revelation he has received; otherwise it would be 'really to leave out God, and to blow hot and cold in the same breath'.[2] Every Scripture is inspired of God; it is God-breathed. It may be acknowledged that the precise way God brings about this result is beyond us. 'Speculation into the "how" of inspiration is a prying into what is not revealed, and therefore unwise and unbecoming.'[3] Kelly however has a long section—chapter four— in which he seeks to show that this high view of inspiration does not exclude the human element. 'Nobody doubts', he says, 'that Scripture without exception has a human element. In it God speaks and writes permanently to man, and therefore in human language.'[4] By this stress he contends 'the reproach "mechanical" is unfounded, no less than the setting up of "dynamical" is cold and insufficient'.[5] He elucidates by adding, 'The inspired are through His goodness far beyond being His pen or even His penmen, as it has been said. Their minds and affections He uses as well as their language'.[6] Kelly proceeds to an examination of every book in the Canon with a view to showing the evidences therein of its 'Divine design'. Having fulfilled this task he remarks about the result, 'As it already exceeds 600 pages, I think it better to let the positive truth produce its own impression, which difficulties of the kind have no real title to destroy seeing that the most certain truth, save in matter or in abstract forms, is necessarily open to such questions. It ought not to be where God has spoken or caused His word to be communicated to writing.'[7]

The position of James Orr as stated in what the *Expository Times* called his 'courageous' book[8] is well known. Orr was a careful scholar. Beginning with a chapter of 'Revelation and Inspiration in Current Thought', Orr seeks to show how a certain confusion has been introduced into the discussion by the failure to state exactly the precise significance of each term. He

[1] W. Kelly, *Inspiration of the Scriptures*, 1907, second edition, pp. 31-2.
[2] *Ibid.*, p. 34.   [3] *Ibid.*, p. 38.
[4] *Ibid.*, p. 47.   [5] *Ibid.*
[6] *Ibid.*   [7] *Ibid.*, p. 597.
[8] *Expository Times*, Vol. XXI, 1909–10, p. 373.

then makes a study of the subject of revelation and concludes this investigation with the assurance that a real revelation of God has been given. But this revelation is made permanent and available to every generation in its record. Thus for all practical purposes the revelation is to be identified with the record.

Inspiration is the distinctive characteristic of the record. The Scriptures are the result of God's working in and upon the writers. But it is not 'mechanical' since 'inspiration does not annul any power or faculty of the human soul, but raises all powers to their highest activity, and stimulates them to their freest exercise'.[1] He believes that the Bible in its Old and New Testaments claim, and make good their claim, to be inspired. He notes the ambiguity attaching to the phrase 'verbal inspiration' but he considers, however, that it 'expresses a true and important idea'.[2] It correctly, he maintains, opposes the theory which would limit revelation and inspiration to thoughts and ideas, leaving the language altogether to the unaided faculties of the sacred penmen. Such an idea Orr considers defective. 'Thought of necessity takes shape and is expressed in words', he remarks. 'If there is inspiration at all, it must penetrate words as well as thought, must mould the expression, and make the language employed the living medium of the idea to be conveyed.'[3]

The doctrine of inspiration which these books expound is the same as that which traditionalists, as some call them, or as conservative evangelicals, as they prefer to call themselves, continue to maintain. It is the view stated again by R. B. Girdlestone a few years after Orr wrote. 'Inspiration', declares Girdlestone, 'is thus to be regarded as the handmaid of revelation.'[4] It is the Spirit's work which results in an inspired Scripture. 'The conclusion we are brought to is that the Scriptures of the Old Testament are believed to be the inspired Word of God, not only because of their contents, which are so largely of the nature of revelation, but also because the writers, who so far as we are able to trace them were prophets, were Divinely commissioned either to speak or to write.'[5] So, too, is

---

[1] James Orr, *Revelation and Inspiration*, 1910, reprint, 1952, p. 169.
[2] *Ibid.*, p. 209.   [3] *Ibid.*
[4] R. B. Girdlestone, *The Building up of the Old Testament*, 1912, Excursus on Inspiration, p. 297.   [5] *Ibid.*, p. 302.

it with the New Testament. But Girdlestone would caution the student against certain assumptions. The book is inspired, but this does not mean that those who copied them were kept free from error; the same is true of translators. A book in the Bible, although surely inspired, does not on that account mean that all the opinions and the conduct it records are approved of. 'The candour of the Bible is pre-eminent.'[1] The theological and moral ideas of some books are not final or complete because they are inspired. Inspiration does not obliterate the national and personal characteristics of the writer nor yet does it necessarily imply originality. It is, however, Girdlestone's conclusion that 'The books of the New Testament are in the same position as those of the Old, and the whole Bible may be unhesitatingly described as "God's word written" '.[2] Girdlestone adds that the writers were not acted upon mechanically; there was room left for much that was natural and personal.[3]

W. E. Vine in like manner defends the Bible as an inspired Book. The contents of the Bible, he argues, have proved their inspiration, by their power to probe the conscience, to penetrate to the inmost depths of the soul, and to appeal from every page to the heart of men. Vine underlines the fact of the human element in the process and insists that in inspiration 'God raised His human agents into co-operation with Himself, not excluding the natural factor, but developing and expanding their faculties'.[4] The evidences that God in no way set aside the human in the activity of His inspiring are abundant. The writers of the Bible were clearly men of like passions with ourselves. At the same time, 'the Divine and human are combined in the Scripture records, that is to say, that they were neither mere machinists nor solely responsible for what they wrote'.[5] Vine is, of course, assured that the only valid inspiration is that which relates to the words. 'The Inspiration of Scripture is the Inspiration of its words, and the words themselves must be taken to express its real intention.'[6] He believes, too, that this assures accuracy.[7] Vine seeks authority for this understanding

[1] R. B. Girdlestone, *The Building up of the Old Testament*, 1912, Excursus on Inspiration, p. 306.
[2] *Ibid.*, p. 310. Cf. Article 20 of the Thirty-Nine Articles of the Church of England. [3] *Ibid.*
[4] W. E. Vine, *The Divine Inspiration of the Bible*, 1923, p. 18.
[5] *Ibid.*, p. 19. [6] *Ibid.*, p. 23. [7] *Ibid.*; cf. pp. 30 and 69 f.

of inspiration in the testimony of Christ. He endorsed the Old Testament and gave testimony to the inspiration of its words.[1] Passage after passage from both Testaments are adduced to show the emphasis which is placed upon their words. The book concluded with a section in which 'Some Objections' are considered. Questions relating to moral, scientific, and historical problems are dealt with. Problems, as for example, 'How can wrong utterances be inspired?' have not been avoided. This particular query is answered by stating that such statements as the mistaken utterance of Job's friends, the falsehoods told by Peter in his denial of the Lord, the speech of the town clerk in Ephesus, the oration of Tertullus, and the like 'were certainly not inspired in the lips of those who made them, but the records of their words by the writers of Scripture are inspired, and that these records are faithful and accurate has not been disproved'.[2]

Conservative writers, then, are agreed that inspiration is not something done *on* man, nor yet is it merely something done *in* man. They wish to focus attention on the writings themselves: and thus they see the Scriptures as something done by man and for man: yet as something done so decisively by God that the result of their work is rightly to be designated the Word of God. They see little value in probing the psychical reactions of a prophet to whom the word of the Lord came. Their interest is in the word which has come. 'When we speak of the *Scriptures*', F. F. Bruce declares, 'we use a word which etymologically denotes the writing and not the material.'[3] Without writing, he adds, there would be no Bible at all 'for the Bible is God's Word *written*'. Basil F. C. Atkinson, too, insists upon the doctrine of an infallible and inspired book. The Bible is, he maintains, an inspired volume. It is the result of the Holy Ghost's action. 'His inspiring work had not only the negative side of preserving them from error as they directed their thoughts to their books and wrote them. Greater still was His positive work of bringing to bear through their varied minds, the message that God intended to deliver to men.'[4] Atkinson compares the union of the human in inspiration with the human in our Lord's nature and concludes

---

[1] W. E. Vine, *The Divine Inspiration of the Bible*, 1923, pp. 32 ff., esp. p. 38 f.
[2] *Ibid.*, p. 110.
[3] F. F. Bruce, *The Books and the Parchments*, 1950, p. 15 (italics in original).
[4] Basil F. C. Atkinson, *The Christian Use of the Old Testament*, 1952, p. 12.

that just as Christ was sinless so, too, must be the Bible.[1] The Old Testament, he urges, stakes a claim to be inspired and authoritative and this claim is vindicated by our Lord Himself and the writers of the New Testament. He would maintain 'the highest view of inspiration. because such only, he believes, is consistent with the facts.

We can reach a conclusion of this investigation with a reference to a slender but scholarly booklet by T. C. Hammond. In it Hammond rejects, equally with those whose works have concerned us in this section, the mechanical view of inspiration. Had God proposed to deliver to us a mechanical message, he suggests, he would most certainly have chosen mechanical means. 'If man can teach a parrot to talk, and produce the sounds of the human voice on a revolving disc, God, it is to be assumed, could deliver a message of mere words, without soul or mind behind them.'[2] But God did not choose to do this. He spoke through men. 'The Divine message was formulated under the guidance of God in those conditions which are incidental to the development of human thought.'[3] The Divine influence did not nullify human peculiarities. Hammond, however, insists that inspiration is essentially verbal. We have an inspired Scripture. Thoughts without words, ideas without language, have no significance for others. 'If all God's teachers had heard only unspeakable words, there would be no Bible.'[4] Therefore, concludes Hammond, it is not accurate to say, as is popularly said, that 'the men indeed were inspired but not their utterances'.[5] Hammond is in agreement with Orr and Girdlestone as to the general veracity of what has been preserved. 'The message of God has been preserved in verbal form with substantial accuracy.'[6] It is in this way that Hammond regards the various accounts of our Lord's words. The evangelists were directed to record the words as they heard them or as they had come to them. They were not 'newspaper verbatim reporters'.[7]

---

[1] Basil F. C. Atkinson, *The Christian Use of the Old Testament*, 1952, p. 11 f. Cf. 'How was this inspiration brought about? We cannot exactly tell, just as we cannot exactly tell how the Lord Jesus Christ became a man except that it was by the operation of the Holy Spirit'. Basil F. C. Atkinson, *Is the Bible True?* 1933, third edition, 1934, p. 20.

[2] T. C. Hammond, *Inspiration and Authority*, 1935, Inter-Varisity Papers, No. 3, p. 23. [3] *Ibid*. [4] *Ibid*., p. 17.

[5] *Ibid*. [6] *Ibid*., p. 37. [7] *Ibid*., pp. 35–6.

An understanding of the position contended for by conservative writers has now been reviewed. It was emphasized thoughout that inspiration is not simply a subjective phenomenon, not merely the stirring of the inner life of a legislator, a preacher, a poet, a prophet or an apostle. The significance of inspiration lies in its result—in a Book which gives to men in human language the message of God. In a very real sense the claim is made that the words of the Bible are the words which the Holy Ghost taught men to speak from God.

It should be pointed out, however, that there were writers who tended to overstate their case and consequently gave some justification to those who credited the traditionalists with a mechanical theory of inspiration. This undue emphasis upon the action of God, which gave the impression of virtually obliterating the human agents of inspiration, can be seen in three important volumes of our period. C. Wordsworth, in his book on the subject, does at times make statements, which seem to border on the idea of a mechanical dictation, although he seeks to correct this conclusion by urging that the writers were spontaneous and free and that the human element had its genuine place in the process.[1]

L. Gaussen's book translated into English by David Scott in 1863 exercised a profound influence. Gaussen states boldly that 'the miraculous operation of the Holy Ghost had not the sacred writers themselves as the object . . . but that the objects were the holy books themselves'.[2] Taken by itself such an utterance could be, and indeed was, misunderstood. It was concluded by some that he regarded the writers as machines. Yet strongly as Gaussen expresses himself, it is but justice to observe that he does admit the interplay, in the process of inspiration, of the human personality.[3]

Constant reference is made to the famous sermon preached by J. W. Burgon at Oxford in 1860, which Alan Richardson wrongly quotes as a classical statement of 'Fundamentalism'. 'The Bible is none other than the *voice of Him that sitteth upon the Throne!* Every book of it, every chapter of it, every verse of it, every word of it, every syllable of it (where are we to stop?),

---

[1] C. Wordsworth, *The Inspiration of the Bible*, 1861, p. 5.
[2] L. Gaussen, *Theopneustia: The Plenary Inspiration of the Holy Scriptures* (trans. David Scott, 1863), p. 24; cf. p. 281.   [3] *Ibid.*; cf. pp. 38 ff.

every letter of it, is the direct utterance of the Most High! *Pasa graphe theopneustos.*[1] Such a statement has been much used by those who see verbal inspiration to be one and the same with a mechanical process. Perhaps the passage has not been fairly used, since as J. I. Packer justly points out, 'This is nothing more than a rhetorical affirmation of the divine origin of all Scripture. Burgon is affirming the fact of inspiration; he is not discussing the mode of it, and the passage contains not a word to suggest that dictation was the method whereby Scripture was given'.[2] In actual fact, Burgon later explicitly repudiates the mechanical theory and admits quite frankly that the method of inspiration is one of the many things he cannot understand.[3]

We would ourselves want to insist that there must be in any acceptable and sufficient account of inspiration, adequate emphasis given to the double aspect: the Divine and the human; the outward and the inward; the Spirit and the letter. It is, indeed, in the combination of these that the very essence of the process consists. The relation between the Divine and the human is not easy to comprehend, but it is a fact to which all genuine Christian experience bears abundant witness. Of the possibility, indeed, of the reality of such a combination the believing man has his own certain awareness. And the combination of the Divine and the human in inspiration is a special instance of this interplay for a particular spiritual purpose.

Men of faith will not regard it as something impossible with God who is Lord of all life, for the fulfilment of His plan of grace, to deal thus with chosen men for the sake of humanity. 'To enlarge or inform any faculty is evidently a secondary operation of the same power by which it was first given and quickened.'[4] This does not mean that the human faculties of the selected messengers do not act according to their natural laws even though they are supernaturally strengthened. The man is not converted into a machine, even in the hand of God. It is in that required union of the Divine and the human that the message of God is given. But to be complete the message must find its fulfilment in language. Without it the mysteries unveiled

---

[1] J. W. Burgon, *Inspiration and Interpretation*, reprint, 1905, p. 86.
[2] J. I. Packer, *'Fundamentalism' and the Word of God*, 1958, p. 180.
[3] Cf. J. W. Burgon, *Inspiration and Interpretation*, 1905, reprint, pp. 122 ff.
[4] B. F. Wescott, *Introduction to the Study of the Gospels*, 1882, p. 36.

before the eyes of the seer would remain confused shadows, but with it they become permanent and authoritative for human life. When addressed to the man, the human element becomes a part of the Divine message, since the Divine message can be grasped only when defined and moulded according to the laws of his own nature. This means, quite emphatically, that the Book is rightly said to be inspired no less than the prophet. The Book will, of course, reflect and perpetuate the peculiar idiosyncrasies of each prophet but it does not create them. The prophet is not merely a man who sees, he is one who sees and speaks what he sees: he is in a profound sense a speaking man. He *is* his language: 'between being and the word there does exist an irrefragable unity', says Gabriel Marcel. Elsewhere we have drawn attention to a distinction which may be made between 'use-language' and 'being-language'. It is 'being-language' which is declarative and convictive. 'Ultimately we are what we say. The prophets were men who spake from God. And it was their speech which betrayed them, which showed them to be God's men. There is a very vital relationship between the person and the word. Nowhere is this unity seen so effectively and so significantly as in the One of Whom it is declared that He is the Word made flesh. In Him there is no disharmony between language and life. Here the language-of-being is the Divine Word in human form —truly Divine and truly human. In Him the "I am" and the "I utter" are one and the same. Here is *Homo Confessor* and *Deus Loquens*.'[1]

In the Scriptures we have not just what the prophets thought, but we have the declarative and the convictive language of what was given them from above. Unless this is so there is an end of all certainty. The writing does not introduce any limitation into the representation which does not belong to the first conception and expression of it. For man the purely spiritual and absolute is but a vague thing—a dream perchance. It is language which is the condition of our being, the determining factor and the essential medium of ideas which are divine in their origin. In the process of Biblical inspiration, then, there is combined harmoniously the two factors, the Divine ideas and the human language. 'Each element performs its perfect work. . . . The

[1] H. D. McDonald, 'Is Speech the Key to the Riddle of Man? Language as Tool and Mirror', *The Baptist Times*, October 6, 1960.

letter becomes as perfect as the spirit; and it may well seem that the image of the Incarnation is reflected in the Christian Scriptures, which, as I believe, exhibit the human and the divine in the highest form, and in the most perfect union.'[1]

[1] B. F. Wescott, *Introduction to the Study of the Gospels*, 1882, p. 41.

CHAPTER EIGHT

The Problem of Biblical Authority

The conflict over the Bible initiated by the higher criticism made inevitable a discussion of the precise nature of its authority. If the inerrancy of the record and the inspiration of the words are renounced, then what is to be made of its infallibility? The question must be faced, In what ways and in what words can its authority be expressed? Such was to become and to continue the central problem of the discussion of the subject of revelation. 'Nothing is more remarkable', it was stated in an article in an issue of the *Speaker* for the year 1891, 'than the ubiquity of the question as to criticism and the authority of the Scriptures.'[1]

For centuries the authority of the Bible had remained secure in the Church. There had been, indeed, attacks made on it from without, by sceptic and deist; but it had held its place of supremacy. Even from within there had been movements, such as those which can be classed under the general heading of Enthusiasm, which tended to undermine the objective authority of the Bible and enthrone in its place an individual subjectivism,[2] but even these movements did not greatly affect the general estimation of the Bible as fully and finally the external truth of God to man, and for man.

But the first and fundamental result of criticism was to shift the emphasis from the external to the internal and to set up the claim that the principle of authority was to be sought within, not without. It was maintained that this subjective emphasis was the outcome of the Reformers' position. This is, perhaps, too bold a claim. Luther to begin with certainly envisaged the problem of authority in terms of the supremacy of Scripture. Luther had

---

[1] 'The Churches and the Scriptures', *Speaker*, iii, 1891, pp. 724–5.
[2] H. D. McDonald, *Ideas of Revelation*, 1959, Chapter IV.

discovered the Bible through his own profound religious experience. But it soon became evident that it did not in all points tally with his experience. This led Luther to seek for the 'Bible within the Bible'. Concerning the New Testament, in particular, he asked, What is the Word of God? and gives for his answer that that is the Word of God which preaches Christ. It was statements such as this, which made Sabatier enter the claim that Luther 'moved the seat of authority from the Church to the Christian consciousness'. But R. E. Davies in his study of the matter has convincingly shown that this is not an accurate account of the case. He grants that it was the *tendency* of Luther's teaching, but it certainly was not his purpose. For Luther, the Word of God as religiously defined continued to be regarded as an external infallible authority.[1]

John Oman seems ready to admit another origin for the subjective emphasis. He refers to the parallel movement of the Reformation, the Renaissance, and contends that 'Its distinctive work was the conscious rejection of all external, authoritative infallibilities'.[2] It was the Aufklärung which renounced all objective authority and gave supremacy to the subjective. Revelation is not to be conceived as something *ab extra*, something standing, so to say, over against the individual. Revelation is the movement of God within, and such a revelation is its own sufficient authority. To seek an external infallibility is to seek what does not exist: indeed, declares Oman 'all infallibilities presuppose an idea of grace mechanically irresistible'.[3]

Without however pursuing this matter further it will have become evident that criticism did shift the locus of authority

---

[1] Cf. R. E. Davies, *The Problem of Authority in the Continental Reformers*, 1946, p. 39 f. Cf. G. H. Hospers, *The Reformed Principle of Authority*, 1924; P. L. Lehmann, 'The Reformers' Use of the Bible', *Theology Today*, Vol. 3, pp. 328–44, October 1946; A. M. Renwich, 'The Authority of the Bible, "The Attitude of the Reformers" ', *The Evangelical Quarterly*, Vol. 19, pp. 110–26.

Cf. the following quotation from Luther's Lectures on the Psalms, 1513–15. 'What pasture is to the beast, the nest for the birds, the stream for fish, the Scriptures are for believing souls. . . . They give everything the soul needs, and it is to tempt God, if anyone will not be satisfied with the Scriptures . . . God's will is completely contained therein; so nothing should be presented which is not confirmed of both Testaments and agrees with them. It cannot be otherwise, for the Scriptures are divine; and in them God speaks and they are His Word.'

[2] John Oman, *Grace and Personality*, 1925, second revision, pp. 3–4. Cf. A. Lecerf, *An Introduction to Reformed Dogmatics*, 1949, pp. 99 ff.

[3] *Ibid.*, p. 14.

from without to within. C. J. Cadoux notes the significance of what he calls the 'critical victory' in the areas of Christian morals, devotion, and especially theology. Although not always realized, he observes, its result was to give tacit recognition to the ultimate authority of the subjective powers conferred on man by God. Here is the sovereignty, by which all is to be tested. There is no need to hanker after objective authority. The claim of liberal theology, he says, rests upon 'the legitimacy of the inner light'. 'What ground is there for positing Revelation in any writing other than the fact that we find inspiration in it?' he asks.[1] The ultimate is the inward and here authority is to be discovered.

Cadoux may be stating the case in too extreme a way for the period in which he wrote, since there appears to be more readiness recently to give an external significance to the Bible than was the case in earlier days. The immediate reaction to criticism seems to have been to discard the objective authority of Scripture altogether. 'It is a sign of conservatism', was the verdict, 'not to believe in the authority of Scripture at all.'[2]

Criticism had forced some to accept the new estimate of the biblical records. And in this context our Lord's conception of the Bible was valuated. Was it possible any longer, it was seriously asked, to credit any authority to this patchwork volume? The Bible is a record of revelation, and authority really belongs to the revelation, not to the record. So it came about that the problem opened out into the wider question of where the seat and source of religious authority are to be found. If religion is to be allowed as an authentic experience, if it is to be seen as other than a paralyzing neurosis, a hollow illusion, or even a valuable emotion, then it must be asked, Wherein lies its authority? The problem of revelation is, indeed, the dominant one in contemporary religious thought. But with the wider

[1] C. J. Cadoux, 'Scripture and Theology', *The Congregational Quarterly*, Vol. 25, January 1947, p. 26. Cf. his *A Case for Evangelical Modernism*, A Study in the Relation between Christian Faith and Traditional Theology, 1938, in which the position is given a more elaborate statement.

[2] *Expository Times*, Vol. IX, 1897–8, p. 481. Cf. 'One of the most earnestly debated questions of our day is Authority. The feeling is that old authorities—especially of the Church and the Bible—are no longer authoritative. And there are those who assert that no authority whatever is left.' *Expository Times*, Vol. XXIV, 1912–13, p. 517 (comment on E. Y. Mullins's *Freedom and Authority in Religion*, 1913).

issues concerning its meaning and media goes the more fundamental, if narrower one, of authority. Indeed, as H. Wheeler
Robinson has said, the discussion of the principle of authority
is 'the nodal point, since authority must always be characteristic
of the Christian revelation'.[1]

At the present our concern is with the special subject of the
authority which is to be allowed to the Bible since it is agreed
by all that it has some connection with the Christian revelation.
To those who sought authority within, the Bible was conceived
to be, to begin with, a record of the insights of religious men. It
was their insights into, and experience of God's saving acts in
history, which are of ultimate significance for us. The Bible is the
self-authenticating record of such experiences; thus, it was
declared, its authority lies 'in the reality of the experiences of
men who stood in situations like our own'.[2] As time went on,
however, the individual's own personal experience was taken
into account as a vital factor, and the Bible was credited with
authority in so far as it authenticated itself in the inner spiritual
life of the one who makes the personal response of faith to God's
saving acts in history. But, in whichever way the position was
stated, there was virtually a rejection of the Bible as an outside
infallible standard: 'the authority with which the Bible comes to
us' says R. H. Lightfoot, 'can no longer be wholly or primarily
external'.[3]

Those who maintained that the Bible was an inspired Book,
it will be understood, insisted that it must, on that account, be
accepted as an infallible guide and an authoritative Scripture.
The position, then, on the question of the authority of the Bible
will be seen to follow the same pattern which we observed with
regard to inspiration. There is, on the other hand, the focus
within, and, on the other hand, the focus without. Some contend
that real authority is to be found in the experience of which the
Scriptures bear witness, and that whatever authority belongs to
the Bible derives from that experience. Others are just as
emphatic that the Bible holds its authority apart from
experience.

[1] H. Wheeler Robinson, 'The Principle of Authority in the Christian Religion'.
Ernest A. Payne, *Henry Wheeler Robinson*, 1946, p. 170.

[2] J. M. Graham, 'After Fifty Years', *Expository Times*, Vol. I, 1938–9, p. 539.

[3] *The Interpretation of the Bible* (ed. C. W. Dugmore), 1944, p. 90. Cf. A. Peel
in same, p. 52.

Something by way of detail concerning these two opposed views must now be given.

A. THE AUTHORITY OF THE BIBLE
BASED UPON EXPERIENCE

A beginning here may be made by noting how definitely some writers have maintained that spiritual experience is the sole and sufficient ground of religious authority. H. Hensley Henson, in his volume *The Value of the Bible*, sees this value as so founded. If we are Christians in fact as well as in name, he says, 'we, no less than the writers of the New Testament build the fabric of belief on the foundation of experience'. The new scholarship has brought us 'to understand that the Bible has been extensively misconceived by the Church, and we are not a little embarrassed by the fact that the place which the Bible holds in the system and custom of the Church was determined to no small extent, by that misconception'.[1] Henson refers to what he calls an 'inner certitude' which exempts us from 'fear from the most searching criticism of the historical memorials of our Master's life'. Authority is something within; indeed, he informs us, 'A faith which is based upon external authority, whether of miracles, or of the Church, or the senses, is in itself a poor thing'.[2] Although in this particular passage the Bible is not included, it is his position that external authority no more belongs to it than to the other items mentioned, since, as he quotes Coleridge to express his view, 'Faith is subjective'.[3]

The phrase, 'inner certitude' used by Henson, is a significant one and may be taken as the key to the whole position. R. H. Strachan boldly declared for the ultimacy of this 'inner certitude' in his book, *The Authority of Religious Experience*, being the Alexander Robinson Trust Lectures of the University of Glasgow for the year 1929. Strachan places authority squarely on the individual Christian conscience. He does however seek to safeguard his subjectivism from the vagaries and vagueness to

---

[1] H. Hensley Henson, *The Value of the Bible and other Sermons*, 1902–4, with a Letter to the Lord Bishop of London, 1904, p. 26.

[2] *Ibid.*, p. 196.

[3] *Ibid.*, p. 197. Note Henson's quotation of the passage from Coleridge, which refers to the Bible revealing its authority by the way its words 'find me at greater depths of my being' than any other book (pp. 33–4).

which unrestricted individualism is prone. He thus gives some respect to the religious community and to historical revelation. He is, however, sceptical about reliance upon any mere external authority, whether it be that of the Bible or the Church. A reading of the volume will show that when once the idea of the individual's religious consciousness is taken as the key to the problem of authority, it is difficult to keep out of the abyss of subjectivism. Strachan does indeed recognize that the historical side of Christianity is a datum preceding individual experience which the experience itself does not create, but has to accept and interpret. This fact, however, admitted on one page is actually contradicted on another.

In a similar way, Sidney Cave in his *Doctrine of the Christian Faith* (1931) stresses the experience of the gospel as the way to an understanding of Scripture. Religion is essentially a matter of experience, he argues. 'God has not willed', it is declared, 'to give to men a book of indubitable facts and clearly formulated teachings. A religion based upon an infallible handbook of religion and ethics would be a religion, static and legalistic. Christianity is not founded on a book, but on a personal revelation of the living God.' The Bible is to be regarded as the classic record of religious experience and authenticates itself as a 'true' witness, by the Spirit in believing hearts.

Two interesting statements of the inward nature of authority are worthy of mention. The one comes in a religious biography and the other in a paper delivered before a Church group. The first concerns the story of the life and experiences of Charles Hargrove by L. P. Jacks and is entitled *From Authority to Freedom* (1920). Hargrove had been, in his early life, a member of the Brethren and had accepted the authority of an infallible Bible. He later seceded to the Roman Church and submitted to its authority. But soon he became dissatisfied with this external authority. Thereupon he became a Unitarian and accepted the invitation to the pastorate of a congregation in Leeds. He found what authority he needed within his own 'enlightened' soul. Here is discovered the religion of the spirit in contrast with the religions of authority. Man is 'left to the guidance of his own conscience and the stars', he declared. It is noteworthy, however, that Hargrove in stating his position makes no reference to the Holy Spirit; and for that matter neither does his biographer.

In a paper on 'Authority in Religion' read at the Modern Churchmen's Congress, July 1949, W. R. Inge stated that Paul must be regarded as the founder of Christian mysticism. As he develops his thesis he virtually dismisses the Bible and the Church as unworthy of consideration. Reason likewise cannot be taken as the ground of authority. 'How can we pray to a mathematical God?' he asks. The centre of gravity has shifted, he urges, 'from external authority to inward experience' and he thinks rightly. 'My conviction is', he adds, 'that this inner authority is strong enough to take the place of those external authorities which, as perhaps most of you will agree with me, have lost most of their cogency.'[1]

This subjective approach to the problem of authority may be illustrated in the works of a number of writers over our period. John Clifford, having freely acknowledged 'errors and mistakes' in the Bible, raises the question, What and where, then, is its authority? His answer broadly is that the authority of the Bible lies in the elevation and universality of its religious ideas, and in the experience of Christ through which these ideas are vivified, applied and used. He makes reference to several kinds of authority and concludes that mere external and mechanical authority is less significant than that which operates between persons. The authority of the Bible is that of truth, wherein the witness is within ourselves.[2] But ultimately Christ is the Truth; consequently, 'the authority of the Bible is the authority of Jesus'. This means that 'the authority is personal rather than literary'.[3] Secondary authorities, such as Christian preachers and the Church, do exist, but these must not be elevated into the position of absolutes. Yet 'the crowning certainty is secured through these forces by the work of God in the spirit of man'.[4]

---

[1] W. R. Inge, 'Authority in Religion', Paper read at Modern Churchmen's Congress, July 1949. Cf. his earlier *Authority and the Inner Light*, Liverpool Diocesan Lecture, 1912. See also his Introduction to his *Everyman's Bible, An Anthology*. Here Inge asks, How is the will of God communicated? He suggests three possible ways: the Church, the Holy Scriptures and the Inner Light. He seems to desire a blend of the three but adds, that 'in the interpretation of the inspired books we have to depend on the inner light, on the wisdom which is from above'. W. R. Inge, *Everyman's Bible, An Anthology—Arranged with an Introduction*, 1931, p. xxv.

[2] John Clifford, *The Inspiration and Authority of the Bible*, third edition, 1899, pp. 83–4.   [3] *Ibid.*, p. 85.

[4] *Ibid.*, p. 89.

Robertson Smith had argued for this idea of biblical authority. 'The persuasion that in the Bible, God Himself speaks of love and life to the soul is the essence of the Christian conviction of the truth and authority of the Scripture', he had stated. It is the personal assurance of the Spirit bearing witness with our spirit, which is the source of individual certainty and which lifts faith out of the region of probable evidence and into the sphere of divine confidence. This statement of the case for the authority of the Bible was given more elaborate exposition by following writers.

H. Wheeler Robinson relates how in his own experience he came to a period when the idea of the Bible as a book of objective infallible truths failed to satisfy the needs of his soul.[1] In the title of his book *The Christian Experience of the Holy Spirit*, we have a succinct statement of his concept of religious authority. He sees in this 'neglected doctrine' the key to the understanding of the place of the Bible. He refers to what he calls a 'kenosis' of the Spirit in a passage in which he contends 'that we can have no properly theological doctrine of fellowship with Christ without full recognition of the doctrine of the Holy Spirit, involving Christian experience. Within that experience, our knowledge of Christ will be conditioned by our growth in grace; historical objectivity has to be partly surrendered to secure vitality, and there is a *kenosis* of the Spirit as well as of the Son'.[2]

In a series of articles under the general title *Things Most Surely Believed*, to which he with others contributed, he makes the point that the reality of moral authority, however mediated, lies in our being 'possessed'. 'The authority of the gospel always operates through the value-judgement of the individual believer. That authority rests on the intrinsic worth of the revelation of God in Christ.'[3] He returns again to the same idea in his article on 'Canonicity and Inspiration'. Having argued against the absoluteness of the *consensus ecclesiae* in reference to the formation of the Canon, he states that it 'cannot be objectivied and

---

[1] H. Wheeler Robinson, *The Christian Experience of the Holy Spirit*, 1928, p. 4. Cf. Ernest E. Payne, *Henry Wheeler Robinson*, 1946, pp. 56–7.

[2] H. Wheeler Robinson, *The Principle of Authority in the Christian Religion* Ernest E. Payne, *Henry Wheeler Robinson*, p. 177.

[3] H. Wheeler Robinson, *Things Most Surely Believed*, ii, *Expository Times*, Vol. XLVI, 1934–5, p. 55. See also H. R. Mackintosh under same title, vi, *op. cit.*, p. 246 f. Cf. F. R. Barry, *The Relevance of Christianity*, 1931, p. 142.

isolated in any external and material object'. Reference is made once again to the authentication within experience of the Books of the Bible as witnessed by the individual's own response to their message under the guidance of the Spirit. 'The authority of Scripture', it is then concluded, 'needs no testimony from man, because it rests on the testimony of the Holy Spirit Himself confirming His truth without by the creation of an echoing truth within.'[1]

The subject of authority was an important and recurring one for Wheeler Robinson. It could not be lightly dismissed, since he regarded it as the most urgent, as well as the final issue of the Church. He insisted that 'confusion on the question of authority means a partial paralysis of energy, a lack of conviction in utterance, even of doubt whether some other type of Church (he was in this instance addressing a company of Baptist Ministers) with a more plausible emphasis on apparently external and objective authority, might not be a better basis for preaching and worship and pastoral oversight'.[2]

There is no vital difference, he contends, among Christians about the source and the content of revelation. The real problem concerns its media. Robinson refers to three ways in which revelation may be said to be mediated. First, the historical—the tradition of events, which are interpreted as the mighty acts of God; and so interpreted, become Christian facts and the foundation of faith. Then the social or corporate organization of the Church, which, whatever else it is, is obviously a form of society made inevitable because of the inherent sociality of man. And, thirdly, of course, the individual, because every form of Christian faith must demand some kind of personal response. It is the reality of this personal experience, which can be revised and enlarged by contact with other experiences which delivers revelation, and consequently authority, from being merely subjective. In this way, 'The revelation, and therefore the authority, is both subjective and objective, and necessarily so'.[3] It is, he argues, only as the events of history are interpreted by faith that they become facts and factors for revelation. Like

---

[1] H. Wheeler Robinson, *Canonicity and Inspiration, Expository Times*, Vol. XLVII, 1935–6, p. 123.

[2] H. Wheeler Robinson, *The Principle of Authority in the Christian Religion*, Ernest A. Payne, *Henry Wheeler Robinson*, 1946, p. 125.

[3] Ernest A. Payne, *Henry Wheeler Robinson*, 1946, p. 178.

William Temple, Wheeler Robinson sees revelation as the product of event and interpretation, as an interfusion of history and meaning. Thus may the authority of Christian experience be regarded as, at the same time, both subjective and objective; and it is in this 'duality lies its continued vitality', he says.[1] Ultimately, however, the emphasis is put upon the subjective, since it is the Spirit within as 'the active partner and director' which is finally authoritative. In this context the Bible (and the Church) will be understood. They will be reverenced as 'subordinate authorities' by which the events of history become interpreted to us.[2] Both the Bible and the Church are 'secondary and delegated authorities in religion'. It is in 'the prophetic consciousness and its continuance in personal religion that there is found the ultimate sanctuary, in which the voice of God is still heard, the sanctuary in which the ancient Scriptures are still transformed into living oracles'.[3]

We have made particular reference to Wheeler Robinson's teaching at this point, because he was the dominant figure of the period on this side. He was, indeed, as Alexander McLaren is reported to have drily remarked, 'an able man And he knows it!'[4] There were, as we shall see, those before him who stated the same ideas, but they did not, and probably could not, do so with the same clarity of style and the same profundity of scholarship as were his. Others followed and took their cue from him, but in many cases they were mere echoes of the Oxford teacher. Wheeler Robinson was in fact the powerful spokesman of the thesis that the authority of the Bible gets its effect from the religious experience of the Spirit.

It remains, however, a fact that the uncertainty which was evident with regard to the authority of the Bible before Wheeler Robinson had written was not magically removed by what he had to say. While the question of inspiration was the immediate issue resulting from the controversy initiated by the higher criticism, it is the subject of authority which was destined to gather momentum, and to become, during the last three decades,

[1] H. Wheeler Robinson, *Inspiration and Revelation in the Old Testament*, 1938, p. 198. Cf. his 'The Bible and Protestantism', *Congregational Quarterly*, Vol. 16, January 1938, pp. 40–50, esp. p. 47.
[2] Ernest A. Payne, *Henry Wheeler Robinson*, 1946, p. 179.
[3] H. Wheeler Robinson, *Inspiration and Revelation in the Old Testament*, p. 198
[4] Ernest A. Payne, *Henry Wheeler Robinson*, p. 56.

the most pressing, as well as the most perplexing, of theological problems. When, in the year 1951, Alan Richardson and W. Schweitzer edited the volume *Biblical Authority for Today*, the appropriate comment was made in the *Expository Times*: 'There is no more important subject at the present than the Nature of Biblical Authority'.[1] But while all those to whom we are making reference agreed that the 'old' doctrine of the Bible as an external authority could no longer commend itself, and that, therefore, the focus must be within, there was no real agreement as to the precise way the 'new' doctrine was to be stated.

This fact may be illustrated by drawing attention to two Church conferences which met within a couple of years of each other towards the end of the nineteen-twenties. In 1927 there was the Oxford Conference in which Congregationalists dealt with the subject 'The Christian Faith in the Light of Modern Science and Criticism'. An examination of the papers read at this conference will reveal that the urgent concern was with the problem of authority. R. F. Horton posed the question, 'What are we Congregationalists to present as our authority?' Certainly neither an infallible Church nor an infallible Bible, he replies. Yet to rest on the idea of the self-authenticating significance of truth is not satisfactory, since this involves the further question, What is truth and how are we to distinguish it from error? It is not enough, either, to state that our authority is Christ *qua* Christ. The answer must be Christ is the authority because He is the Truth. Christ must be; but why? and, how? To these inquiries there is no answer given. Nathaniel Micklem took the same line. 'In religion as a whole', he declares, 'there is no infallible authority except Christ Himself.' But still all is not clear. Micklem later states that 'Our authority is our personal consent to the faith of the Church as it comes to us through the Christian community and is for us corroborated in the Gospels'.[2]

The sheer fact appears to have been that there was a prevailing uncertainty as to what is the foundation upon which faith was

[1] *Expository Times*, Vol. LXIII, 1951–2, p. 97.

[2] Cf. *The Congregational Quarterly*, Vol. V, 1927. In 1928 the Congregationalists returned once again to a discussion of the subject 'Authority'. Note two papers read at a later Oxford Conference in 1934: R. S. Birch on 'The Holy Spirit and Individual Experience', and N. Micklem on 'The Holy Spirit and the New Creed', *The Congregational Quarterly*, Vol. 12, 1934, pp. 510 f. and 545 f. Cf. also G. B. Storr, 'The Final Authority in Conduct', *The Congregational Quarterly*, Vol. 18, 1940, p. 283 f. The 'ultimate responsibility is with the individual' it is concluded (p. 289).

to take its stand. There was, indeed, evidence enough of a grim desire to stand on something if one could be sure what it was. But no one was quite sure.

About two years later the Sixteenth Annual Conference of Modern Churchmen was held at Cambridge and the subject discussed was 'Authority in Religion'.[1] These papers, too, show the same sort of hesitancy; the general tendency seems to be either to find authority in individual experience, or, with more assurance, in the community experience of the Church. Commenting on this Conference and on the fact that the Congregationalists had been 'twice already' concerned with the subject, the *Expository Times* remarked that 'on the showing of these papers (at Girton College, Cambridge) it may be hazarded that the modern Churchmen have not been much more successful'[2] in coming to a confident pronouncement respecting the seat of authority in religion.

As far back as 1891, W. T. Davidson, in his paper to the Wesleyan Ministers, had sought to establish the authority of the Bible upon faith in Christ and in doing so expressed dissatisfaction with the complete subjectivism contained in the famous dictum of Coleridge. 'In establishing its (i.e. the Bible's) authority', he says, 'we must go to the Lord Jesus Christ and make the doctrine of Scripture Christo-centric.' It is faith in Christ which gives authority to the Scriptures. 'For those who believe in Jesus Christ as the Son of God, there is an irremovable basis for the doctrine of Holy Scripture as a sufficient, complete, infallible guide in things pertaining to God, the sole authoritative rule of faith and practice.'[3]

In the same year V. H. Stanton wrote his book *The Place of Authority in Matters of Religious Belief*. He sought to escape from an excessive subjectivism by arguing that religious authority

---

[1] Cf. *The Modern Churchman*, October 1930.

[2] *Expository Times*, Vol. XLI, 1929–30, p. 97.

[3] T. W. Davidson, *Inspiration and Biblical Criticism, ad. loc.* In a chapter on 'Revelation and Authority' in *The Chief Corner-Stone, Essays Towards an Exposition of the Christian Faith for Today*—a symposium of which Davidson was the editor, says, 'Protestants should remember the rock whence they were hewn. The Bible is indeed "the religion of Protestants", but its authority is spiritually discerned, and the response to its appeal must be spiritual, given in the exercise of personal trust and personal activity of mind and conscience. No language can be too strong to describe the worth of the Bible as a spiritual guide' (p. 47).

arises out of a combination of the Church, the Bible and private judgement.

Actually a year earlier James Martineau's *magnum opus*, *The Seat of Authority in Religion* (1890), had appeared, but its critical position was so extreme that it was not received with general favour. Under the influence of Schleiermacher, Martineau maintained that authority belongs to the individual conscience. The Christian religion, he argued, has been false to its essential message by first crediting authority to the Church and after that to the Bible. Authority belongs to neither, but rather to the religious consciousness as that is stimulated and inspired by the challenge and example of Jesus.

To a book by a Frenchman may be attributed one of the most effective statements of authority as having its focus within. In 1900, Auguste Sabatier wrote his famous work, which was later translated into English under the revealing title, *The Religions of Authority and the Religion of the Spirit*. There is a profound difference to be noted between this volume of Sabatier's and that of the earlier Martineau, but there is agreement of emphasis with regard to the seat of authority within the quickened conscience. Sabatier rejected all external infallibilities although he is ready to grant that both the Bible and the Church may be regarded as possessing a relative and preparatory, as distinguished from an absolute and external authority. Sabatier did not feel it any stigma to be charged with opening the door to an 'unlimited subjectivity'. Indeed, in his Socratic dialogue with Adelphi, he brings the charge against himself and then seems to take special delight in his own condemnation. 'At last the great word is out, the scarecrow with which men think to reply to everything and ward off all dangers. We must avoid subjectivism, and for that reason we will not have a subjective criterion.' Then Sabatier asks, so as to call forth a negative reply, 'But can there be any other?'[1]

Almost immediately the idea of Sabatier was popularized by two influential scholars. We have already had occasion to refer to John Oman and to quote from his *Grace and Personality*. But it is in his *Vision and Authority* that this profound thinker sought to justify his thesis that authority is grounded on man's own

[1] Auguste Sabatier, *The Religions of Authority and the Religion of the Spirit*, 1900 (trans. L. E. Houghton), New York, 1904, p. 261.

conscience. All external authorities are of no use to the saving of man from the blight of fear and the burden of uncertainty. 'Every man's authority is within his own soul', he states.[1] An historical revelation there must be, but it is the inward vision and understanding of it which give it authority. Oman's book is a vigorous one and 'remains a spiritual and intellectual classic which cannot be neglected'.[2]

T. B. Strong in his *Authority in the Church* (1903) stresses the need for the subjective emphasis. All authorities must be personally accepted and individually appropriated. But Strong allows for the existence of a 'deposit of faith' which has normative value for the Church. It is, indeed, this deposit which provided an authoritative basis for the teaching ministry of the Church. Beyond this essential norm, there lies a wider area of inherited Church customs, some of which, like the two sacraments, are essentially binding, while others remain to us to be used or disused to suit need or taste.

In 1908, Edward Grubb published his *Authority and the Light Within*, in which, although he was critical of the Quaker position, yet comes out for an idea in general agreement with it. He sees authority as the opening of the inward eye to the light of Christ —the light which lighteth everyman coming into the world. He returns to the same emphasis in a pamphlet on *The Problem of Authority in Religion* (1911). In 1924 in his *Authority in Religion*, he omits his critical exposition of the Friends and goes on to assert in a positive way, 'Divine Authority is Inward Authority'. Grubb contends that when the word 'authority' is used it is generally taken to refer to something 'outward'.[3] He seeks instead an authority which 'compels us by its own inward force to acceptance of what presents itself to us as True, and Beautiful, and Good, is the Light Within of which the Mystics speak'.[4] Grubb seems in a closing chapter to equate the authority of the inner light with that of the *internum Spiritus sanctus*. He suggests that the Society of Friends shows the way to a real understanding of authority. 'That body' he observes, 'has tried to rest its whole Church polity on experience of Divine guidance,

[1] John Oman, *Vision and Authority*, 1902, p. 49.
[2] R. R. Williams, *Authority in the Apostolic Age*, 1950, Burrough Lectures at Leeds University, 1948, p. 118.
[3] Edward Grubb, *Authority in Religion*, 1924, p. 3.
[4] *Ibid.*, p. 4.

individual and collective, and, while maintaining this trust in the authority of the Spirit, it has kept together.'[1]

H. B. Swete, in his chapter in the *Cambridge Theological Essays*, stresses the religious significance of the Bible. He defines religion 'as the recognition on man's part of the bond which unites him to God'.[2] He then regards the Bible to be the witness to this assurance. It is his conviction that the value of the Bible is apprehended through its experiences of life and is 'proved by the experiences of the religious life'.[3]

In 1909, J. H. Leckie, in his *Authority in Religion*, strongly, urged that the question of authority is ultimately the question of conscience. Whatever is not of conscience is not of faith.

A. S. Peake made it clear that he regarded the older Protestant view of the Bible as an infallible authority as no longer tenable. The newer theory of Scripture, he contends, has not brought perplexity only but also the feeling of relief.[4] 'It is', he says, 'one of the infirmaities of human nature to desire an infallible authority.'[5] But with the rejection of the external infallibility of a Book, does this mean, he asks, that we are to seek God in our own soul. This leads him to discuss the significance of mysticism; but he finds it unsatisfactory since it gives exclusive emphasis to the emotions. Here 'feeling is private and dumb, and unable to give an account of itself, declines to justify them rationally, and on occasions is willing that they should pass for the paradoxical and absurd'.[6] Mysticism is open to the charge brought against it by William Temple of involving a 'scepticism of the instrument', denying, that is, the objectivity of value, thereby rendering 'all conviction impossible and all opinion temerarious'.[7] Mysticism, indeed, Peake sees 'weakens the rational and practical side of religion and inclines to substitute pantheistic absorption for spiritual communion'.[8]

---

[1] Edward Grubb, *Authority in Religion*, 1924, p. 112. Cf. G. K. Hibbert, *The Inner Light and Modern Thought*, The Swarthmore Lecture, 1924, in which sensitive appreciation of the authority of the 'inner light' is given in this tercentenary tribute to George Fox.

[2] H. B. Swete, Cambridge Theological Essays, *Essays on some Biblical Questions of the Day*, by members of the University of Cambridge (ed. H. B. Swete), 1909, p. 545.   [3] *Ibid.*, p. 556.

[4] A. S. Peake, *The Bible, Its Origin, Its Significance, Its Abiding Worth*, 1913, second edition, p. 447.   [5] *Ibid.*, p. 446.

[6] William James, *Varieties of Religious Experience*, 1902, sixteenth edition, 1909, p. 432.   [7] William Temple, *Nature, Man and God*, 1949, p. 255.

[8] George Galloway, *The Philosophy of Religion*, 1914, p. 161.

From a consideration of mysticism, Peake turns to investigate the claims of the Church to be an authoritative guide. It has, he argues, the merit of recognizing the collective consciousness and it must be welcomed as a corrective to the freelance spirit and self-assertive individualism in religion. 'Loyalty to the Church and enthusiasm for it are indispensable if we are to win for our religion the inward strength and outward victory for which we profess to be eager.'[1] But withal, the Church is not an infallible authority. The Bible belongs to the Church but this does not mean that it is to be conceived merely as the crystallized mind of the Church. Although the Church is responsible for the formation of the canon and its life is the presupposition of its writings, yet the collective consciousness is not expressed in them; it is guided by them. 'It was not the collective consciousness of Christians which guided Paul to pen his immortal expositions of fundamental Christian truth.'[2] Peake contends, however, that the Bible does become an objective standard because here we have stated the spiritual insight and experience of its writers. 'If the subjective illumination', he remarks, 'experienced by the saint is committed to writing or expressed in oral utterance, then the same kind of authority might be claimed for the outer expression as for the inward certainty.'[3] There may be a certain vagueness, he grants, in his thesis, but in the things which it most concerns us to know, the Bible carries 'its own witness within itself and is recognized by our inward faculty'.[4] Revelation must needs be verified within experience, limited though individual experience must be allowed to be. 'The individual', he argues, 'verifies the New Testament by the immediate response which it awakens within him.'[5] Herein indeed is the permanent value of the Scripture.[6] He then concludes with the remark: 'However high credentials may be they ought not to win assent unless they are ratified by experience. And this test also it satisfies. Not only did the theology take its rise in experience, but its truth is always being verified in new experience, and will, therefore, I believe, continue to be verified. Deep still calls to deep as his experience is answered in our own'.[7]

[1] A. S. Peake, *The Bible, Its Origin, Its Significance, Its Abiding Worth*, p. 457.
[2] *Ibid.*, p. 458.   [3] *Ibid.*, p. 459.   [4] *Ibid.*, p. 463.
[5] *Ibid.*, p. 476.   [6] *Ibid.*; cf. pp. 479 ff.   [7] *Ibid.*, p. 503.

It is almost an impertinence to put P. T. Forsyth's mighty volume *The Principle of Authority*—of the same date as Peake's —in the same context and to dismiss it in a few summary sentences. What are supposed today to be new theological 'insights' were commonplaces in the thought of this gifted writer. His book is the result of much reflection on the problem of authority in matters of faith and ethics. A few years before its appearance, Forsyth had given an indication of his views in two powerful addresses delivered when he was Chairman of the Congregational Union in 1905, under the suggestive titles 'A Holy Church, the Moral Guide of Society' and 'The Moral Authority of the Church'.

It would be altogether wrong to give the impression that Forsyth's rightful place is among those who seek authority within religious experience. He was, in fact, unhappy about looking within the shifting soul of the individual for such. 'An authority which has its source in ourselves', he says, 'is no authority. In us authority can have but its sphere and its echo, never its charter.'[1] Yet while Forsyth refuses to ground authority within, he does seek in a way with which we would ourselves agree, to emphasize the inward. It is, he contends, within the sphere of experience only that authority has its reality, however much he insists that the autonomy and finality of mere experience is an end of all authority. 'A real authority' he declares, 'is indeed *within* experience, but it is not the authority *of* experience, it is an authority *for* experience, it is an authority experienced.'[2] The ultimate authority is the grace of God as revealed in the gospel.[3] It is therefore something essentially redemptive and moral. The keynote of this ethical salvation experienced in the gospel of the holy God is appropriation, not verification.[4] 'The faith we are born into must become personal, and that is only done by its appropriation in a moral act or process. We do not take it on the strength of external

[1] P. T. Forsyth, *The Principle of Authority*, 1913, second edition, 1952, p. 299.
[2] *Ibid.*, p. 75. Cf. 'We do not believe things *because* of an experience, but we do *in* an experience. They are true not *by* experience, but *for* it. . . . Faith is a religious experience, but religious experience is not faith' (p. 27).
[3] Cf. 'The Authority of the Cross', A Paper of 1906 by Dr Robert Mackintosh with Annotations by P. T. Forsyth, *The Congregational Quarterly*, Vol. 21, 1943, July 1943, pp. 209 ff.
[4] P. T. Forsyth, *op. cit.*; cf. pp. 334 ff.

authority; i.e. the belief of others is no sufficient ground for ours at last, though it is an essential school.'[1] But the Bible has its moral authority for life. It is not the mere classic of the faith of 'eminent Christians'. The New Testament especially is not to be thought of as mainly made up of ideas which grew upon the apostles out of their personal faith, their private and tentative interpretation of their religiosity. The question to be asked about the Bible is, 'Have we here men's thoughts or God's Word?'[2] Forsyth declares that at the very heart of the Bible, so to speak, there is the final revelation of the gospel of God. In the Scriptures is laid down once and for all and once for all, the meaning of the Christian fact and the sole principle of positive faith, which the true Christian experience could only ripen and explicate but never outgrow. Herein is to be found the finality and autonomy of the Bible for faith. 'The Christian experience is not something we bring rationally to the Bible to test scriptural truth; it is something miraculously created in us by the Bible in response to divine power acting as grace; and it can therefore be in no collision with the authority which makes the Bible what it is, the authority of the Gospel, of the Redeemer felt and owned as Redeemer.'[3] So it comes about that Christian experience is the experience of the authority of the gospel; it is not an experience which becomes the authority for the gospel.

In his book, *The Theology of Experience* (1916), H. Maldwyn Hughes puts great stress upon the creative significance of religious experience as the ground of an 'inner certitude'. Experience is the fundamental necessity, he argues; yet the preacher cannot make his own experience the test and limit of truth. His experience is not real and effective independently of the Bible and the facts of history.

In his contribution, K. Fullerton makes immense claims for the modern reconstruction of the Bible and its bearing on authority. The subtitle 'A Study in the History of the Doctrine of the Inspiration of Scripture' gives a more exact statement of its content. Fullerton regards the subject of prophecy as having decisive significance in testing the old and the new view of Scripture. The predictive element in prophecy, he thinks, on the old view, is to be interpreted as 'the result of a direct revelation

[1] P. T. Forsyth, *The Congregational Quarterly*, Vol. 21, 1943, July 1943, p. 335.
[2] *Ibid.*, p. 333.   [3] *Ibid.*, pp. 333–4.

from heaven which was *psychologically unmediated*'.[1] Thus the whole process must be regarded as mechanical and the writers as passive agents, each of which is a 'calamus', a penman, an amanuensis of the Holy Spirit. He objects to such a view because it is non-moral in character.

The modern reassessment of the Bible has changed all this. The prophet 'receives his revelations and as a man he gives them'.[2] Prophecy is, he contends, virtually unconcerned with the predictive element: it seeks to understand 'the relationship of the Prophet to the Spiritual and Moral needs of his own day'. A typical example is the Book of Daniel—'the modern scholar asks what possible meaning there is in Daniel's prediction to the Jews of deliverance from the persecutions of Antiochus Epiphanes at a time when all they desired was to be delivered from the tyranny of Babylon. To compare small things with great, it is as if a dentist should undertake to comfort a patient suffering with a violent toothache by telling him that he would eventually recover from a far worse attack five years later.'[3]

The modern view, Fullerton believes, emphasizes the moral element by connecting it with the spiritual experience of the prophet through whom it was delivered, thus giving a moralized view of inspiration, and with the needs of the people to whom it was originally given so stressing a moralized function of prophecy. Fullerton would eliminate an emphasis on the supernatural. But he seeks to answer the question concerning the authority of the Bible. Its authority is that of the spiritual insights of its prophets. They were the great discoverers of truth. They read the signs of their own day and called for justice, truth and righteousness. They announced that goodness was sovereign and must prevail.

The whole thesis is shot through with the optimism characteristic of the immediate post-First World War period which was supposed to witness the establishment on earth of the Kingdom of God, all bright and fair: 'not the reign of a thousand years, but the *City of God*, a broad and beautiful city which shall gradually enlarge its gracious borders till they are one with the confines of the habitable earth. In the building of this city man joyfully co-operates with God because he has faith in its ultimate

[1] K. Fullerton, *Prophecy and Authority*, 1919, p. 191 (italics in original).
[2] *Ibid.*, pp. 191–2.   [3] *Ibid.*, p. 193.

completion, a city purified of sin and all injustice, a city crowned with the presence of the Lord, a city called into being not by the magic rub of an Aladdin's lamp, but by the moral efforts of the race, as they are guided and inspired by the Spirit of God'.[1] Fullerton's picture was indeed a glowing one and breathes hope and confidence in man. The only trouble is that man does not seem to have co-operated in the great way that was expected.

An exposition of the 'new view' of the authority of the Bible, which caused much controversy and concern comes in the article with which E. Griffith-Jones opened Peake's *Commentary on the Bible*. Our own observation would want to be, 'Alas master, for it was borrowed!' There is no doubt that much of what is said is drawn from Garvie and Peake. After the assurance that the Bible 'brings man near to God' and, 'God home to man', Griffith-Jones proceeds to the usual criticism of the 'old view' of inspiration. Considered to be 'mechanical' or 'dictation', it makes the author 'the "pen" of the Holy Spirit'.[2] Griffith-Jones writes enchantingly about the 'baleful' and 'unfortunate and mis- chievous results' of such an idea. He therefore suggests the 'dynamical' theory which in his understanding of it 'transfers the problem from the form of the Bible as literature to the personalities of the writers'.[3] It was really because these men had sensitiveness and appreciation that they were inspired. They were supremely men who *felt*. Above all they were spiritual artists and seers; and 'The artist may not be a good historian; the seer may be a poor logician'. With these ideas Griffith- Jones sets out on his discussion of the 'authority of the Bible'.[4] 'There is', he says almost in the words of Peake, 'an instinctive craving in the human soul for a standard of belief and conduct which shall be accepted as infallible.'[5] But no such guide has been given. Thus the mystic claim and the ecclesiastic boast are to be dismissed. And the Bible long held by Protestants as an infallible authority is no longer able to maintain this position.

Yet there is 'something' about the Bible which clothes it with some sort of compelling atmosphere: it emits, we might say, a virtue. From whence does this come? It is to be found in the

---

[1] K. Fullerton, *Prophecy and Authority*, 1919, p. 205.

[2] E. Griffith-Jones, '*The Bible: Its Meaning and Aim*', Peake's *Commentary on the Bible*, 1919, new edition with supplement, reprint, 1948, p. 3.

[3] *Ibid.*, p. 4.   [4] *Ibid.*; cf. pp. 7 ff.   [5] *Ibid.*, p. 8.

gospel which is enshrined therein. It is in the experience of that
saving message that true authority lies. We are not bound
perpetually by 'mere literalism; "My words", He said, "they
are spirit and they are life" '.[1] It is not then in abstract terms but
in living practice that the problem of authority is 'solved'.

The position occupied by Charles Gore on the authority of the
Bible will be seen to follow from what he had to say with regard
to its inerrancy and inspiration. A key, perhaps, to his view is
provided by the fact that in the last of his three books which
make up the composite volume, *The Reconstruction of Belief*, he
gives a chapter to the subject of the authority of the Church
before he comes to discuss the Bible. It would seem correct,
therefore, to deduce from Gore's treatment that he attached a
great importance to the Church and its established traditions. In
matters of discipline, he asserts, the Church can act freely, and
give injunctions of binding force, as circumstances require, on
its own authority.[1] He rejects the Roman theory of infallibility
and contends for the necessity of free thought. He refers to the
'doctrinal and sacramental authority' of the Church which is
'relative to its moral and social mission'.[2]

Coming to the discussion of the authority of the Holy
Scriptures, he makes the revealing remark that he has sought 'to
build up a constructive doctrine of God and Christ and the Holy
Spirit in the Church without using the books of the Bible except
as historical documents'.[3] But he has referred earlier to 'a curious
question' which has to be faced. Was the ancient Church right
in elevating the written books of the New Testament to a throne
of solitary supremacy?[4] Certainly the Church came to believe
that they were written under the inspiration of the Holy Ghost.
It was 'this root conviction', which 'expressed itself in the
doctrine that every book and every sentence of the Bible is
infallibly true'.[5] Our Lord, however, did not fall a victim, as did
the early Church, to the prevailing notion of 'a strict doctrine of
the infallibility of the sacred books in all their details'.[6] He did
not accept 'the current Jewish interpretation of the meaning of
inspiration'.[7] Elsewhere, however, he has argued that Christ did

[1] C. Gore, *The Reconstruction of Belief*, 1921–4, new edition in one volume, 1926,
reprint, 1945, p. 792.   [2] *Ibid.*, p. 781.
[3] *Ibid.*, p. 874.   [4] *Ibid.*, p. 872.   [5] *Ibid.*, p. 874.
[6] *Ibid.*, p. 877.   [7] *Ibid.*

accommodate Himself to the popular ideas of biblical authorship and the only reason for his refusal to allow that He did not fall in with the popular view of inspiration is that Gore wishes to use Christ's authority for his own theory of the Holy Scriptures. Like Hebert later, Gore favours the mystical sense of Scripture and he would limit the scope of its inspiration to 'the things of faith and morals'. He rejects what he calls 'the power of naked appeal to the infallible book',[1] and thus states that experience is the ultimate test whereby the word of God can be verified. The scholar may seek, by reason of his special vocation, to test the Bible in the field of critical history, but for most men the testing must be mainly practical. 'Put to account by faith, the claim verifies itself as divine in moral and spiritual experience.'[2]

The problem of religious authority had, over an extended period, special interest for A. E. J. Rawlinson. In 1923, he delivered his Paddock Lectures on the subject and there made explicit some of the ideas he had already expressed as far back as 1912 in his essay contributed to the volume *Foundations*.

In this earlier work, Rawlinson contended that there is no ultimate opposition between the religion of authority and the religion of the Spirit. The trouble has been the way the concept 'authority' has been 'popularly confused with infallibility'.[3] He considers the Infallibilist view of authority to have developed as a logical corollary of an over-mechanical idea of inspiration. 'The legal spirit reacted with transforming effect upon the conceptions alike of authority and inspiration.'[4] All infallible authorities are therefore due to a false emphasis. Papal infallibility is the result of the logical outcome of a one-sided development, while Protestantism reveals a position equally one-sided. 'Its intellectual basis, that is to say, was equally authoritarian with that of Rome, from which it differed merely in the substitution of the infallible Book for the infallible Church: a substitution which in itself was by no means an improvement.'[5] Both ideas, according to Rawlinson, have been finally discarded: 'the infallible Book has gone the way of the infallible Church'.[6] Some would, however, fall back on the 'witness of the Spirit', but this is considered

---

[1] C. Gore, *The Reconstruction of Belief*, 1921–4, new edition in one volume, 1926, reprint, 1945, p. 889.　　　　[2] *Ibid.*, p. 894.

[3] A. E. J. Rawlinson, 'The Principle of Authority', *Foundations* (ed. N. H. Streeter), 1912, reprint, 1922, p. 365.　　　　[4] *Ibid.*, p. 366.

[5] *Ibid.*, pp. 371–2.　　　[6] *Ibid.*, p. 372.

inadequate by Rawlinson. 'What is needed is rather a restatement of the principle of authority which shall avoid either confusing it with infallibility or legalizing it as despotism.'[1]

Rawlinson then examines the word 'auctoritas' in its classical meaning and contends that it would be best understood by such a phrase as 'corporate' or even 'inspired' witness. He points out that in actual religious psychology, a beginning is made by the acceptance of truth 'on authority'. This 'bondage to authority' period is, however, soon passed, when the right to criticize, or even to deny, is asserted. But there is the final stage which Rawlinson calls 'concrete freedom' to be gained; here comes voluntary assent 'on the ground of reason' to what was formerly believed 'on authority'. The critical stage, is, he thinks, the second. And it is just here that the authority of the Church, which is none other than 'the corporate witness of the saints to the validity of the spiritual experience on which their lives are based' is to be taken into account. It is thus concluded that 'the function of authority in religion (is) neither to compel assent nor to override reason, but to testify to spiritual experience'.[2]

In the Paddock Lectures, these views are given more precise statement, although meanwhile Rawlinson has reiterated something of what he has said in his essay on *Foundations* in his volume *Dogma, Fact and Experience*. The title given by Rawlinson to the Paddock Lectures, *Authority and Freedom*, would lead us to expect a clear statement of his position. He argues that real authority can exist only where there is complete freedom of thought. Authority lies in the truth of a self-evidencing revelation plus the accumulated experience of the ages. He thinks that the future belongs to what he calls 'Evangelical Catholicism', and that it is within this 'revived' New Testament 'Catholicism' that freedom and authority are reconciled.[3] He stresses the authoritative function of the sacraments in the life of the Church. In his article on 'Criticism and the Authority of the Bible' in *The Anglical Communion* (1929),

---

[1] A. E. J. Rawlinson, 'The Principle of Authority', *Foundations* (ed. N. H. Streeter), 1912, reprint, 1922, p. 373.   [2] *Ibid.*, p. 380.

[3] Cf. the later remark of R. B. Owen: 'Not all the philosophy in the world has yet succeeded in resolving the paradox (of freedom and authority). Yet in actual experience we know that freedom is born of an inner authority, a sense of compulsion within the soul of man himself.' *Expository Times*, Vol. LX, 1948-9, pp. 50-1.

Rawlinson gives emphasis to this idea in his apology for the self-evidencing reality of biblical doctrine as experienced within the 'Catholic tradition' of the Anglican communion.

Rawlinson deals with the subject of authority again in his contribution to *Essays Catholic and Critical*, a volume which is 'in its way, a new *Lux Mundi* which may be regarded as a manifesto of the Anglo-Catholic party'.[1] It seems that in this essay, which is entitled 'Authority as a Ground of Belief', Rawlinson puts greater emphasis than elsewhere on the authenticating significance of experience, although the importance of the Church is still much insisted upon.

Rawlinson begins by asserting that the Church is a divine institution, the Spirit-filled Body of Christ. It is, therefore, not irrational for a man to submit his judgements to its authority. Yet authority is never its own guarantee: its claims must be verified. The point is made by a quotation from F. Heiler's *Das Gebet* to the effect that the idea of authority is rooted in the revelational character of the prophetic type of religion.[2] Our Lord, it is observed, as a matter of actual historical fact, astonished the people by teaching independently of scribal tradition, with the unhesitating 'authority' of immediate inspiration.[3] The conclusion then to which he is lead is that 'final authority is not anything which is either mechanical or merely external, but is rather the intrinsic and self-evidencing authority of truth. It means that authority as such can never be ultimately its own assurance, that the claim of legitimate authority must always be in the last resort verifiable claims. The final appeal is to the spiritual, intellectual and historical content of divine revelation, as verifiable at the threefold bar of history, reason and spiritual experience'.[4]

In the same volume, it may be noted here, W. L. Knox writes on 'The Authority of the Church'. The idea of an infallible Bible is vigorously denied and set aside as the only source of authority. Yet it is allowed that 'all Christians would agree that in some sense the Bible possesses a permanent authority in matters of belief and conduct'.[5] The authority which the Bible has derives

---

[1] *Expository Times*, Vol. XXXVII, 1925–6, p. 532.
[2] A. E. J. Rawlinson, *Essays Catholic and Critical* (ed. E. G. Selwyn), 1926, third edition, 1931, p. 86.
[3] *Ibid.*   [4] *Ibid.*, p. 95.   [5] *Ibid.*, p. 101.

from its nature as it is realized and tested in Christian experience as found within the tradition of 'Catholic' Christianity. The Church is, indeed, the custodian of the Scripture and the organ of its permanent message.

This reference to W. L. Knox seems a good place to draw attention to another work to which he with A. R. Vidler contributed, namely, *The Gospel of God and the Authority of the Church* (1937). There is general agreement between what is to be found in this volume and the essay in *Essays Catholic and Critical*. The emphasis, however, of the book is strictly not on the question of the authority of the Church but rather on that of in what sense is the *teaching* of the Church authoritative. Authority is defined as 'title to be believed', and consequently to be distinguished from infallibility. The Church's understanding of the gospel is stated to be not a final or intellectually adequate statement of revelation, but rather 'the best available account of it'—a working hypothesis which is being constantly confirmed, a guide which is sufficient for the practical purposes of leading to the experience of the revelation of God in Christ. This does not leave the question of authority precarious, the authors affirm, by making experience the final confirmation of doctrine. It may be granted that in some instances errors are to be admitted, but 'as a developing whole Christian doctrine is entitled to be accepted as providing . . . adequate guidance to the practice of the Christian life'.

Authority in the Church (1928) by T. A. Lacey is a closely reasoned volume in which patterns of authority are noted, moving down from the ultimate authority of God Himself through the Bible and the Church. Thus while God is the source of authority, these other two are special media of it.

On the publication of C. H. Dodd's important book, *The Authority of the Bible*, a reviewer remarked 'one who is seeking in the Bible an external and infallible authority will get little comfort from Professor Dodd'.[1] Not only is this a correct observation, but it would, we think, be true to say that Dodd gives even greater emphasis to the subjective and the focus within than most. 'The criterion lies within ourselves', he remarks, 'in the response of our spirit to the Spirit that utters itself in the

---

[1] *Expository Times*, Vol. XL, 1928–9, p. 147.

Scriptures.'[1] And he contends that the 'inner witness of the Holy Spirit', of which the Reformers spoke, 'is in effect the "subjective" criterion of which we are speaking'.[2]

It is Dodd's purpose all through his book to establish the validity of the subjective principle by which to assess and attest Scripture. In the Preface, he states that 'the measure of any authority which the Bible may possess must lie in its direct religious value, open to discovery in experience'.[3] When he comes to the end he is able to look back and maintain, 'All through our study it has been clear that anything we can say about revelation is relative to the minds that receive it. Nowhere is the truth given in such purely "objective" form that we can find a self-subsistent external authority'.[4]

Dodd is convinced that the use of the Bible as a dogmatic authority has been undermined by criticism.[5] The whole notion of an external infallibility is beset with insuperable difficulties. The ultimate authority is truth itself as it reveals itself in experience and compels assent. The argument, that since the Bible is the Word of God, it must, therefore, be an infallible authority is no longer valid, since we have come to see that it merely 'mediates' the Word of God and that it is what finds us within it, is true.[6] In religion, it is asserted the attainment of truth imperatively calls for the sharing of a personal experience. It is, therefore, 'in this sense we find a religious authority in the Bible—the authority of experts in the knowledge of God, masters in the art of living; the authority of religious genius'.[7] Yet all the Bible is not the product of such genius. There are areas of the Bible, the greater part indeed, wherein the 'authentic marks of personal inspiration' do not appear. What authority belongs to such parts? Here Dodd calls for a widening of the understanding of what is implied in religious experience. It is never simply private and individual: it takes place in and is related to a much wider context of living.[8] And in this connection there is illustrated for us the effect of religion in the

---

[1] C. H. Dodd, *The Authority of the Bible*, 1928, p. 296.   [2] *Ibid.*, p. 297.
[3] *Ibid.*, Preface, p. ix.   [4] *Ibid.*, p. 289.
[5] *Ibid.*; cf. pp. 8 ff.   [6] *Ibid.*; cf. pp. 15 f. and 289 f.
[7] *Ibid.*, p. 24; cf. p. 133.
[8] *Ibid.* Cf. 'A religious man is not one who has "experiences" which he can describe with particularity, in class-meeting, or in reply to a psychological *questionnaire, as* the case may be, but one who takes all life in a religious way' (pp. 135–6).

larger areas of secular and common life. The value of the Bible in this wider context of human affairs wherein truth reveals itself will be obvious. Herein is indicated for us something more than transient and individual 'religious experiences' as the basis of faith.

Dodd has some observations to make about the authority of the gospels which he regards as a product of the experiences of the early Church and yet which enable us to go beyond that experience to the events which created it. It is useless, he states, to attempt to find in the words of Christ the last refuge of an infallible external authority. Still there is eternal truth which makes its impact upon the mind through its external expression.[1] Right through Dodd again and again insists upon the subjective necessity. 'Thus in every way', he adds once more, 'we are brought back to the importance of the "subjective" factor. Granted that religious authority somehow resides in the Bible, how does it become authoritative *for me?*'[2] It is, then, finally, according to Dodd, what authenticates itself within experience is authoritative. There is strictly no objective infallibility, not even the words of Jesus.

It may be saying too much to suggest that Dodd's subjectivism is less pronounced in his later studies. At any rate in his 'course of "open lectures" given under the auspices of the Divinity Faculty of the University of Cambridge' in 1945, there seems to be a greater recognition given to the Bible as an objective 'authority'. 'The Scriptures of the New Testament, or in other words, the documents of the New Covenant', it is stated, 'are the authoritative record of that act of God by which He established relations between Himself and the Church; and they are the charter defining the status of the Church as the people of God, the terms upon which that status is granted, and the obligations it entails.'[3] He goes on to declare concerning the Bible that the Church 'offers this book to us as "revelation" of God'.[4] Dodd has not, of course, been forgetful of his earlier insistence upon experience, he thus refers to the prophetic experience of the Old Testament prophets and the New Testament apostles as giving truth its authority.[5]

[1] C. H. Dodd, *The Authority of the Bible*, 1928, cf. pp. 231 ff.
[2] *Ibid.*, p. 290.   [3] C. H. Dodd, *The Bible Today*, 1946, p. 8.
[4] *Ibid.*, p. 12.   [5] *Ibid.*; cf. pp. 102 ff.

In 1930 Bertram Lee Woolf published his work on *The Authority of Jesus*. He had, however, given a fairly good indication of what could be expected in this volume by an article he had written earlier on 'The Authority of the Risen Lord' in an issue of the *Congregational Quarterly* for the year 1928. In this article Woolf argued that the resurrection of our Lord was decisively significant in the experiences of the disciples. They were caught up into a new relationship with the living Christ and here lay for them divine authority. It was through Pentecost that the resurrection was vitalized in their experiences. Thus the authority of Jesus was founded upon His immediate influence upon individuals and upon the believing society. Through the Spirit they became vividly and vitally conscious of a new life, power and personal communion with Christ as living Lord. So is it today: the authority of Jesus 'is only to be found in the inmost experience of the believing soul'. Jesus is indeed to be regarded as the ultimate spiritual authority, because He lives as everpresent in redeeming action as Lord of life.

These are the ideas which Woolf works out with fuller detail in his later thesis on *The Authority of Jesus*. The 'discovery of the ultimate freedom is the discovery of final freedom to live our lives', he urges.[1] And to live our lives in freedom is to know the redeeming inwardness of the living Christ. Writing in one section of 'Authority of the Christian Faith', he says, 'The Christian certainty of the supremacy of Christ is based upon the superior quality of the experience which believers enjoy'.[2] He expresses sympathy with Schleiermacher's emphasis upon religious feeling although he seeks to defend him from the charge of founding religion upon it. He allows that Schleiermacher does give to religious experience its own peculiar form of authority, and with that Woolf profoundly agrees.[3] He is able therefore to say: 'it is this constant and ever-renewed appeal to experience which constitutes the active authority of the Christian religion, where all authority is real in proportion to the vividness and the transforming power of the experience'.[4] He grants that personal experience 'to the one who is used to the important but secondary support of church, or tradition or

---

[1] B. L. Woolf, *The Authority of Jesus*, 1930, p. 39.
[2] *Ibid.*   [3] *Ibid.*; cf. pp. 21-2.
[4] *Ibid.*, p. 23.

scripture may feel this authority is too slender or delicate, and quite unable to bear the demands that will be made upon it'.[1] Woolf cannot grant that this is so. Experience is, he is certain, 'the only authority which has ultimate and effective ethical or religious power', so that as an individual becomes 'accustomed to its purity and its grace' so he 'becomes more aware of its strength'.[2] Jesus is, after all, the contemporary of every era. He is always modern. Thus the authority of Jesus is the authority of His active and living presence in every age. 'The authority of Jesus, in so far as it is felt to be modern, authenticates itself to be the authority of the Lord of Life.'[3]

The same focus upon the inward nature of religious authority comes in one of J. A. Chapman's *Fellowship of the Kingdom* pamphlets.[4]

C. J. Wright seeks to identify the self-witnessing nature of truth with the doctrine of the inner witness of the Spirit. In the past, he states, both the Roman and Protestant Churches, each in their own way, have sought to impose an external authority. He asks the question, 'Is Christianity concerned with "truths", or with "truth"? In other words, with doctrines which are held to be in accord with ultimate reality, or with an ethical attitude of heart and mind?'[5] He is prepared to admit that religious authority is concerned with both. With regard to the second, he argues, Christianity is certainly concerned with 'truth' in the sense of a personal ethical attitude and a personal spiritual insight. 'In the Gospels the test of real truth is never submission to external authority or ceremonial or precept.'

There is, however, the other aspect of the matter in which Christianity is not only bound up with the question of the 'authority' of one's personal attitude, but with the question of 'Authority' itself. Here arises the problem of 'absolute truth'. According to Wright, absolute truth is one and the same with the authority of the truth itself. He then asks, 'What precisely are these truths for which Christianity stands: and further, How can we know them to be true?'[6] The fundamental truth, which is the very essence of the gospel itself, is that of the grace of God.

---

[1] B. L. Woolf, *The Authority of Jesus*, 1930, p. 285.   [2] *Ibid.*   [3] *Ibid.*
[4] J. A. Chapman, *Authority*, 1930.
[5] C. J. Wright, *The Question of Authority in Religion, Expository Times*, Vol. XLIV, 1932-3, p. 440. Cf. *ibid.*, W. J. Sparrow-Simpson, *Modern Witnesses to the Value of Authority in Religion*, pp. 444 ff.   [6] C. J. Wright, *op. cit.*, p. 442.

This supreme truth which ultimately includes all others can be verified as true only in the actualities of experience. Here all things are proved. Divine truth wins its way into the heart and soul. Those who are persuaded and possessed will be ready to claim that the Divine Spirit has authenticated the Divine word within the depths of the human soul. 'What else', he asks as his conclusion, 'is the doctrine of the *Testimonum Spiritus Sancti* but the religious side of the philosophical doctrine of the self-evidencing nature of Truth?'[1]

A. E. Garvie seeks to rescue himself from the hopeless subjectivism to which all his theological writings shows him to be prone. Writing on 'The Value of the Old Testament for the Christian Church', he, too, gives a supreme place to the inner witness of the Spirit. 'Nor is this conviction solely *subjective*', he hastens to add, 'There are objective facts to sustain it'. These objective facts, however, turn out to be themselves subjective. We are to believe, it is told us, that the Holy Spirit 'moved' the 'prophetic consciousness' of the Bible prophets. But the reason for this belief is due to the fact that the Bible has become so assured within experience. The prophetic consciousness through the prophetic succession is the core of revelation, it is stated, and it is in the unfolding content of that prophetic consciousness that Garvie places the authority of the Bible.[2]

Two years after the appearance of his lectures on *Inspiration*, R. H. Malden added another book with the title, *The Authority of the New Testament* (1937). Critical scholarship, he assures his readers, has not impaired the New Testament as the final authority in the areas of faith and morals. Whatever truth there may be in the Bible, and whatever degree of probability is to be allowed to the evidences for its highest religious assurances, ultimately, it appears, for Malden, as for Hort, whose words we may quote here, the authority of the Bible 'is to be found in the light which it brings, far more than in any light which it reveals'.[3]

[1] C. J. Wright, 'The Question of Authority in Religion', *Expository Times*, Vol. XLIV, 1932–3, p. 443.

[2] A. E. Garvie, 'The Value of the Old Testament for the Christian Church', *Expository Times*, Vol. XLVIII, 1936–7, p. 375 f. Cf. 'The Synthesis of History, Experience and Reason in the "Knowledge of God".' *Ibid.*, Vol. XLIII, 1931–2, pp. 103 ff. Cf. also his *The Preachers of the Church*, 1926, and 'The Nature of Religious Authority and the Certainty of Christian Faith' in Mansfield College Essays Presented to A. M. Fairbairn, November 4, 1908, 1909, pp. 161 ff.

[3] F. J. A. Hort, *The Authority of the Bible*, n.d., p. 11.

In an article on 'The Authority of the Bible Today', H. Hodkin argued for, what he calls, the 'propaedeutic' authority of the Scripture. 'The Bible offers these twin truths to us', he writes, 'the truth about life and the truth about God. It does not call upon us to accept them merely because they stand written or because someone else has said that we ought to, but to verify and prove them for ourselves. If experience and testing bears out and establishes these truths, if the acceptance of them gives to the heart and mind that joy, power, and repose which only truth can give, then the authority of the Bible is vindicated. This authority is now seen to be essentially propaedeutic.'[1]

In his *Signposts to God* (1938), W. R. Matthews gives, we think, his clearest statement of religious authority. The title for another of his books, *God in Christian Thought and Experience*, will lead us to expect an emphasis upon the vindicating reality of experience. Matthew begins his less pretentious volume by specifying several kinds of 'signposts' to God, such as nature, history and conscience. Concerning conscience he remarks with the words of John Knox to Mary Queen of Scots, 'Conscience, Madam, requires knowledge'. The voice of authority is, Matthews declares, another and a most important 'signpost'. Some would argue that they listen to no authority. Whoever will not listen to authority, he replies, is 'bound to end up with a meagre and shallow creed'. The individual's own conscience is necessarily very limited. The pressing question is, Where does religious authority exist? There 'is a kind of authority in religion', he answers, 'which is rather like the authority of the people who appreciate art and music. . . . There seem to be persons who have a peculiar sensitiveness of the spiritual world. These are the creative individuals in the history of redemption'. The Bible is authoritative, he concludes, because it contains testimonies to the reality of man's religious experience of God to the Church which enshrines and interprets them.

A careful statement of the problem of authority is given by N. P. Williams. Williams sees the history of Israel as the '*praeparatio evangelica*' leading up to the 'temple of Christian faith'. He then adds, 'Of that temple, "other foundation can no man lay than that which is laid, which is Jesus Christ" '. He, therefore, and no other, is the primary authority for Christian

[1] *Expository Times*, Vol. XLIX, 1937–8, pp. 232–3.

faith, and the Old Testament is precious in our eyes because 'these are they which bear witness of me'.[1] We still have, however, to seek a 'secondary authority' to give us relative information and correct interpretation of Christ's teaching. In some sense the New Testament is to be regarded by all as providing these. But the question of how that teaching is to be derived from this source remains as the vital problem since 'the New Testament though unique as a historical authority' 'seems to refer us beyond itself for our ultimate doctrinal authority'.[2] What is this ultimate authority? Williams apparently regards it as continued Christian tradition which throughout the changing centuries has remained faithful to the primitive 'kerygma'. 'It is, surely, to the indivisible, yet real, weight and pressure of the central Christian tradition, rather than to an indefinite series of coincidences in the construction of inferences from the written page, that the unity of belief manifest at Lausanne and Edinburgh is due. And, whilst mere posteriority in time is in itself no guarantee that a particular phase of religious thought is more authoritative than the phase which preceded it, the conception of the corporate mind of the people of God, slowly growing through the centuries and clarifying the fundamental ideas of its revelation under the guidance of that Spirit who leads men into all truth, will provide us with the clue to the tangled history of Christian theology and with criteria whereby "false starts" and "blind-alley" developments in the interpretation of the deposit of faith may be distinguished from the true and Divinely-intended course of dogmatic evolution.'[3]

[1] N. P. Williams, 'Authority in Matters of Religious Belief', *Expository Times*, Vol. LI, 1939-40, p. 407.

A more 'High Church' statement of the same idea is found in G. W. Broomfield's book, *Revelation and Reunion* (1942). Broomfield contends that the 'authority behind the two creeds' (the Nicean and the Chalcedon) 'is essentially the same as that behind the formation of the New Testament canon'. That authority is, the Holy Spirit inspired Church. What is the real seat of authority, and What is the relation of the Holy Spirit to the Church? he asks. Authority, he urges, and all will agree with him here, is 'from above'. The crucial question is how does it come to us? Through what media is it channeled? Broomfield, and fewer will agree with him here, would restrict authority to the Church as ordered by its bishops; an authority, that is, which is derived by descent from the apostles.

A less forbidding account of the relation of authority to his own Church is given by E. C. Rich in his *Spiritual Authority and the Church of England* (1953). Rich is less inclined to grant to the Church the claim which Broomfield makes for it. His emphasis is upon the 'spiritual' aspect of authority.

[2] *Ibid.*, p. 408.   [3] *Ibid.*, p. 410.

Repeated references have been made in earlier pages of this work to the writings of A. G. Hebert which relate to our subject. Hebert, as we have seen, disavows the idea of an infallibly inspired Bible. The Bible is doubtlessly inspired, but so, too, are 'other books on religious and on "secular" subjects'.[1] They also are in some way born of the Spirit. Consequently if 'the Bible is authoritative because the Holy Ghost spoke through it, those other books should owe whatever authority they possess to the same cause'.[2] What marks a book as authoritative is the approximation to the knowledge of its subject and the wisdom it embodies. The 'difference between the Bible and other books should then be due to their respective subject-matter'.[3] According to Hebert, the main matter of the Bible concerns the Kingdom of God. The Bible is therefore the authority of the Kingdom. It has authority for us 'as the record of a divine Purpose worked out in history'.[4] The Kingdom of God can be considered under three aspects, represented by the Greek words ἀρλή and λόμος and τέλος. These words apply to the idea of the kingdom in its fundamental purpose, its outworking, and ultimate effect. As unfolding the developing Purpose of grace in all these phases, the Bible alone for the Old Israel and the New, is our 'authority'. Yet no infallibility can be claimed for the record. Imperfect though it may be, it does still contain 'a hard core' in which and through which the saving purpose of God can be traced. In the events of their history the prophets of the Old Testament saw something of the salvation of their God. In every phase of its disclosure of the Kingdom, the Bible bears an 'authoritative testimony'. Yet it is not the testimony of an infallible account, but the conviction of a sure faith. The stories of the Old Testament are 'designed for a specific purpose', they 'cannot be recognized'—he here quotes with approval Pythian-Adam's book *The Call of Israel*—as 'what *we* should call historical'.[5] It is only when we ourselves have penetrated behind the immediate purpose of the individual writer and the garb in which he has clothed it can we get an understanding of the facts 'which may not (the words are again Pythian-Adam's) be by any means recognizable in the *form* in which they are presented'.[6] But ultimately this penetrating activity is ours:

---

[1] *The Authority of the Old Testament*, 1947, p. 49.   [2-6] *Op. cit.*

apparently the Bible cannot be taken at its face value, there is a 'theological' and 'mystical' meaning which they of the Kingdom will appreciate, since, 'The Bible is the Book of the Faith, the Book of the divine Kingdom'.[1]

Following a section on 'The Inner Witness of the Holy Spirit', in his *Christian Apologetics*, in which he has maintained the fundamental necessity for this inner certitude, Alan Richardson then deals with the subject, 'The Divine Authority of the Bible'. The conclusions for which he has argued are substantially those for which he has contended in his *A Preface to Bible-Study*. He expresses the same dissatisfaction with the idea that the authority of the Bible is simply that of religious genius. 'To ascribe to the writers of the Biblical books an authority which is merely that of religious geniuses does not account for the undeniable fact that the Bible comes to Christians in the Church, not merely as possessing the highest human authority, but as the unconditional demand and gracious invitation of God Himself; nor does it in the least help us to understand why such a remarkable succession of "religious geniuses" should have "happened" in Israel and nowhere else.'[2] In the Bible we have not the record of man's search for God but God's search for man. It is from this point of view that its authority must be understood. The authority of the Bible is not to be 'looked upon as a "blind authority" which bludgeons the reason of men into unquestioning acquiescence or which asks of men a "blind faith" '.[3] It is the authority, we might say, of a gracious persuasion and of a divine winsomeness. Richardson stresses the need for the inner illumination of the Spirit since it is by the quickened intuition that the divine truth is apprehended.[4] The sum of the matter is, as his own words declare, 'It was the divine enlightenment of the eyes of the prophets and apostles which enabled them to understand and to interpret the events of the biblical history, and it is still this divine enlightenment which enables Christians today to believe and understand the message of the prophets and apostles, their testimony to Christ which the Bible contains'.[5]

H. Cunliffe-Jones takes a position on the authority of the

---

[1] *The Authority of the Old Testament*, 1947, p. 74.
[2] Alan Richardson, *Christian Apologetics*, 1947, p. 221.
[3] *Ibid.*, p. 222.   [4] *Ibid.*; cf. pp. 225–6.   [5] *Ibid.*, p. 220.

Bible somewhat akin to that of Hebert. He makes the point to begin with, with which all Christians will agree, that the ultimate authority must be God Himself. But the authority of God is not, however, that of God in the abstract, but that of God as clothed in His gospel.[1] 'The authority under which all men live which is acknowledged truly in the Christian faith is the authority of God in his revelation.'[2] To this authority of the gospel the Bible is 'the indispensable witness'. But it is God in His revelation in Jesus Christ who is the authority for the Christian. This means that 'What is ultimately authoritative for the Christian theologian is not the Bible as such, but the gospel of God to which it testifies'.[3] This declaration involves a discussion of the relation between 'The Gospel, the Church, and the Bible' which is Cunliffe-Jones's concern in chapter two of his book. It is the gospel as the revelation of the grace of God in Christ which is the final fact for Christian faith.

It is, however, the 'acknowledgement of the authority of God in his revelation which is life under the gospel is life in the Church'.[4] Indeed, life under the gospel involves churchmanship. It is in and through the Church that the individual believer is nourished. The question remains as to the place of the Scriptures; 'what is the function of the Bible, and what is the nature of its authority?'[5] Clearly the Bible is not a primary authority; its authority derives from the gospel to which it is a witness. A distinction is drawn between the theologians and churchly use of the Bible, and it is contended that in the case of the latter the Bible must be used as it stands. The historical approach has had the effect of destroying 'the old common believing use of the Bible, and has not yet enabled a common believing use, which takes for granted the general results of historical study, to govern the use of the Bible in the Church'.[6] It is in this way Cunliffe-Jones admits a sort of double standard of the authority of the Bible and accounts for the prevailing uncertainty concerning its position and place by the inability of the Church to accept the assured results of Biblical criticism in a believing way. Stress is given by Cunliffe-Jones to the witness of the Spirit[7] and it is asserted that 'The continued reappropriation of what the

---

[1] H. Cunliffe-Jones, *The Authority of the Biblical Revelation*, 1948, p. 7.
[2] *Ibid.*   [3] *Ibid.*, p. 13.   [4] *Ibid.*, p. 16.
[5] *Ibid.*, p. 18.   [6] *Ibid.*, p. 35.   [7] Cf. Chapter XI.

Bible says has very great relative authority for the Christian that he may truly submit himself to the absolute authority of God'.[1]

The year 1949 saw two important discussions of the subject of the authority of the Bible. J. W. C. Wand is insistent that the Bible possesses no 'infallible authority' in itself, and he acknowledges the sense of disappointment the declaration 'that there is no such infallible authority either in the Bible or elsewhere' will occasion. He, however, contends for its relative value and goes on to investigate what he regards as its sphere, source and nature. He finds the source of its authority in three particulars: first, in the writer's own spiritual genius and his humble recognition of the sources from which he draws. Its writers were good men, and 'Goodness is its own authority, and it is their goodness, as well as their ability to assess and present facts, which forms the first element in the authority of the writers and so of the Scriptures'.[2]

The second particular is the Church, in which, and for which, the Bible was produced. 'The Church authorized the Bible; and the Bible vindicates the Church.'[3] Finally, there is God Himself. Thus, remarks Wand, 'in the last resort a large part of the authority of the Scriptures must lie in the appeal that they make to our own conscience'.[4] They awaken a response, and in the response, the authority of the Bible is made effective. Ultimately the authority of the Bible lies in its persuasive appeal. It is not therefore an imperative authority like a military order which must be obeyed. Nor is it an exclusive authority. It does not extend to the whole range of thought but is limited to the necessities of man's salvation. It is not a universal authority, because there are other truths outside it which can be accepted:

---

[1] H. Cunliffe-Jones, *The Authority of the Biblical Revelation*, 1948, p. 21. A position something akin to this will be found in an article by E. C. Blackman, 'The Authority of the Old Testament: Is it Christian Scripture?' He, too, sees the authority of the Old Testament (that is his particular concern) focused in the 'gospel' which it enshrines. 'What we need from our teachers and guides is to be led through the details to this central truth' (p. 24). About the rough swaddling bands in which the Christ is laid we need not be ashamed or preoccupied. The 'dubious history and sub-Christian morality need cause no embarrassment' (p. 23). Cf. *The Congregational Quarterly*, Vol. 24, 1946, January 1946, pp. 13–24.

[2] J. W. C. Wand, *The Authority of the Scriptures*, 1949, p. 107.

[3] *Ibid.*, p. 108.　　　　　　　　[4] *Ibid.*, p. 109.

and it is certainly not compulsive. We must therefore boldly acknowledge 'that the authority of the Scriptures cannot be quite so clear-cut as one might otherwise have thought'.[1]

It is H. H. Rowley's conviction in his Third Joseph Smith Memorial Lecture on *The Authority of the Bible* (1949), that the idea that authority is guaranteed by the inner witness of the Spirit in man comes near to 'the delusion of mere subjectivism', and he consequently pronounces it as 'unsatisfying'. Rowley quotes Millar Burrow's statement that 'what is ultimately authoritative for us is that which commends the assent of our own best judgement, accepted as the witness of the Spirit within us. The only ultimate basis of assurance is the witness of the Spirit with the believer's own spirit'. Such a view Rowley quite rightly observes would make the Bible authoritative for one individual and not for another. Equally to be rejected with this excessive subjectivism is the Roman Catholic view which rests the authority of the Bible on that of the Church. Such a theory, by making the Church primary and final, must justify its claims at the bar of reason. This does not make man a mere creature of reason, since he allows that there is a necessary non-rational element in religion. In man's belief in the authority of the Bible there may be indeed a non-rational element, but if it were wholly non-rational it could approve itself to reason. 'What is first of all in question', therefore, contends Rowley, 'is whether a belief in the authority of the Bible can approve itself to reason, when reason is free and unfettered.'

Rowley argues that there is an authority behind the Bible which remains valid independently of any individual's recognition of it. 'The supreme revelation of God was in the Person of Christ, and while the *story* of that revelation is given in the Bible, the revelation itself lay outside the Bible', he states. This means that the Bible is to be regarded as the record of the revelation. There is, however, something in the sacred history which stamps it as an authentic Divine revelation. There is, throughout, the account of God's grace in deliverance and salvation in which 'we have a complex of human and non-human factors, and neither could determine the other, and *the only possible common source of both is God*'. Throughout both the Old Testament and the New, this same complex pattern, in which the

---

[1] J. W. C. Wand, *The Authority of the Scriptures*, 1949, p. 115.

human and non-human interweave, can be observed. Rowley considers the story of the deliverance of Israel from Egypt by Moses the first significant illustration of this complex of history. 'The confidence', he says, 'of Moses that he was divinely moved to promise deliverance and the manner of his justification; the immense fruitfulness of his work in the religious development that emerged from it; the wide variety of hopes expressed by Old Testament prophets that converged to find their fulfilment in Christ and His Church; the confidence of Christ and the early Church that in them their fulfilment was to be found, in days when the world thought that confidence ludicrous, and the vindication of that confidence in objective fact—all this provides solid evidence that can deliver the Christian from any sense of intellectual shame in finding the hand of God in the Bible and in the history it records and in the persons concerned in it all.'

This view is certainly commendable for the reason that it refuses to base the authority of the Bible upon the idea of the sublimity of its teaching or the mere spiritual insights of its readers. It does seek to build it upon the conviction of God's activity in history. The weakness lies in the fact that this alleged action of God is justified only from the Bible itself. The question which still has to be pressed, But supposing the historical foundations are insecure, or the interpretation of its writers mistaken, What then? The revelation seen as God's acts in history is divorced from the Bible, and yet, it is obvious, we can know of such a revelation only from its pages. Rowley himself may be able to find the certain, solid, historical truth within the record, but then he may have the adequate equipment. What of the ordinary man? He has not the sight and the sense of the 'able historical critic'. Must he be left ultimately to the 'authority of the experts'?

To his Burroughs Lectures of 1948, R. R. Williams adds, for publication, two essays on the modern problem of authority. The lectures themselves are concerned with the concept of authority in the apostolic Church. And what he has to say in this respect is summarized in this way. He has argued that 'the authority recognized in the apostolic age was the authority of God, asserted in history by Christ, His vice-regent. This was conveyed to individual Christians and Christian groups in a variety of ways. There was the record of Christ's deeds and words, which could be personally known and increasingly appropriated by all. There was the existence of a ministry felt to be commissioned by Him. There was, too, the sense of His immediate presence, made real and vivid by His indwelling Spirit. Every man had to be fully persuaded in his own mind concerning his own actions, but actions which concerned larger groups and more far-reaching issues called for more formal decision, which was reached either by apostolic fiat or by conciliar discussion with prayer for the guidance of the Spirit. No one channel could be regarded as monopolizing the right to mediate Christ's authority. The right, if it lay anywhere, lay in the whole Church, and then only in so far as the whole Church was obedient and responsive to the Spirit. Life in the apostolic Church was life in a complex of relationships, through each and all of which Christ's authority was to work. No one aspect of it could have been easily isolated from the others'.[1]

In the first of his two supplementary essays, Williams seeks to give 'An Account of the Modern Discussion of Authority in Religion and in the Church'. He makes reference to about half a dozen books in which there is revealed in some of them a tendency to accentuate the religion of the spirit and in others of them to stress the religion of authority. Dealing then with 'The Contemporary Problem of Authority' he has some remarks to make on that of the Scriptures in particular. They have an authority because they are 'the classical, normative account of Christian origins'.[2] And although, according to Williams, they are not our only historical source (he specifies The Eucharist, as 'itself part of the historical tradition'), they are the written documents which give permanency and stability to the historical tradition. The Scriptures have an authority, besides, because they act as 'a salutary check on the Church's waywardness'.[3] Then, too, in harmony, as he maintains, with Augustine, Luther, Sabatier, Barth, the Bible is authoritative because through its pages God speaks to men and to His Church in every age. In the end, however, it is the saving action of God in Christ, recorded in the Scriptures, summarized in the Creeds, dramatized in the sacraments, where exists the locale of authority. 'It is the Holy

---

[1] R. R. Williams, *Authority in the Apostolic Church*, 1950, pp. 112–13.
[2] *Ibid.*, p. 132.   [3] *Ibid.*

Spirit who brings home to Church and to Christian the authority of God in Christ. The Lord is the Spirit.'[1]

The very title of the symposium edited by Richardson and Schweitzer, *Biblical Authority for Today* marks it down for comment here. The reference in the Preface to 'the tentative character of the document' has been already noted.

Apart from one or two of the writers, the idea of an infallible Bible is denied. Regin Prenter giving the Lutheran view of the subject states that 'Fundamentalism' deriving from traditionalism, by making the Scriptures infallible 'actually turns Scripture itself into a tradition'.[2] As revelation is the *living* Word of God, the Bible and tradition witness to the fact, and it is the realization of this, which prohibits us from regarding the Bible 'as if it were a collection of supernaturally revealed truths'.[3] Stressing the testimony of the Holy Spirit, he declares that the 'Church must have the courage to preach the message of God's revelation without possessing an infallible Bible and an infallible interpretation of the Bible'.[4] Thus the authority of the Bible is not the authority of a book, nor indeed the authority of its authors, but the authority of the content of its message, the authority of the witness of the self-revealing action of the triune God, who is Himself the real authority for the validity of the Bible.

Barnabas Nagy, for the Reformed Church, maintains that the authority of the Bible is the living concrete authority of Jesus Christ who speaks by means of it. In this sense all other authorities are relative and limited. The unconditional authority of the Bible as God's words is above that of the Church and the inner witness of the Spirit. 'The position of these two authorities must never be reversed, nor may they be put on the same level.'[5] The Bible, in theory and practice, first and last, is exalted high above all human attempts to control it. But it is the Holy Spirit who 'makes the letters, the words, the texts of the Bible into a living witness, so that the living Lord Jesus Christ stands before us: God's Word in the human word'.[6]

---

[1] R. R. Williams, *Authority in the Apostolic Church*, 1950, p. 141.

[2] *Biblical Authority for Today* (ed. A. Richardson and W. Schweitzer), 1951. A World Council of Churches Symposium on 'The Biblical Authority for the Churches' Social and Political Message for Today', p. 110.

[3] *Op. cit.*, p. 111.   [4] *Op. cit.*   [5] *Op. cit.*, p. 89.

[6] *Op. cit.*, p. 91.

Clarance Tucker Craig, giving the Methodist contribution, shows a thorough dislike for the word 'authority'. He prefers to speak of the Bible as the primary 'source of guidance'.[1] Authority rests ultimately, he says, on the will of God and in the discovery of that will, authority is found. 'When faith responds to the testimony of the Bible that its witness is true, then the Bible has for that person a position for which the word "authority" is not too strong a word.'[2]

Panyotis I. Bratsiotis, speaking for the Orthodox communion, sees the Bible as 'the authoritative written expression of what God does and will do for the salvation of man, for the establishing and triumph of His own kingdom'.[3] The other writers, each with his own particular emphasis, reiterate the same general theme.

The article on 'The Bible: Its Significance and Authority', by H. H. Farmer in *The Speaker's Bible* is of some importance. The Bible is, he argues, certainly a standard and norm, but there are, he states, two types of such: an extrinsic or static, and an intrinsic or dynamic one. The Bible is of the latter sort. Yet while 'it is true that we cannot rightly apprehend the essentials of the Christian faith and life without using the Bible as an authoritative source and norm, it is equally true that we cannot apprehend the Bible as such a source and norm, still less rightly use it, apart from a living participation in the Church's faith and life'.[4] Having stressed that the essence of the faith is harmonious with the content and structure of the Bible, Farmer comes to discuss the question of the normative function of the Bible within the Church.

The creative and constructive principle of the Church is the living Christ Himself, who in all things rules and directs its faith and life through the Holy Spirit. But while Christ is the final and absolute authority the Bible is in some sense the supreme standard and norm. The crucial question concerns the relation of the authority of Christ to that of the Bible. The Bible, contends Farmer, 'indispensably participates in the authority of the living Christ'. Through it an encounter can be continually re-enacted with the historic Saviour.

[1] *Biblical Authority for Today* (ed. A. Richardson and W. Schweitzer), 1951. A World Council of Churches Symposium on 'The Biblical Authority for the Churches' Social and Political Message for Today', p. 35; cf. p. 41.

[2] *Op.cit.*, p. 32. [3] *Op. cit.*, p. 20.

[4] H. H. Farmer, 'The Bible: Its Significance and Authority', *The Speaker's Bible*, 1952, p. 5.

The authority of the Bible is then not different from that of Christ.[1] Wherein then lies the authority of Christ? It is significant that Farmer quotes from John Oman's *Vision and Authority* in developing his answer.[2] Just here is the key to his position. The authority of Jesus, Oman teaches, was no external authority; it was the authority of an inward appeal. Thus, writes Farmer, 'it is a most grave disloyalty to Christ, and to the Scriptures which He uses to speak to men, to turn the latter into an over-riding authority of the extrinsic "yardstick" sort'.[3] Farmer seeks to answer objections to this account of the authority of the Bible which puts the focus within. He will not allow that to accept in the Scripture only that which compels our assent is to be exposed to the danger of an unchecked individualism. He retorts: 'It is to the insight of the individual Christian that Christ speaks, but to picture the individual Christian to whom Christ thus speaks as an isolated and self-contained unit shut up within the circle of his own mental processes is to deny in effect the two truths thus stated'.[4] These two truths which he has maintained are, first, that the new man in Christ has become incorporated in the new covenant community, and, secondly, that it is only as such he can understand and use the Scriptures. Farmer contends, too, that by throwing the Christian believer back on his own inward sense of truth, he does not overlook the fact of sin. In truth, he claims that the clamour for an authoritarian direction, which should dispel all our doubts and perplexities and exempt us from ever making mistakes, is itself a form of anxiety which betrays unbelief and lies somewhere at the very heart of sin. Closing with a section on 'The Bible the Authoritative Basis of Preaching' he returns once again to make the subjective emphasis.[5]

A reference is required concerning the paper prepared for a Joint Theological Commission in South India, under the chairmanship of L. Newbigin, by J. R. Macphail and others, with the title 'The Authority of the Bible'. The trite remark is made at the beginning that Jesus did not leave behind Him a single written word. The paper puts as the first regard a discussion of 'The Primacy of the Church'. It goes on to state that while the

---

[1] H. H. Farmer, 'The Bible: Its Significance and Authority', *The Speaker's Bible*, 1952, p. 24.   [2] Cf. *ibid*.   [3] *Ibid*., p. 25.
[4] *Ibid*.   [5] *Ibid*.; cf. p. 31.

original witnesses of the saving acts of God in Jesus survived, there was no need for any other authority in the Church except the apostolic men and the Old Testament. But as 'the last living witnesses were taken one by one from among men, the Church set itself carefully and patiently to gather and to set apart a little library of books in which their testimony was preserved'.[1] This 'unique book', into which the collection was brought together, is so 'not because it is better than other books in the same way but because it is the original record of a unique story'.[2] Its contents derive their meaning from the fact that it is concerned with Christ. Unique, however, as it is, it is not a book without mistakes. And although its writers were indeed helped in their work by the Holy Spirit of Promise, they had still to use their own memory, imagination, knowledge, judgement and concentration of will. They were not 'mechanical instruments of supernatural power' rendered incapable of all error. Yet 'in spite of their mistakes, God's word is spoken and heard and done'.[3] Essentially, however, the reader of the Bible must be 'as truly inspired as the original writing of it was'.[4] But in the end the Bible has no authority but its own; the authority, that is, of the truth which it proclaims. Christ is the Truth and it is in the Bible's power to bring us face to face with Him 'that it becomes truth to us'.[5]

J. K. S. Reid's book *The Authority of Scripture*, lays stress upon Christ's authority as ultimate and final. And once again there is emphasis put upon the inner witness, which gives the Bible its validity and its relative authority. Raymond Abba is prepared to admit that the 'Fundamentalists' rendered 'valuable service to the Christian Church' in preserving 'the great supernatural facts of Biblical religion'.[6] No longer do they seem to be dismissed under the odious stigma of obscurantist. It is by reason of their continued insistence on inerrancy and verbal inspiration that they must be held outside the pale of the theologically respectable and the intellectually open. Abba, as we have seen earlier, castigates 'Fundamentalism' on these counts.

[1] J. R. Macphail and Others, 'The Authority of the Bible', *The Scottish Journal of Theology*, March 1956, p. 18.
[2] *Ibid.*   [3] *Ibid.*, p. 23.
[4] *Ibid.*   [5] *Ibid.*, p. 29.
[6] Raymond Abba, *The Nature and Authority of the Bible*, 1958, p. 65.

It is his view that the ultimate authority for the Christian is Christ Himself. And certainly no voice will be raised against such an assertion. It is to Him that both Church and Bible point. The question however remains as to the nature of Biblical authority. 'The nature of the authority of the Bible is determined by the nature of the Bible itself', he declares.[1] The Bible is not however a 'faultless and inerrant oracle'. It is such a notion, we are told, which is the reason for the Fundamentalist's dilemma. He begins with the 'unbiblical assumption' of the inerrancy of Scripture, and finds himself driven to sacrifice intellectual integrity in an attempt to vindicate every factual statement in the Bible, or he is compelled to abandon all belief in biblical accuracy.

The authority of the Bible, it is reiterated, is Christ in the Scriptures. This means that it is 'essentially a *religious* authority'.[2] It is the introduction of the divine–human encounter in which God confronts man in succour and demand. The authority of the Bible is, in fact, an 'accepted' authority, recognizable only within a faith-situation. 'The authority of the Bible, therefore, has to be experienced to be known.'[3] Abba, however, seems to place the Bible in the same category as the Church and the Inner Light. Authority, he says, is 'a cord with three strands' in which each of these has its place: 'the Bible needs to be read in the light of the living faith of the Church and authenticated in the heart of the believer by the inward testimony of the Holy Spirit'.[4]

The symposium, *On the Authority of the Bible* (1960), to which L. Hodgson, C. F. Evans, J. Burnaby, G. Ebling and D. E. Nineham contribute is in outlook and conclusion in general accord with the fundamental principles outlined in the main writings above.

Looking back over how one and another writer referred to in the previous section stated his understanding of the Bible, one is impressed by the strength and the weakness of the emphasis. It was a right and proper thing to give attention to the subjective necessity in validating the authority of the Scripture. The point had to be made in view of the tendency, which had earlier prevailed, to regard Christian faith as a sort of mental assent to a

---

[1] Raymond Abba, *The Nature and Authority of the Bible*, 1958, p. 304.
[2] *Ibid.*, p. 306.   [3] *Ibid.*, p. 308.   [4] *Ibid.*, p. 307.

body of 'Biblical doctrines'. Revelation, some had conceived to
have been given in the form of a series of cold and calculated
propositions. Against such there was a hearty reaction, In this
Schleiermacher had earlier led the way, and those who followed
him, appear, no more than did Sabatier, to be unduly perturbed
by their subjectivism. They no doubt realized the necessity for,
as well as the strength of, their position.

At the same time, it was not sufficiently grasped, that it was
no adequate foundation for a robust faith, to build theology on
changing experience, even if it be designated 'religious' or even
'Christian' experience. It is one thing to say that the knowledge
of God is discovered by experience, but it is quite another to
maintain that it arises out of experience. It should, of course, be
allowed that authority has no final meaning unless it is
experienced through surrender and obedience. It was, however,
a rightful protest which Forsyth entered against the 'cult of
experience', to insist that God alone speaks of God and that God
is known through God alone. There must therefore be an
authority for the redemptive experience, not merely psychological, but historical, at least in the sense of *Geschichte*,
Forsyth contended; and 'it must be', he adds, 'the Christ of the
historical and redeeming cross'.[1]

Objective authority in religion, it had been asserted, was
essentially a false note. It was a transgression of man's fundamental freedom and corrupting of his rightful autonomy. A book
religion would be a hurtful burden because it means the dictating
of truth *a priori*. Thus special delight was taken by writer after
writer in making the observation that Jesus never left any
written authority. Had He given to us a dictated volume, it was
bluntly stated by Percy Gardner, it would have become 'a
crushing weight on the Church'.[2]

By stating the case in the way they did, so as to repudiate the
Scripture as an essential standard, several writers overstepped
the bounds of the required emphasis. By turning within for the
grounds of religious authority they were left with no ultimate
standard by which religious experience itself could be sifted and
settled. The only test for a genuine religious experience seems
to be its quality or its vividness or its clarity. But the strength of

[1] P. T. Forsyth, *The Principle of Authority*, 1913, second edition, 1952, p. 63.
[2] Percy Gardner, *Modernism in the English Church*, 1926, p. 105.

an experience is no guarantee of its authenticity. The fact is, that when revelation or authority is made conterminous with religious experience the whole content of both is destroyed. To read authority in terms of experience is to leave no possible escape from an unhealthy subjectivism.

There must be a revelation having truth-content if there is to be valid authority in religion. Revelation or religious authority, for they are two sides of the one reality, is not something *made*; it is something *given*. If a real objective revelation is denied, then the reality of authority is destroyed.

Many writers did seek a way of escape from the morass of subjectivism to which their revelational theory had brought them. Reference was made, for example, to the check of social experience, to the voice of truth itself, and so forth. 'By some sort of dance-step', charges Bernard Ramm, 'the objective is brought into the subject of religious authority without waltzing to the orthodox tune.'[1] The ideas were urged that, seen from the philosophical point of view, religious experience is the only means by which the Object of religion is grasped; and that the subjective experience thus asserted reached its apex in the life of Jesus Christ and that consequently His life is, then, to be reckoned as the 'objective' test whereby all subjective experience can be tested.

But this only raises the further question, as Ramm was not slow to observe, How does the life of Christ become such a valid, objective revelation? It can only be as it is properly documented. This means that that which exercises authority over Christian experience can be objective only because it is historical. It is no longer, then, merely 'of the spirit': it is the authority of a documented life. It is only an objective revelation which is historical and vice versa. 'The inner piety of Jesus is private, and it is available to neither contemporary nor historian unless it is communicated. The inner life of Christ can be known only if it is documented. Even if one insists that the revelation *per se* was private to Christ, yet the recorded documentation of that life of ideal piety must stand authoritative for Christian experience.'[2]

The sheer fact is that we know nothing of Jesus except through His words. It is by His words He is known and understood. This means that if the words of Jesus are true then the

[1] Bernard Ramm, *The Pattern of Authority*, 1957, p. 81.   [2] *Ibid.*, p. 82.

Church does possess an authoritative truth, but if we cannot trust His words then we have no key to an understanding of His filial piety. It is indeed a surprising fact how much the radical subjectivists profess to know about the 'consciousness of Jesus'. But the only way to an understanding of that consciousness is by way of His words.[1] 'Religious liberalism was so careful to protect the human spirit from unhealthy authoritarianism, to defend its freedom, to emphasize the necessity of experimental appropriation of religion, that it lost the Object of religion and His freedom to speak to man as He pleased. . . . In so carefully setting forth how religious truth is to be appropriated, religious liberalism in practice confuses religious experience, religious authority, and the Object of religion.'[2]

Readers will no doubt be confused by the contradictory claims made to support the same general thesis. There are those who, in expounding the idea of Biblical authority as based on experience, contend that this was the view of the primitive Church: others, however, argue that it was not. Some, too, have maintained that it has its origin in the Reformation, while others take the opposite position. Thus, to take only one example, A. L. Lilley, in a reference to Luther, states: 'No Christian doctor of the first rank ever disparaged the revelational role of the Scripture more consistently than the great reformer'.[3] On the other side, F. R. Barry puts Luther and Calvin together and asserts that 'In their zeal for the newly discovered Scriptures . . . the Reformers allowed themselves to become intoxicated with a crude and fanatical bibliolatry'. Disastrous results, he contends, have followed from their Bible worship; 'the authority of an infallible Scripture has proved to be more sterilizing in morals than the autocracy of an infallible pope'.[4]

Here are two writers who are to be found attributing to the Reformers opposing doctrines. 'On the one hand there are those who believe that the Fathers of the Reformation', to quote what we have written on this strange inconsistency elsewhere, 'rejected all external authority in the rediscovery of the freedom of the Spirit. On the other hand, there are those who stigmatize

[1] Cf. James Orr, *The Christian View of God and the World*, 1893, third edition, 1897, pp. 405-8.

[2] Bernard Ramm, *The Pattern of Authority*, pp. 83-4.

[3] A. L. Lilley, *Religion and Revelation*, 1932, p. 79.

[4] F. R. Barry, *The Relevance of Christianity*, 1931, revised edition, 1932, p. 24.

them because they substituted a new authority—an infallible Bible for an infallible Pope. They are thus supposed to be, at the same time, the creators of a new subjectivism and a new scholasticism. They are commended by some because they were "liberal" in their attitude to the Bible; and they are condemned by others because they were "bibliolaters".'[1]

Sometimes, too, it will have been noted, the opposers of the subjectivist emphasis are spoken of as Traditionalists, as for example, by Gore and Hebert. On the other hand, they are believed to be innovators of a new theory. R. R. Williams, for instance, says 'After the Reformation (comes) a new orthodoxy, an almost Judaistic reverence for the letter of Scripture. This was something new, not paralleled in either Medieval or Reformation times. It is known today as Fundamentalism, through the name given to all anti-modernists in America'.[2]

It will be hard for the student who seeks an understanding of this subject to reconcile all these contradictions. He must be forgiven if he remains uncertain as to the precise facts if he limits himself to these writings. Or he may, perhaps, see for himself in such contradictions an illustration of the subjective principle of authority and the uncertain results to which it leads if taken as the only criterion of truth.[3]

B. THE AUTHORITY OF THE BIBLE AS EXISTING APART FROM EXPERIENCE

Under this heading we do not intend to refer again to the volumes already reviewed in which the idea of a verbal inspiration of Scripture is stated and defended, and in which revelation was identified, for all practical purposes, with the written word. It will be sufficient to point out that all who take this position are at one in maintaining that the Bible is the objective standard of all religious truth and trust. It possesses in itself an

---

[1] H. D. McDonald, *Ideas of Revelation*, 1959, p. 207.

[2] R. R. Williams, *Authority in the Apostolic Age*, 1950, p. 131.

[3] An interesting example of the same effort to have the argument both ways may be noted in the methods by which the Roman Catholic controversialists sought to dispose of the Reformers' doctrine and preaching of justification by faith. To begin with they were charged with introducing a 'novelty' into the traditional teaching of the Church. Then, in order to regain their hold, it was contended that it was the 'old doctrine' of the Church—thus, says Luther in indignant sarcasm, these 'Popish writers pretend that they have always taught what they now teach . . . thus the wolf

authority which is independent of experience. Its authority, to be sure, must become effective within experience but it is not credited with an authority on that account. There must be the witness of the Spirit, but apart from that witness, the Bible is declared to be, objectively, and in itself, the word of God. The Spirit, it is argued, can only bear testimony to that which is true. And He leads to Him who is the Truth, even Christ, but He does it through the Scriptures, and for this reason, it is maintained, the Bible is the Word of truth. The authority of the Bible, no more than its inspiration, it is contended, cannot be abstracted from the words. In a very real sense its language is the language of the Holy Spirit and consequently its authority is not 'made' in the context of human experience.

It does, however, seem to be required that those who contend for this understanding of the authority of the Bible should be permitted to give some account of themselves. And to meet this necessity we have thought it best to allude to a few statements of the case to which reference has not been hitherto made.

A 'generous and well-informed apology for Bible infallibility', so a contemporary issue of the *Expository Times* describes D. M. McIntyre's volume *The Divine Authority of the Scriptures of the Old Testament* (1906). McIntyre argues that Christ's authority is a sufficient assurance of the authority of the Bible. But lest it be concluded that he conceived of faith as a mere assent of the truth of a writing, he added another volume sometime later on *The Spirit in the Word* (1908). In this attention is given to the supplementary inward action of the Spirit who makes the Word a living reality.

An article appeared in a 1908 edition of *The Record* in which H. Wace, Dean of Canterbury, dealt with 'The Authority of Holy Scripture'. It is vigorously maintained that the whole Bible is a reliable external authority. The Old Testament was certainly so to our Lord, and must consequently be so for us. Christ indeed submitted Himself to its authority, he argues by

puts on the sheep's skin till he gains admission into the fold'. Upon which summer-saulting James Bannerman commented, 'That their original charge against the Protestant doctrine as a "novelty" and their subsequent claim to it as the "old doctrine" of the Church, could not both be true, is evident, for they are manifestly contradictory; and it might seem incredible that they could have been adopted by the same parties in good faith'. James Bannerman, *Doctrine of Justification by Faith*, 1867, reprint, 1955, p. 135; cf. pp. 138–41.

reference to five separate passages in the New Testament. As regards the New Testament itself, although Christ's example and words cannot be appealed to, yet 'It is no less unquestionable, that the Scriptures of the New Testament were, from the first, treated by the Church as similarly authoritative'. His assurance is, then, that in the Jewish Church in the period of Christ, and the Christian Church for the first two centuries, as well as for the apostles and Christ Himself, the Scripture of both Testaments were conceived to be historically true and divinely authoritative. This 'uniform belief of the Church in early ages', he concludes, cannot be considered ill-founded. The books which have come into our hands 'have been preserved under the Divine control, and consequently carry Divine authority'.

In the popular one volume *New Bible Commentary*, published under the auspices of the Inter-Varsity Fellowship, there will be found a carefully written article by G. W. Bromiley on the subject, 'The Authority of Scripture'. Bromiley opens up his statement with an investigation of the Bible's witness to its own authority. He then faces the charge that to claim for the Bible a unique authority by an appeal to its own testimony is an outrageous form of question-begging. He vigorously repudiates the suggestion. 'If the Bible did not make that claim', he says, 'we should have no call to believe it. And we could have no general confidence in the teaching of Scripture. But if the Bible stands before us as an authoritative Word of God, a Word which itself claims authority, then it is as such that we must reckon with it, receiving that Word and the authority of that Word, or resisting it.'[1] Both Testaments, he contends, everywhere in an implicit way, and in many places in open and direct expression, claim themselves to be more than of human origin. A definite authority belongs to the written words of the Bible. 'When we come to the apostles we find that their testimony to the divine authority of the Bible is equally clear.'[2] Certain passages, for example, II Tim. iii. 15–16; II Peter i. 21 and iii. 16, are evidences that 'the written word was itself treated as the inspired and authoritative form in which the content of divine revelation had been expressed and handed down'.[3]

---

[1] G. W. Bromiley, 'The Authority of Scripture', *The New Bible Commentary* (ed. F. Davidson, A. M. Stibbs and E. F. Kevan), 1953, p. 15.
[2] *Ibid.*   [3] *Ibid.*, p. 16.

Having dealt with some implications of this witness, he concludes that, in spite of certain difficulties, 'the Bible does lay serious claim to a divine origin, status and authority'.[1] Through its human writings may be traced the authorship of the Holy Spirit. In both the prophetic utterance and the historical events the supernatural are accepted. No artificial distinction is made between the inward content of the Word of God and the outward form. It comes with challenge to belief or unbelief and thus authenticates itself as God's written Word.

This view of the authority of the Bible is, Bromiley believes, in substantial agreement with the Reformed position. The leaders of the Reformation considered the Bible to be inspired and authoritative and the 'sole-sufficient' in matters of faith and conduct.[2] 'They did not take any radical step when they propounded this view' he adds. Such had always been the understanding of the Church with regard to its Scriptures. The Reformers emphasized the importance of the very letter of Scripture,[3] yet they did not do so at the expense of a clear doctrine of the sovereignty of the Spirit. They did, indeed, make much of the inner witness of the Spirit, but not as operating apart from the written Word, but as the indispensable counterpart of God's outward revelation. By 'that emphasis upon the Lordship of the Holy Spirit the Reformers safeguarded themselves against dead literalism and scholastic rationalism in their understanding of Holy Scripture. They yielded to none their loyalty to the given form of the Bible. They had a high view both of the Bible itself and also of its inspiration. They believed the Bible itself is inspired truth. They believed that it is the Word written, a Word given and applied by the Holy Spirit. They taught that that Word must always be respected and received and obeyed. Yet they remembered always that God is the Lord of Scripture, and that it is His voice which must be heard if the

---

[1] G. W. Bromiley, 'The Authority of Scripture', *The New Bible Commentary* (ed. F. Davidson, A. M. Stibbs and E. F. Kevan), 1953, p. 17.

[2] It will be of interest in this connection to compare two recent books in which the theological standpoint of each writer is not the same. Cf. R. C. Johnson, *Authority in Protestant Theology*, 1959, and John Murray, *Calvin on Scripture and Divine Sovereignty*, 1960, Chapters I and II. Both would confirm Bromiley's contention.

[3] Cf. 'There is no hint anywhere in Calvin's writings that the original text contained any flaws at all'. E. A. Dowey, *The Knowledge of God in Calvin's Theology*, 1952, p. 100.

Bible is to do its work. The Bible is not an academic textbook of divine truth, the Euclid of the Christian faith. The text is indeed given by God, but it is always in the hands of God and always applied by God. The Bible must be respected and received and obeyed not because it is a fixed and static letter, but because under the Holy Spirit that letter is the living Word of the living God both to the individual and to the Church'.[1]

Bromiley deals with certain modern trends and sees inadequacies in the Roman Catholic, liberal Protestantism and Barthian views. Concerning the last, he says, 'Barth has performed a useful service by showing that the categories of a dead (as opposed to a living) orthodoxy simply will not do. An abstract objectivism, or a mechanical conception of revelation, is as far from the truth on the one side as is a pure subjectivism or naturalistic view of revelation on the other'.[2]

He considers that the Incarnation provides the key to the correct understanding of the Bible. The ultimate problem concerns the proper relation between the divine and the human. In the case of the Bible, he asks, 'Ought we to think that the Bible is trustworthy merely because we can demonstrate its historical accuracy? Ought we to think it authoritative merely because we have come to know the truth of its message through the Holy Spirit, and irrespective of the historical reliability or otherwise? Ought we not to see the authority of the Bible in the balanced relationship of a perfect form (the objective Word) and a perfect content (the Word applied subjectively by the Holy Ghost)—the form holding the content, and the content not applied except in and with the form?'[3]

It is Bromiley's conviction that the Bible should be seen in this light and for this reason he finds help in the relationship between the divine and the human in Christ. In Him, these two are distinct, yet one. So is it with the Word written, which is the witness to Him. 'It is not enough to deny the divine, to see only a man here, a book there. But it is also not enough to ignore the human, to see only a God here, an oracle there. It is a true paradox (i.e. it is not irrational) that the man Jesus is the Son of

---

[1] G. W. Bromiley, 'The Authority of Scripture', *The New Bible Commentary* (ed. F. Davidson, A. M. Stibbs and E. F. Kevan), 1953, p. 19.   [2] *Ibid.*, p. 22.
[3] *Ibid.* Cf. G. W. Bromiley, 'The Authority of the Bible: The Attitude of Modern Theologians', *The Evangelical Quarterly*, Vol. XIX, No. 2, April 1947, pp. 127–36, esp. p. 136.

God (and faith by the Holy Ghost knows Him to be so). So too
is it a true paradox (i.e. it is not irrational) that the book, the
Bible, can be and is the revelation of God (and faith by the Holy
Ghost apprehends it as such).'[1] The parallel between Christ and
the Bible, he agrees, must not be pressed too far, since the Bible,
however highly regarded, is still 'a creature'. At the same time,
taking the Incarnation as our guide, it will help us to a truer and
fuller understanding of the authority and integrity of the
Scripture, not only in reference to its content, but also as
regards its historical form.

In the Introduction to his published series of addresses on
Authority delivered at a Conference of the General Committee of
the International Fellowship of Evangelical Students in 1957,
D. Martin Lloyd-Jones remarks, 'If I understand the modern
religious situation at all this whole question of authority is one
of the most important problems confronting us'.[2] He is aware,
on the one hand, of the success following the claim to possess
such authority, and, on the other hand, of the need for an
authentic authority if Evangelical faith is to press forward
vigorously and victoriously.

The first of his three lectures argues for the final and supreme
authority of the Lord Jesus Christ. 'Jesus Christ is not one in a
series, He does not represent one authority among a number of
authorities. He stands alone. In the New Testament He is the
sole authority.'[3] He then turns to consider the authority of the
Scriptures. He sees this bound up with the assertion of the
finality of Christ. 'In any consideration of final authority of the
Lord Jesus Christ Himself (with which we have already dealt)
we are driven of necessity to a consideration of the authority of
the Scriptures.'[4] Lloyd-Jones contends that it was the immediate
effect of the Higher Criticism to instil doubt about the authority
of the Bible. Since then the charge has been levelled against the
Conservative Evangelical that he is a 'Bibliolater'. It is claimed
by those who utter this condemnation that they have freed themselves from the crippling burden of an infallible book. For them,
not the Bible, but Christ Himself is their authority, they say. But

---

[1] G. W. Bromiley, 'The Authority of Scripture', *The New Bible Commentary* (ed.
F. Davidson, A. M. Stibbs and E. F. Kevan), 1953, pp. 22–3.
[2] D. Martin Lloyd-Jones, *Authority*, 1958, p. 7.
[3] *Ibid.*, pp. 26–7.   [4] *Ibid.*, pp. 32–3.

impressive as this may sound it does not meet the demands of the situation. Lloyd-Jones asks of them the question, 'How do you know the Lord? What do you know about the Lord, apart from the Scriptures? Where do you find Him? How do you know that what you seem to have experienced concerning Him is not a figment of your own imagination, or not the product of some abnormal psychological state, or not the work perchance of some occult power or evil spirit?'[1] It may sound impressive to say that you go directly to Him, but there is no going to Him without the practical possession of certainty respecting His authority.

Bromiley had maintained with regard to the unique authority of the Bible that 'in the last analysis we accept that authority by faith',[2] and this is a special point made by Lloyd-Jones.[3] Faith does not begin with supplying an answer to the question of the authority of the Bible, it springs out of belief in and submission to that authority, as it is made real by the *testimonium Spiritus internum*. The authority of the Bible is not a matter to be defended, so much as to be declared. It is the presupposition of true biblical teaching and preaching. It is the whole Bible which is the Word of God and it must be viewed as a whole. Lloyd-Jones refers to the 'great army of powerful and convincing arguments from the Scripture itself' used by the Protestant Fathers and the dogmaticians of the seventeenth century, to establish the authority of Scripture. Yet these arguments are not to be considered primary, they occupy a secondary position in order to strengthen faith. Although Lloyd-Jones gives a brief summary of these arguments, he sees greater weight attaching to the Scripture's own claim for itself.[4] Our Lord's teaching, the New Testament view of the Old, and the authority of the Apostles, unite to establish the unique authority of the Bible. The authority, therefore, for which Lloyd-Jones contends, as final for the Christian and the Church, is the authority of Christ as that is documented and expressed in what he refers to, without acknowledgement to Gladstone, as 'the impregnable Rock of Holy Scripture'.[5]

[1] D. Martin Lloyd-Jones, *Authority*, 1958, p. 36.

[2] G. W. Bromiley, 'The Authority of Scripture', *The New Bible Commentary*, p. 15.

[3] D. Martin Lloyd-Jones, *op. cit.*; cf. pp. 38 ff.

[4] *Ibid.*; cf. p. 50 f.   [5] *Ibid.*, p. 60.

In his final lecture, emphasis is placed upon the authority of the Holy Spirit. It is He who is authoritative to lead, to strengthen, to convert and so forth. History has witnessed, however, a fatal one-sidedness in the matter of the relation between the Scriptures and the Spirit. There have been those who have so stressed the inner witness, the inner light, the inner experience, to such an extent that they have displaced the Scripture. While, on the other side, there have been others who have neglected the influence and authority of the Spirit in an exclusive emphasis upon the finality of the Bible. This is, adds Lloyd-Jones, 'a thoroughly artificial and false emphasis'.[1]

It is an undoubted fact that in the last couple of centuries of Christian history there has been, at one time, an overstress on the outward aspect of revelation and authority at the expense of the inward, and, at another time, the virtual disregard of the outward in the interests of the inward. Sometimes there has been a feverish effort revealed to make the objective authoritative in religion, and then there has come a reaction, with an equally frantic attempt to state the subjective as ultimate and final. The tendency to one-sidedness has been throughout recent theological discussion all too evident.

The right relation between the objective and the subjective in religion is an issue of the most fundamental importance and an enquiry demanding the greatest urgency. Whenever the balance between these two becomes upset, then some element of the full truth is inevitably lost. This fact is true over the whole field of epistemology, and such theological realities as divine revelation and religious authority are no exception. 'Theology is certainly a human enquiry, whether or not it be more, whatever its assurances of a more than human reference and validity in the objects with which it deals or the methods by which it deals with them. It is to be expected, therefore, that theology, too, will share in such human error which is common to humanity, and that sometimes such error will be the result of a disproportion of the subjective and objective factors in its special kind of knowledge.'[2]

---

[1] D. Martin Lloyd-Jones, *ibid.*, p. 63. For the same understanding of authority see *Evangelicalism*, Essays by members of the Fellowship of Evangelical Churchmen (ed. J. Russell Howden), 1925, Chapters VI and VII; and also Douglas Johnson, *The Christian and His Bible*, 1953.

[2] James Brown, *Subject and Object in Modern Theology*, The Croall Lectures, University of Edinburgh, 1955, p. 12.

For our own part we are convinced that the fullest account must be given to both necessities in revelation and authority. There must be no divorce set up between the Spirit and the Scriptures. No ultimate antithesis between 'Spirit' and 'Truth' is possible.[1] A one-sided relationship and emphasis cannot meet the demands of the situation or the needs of the soul. A much more intimate connection would appear to be demanded between the Scripture and the Spirit than the protagonists of the opposing views seem to permit. We are not, of course, suggesting the application of the Greek maxim μηδὲν ἄγαν 'nothing too much'; rather we would suggest both, very much. It is not a case of the Spirit without the Scriptures, nor is it a case of the Scriptures without the Spirit. The Spirit cannot do His work without the Scriptures and the Scriptures cannot do theirs without the Spirit. Revelation is not a matter of Spirit only, but of Spirit and Truth. God's word is 'truth', God's work is by the 'Spirit'. The two go together. It is the Scriptures themselves on their side, which give witness to the reality and actuality of the Spirit; they give the assurance that the Holy Spirit has come. It is their assertion, further, that the Spirit will vivify and verify to our understanding the truth of that which the Scriptures themselves declare. On the other hand, the Spirit authenticates to us through the reality of the Scriptures the fact that the Christ has come. But it is through the record, and through it alone, that we have our confidence in Him. It is, then, the Spirit who gives witness to the truths already documented and declared in the Scriptures. It is when the Spirit breathes upon the Word that the truth comes to sight.

To deny the inner activity of the Spirit would be to reduce Christian faith to a mere intellectual assent to the letter of a written Book. 'It is a well-known fact', stated Philip Melanchthon long ago, 'that the herd of Sophists call faith the assent to those things set forth in Scripture. Hence then, that is faith even what the impious possess.'[2] But such is not the true 'fiduciary'

---

[1] Cf. H. D. McDonald, *Ideas of Revelation*, 1959, pp. 284–5.

[2] Philip Melanchthon, *The Loci Communes*, 1521, 'On Justification and Faith', Section 2. Cf. '. . . it is not enough, nor is it Christian, to preach the works, life, and words of Christ as historical facts, as if the knowledge of these would suffice for the conduct of life, although this is the fashion of those who must today be regarded as our best preachers. . . . Rather ought Christ to be preached to the end that faith in Him may be established, that He may not only be Christ, but be Christ

faith of the gospel. It is a mere rational affair against which the
Epistle of James so strongly protests. On the other side, there
are those who conceive of faith as a direct and immediate
inspiration of God and deny the need for Scripture. Such an idea
is to equate faith with a sort of mystic feeling and to
miss altogether its truth-content, and the basic 'propositional'
requirements out of which faith, created by the Spirit, takes its
rise. 'Happily, however, we are not confined to the two extreme
theories; the elements of truth on which they are respectively
based are opposite indeed, but not contrary. If we combine the
outward and the inward—God and man—the moving power and
the living instrument—we have a great and noble doctrine, to
which our inmost nature bears it witness. We have a Bible
competent to calm our doubts, and able to speak to our weakness.
It then becomes, not an utterance in strange tongues, but in the
words of wisdom and knowledge. It is authoritative, for it is the
voice of God; it is intelligible, for it is in the language of men.'[1]
Thus a Scripture without the Spirit makes for a fruitless faith,
while the Spirit without the Scriptures makes for an undisciplined faith. The one makes for a dead orthodoxy, while the other
leads to an unrestrained enthusiasm. The first gives lifelessness
to the Church; and the second, licence to the individual.

The reality of the Spirit's activity through the Scriptures must
be taken with the utmost seriousness. His sovereignty must be
unquestionably recognized. But so, too, must the instrumental
adequacy of the Scriptures be accorded its absolute place in the
scheme of God's redemptive act. It is not the Church, we would
even dare to maintain, but the Scripture, which is 'the extension
of the Incarnation', if anything is to be rightly so designated.[2]
The authority of the Bible, as a real objective reality, must be
given definite and decisive significance. It is still a valid procedure for the Church and the Christian to say: 'To the Law and

for thee and for me, and that what is said of Him, and what His name denotes may
be effectual in us. And such faith is produced and preserved in us by the preaching
why Christ came, what He brought and bestowed, and what benefit it is to us to
accept Him'. Martin Luther, *A Treatise on Christian Liberty, ad. loc.*

[1] B. F. Wescott, *Introduction to the Study of the Gospels,* 1882, p. 33.

[2] In such statements as the following, the Church is accorded a place which, we
believe, does not belong to it. We would ourselves contend that if the Bible were
substituted for the Church in these passages, then they might stand as nearer to the
truth of the matter. 'We can say that Christ and His Church are inseparable entities.'
Anders Nygren, *Christ and His Church,* 1956, p. 90. 'Christ and the Church belong

to the Testimony if they speak not according to these is it because there is no life in them'. The simple fact is, as Luther declared, 'there is no other testimony on earth to Christian truth than the Holy Scriptures'. The Church and the Christian must, indeed, try the spirits to see which are of God. But both will find that He will be authenticated to them as the Holy Spirit, the Spirit which is of God, makes the letter of the Bible the Word of the living God. By authentication of Himself as such, in this way, there will be validated at the same time the authority of the Bible as one with the authority of God. Only so can we declare that our faith does not stand in the wisdom of man, but in the power of God. In this connection there is a profound truth in some words of the 'old Luther' which show that in this particular the position was the same as that of the 'young Luther'. 'Dear Lord God,' he wrote, 'if the Christian faith were to depend on men, and be grounded on words of men, what need do we have for the Holy Scriptures, or why has God given them?'[1]

It may well have been, as Martensen thinks, that the older Protestantism gave undue prominence to salvation as solely and exclusively the reference and design of Scripture and as a result tended to a too individualistic use of the Written Word. Certainly the Scripture does contain much more than the individual needs to know for his own salvation. There is, therefore, a correct emphasis to be put upon the place and purpose of the Bible within the Church. But even here, as Martensen rightly insists, the Holy Spirit acts by means of the Scripture.

'The necessity of Scripture', he then declares in words which sum up the view of the matter with which we wish to end this chapter, 'is not *principally* for the individual, but for the Church; and its full import and design is stated rather in the assertion, that it contains all truth necessary for the preservation of the Church, and for its progressive development towards its final consummation. This again is to say, that by means of the Holy Scripture, under the guidance of the Holy Spirit, the Church not

---

together. They cannot be separated from each other.' 'The Church is a revelation of the invisible Lord, a continued incarnation of Christ on earth.' Gustaf Aulén, *Church, Law and Society*, 1948, New York, pp. 15 and 16. 'The Church is Christ, by reason of the fact that since His resurrection He is present with us and meets us on earth.' *This is the Church* (ed. Anders Nygren), 1952, p. 10.

[1] Quoted by R. C. Johnson, *Authority in Protestant Theology*, 1959, p. 41.

only may be kept in purity of doctrine and true worship, but that in the whole course of her development there can be no new practice or law established, be it in relation to doctrine or to life, which she cannot abolish by means of the eternal principle of truth and life laid down in the Holy Scripture: moreover, that on the one hand, all critical and cleansing activity of the Church, and on the other hand, all building up, edifying and strengthening activity (taking this expression in the widest sense), must find its governing type for all times in the Holy Scriptures. Maintaining as we do that the Holy Ghost guides the Church into all truth by means of the Scripture, we attribute to the Scripture perfect sufficiency and clearness (*sufficientia et perspicuitas*); in so far, that is, as the Church is given through the Scripture the revelation of the Spirit concerning what is advisable or useful for *any particular time*, while Scripture itself must be looked upon for *all times*—much that it contains not being perfectly accomplished until the latter days. Experience, moreover, teaches that whenever a true reform has been accomplished in the Church, the word, *It was not so in the beginning*, has been spoken with telling power against a lifeless ecclesiasticism, because it has spoken in the strength of the Holy Scripture. This holds good not only of the great Reformation of the sixteenth century, but of the many successive protests which have been made in the Middle Ages and in modern times. For as the Church has, in every age, triumphed over that false *gnosis*, which resolves Christianity into merely human reason, by the Word of Scripture, this same word has been a safeguard against a barren orthodoxy, which has built up ecclesiasticism at the expense of Christianity; and it has continually led back to an illumination inseparable from edification, because the apostolic illumination is in itself an enlightenment which leads to salvation.'[1]

[1] H. Martensen, *Christian Dogmatics* (E.T. 1866), pp. 405–6.

CHAPTER NINE

Revelation and Authority

The ultimate issue which emerged from the long and lively discussions and controversies of the past century, which our previous chapter was intended to make clear, concerns the problem of authority. The question of revelation passed into that of authority, and to discover the locus of revelation is to find the seat of authority. In the words of F. W. Camfield, to which we may refer again, it was agreed that 'We must find authority in Revelation, for authority is its hall-mark'. It seems, therefore, a matter of indifference whether we talk of the understanding of revelation or of authority. In the context of religion and religious faith, to say, Here is Revelation, is the same as to say, Here is Authority.

A. THE REVELATION OF AUTHORITY

Under this heading we may summarize, in a very few words in view of all we have said, the dominant ideas of the century. R. E. Davies, in his study of *The Problem of Authority in the Continental Reformers*, concludes that they all, Luther no less than Calvin, failed to emancipate themselves from 'the mediaeval error that the source of authority is necessarily to be found in some place wholly outside the individual'. Without discussing here the historical and theological accuracy of this statement, it may be safely maintained that the present century has witnessed an all-out bid to free itself from this suggested 'mediaeval error'. In the earlier part of our era, any view which identified revelation with its record was strongly resisted. It was, in fact, characteristic of the times to draw a sharp line of distinction between the two. More recent days have seen an equally definite divorce made between the Word and the Words. The significant emphasis of the present is that 'Jesus Christ, the Word made flesh' is 'recognized and acclaimed as the sole Word of God', thus necessitating, as a speaker at the Amsterdam Assembly of 1948 declared, a 'new understanding of the Old and New Testaments'.[1] This 'new understanding' is boldly referred to by Edwin Lewis as 'The Emancipation of the Word of God'.[2]

Lewis remarks, with the statement made at Amsterdam in mind, that 'Christ as "the sole Word of God"; in consequence, "a new understanding of the Bible"—this fairly describes "the new Biblicism"; but the difference from the old Biblicism is nothing less than radical. The old Biblicism shackled the revelation; the new Biblicism would set it free. The old Biblicism was concerned to take the Bible "as is". The new Biblicism is critical, discriminating, unafraid. The old Biblicism yielded a static authoritarianism. The new Biblicism promises to issue in the creation of a dynamic spiritual freedom'.[3]

Freedom from external authority is then the great discovery of our century. But, as even Lewis's own chapter reveals, this freedom from authority resulted in a crop of new theological 'reconstructions' in which each man was his own master, and each believed that to be right which was good in his own eyes. The student of historical theology will be able to add considerably to the list of extraordinary and eccentric consequences following from these new approaches unhampered by historical considerations and no longer bound by the 'mediaeval error' of seeking the source of authority outside and especially in the 'old Biblicism' which 'shackled the revelation'.

But the idea of authority cannot be allowed to pass. It must be sought, then, in the revelation to which the Bible, for the Christian at all events, has some sort of relation. It will be better, therefore, not to speak of the authority of revelation for then the idea of revelation is made to be something external and static. It will be more appropriate to think of the revelation of authority.

Revelation, and consequently authority, was conceived in a radical manner by some to be located in the sensitive conscience.

---

[1] Cf. *Man's Disorder and God's Design*, Vol. 1, 1949, p. 101.
[2] Edwin Lewis, *The Biblical Faith and Christian Freedom*, 1953, Chapter III.
[3] *Ibid.*, p. 31.

Conscience makes Christians of us all, the new gospel announced. Whatever is not of conscience is not of faith. Conscience, God immanent within, is the guide of life; here is that inner light of the soul to which if a man gives heed, he shall do well. To be sure Herbert Spencer had sought to explain conscience in a naturalistic way as the deposit left in the human race by its age-long struggle for existence, as a sort of 'hindsight' which for the next stage in the development becomes 'foresight' by which the upward moving man learns to avoid what frustrates his happiness and impedes his progress. Such a view was rejected as being no sufficient explanation of man's sense of the divine 'ought'. Rufus Jones notes that although Jesus, according to the gospel records, never used the term 'conscience', yet 'that inner tribunal which we name by that word is nowhere more clearly in evidence than in the stages of the decision that carried Jesus to the cross, in dedication to the untried, but ultimately irresistible power of redeeming love'. By His emphasis 'on the nearness of the divine to the human in man', he goes on to urge, Jesus showed that 'the Kingdom of God is an interior spirit and not an external power'.[1] Jesus stressed specially the idea of the Brotherhood of Man, and it was this thought which enlightening the conscience of men has been the reason for the undermining and destroying of long established evils such as Slavery and Feudalism; and by its authority War itself will one day be made to cease.

Conscience, the voice of God in the soul, the light which lighteth every man that cometh into the world, is, therefore, the ultimate locus of revelation and the final seat of authority. By conscience all must be tested: at this bar the 'morality' of the Old Testament is to be judged and rejected. A more sensitive conscience had now been developed under the influence of education and enlightenment. Paul is even quoted by some as a witness to the view, it would be a contradiction in terms to say as an authority: 'By manifestation of the truth commending ourselves to every man's conscience in the sight of God'.[2] And the

---

[1] R. M. Jones, *The Nature and Authority of Conscience*, 1920, pp. 21–2.

[2] II Cor. iv. 2. The Greek term 'syneidesis' rendered 'conscience' is used in the New Testament for what Kant called the 'practical reason' (cf. Acts xxiii. 1; xxiv. 16; Rom. ii. 15; ix. 5; I Cor. viii. 7, 10–11; II Cor. i. 12; iv. 2; I Tim. i. 5, etc.). The word may be an instance of the influence of the Stoic ethic on the moral vocabulary of the civilized world at the time of the Christian era. But the 'conscience'

place of Jesus in the scheme we shall not, we think, be far wrong in saying that He may be regarded as the greatest educator of conscience.

Not all by a long way could concur in this way of stating the case for the source of authority within the individual. There were those who preferred to see revelation supremely as the insights of religious geniuses. The great prophets of religion were not just men of tender conscience in their day; they were essentially men of vision. They were men who could see. For the thousand people who can talk, observes John Ruskin somewhere, there are only a hundred who can think; but for the hundred who can think there is only one who can see and can tell what he sees in a convincing and challenging way. Revelation is, then, a thing of profound spiritual insight by men who had what Clutton-Brock calls a 'scent for truth'. They were men with the gift of apprehension and the grace of appreciation. They saw the movements of God in the dramas of human history; and what they saw they sought to interpret to others. What to less penetrating eyes were but happenings were to the prophets the acts of God. And they sought to persuade their own day and ours that God is real and living and by thus believing they are blessed.

It was, of course, stressed that faith here is not simply believing the prophets' beliefs. It is not a blind submission to any outward authority. It is rather an 'inward beholding', or, as it has been put, 'a keen-eyed response to the *inward* authority with which God speaks to man through Nature, through Conscience, through History and most of all through Jesus Christ'.

The prophet, it is explained by W. R. Inge, 'commends his message to us by awakening a response in our hearts. This is in reality the only way in which a revelation is or can be made to us'. When these men of 'strong soul'[1] speak 'Our hearts leap out to meet their words; we recognize that this is what we wanted; that here is the truth which we could not find for ourselves, the good news which we should not have dared to believe'.[2]

as the New Testament conceives it is not the clear-eye of the soul which some have supposed. It may be purified by grace (cf. I Tim. iii, 9), but it can also be defiled (cf. I Cor. viii. 7).

[1] V. H. Stanton, *The Place of Authority in Matters of Religious Belief*, 1891, p. 32.
[2] W. R. Inge, *Faith and its Psychology*, 1910, p. 81.

Such a conception many writers were not slow to identify with the inner witness of the Spirit. Inge himself had, indeed, maintained that 'it is the indwelling Christ who is the primary authority',[1] and this expression about sums up what a large number of influential writers maintained as the truth of the matter. We have seen how the idea appealed to H. Wheeler Robinson. He found revelation and the authority which goes with it in the inner actuality of the Spirit. The testimony of the Spirit was regarded by many as the final reality both for the Church and the individual Christian. The Church was founded as a community of inspired people, the declaration went. The individual believer had his own inner certitude. It was only as the Spirit of God moved within his soul that the words 'Let there be light' could have their own individual illuminating certainty.

The idea was given an almost 'pantheistic' stress by some teachers. John Caird, for example, in his Gifford Lectures argued that our belief in Christ does not stand or fall 'with the proof of the authenticity of ancient documents'.[2] It has 'a more impregnable foundation than historic tradition—even on the inward witness of a spiritual presence here and now . . . the inward witness of the presence of that redeeming, purifying, hallowing Spirit that was incarnate in Him, and that is still and for ever living not only *for* us, but *in* us, and in all who open their spirits to its life-giving power'.[3] There is no need, he maintains, to bring Christ down from above, or back from a dim and vanished age with painful research. The divine is around and about and those who open their lives to the 'redeeming, hallowing, saving spirit' have 'the irrefragable proof' in themselves.[4] 'The Divine Spirit that was embodied in the life of Christ, and which realizes itself in every soul that yields to its transforming power, wherever and whenever it takes possession of human spirits, is in essence one and the same in all.'[5]

Some sought escape from the pantheistic and subjectivist drift of such a teaching by contending, on the one hand, for the 'sacredness of the human personality' and, on the other hand, by putting emphasis upon the corrective restraints of the 'inspired

---

[1] W. R. Inge, *Faith and its Psychology*, 1910, p. 136.
[2] John Caird, *The Fundamental Ideas of Christianity*, 1899, Vol. II, p. 97.
[3] *Ibid.*   [4] *Ibid.*; cf. pp. 98–9.   [5] *Ibid.*, p. 252.

community'. It was, however, the bold contention that authority is 'not to be sought by any mechanical reference to the letter of His (i.e. Christ's) words on earth, but by seeking and following His Spirit in the heart'.[1] Revelation is an affair of the heart, the Spirit's internal witness within the soul. And here is authority, not mechanical, not external, not static, but spiritual, and inward and dynamic.

That there is truth here must not be denied: indeed, we may say one 'half' of the truth is here. Of the other 'half' there was no clear recognition. It was not made evident, in fact it was not well understood, that there are two that bear witness on the earth, the Spirit and the Scriptures and these two agree in one.

It was not enough to repudiate the intolerable abstract intellectualism of scholasticism by finding relief in a sort of pietism which dwelt much on the mystical union of the soul with Christ, and construe that in the terms of a spiritualizing imagination. The tendency always is to seek escape from a barren dogmatic system by finding satisfaction in a spiritual subjectivism. Christianity, whenever it becomes scholastic, lacks the inspiration of the Spirit; when it becomes mystical it lacks the reality and balance of historical truth. Thus it came about that from the beginning of the present century an effort was made to find the Jesus of History. Revelation must be somehow centred upon and authority grounded in Him. Few saw more clearly than did D. W. Forrest the need to have some historical foundation for the illuminating and enlightening experience of the Spirit which had been set forth as the locus of revelation and the seat of authority. 'It sounds very heroic to affirm', he states at a time when his own words may be considered 'heroic', 'that that faith does not hang upon records, upon the accident of the preservation of the Gospels; that if God's Son entered our humanity and revealed Himself to a few souls in His own generation, who after His death beheld Him as the risen Lord and experienced the outpouring of His Spirit, then that same Spirit could continually work through regenerated men to the spiritual conversion and quickening of human souls, even though the traditions of Christ's humanity had vanished. But, however heroic this proposition may be, it is in the last degree absurd,

[1] Edward Grubb, *Authority in Religion*, 1924, p. 88.

because it is impossible to conceive such a contingency.'[1] Forrest, indeed, goes on to suggest that not only is the idea absurd, it is also, 'dangerous'. It is pleaded that 'faith is founded on an inward experience of your own, corroborated by the similar experiences of other people'. The historical element may as well be dropped. But it is, Forrest argues, exactly this direct touch with the historical Jesus which the simplest believer knows to lie at the root of his confidence.[2] In another volume Forrest seeks to demonstrate in more precise fashion the meaning and measure of Christ's authority. In his book *The Authority of Christ* (1906), he seeks to elaborate the thesis that after all that can be questioned by criticism has been set aside there remains an adequate 'historical residue' sufficient to tie faith to a genuine reality of history. Forrest's was a commendable effort to provide for faith some factual foundation.

At the same time, one is not fully carried by his endeavours, convinced as we are of the absolute need for faith to be firmly grounded in history. Forrest's lot was cast in the period when it was an urgent thing to provide for the claims of Christian experience an historical basis, but it was a day, none the less, when that was virtually impossible to discover. The New Testament had been so torn to shreds in the recent past that there was little which could be confidently pronounced factual. This was not just because Jesus was, as Matthew Arnold says, 'above the heads of His reporters',[3] but because critical analysis had already flowed over into the New Testament and applied to it the same presuppositions which had already weakened faith in the Old. Forrest, in both of the books to which we have made reference, appeared to be acutely aware of the difficulty when he remarks, 'One of the greatest problems is to disentangle the everlasting truth it contains (i.e. the "historical" report) from its accidental embodiment'.[4] The dilemma is then a real one. It appears that it is only by the application of subjective criteria that it is possible to arrive at any acceptable data, to find 'the everlasting truth' embodied in 'its accidental forms', for an historical account. It is in this way that the wheel comes full circle.

---

[1] D. W. Forrest, *The Christ of History and of Experience*, 1906, fifth edition, p. 329.   [2] *Ibid.*; cf. p. 330.
[3] Matthew Arnold, *Literature and Dogma*, 1873, Chapter VI.
[4] D. W. Forrest, *The Christ of History and of Experience*, p. 334.

Rejecting the records as altogether historically factual, there had to be eliminated from them whatever the conscience could not verify, or the reason could not explain or the spiritual sensitivity could not authenticate. The actual result was that there was no possible agreement as to what was to be accepted, because conscience and reason and spiritual sensitivity varied from writer to writer. In the end the much acclaimed 'historical sense' turned out to be even more subjective than the subjectivism which it set out to correct. The authority of Jesus came to be nothing other than that of the individual critic's ingenuity, or imagination or intuition, as the case may have been. The many volumes each supposed to present us with the authority of the Jesus of history were but the outcome of each writer's own uncontrolled dream or unrestricted daring.

The real truth of the matter is that the Authority of Jesus was lost because there was hardly any data left for a picture of a Jesus who could be authoritative. It was allowed as a sort of grudging apologetic that He saw more deeply into the truth of things than other men and therefore that it was proper to speak of His authority as greater in degree than that of other men. The idea is put by one writer with admirable frankness: 'the authority with which Jesus of Nazareth speaks of God, of sin, of forgiveness and of righteousness, is the outcome of that wondrous clearness of spiritual vision which shines everywhere on the Gospel pages, and which can only have been possible for One who lived ever in perfect communion with God. His authority covers the matters concerning which He had special knowledge, not those of which He had not. To quote His words in support of traditional theories about the Old Testament is to miss His true significance, to go back from the light and freedom of the Gospel to the darkness and bondage of the Scribes and Pharisees. He is our highest outward Authority in Religion; but no outward Authority can ever be final and absolute.'[1]

Was it as a revolt from such a conclusion that the Dialectical-Crisis theologians renounced all attempts to find revelation and authority in any measure in the historic Jesus? Harnack and company wanted an historical Jesus but could not find one: Barth and company are in a better position to have such but do not want one. The Barthians, it is well known, and we have

[1] Edward Grubb, *Authority in Religion*, 1924, pp. 80–1.

referred to the fact on a number of occasions, constantly repudiate what one writer refers to as a 'blind credulity of unimaginative verbalism'. The revelation of which the Bible speaks, it is asserted, is not to be 'mechanically equated with the total Biblical language'. The Word, the only Word, is the living Christ; and here is God's final redemptive Act. The gospels are not properly spoken of as the Word of God: the Word is He who became flesh.[1] Brunner especially insists that it is the Word of God that is the Revelation of God, and it is in the reality of the 'Divine–Human Encounter' that revelation becomes effective and authority dynamic. Thus has the Word of God been emancipated in the 'new biblicism'. The Word is to be sharply distinguished from the words. The Word is 'of God'; the words are 'of men'. Revelation and authority are not 'of men', but 'of God'. They are discovered in the 'encounter' with the living Word. The truth in this Barthian thesis must be acknowledged and appreciated. But it fails, we think, to give right significance to the words in its exclusive emphasis on the Theology of the Word. It will be sufficient, at the present, to re-echo a statement made above. Here we would state it like this: there are two that bear witness in heaven, the Word and the words, and these two agree in one.

Authority, then, we have seen, varies according to the understanding of revelation. Indeed, as revelation is, so is authority: there is the authority of conscience, of religious genius, of the experience of the Spirit, of the historic Jesus, or of the encountered Christ. We may perhaps appreciate anew the famous witticism of the thirteenth century of Alanus of Lille when he said, *'Auctoritas cereum habet nasum id est, in diversum potest flecti sensum'*: 'Authority has a wax nose; it can be twisted in different directions'.

B. THE AUTHORITY OF REVELATION

In a reference to the subject of revelation Karl Barth remarks that 'It is possible to speak in an original manner on every subject in the whole wide world except this one. Of this subject it is possible only to speak faithfully, i.e. exegetically'.[2] Conse-

---

[1] Cf. Edwin Lewis, *The Biblical Faith and Christian Freedom*, 1953, p. 45.

[2] Karl Barth, *God in Action*, 1936, p. 7. The cynic might be forgiven if he were

quently, while no claim to originality is made in what follows, it is our desire to give as faithfully, if not quite exegetically, as we can some positive statement of our own understanding of the topic of our heading.

It is frequently declared in present-day discussions of the subject that the ultimate seat of authority in religion is God Himself. And this is a most necessary truth upon which constantly to insist. It is, indeed, a fundamental fact that there can be nothing finally binding upon human beings, whose chief end is to glorify God, but God's holy will. Only that which is clearly and convincingly of Him can be decisive for religious faith. It is in the reality of and the response to the authority of God that man finds his freedom and fulfils his destiny. Man is essentially a responsible being before God. In the presence of God he discovers that his rightful attitude is that of a suppliant not a sovereign. Here he becomes aware that he does not exercise authority, he merely recognizes it. Before God the human understanding can find no reasons for owning God's authority. Here the will knows its own Master and the heart its Lord. 'God is His own authority for the religious, and therefore the last for the race; and He is the only Authority we have in the end.'[1] God remains for ever the Object of Man's authority, not the Subject for man's contemplation. God is holy imperative. Man, on the other hand, has a receptivity for authority. Herein is his distinctiveness, his essential greatness. He has power to *own* authority. This is the *a priori* in man, not itself an authority, but the capacity for authority. It cannot, therefore, be too emphatically declared that God is His own Authority for the religious. But this unqualified declaration, true and vital as it is, does not get us very far. The questions which immediately arise are, Where is this authority to be found? and, How does it come to us?

To answer such questions we will first of all venture the proposition that authority is located in the revealed will of God. In an age past Augustine wrestled with the problem of authority and urged on by the momentum of his own profound religious experience he came to realize that revelation and authority are correlatives. It is in His self-disclosure that God's authority is to

to urge that Barth in his *Church Dogmatics* has used much space about that which it is impossible to speak of in an original manner!

[1] P. T. Forsyth, *The Principle of Authority*, 1913, second edition, 1952, p. 146.

be found: God's authority is expressed in His revelation. This means that 'Revelation is the key to religious authority'.[1] There can be no authority of God unless there is revelation; for in the locus of revelation is the seat of authority. Revelation is the Object of religion disclosed as authority. God is known only in revelation. And in revelation God is disclosed not as an Object of leisurely, theoretic investigation. God is known in revelation as urgent, demanding and authoritative.

In revelation the main thing is not that God gives Himself to us to be *known* but He gives Himself to be *owned*. Herein is the contrast between religious knowledge and science. 'In religion the fundamental movement of the knowledge is in the reverse direction from that of science. In science we move to the object of knowledge; in religion it moves to us.'[2] Essentially then religion is only possible by revelation. And in revelation God as Ultimate Authority speaks to man who has a receptivity for authority. It is important, therefore, to insist that 'authority can only be found in the revealed will of God'.[3]

Yet even this statement of Griffith-Jones leaves the issue too vague. Something more definite and precise is called for. Authority is located in the revealed will of God, but where is that will revealed?

Revelation has, of course, a specific meaning. The word itself means 'a drawing back of a veil'. And this is exactly what God does in His revelation. In a general way, from Nature, from the movements of history, from the spiritual constitution of man, we may gain an idea that there is, so to speak, Something, perhaps Someone, behind the curtain. But revelation is God drawing back the curtain and showing Himself. In revelation God is not just giving us information about Himself; He gives Himself. He, actually, dramatically and savingly comes forth, disclosing His own being and character as the Triune God of all grace.

Christians believe that there was a preparatory revelation, a preparation of the stage, an announcement, so to say, of God's real forthcoming. There was a disclosure made to selected

---

[1] Bernard Ramm, *The Pattern of Authority*, 1957, p. 20.
[2] P. T. Forsyth, *The Principle of Authority*, 1913, second edition, 1952, p. 150.
[3] E. Griffith-Jones, 'The Bible: Its Meaning and Aim', Peake's *Commentary on the Bible*, 1919, new edition with supplement, reprint, 1948, p. 7.

persons before there was the Self-disclosure in a special Person.
Revelation by proclamation preceded revelation by incarnation.
In this preparatory revelation, however, there was a Word of
God given. There were chosen spokesmen of a divine unveiling.
And it was the revelation which gave them their authority. Their
authority was not in their own person, but in the word uttered.
No subjective experience, no inner light, no illuminated imagination gave them their authority. The word was their authority,
the word which in coming to them reconciled them and recreated
them and made them God's ambassadors. The word they heard
was not for themselves alone or indeed for themselves
supremely. It was a word which could not be hidden in their
hearts; it had to be uttered forth. The word was the revelation
and consequently the authority for those to whom it came, for
here was the revealed will of God. For the Old Testament
believers, their authority was the Word of God which came to
them through the spokesmen of the divine disclosure. Thus it
was that to disbelieve the utterance of the messenger of God was
to disbelieve God and to disobey him was to disobey God. Their
authority was not what appealed to them but what was declared
to them. For no moral being is his own ultimate authority: in
truth, that only can be our authority which has no authority
beyond itself, which is its own authority. 'An authority which
has its source in ourselves is no authority. In us authority can
have but its echo, never its charter.'[1]

But for the Christian it is his assertion and assurance that
God's revelation is to be found fully in Christ. Here has been
embodied and expressed God's will in His purposes of pardon
and grace. Christ stands as the final Exegete of God. True it is
that 'We cannot make any mistake about God after we have
known Jesus'.[2] For the Christian, then, the ultimate seat of
authority is God's will revealed in Christ.

In an article on 'The Authority of Christ', James Denney has
drawn attention to the fact that the first recorded comment on
the teaching of Jesus is that, 'They were astonished at his
doctrine for he taught them as one having authority and not as
the scribes'. The scribes appealed to tradition, but He made no
such appeal. It was evident that He was Himself the authority.

---

[1] P. T. Forsyth, *The Principle of Authority*, p. 299.
[2] Otto Borchert, *The Original Jesus* (E.T. 1953), p. 460.

All His teaching bears the character of this divine authority and the absoluteness of His authority in the sphere of ultimate knowledge of God is asserted in Matt. xi. 27: 'in the work of revelation and especially in the revelation of Himself as Father, God has no organ but Christ, and in Christ, He has an adequate organ'.[1]

The essential purpose of the divine revelation is redemptive; it is to give that knowledge of God in which consists eternal life. The 'chief end of revelation' is not philosophy, though it has a philosophy profound and worthy. It is not doctrine, though it has a doctrine satisfying and inspiring. It is not enjoyment, though it has its experience precious and lasting; it is not even morality, though it has its ethic unique and powerful. Christianity *has* all these, but *is* far more than them all. It is the religion of redemption, including salvation from sin, equipment for holiness, and provision for life to be lived in fellowship with God and for His glory.[2] God's revelation His of grace and truth; this means, as Warfield says, that 'God's authoritative revelation is His gracious revelation; God's redemptive revelation is His supernatural revelation'.[3] And echoing the words of Ramm, we would contend that the saving action of God in the world and in experience is an action of divine grace. God's imperial authority is most graciously expressed. When God binds His authority on men it is an act of grace. In God's supreme revelation in His Son, there is the epitome of revelation as grace and truth.[4] It is perfectly in accord with the requirements of the case then for Gore to assert that 'Jesus Christ is the summary of authority in religion. He is this because He reveals God, as being His image'.[5] It is central in the Christian Gospel and vital for Christian experience to give unhesitating stress to our Lord's finality and authority. But it is just here the real issue comes. 'To say vaguely that the revelation is Christ, or that Christ is its centre, is the source of all our confusion.'[6] The question may be immediately pressed, What Christ is this who is authoritative?

[1] James Denney, *Hasting's Dictionary of Christ and the Gospels*, ad. loc.
[2] Cf. W. H. Griffith Thomas, *Hastings Dictionary of the Bible*, one volume, p. 797.
[3] B. B. Warfield, *The Inspiration and Authority of the Bible*, reprint, 1948, p. 100.
[4] Cf. Bernard Ramm, *The Pattern of Authority*, 1957, p. 21.
[5] Charles Gore, *Incarnation*, Bampton Lectures, 1891, p. 172.
[6] P. T. Forsyth, *The Person and Place of Jesus Christ*, 1909, fifth edition, 1946, p. 151.

In answer to this we would enter our second proposition to the effect that the authority which is located in Christ as revealing the will of God is interpreted for us through chosen media. There is only one Christ who is authoritative. It is not the mere Figure of the gospel narratives. The fact is, of course, that there is no understanding of the historic Jesus apart from faith's affirmations, and at the same time, lest we fall a victim to the opposite error, we would stress that faith's affirmations are of a Figure who is genuinely historical. 'It is the whole Biblical Christ that is truly and deeply historical Christ.'[1]

It is often pointed out that Jesus never wrote a book even though we acknowledge Him as having for us the authority of the revealed will of God. But the fact is that this interpretation of the fact of Christ has come to us through His chosen apostles. Their business was to interpret Him. The apostles were men with a unique vocation; they were God's 'elect and providential personalities'. They were not corruptors of the self-disclosure of God in Christ: they were its conveyors. Their words were not an intrusion upon the revelation but part of the scheme of revelation. This means for us that the Christ who is authoritative is the Christ who is interpreted.

Gore has argued that 'the first Christians looked to two kinds of authority—the authority of the Old Testament and the authority of apostolic teaching or tradition'.[2] This is but another way of stating that the Christ who is authoritative is the whole biblical Christ: in the Old Testament prefigured, and in the New presented. It is impossible to speak of an authoritative Christ apart from the Bible in which He is set forth. The historical preparation and the apostolic interpretation are essential to a full estimate of the Saviour who alone is absolute. The Old Testament preparation for the revelation in Christ is not a mere ornamental prefix to it, nor is the apostolic understanding of God's revealed will in Christ a mere addition to it. They are part of it. In the one revelation is figured, in the other it is finalized. When, therefore, it is said that Christ is authoritative it must be understood that this is the Christ who is so.

The apostolic interpretation was not the result of human musings upon the fact of Christ. It was a part of the revealing act.

---

[1] P. T. Forsyth, *The Person and Place of Jesus Christ*, 1909, fifth edition, 1946, p. 169.   [2] Charles Gore, *The Doctrine of an Infallible Book*, 1924, p. 33.

The apostolic men stood in close contact with Christ and for this reason they held a position historically unique; yet it was not merely their proximity to Jesus which gave them their interpretation. Neither was it the outcome of unusual insight nor religious genius. They were men instructed by the Spirit, men who received the gift of interpreting knowledge from the ascended Lord. Their interpretation was His instruction. 'The compilation of the New Testament out of the "Gospels", with their Apostles, and the "Apostolus", is clearly the expression of two convictions: (A) that in a certain sense the apostles are equal to Christ in that they, being chosen not only to be witnesses, but also dispensers of His power, are His continuation; and (B) that the *attestation* of a revelation is not less important than its *content*.'[1]

It will be observed how the ethical injunction of the apostles become authoritative because the New Testament knows no ethics save that of Christ redeemed lives. Paul, for example, charges his readers to bear one another's burdens. We have no precept of Christ's to this effect and yet he says to obey this word is to fulfil the law of Christ.[2] 'I am not obliged to obey Paul', remarks Kierkegaard, 'because he is clever, or exceptionally clever, but I must submit to Paul because he has divine authority.' It must then be insisted that 'the word of the apostles itself forms part of the revelation of God through Jesus Christ. The act of the historical divine revelation is completed only where, in the spoken word of the apostles, it becomes the knowledge of faith, the confession of faith, and the witness which creates faith. Only after Jesus Christ has revealed Himself to an Apostle has the divine revelation reached its goal; the circuit is now complete'.[3]

Geldenhuys has convincingly shown that a unique authority is involved in the very title 'apostle'. The Apostle was one set forth and sent out for a definite purpose. Commenting on several passages in his epistles, Geldenhuys concludes that 'Paul thus unequivocally declares that the preaching of the Gospel by him and by the other apostles has an ἐφάπαξ, once-for-all character, because Jesus Himself gave them the authority and the equipment

[1] Adolf Harnack, *The Origin of the New Testament*, 1914 (E.T. 1925), p. 44.
[2] Gal. vi. 2.
[3] Emil Brunner, *Revelation and Reason* (E.T. 1946), p. 122.

362 THEORIES OF REVELATION

to act and teach as His שְׁלוּחָ֫ים '.[1] It was, then, through God's chosen media that the Church was given a normative gospel and a formative word.

Gore is therefore bound to give some qualifications to the bald assertion that 'The Christian authority is simply Jesus Christ'. He adds significantly that 'for the external knowledge of our Lord, the knowledge of what He taught and was, we are dependent, by His deliberate intention, upon the witness of His apostles'. Believers in Christ, he contends, will regard the apostles as something more than mere witnesses, they were, indeed, witnesses qualified for a unique function by a special inspiration. It was their call and prerogative to take of the things of Christ and declare them unto us. Wescott marks the position of the apostles as unique and so also by implication the office of the apostolic writings as a record of their teaching. 'Christians', states Gore, 'believe then that the apostles were specially enlightened to present to us without distortion the person and teaching of our Lord, and familiarity with their writings through nineteen centuries has confirmed that belief. We cannot as a matter of historical enquiry go behind the apostles, for our Lord wrote nothing Himself; as a matter of fact we do not need to go behind it. In the apostolic teaching, then, we find the ultimate court of appeal in respect of "the faith once delivered to the saints". He that heareth them, heareth Him.'[2]

The authority for religion rests in God but it has become a genuine reality for us because located in the divine revelation: and for the Christian that is Jesus Christ, the Word made flesh. But the Christ who is thus authoritative is the Biblical Christ, the Christ, that is, indicated and interpreted by divinely chosen and commissioned representatives. A further stage in presenting the position must now be taken. The proposition must consequently be advanced that the authority of revelation is perpetuated by the Written Word.

[1] N. Geldenhuys, *Supreme Authority*, 1953, p. 77. Cf. 'it is clear on what the apostles based their claim that they, and they alone, are the שְׁלוּחָ֫ים of the Lord; namely, they saw the risen Jesus and He Himself chose, commissioned and equipped them to be His "apostles". . . . Never again could or can there be persons who possess all these qualifications to be שְׁלוּחָ֫ים of Jesus. Just as the revelation of God in Christ is ἐφάπαξ, "einmalig" (once for all), the action of the risen Lord in and through His apostles in laying the foundations of His Church for all time is once and for all'. *Op. cit.*, pp. 73–4.

[2] Charles Gore, *Incarnation*, 1891, pp. 188–9.

It has been observed that Christ wrote no book: this fact has been taken by some to argue that it was never His purpose to give to His Church authoritative records. But the simple fact is, of course, that our Lord could not have expanded and expounded the redemptive significance of His coming until the crowning event itself had been accomplished. It is, however, our conviction that He has fulfilled this necessity in the words of the apostles. True, He wrote no book, except through them: they were in a very definite sense His posthumous penmen. What He was unable to teach them in the days of His flesh He as the ascended Lord, by the power of His Spirit, spoke to them.

It was not possible that His whole enterprise of grace could be allowed to pass. Unless some adequate provision for its preservation were made His work would have been tragically stillborn. But an open-minded reading of the New Testament makes it certain that He did make provision, not only for the elucidation and finalization of His revelation to the people for the first days, but also for its perpetuation for all days.

Calvin puts this conviction with telling cogency when he observed that 'since no daily responses are given from heaven, and the Scriptures are the only records in which God has been pleased to consign His truth to perpetual remembrance, the full authority which they ought to possess with the faithful is not recognized, unless they are believed to have come from heaven, as directly as if God had been heard giving utterance to them'.[1]

The Scriptures give us God's word written. Here is the embodied account of the revelatory fact. And the authority of God belongs as much to the interpretation and application of God's self-disclosure in grace as it does to the actuality of the event itself. 'The apostles were recognized in the Church', says Leitzmann without hesitation, 'as the only unconditional legitimate vehicles of the Spirit. Everything which claimed to be the working of the Spirit was tested by their messages. In this way their writings were regarded as inspired by the Spirit, and therefore of final divine authority. They came to be regarded as equal in origin to the documents of the Old Testament, or, to speak more accurately, as a necessary complement at its side and bringing it to a completion; they also were "Holy Scriptures". A New Testament came to stand along with the Old and it

---

[1] John Calvin, *Institutes of the Christian Religion*. Berridge's Trans., Vol. I, p. 68.

became customary to appeal to it by using the solemn words
"It is written", in a way similar to that which at an earlier date
had been applied only to the Old Testament.'[1]

The early Church had no doubt but that the ascended Lord
fulfilled Himself in the words of the apostles, and consequently
they regarded their words as His. These were the men who
spoke in His Spirit and by His Spirit. In them the promise to
lead into all the truth was made good. So certain was this to the
first Christians that Harnack can say, 'the Holy Spirit and the
Apostles became correlative conceptions, with the consequence
that the Scriptures of the New Testament were indifferently
regarded as composed by the Holy Spirit or the Apostles'.[2]

Revelation is then incomplete apart from the apostolic interpretation. In fact, in the apostolic interpretation we see the Christ
explaining Himself. He as living and unsilenced unfolds the
fulness of the conquest He has achieved. Having the Apostles'
Word we do not lose God's Word: we gain it, we receive it. It
is for this reason, and only for this reason could the apostles
claim 'for their words, especially on eternal truth, a like
permanent authority with Christ's. They even ignore His
precepts, which they seldom or ever quote to their Churches;
they make their own, and they expect from them the obedience
due to Christ'.[3] This fact must be taken quite seriously. The
apostles regarded their words on a level with Christ's because
they believed that He spoke through them. Without this
certainty it would have been nothing short of blasphemy from
them to enter the claim they did; it would be tantamount to
putting the redeemed above the Redeemer, and the servant
above his Lord. Those to whom the word came were not bibliolaters when they received the apostolic proclamation, not as the
mere desires of respected religious advisers, but as the authoritative statements of the divine will, as much His words as if He
Himself had spoken or written.

The indicators and interpreters of God's revelation were not
just a religious élite group. They knew themselves to be men

[1] H. Leitzmann, *The Foundation of the Church Universal*, 1938, p. 127. Cf. his
Beginning of the Christian Church, 1937, p. 92.
[2] A. Harnack, *The Origin of the New Testament*, 1914 (E.T. 1925), p. 49
(footnote).
[3] P. T. Forsyth, *The Person and Place of Jesus Christ*, 1909, fifth edition, 1946,
p. 165.

inspired of God. Their inspiration did not just give them religious ideas. An inspiration which is limited to thoughts may be a thrilling private luxury, but it has no significance, no relevancy and no permanency, unless it is embodied in language as the living medium of communication. In inspiration God's concern was not to excite the souls of the few but to transmit His thoughts to the many. An inspiration which is not conveyable and not conveyed is of no use. An inspiration which has no reference to its vehicle of communication would seem to be precarious. Floating notions, like 'songs without words', have no stability. It is when they take shape that they become significant. It is a serious question for faith whether we have inspired ideas in the past or an embodied inspiration in the present. It is not simply that holy men thought as they were moved by the Holy Spirit, but that they spake. It must be confidently asserted that not only were their ideas Spirit-given but that their verbal expression was under the guidance of the same Spirit. Under the superintendency of the divine Spirit the language which faithfully reproduced the thoughts was secured. There is no suggestion here, it must be urged, of a process. Our Lord Himself stated that the words which He spoke were not His own but those given to Him by the Father who sent Him. There is no idea of the method which brought about this result in His declaration. The fact is asserted but the process is not described. It would not be sufficient to say that Jesus had God-given thoughts. The truth is rather that the words He spoke matched His thoughts in a divinely adequate way. The disciples were not called upon to read His thoughts but to hear His words; and the words He spake they are spirit and they are life. No less is it the case with the words spoken by His apostolic men. It is in the union of the divine and the human that the essence of inspiration lies. It is not possible to comprehend this interplay, but all genuine Christian experience is a witness to its reality and actuality. In the process the man is not turned into a machine. But the whole process is completed only in the result, in its fulfilment in language. Without that the mysteries unveiled before the eyes of the seers and the ideas brought to the minds of the prophet and apostle, would remain confused shadows and vague notions. When they are expressed in an adequate language they become clarified, permanent and authoritative.

When addressed to man the human element becomes part of the Divine message, since the Divine message can be grasped only when defined and moulded according to the laws of man's being. This means quite emphatically that the Bible is rightly said to be inspired no less than its prophets and apostles. It is not simply that they had holy thoughts, but that they uttered divine words. Of course the Bible will reflect and perpetuate the peculiar idiosyncrasies of each prophet and apostle, of his time and his environment, but they do nevertheless give forth a divine word which is for all time and for all circumstances. Not only did the creators of the Bible see and hear, but they set forth what they saw and heard. They are in a profound sense God's spokesmen —God's penmen.

To remain Christians we must reproduce the Christianity of the apostolic gospel and the apostolic Church, but 'it is only through the apostles that we have received Christianity and that Christianity *only* is genuine, which can show itself to be *Apostolic*'.[1] But to reproduce this apostolic Christianity we are shut up to the written word as the only guarantee of that Christianity: 'For the Christian Church is the company of all those who, on the basis of the Biblical testimony, recognize and believe that Jesus is the Christ, i.e. the Messiah of Israel, the Son of the living God, the Saviour of the world.'[2] Being shut up to the written word, we are, *ipso facto*, bound by its pages as our authority. We have no real authority apart from the Biblical Christ, the Christ who reveals the will of God.

It was only when the conception of the Church changed from a fellowship of redeemed people into an institution in which the rule was vested in the few that the Bible was dethroned from its proper place. The first Church regarded the written Scriptures, not as the first word in an evolutionary process, but as the final word in the revelatory fact. To the redeemed community it was the word of God in which and through which it found its life, its authority and its nourishment. When the Church built up its sacerdotal system, it found itself unable to justify its accretions from the Scripture, consequently it adopted tradition as a sufficient warrant. The authority of the Bible was lost in the

---

[1] H. Martensen, *Christian Dogmatics* (E.T. 1866), p. 25.
[2] Wilhelm Vischer, *The Witness of the Old Testament to Christ* (E.T. 1949), Vol. I, p. 7.

Church when the Church had ceased to be that of the New Testament. Without the security of a written Scripture the mediaeval Church virtually lost Christ: saints and relics took the place of the Saviour and the Redeemer. 'The specific appeal to the Scriptures of the New Testament to verify or correct current tendencies is gone . . . the safeguard has vanished.'[1] The tie, as H. R. Mackintosh remarks, between the Scriptures and the Saviour is an absolutely vital tie. Only when Christ is seen and heard can He be worshipped and obeyed, and it is in and through the Scriptures that He is seen and heard.

This puts the relation between the Bible and the Church in right perspective. The Bible is, to be sure, in the custody of the Church but it is not in its control. The contention that since the Bible is a product of the Church, then the Church is to be regarded as the supreme authority does injustice to the facts. To acknowledge the historic fact that the Church was prior to the records is not to admit that the Church is pre-eminent to the records. To be first does not mean to be final. To be anterior does not prove an event to be superior. The truth is, of course, that the Church was itself the product of the apostolic word. It was the oral message which created the saved communities in which the apostolic word was regarded as authoritative. 'As long as the Apostles' teaching was available nothing was required, but as time went on it was necessary to embody the Apostolic message in permanent form. Thenceforth to all eyes its written Word became equivalent to the spoken Word as the seat of authority. The fact is the same throughout; the form alone has changed. Thus, the Apostles were the seat of authority at the first, and they have continued so to this day, the only difference being between their spoken and the written Word. The Word created the Church, not the Church the Word'.[2] Christ's work in its revelatory significance is transmitted and communicated by the written word. If salvation comes to men apart from the Word, if it is indeed found in the Church, then the necessity for the Bible has gone. 'If, in fact, the Church be

---

[1] Charles Gore, *The Body of Christ*, 1901, p. 33.

[2] W. H. Griffith-Thomas, *The Principles of Theology*, 1930, pp. 125–6. Cf. 'The Books of the Bible were given *to* the Church more than *by* it, and they descended on it rather than rose from it. The Canon of the Bible rose from the Church, but not its contents.' P. T. Forsyth, *The Person and Place of Jesus Christ*, 1909, fifth edition, 1946, p. 140. Cf. *The Principle of Authority*, pp. 96, 142, 146–55.

infallible, it is impossible to understand why the Bible was given.'[1]

The position adopted here can now be given a summary statement. God in His revelation is authoritative for religious faith. But that revelation which has been finalized in Christ has been interpreted by the apostles to become available for all following generations in the Scriptures. The Scriptural word, then, becomes the authority for the faith, life and guidance of the Church and for the individual believer. The Scriptures are the divinely inspired statement of God's revealed will and especially as that is demonstrated in the Person of Christ, His Son, our Lord. As the Old Testament prepared the way, so the New Testament proclaims the reality, gives the interpretation and assures the continuity of God's redemption. This action of God comes new to every age in the words of Scripture as it is read or heard, understood, received, believed and lived. Here God actually speaks forth His will which is authoritative for every generation. The authority of revelation is not however the characters of the alphabet printed upon a page but the authority of the Lord God Himself who has spoken, and speaks again, in, with and by the Holy Scriptures. The Apostles, therefore, 'were not panes of bad glass, but crystal cups the Master filled. They were not mere mediums even, but sacraments. They were not mere channels but agents, not vehicles of Christ but members of Him. They did not merely take their departure from Jesus, they had their life, and function, and truth in Him always. We have no testimony but theirs, in which also the fact itself touches us. The fact works upon us only in their interpretation'.[2]

A further proposition must be added here since it must be insisted that authority is mediated by the Holy Spirit. The Scriptures are authoritative for the Christian and in the Church, because it is part of the organism of revelation. But its authority is an authority which finds meaning and possibility only through the Spirit. Here is one of the important emphases made by the Reformers. It was neither the Bible alone as something to be

---

[1] G. Salmon, *The Infallibility of the Church*, 1888, reprint, cheap edition, 1933, p. 117. Cf. '. . . the Scripture as the product of the Spirit's interpretation gives testimony to the believer and lends authority to the Church instead of receiving from the Church its authority'. John Macpherson, *The Westminster Confession of Faith* with Notes and Introduction, second edition, 1882, p. 36.

[2] P. T. Forsyth, *The Principle of Authority*, 1913, second edition, 1952, pp. 134-5.

mechanically followed nor the Spirit alone as an inner impulse to be acted upon, that they stressed. A religion of the fixed word without the free Spirit is notional and a religion of the free Spirit without the fixed word is nebulous. The Spirit and the Word go together. This 'duality' of Spirit and Word, as it has been called, must never be lost. It is rightly declared that the Scriptures function in the ministry of the Spirit and the Spirit functions in the Word 'The *duality* of the Word and the Spirit must always be maintained, for it is in this *duality* that the Protestant and Christian principle of authority exists.'[1] The fullest insistence must be given to this union of Scripture and Spirit: it is not, indeed, a case of one above or prior to the other; but both together. 'These two principles must always be held together, so that it may be said either that: (1) our authority is the Holy Spirit speaking in the Scriptures, or, (2) our authority is the Scriptures sealed to us by the Holy Spirit.'[2] The Voice that said to the Apostle, 'Write', was the Voice of the Spirit, and what is written is then the Spirit's Voice; and he who hears the Voice has understood the living authority of the Scriptures.

It will conclude our conception of the stages of authority if a few remarks are added on the final proposition: authority is appropriated within Christian experience. This works out in three spheres, in the individual experience of the believer, in the community experience of the Church, and in the crystallized experience of the creeds.

Without expanding these ideas here, each one of which demands a volume on its own, the general drift of our point of view can be put in short compass. Real authority it must be clearly understood always exists independently of any personal appropriation of it, yet it must be recognized and received if it is to become a decisive reality within experience. In Christian experience God's redemptive will becomes our spiritual authority by faith. Indeed faith might be defined, in line with the duality of the Spirit and Scripture, as the illumination of divine authority by the Spirit and the recognition of divine authority in the Word. Faith is the mode by which authority is appropriated. The two, the existing authority and the personal appropriation, must not be confused. 'If the living God has spoken, His word of

---

[1] Bernard Ramm, *The Pattern of Authority*, 1957, p. 30.
[2] *Ibid.*, p. 29.

revelation is the authority in religion. If this word is made permanent through writing, then the written revelation is our authority in religion. A man accepts this written revelation as his authority in religion by personal appropriation. But whatever the subjective ground for receiving this revelation might be, it neither constitutes nor compromises the authority of the divine revelation.'[1]

Freedom in religion is the wisdom of obedience: it is the realization of authority and its appropriation in personal dedication. Absolute obedience, as Forsyth remarks, is the condition of entire freedom. The appropriation of God's redemptive revelation is at once the end and the limit of personal freedom.

It must be stressed that the mode of appropriation, or, indeed, the individual's own act of appropriation, does not itself make authority. The ground for the personal reception of authority is not in its turn another authority. To make the individual his own authority is to be guilty of confusing the appropriation with the actuality. Herein is the error of all who seek authority in the religious experience itself, or in spiritual insight or in inner vision and so forth. Every believing man must see his authority in the revealed will of God as that is centralized in the life and work of Christ and finalized and perpetuated in the Holy Scriptures. It is certainly true that this authority must be personally appropriated. God's revelation is a revelation of grace and truth and the one who has been apprehended by divine grace and truth has the witness in himself. Such can say, 'I know whom I have believed'. For such the authority of God has become an appropriated reality, an authority experienced. So has the authority for experience become the authority within experience. 'Christian obedience means actual obedience to an authority we have found, and found only because it first finds us.'[2]

The Church rightly understood is the company of those, each one of whom has appropriated the authority of God's revelation within experience. And the richness of the experience of the many is greater and fuller than that of the one. There is therefore a vital sense in which this wider community appropriation

---

[1] Bernard Ramm, *The Pattern of Authority*, 1957, p. 41.
[2] P. T. Forsyth, *The Principle of Authority*, 1913, second edition, 1952, p. 272.

of authority must affect the individual. To turn towards the One, says Berdyaev, is not to turn away from the Many. The devil alone is the Great Neutral. Wesley in one of his sermons makes the revealing remark that there are no friendships in hell. Thus arises the paradox: religion to be vital must be personal, but a purely individualistic religion is false to the essential nature of faith. 'The knowledge of God creates community, and indeed community is the aim of the divine revelation.'[1] The Reformation made religion personal, but it never made it individualistic. In the Church, however, the individual will find support for his faith. The believer will here realize that his is not a lone figure, an isolated unit, but that others share with him in his communion with the same Lord. In a very special sense, too, the Church can be said to be a reservoir of faith. In the religious community, as de Wette says, 'ideas and feelings which emerge in the individual are passed on, become common property, create a community in which these ideas are stored up, bequeathed to posterity and continually increase. And thus is formed an association, in which religion can develop historically, can assume shape, in which there is now also scope and sphere of action for the emergence of individuals of supreme distinction.'[2]

At the same time the Church must act as a corrective of faith. 'The necessary price paid for social worship is that spontaneity must accept the fetters of regularity, but that is itself a necessary part of religious education.'[3] Thus must be avoided a mere individualism which is the perpetual fallacy of mysticism, as it is the constant danger of Protestantism, and, on the other hand, a mechanical institutionalism which would suppress individual initiative. The extremes, 'all authority belongs to the Church', and 'no authority belongs to the Church', are ultimately false to the essential nature and experience of religion.

The great creeds of the Church arose out of the living experience of God's revelation in Christ. They were an attempt to put into a form of sound words what had been discovered by the appropriation of the Divine grace and truth of God's Self-disclosure. The creeds are in a sense the Church confessing its experience of Christ's authority. It is on this account that they

[1] E. Brunner, *Revelation and Reason* (E.T. 1946), p. 27.
[2] Rudolf Otto, *The Philosophy of Religion* (E.T. 1931), p. 199.
[3] H. Wheeler Robinson, *Redemption and Revelation*, 1942, p. 100.

have and must have our interest and a certain significance for the individual. Credal indifference in the backbone of the Church is a fatal disease. No Church and no believer can afford to repudiate the historic expression of the faith in the form of the creeds. It may be true that the Church does not merely preach dogma, yet it cannot really preach without it.

It is, of course, understood that to repeat the creeds in perfection is not saving faith. The creeds are signs not steam-rollers. Calvin was certainly right at the Council of Lausanne to oppose Caroli who had contended that whoever could not express his faith in the exact words of the three ancient creeds could not be saved. Calvin challenged Caroli to repeat the Athanasian symbol and in doing so he broke down at the fourth clause. Calvin retorted, 'you yourself do not hold that faith; you do not express it in the exact words of the creed. Should you die suddenly the Devil must demand your eternal damnation for your inability to repeat the exact formulae'. Calvin was true to the great Reformation rediscovery of the Biblical understanding of faith as 'fiduciary' in repudiating the idea that the object of faith is always *articuli fidei*. The Reformed Churches, as Brunner has observed, refer to its formulated doctrine, not as dogma, but as Confession. It is the expression of the faith. Thus, he argues, the Confession is a 'Banner'; it is not a sign for the world but a flag to which it rallies. The Church has a confession because it believes, not in order to believe. The Roman Church has a 'password'. A banner rallies, but a password separates. The creed is a 'sign'. It is a 'norm' by which every individual member of the Church ought to examine himself to find out whether 'he belongs to it'. The creeds contain what the Church has understood of its appropriation of the revelation in Christ. They are not themselves a final authority any more than the community experience of the Church or the individual experience of the believer. They possess, like these, a derived authority, an authority which is only real in so far as it derives from God and has its authentication in the Scriptures known and understood through the Spirit.

'The final authority is a gracious God in salvation—mira-culous, because if we would explain this act He would cease to be an authority, and the authority would then be the explanatory principle.

'All other authorities for the soul stand ranged into a hierarchy as they are near to this God, necessary for His purpose or full of His action. The authority of the first degree is therefore religious. It is God as actually and historically experienced, God in Christ, Christ in the Holy Spirit, through a Church. The authority of the second degree is theological. It is the witness, not of our soul's instincts or our heart's voice, but of the experienced nature and action of the prime authority. And it is given us first in the Apostles, and second in their prolongation in the shifted and select experients of the Church. Apostolic authority rests on the fact that in the Apostles we have something beyond ideas which grew out of their faith, ideas making them, at the lowest, tentative interpreters of their subjective faith, or at the highest, classics and no more. It rests on the fact that we have in them interpreters of God's revelation, who had this for their unique vocation, and were equipped by God accordingly, to open up Christ's wealth of significance once for all time. And the authority in the third degree is ecclesiastical, though not officially so. It is the Church of the experients as the social creation of the Gospel, the Church of worshippers, of the hymns and liturgies, the graces and virtues, the saints, martyrs, and blessed ministrants, rather than the creeds. It is not the Church as an institution prescribing faith, but as a community confessing and giving effect to every kind of faith. It wields an ample and intimate experience, and not prescriptive knowledge or impressive thought. Its power is felt in our heart and conscience, and owned in love, service and patience.'[1]

---

[1] P. T. Forsyth, *The Principle of Authority*, 1912, second edition, 1952, p. 30.

INDEX OF NAMES

Abba, R., 209 n., 254–5, 330–1
Acton, Lord, 83
Adler, A., 24
Alanus of Lille, 355
Alexander, W. L., 108
Andersen, F. I., 107 n., 171 n.
Anderson, R., Sir, 130–1
Aquinas, 255 n.
Arndt, 107
Arnold, M., 45, 65, 264, 353
Astruc, 155
Athanasius, 147
Atkinson, B. F. C., 282–3
Augustine, 326, 356
Aulen, G., 33 n., 163 n., 345 n.

Babbage, C., 50
Bacon, F., 199
Baillie, D. M., 66, 83 n., 86, 92 n., 97 n., 98
Baillie, J., 162, 166, 168, 172–3, 208 n.
Balfour, A. J., 118 n.
Bannerman, J., 184 n., 225 n., 260, 263–5, 336 n.
Barclay, R., 246 n.
Barry, A., 15, 230–1
Barry, F. R., 295 n., 334
Barry, G. D., 239–40
Barth, K., 26 n., 27 n., 38–40, 87, 88 n., 90–2, 163, 169, 173, 178, 214, 257, 326, 339, 354, 355
Baxter, W. R., 122–3
Beidermann, 153
Berdyaev, N., 371
Berkhof, L., 170
Berridge, J., 205
Bevan, E., 97 n.
Binley, T. H., 242
Blackman, E. C., 323 n.
Blake, B., 137 n., 143
Borchert, O., 358 n.
Bosanquet, B., 74
Boyce, W., 102–3
Bradley, F. H., 73, 74
Bratsiotis, P., 328
Briggs, C. A., 121, 201, 213 n.
Brockington, A. A., 64 n.

Bromiley, G. W., 211, 214–16, 337–8, 339, 340, 341
Brook, R., 222
Bromfield, G. W., 319 n.
Brown, H. D., 156
Brown, J., 242 n.
Bruce, A. B., 45, 47, 51 n., 58 n., 60 n., 63–4, 107, 147, 163, 167, 201, 203
Bruce, F. F., 160 n., 282
Brunner, E., 26 n., 87, 90–2, 93, 163, 167, 168, 169, 170, 173, 178, 246 n., 257, 355, 361 n., 371 n., 372
Buler, J., 57, 197, 199
Bulgakoff, S., 183
Bultmann, R., 93, 94, 96, 97
Bunsen, P., 28
Burgon, J. W., 284, 285
Burnaby, J., 211 n., 212 n., 224, 249, 250 n., 331
Burrows, M., 324
Butler J., 57, 197, 199.

Cadoux, C. J., 183 n., 290
Caird, E., 72, 73
Caird, J., 72, 181 n., 351
Cairns, D. S., 67
Cairns, J., 225
Caldecott, A., 277 n.
Calvin, John, 179, 334, 338 n., 347, 363, 372
Camfield, F. W., 91, 168, 347
Campbell, R. J., 73
Carlyle, J. C., 184 n.
Carnell, E. J., 86, 170 n.
Caroli, 372
Carpenter, J. E., 103, 113, 115, 116, 117, 164
Cartwright, J., 181
Cave, A., 33, 99, 100, 102, 184–5, 270–1
Cave, S., 293
Chapman, J. A., 240, 316
Cheyne, T. K., 33, 99, 102, 105–6, 107, 111, 115, 120, 121, 129, 142–3, 152, 274
Christlieb, T., 62–3
Church, R. W., 48

Clapperton, J. A., 147, 148–9
Clement, C., 132
Clifford, J., 202, 203, 205, 221, 294
Clifford, W. K., 20, 43, 73
Clutton-Brock, 350
Colenso, J. W. P., 29, 30, 40, 102, 103, 235
Coleridge, S. T., 36, 96, 166, 176, 177 n., 184 n., 192, 222, 246, 255, 259, 264, 267, 292 n.
Comte, Auguste, 30
Cook, S. A., 81, 113
Cornhill, 108, 125
Coulson, C. A., 9
Craig, C. T., 251, 328
Cumming, J. E., 119, 152
Cunliffe-Jones, H., 168, 174, 179, 189, 247, 321–3
Curteis, C. H., 50
Cyril of Alexandria, 140

Dale, R. W., 201
Danby, H., 118
D'Arcy, C. F., 195 n.
Darlow, T. H., 131, 259 n.
Darwin, C., 8, 15, 16, 19, 20, 69, 80, 196, 198, 201
Davidson, A. B., 105, 106, 107
Davidson, S., 103–4, 108, 200, 224
Davidson, W. T., 228–9, 271, 299
Davies, O., 109
Davies, R. E., 289, 347
Delitzsch, F., 51, 130
Denney, J., 67, 192–3, 259, 358
Devadutt, V. E., 250
De Wette, 371
Dewey, E. A., 338 n.
Dickie, E. P., 168, 179 n.
Digges La Touche, E., 38
Dionysius, 97, 171 n.
Dodd, C. H., 162, 173, 182, 183 n., 209 n., 222 n., 227 n., 312–14
Dods, M., 64, 199, 200 n., 203, 222–3
Dorner, J. A., 234, 262
Dotterer, R. H., 74
Driver, S. R., 99, 100, 107, 109, 111, 113, 114, 115, 116, 120, 121, 131, 141–2, 148, 220, 238–9, 270
Duff, A., 104
Duns Scotus, 73

Ebling, G., 331
Eckhart, 71

Eichhorn, J. G., 102, 155
Eliot, G., 43
Ellicott, C. C. J., 101, 119, 151–2
Elliott-Binns, L. E., 14, 34, 64, 75, 79, 82
Elmslie, W. G., 185
Emerson, R. W., 59
Erasmus, 52
Erigena, John Scotus, 97
Ervine, A., 195 n.
Evans, C. de B., 71
Evans, C. F., 33
Evans, L. T., 20
Ewald, G. H. A., von, 227
Ewald, H., 227
Euchen, R., 77

Fairbairn, A. M., 34, 68, 112, 150
Farmer, H. H., 49, 52, 56, 328–9
Farrar, F. W., 131, 180, 181, 219, 225, 226, 232, 234, 275
Farrer, A., 171–2
Ferré, N. F. S., 170 n., 178
Finlayson, R. A., 172
Fisher, G. P., 71, 179
Fitchett, W. H., 241
Flint, R., 71
Floroosky, G., 250
Forrest, D. W., 252–3
Forsyth, P. T., 57, 68, 83, 87–9, 90, 92, 150, 154, 237, 304–5, 332, 356, 357, 359 n., 364 n., 367 n., 368 n., 370, 373
Fox, H. E., 156–7
Frazer, D., 81, 218 n., 259 n., 260 n., 265–6
Freud, S., 24
Fullerton, K., 305–7
Fullerton, W. Y., 184 n.

Galloway, G., 302 n.
Gardner, P., 139, 332
Garvie, A. E., 76, 221, 307, 317
Gaussen, L., 284
Geldenhuys, N., 361, 362 n.
Gibson, B., 76
Gibson, I., 116
Gibson, J. M., 237
Girdlestone, R. B., 127–8, 280–1
Gladstone, W. E., 51, 137, 341
Glover, W. B., 81, 270 n.

Goethe, 249
Goode, W., 155
Goodwin, C. W., 28
Gore, C., 33, 34, 35, 66, 75, 138, 140, 141, 142, 148, 201, 203, 208, 209, 210 n., 212, 220, 227, 228, 240, 308–9, 335, 359, 360, 362, 367 n.
Graham, B., 209
Graham, J. M., 291 n.
Grant, W. M., 242
Green, T. H., 74, 75, 139
Green, W. H., 116, 259
Griffith-Jones, E., 307, 357, 359
Grubb, E., 301–2, 352, 354 n.

Haeckel, 80
Hagenbach, K. R., 180
Haldane, R., 75, 261
Hamann, 68
Hammond, T. C., 159, 283
Hare, J., 264
Hargrove, C., 293
Harnack, A., 9, 37, 38, 40, 54, 71, 83, 85, 354, 361, 364
Harris, C., 58
Harris, H., 131
Harrison, F., 29, 43
Harvey, 205
Hay, D. W., 195 n.
Hebert, A. G., 159–60, 166, 170, 177, 209, 210–11, 212, 213, 214, 218 n., 228, 247–8, 309, 320–1, 322, 335
Hegel, 18, 72, 73, 74, 81
Heiler, F., 311
Hendry, G. S., 168
Henry, C., 173
Henson, H. H., 292
Herder, 215
Herrmann, W., 54, 71, 117
Hibbert, G. H., 302 n.
Hiralel, H., 72
Hodge, A. A., 260
Hodgson, L., 66, 67
Hodkin, H., 318
Holden, J. S., 208
Hommel, 123
Homrighausen, E. G., 170
Hooke, S. H., 249 n.
Hort, F. J. A., 317 n.
Hort, R. F., 27, 64
Horton, R. F., 167, 181, 182, 184, 186, 202, 203, 207, 226–7, 274, 298

Horton, W. M., 183
Horwill, H. W., 143–4
Hospers, G. H., 289 n.
Howison, G. H., 74
Hügel, F. von, 44, 71
Hughes, H. M., 305
Hume, D., 45, 47, 49, 79
Hunzinger, 52
Huxley, T. H., 17, 42, 47, 69

Illingworth, J. R., 34, 45
Inge, W. R., 71, 294, 350, 351

Jacks, L. P., 293
James, W., 21, 44, 73, 78, 126, 302 n.
Jeremie, 277
Joad, C. E. M., 23, 24
Johnson, D., 240
Johnson, H., 209 n.
Johnson, R. C., 39, 338 n., 345 n.
Jones, H., 74
Jones, J. C., 131
Jones, J. D., 109
Jones, R. M., 71, 349
Jowett, B., 28, 29, 200
Jowett, J. H., 208
Joyce, G. C., 238
Jung, C. G., 24

Kant, 36, 72, 73, 349 n.
Kayser, 155
Kegel, M., 241
Kelly, J., 103
Kelly, W., 278–9
Kennedy, A. K. S., 81, 100
Kennedy, J., 204
Ker, J., 125
Kiel, 121
Kierkegaard, S., 7 n., 25, 39, 90, 91, 361
Killen, R. A., 95 n.
Kingsley, C., 17
Kirkpatrick, A. F., 113, 114, 115, 148, 216, 222, 229–30, 238, 239 n.
Kittel, R., 162
Knight, H. T., 116
Knox, E. A., 240
Knox, J., 96, 97, 318
Knox, W. L., 203, 210 n., 251, 311, 312
Kröner, R., 97, 171 n.
Kuenen, A., 155, 226

Lacey, T. A., 312
Langmead-Casserly, J. V., 36
Law, E., 102
Law, W., 178 n.
Leathes, S., 121, 128, 181 n., 225, 226
Lecerf, A., 289 n.
Leckie, J. H., 302
Lee, W., 140, 166, 260, 262, 263, 267
Lehmann, P. L., 215, 289 n.
Leibniz, 62, 73–4, 79
Leitzmann, H., 363, 364 n.
Leon, P., 21
Lessing, 27, 79, 88, 215
Lewis, C. S., 49
Lewis, E., 20, 348, 355
Lias, J. J., 121, 128
Liddon, H. P., 36, 100, 151, 205
Lightfoot, R. H., 96, 97, 104, 176, 277, 291
Lindsay, J., 131
Lindsay, T. M., 32, 182
Lloyd-Jones, D. M., 340–2
Loofs, F., 83
Lotze, H., 35, 75
Luther, Martin, 179, 288, 326, 334, 335 n., 344 n., 345, 347

Macgreggor, J., 271–3
Mackay, A. M., 222, 223
Mackintosh, H. R., 66, 150, 295 n.
MacNaughton, 264
MacPhail, J. R., 329–30
Macpherson, J., 368 n.
Maine, C. P., 203, 239
Malden, R. M., 242, 243, 317
Mansel, H. L., 49, 73
Manson, T. H., 183–4
Marcel, G., 286
Marchant, J., 185 n., 202 n.
Margoliouth, D. S., 128–9
Mark, T., 240–1
Martensen, H., 193, 194, 234, 345, 346, 366 n.
Martin, H., 33
Martineau, J., 164–5, 300
Marvin, F. S., 81
Marx, K., 18
Matheson, D., 15
Matthews, W. R., 318
Maurice, F. D., 17, 30, 40, 82, 96, 166, 176, 178 n., 237, 264
McCaig, A., 261 n., 273–6

McDonald, H. D., 7, 51, 68, 91, 166, 174, 193, 197 n., 212 n., 247 n., 255 n., 286 n., 325 n., 343 n.
McFadyen, J. E., 117, 236, 241–2
McIntosh, H., 153–4, 155
McIntyre, D. M., 336
McLaren, A., 297
McNeile, A. H., 158–9
Melanchthon, 343
Meland, B. E., 177 n.
Metz, R., 20
Meyer, F. B., 208
Micklem, N., 168, 183 n., 298
Mill, J. S., 73
Moberley, R. C., 34
Moore, A., 14, 46, 70
Moorhouse, 142
Morgan, G. C., 195 n., 208
Morley, J., 27, 28
Morrell, J. D., 166, 262 n., 264
Morton, W. H., 86, 168, 170
Moss, C. B., 168
Moule, H. C., 130, 157, 205
Mowell, 155
Mozley, J. B., 27, 28, 46–8, 58
M'Quot, J. E., 235–6
Mullins, E. Y., 290 n.
Murray, J., 338 n.
Myers, F. W. H., 43

Nagy, B., 327
Nestorius, 258
Newbigin, L., 329
Nicholls, W. R., 105, 110, 128, 162, 163, 178 n., 200 n., 259
Niebuhr, H. R., 33 n.
Niebuhr, R., 92, 93, 94, 97
Nineham, D. E., 331
North, C. R., 175
Nygren, A., 344 n.

Olver, G. W., 170 n., 199, 225
Oman, J., 80, 206, 289, 300–1, 329
Origen, 246
Orr, J., 66, 126–7, 129–30, 159, 175–6, 184, 236, 238, 247, 255 n., 257, 260, 263, 279–80, 334 n.
Ottley, R. L., 132, 147–8
Otto, R., 371

Packer, J. I. L., 160, 172, 190, 209 n., 211–12, 213, 214, 257 n., 259 n., 285

Paget, S., 36
Paley, W., 57, 60
Parker, J., 185–6, 205, 207
Paterson, W. P., 179 n.
Pattison, M., 28
Paulin, G., 18
Paulus, 155
Payne, E. A., 33, 108, 291 n., 295 n., 296 n.
Peake, A. S., 106, 116, 117, 123, 167, 188–9, 200 n., 225–6, 261, 302–3, 304, 307
Peake, L. B., 109
Pearson, K., 21
Peel, A., 176, 179
Peloni, A., 50
Perowne, J. J. S., 102, 229
Perry, V., 218 n.
Pfeiffer, F., 71
Philo, 165
Picton, J. A., 225 n.
Plummer, A., 142
Pope, H., 255 n.
Powell, Baden, 45
Powell, H. C., 137, 148
Prenter, R., 327
Preus, L., 161, 179
Priestley, J., 102
Pringle-Pattison, A. S., 76
Pusey, E. B., 109

Quiller-Couch, 73

Rainey, R., 33, 184, 221 n.
Raleigh, A., 201
Ramm, B., 333, 357, 369 n., 370 n.
Randle, M., 216
Ranke, 84
Rashdall, H., 61, 75, 76, 81, 82
Rawlinson, A. E. J., 309–11
Rawlinson, G., 121
Reich, E., 118, 119, 128, 129
Reid, J. K. S., 180, 209 n., 254, 330
Renan, A., 65
Renwick, A. M., 289 n.
Reu, M., 179 n.
Rich, E. C., 319 n.
Richardson, A., 219, 243–4, 250, 258, 284, 298, 321, 327
Richardson, C. A., 77
Ritschl, A., 30, 53, 54, 71, 92, 94, 177 n.
Robertson, J., 120

Robinson, H. Wheeler, 35, 113, 114, 162, 167, 175, 244–6, 247, 251, 291, 295, 297, 351, 371
Robinson, T. H., 115, 194, 255 n.
Rogers, A. K., 74, 79
Rogers, H., 198–9
Rooke, T. G., 232–5
Rouse, G. H., 143
Rousseau, 57
Row, C. A., 48–9, 60–1
Rowley, H. H., 117, 134–5, 136, 251, 254, 255 n., 324–5
Ruskin, J., 350
Rutherford, Lord, 10
Ryle, H. E., 116
Ryle, J. C., 205, 206, 207

Sabatier, A., 54–5, 289, 300, 326, 332
Salmon, G., 368 n.
Salmond, S. D. F., 107, 164, 166
Sanday, W., 125, 140, 145, 146, 147, 165, 231–2
Saphir, A., 132–4, 135, 136
Saussure, J. de, 191
Sayce, A. H., 109, 112, 119
Schiller, F. C. S., 77
Schleiermacher, 55, 78, 91, 94, 95, 96, 102, 166, 177 n., 215, 262, 300, 315, 332
Schmiedel, P. W., 37, 38, 40
Schmidt, N., 130
Schwartzkopff, P., 153
Schweitzer, W., 250, 298, 327
Scott, D. H., 18
Scott-Holland, H., 36
Seeley, J. R., 83
Selby, W. B., 118
Selwyn, E. G., 277
Seth, J., 76
Shakespeare, W., 223, 249
Sharr, F. F., 271
Shearer, W. C., 149–50
Simeon, C., 8
Smethurst, A. E., 9
Smith, G. A., 31, 110–11, 112, 116, 124
Smith, H. P., 20
Smith, J., 123–4
Smith, T. S., 241
Smith, W. Robertson, 30, 31, 32, 33, 40, 45, 82, 101, 105, 106, 121, 123, 124, 166, 182, 266, 270, 274, 295
Smyth, N., 49, 171 n.

Snaith, N. H., 244
Snell, B. J., 200 n., 242
Snell, J. B., 132
Söderbloom, N., 98
Sorley, W. R., 76
Sparrow-Simpson, W. J., 316 n.
Speer, R. E., 83
Spencer, H., 16, 80, 349
Spinks, G. S., 69, 78
Spinoza, 74, 140
Sprott, T. H., 236-7
Spurgeon, C. H., 109, 184, 185, 205, 207
Stanford, E. G., 27
Stanton, V. H., 299-300, 350 n.
Stephen, L., 79, 196
Stirling, T. H., 72
Storr, G. B., 298 n.
Storr, V. H., 78, 84, 158, 159
Stott, J. R. W., 209 n., 218 n.
Stout, G. F., 77
Strachan, J., 255 n.
Strachan, R. H., 292-3
Strauss, 65, 93, 155
Strong, A. H., 263
Strong, T. B., 301
Sturt, H., 71
Swainson, 277
Swayne, W. S., 142
Swete, H. B., 255 n., 302
Swinburne, 43
Symonds, J. A., 23

Tasker, R. V. A., 160
Taylor, A. E., 76
Taylor, V., 150
Temple, F., 27, 49-51, 53, 62
Temple, W., 33, 76, 162, 163, 169, 209 n., 297, 302
Tennyson, A., 28
Tertullian, 140
Theodoret, 140
Thomas, G. F., 173
Thomas, W. H. Griffith, 192-3, 367 n.
Thompson, W. R., 19
Thomson, P., 53
Thornton, L. S., 187
Thornton, L. E., 174
Townsend, L. T., 131
Troeltsch, E., 38
Tyrrell, G., 71, 85

Underhill, E., 71
Underwood, A. C., 185 n.

Urquhart, J., 155, 276

Vaihinger, H., 178
Vatke, W., 155
Venn, H., 205
Vidler, A. R., 312
Vine, W. E., 281-2
Virgil, 249
Vischer, W., 366 n.

Wace, H., 121, 336
Wand, J. W. C., 186, 248-9 255 n., 323-4
Ward, J., 76-7, 80
Warfield, B., 218 n., 254, 259, 260, 359
Warren, W. P., 72
Warschauer, J., 139
Watkins, H. W., 103, 104
Watson, F., 121, 277-8
Watts, R., 266-7
Watts-Durton, 70
Weatherhead, L. W., 240
Webb, C. C. J., 42, 68, 69, 76, 81
Wellhausen, J., 121, 122, 123, 124, 130
Wells, H. G., 74
Wendland, J., 49, 51
Wenham, J. W., 160
Wesley, J., 8, 79, 196, 197 n., 371
Wescott, B. F., 59, 66, 104, 256, 259, 285 n., 287 n., 344 n.
White, E., 181 n., 225-6
Whitehead, W. N., 55
Whitehouse, O. C., 105
Whitelaw, T., 124-6, 153
Whitman, W., 13
Wieman, N. H., 177 n.
Wilberforce, S., 29, 30
William of Occam, 73
Williams, D. D., 91
Williams, N. P., 318-19
Williams, R., 28
Williams, R. R., 310 n., 325-6, 335
Wilson, D., 262
Wobbermin, 88
Wood, A., 42
Woods, F. H., 43, 100, 145-6
Woolf, B. L., 315-16
Woolley, H., 241
Wright, A., 169
Wright, C. J., 316-17
Wright, G. E., 26

Young, E. J., 213-14 n.

INDEX OF SUBJECTS

Abraham, historicity of, 112, 127, 129
Absolute, 73, 75, 76
'Accommodationist' Theory, 140–5, 146, 148, 150, 156, 189, 309
Activism, 167 n., 169, 170
Afflatus, 232, 233, 238, 239
Agnosticism, 42–3, 44, 68, 145, 242
Airdale College, 265
Allegorical interpretation, 210
Altruistic Theory, 147, 148–9
Amos, 238
Animism, 81
Anthropogeography, 80
Apollinarianism, 146, 257
Apologetic, 46, 56, 57, 59, 60, 70, 176, 196, 199, 202, 236
Assembly's College, Belfast, 266
Atheism, 29, 45
Atonement, 200
Authority—of the Bible, 9, 53, 99, 137, 151, 154, 155, 173, 175, 182, 203, 205, 209 n., 210 n., 216, 217, 228, 230, 233, 236, 237, 238, 239, 240, 244, 247, 248, 249 250, 252, 253, 254, 260 n., 264, 265, 274, 288–373

Bible, as 'containing the Word of God', 30, 167 n., 180–1, 182 n., 185–6, 187, 188, 189, 190, 192, 193, 194, 262, 275, 320
   as 'a record', 166, 167, 168, 174, 175, 176, 186, 244, 251, 271
   as 'a witness', 116, 130, 164, 167, 168–9, 176, 179, 182, 193, 207, 214, 322
   its unity and diversity, 133, 134, 135, 136, 156, 199, 230, 250, 252, 262, 290
Biblicism, 92, 96, 348, 354–5
Bibliolatry, 174, 176, 178, 211, 219, 235, 276, 334–5, 340, 364

Canon, of Scripture, 113, 192, 226, 246 n., 247, 269, 279, 303, 319 n., 367 n.
Canonicity, 247, 248, 295

Coleridgean School, 177, 182
Comparative Religion, 81, 82, 83
Conscience, 348–50
Conservative Evangelical, *see* Evangelicalism
Continuity, principle of, 16, 17, 79, 83, 87
Creation, accounts of, 28
Criticism (German, Higher, New, Modern) 28, 30, 31, 32, 33, 36, 37, 38, 43, 45, 83, 84, 88, 90, 91, 99, 100, 101, 102, 103, 104, 105 ff., 137, 140, 142–3, 145, 150, 155, 156, 157, 158, 165, 177, 180, 184, 199, 200, 201, 216, 218, 220, 221, 223, 226, 228, 230, 237, 238, 243, 249, 258, 270, 274, 277, 288, 289, 298, 309, 310, 312, 313, 317, 322, 353
   Historical, 101, 102, 111, 112, 115, 121, 199, 226, 242
   Textual, 235

Daniel, historicity of, 131, 236, 306
Darwinianism, 15–17, 18, 19, 20, 25, 43, 69, 70
Deism, 8, 25, 45, 57, 69, 163, 196, 197, 288
Demythologization, 93 n., 94, 353
Deuteronomy, 120, 157, 236
Dialectical theology, 87, 93, 183, 354
Docetism, 86, 262, 278
Dogmatism, 92, 313
Dualism, 73
Dynamical theory, 222, 231, 234, 260, 262, 264, 275, 279, 307

Ecclesiastes, 181, 186
Election, doctrine of, 133, 135, 227, 249, 250
Empiricism, 78
Encounter, Divine-human, 27, 31, 38–9, 40, 87, 97, 162, 163, 166, 173, 331, 355
Enlightenment, 79
Enthusiasm, 70

Erastianism, 83

Evangelicalism, 100, 117, 133, 159–60, 172, 175, 184, 190, 205, 206, 208, 211, 212, 218 n., 241, 242, 247, 248, 258, 270 n., 271, 280, 284, 340

Evolutionary development of religion, 25, 28, 31, 40, 49, 81, 82, 113, 164, 201, 243

Evolutionism, 8, 15, 16, 17, 21, 41, 44, 49, 75, 80, 183, 196, 199, 243, 349

Existentialism, 24

Exodus, 119, 124

Exorcism, 144

Ezra, 151

Fatherhood of God, 38

Finiteness, 74, 76

Form-Geschichte, 92–3

Freedom, of man, 48, 49, 59, 77–8, 239, 273, 310, 332, 334, 356, 370

Fundamentalism, 86, 100 n., 174, 178, 186, 190 n., 209, 211, 242, 258, 259 n., 284–5, 327, 330, 331, 335

Genesis, 16, 17, 28, 100, 131, 185, 201 n., 213 n., 235, 268

Geschichte, 86–7, 88, 89, 90–2, 332

Gnosticism, 85

Grace of God, 39, 135, 167, 230, 253, 285, 289, 304, 314, 316, 320, 321, 324, 359

Graf-Wellhausen theory, 30, 185, 270

Hackney College, 267

Hagiographia, 268, 269

Hegelianism, 18, 75, 108, 132

Heilsgeschichte, 26, 90

Hexateuch, 100, 116, 125

Historicism, 78–86

Historie, 88–9

History, idealization of, 35, 115, 116, 242

as a natural process, 45, 114

as revelation, 25, 26, 32, 40, 88, 97, 126, 128, 133, 161, 162, 169, 175, 221, 222, 224, 229, 237, 241, 296, 320, 325

Holy Spirit, 7, 8, 32, 34, 95–6, 110, 151, 164, 167 n., 169, 173, 175, 183, 188, 191, 192, 200, 203, 224, 225, 226, 229, 230, 232, 233, 239, 246, 249, 250, 251, 254, 256, 262, 263, 264, 267, 295, 296, 297, 300, 302,

306, 320, 326–7, 338, 339, 342, 343, 345, 348, 352, 363, 364, 365, 368, 369, 373

indwelling of, 96, 221, 326, 350–1

witness of, 31, 172, 301, 309, 313, 316, 321, 322–3, 324, 327, 330, 331, 341, 342, 343, 351, 352, 369

Humanism, 22, 43

Idealism, 68–73, 74, 77, 81

Illumination theory, 234, 256, 261, 275, 352, 358

Images and revelation, 171–2

Immanence, divine, 25, 26, 34, 55, 56, 59, 70, 96

Immanentism, 69, 73

Incarnation, 26, 34–5, 40, 61, 65, 66, 85–6, 126, 137, 140, 145, 147, 148, 156, 234, 251, 257, 339–40, 358

Individualism, 14–15, 59, 75, 76, 273, 293, 303, 345, 371

Inerrancy, 9, 31–2, 33, 36, 77, 99, 154, 161, 167, 178, 196–217, 218, 248, 250, 252, 271, 276, 308, 331

Infallibility, of the Bible, 36, 96, 139, 147, 153, 154, 155, 156, 161, 167, 178 n., 181, 196, 200 n., 201, 203, 204, 205, 207, 208, 209, 212, 213, 214, 216, 219, 228, 231, 241, 242, 249, 250, 254, 255, 256, 259, 263, 272, 282, 288, 289, 291, 295, 302, 307, 309, 311, 312, 314, 320, 323, 327, 336, 341

of the Church, 242, 303

Insight theory, 237, 253, 261, 370

Inspiration, 9, 28, 29, 31, 99, 103, 110, 135, 155, 191, 192, 202, 210, 215

degrees of, 224–6, 251, 252, 260 n., 262, 277, 279

dictation theory of, 96, 178 n., 188, 212 n., 213, 218, 219, 220, 222, 223, 225, 227, 230–1, 232, 237, 241, 244, 248, 259, 260, 261, 266, 267, 272, 275, 276, 280, 281, 283, 284, 285, 307, 309, 311, 330

plenary, 260, 261 n., 264, 266, 274, 275, 276, 279

verbal, 96, 221, 225, 226, 227, 238, 241, 242, 251, 254, 258, 260, 261, 264, 265, 266, 267, 271, 273, 274, 276, 283

Intellectualism, 108, 343, 352

Isaiah, 105, 236, 268

Israel, development of religion, 30, 31, 126
  history of, 119, 123
  significance of the history of, 26, 31, 112, 124, 130, 133, 134, 135, 175, 227, 229, 325

Jesus, His authority, 139, 141, 152, 160, 229, 242, 298, 299, 314, 315, 316, 318, 327, 328, 329, 336, 340, 341, 351, 353, 354, 358-9
  His knowledge, 35-6, 66, 111, 121, 138, 139, 140-60
  of history, 37, 38, 40, 67, 84, 86, 87, 88, 89, 90, 92, 93, 94, 95, 96, 97, 130, 352, 353, 354, 360
  His teaching, 37, 85, 358-9
Joshua, 29, 61

Kenotic theory, 35, 66, 138, 149, 150, 151, 152, 154, 157, 158, 295

Liberalism, 37, 84, 86, 183, 184, 207, 208, 215, 226, 242, 334, 339
'Limitationist' theory, 145-7, 148, 156, 157, 158
Logos, 61, 82, 170

Malachi, 268
Marxism, 18
Materialism, 15, 41, 42, 44, 45, 53, 75, 76, 80, 81, 132, 186
Mechanical theory of the universe, 43, 44, 45, 48, 49
Messiahship, 63, 64, 110, 142, 151, 157, 164, 366
Metaphysics, 71, 128
Metapsychosis, 144
Miracles, 16, 29, 44-64, 65, 66, 67, 70, 95, 199
Monism, 73, 74
Monophysitism, 96, 178 n.
Monotheism, 104, 123
Mosaic authorship, 29, 102, 103, 140, 141, 144, 153, 268, 269
Moses, historicity of, 112
Mysticism, 68, 69, 71, 72, 93, 96, 294, 301, 302-3, 307, 371

Naturalism, 17, 21, 22, 25, 44, 45, 51, 68, 69, 70, 72, 80, 81, 113, 114, 131, 349
Natural theology, 39-40
Neo-criticism, 156, 157

Neo-Hegelianism, 170
Neo-Liberalism, 184
Neo-Orthodoxy, 86, 92, 93, 94, 98, 173
Neo-Platonism, 97
New College, Edinburgh, 263
Nominalism, 73, 173 n.
Numbers, 30

Obscurantism, 118, 134, 150, 206, 259, 273, 330
Optimism, 20-4, 117, 236, 306-7, 349
Original sin, 15, 200

Pantheism, 34, 71, 72, 73, 302, 351
Pastors' College (Spurgeon's), 273
Pentateuch, 29, 30, 108, 116, 117, 131, 153, 236, 259 n., 270 n.
Personalism, 75, 76, 77
Pessimism, 22-3, 186
Pluralism, 73, 74, 75, 76, 77, 78, 79
Polytheism, 180
Pragmatism, 77, 240, 257
Prophecy (and prophets), 107, 113, 114, 119, 120, 123, 125, 134, 145, 177, 216, 220, 223, 238, 239, 244-5, 246, 252, 256, 264, 268, 269, 278, 280, 286, 317, 320, 321
Propositional revelation, 31, 32, 58, 97, 134, 162, 163, 166, 167 n., 168, 169, 170, 171, 172, 176, 188, 224, 226, 237, 238, 244, 331-2, 338-9, 344
Psalm cx, Davidic authorship of, 35, 137-8, 141, 142, 143, 144, 146, 151, 157, 159, 181
Psalms, 125, 126, 140, 143, 153, 237, 268
Psychology, 78, 238, 244-5, 246, 248, 282, 306, 310
Puritan doctrine, 206, 209

Radicalism, 92, 98, 139, 164, 165, 205
Rationalism, 68, 83, 106, 108, 109, 131, 215, 338
Rawdon Baptist College, 232
Reconstructionist theories, 92-3, 118, 119, 130, 139, 227, 228, 231, 253, 255, 348
Redemption, 64, 65, 68
Redemption (and revelation) 26, 62-4, 142, 166, 173 n., 193, 244, 247, 304, 305, 315, 318, 326, 330, 344, 355, 359, 366, 368, 369

Reformation, 179, 289, 334, 335, 346
Reformers' doctrine, 100, 168, 179, 180, 204, 214, 215, 242, 254, 255 n., 288–9, 313, 335, 338, 347
Religious experience, 51, 52, 53, 54–5, 72, 77, 78, 82, 94, 95, 96, 161, 164, 168, 176, 177, 187, 204, 219, 220, 222, 227, 240, 242, 243, 244, 247, 251, 252, 253, 255, 256, 290, 292, 293, 304, 313, 314, 315–16, 318, 332–3, 370
Religious geniuses, 77, 111, 161, 222, 223, 224, 229, 239, 244, 253, 255, 256, 275, 291, 313, 318, 321, 323, 350, 361
Resurrection, 49, 51, 91, 152, 200, 315
Roman Catholicism, 85, 246, 308, 309, 324, 335 n., 339, 372

Scepticism, 33, 82, 92, 101, 104, 109, 111, 119, 288, 302
Scholasticism, 73, 86, 168, 255 n., 335, 352
Science, influence of, 29, 34, 42, 49, 50 53, 55, 61, 79, 229, 298
as divine, 21
methods of, 9, 42, 44, 46, 69, 80, 119, 130, 357
Self-disclosure, divine, 162, 163, 167, 168
Subjectivism, 33, 38, 53, 55, 77, 78, 91, 94, 95, 98, 183, 204, 207, 215, 231, 247, 255 n., 256, 257, 289, 292, 296, 299, 300, 303, 304, 312–

14, 317, 324, 329, 332–3, 335, 351, 352, 353–4
Supernatural, in religion, 30, 43, 44, 46, 47, 58, 62, 65, 69, 95, 114, 220, 240, 264, 265, 269, 285, 306
Synoptic Gospels, 89, 90

Theism, 15, 17, 58, 69, 77
Traditionalism, 37, 67, 124, 127, 131, 151, 203–4, 205, 218, 232, 248, 249, 259, 260, 270, 271, 280, 284, 327
Transcendence, divine ('Otherness' of God), 25, 34, 59, 68, 87, 91, 96, 244

Ultra-Darwinianism, 16
Utopia, 22

Valuation, religious, 113, 115, 122, 132, 229, 272, 313, 314
Value, category of, 53, 76, 78, 91
Value-judgement, 245, 246, 295
epistemology, 44, 94

War, influence of, 22, 24, 25, 236, 306
Word: (words) of God, 89, 90, 91, 96, 97, 98, 110, 154, 155, 159, 168, 170, 172, 174, 176–94, 195 n., 206, 212, 213, 214, 218 n., 219, 221, 225, 230, 234, 241, 250, 261, 262, 265, 266, 267, 273, 277, 282, 286, 289, 327, 333, 337, 339, 343, 345, 346, 348, 354, 362, 365, 367

twin brooks series BOOKS IN THE SERIES

THE ACTS OF THE APOSTLES ....Richard B. Rackham
APOSTOLIC AND POST-APOSTOLIC TIMES (Goppelt) ....Robert A. Guelich, tr.
THE APOSTOLIC FATHERS ....J. B. Lightfoot
THE ATONEMENT OF CHRIST ....Francis Turrettin
THE AUTHORITY OF THE OLD TESTAMENT ....John Bright
BACKGROUNDS TO DISPENSATIONALISM ....Clarence B. Bass
BASIC CHRISTIAN DOCTRINES ....Carl F. H. Henry
THE BASIC IDEAS OF CALVINISM ....H. Henry Meeter
THE CALVINISTIC CONCEPT OF CULTURE ....H. Van Til
CHRISTIAN APPROACH TO PHILOSOPHY ....W. C. Young
CHRISTIAN PERSONAL ETHICS ....Carl F. H. Henry
COMMENTARY ON DANIEL (Jerome) ....Gleason L. Archer, Jr., tr.
THE DAYS OF HIS FLESH ....David Smith
DISCIPLING THE NATIONS ....Richard DeRidder
THE DOCTRINE OF GOD ....Herman Bavinck
EDUCATIONAL IDEALS IN THE ANCIENT WORLD ....Wm. Barclay
THE EPISTLE OF JAMES ....Joseph B. Mayor
EUSEBIUS' ECCLESIASTICAL HISTORY
FUNDAMENTALS OF THE FAITH ....Carl F. H. Henry, ed.
GOD-CENTERED EVANGELISM ....R. B. Kuiper
GENERAL PHILOSOPHY ....D. Elton Trueblood
THE GRACE OF LAW ....Ernest F. Kevan
THE HIGHER CRITICISM OF THE PENTATEUCH ....William Henry Green
THE HISTORY OF CHRISTIAN DOCTRINES ....Louis Berkhof
THE HISTORY OF DOCTRINES ....Reinhold Seeberg
THE HISTORY OF THE JEWISH NATION ....Alfred Edersheim
HISTORY OF PREACHING ....E. C. Dargan
LIGHT FROM THE ANCIENT EAST ....Adolf Deissmann
NOTES ON THE MIRACLES OF OUR LORD ....R. C. Trench
NOTES ON THE PARABLES OF OUR LORD ....R. C. Trench
OUR REASONABLE FAITH (Bavinck) ....Henry Zylstra, tr.
PAUL, APOSTLE OF LIBERTY ....R. N. Longnecker
PHILOSOPHY OF RELIGION ....D. Elton Trueblood
PROPHETS AND THE PROMISE ....W. J. Beecher
REASONS FOR FAITH ....John H. Gerstner
THE REFORMATION ....Hans J. Hillebrand, ed.
REFORMED DOGMATICS (Wollebius, Voetius, Turretin) ....J. Beardslee, ed., tr.
REFORMED DOGMATICS ....Heinrich Heppe
REVELATION AND INSPIRATION ....James Orr
REVELATION AND THE BIBLE ....Carl F. H. Henry
ROMAN SOCIETY AND ROMAN LAW IN THE NEW TESTAMENT ....A. N. Sherwin-White
THE ROOT OF FUNDAMENTALISM ....Ernest R. Sandeen
THE SERVANT-MESSIAH ....T. W. Manson
STORY OF RELIGION IN AMERICA......................................Wm. W. Sweet
THE TESTS OF LIFE (third edition) ....Robert Law
THEOLOGY OF THE MAJOR SECTS ....John H. Gerstner
VARIETIES OF CHRISTIAN APOLOGETICS ....B. Ramm
THE VOYAGE AND SHIPWRECK OF ST. PAUL (fourth edition) ....James Smith
THE VIRGIN BIRTH ....J. G. Machen
A COMPANION TO THE STUDY OF ST. AUGUSTINE ....Roy W. Battenhouse, ed.
STUDIES IN THE GOSPELS ....R. C. Trench
THE HISTORY OF THE RELIGION OF ISRAEL ....John Howard Raven
THE HISTORY OF CHRISTIAN DOCTRINE (revised edition) ....E. H. Klotsche
THE EPISTLES OF JUDE AND II PETER ....Joseph B. Mayor
THEORIES OF REVELATION ....H. D. McDonald
STUDIES IN THE BOOK OF DANIEL ....Robert Dick Wilson
THE UNITY OF THE BOOK OF GENESIS ....William Henry Green
THE APOCALYPSE OF JOHN ....Isbon T. Beckwith
CHRIST THE MEANING OF HISTORY ....Hendrikus Berkhof